INSTRUCTOR'S RESOURCE GUID

JOHN R. BROOKS, JR.
Houston Baptist University

KELLYE K. BROOKS
Houston Baptist University

to accompany

◆ ◆

GLOBAL MARKETING MANAGEMENT

◆ ◆

MASAAKI KOTABE
The University of Texas at Austin

KRISTIAAN HELSEN
Hong Kong University of Science and Technology

JOHN WILEY & SONS, INC.
New York Chichester Weinheim Brisbane Singapore Toronto

ISBN 0-471-19385-2

Printed in the United States of America

10 9 8 7 6 5 4 3 2 1

Printed and bound by Victor Graphics, Inc.

Contents

Test Bank
Contents

INSTRUCTOR'S RESOURCE GUIDE
GLOBAL MARKETING MANAGEMENT
Masaaki Kotabe and Kristiaan Helsen

HOW TO USE:

Kotabe/Helsen's *Global Marketing Management* has a complete set of supplemental learning and teaching aids. The Instructor's Resource Guide plays a central role in organizing this package. This guide has been designed so the instructor can plan lectures, demonstrations, discussions, visual presentations (including video presentations), case evaluations and discussions, and written/project/Internet assignments that will stimulate student learning and creative thinking.

All 18 chapters of the textbook have been carefully reviewed in order to develop the most logical and helpful guide for classroom use. Primary features of the chapter reviews are presented below. Evaluations of special sections of this guide follow the chapter review explanation.

CHAPTER OBJECTIVES

To facilitate learning, chapter objectives have been included in each chapter review. These objectives have been derived from those included in the text book. These objectives may be used to focus attention toward the primary features of the chapter and as guides to the learning experience. The instructor may plan learning objectives around these critical points.

CHAPTER OVERVIEW

Each chapter of the text book is summarized in the Chapter Overview. This portion of the *Instructor's Resource Guide* provides the instructor with a summarized version of the critical information included in the chapter. This summary of material is especially helpful in planning chapter sequence presentation. In addition to helping the instructor plan introductory lecture remarks, it is a good quick reminder of material that can be reviewed prior to the start of the lecture.

CHAPTER OUTLINE

This section of the *Instructor's Resource Guide* is the most important learning and preparation aid for the instructor. This teaching outline is a thorough summarized description (specifically tied to the actual phrases and definitions used in the master text book) of the primary material from the text book chapters. This outline includes major (shown in **Bold**) and minor (shown in *Italic Bold*) headings from the text book. This makes it easier to associate this material with the material from the text book.

The instructor will note special information sections that appear periodically in body of the outline. This material is indicated with **bold type** and **bold asterisks (*****)**. The purpose of these special information sections or blocks is to make the instructor aware of where key material appears in the text book and when to use teaching aids. These information blocks may contain the following items of information: **Exhibits (identified by Exhibit # from the text book); Global Perspectives (identified by Global Perspective # and title from the text book); Review Questions (identified by # from the text book); Discussion Questions (identified by # from the text book).**

It is recommended that instructor carefully review the Chapter Outline prior to preparing a chapter lecture. This review will help in coordinating the learning activities that are available with the text book.

REVIEW QUESTIONS

The review questions are listed in **bold** as they appear in the text book. These review questions are meant to challenge the student to think about material presented in the chapter and then formulate a creative answer to the review question. Though most of these questions are factual in nature, many of the answers require judgments rather than line-by-line quotation of facts. The answers provided in this *Instructor's Resource Guide* are meant to provide stimulation of creative answers by the students.

DISCUSSION QUESTIONS

The discussion questions are listed in the individual chapters in the text book. These questions are not repeated in the *Instructor's Resource Guide*. Instead, they are referred to by number (since many of the questions are very lengthy). The proper placement of these discussion questions is up to the instructor, however, suggestions are made within the body of the chapter outline provided for each chapter of the text book. Suggestions for answering and discussing the questions is presented in this section of the *Instructor's Resource Guide*. Remember, many of these questions require student opinion, reaction, and judgment. Therefore, some latitude should be given to responses.

STUDENT PROJECTS and INTERNET FOCUS

This section suggests several projects that may be assigned to the students for a specific class or for several class periods. Since these projects do require time and outside preparation, they should be assigned prior to the assignment of the chapter. The projects may be assigned to individuals or to groups. Format for discussion or written comments is up to the instructor.

All the material contained in this section has been written in a student assignment format (each phrase may be given directly to the students without rewording).

A special feature of this *Instructor's Resource Guide* is the Internet Focus section. Each chapter has three Internet discovery projects that are tied to the material from the individual chapters. This material does not appear in the text book. These projects require the students to both use and understand the Internet. If the students do not understand how to use the Internet, explanation should be given before these projects are undertaken. The Web sites provided were current at the time of this writing. However, since Web addresses change frequently, the instructor should re-affirm the site address and the content of the site before making an assignment. Another hint: if the Web address does not work, try using only the primary address instead of the sometimes lengthy specific address. Sometimes the only thing that has changed is some component of the lengthy address.

The assignments familiarize the students with using search engines, doing research from private, library, and government sources, and reviewing some to the most dynamic private business sites present on the Web. The Internet Focus is a great learning experience for the students the Kotabe/Helsen team hopes that you enjoy the experience.

GLOBAL CASES

Global Case comments appear in a special section at the end of the *Instructor's Resource Guide*. As an aid to coordinating these cases with specific chapters from the text book, an instructor's information sheet is provided at the beginning of this section. This guide was prepared by the authors of the text book and indicates some useful hints for case application. Following the guide, each case has extended Case Notes that can be used to aid the case learning experience. In most instances, the Case Notes are from the original authors of the various cases. A variety of case solution formats are used. The instructor may select the format that best fits the educational needs and skill level of the students. Discussion questions are presented.

VIDEO CASES

Video Case comments appear in a special section at the end of this *Instructor's Resource Guide*. As an aid to coordinating these cases with specific chapters from the text book, an instructor's information sheet is provided at the beginning of the section. This guide indicates some useful hints for case application. Following the guide, each case has a series of summarized notes that explain and summarize the video clip. In addition, this section provides Pre- and Post-viewing questions and answers that may be used with each Video Case. As a caution, the instructor should always view the video clip prior to usage in a class to make sure that the material is appropriate for the learning experience at hand.

POWERPOINT SLIDES

Available on the book website (www.wiley.com/college/kotabe), the transparencies were selected from Exhibits in the text book. These slides should help to stimulate the students' visual perception of the material from the lecture and the chapters. To identify the proper place to use the chapter slide masters, look for the proper Exhibit # in the Chapter Outline.

CHAPTER 1

GLOBALIZATION IMPERATIVE

CHAPTER OBJECTIVES

1. Answer the basic question "Why Global Market Imperative?"

2. Understand the process of globalization of markets and competition.

3. Be able to describe the evolution of global marketing.

CHAPTER OVERVIEW

Marketing products and services around the world, transcending national and political boundaries, is a fascinating phenomenon. The interest in the phenomenon is growing rapidly because world trade has grown from $200 billion to over $4 trillion in the past two decades. Though the tremendous amount of money spent on international trade may be new, the trade itself is as old as man. Early recorded history is full of stories of travel and trade adventures.

Companies from Western Europe, the United States, and Japan collectively produce probably more than three times as much in foreign markets as they export. About a third of their exports and imports are transacted on an intra-firm basis between their parent companies and their affiliated companies abroad or between the affiliated companies themselves.

The chapter points out that it is almost impossible for domestic company executives to consider their domestic markets and domestic competition alone. International markets today are so much more than mere importing and exporting. The markets are so intertwined that separating international from domestic business may even be a futile mental exercise.

Historically, international expansion has always been a strategy consideration after domestic marketing, and has therefore been reactionary to such things as a decline in domestic sales and increased domestic competition. Global marketing is a proactive response to the intertwined nature of business opportunities and competition that know no political boundaries. It is a company's willingness to adopt a global perspective instead of a country-by-country or region-by-region perspective in developing a marketing strategy for growth and profit that will sustain growth efforts in the rapidly approaching 21st century.

CHAPTER OUTLINE

A. Why Global Marketing Imperative

1. Do the terms global, international, or multinational have different meanings or are they just play on words?
   a. Competition has changed in the last twenty years.
   b. Old companies have declined and new ones have emerged primarily because of global influences.
2. By examining the top 100 companies in the world, profound changes can be observed.

*****Use Exhibit 1-1 Here*****

   a. In 1970 sixty-four of the world's top companies were from the United States.
   b. In 1995 only twenty-four were from the United States.
   c. During the same time period, the Japanese have increased their rankings from eight to thirty-seven.
   d. United States dominance has been under increasing pressure from abroad.
   e. It is not so much that the United States is doing poorly as the rest of the world is doing better.
3. The changes observed in the past 25 years simply reflects that companies from other parts of the world have grown in size relative to those of the United States.
   a. Pressure is on executives in all countries to do better in the upcoming decade.
   b. Political and economic events have also had an impact on the nature of global competition:
      1). The demise of the Soviet Union.
      2). The establishment of the European Union.
      3). The establishment of NAFTA.
      4). The deregulation and privatization of state-owned industries.
   c. Growth of Eastern Europe and Southeast Asia will also eventually have an impact on global marketing and business.
4. The term "global" epitomizes both the competitive pressure and the expanding market opportunities around the world.

*****Use Review Question #1 and Review Question #3 Here*****

B. Globalization of Markets and Competition

1. It takes an annual income of about $10,000 to have a disposable income sufficient enough to have any real purchasing power.
   a. Below $10,000 people tend the subsistence oriented.
   b. Marketers carefully tract the increasing number of international consumers that earn more than $10,000 per year.

2. International wants and desires (for example, the want or desire for Nike tennis shoes) tends to transcend cultural and international boundaries.
3. At present, the United States is the single most important market for foreign as well as for domestic companies.
   a. The United States has the highest per capita income level.
   b. The United States has an almost insatiable demand for foreign products.
   c. This demand has created a trade deficit.

*****Use Exhibit 1-2 Here; Use Review Question #4 Here*****

4. The trade deficit is not just a result of declining United States productivity.
5. *International Trade vs. International Business.*
   a. International trade consists of exports and imports between nations.
      1). If imports exceed exports, a trade deficit would occur.
      2). If exports exceed imports, a trade surplus would occur.
   b. International business is a broader concept that includes international trade and foreign production. Marketing can occur in three ways:
      1). Export products.
      2). Invest in foreign production and manufacture domestically.
      3). Contract out manufacturing through licensing or joint ventures.
   c. Foreign production constitutes a much larger portion of international business than international trade.
   d. Global reach is the extensive penetration of U. S. and other countries.
      1). Figures show that experienced companies tend to manufacture overseas much more than they export.
      2). Japanese firms have only recently begun to do this.

*****Use Discussion Question #1 and Discussion Question #2 Here*****

6. *Who Manages International Trade?*
   a. Multinational companies are increasingly managing the international flow within themselves. This is called intra-firm trade.
      1). This form of trade makes statistics more difficult to understand.
      2). Most of the large industrialized countries have about 30% intra-firm trading.

*****Use Review Question #2 Here*****

C. **Evolution of Global Marketing**

1. *What is Marketing?*
   a. Marketing is essentially a creative corporate activity involving the planning and execution of conception, pricing, promotion, and distribution of ideas, products, and services in exchange that not only satisfy customer's present

needs but also anticipate and create their future needs at a profit.

   1). Marketing is much broader than selling.
   2). Marketing must focus on customers and competition to be successful.
   3). One must be careful not to gain customers at the expense of losing markets.
   b. Increasingly, firms are drawn into marketing activities outside their domestic environment.
   c. Firms generally develop different marketing strategies depending on the degree of experience and the nature of operations in international markets.
   d. Many researchers believe that firms evolve over time into international companies and organizations.
   1). Actual evolution depends on the economic, cultural, political, and legal environments of various country markets in which the company operates as well as on the nature of the company's offerings.
   2). A key point here is that many companies are constantly under competitive pressure to move forward both reactively (responding to the changes in the market and competitive environments) and proactively (anticipating the change).
   e. Knowing the dynamics of evolutionary change is important for two reasons:
   1). It helps in the understanding of how companies learn and acquire international experience and how they use it for gaining competitive advantage over time.
   2). With this knowledge, a company may be able to compete more effectively by predicting its competitors' likely marketing strategy in advance.

*****Use Exhibit 1-3 Here*****

2. *Domestic Marketing.*
   a. Domestic marketing is the first stage of evolution of marketing across international boundaries.
   b. Companies focus on domestic sales and markets.
   c. This strategy is based on domestic needs and domestic competition only.
   1). Marketers are ethnocentric and pay little attention to what is going on in the international market place (such as changing customer demand).
   2). All strategic actions are tailored to domestic responses.
   d. As a result, these companies are vulnerable to sudden changes forced on them from foreign competition.
3. *Export Marketing.*
   a. The second stage is export marketing.
   b. Usually, this stage begins from unsolicited orders from markets or distributors located abroad.
   1). Companies learn to benefit from this business.
   2). Strategy is reactive rather than proactive.
   3). Businesses have many uncertainties and unknowns in the unfamiliar international market.

    c. Companies advance once they satisfy the following conditions:

        1). The management of the company obtains favorable expectations of the attractiveness of exporting based on experience.

        2). The company has access to key resources necessary for undertaking additional export-related tasks.

        3). Management is willing to commit adequate resources to export activities.

    d. Difficulties experienced include:

        1). Import/export restrictions.

        2). Cost and availability of shipping.

        3). Exchange rate fluctuations.

        4). Collection of money.

        5). Development of distribution channels.

    e. If companies do not have a favorable experience at this level, it will retard advancement along the continuum.

    f. Many forces may make the company consider this alternative, but they still tend to take an ethonocentric view toward strategy formulation.

4. *International Marketing.*

    a. Once export marketing becomes an integral part of the company's marketing activity, it will begin to seek new directions for growth and expansion.

    b. A unique feature of the international marketing phase is its polycentric orientation with emphasis on product and promotional adaptation in foreign markets.

        1). The company must begin to defend its position in foreign markets against local competition.

        2). The international marketer will need to adapt their products to overcome the inherent advantage of the domestic marketer.

        3). The company can begin to allocate a certain portion of its manufacturing capacity to its export business.

        4). Or, because of transportation costs, tariffs and other regulations, and availability of human and capital resources in the foreign markets, the company may even begin manufacturing in the foreign environment.

    c. The extreme of this phase is to establish an independent foreign subsidiary in each and every foreign market and have each of the subsidiaries operate independently of each other without any measurable headquarters control. This is known as multi-domestic marketing.

        1). Few economies of scale result.

        2). Useful when there are wide differences between markets.

*****Use Review Question #6 and Review Question #7 Here*****

5. *Multinational Marketing.*

    a. In this phase the company markets its products in many countries around the world.

    b. Because of efficiencies and economies to earned, the company consolidates on a regional basis.

1). This regiocentric approach suggests that product planning may be standardized within a region but not across regions.
2). Regional advertising might be accomplished.
3). Regional brands might be developed.
6. ***Global Marketing.***
a. The international (country-by-country) or multinational (region-by-region) orientation, while enabling the consolidation within countries or regions, will tend to result in market fragmentation worldwide, nonetheless.
b. Operational fragmentation costs are often high.
c. It is argued that the multinational and global corporation are not the same thing.
d. Global marketing refers to marketing activities by companies that emphasize:
1). Reduction of cost inefficiencies and duplication of efforts among their national and regional subsidiaries.
2). Opportunities for the transfer of products, brands, and other ideas across subsidiaries.
3). Emergence of global customers.
4). Improved linkages among national marketing infrastructures leading to the development of a global marketing infrastructure.
e. Most researchers do agree that some standardization is all right, however, what is really called for is a company's proactive willingness to adopt a global perspective when developing marketing strategy.
f. While many companies are along way from this concept, they are making progress with their subsidiaries.

*****Use Global Perspective 1-1 "Globalizing the Business Terms before Globalization of the Firm" Here; Use Review Question #5 Here; Use Discussion Question #3 and Discussion Question #4 Here*****

g. Rather than becoming more simplistic, the world economic and marketing environment is becoming more sophisticated and complex.

*****Use Chapter Appendix Here (for additional information about international trade and investment). This material is outlined following this chapter.*****

REVIEW QUESTIONS

INSTRUCTOR'S NOTE: The following chapter review questions are meant to challenge the student to think about material presented in the chapter and formulate a creative answer to the review question. Many of the answers require judgments rather than specific line-by-line quotation of facts. The answers provided are meant to provide stimulation of creative answers.

1. Discuss the reasons why international business is much more complex today than it was 20 years ago.

Among the commonly cited reasons for increasingly complex international business environments are:

a. More sophisticated consumers.
b. More consumers and markets to analyze.
c. Increasing international competition that impacts the international as well as the domestic environment.
d. Expanding international opportunities.
e. Political and governmental barriers.
f. Ethical and moral concerns.
g. Cultural barriers.
h. Shifting multinational environments.
i. Newly emerging nations and new strategic alliances.

2. What is the nature of global competition?

The new view toward global competition is that it includes domestic as well as foreign competitors. Large multinationals have expanded to the extent that they can begin to think globally rather than on a country-by-country or region-by-region basis. In order to do this, new formats for strategies and subsidiaries are being developed. Products and services are being adapted or standardized (as the market dictates). Proactive strategy is replacing reactive strategy.

3. Does international trade accurately reflect the nature of global competition?

If the marketer only thinks in terms of exports and imports, the answer is no. If the marketer does not consider the amount of business that is being done between the subsidiaries of the same multinational or global firm, then the answer is no. If the global competitor truly is designing strategy and policy to fit the current international trade environment, the competitor uses international trade as a component of the firm's strategy formulation process.

4. Why is consumption pattern similar across industrialized countries despite cultural differences?

As country or a market's disposable income increases, research has shown that more of the discretionary income is spent on non-subsistence goods and services. Once the average person passes about $10,000 per capita income per year, that person begins to become a viable prospect for non-subsistence goods. The need for goods in general is similar. The need for specific goods may be affected by cultural differences.

5. How is global marketing different from international marketing?

Global marketing is a more advanced phase of international marketing. Once export marketing becomes an integral part of a company's marketing activity, it begins to seek growth and expansion through international marketing. The emphasis is polycentric (emphasis on product and promotional adaptation in foreign markets--wherever necessary). In global marketing, fragmentation caused by international marketing is overcome.

Global marketing refers to marketing activities by companies that emphasize:
1). Reduction of cost inefficiencies and duplication of efforts among their national and regional subsidiaries.
2). Opportunities for the transfer of products, brands, and other ideas across subsidiaries.
3). Emergence of global customers.
4). Improved linkages among national marketing infrastructures leading to the development of a global marketing infrastructure.

6. Why do think a company should or should not market the same product in the same way around the world?

Students should be encouraged to think about the standardization versus the adaptation alternative. Standardization has the advantages of efficiencies in production and communication as well as economies of scale. Adaptation has the advantages of customization, matching the true unique desires and wants of the customer, and the ability to compete against local competition more effectively.

Students should be encouraged to think of product examples for standardization and then adaptation. Try to make a case for each form being effective. What is the most deciding factor?

7. What is proactive standardization?

In global marketing, the trend may be to see the world as one giant market. The trick to being successful in more than one market (while still retaining the advantages of production economies of scale) may be in finding products that everyone needs (with little adaptive change). This response to true global competitors may be a very good defense against market erosion.

DISCUSSION QUESTIONS

INSTRUCTOR'S NOTE: Discussion Questions are found at the end of each chapter in the text. These questions (in many cases) are too lengthy to repeat in this manual. Suggestions for answering and discussing the questions are presented in this section. Many of the questions require student opinion and judgment.

1. This question focuses on whether or not corporations and the media (because of stability of imports and exports as a percentage of GNP for many countries has changed little over the past three decades) may be over-emphasizing globalization. Most students should see that the world is growing. As growth occurs within individual economies GNP will grow. Even if imports and exports remain constant, they actually increase because of increasing GNP. If anything, the corporations and media of the world should be placing more emphasis on globalization. It probably is the one true secret to expanding and succeeding in the next century.

2. Merchandise (though only 2 percent of foreign exchange) is still a significant factor in world trade. As world consumers continue to increase their disposable income, more merchandise will be demanded. This merchandise will come from domestic and international sources. Merchandise is the end result of procuring raw resources and conducting manufacturing. With this in mind, it would be correct to state that the impact of merchandise cannot be considered alone. It must be considered in a broader context. It is, ideally, what most nations would like to trade. It is also where a nation can succeed by having a comparative advantage.

3. This question assumes the format of a small case. After reading the material contained in the question, the student is asked to formulate an opinion on three basic questions with respect to market entry into the Indian market. These questions deal with the questions of standardization versus adaptation, positioning with respect to culture and life style habits, and choices made in encouraging the development of brand equity. To answer each of these questions the student should assume the role of a brand manager. First, the student should re-read the section of the chapter that discusses standardization versus adaptation. Second, the student should review the material found in the Appendix to Chapter 1. By reviewing this material the student should be better prepared to analyze positioning strategy and the concept of brand equity. Lastly, the student should be encouraged to consider whether policies that are successful in one country or market (in this case China) can be directly transferred to another market or country (in this case India). Globally, customization is needed in many instances. What areas can be standardized?

4. This question assumes that global marketing is an accepted practice and a worthy goal. The difficulty comes in finding managers who are either familiar with how to manage globally or are good at managing globally. This is certainly a common problem. One could ask the question "Where will our global managers come from?" Do the managers come from domestic operations or from foreign subsidiaries? At this point the answer is unclear. What is clear, however, is that the manager of the future must be familiar with

marketing in a global atmosphere. If they are unfamiliar, they will not be successful in designing or implementing global strategy. Many firms may be making mistakes today because of a lack of managerial expertise, however, they are learning and will not make mistakes tomorrow.

STUDENT PROJECTS and INTERNET FOCUS

1. Identify three companies that you believe have a global marketing focus. Provide supporting evidence or arguments that justify selection of these firms.

2. Using Exhibit 1-3 and the descriptive material in the chapter as your guide, identify a company that fits each of the categories mentioned. Provide supporting evidence or arguments that justify selection of these firms.

INSTRUCTOR'S NOTE: The following projects require the students to both use and understand the Internet. If students do not understand how to use the Internet, explanation should be given before these projects are undertaken. The Web sites provided were current at the time of this writing. However, since Web addresses change frequently, the instructor should re-affirm the site address and the content of the site before making an assignment.

3. Go to Toyota Motor Company's world wide web site at (**http://www.toyota.com**). By investigating the material that you find on their web pages, construct evidence that would support your contention that Toyota (1)standardizes or (2) adapts its world wide products.

4. Using either the *Global Business Forum* (**http://www.pragmatix.com/gbf**) or the *Export Process Assistant* (**http://venture.cob.ohiostate.edu:1111/tutorial/openingscr.html**)web sites, investigate the export process. What types of information can be obtained from these free sites? Could a small business person begin an export process by using information found on these sources? If not, what would be necessary?

5. Go to the *International Trade Administration (US Dept. of Commerce)* web site (**http://www.ita.doc.gov/itahome.html**). Find an announcement or a trade article that you think might be interesting to bring to class. Download the material, abstract it if necessary, and discuss the material in class. Besides articles and news flashes, what other information can be obtained from this site?

APPENDIX TO CHAPTER 1

APPENDIX OVERVIEW

Theories are a simplification of the complex realities one way or the other. This appendix examines three theories that help to explain the background and economic forces that have shaped contemporary international business and global marketing. These theories, rather than being independent thoughts, supplement one another.

Comparative advantage theory is useful when managers think broadly about the nature of industrial development and international trade. The international product cycle theory helps to explain why and how a company initially extends its market horizons abroad and how foreign competitors shape global competition over time and place. Internalization or transaction cost theory provides some answers to how to manage multinational operations in a very competitive world. These theories provide foundations upon which to build sound strategy and policy in the international arena.

APPENDIX OUTLINE

A. Comparative Advantage Theory

1. Countries trade with one another for fundamentally the same reasons that individuals trade with one another--mutual benefit.
2. Comparative advantage theory is a arithmetic demonstration made by the English economist, David Ricardo, almost 180 years ago.
   a. The idea was that a country can gain from engaging in trade even if it has an *absolute* advantage or disadvantage.
   b. Examine what trading partners can produce *relatively* more efficiently.

*****Use Exhibit 1-4 Here for a demonstration of comparative advantage theory*****

3. An example concerning trade between the United States and China shows that trade might be prohibited because the United States has an *absolute advantage*.
4. However, upon close inspection, one observes that trade can take place (for example in PCs and desks) because of *comparative advantage*.
   a. This suggests that the two trading partners should specialize.
   b. A mathematical demonstration is provided that indicates degree of specialization required to make trade beneficial.
   c. *Commodity terms of trade* (a price of one good in terms of another) must be agreed upon.
5. In reality, trading members rarely trade one good for another. Instead, they use

foreign exchange.
   a. Actual exchange rate will be affected by consumer demands.
   b. They are also determined by the money supply situations in the affected countries.
6. General *principles of international trade* include:
   a. Countries benefit from international trade.
   b. International trade increases worldwide production by specialization.
   c. Exchange rates are determined primarily by traded goods.
7. The *factor endowment theory* indicates that:
   a. A capital-abundant country tends to specialize in capital-intensive industry and export capital-intensive products and import labor-intensive products.
   b. A labor-abundant country tends to specialize in labor-intensive industry and export labor-intensive products and import capital-intensive products.

*****Use Global Perspective 1-2 Here*****

   c. Be careful of assuming that labor productivity alone shows industry competitiveness.
8. The comparative advantage theory is useful in explaining *inter-industry* trade between country that have very different factor endowments.
   a. It suggests efficient allocation of limited resources across national boundaries by specialization and trade.
   b. It does not explain trade where there is no competition.
   c. It also fails to explain trade between countries with similar factor endowments.
   d. *Intra-industry* competition cannot be explained by comparative advantage theory.

B. International Product Cycle Theory

1. Intra-industry competition is addressed in the international product cycle theory.
2. Speculations must be made:
   a. A large domestic market (such as in the United States) makes it possible for domestic firms to enjoy *economies of scale*.
   b. Low cost producers can engage in international trade.
   c. *Economies of scope* allows the firms to extend there advantages beyond the domestic market into foreign ones.
   d. Technological innovation can provide an innovative company a competitive advantage, or *technological gap*, over its competitors both at home and abroad.
      1). The firms may temporarily have *monopoly power*.
   e. It is generally the per-capita income level that determines consumers' *preference similarity*, or consumption patterns, irrespective of nationality.
3. These ideas have been combined with the theory of comparative advantage.
4. International product cycle theory suggests that new products are developed primarily to address the needs of the local consumers, only to be demanded by

foreign consumers who have similar needs with a similar purchasing power.

*****Use Exhibit 1-5 Here to observe the pattern and stages of the international product cycle*****

5. The stages include:
   a. The *introductory stage* where a company innovates on a new product to meet domestic consumers' needs in the domestic market.
   b. The *growth stage* has product standards emerging and mass production becomes feasible.
   c. In the *maturity stage,* many companies vie for market share and prices fall and product differentiation occurs.
   d. In the *decline stage*, companies in developing countries also begin producing the product and marketing it.
6. As an explanation of international business behavior, international product cycle theory has limited explanatory power.
7. It does, however, describe initial expansion in the international market.

C. Internalization/Transaction Cost Theory

1. Companies must be managed across international borders.
2. A primary objective of multinational firms is to keep their market positions from being eroded.
3. Most firms have some proprietary expertise that makes is different from its competitors. This investment in research, information, and managerial expertise can be seen as *internalization/transaction cost theory*.
4. Today's company expertise can be channeled through three routes to garner competitive advantage:
   a. *Appropriability Regime*--the aspects of the commercial environment that governs a company's ability to retain its technological advantage.
   b. *Dominant Design*--a narrow class of product designs that begins to emerge as a "standard" design. A company that has won a dominant design status has an absolute competitive advantage over its competition.
   c. *Manufacturing and Marketing Ability*--required in almost all cases for successful commercialization of a product innovation.
      1). It is clear that innovative companies committed to manufacturing and marketing excellence will likely remain strong competitors in industry.
5. It can be assumed that the above sources of competitive advantage are not independent of one another.
6. To gain all advantage possible in the ever-expanding international competitive environment, an increasing number of firms have entered into strategic alliances so as to complement their competitive weaknesses with their partner's competitive strengths.

CHAPTER 2

GLOBAL ECONOMIC ENVIRONMENT

CHAPTER OBJECTIVES

1. Understand the intertwined relationships within the world economy.

2. Classify the characteristics of the economic environment within a nation.

3. Demonstrate an understanding of the role of the General Agreement on Tariffs and Trade (GATT) and the World Trade Organization (WTO).

4. Explain the U. S. position in foreign direct investment and trade.

5. Observe the role of information technology and changing nature of competition on contemporary business practice.

6. Classify regional economic arrangements.

7. Describe the multinational corporation.

CHAPTER OVERVIEW

In no other time in the economic history of the world have countries been more economically interdependent than they are today. The world economy is getting increasingly intertwined and virtually no country that has a steadily rising standard of living is independent of the economic events in the rest of the world. Today a country has to participate in the world economy, however, participation has risks because forces beyond the control of the individual country may have serious effects on their individual economy. For example, many countries were affected by the Mexican financial crisis of 1994.

Growth in international financial flows (which include foreign direct investment, portfolio investment, and trading in currencies) has achieved a life of its own. The annual trade in goods and services totaled nine trillion dollars in 1995. Daily financial flows now exceed a trillion dollars daily. These numbers are expected to increase as barriers to international trade and financial flows get lower and lower.

Some of the factors that have lead to interdependency and integration are transportation and communications. These areas are making information acquisition faster, cheaper, and more widely accessible. The nature of value adding activities is changing in the advanced countries from manufacturing to services and information manipulation. All countries are attempting to remain competitive by adding to and increasing their telecommunications effort.

For all practical purposes, the capital markets of the world are already integrated. This integration affects exchange rates, interest rates, investments, employment, and growth across the world. Multinational corporations are common. The world is becoming a true global village. The challenge for the next century will be to manage this increasingly interconnected environment for the betterment of all mankind.

CHAPTER OUTLINE

A. Intertwined World Economy

1. Despite the relative insularity of the U. S. economy, it is getting increasingly integrated into the world economy.

*****Use Exhibit 2-1 Here*****

2. Over the next two decades, the markets that hold the greatest potential are to be found outside the traditional trading sphere and in Big Emerging Markets (BEMs).
   a. The Chinese Economic Area (CEA--including China, Hong Kong, and Taiwan).
   b. India.
   c. South Korea.
   d. Mexico.
   e. Brazil.
   f. Argentina.
   h. South Africa.
   i. Poland.
   j. Turkey.
   k. The Association of Southeast Asian Nations (ASEAN--including Indonesia, Brunei, Malaysia, Singapore, Thailand, the Philippines and Vietnam).
3. The World Economic Forum's global competitiveness report placed Singapore and Hong Kong among the world's top four economies along with the U. S. and Japan.
4. World trade as a percent of GNP varies from country to country. It is an important calculation.
   a. The percent has risen from 10 percent in 1970 to 23 percent in 1995 for the United States.
   b. For Holland the percent runs as high as 60 percent.
   c. Developing nations percentages are increasing as they lower trade barriers and

begin to participate in the world economy.

5. Intertwining of economies by the process of specialization due to international trade leads to job creation in both the exporting country and the importing country.

6. A nation that is a successful trader displays a natural inclination to be competitive in the world market.
   a. Competition is an incentive rather than a threat.
   b. Technology investment increases.

7. *Foreign Direct Investment.*
   a. This concept means that a firm invests in manufacturing and service facilities in a foreign country.
   b. It is an alternative to exporting.
   c. This is on the increase because of wooing from governments.
   d. Foreign direct investment can also result from trade friction (you can invest with me if I can invest with you).

8. *Portfolio Investment.*
   a. This is sometimes called indirect investment (investments can be withdrawn on short notice).
   b. With respect to this concept, international borders have disappeared.
   c. In today's international financial markets, traders trade currencies most of the time without an underlying trade transaction.
   d. The increase in trading makes nations vulnerable to currency fluctuations. The effect may be to deter trading because of the high cost of money.
      1). This may, however, encourage central banks to lower interest rates to encourage trade.
   e. Even though integration is a fact of international life and trade, the United States seems to be more insulated than most of its competitive trading partners.
   f. About 90 percent of what Americans consume is produced in America.
   g. The dominant feature of the global economy is that the share of the world output from the developing nations is rising in a sustained manner and has been estimated to overtake the share of the present rich nations before the year 2000.
      1). China and India will be responsible for the largest amount of the increase.

*****Use Review Question #1 Here*****

B. Economic Environment within a Nation

1. While the world economy is getting increasingly integrated, there are significant differences among the economies of individual nations which are likely to persist for some time.

2. One way to visualize the differences is to look at the method of resource allocation and control and the type of property ownership in an economy.

a. The method of resource allocation and control refers to where the national economy lies in a continuum between a market economy and a command economy.

b. In a pure market economy the supply and demand of goods determine the price and the role of the government is minimal.

c. In the command economy the government determines the supply and the prices and, therefore, the demand.

*****Use Exhibit 2-2 Here*****

d. Countries such as the United States fall at the market-private end of the table while North Korea and Cuba would be at the command-public end of the table.

   1). Western societies have moved toward the market-private model while totalitarian societies have moved toward the command-public model.

   2). The weaknesses of this model can be found when applied to societies that are mixed (such as Japan--Western yet closed from the West).

   3). Governmental policy might alter the mixes (such as the Robinson-Patman Act in the United States).

   4). "Keiretsus" (groups of firms bound together by strong informal ties and interlocking ownership) in Japan would be discouraged in the West.

   5). Many countries have differing views on formulating a governmental "industrial policy."

e. There is common agreement that a telecommunications infrastructure is essential for sustained economic growth.

   1). Underdeveloped countries are opening traditional monopolies in the hopes of developing this infrastructure quicker.

   2). Opening these structures is a major determinant of the flow of economic activity.

*****Use Exhibit 2-3 Here*****

C. Role of the General Agreement on Tariffs and Trade (GATT) and the World Trade Organization (WTO)

1. *GATT.*

   a. The first attempt (in the modern era) at ensuring free trade among nations through negotiated lowering of trade barriers was the *International Trade Organization (ITO).*

   b. When the ITO failed, most of the signatories agreed to operate under the informal aegis of the *General Agreements of Tariffs and Trade (GATT).*

      1). GATT provided a forum for multilateral discussion among countries to reduce trade barriers.

      2). The main operating principle of GATT was the concept of *Most Favored Nation (MFN)* status.

3). MFN meant that any country which was a member state to a GATT agreement and which extended a reduction in tariff to another nation would have to automatically extend the same benefit to all members of GATT.

4). It should be noted, however, that there is no enforcement mechanism.

*****Use Global Perspective 2-1 "Trade Barriers, Hypocrisy and the United States" Here*****

c. Some weaknesses have been observed with GATT.

1). The initial lowering of barriers only applied to products (not to services).

2). GATT has not dealt successfully with non-tariff barriers.

3). Knowledge based economies have sought to bring intellectual property to the accords.

*****Use Review Question #2 Here*****

2. *WTO.*

a. The Uruguay Round of GATT (held from 1986-1993) agreed to set up an international body called the *World Trade Organization (WTO)*.

1). This body would have statutory powers to adjudicate trade disputes among nations.

2). It provides a framework for governments to frame and implement domestic trade legislation and regulations.

b. One of the attempts of this form of negotiation is to get certain nations to agree to honor intellectual property rights. This is still a very difficult issue in trade relations.

*****Use Exhibit 2-4 Here*****

c. WTO is not just an extension of GATT. It is an entity unto itself.

d. The WTO settlement mechanism is faster, more automatic, and less susceptible to blockages than the old GATT system.

*****Use Global Perspective 2-2 "WTO dispute panel works despite blocks" Here; Use Review Question #3 Here*****

e. *Financial Services in WTO/GATT.*

1). Key developed powers (excluding the United States) have extended WTO/GATT to financial services.

2). The attempt is to control banking, insurance, and securities.

3). The European Union is the main promoter.

4). The United States argues that the pact does not go far enough.

5). For the finance industry in most industrialized nations, the accord would bring guaranteed access to fiercely-protected domestic markets.

6). 1997 will bring a review that promises more access.

7). The United States is still trying to form a model that they would be willing to join.

D. U. S. Position in Foreign Direct Investment and Trade

1. The United States has been a significant overseas investor since 1945.
   a). The Marshall Plan in the 1950s helped to rebuild Europe after World War II.
   b). Investment grew overseas with the appreciation of the dollar.

*****Use Exhibit 2-5 Here*****

   c). Most United States investment has been concentrated in Europe (particularly in Britain.
   d). The most recent investment surge has been directed towards Asia.
2. *Foreign Direct Investment in the United States.*
   a). Before the 1980s, foreign investment in the United States was modest.
   b). Investment was spurred by a fall in the value of the dollar in the 1980s.

*****Use Exhibit 2-6 Here*****

   1). This is also the period in which the United States ran its largest trade deficits.
   c). The largest investors have been Britain and the Netherlands (though the Japanese have also increased their investment and interest).

*****Use Exhibit 2-7 Here*****

3. *Balance of Payments Position.*
   a). The United States has run a persistent deficit on the current account since the first oil shock 1973.
   b). Through the same time period the United States has run a consistent surplus on services.
   c). There is consistent concern that conventional measures do not accurately reflect a country's transactions with the rest of the world.
   1). Most measures do not account intra-firm transfers correctly.

*****Use Exhibit 2-8, Exhibit 2-9, and Exhibit 2-10 Here*****

   d). Even though the trade deficit remains substantial, it has declined substantially as a percentage of the sum of imports and exports and as a percentage of of the GDP since 1987.

*****Use Review Question #4 and Review Question #6 Here*****

E. Information Technology and Changing Nature of Competition

1. Industrialized nations are focusing more on Trade Related Intellectual Property (TRIPs).
   a. Information related products such as software, music, movies, and publications are important sources of revenue.
   b. Copying did not present problems in the past because of poor reproductive technology.
   c. Today, individuals can copy easily.
2. *Value of Intellectual Property in Information Age.*
   a. Using the Internet, material can almost instantly be copied.
   b. Since most developing nations are interested in value creation (especially in intellectual property), there is strong pressure on intellectual property laws.
   c. Technology based protection of electronic information through hardware, software or a combination thereof in the form of encryption and digital signatures have been suggested as the means of circumventing the problem of unauthorized copying.
   d. Controlling copies has become a complex challenge.
   e. The trick may be to control not the copies of the firm's information product but instead a relationship with the customers through subscriptions or membership. Marketing's role will increase in importance.
   f. Other problems center around a truly efficient market for information.
      1). Information products can now be created that are somewhat standard.
      2). Upgrades of many informational products are almost free.
   g. The regulation of international commerce is still open to question as are the governments that attempt to accomplish the regulation.

*****Use Global Perspective 2-3 "The Real Truth about the Economy" Here*****

   h. Some nations are attempting to regulate the infrastructure of and access to the electronic network.

*****Use Review Question #7 Here; Use Discussion Question #1 Here*****

F. Regional Economic Arrangements

1. An evolving trend in international economic activity is the formation of multi-national trading blocs.
   a. These blocs take the form of a group of contiguous countries which decide to have common trading policies for the rest of the world in terms of tariffs and market access but have preferential treatment for one another.
   b. These arrangements can take many forms and names:
      1). European Union.
      2). North American Free Trade Agreement.

3). MERCOSUR (Southern Cone Free Trade Area).
4). Andean Group in South America.
5). The Gulf Cooperation Council in West Asia (GCC).
6). The South Asian Agreement for Regional Cooperation in South Asia (SAARC).
7). Association of South East Asian Nations (ASEAN).

*****Use Discussion Question #4 Here*****

2. *Categories of Regional Groups.*
   a. *Free Trade Area.* This form has a higher level of integration than a loosely formed regional cooperation and is a formal agreement among two or more countries to reduce or eliminate customs duties and non-tariff barriers among partner countries.
      1). NAFTA is an illustration.
      2). The free trade area is not free of all trade barriers.

*****Use Global Perspective 2-4 "NAFTA Promising Freer Trade May End Up Less Free" Here*****

   b. *Customs Union.* When members of a free trade area add common external tariffs to the provisions of the free trade agreement then the free trade area becomes the customs union.
      1). ASEAN is an example.
   c. *Common Market.* A common market eliminates all tariffs and barriers to trade among members of the common market, adopts a set of external tariffs on non-members, and removes all restrictions on the flow of capital and labor among member nations.
   d. *Monetary Union.* In this form member nations move to a common currency and a central bank.
      1). The European Union is attempting to achieve this step (slowly).
   e. *Political Union.* In this phase new nations are created. Integration is achieved on a voluntary basis. A loose political union normally comes first (such as the British Commonwealth).

*****Use Global Perspective 2-5 "Crossing National Borders is Easier than ever in the European Union" Here; Use Review Question #5 and Discussion Question #5 Here*****

G. **Multinational Corporation**

   1. Multinational corporations have a definite influence on the world's economy.
   2. The forces of economies of scale, lowering trade and investment barriers, the need to be close to markets, internalization of operations within the boundaries of one firm, and the diffusion of technology will continue to increase the size

and influence of multinationals.

3. Sovereignty of nations may weaken as a result of multinational influence.
4. The size problem has yet to be solved by the multinational.
5. All multinationals are more multinational than ever before and the trend is expected to continue.

*****Use Review Question #8 Here; Use Discussion Question #2 and Discussion Question #3 Here*****

REVIEW QUESTIONS

INSTRUCTOR'S NOTE: The following chapter review questions are meant to challenge the student to think about material presented in the chapter and formulate a creative answer to the review question. Many of the answers require judgments rather than specific line-by-line quotation of facts. The answers provided are meant to provide stimulation of creative answers.

1. What are some of the visible signs that reflect the current increased economic interdependence among countries? What are some reasons for this growth in interdependence and for the rise in global integration?

Some of the signs that reflect current increased economic interdependence among countries are:

Increased trading activity among the ten Big Emerging Markets, the Chinese Economic Area, and the Association of Southeast Asian Nations.

Increasing foreign direct investment.

More attention to portfolio investment in foreign countries and with money flows in international financial markets.

Reasons for the increases might be the number of countries that are insulated from the global economy are decreasing, new markets are emerging, the disposable income is rising in countries where only poverty ruled, and monetary and communication links are making a the world market a viable opportunity.

2. What is GATT and what is its role in international transactions?

The General Agreements of Tariffs and Trade (GATT) provides a forum for multilateral discussion among countries to reduce trade barriers. Nations met periodically to review the status of world trade and to negotiate mutually agreeable reductions in trade barriers.

The main operating principle of GATT was the concept of Most Favored Nation. The MFN status meant that any country which was a member state to a GATT agreement and which extended a reduction in tariff to another nation would have to automatically extended the same benefit to all members of GATT.

3. How is the WTO different from GATT? What functions is WTO expected to perform?

The World Trade Organization (the WTO) is different from GATT in that it has statutory powers with authority to adjudicate trade disputes among nations. The WTO is the new legal and institutional foundation for a multilateral trading system. It provides the contractual obligations determining how governments frame and implement domestic trade legislation and regulations.

WTO is not just an extension of GATT. The GATT was a multilateral agreement with no institutional foundations. WTO is a permanent institution with its own secretariat. WTO is legally binding. The WTO dispute settlement mechanism, is faster, more automatic and therefore much less susceptible to blockages than the old GATT system.

4. In what way have the U.S. foreign direct investment and trade patterns changed over the past decade?

As shown in Exhibit 2-5, the United States continues to invest in Europe (as it has in the past). New investment is occurring in increasing amounts in Asian countries. This is expected to continue into the future.

Historically, investment in the United States had been modest. However, the 20th century brought a sharp increase in outside investment (especially since the 1980s). Reasons have been attributed to the fall in the price of the dollar (as measured against other currencies) and because of a persistent trade deficit the government has increased pressure on trading partners to invest in the country through a variety of channels. The United States is predicted to be a prime investment for several years to come.

5. Cooperative inter-relationships between countries (regional groupings) can be classified into five broad categories. What are these categories and how do they differ from each other?

    a. *Free Trade Area.* This form has a higher level of integration than a loosely formed regional cooperation and is a formal agreement among two or more countries to reduce or eliminate customs duties and non-tariff barriers among partner countries.
       1). NAFTA is an illustration.
       2). The free trade area is not free of all trade barriers.
    b. *Customs Union.* When members of a free trade area add common external

tariffs to the provisions of the free trade agreement then the free trade area becomes the customs union (ASEAN is an example).

    c. *Common Market.* A common market eliminates all tariffs and barriers to trade among members of the common market, adopts a set of external tariffs on non-members, and removes all restrictions on the flow of capital and labor among member nations.

    d. *Monetary Union.* In this form member nations move to a common currency and a central bank.

        1). The European Union is attempting to achieve this step (slowly).

    e. *Political Union.* In this phase new nations are created. Integration is achieved on a voluntary basis. A loose political union normally comes first (such as the British Commonwealth).

6. Do current measures of balance of payments accurately reflect a country's transactions with the rest of the world? What are the concerns?

In the context of trade deficits, there is increasing concern that the conventional measures of the deficit may not be an accurate reflection of a country's transactions with the rest of the world. America's National Academy of Sciences (NAS) for example has suggested measuring trade entirely on the basis of ownership. It defines exports as the sum of three numbers: cross border sales to foreigners; net sales to foreigners by subsidiaries abroad and sales by American firms to American subsidiaries of foreign firms.

This view probably more accurately reflects the problem of accounting for sales to subsidiaries that most traditional measures do not account for. As multinationals spread throughout the world and a substantial proportion of international trade consists of intra-firm transfer, this question will assume increasing importance in the future.

7. What challenges do the content creators and information providers face due to the advent and popularity of the electronic media? Are there current mechanisms to protect their rights? What are the macro-economic implications for industrialized countries?

With advent of the information age, firms are faced with new situations. Not only is it easy for individuals to make duplicates of many works or to re-use their content in new works, but the physical manifestation of content is almost irrelevant. The United States, in an attempt to protect intellectual property rights, has insisted that intellectual property rights be dealt with in GATT and WTO. Technology based protection of electronic information through hardware, software, or a combination thereof in the form of encryption and digital signatures have been suggested as a means of circumventing the problem of unauthorized copying.

Controlling copying is a difficult problem. The solution may be in not controlling the copies but instead controlling the relationship with the customers through subscriptions or membership. Other larger questions also hurdles to be overcome. First, is the rise of a truly efficient market for information. Second, is the attempts by governments to regulate international commerce.

8. What are some of the forces influencing the increase in size of multinational corporations? Are there any forces which are influencing them to downsize?

Authorities believe that the forces of economies of scale, lowering trade and investment barriers, need to be close to markets, internalization of operations within the boundaries of one firm, and the diffusion of technology will continue to increase the size and influence of multinationals. The sovereignty of nations will perhaps continue to weaken due to multinationals and the increasing integration of economies but the threat to sovereignty may not assume the proportions alluded to by some researchers. Multinationals have yet to solve the problem of size.

Currency movements, capital surpluses, faster growth rates, and falling trade and investment barriers have all helped multinationals from a variety of countries dictate movement of trade goods beyond the control of national governments.

DISCUSSION QUESTIONS

INSTRUCTOR'S NOTE: Discussion Questions are found at the end of each chapter in the text. These questions (in many cases) are too lengthy to repeat in this manual. Suggestions for answering and discussing the questions are presented in this section. Many of the questions require student opinion and judgment.

1. Patent life is a very controversial question. Students should be encouraged to argue both pro and con on this issue. As stated in the Discussion Question, the issue has supporters and detractors in the U.S. Senate. Students should be reminded to look at this issue not only as a consumer but as a business person before formulating a response.

The second issue in this question is how to deal with this issue internationally. Would the United States impose its law on patents held in foreign countries? Would the United States require that foreign countries cater their development process to match ours? Students should be encouraged to take the role of the United States trade negotiator who believes in U.S. control and the foreign business producer who believes in sovereignty of patents. Give creative statements to support both positions.

2. In this question the student is asked to formulate a position that reaches toward the core of a huge policy trade issue. What is the role of the multinational corporation in America's future and how should they be regulated? Most students will probably agree that the United States multinational is not the same as a foreign international firm and is in most cases still primarily a U.S. based firm. Foreign multinationals that supply jobs in the United States are valuable contributors to the United States economy. Therefore, those that argue the multinationals are bad and uncontrollable cannot have it both ways.

they cannot condemn the multinationals but still enjoy the economic benefits of jobs gained (even though they will look carefully at jobs lost).

3. This question is somewhat similar to Discussion Question #2 above. As jobs move across borders, they are not always blue collar jobs. In fact, many of those jobs are white collar jobs (especially in high tech areas or in information technology). Wage rates and productivity are always issues. However, as our world becomes more sophisticated and smaller (in terms of communication and technology), jobs will move to where they can be done the cheapest, with the highest quality, and with speed. The trick is to be the country that will attract those jobs. Students should be encouraged to discuss how the United States can position itself to attract white collar work from overseas.

The second issue in this question deals with the ability to control information across borders. As indicated in the chapter, this is a new frontier and at present control of information flow is very primitive. There is even the question as to whether control should even be allowed. Students should be encouraged to discuss under what circumstances control should be encouraged and discouraged.

4. This question asks students to take a stance on the advisability of trading blocs. Considerations in taking a pro or con position would include the benefits of trading blocs, tariff reduction, trade barriers erected, efficiencies gained, prohibitions of competition, relationship of governments and multinationals, and future trends. By examining each of these areas within the context of the material presented in the chapter, the students should be able to formulate an opinion of trading blocs. It might be useful to break the class into teams and assign different roles to them, ask them to defend their position, and rebut the other teams position.

5. It would appear based on data presented in this question that total capital outflows from the United States are beginning to balance and do reflect a regionalization of the world economy. It would also indicate that some regions are gaining in importance (as opposed to their past performance) and are receiving increased attention in the world economy. The data could also be interpreted to mean that trading relationships are strengthening and new alliances are being formed. New regional associations such as NAFTA might result from the increased attention to certain markets. As the European Union achieves a common currency, new effects are sure to be felt.

STUDENT PROJECTS and INTERNET FOCUS

1. Go to the library and research the subject of trading blocs. Find a current article on one of the numerous trading blocs around the world (these trading blocs could also include new trade alliances or treaties such as NAFTA). Determine from the article who the members are, what are the strengths and weaknesses of the trading bloc, and what is the overall purpose of the trading bloc. You may also use other references to aid you in your discovery process. Report your findings.

2. Investigate the issue of intellectual property rights as applied to the international environment. Pick any area (such as movies, books, software, inventions, or patents) and demonstrate the problems that are currently occurring, what is being done to curtail the abuses, who the chief abusers are, and the amount of money that is in question. Present your own ideas for stopping intellectual property rights abuse in the international market place. Have you ever been a member of copying or duplication process? Explain how? What would you do to stop yourself?

INSTRUCTOR'S NOTE: The following projects require the students to both use and understand the Internet. If students do not understand how to use the Internet, explanation should be given before these projects are undertaken. The Web sites provided were current at the time of this writing. However, since Web addresses change frequently, the instructor should re-affirm the site address and the content of the site before making an assignment.

3. Go to the following Web sites and determine which of the following firms would be classified as multinationals. Please explain what information you obtained led you to that conclusion. Remember this appraisal should be based on what you found not what you think (or previously thought).

a. Aetna   (**http://www.aetna.com**)

b. British Telecom   (**http://www.btglobal.com**)

c. Caliber System   (**http://www.calibersys.com**)

d. Fujitsu   (**http://www.fujitsu.com**)

e. U.S. Robotics   (**http://www.ust.com**)

4. Using the Web site for *The Economist* find an article about trade blocs or multinationals and their effect on the world economy. Summarize the material and give a brief overview to the class. The Web site is (**http://www.economist.com**).

5. Go to the Web site for *The U.S. Patent and Trademark Office.* This site will provide information on how the office classifies information, facts about international intellectual property, and publication lists. In addition, there is information on how to protect your intellectual property. Using this information, formulate a strategy for protecting intellectual property (you may choose from a movie, a piece of music, software, or a creative idea or patent). Relate your strategy to the class. The Web site address is (**http://www.uspto.gov**).

CHAPTER 3

FINANCIAL ENVIRONMENT

CHAPTER OBJECTIVES

1. Understand the historical role of the U.S. dollar in trade and international affairs.

2. Review the historical role of the gold standard and its affect on international trading.

3. Understand the interwar years of 1919-1939 as they historically affect trading relationships.

4. Document the development of the current international monetary system's role in international economics.

5. Review the affect of fixed versus floating exchange rates on international policy.

6. Analyze foreign exchange and foreign exchange rates from the perspective of a marketing manager.

7. Review the trends in the balance of payments issue.

CHAPTER OVERVIEW

The international financial environment is constantly changing as a result of income growth, balance of payments position, inflation, exchange rate fluctuations, and unpredictable political events in various countries. This chapter analyzes and examines international trade in monetary terms.

Given the drastic realignment in recent years of exchange rates of major currencies, the current international monetary system may well be in for a major change. The affect of the International Monetary Fund and the World Bank is analyzed within this context. It has been found that a change in a country's balance of payments position is an immediate precursor to its currency rate fluctuation and subsequent instability in the international financial market.

Thanks to the huge domestic economy and the international transaction currency role of the U.S. dollar, many U.S. companies have been shielded from the changes in the international financial market during much of the postwar era. However, as the United States economy increasingly depends more and more on international trade and investment for its livelihood, few companies can ignore changes and trends that are

28

occurring. Other countries and companies (such as those in Japan and Europe), seem better prepared (because of past experiences) to deal with monetary fluctuations.

International marketers should be aware of the immediate consequences of exchange rate fluctuations on pricing. Pricing is a central part of international competition. This chapter explores some of the tools that are available for predicting changes in price and the effects of those pricing changes.

CHAPTER OUTLINE

A. Historical Role of the U.S. Dollar

1. All international transactions must take place within the context of an international monetary system, or a set of procedures for making and receiving international payments.
2. Each country has its own currency via which it expresses the value of its products.
   a. Given the absence of a universal currency, countries develop a system which allows for the transfer of purchase power between countries with different national currencies.
   b. This is accomplished through foreign exchange markets.
3. Periodically, countries have to review the status of their economic relations with the rest of the world.
   a. In the post World War II period, a number of institutions came into existence to monitor and assist countries as necessary in keeping their international financial commitments.
   b. The dollar has become the common denominator in world trade (valued at $35 per ounce of gold).
   c. Fluctuations in the dollar in the 1970s and 1980s caused U.S. exports to become costlier, and foreign imports to become cheaper, resulting in an adverse trade balance.

*****Use Review Question #1 Here*****

B. The Gold Standard

1. The Gold Standard stretched from the 1880s to 1914.
   a. Under the Gold Standard, the major nations of the world issued paper money backed by gold.
   b. Each country declared a par value for its currency in terms of this metal.
2. The gold standard had three major features:
   a. It established a system of fixed exchange rates between participating countries.
   b. The gold standard limited the rate of growth in a country's money supply.
   c. Gold served as an automatic adjustment tool for countries experiencing Balance of Payment problems.

3. World War I effectively closed the Gold Standard.
    a. The gold supply stopped growing.
    b. The gold supply could not keep pace with the demands and needs of commerce.
4. This system effectively limited government's ability to decide their own independent monetary policies.

C. The Interwar Years of 1919-1939

1. The 1920s and 1930s were a tumultuous period for the international monetary system.
    a. The British Pound could no longer be counted on as a stable currency.
    b. The U.S. Dollar suffered on the Gold Standard up through the Great Depression.
2. The effect of the turmoil was for countries to adopt isolationist and protectionist policies.
    a. Markets were closed to foreign producers.
    b. Currency devaluations were common.
3. By the early days of World War II, international trade had ground to a halt.

D. Development of Today's International Monetary System

1. *The Bretton Woods Conference.*
    a. There was a strong desire to avoid the mistakes (punishing the losers) following World War I.
    b. There was a desire to bring about a new era of economic prosperity following World War II.
    c. Recommendations at the Bretton Woods Conference were:
        1). Each nation should be at liberty to use macroeconomic policies for full employment--do not return to the Gold Standard.
        2). Free floating exchange rates could not work.
        3). A monetary system was needed that would recognize that exchange rates were both a national and international concern.
    d. The Bretton Woods conference provided an adjustable peg.
        1). Currencies were to establish par values in terms of gold, but there was to be little if any convertibility of the currencies for gold.
        2). Central banks were to intervene if problems developed.
    e. Under the recommended system, a country could defend its system by purchase or sell its currency to achieve stability.
    f. The International Monetary Fund (IMF) was established at the conference to oversee the system.
        1). Adjustments beyond 10% required IMF approval.
        2). The United States first experienced problems with this system in the 1960s.
        3). Dealing in gold and U.S. Dollars became real problems and contributed to payments problems and devaluations with the United States.
        4). Gold flowed out of the United States at an alarming rate.

5). Richard Nixon suspended the convertibility to gold in 1971 and effectively ended Bretton Woods.

2. ***The International Monetary Fund.***
   a. The purposes of the IMF were defined in the following terms:
      1). To promote international monetary cooperation.
      2). To facilitate expansion and balanced growth of international trade.
      3). To promote exchange stability.
      4). To assist in the establishment of a multilateral system of payments in respect to current transactions. To reduce exchange restrictions.
      5). To give confidence to members by making the general resources of the fund available on a temporary basis.
      6). To shorten the duration and lessen the degree of disequilibrium in the international balance of payments to members.
   b. As time passed it became evident that the resources of the IMF were inadequate to solve the world's problems.
      1). The fund created special drawing rights (SDRs) in 1969.
      2). These were designed to aid in providing liquidity to support growing world trade.
      3). These privileges may be used for spot transactions.
      4). The IMF makes a unique contribution to the stability of the world's financial markets.

3. ***The International Bank for Reconstruction and Development.***
   a. Another creation of the Bretton Woods Conference was the International Bank for Reconstruction and Development (more popularly known as the World Bank).
   b. This entity was intended to aid in postwar reconstruction and infrastructure development.
   c. Recently, it has become involved in resolving debt problems.

4. ***The Twin Crises: Oil Prices and Foreign Debt.***
   a. Oil prices has produced huge inflation.
   b. These crises have resulted in a recycling of dollars from the developing nations back to them (with the addition of hefty interest and finance charges).

*****Use Review Question #4 Here*****

E. Fixed vs. Floating Exchange Rates

1. Since the 1970s all major nations have had floating exchange rates. Problems that have materialized include:
   a. Balance of payments has not occurred (in fact they have worsened).
   b. Currency speculation has increased.
   c. Exchange rate imbalances have increased.
   d. Autonomy in economic and monetary policy has not been maintained.
2. There are two kinds of currency float:

a. The free (clean) float is the closest approximation to perfect competition, because there is no government intervention and because billions of units of currency are being traded by buyers and sellers.
b. A managed float allows for a limited amount of government intervention to soften sudden swings in value of a currency.
   3. Despite occasional problems and sharp changes in the relative values of currencies, the floating rates system has not collapsed.

*****Use Exhibit 3-1 Here; Use Review Question #3 and Review Question #5 Here*****

   4. *Currency Blocs.*
a. The major trading countries of the world (the U.S., Britain, Japan, etc.) float their currency value against one another and against the European Currency Unit (ECU). Developing nations are also tied to this system.
b. There seem to be three major currency blocs today:
      1). The U.S. dollar.
      2). The Japanese yen.
      3). The German mark.

*****Use Review Question #2 and Review Question #6 Here; Use Discussion Question #4 and Discussion Question #6 Here*****

F. **Foreign Exchange and Exchange Rates**

   1. Foreign exchange refers to the exchange of one country's money for that of another country.
   2. *Purchasing Power Parity.*
a. This theory states that the exchange rate between the currencies of two countries is in equilibrium when it equates the prices of a basket of goods and services in both countries (or the value of the currency is determined by what it can buy).
b. The McDonald's Big Mac hamburger index (equates currencies around the world) is shown in Exhibit 3-2.

*****Use Exhibit 3-2 Here; Use Review Question #7 Here; Use Discussion Question #3 Here*****

   3. *Forecasting Exchange Rate Fluctuation.*
a. Actual exchange rates can be very different from the expected rates.

*****Use Exhibit 3-3 Here*****

b. Factors that influence the value of a floating currency include:
      1). The nation's inflation rate relative to its trading partners.

2). The nation's balance of payments situation.

3). World political events.

c. Exchange rate fluctuations have an enormous direct impact on the bottom line for the company--profitability.

4. ***Coping with Exchange Rate Fluctuations.***

    a. For many countries, foreign currency must be obtained (bought) before the companies of that country can by international products (since the selling company would like to have payment in their currency). This can make many products very expensive if the country's currency is not worth much with respect to the currency of the selling company.

    b. In order to solve this disadvantage problem, some countries implement exchange controls.

    c. Currencies can appreciate or depreciate relative to other currencies.

    d. Many countries attempt to maintain a lower value for their currency in order to encourage exports.

    e. Directly related to the issue of floating currency is the concept of transaction gain or loss on the import or export of merchandise.

5. **Spot vs. Forward Foreign Exchange.**

    a. If payment on a transaction is to be made immediately, the purchaser has no choice other than to buy foreign exchange on the spot (or current) market.

    b. If there is enough time for a forward date, the purchaser has the option of buying foreign exchange on the forward market.

    c. Many multinational companies actively buy and sell the foreign currencies of the countries in which they do business.

    d. Forward currency markets exist for the strongest currencies.

*****Use Review Question #8 Here******

6. **Exchange Rate Pass-Through.**

    a. Dramatic swings in the value of the dollar are common.

    b. Some companies (countries) use this to their advantage (particularly the Japanese).

    c. Target exchange rates are used. See the Japanese example below.

       1). A particularly unfavorable exchange rate (hypothetically appreciated yen environment) is used for a costing strategy in order to make sure that they will not be adversely affected should the yen appreciate.

    d. The extent to which a foreign company changes dollar prices of its products in the U.S. market as a result of exchange rate fluctuations is called exchange rate pass-through.

*****Use Review Question #9 Here*****

G. Balance of Payments

1. The balance of payments of a nation summarizes all the transactions which have taken place between its residents and the residents of other countries over a specified time period.
2. The transactions are recorded in:
   a. The current account.
   b. The capital account.
   c. The official reserves.
3. The balance of payments record is made on the basis of debits and credits, similar to those in business accounting.
   a. Exports are credits.
   b. Imports are debits.
4. Double entry accounting is used. Therefore, balance must be maintained.
5. The balance of payments in goods account (trade balance) shows trade in currently produced goods as well as unilateral transfers of merchandise. This is an indicator of the health of a country's international trade position.
6. The balance of payments in current account (current account balance) shows trade in currently produced goods and services, as well as unilateral transfers of merchandise.
7. The balance of payments in capital account (capital account) summarizes financial transactions and is divided into two sections--short and long capital accounts.
8. Direct investments are those investments in enterprises or properties that are effectively controlled by residents of another country.
   a. Portfolio investment includes all long term investments that do not give the investors effective control over the investment.

*****Use Review Question #10 Here*****

9. Three important balances are:
   a. Balance of the merchandise trade account.
   b. The current account.
   c. The basic balance.

*****Use Global Perspective 3-1 "Balance of Payments and Competitiveness of a Nation" Here; Use Discussion Question #1 Here*****

10. *The Internal and External Adjustments.*
    a. According to the theory of international trade and balance of payments, a surplus or a deficit in a country's basic balance should be self-correcting.
       1). This is accomplished through the internal and external market adjustments.
       2). The internal market adjustment refers to the movement of prices and incomes in a country.
       3). The external market adjustment concerns exchange rates or a nation's currency and its value with respect to the currencies of other nations.

b. Adjustments are a complicated issue and often topics of discussion in international trade conferences between nations.

*****Use Discussion Question #2 Here*****

REVIEW QUESTIONS

INSTRUCTOR'S NOTE: The following chapter review questions are meant to challenge the student to think about material presented in the chapter and formulate a creative answer to the review question. Many of the answers require judgments rather than specific line-by-line quotation of facts. The answers provided are meant to provide stimulation of creative answers.

1. How did the U.S. dollar become the international transaction currency in the post World War II era?

Because of the strength of the military, economic, political, and fiscal power of the United States following World War II, the United States agreed to exchange the dollar at a rate of $35 per ounce of gold. With the value of the dollar stabilized, countries could deal in dollars without being constrained by currency fluctuations. Thus, the dollar became the common denominator in world trade.

2. Which international currency or currencies are likely to assume increasingly a role of the international transaction currency in international trade? Why?

Today, the global economy is increasingly dominated by three major currency blocs. The U.S. dollar, the Japanese yen, and the German mark each represent their "spheres of influence" on the currencies of other currencies in the respective regions. Each of these currencies have become the standard within their regions of the world (and thereby have also become international trading currencies).

3. Why is a fixed exchange rate regime that promotes the stability of the currency value inherently unstable?

The real rate of stability of currency value depends on the stability of economic and financial conditions. History has shown that these variables fluctuate. Government intervention is always a reality, therefore, instability must be managed if exchange rates are to be stable.

4. Discuss the primary roles of International Monetary Fund and World Bank.

The International Monetary Fund (IMF) was created at Bretton Woods to oversee the newly created monetary system. The IMF was a specialized agency within the United Nations established to promote international monetary cooperation and to facilitate the expansion of trade, and in turn to contribute to increased employment and improved conditions in all member countries.

Another creation of the Bretton Woods conference was the International Bank for Reconstruction and Development, known as the World Bank. The World Bank (as different from the IMF) was initially intended for the financing of postwar reconstruction and development and later for infrastructure building projects in the developing world. More recently, the Bank has begun to participate actively with the IMF to resolve debt problems of the developing world and may also play a major role in bringing a market economy to the former members of the Eastern bloc.

5. What is managed float?

A managed float allows for a limited amount of government intervention to soften sudden swings in value of a currency. If a nation's currency enters into a rapid ascent or decline, that nation's central bank may wish to sell or buy that currency on the open market in a countervailing movement to offset the prevailing market tendency. This is for the purpose of maintaining an orderly, less volatile foreign exchange market.

6. How does a currency bloc help a multinational company's global operations?

The currency bloc helps a multinational within a regional area because a particular currency will be pegged as the currency to trade in and some degree of stability will occur. The currency bloc medium (a particular currency) will probably be more stable than the currency of any particular country (especially if it is a developing country). The currency bloc phenomenon encourages trade within a particular region.

7. Using the purchasing power parity argument, estimate whether the U.S. dollar is overvalued or undervalued vis-à-vis the German Mark, the French franc, and the Japanese yen.

To answer this question, the students should use the formula:

$$Rt = R0 * \frac{(1+ \text{Infl Ger})}{(1+ \text{Infl US})}$$

where

R= the exchange rate quoted in DM/$,
Infl= the inflation rate,
t= time period.

Use Exhibit 3-2 for an interesting example comparison.

8. Describe in your own words how the knowledge of spot and forward exchange rate market helps international marketers.

In order to answer this question, students should refer to the definitional material in the chapter. A summary of this material is presented below.

If payment on a transaction is to be made immediately, the purchaser has no choice other than to buy foreign exchange on the spot (or current) market, for immediate delivery. However, if payment is to be made at some future date, the purchaser has the option of buying foreign exchange on the spot market or on the forward market, for delivery at some future date. The advantage of the forward market is that the buyer can lock in an exchange rate and avoid the risk of currency fluctuations; this is called hedging, or protecting oneself against potential loss.

9. Why is the exchange rate pass-through usually less than perfect (i.e., less than 100%)?

The extent to which a foreign company changes dollar prices of its products in the U.S. market as a result of exchange rate fluctuations is called exchange rate pass-through. It is usually less than perfect because it requires an estimate of the average increase with respect to dollar prices (with respect to the currency of the trading country or company).

10. Define the four types of balance of payments measures.

a. The balance of payments in goods account (trade balance, for short) shows trade in currently produced goods as well as unilateral transfers (private gifts) of merchandise.

b. The balance of payments in current account (current account balance) shows trade in currently produced goods and services, as well as unilateral transfers (private gifts and foreign aid) of merchandise.

c. The balance of payments in capital account (capital account) summarizes financial transactions and is divided into two sections, short and long capital accounts.

d. Subaccounts include direct investments and portfolio investment. Direct investments are those investments in enterprises or properties that are effectively controlled by residents of another country. Portfolio investment includes all long term investments that do not give the investors effective control over the investments.

DISCUSSION QUESTIONS

INSTRUCTOR'S NOTE: Discussion Questions are found at the end of each chapter in the text. These questions (in many cases) are too lengthy to repeat in this manual. Suggestions for answering and discussing the questions are presented in this section. Many of the questions require student opinion and judgment.

1. The balance of payments of a nation summarizes all the transactions which have taken place between its residents and the residents of other countries over a specified time period, usually a month, quarter or year. Countries seek to export but they also have to import to maintain good trade relationships and attract investment. Balance helps to support commercial activity, keep down interest rates and inflation, and maintain a growing domestic economy. Measurements can be difficult because they usually only account for trade between countries rather than trade between subsidiaries.

2. Reasons for the Japanese preferring to trade (and establish contracts) in dollars only could be:

a. A basic belief in the soundness of the dollar.
b. Its wide acceptance.
c. Its managed fiscal nature (primarily by the Federal Reserve).
d. It does not fluctuate as wildly as other currencies (such as the Yen).
e. It seems to be the currency that most trust in.

3. Some considerations that might draw suspicions on the Big Mac Index are:

a. The question of value (all may not value the Big Mac).
b. It does not explain big ticket items.
c. It does not deal with services.
d. It does not account for subsidiary trading.
e. It may not really closely monitor value and overvalue.

4. The question of investing in Brazil is a question of confidence. Brazil is the midst of a building boom in infrastructure and trade. Inflation is bound to occur. If the companies deal primarily in dollars (given relative stability in the exchange rate) they should find that their investment is protected. However, foreign investment is always risky. The reward, however, can be huge profits and large market share.

5. In the case mentioned, the marketing manager would probably look at the situation differently. In one case, the Mexican Peso must be carefully considered in the future of the marketing effort. In the other case, the dollar will probably be the medium of exchange and the fluctuations of the peso may not so seriously affect the company's performance. Having manufacturing locations in Mexico or in the United States will obviously be an important consideration.

STUDENT PROJECTS and INTERNET FOCUS

1. Go to the library. Find an article that discusses the United States balance of payment problems. Read and abstract the article. Give a short report to the class on your findings. From your reading develop an opinion on the difficulties faced by the United States with respect to the balance of payments. What strategies can you recommend for correcting the problem?

2. Pick a product of your choice. Illustrate the difficulties faced by the international marketer with respect to fluctuating exchange rates. Using the rationale presented in your chapter, show how rates between currencies might adversely affect the sale of your product. The currencies that you should use for your illustration should include (a) the Mexican Peso, (b) the British pound, (c) the Japanese yen, and (d) the German mark. What strategies might you employ to prevent fluctuating currencies from affecting the sale of your product? Hint: You might use the Big Mac chart as a format for constructing your example (See Exhibit 3-2).

INSTRUCTOR'S NOTE: The following projects require the students to both use and understand the Internet. If students do not understand how to use the Internet, explanation should be given before these projects are undertaken. The Web sites provided were current at the time of this writing. However, since Web addresses change frequently, the instructor should re-affirm the site addresses and the content of the site before making an assignment.

3. Go to *Welcome to the International Monetary Fund (IMF)* site at (**http://www.imf.org**). This site provides country reports, working papers, and information on briefings and happenings at the IMF. Pick one of these reports and abstract the data. Give a brief report to the class from your abstract.

4. An interesting Web site to visit is *The World Bank* Web site. The Web site address is (**http://www.worldbank.com**). Go to the site and find the latest news about happenings at the World Bank. Pick a news story and abstract the material. Give a brief report to the class concerning the events from your abstracted article.

5. Two interesting Web sites to visit are the *GNN/Koblas Currency Converter* and the *Daily Foreign Exchange Converter.* Go to either (or both) of these sites and convert the U.S. dollar to seven (7) different currencies. Try to pick at least one currency from all the major continents or trading bloc areas. After having gone through this process, what did you learn? Bring list of conversions to class for discussion. The Web addresses are as follows:

a. GNN/Koblas Currency Converter   (**http://bin.gnn.com/cgi-bin/gnn/currency**)

b. Daily Foreign Exchange Converter   (**gopher:caticsuf.csufresno.edu**)

CHAPTER 4

GLOBAL CULTURAL ENVIRONMENT

CHAPTER OBJECTIVES

1. Be able to define culture.

2. Be able to identify the elements and unique aspects of culture.

3. Be able to compare cultures around the world by examining similarities and differences.

4. Demonstrate how adapting to cultures is an art that should be learned in business.

5. Understand the primary points of cross-cultural negotiations.

CHAPTER OVERVIEW

Global marketing does not operate in a bubble. To be able to successful market in a dynamic world environment, the firm must understand that culture is an intrinsic part of the global community. The successful firm must be able to identify, appreciate, and adapt to the cultural diversity present in most foreign markets. This diversity should be looked upon as being the cornerstone of opportunity rather than an anchor of weakness. The challenge is, however, great. Avoiding cultural mishaps is a skill that needs to be acquired by the firm that seeks expansion through the international marketplace.

One of the best ways to learn a foreign culture and its impact on the marketing of goods in that environment is to be culturally sensitive. "Do as the Romans do" means exactly what is says. However, the world environment with respect to culture is constantly changing because of the merging of ideologies and the spread of international trade. For example, the face of Europe is changing because of the growth of the European Union and the fall of communism in eastern Europe.

In this chapter culture is defined. In addition, several elements of culture along with cultural differences are presented. The reader will note several procedures for making cultural adjustment and how to interface so that cross-cultural negotiations can take place. The rule of thumb with respect to culture is to be empathetic--see the world from someone else's perspective.

CHAPTER OUTLINE

A. Introduction

1. Buyer behavior and consumer needs are largely driven by cultural norms.
   a. Global business means dealing with consumers, strategic partners, distributors and competitors with different cultural mindsets.
   b. Foreign cultures are intrigue.
2. From a global marketing perspective, the cultural environment matters for two main reasons:
   a. Cultural forces are a major factor in shaping a company's global marketing mix program.
   b. Cultural analysis oftentimes pinpoints market opportunities.

*****Use Global Perspective 4-1 "Selling U.S.-Style Fast Food in Asia" Here*****

3. Consider the central role of culture in consumer behavior in the marketplace.
4. Consumption processes (within a given culture) can be described by the sequence of four stages:
   a. Access.
   b. Buying behavior.
   c. Consumption characteristics.
   d. Disposal.

*****Use Exhibit 4-1 Here*****

B. Defining Culture

1. There are numerous definitions of culture.
2. In this text, culture (in a business setting) is defined as being a learned, shared, compelling, interrelated set of symbols whose meanings provide a set of orientations for members of society. These orientations, taken together, provide solutions to problems that all societies must solve if they are to remain viable.
3. Common elements to all definitions include:
   a. Learned by people.
   b. Interrelated.
   c. Shared by individuals.
4. Cultures may be defined by national borders.
   a. Most nations contain subcultures.
   b. These subcultures can be linguistic or religious.

C. Elements Of Culture

1. *Material Life.*

a. Material life refers primarily to the technologies that are used to produce, distribute and consume goods and services within society.

b. These differences partially explain differences in demand for many consumption goods.

c. To bridge material environment differences, marketers are often forced to adapt their product offerings.

d. Technology gaps also affect investment decisions.

2. *Language.*

a. Language (because it is used to communicate and to interpret the environment) is often described as the most important element that sets human beings apart from animals.

b. Two facets of language have a bearing on marketers:

   1). The use of language as a communication tool within cultures.

   2). The huge diversity of languages across and, often, within, national boundaries.

c. Language can be spoken or silent (non-verbal gestures).

d. Language is often described as being a mirror of a culture.

e. Meanings and expressions can differ widely across the language spectrum.

f. Language blunders are embarrassing and often unnecessary.

*****Use Review Question #1 Here*****

3. *Social Interactions.*

a. Social interplay refers to the manner in which members of society relate to one another.

   1). The most critical expression of this type is kinship.

   2). In Western countries, the nuclear family (parents and children) form the basis of kinship.

   3). In other countries, the extended family is just as important.

b. Countries vary in decision-making authority (the role of males and females in the family purchase process).

*****Use Exhibit 4-2 Here; Use Discussion Question #3 Here*****

c. Another important form of social interactions are the individual's reference groups (the set of people to which an individual looks for guidance in their values and attitudes). Types include:

   1). Membership--groups one belongs to.

   2). Anticipatory--groupings of which one would like to be a part of.

   3). Dissociative--groups the individual does not want to be a part of.

d. Reference groups are especially influential for consumer products that are socially visible.

*****Use Review Question #2 Here*****

4. *Religion.*
   a. To appreciate people's buying motives, customs and practices, awareness and understanding of their religion is often critical.
   b. Religion refers to a community's set of beliefs that relate to a reality that cannot be verified empirically.

*****Use Exhibit 4-3 Here; Use Discussion Question #5 Here*****

   c. Religious taboos often force companies to adapt their marketing mix program.

*****Use Global Perspective 4-2 "The Golden Arches in India--No Pork, No Beef" Here*****

   d. The role of women in society is sometimes largely driven by the local religion.
   e. Religious norms influence advertising campaigns.
5. **Education.**
   a. Education is one of the major vehicles to channel culture form one generation to another. Primary considerations are:
      1). The level of education.
      2). The quality of education.
   b. One powerful indicator of the education level in a country is the literacy rate.
   c. Education factors affect the marketers use of labels, print ads, and survey research.

*****Use Exhibit 4-4 Here*****

6. *Value Systems.*
   a. Value systems shape people's norms and standards.
   b. These norms influence people's attitudes towards objects and behavioral codes.
   c. Value systems are deeply rooted and vary widely across cultures.
      1). Monochronic cultures do one thing at a time.
      2). Polychronic cultures do more than one thing at a time.
   d. A culture's attitude toward change is important. Suggestions to be used for resistance to change include:
      1). Identify roadblocks towards change.
      2). Determine which cultural hurdles can be met.
      3). Test and demonstrate the innovation's effectiveness in the host culture.
      4). Seek out those values that can be used to back up the proposed innovation.
   e. Cultural norms can dictate selling approaches.

*****Use Review Question #3 Here; Use Discussion Questions #1 and #2 Here*****

D. **Cross-Cultural Comparisons**

1. *High- versus Low-Context Cultures.*
   a. Cultural complexity refers to the way messages are communicated within a society.
   b. A high-content culture rests heavily on contextual cues (what is left unsaid is often as important as what is said). Japan is an example.
   c. A low-context culture put most emphasis on the written or spoken word. The United States is an example.
   d. The most noticeable differences occur in relation to the use of advertising and business relationships.

*****Use Review Questions #4 and #6 Here*****

2. *Cultural Homogeneity.*
   a. Homophilous cultures--people share the same beliefs, speak the same language, and practice the same religion.
   b. Heterophilous cultures--countries with a fair amount of differentiation.
   c. Differences in cultural homogeneity underlie differences in adoption rates for new products or services.
      1). There is strong evidence that new products diffuse more rapidly in homogeneous countries.
3. *Hofstede's Classification Scheme.*
   a. Power distance--refers to the degree of inequality among people that is viewed as being equitable.
   b. Uncertainty avoidance--the extent to which people in a given culture prefer structured situations with clear rules over unstructured ones.
   c. Individualism--describes the degree to which people prefer to act as individuals rather than group members ("me" versus "we" societies).
   d. Masculinity--considers the importance of "male" values as opposed to "female" values.
   e. Long-termism--the difference between societies that have a long-term orientation versus a short-term orientation.

*****Use Exhibit 4-5 (a) and (b) Here; Use Review Question #5 Here; Use Discussion Question #4 Here*****

E. **Adapting to Foreign Cultures**

1. To function in the global marketplace, companies need to become sensitive to cultural biases that influence thinking, behavior, and decision-making.
2. Lack of cultural sensitivity takes many forms.
   a. Cultural stereotypes.
   b. Cultural blunders.
   c. Cultural misassessments.
   d. Self-reference criterion--people's unconscious tendency to resort to their own

cultural experience and value systems to interpret a given business situation.

3. A four step mechanism for dealing with cultural differences includes:
   a. Define the business problem or goal in terms of your own cultural traits, customs or values.
   b. Define the business problem or goal in terms of the host culture's traits, customs or values.
   c. Isolate the SRC influence in the problem and examine it scrupulously to see how
      it interferes with the business problem.
   d. Redefine the business problem, but this time without the SRC influence, and solve for the "optimal" business goal situation.
4. Avoid ethnocentrism--the believe that one's culture is superior to another.

*****Use Exhibit 4-6 Here*****

5. Techniques that can be used to prepare managers for dealing with international situations and cultural differences include:
   a. Language training.
   b. Humility.
   c. Briefings on values, customs, and attitudes.

*****Use the Culturgram found in the Appendix to this chapter Here*****

F. Cross-Cultural Negotiations

1. Conducting successful cross-cultural negotiations is a key ingredient for many international business transactions.
2. *Stages of Negotiation Process.*
   a. Non-task surroundings.
   b. Task-related information exchange.
   c. Persuasion.
   d. Concessions and agreement.
3. *Cross-Cultural Negotiation Strategies.*

*****Use Exhibit 4-7 Here*****

   a. Employ an agent or advisor.
   b. Involve a mediator.
   c. Induce the counterpart to follow one's own negotiation script.
   d. Adapt to counterpart's negotiation script.
   e. Coordinate adjustment of both parties.
   f. Embrace the counterpart's script.
   g. Improvise an approach.
   h. Effect symphony.

4. To pick a strategy, the following steps ought to be considered:
   a. Reflect on your culture's negotiation practices.
   b. Learn the negotiation script common in the counterpart's culture.
   c. Consider the relationship and contextual cues.
   d. Predict or influence the counterpart's approach.
   e. Choosing a strategy.

REVIEW QUESTIONS

INSTRUCTOR'S NOTE: The following chapter review questions are meant to challenge the student to think about material presented in the chapter and formulate a creative answer to the review questions. Many of the answers require judgments rather than specific line-by-line quotation of facts. The answers provided are meant to provide stimulation of creative answers.

1. How does language complicate the tasks of global marketers?

The huge diversity of languages creates a headache to multinational companies. Language is often described as a mirror of a culture. Differences exist across and within borders. Countries with many languages (such as India) present unique problems.

Even within the same language, meanings and expressions vary a great deal between countries that share the language (for example: the United States and Britain). Language blunders are most often seen on product labels and in advertising slogans.

2. Describe the importance of reference groups in international marketing.

An important form of social interaction is an individual's reference group. Reference groups are the set of people to which an individual looks to for guidance in his/her values and attitudes. As such, reference groups have an enormous impact on people's consumption behavior patterns. Knowledge on reference group patterns can provide an input in formulating product positioning strategies and devising advertising campaigns. Group conformity pressure must also be considered.

3. What can marketers do to launch new products in countries that tend to be resistant towards change?

According to Terspstra and David some guidelines for reducing the hostility towards change might include:

a). Identify roadblocks towards change.
b). Determine which cultural hurdles can be met.

c). Test and demonstrate the innovation's effectiveness in the host culture.

d). Seek out those values that can be used to back up the proposed innovation.

4. How do high-context cultures differ from low-context ones?

For additional information see Exhibit 4-7. To begin a discussion of this area note that cultural complexity refers to the way messages are communicated within a society. High-context cultures (such as Japan) rely heavily on contextual cues (what is left unsaid is often as important as what is said). While low-context cultures (such as the United States) put more emphasis on the written or spoken word (what is meant is what is said).

5. What are some possible issues in applying Hofstede's classification scheme in a global marketing concept?

Hofstede's scheme is presented as having five components:

   a. Power distance--refers to the degree of inequality among people that is viewed as being equitable.
   b. Uncertainty avoidance--the extent to which people in a given culture prefer structured situations with clear rules over unstructured ones.
   c. Individualism--describes the degree to which people prefer to act as individuals rather than group members ("me" versus "we" societies).
   d. Masculinity--considers the importance of "male" values as opposed to "female" values.
   e. Long-termism--the difference between societies that have a long-term orientation versus a short-term orientation.

Exhibit 4-5 portrays how different countries score on the various dimensions mentioned above. One must be cautious with applying these schemes to global buyer behavior. It is important to bear in mind that the five dimensions and the respective country scores that were derived in Hofstede's work were not determined in a consumption context. Questions have been raised about the validity of the measure.

DISCUSSION QUESTIONS

INSTRUCTOR'S NOTE: Discussion Questions are found at the end of each chapter in the text. These questions (in many cases) are too lengthy to repeat in this manual. Suggestions for answering and discussing the questions are presented in this section. Many of the questions require student opinion and judgment.

1. There is ample evidence that America's youth are world-wide trend setters. However, even though foreign youth may mimic trends from America it does not mean that the interpretation is exact. This might explain why Gangsta rap music is popular in Malaysia while at the same time family values are stressed within the family units. The beat of the

music (and not the words or the literal meaning of the words) may be what is attracting the youth. Visuals from MTV may also have an impact. The music (derived from urban ghettos) may take on a completely different context in Asia.

2. Many times products face infrastructural road blocks in foreign markets. Ice cream in South East Asia might have difficulties with transportation and storage facilities. The average consumer might also not have individual refrigeration units at their disposal. Ice might be not existent. Storage and transportation facilities might be devoted to more critical food products. A product such as ice cream (while potentially profitable and pleasurefull) might have great difficulties dealing with the more primitive infrastructure found in most South East Asia markets.

3. To answer this question, the students will have to think carefully about what it means to have only one child in a home (especially where children are revered by parents and grandparents alike). Toys, games, theme parks, bicycles and educational lessons might be just a few of the items that might be targeted toward these children. Students should be encouraged to formulate a list of items that might work. Recent popularity of "Beanie Babies" and watches that ask children to take care of an egg illustrate that Asian children have a need to give affection. What other products could capitalize on this value?

4. As students will recall from the text, individualism describes the degree to which people prefer to act as individuals rather than as group members. In societies that are high on individualism the focus is on people's own interests. In collectivist societies the interests of the group take center stage. The concept relates to the views about the "self" that people hold. In individualist societies, people tend to have an independent view of the self. The norm here is to discover and express one's unique attributes. In collectivist societies, an interdependent view of the self prevails where people desire to be connected with other individuals.

Salesforces would have to recognize whether an individual would make an independent decision or would be influenced by the group (or perhaps by consensus within the group if they were acting as a collective body). Incentive schemes in the individualistic culture would revolve around total number of individuals contacted or sold. In a collective culture groups would have to be sold and attitude change might be very important.

5. Companies must honor traditions and religious taboos when attempting to market in foreign countries. The example presented in this question presents an interesting problem for the student. Before answering they should be encouraged to read Exhibit 4-3 (which give information on the Islamic culture). The best simple answer to the problem formulated is to show hair in drawings, in animation, or in symbolism without showing the hair as actually being associated directly with the female. Written language can also be used rather than pictures.

6. To answer this question, students should be reminded that Japan is a high-context society. Therefore, suggestion and images are very important. Identification with a

product in an abstract way is one way of selling a product. By stating that a product bring you "inner peace", might be a superior concept as opposed to stating that it is "larger," "more colorful," or "stronger." A relationship would have to be developed between communicator and receiver in a society such as Japan. Nurturing trust and long-term relationships would be equally as important.

STUDENT PROJECTS and INTERNET FOCUS

1. Go to the library and find examples of consumer magazines from foreign markets. Photocopy (**DO NOT TEAR OUT**) 5 examples of advertisements for consumer products that you feel have been uniquely adapted to the market by the manufacturer of the product. Present a short discussion outlining why you think the adaptation is unique. What aspects of the "Elements of Culture" (as outlined in this chapter) were important?

2. Go to the library and do research on high- and low-context cultures. Pick one culture from each group and briefly describe what you found that places the culture in the high- or low-context category that you choose. What type of marketing practices might be successful in the two countries. Give an example of two products and how they might be marketed differently in the two chosen countries.

INSTRUCTOR'S NOTE: The following projects require the students to both use and understand the Internet. If students do not understand how to use the Internet, explanation should be given before these projects are undertaken. The Web sites provided were current at the time of this writing. However, since Web addresses change frequently, the instructor should re-affirm the site addresses and the content of the site before making an assignment.

3. Go to the following Web sites and determine if the companies are using any of the "Elements of Culture" presented in the text in their marketing efforts. Make a determination of which elements are being used in each case and report your findings to the class with documentation of the usage. Use the addresses provided below:

a). Bavarian Ministry of Economic Affairs   (**http://www.bayern.de**)

b). Casio   (**http://www.casio.com**)

c). Hitachi   (**http://www.hitachi.com**)

d). Zurich-American   (**http://www.zurichamerican.com**)

4. Go to the *Nomura Research Institute* site at (**http://www.nri.co.jp**). This site is ideal for anyone researching Japanese companies. By using the site, find a Japanese company and report on the following:

a). Values and corporate philosophy

b). Products

c). Markets

d). Any relevant culture information.

5. One of the results of the recent peace efforts in the Middle East is a renewed interest in attracting international trade to the region. Using information from the chapter and the chapter Exhibits formulate a working paper on how to deal with the cultural barriers found in the Middle East. Write your paper as if you were a company trying to find a partner or a market to trade in. Israel might be one of your options. If is, go to *Israel Trade and Investment* Web page at (**http://world.std.com/~neicc**) for further information on this region of the Middle East. Remember look for barriers to be overcome.

CHAPTER 5

POLITICAL AND LEGAL ENVIRONMENT

CHAPTER OBJECTIVES

1. Observe how the political environment of international affairs affects local governments.

2. Observe how the political environment of international affairs is related to social pressures and political risk.

3. Understand how international agreements impact business relationships.

4. Determine the extent to which international law and local legal environments affect international marketing and marketing relationships between firms.

5. Review pertinent international business issues that transcend national boundaries.

CHAPTER OVERVIEW

When doing business across national boundaries, international marketers almost always face what is perceived to be political and legal barriers. It is due to the fact that government policies, laws, and actions can be very different from country to country. History has shown that, in most cases, a foreign company has to accept a host country's government policies and laws. Multinational firms have been accused to trying to influence local governments--this is always a risky venture.

Despite various international agreements brought about by such international organizations as WTO, G-7, and COCOM, which collectively strive toward freer and more equitable world trade, every nation is sovereign an maintains its special interests which may occasionally clash with those of the international agreements. When considering entry, the investment environment, or market entry in foreign countries, risks with respect to the political and legal environment need to be assessed. Multinational firms need to be aware of political risks arising from unstable political parties and government structure, changes in government programs, and social pressures and special interest groups in a host country.

While government policies and laws of a country usually affect business transactions involving that country, increased business activities transcending national boundaries have tested the territoriality of some policies and laws of a country. International marketing managers should be aware that domestic protection usually cannot be extended beyond their national boundary.

CHAPTER OUTLINE

A. Political Environment-Individual Governments

1. Government affects almost every aspect of business life in a country.
    a. National politics affects business environments directly, through changes in policies, regulations and laws.
    b. The political stability and mood in a country affect the actions a government will take--actions which may have an important impact on the viability of doing business in the country.

*****Use Review Question #1 Here*****

2. *Home Country vs. Host Country.*
    a. International marketing executives should be concerned about the host government's policies and their possible changes in the future as well as their home government's political climate.
    b. As companies usually do not operate in countries that have been hostile to their home country, many executives tend to take for granted the political environment of the host country in which they currently do business.
        1). Sweeping political changes (such as in Cuba) can change all this.
        2). International marketers must understand the fluid nature of the host country political climate in relation to the home country policies.
3. *Structure of Government.*
    a. *Ideology.* One way to characterize the nature of government is by its socio-economic ideology.
        1). Communism--the government owns and manages all businesses and no private ownership is allowed.
        2). Capitalism--an economic system in which free enterprise is permitted and encouraged along with private ownership.
        3). Socialism--a government that advocates government ownership and control of some industries considered to be critical to the welfare of the nation.
    b. *Political parties.* The number of political parties influences the level of political stability.
        1). Single party-dominate systems tend to be stable over time. Restrictive foreign policies may, however, result.
        2). A dual party system are not divided by ideologies but rather by constituencies.
        3). A multiple party system usually has inconsistent government policy since the government cannot govern without many compromises from some radically different groups. Coalitions must be formed.

4. *Government Policies and Regulations.*

   a. It is the goal of government to promote a country's interests in the international arena for various reasons and objectives.

   b. Reasons for wanting to restrict or block trade include:
      1). National security.
      2). Developing new industries.
      3). Protecting domestic industries.

   c. *Incentives and Government Programs.*
      1). Most countries use government loans, subsidies, or training programs to support export activities and specific domestic industries.
      2). The major objectives of any state government support are:
         a). Job creation.
         b). Improving the state balance of trade.
      3). Export promotion activities generally consist of:
         a). Export service programs.
         b). Market development programs.

   d. *Government Procurement.*
      1). The ultimate government involvement in trade is when the government itself is the customer.
      2). The government engages in commercial operations through the departments and agencies under its control.

   e. *Trade Laws.*
      1). Trade controls can be broken into the following categories:
         a). Economic trade controls.
         b). Political trade controls.
      2). Both tariff and non-tariff barriers work to impede imports which might compete with locally produced goods.

*****Use Exhibit 5-1 Here; Use Review Question #2 Here*****

      3). Embargoes and sanctions are examples of country-based political trade controls.
      4). Export license requirements are product-based trade controls.
      5). International businesses have a number of reasons to be concerned with trade restrictions:
         a). Trade restrictions may completely block a company's ability to export a country.
         b). Retaliation may occur.
         c). They often do not work in the way they were intended.
         d). They may affect other forms of commerce or businesses other than those originally targeted.
         e). Harmful trade wars may result.
      6). *Investment Regulations.*
         a). *Ownership Controls.* Often happens with natural resources or other

sensitive areas.

         b). ***Financial Controls.*** These government-imposed restrictions can serve as strong barriers to foreign direct investments. Many companies find loopholes around these controls.

    7). ***Macroeconomic Policies.***

       a). Companies search internationally for stable growing markets where their profits will not be deteriorated by exchange loss or inflation.

       b). Currency control would fall under this area.

       c). Government fiscal policies also strongly influence macroeconomic conditions.

       d). Historical considerations, social and political pressures, and the interests of particular constituencies will affect the political environment in important ways.

*****Use Review Question #3 Here*****

B. Political Environment-Social Pressures And Political Risk

1. New social pressures can force governments to make new laws or to enforce old policies differently.

*****Use Global Perspective 5-1 "Russia: Election and Foreign Investment" Here; Use Discussion Question #1 Here*****

2. ***Social Pressures and Special Interests.***
   a. Governments respond to pressures from various forces in a country:
      1). The public at large.
      2). Lobbyists for businesses.
      3). The church.
      4). Sometimes personal interests of the members of the government.
   b. Feelings of national interest can act as a deterrent both to international trade and to foreign direct investments. Boycotts can be organized.
   c. Political history is often used in assessing whether to venture into a country.

*****Use Discussion Question #3 Here****

3. ***Managing the Political Environment.***
   a. International managers must manage the political environment in which the international firm operates.
      1). Learn the customs.
      2). Know which facets to monitor.
      3). Know which facets can be manipulated.
      4). Understand the political factors.
      5). Understand the national strategies and goals of the country.
   b. In order to be welcomed in a host country, the foreign firm has to offer some

tangible benefits that the host government desires.

*****Use Exhibit 5-2 Here; Use Discussion Question #2 Here*****

 c. Evaluate environmental factors.

*****Use Exhibit 5-3 and 5-4 Here*****

 d. Political risk services can be used to aid in information gathering.
 e. Three types of risk occur:
  1). Risks associated with changes in company ownership.
  2). Risks associated with changes in company operations.
  3). Risks associated with changes in transfers of goods and money.
 f. Dangers can include expropriation or confiscation of its property and nationalization of its industry.
 g. These risks can be reduced by forming joint ventures with the host countries businesses and industries. However, domestication of the business can be the result.
 h. Privatization's have somewhat been reduced because the offending country will difficulty in getting loans and investment.
 i. Operating regulations can make production unprofitable. Local-content requirements regulations are examples.
 j. Price controls and restrictions of number of foreign employees can also be restrictive.
 k. Shifts in regulations on the transfer of goods and money can also dramatically affect the profitability of operating in a country.
  1). Interest rate restrictions.
  2). Devaluations.
  3). Input restrictions.
  4). Countertrade is a useful alternative around currency movement.

*****Use Review Question 34 Here*****

C. International Agreements

 1. International politics has always been characterized by the predominance of strong ideological links, centered around, and dominated by, a relatively small number of large powers.
 2. Recently the hierarchical structure of world politics has been challenged by:
  a. The true independence of previously colonial countries has led to a much larger set of nations playing relatively independently on the international stage, entering into contracts and relations with new economic partners.
  b. The loosening of the tight bipolarity in world politics, combined with the decline of the United States as the hegemonic state in the free world and the breakup of the Soviet Union that led the communist world, has created an

increased level of ambiguity in geopolitical stability.

3. Domestic politics cannot be isolated from international politics.

4. The international political environment is determined by a dynamic process of the interactions of players each pursuing their own interests and working together for mutual interests. Coordination is required.

5. *G-7 (Group of Seven).*

   a. G-7 is an economic policy coordination group made up of political leaders from Canada, England, France, Germany, Italy, Japan, and the United States.

   b. Discussions revolve around financial and macroeconomic issues that affect the world trade environment.

6. *COCOM (The Coordinating Committee for Multilateral Controls).* This group was formed to stop the flow of technology from the West to the Soviet Union.

   a. Recently the focus has shifted from just technology to hardware and software products.

   b. Two trends are of note:

      1). Technologies which had primarily military applications were increasingly finding more civilian applications.

      2). The trend of economic liberalization in the newly industrializing and developing countries put further competitive pressure on the Western companies to share technologies which were until then privy to the Western world.

   c. COCOM ceased to function after 1994.

D. International Law and Local Legal Environment

1. Marketing managers should understand the legal environment in each country in which they do business and the more general international legal environment.

2. *International Law.* Defined as the body of rules or laws which is binding on states and other international persons in their mutual relations.

   a. Technically, there is no international enforcement body.

3. International law comes from three main sources:

   a. Customs.

   b. International treaties.

   c. National and international court decisions.

*****Use Review Question #5 Here*****

4. *Local Legal Systems and Laws.*

   a. Many legal systems do not follow the common law system followed in the United States.

   b. The international marketing manager must be aware of the laws which will govern all business decisions and contracts.

   c. *Business Practices and the Legal System.*

      1). Choices relating to legal industry constraints, and various regulations on product specifications, promotional activities, and distribution must be understood in order to function efficiently and profitably.

*****Use Exhibit 5-5 Here; Use Review Questions #7 and #8 Here*****

   2). In recent years countries have started raising legal requirements for environmental protection.
   d. *Types of Legal Systems.*
      1). Common law systems--those which base the interpretation of law on prior court rulings.
      2). Code (written) law systems--rely on statutes and codes for the interpretation of law.
      3). Islamic law system--rely on the legal interpretation of the Koran and the words of Mohammed.

*****Use Review Question #6 Here*****

   e. *Examples of Different Laws.*
      1). Criminal law.
      2). Civil law.
      3). Commercial law.
   f. *Cultural Values and Legal Systems.*

*****Use Exhibit 5-6 Here*****

5. *Jurisdiction.* The key to evaluating an international contract is in determining which country's laws will apply, and where any conflicts will be resolved.
   a. *Planning Ahead of Time.* Clearly state the applicable law in the contract.
   b. *Arbitration and Enforcement.*

E. Issues Transcending National Boundaries

1. *ISO 9000.*
   a. In a bid to establish common product standards for quality management, so as to obviate their misuse to hinder exchange of goods and services worldwide, the International Standards Organization (based in Geneva, Switzerland) has instituted a set of process standards.
   b. The European Union has adopted the ISO 9000 standards.
   c. These standards concern not only manufacturing standards but all the activities of the firm.
   d. Adoption of these standards will be a marketing tool of the future.
2. *Intellectual Property Protection.*
   a. Intellectual property refers to "ideas that are translated into tangible products, writings, etc. and that are protected by the state for a limited period of time from unauthorized commercial exploitation.
      1). Broadly, they include patents, trademarks, trade secrets, and copyrights.

b. These ideas generally involve large investments in creative and investigative work to create the product, but fairly low costs of manufacturing.

    1). They can readily be duplicated by imitators.

c. *Patent.* These laws differ widely among countries.

d. *Copyright.* Most computer programming and software fall under this category.

e. *Trademark.* A trademark is a word, symbol, or device that identifies the source of goods and may serve as an index of quality.

*****Use Global Perspective 5-2 "How to Keep Copyright and Trademark Illegally Used Abroad from Entering the United States" Here; Use Discussion Question #4 Here*****

f. *Paris Convention.* Designed to provide "domestic" treatment to protect patent and trademark applications filed in other countries.

g. *Berne Convention.* The oldest and most comprehensive international copyright treaty.

*****Use Exhibit 5-7 Here*****

3. *Antitrust Laws of the United States.*

a. Foundations are laid in Sherman Antitrust Act, the Clayton Act, the Federal Trade Commission Act, and the Robinson-Patman Act.

b. The Sherman Antitrust Act of 1890 forbids every contract, combination or conspiracy to restrain free and open trade.

c. The Clayton Act of 1914 outlawed exclusive dealing and price discrimination.

d. The Federal Trade Commission Act of 1914 created a commission to watch over

    unfair methods of competition in commerce.

e. Though these acts were originally designed to deal with domestic competition and issues, they have now been applied to foreign issues as well.

f. In 1977 the Justice Department issues guidelines to monitor antitrust in international operations.

4. *U.S. Foreign Corrupt Practices Act of 1977.*

a. Among the many corrupt practices that international marketers face, bribery is considered the most endemic and murky aspect of conducting business abroad.

b. The difference between bribery and local custom can be very grey.

c. The FCPA was designed to prohibit the payment of any money or anything of value to a foreign official, foreign political party, or any candidate for foreign political office for purposes of obtaining, retaining, or directing business.

    1). This act does not prohibit so called "small grease payments" to lower level officials or persons.

    2). The act does not prohibit payments to non-officials, however, ethics do come into play.

*****Use Global Perspective 5-3 "Cultural Relativism/Accommodation--Selling

Out?" Here***

    d. From an ethical point of view, major questions to be answered when making payments to individuals that must be answered are:
        1). Does such an act involve unfairness to anyone or violate anyone's rights?
        2). Must such an act be kept secret, such that it cannot be reported as a business expense?
        3). Is such an act truly necessary in order to carry on business?
    e. It is advised that multinational firms maintain good "corporate citizenship" wherever they do business since long-term benefits tend to outweigh the short-term benefit gained from bribes.

*****Use Discussion Question #5 Here*****

REVIEW QUESTIONS

INSTRUCTOR'S NOTE: The following chapter review questions are meant to challenge the student to think about material presented in the chapter and formulate a creative answer to the review questions. Many of the answers require judgments rather than specific line-by-line quotation of facts. The answers provided are meant to provide stimulation of creative answers.

1. Describe with examples the role of governments in promoting national interests pertaining to business activities.

It is recommended that the student examine current news broadcasts or contemporary news or international periodicals as a source for examples to illustrate this answer. Business has been considered an integral part of economic forces. It is in the best interest of a government to promote the interests its businesses. It has been said in a rather comic way (for example) "What's good for business is good for the USA"

Businesses bring in the trade dollars that are necessary to fuel the economy of a country. Some countries have a very active part in this process (such as Japan) by developing a national industrial and trade policy.

2. What are the different types of trade controls which influence international business? What are their intended objectives?

Exhibit 5-1 illustrates a variety of tariff and non-tariff barriers that affect business and trade relationships. Other forms can be seen in investment regulations (such as ownership and financial controls). Students should be encouraged to examine each of the controls mentioned in Exhibit 5-1 with an eye to understanding and effectiveness.

3. How do host country macroeconomics and fiscal policies affect foreign company operations?

A host country is a country in which foreign companies are allowed to do business in accordance with its government policies and within its laws. Therefore, international marketing executives should be concerned about the host government's policies and their possible changes in the future as well as their home government's political climate.

Companies can face hostility, uncertain economic climates, devaluation of currency, confiscation of assets, and labor controls in foreign countries. Political upheavals are the primary source of these difficulties. International marketers must understand the fluidity of political climate in the host country if successful business ventures are to be accomplished.

4. What are the factors that international managers should consider in determining the economic and political risks associated with a country?

As outlined by the chapter, the primary areas to investigate would be the structure of the host government (including the ideology, government policy and regulations, incentives and government programs, government procurement possibilities, trade laws, and investment regulations) and social pressures and political risk.

Exhibits 5-2 and 5-3 portray levels of risk assessment. Analyze each of these exhibits to determine critical risk assessment factors.

5. International law is derived from three sources. What are these three? Compare and contrast them.

International law is derived from three sources--customs, international treaties, and national and international court decisions. Customs are usages or practices which have become so firmly accepted that they become rules of law. Custom-based laws develop slowly. Treaties and international contracts represent formal agreements among nations or firms which set down rules and obligations to govern their mutual relationships. While treaties and contracts are only binding on those who are members of them, if a great number of treaties or contracts share similar stipulations, these may take on the character of a customer-based law or a general rule. When these rulings offer an unusually useful insight into the settlement of international cases, or when they develop into a series of interpretations consistent with other nation's courts, then national rulings may be accepted as international laws. Arbitration may be called for.

6. Briefly describe the various types of local legal systems. How do differences in these legal systems affect international business?

There are three types of local legal systems from which most others are built. Common law systems are those which base the interpretation of law on prior court rulings. Code (written) law systems rely on statutes and codes for the interpretation of the law. Islamic law systems rely on some interpretation of the Koran and the words of Mohammed.

These systems primarily affect international business when the legal system differs between countries. Culture, customs, and interpretation of the law and rulings would all come into play. This is especially true when religious law (such as Islamic Law) is being used to govern contracts. You might refer to the previous chapter to review material on dealing with Islam.

7. Enumerate some of the legal issues that international business managers need to take cognizance of in host countries.

There can be a wide variety of answers to this question. Legal issues (see Exhibit 5-2) can cover monetary, fiscal, trade, foreign investment, income, or sectoral issues. Others can be pricing policies, production practices, labor issues, industry constraints, regulation, product specifications, promotional activities, and distribution issues. New areas that are of concern are intellectual property rights and ethical issues such as bribery.

8. Describe the various types of barriers to international trade and investment.

The barriers to international trade and investment are best summarized by examining Exhibits 5-1 and 5-5. Notice that the barriers described in Exhibit 5-1 are characterized as tariff and non-tariff barriers. These barriers tend to cause other barriers to be erected. The potential areas for barriers to be erected in Exhibit 5-5 show component marketing mix areas that might be affected by restrictions on trade.

DISCUSSION QUESTIONS

INSTRUCTOR'S NOTE: Discussion Questions are found at the end of each chapter in the text. These questions (in many cases) are too lengthy to repeat in this manual. Suggestions for answering and discussing the questions are presented in this section. Many of the questions require student opinion and judgment.

1. The question of dealing with Russia with respect to trade is still new to most Westerners. To answer this question creatively review the material in Global Perspective 5-1 carefully. In formulating an answer, the student should remember that Russia is aggressively pursuing investment and, therefore, is trying to reduce barriers to foreign trade. No contracts are iron-clad, however, local contacts and representation in Russia would certainly be helpful. Knowledge of the order and political system would be essential. In addition, even though the opportunities are great, so are the risks. It would probably be better to remember that long-term relationships may be difficult to achieve at this point.

2. The marketing observer will note that what is permissible in the United States is not necessarily permissible in most of the world. This is especially true in terms of advertising and promotional material. The examples in this question illustrate a few of the problems. One might note, however, that other countries face the same problem when seeking distribution and promotion in the United States. In some countries, the use of nudity in commercials is not restricted (it is in the United States). In Europe, condom commercials have been seen on television for some time. It has only been acceptable in the United States for a brief amount of time. The general rule of thumb becomes "adapt your promotion" or design it from the beginning so it is acceptable world-wide (this is very difficult to do). Try to cite other examples where acceptability might be in question.

3. When attempting to enter into a foreign market where your product or service is thought to be controversial (even by a small number of people), the best process is to integrate one's self into the cultural fabric of the country or local area with a concentrated public relations campaign. Part of this process would be to examine all the issues objectively (from all sides) and then devise a strategy to meet resistance. Many firms allow the local business people to carry the majority of the promotional effort. For example, in the KFC case, KFC could be de-emphasized and the local merchant's role could be emphasized. Or contributions can be made to the community. Sometimes the product or service must be changed and adapted to the environment (McDonald's does not sell "beef-based" hamburgers in India because of religious problems). Local adaptability and community support are always key to the solution of problems such as those mentioned in this question.

4. In order to answer this question the student should familiarize themselves with this issue. On the surface it appears that most companies can do little to protect their intellectual property rights unless pressure is brought on the host government by the company's home government. However, this situation is beginning to change. The idea of making the piracy legitimate (as stated in the case) may not be a bad alternative considering that the company is getting nothing at present. However, many are finding that publicity and court battles are perhaps worthwhile. The recording and movie industry has been at the forefront of this effort. Software manufacturers are also aggressively pursuing pirates.

5. Anti-dumping laws are now at a high attention level for most industrialized countries. This is not just a question or a finger pointed at Japan. Others have been accused of using the practice. Most governments are now carefully watching dumping efforts. However, proving dumping and collecting fines is somewhat difficult and legally expensive. Joint ventures seem to be a solution to the problem.

In the discussion question, the business person must be aware of anti-dumping laws and also realize that Europe is very protective of its markets. Coming up against a huge competitor may be very dangerous strategically. A better course of action might be to seek a joint venture with the future competitor. This might be advisable because of the scarce resources and limits on being able to fight an extended legal battle or react to aggressive price cutting.

STUDENT PROJECTS and INTERNET FOCUS

1. Go to the library and review recent materials on anti-dumping cases. The easiest way to begin your search would be to look for material on the Japanese cases of years past. Once you have found material on anti-dumping policy, write a two-page paper either pro or con for the anti-dumping laws and practices. Remember to look carefully for material that can justify your position on the subject. Present your findings and opinions to the class. This material could also be organized into the form of a debate if your instructor so chooses.

2. Pick a country of your choice and demonstrate what type of legal or political information you would have to collect to be able to advertise a product within the country. You may pick any kind of product for your example and you may consider any media form for promotion. Now that you have decided what type of material you might need to have to be able to promote your product, tell how you would go about finding the information. Be sure to be specific in your suggestions. Report your experiences either in writing or to the class.

INSTRUCTOR'S NOTE: The following projects require the students to both use and understand the Internet. If students do not understand how to use the Internet, explanation should be given before these projects are undertaken. The Web sites provided were current at the time of this writing. However, since Web addresses change frequently, the instructor should re-affirm the site addresses and the content of the site before making an assignment.

3. Visit The World Factbook 1996 (formerly known as the CIA Factbook) at (**http://www.odci.gov/cia/publications/nsolo**) and observe the wealth of information provided by this recently declassified information source. Most country evaluations are about 3-6 pages in length. Pick a country and download the information. Prepare a brief for the class that identifies what you perceive to be the chief facts that a company would want to know if it were to be interested in establishing a new business venture in the country. What can you determine about the competition that you might meet there? What political situations might affect your proposed business venture?

4. Go to the Trademark Law Web site at (**http://www.law.cornell.edu/topics/trademark.html**). At this site you can read the Lanham Act that describes United States trademark law and review recent Supreme Court decisions regarding this phase of intellectual property rights. Find an interesting article,

download it, and describe the issue to the class. Try to find an issue that is related to the international area.

5. Go to the *International Entertainment and Multimedia Law & Business Network.* This site is located at (**http://www.laig.com/law**). This site provides information related to U.S. federal statutes (includes information on international law) for intellectual property, copyrights, patents, and trademarks. The focus is entertainment and media. After exploring the site find an issue that is of interest to you and report your findings to the class.

CHAPTER 6

GLOBAL MARKETING RESEARCH

CHAPTER OBJECTIVES

1. Analyze how research problems are formulated.

2. Understand the value of using secondary sources to conduct global marketing research.

3. Understand the process for conducting primary research in global marketing.

4. Determine how to assess market size.

5. Review new market information technologies.

6. Understand what the marketing manager must know to effectively manage global marketing research.

CHAPTER OVERVIEW

Given the complexity of the global market place, solid marketing research is critical for a host of global marketing decisions. Skipping the research phase in the international marketing decision process can often prove to be a costly mistake. It is clear that good information will facilitate solid decision making and will aid in gaining a competitive advantage over competition. Doing research (whether in the domestic or international market place) is still a question of benefit versus cost.

The complexities of the global market place are stunning. There are hurdles to be overcome in gathering secondary and primary information. The chapter discusses the processes of gathering information as applied to the international marketing effort.

To make cross-country comparisons meaningful, companies need to adequately manage and coordinate their market research projects with a global scope. Locals (including the markets themselves) are very important to this process. For any meaningful decisions to be reached, the locals must not only be a part of but support the conclusions of the research effort. The local support goes a long way to making overstandardized research instruments and techniques more customized and culturally sensitive.

CHAPTER OUTLINE

A. Introduction

1. Market research assists the global marketing manager in two ways:
   a. By making better decisions that recognize cross-country similarities and differences.
   b. By gaining support from the local subsidiaries for proposed marketing decisions.
2. To some degree, the procedures and methods that are followed to conduct global marketing research are close to those used in standard domestic research.
3. The steps to be followed are generally recognized to be:
   a. Define the research problem(s).
   b. Develop a research design.
   c. Determine information needs.
   d. Collect the data (secondary and primary).
   e. Analyze the data and interpret the results.
   f. Report and present the findings of the study.

*****Use Exhibit 6-1 Here*****

4. Major challenges that global marketing researchers face are:
   a. Complexity of research design due to environmental differences.
   b. Lack and inaccuracy of secondary data.
   c. Time and cost requirements to collect primary data.
   d. Coordination of multi-country research efforts.
   e. Difficulty in establishing comparability across multi-country studies.

B. Research Problem Formulation

1. Any research starts off with a precise definition of the research problem(s) to be addressed.
2. Once the nature of the research problem becomes clear, the research problem needs to be translated in specific research questions.

*****Use Global Perspective 6-1 "Consumer Research at Campbell Soup" Here*****

3. Often in an international marketing research effort, the problem formulation process is hindered by the self-reference criterion.
4. A major difficulty in formulating the research problem is the unfamiliarity with the foreign environment.
   a. To reduce uncertainty, some exploratory research at the early stage is often called for.

b. An omnibus survey can often be useful for this purpose.
   1). Though advantageous, there is the disadvantage in that only a limited amount of company relevant information is obtainable through an omnibus.
   2). These surveys should be done with some frequency so that data can be historically tracked.

*****Use Exhibit 6-2 Here; Use Review Question #1 Here; Use Discussion Question #1 Here*****

C. Secondary Global Marketing Research

1. Assessing the information needs is the next step after the research problem definition.
   a. Information that is already available is called secondary research.
   b. Information that must be originally collected is called primary research.
2. *Secondary Data Sources.*
   a. Researchers in developed countries have been spoiled with a vast amount of information at their disposal.
   b. The underdeveloped portion of the world is a different story with respect to available data.
   c. Computerized services (such as Lexis/Nexis) are aiding in the data acquisition effort.

*****Use Exhibit 6-3 Here*****

d. Researchers will first tap information sources within the company itself.
   e. Several companies specialize in nothing but providing information for the international market place.
   f. As firms move from governmental publications to syndicated data, the richness of the information increases enormously. However, cost goes up also.
3. *Problems with Secondary Data Research.*
   a. Sometimes data is nonexistent. If so, data from previous time periods might have to be used.
   b. Primary problems include:
      1). *Accuracy of Data.* Issues can be quality, sophistication, purpose for the data collection, and coverage of all relevant issues.
      2). *Age of Data.*
      3). *Reliability over Time.* Historical patterns, taking into account sudden changes, and variable measures can cause problems.
      4). *Comparability of Data.* Cross-country research often demands a comparison of indicators across countries (which can prove to be very difficult).
         a). Triangulation (using more than one source) might help.
         b). Functional or conceptual equivalence hinders the research effort.

*****Use Review Question #2 Here*****

        5). ***Lumping of Data.*** Grouping of data can cause the researcher many problems.
   c. A checklist can be useful in assessing the quality of data:
        1). When were the data collected? Over what time frame?
        2). How were the data collected?
        3). Have the variables been redefined over time?
        4). Who collected the data?
        5). For what purpose were the data gathered?

D. Primary Global Marketing Research

  1. Since secondary research seldom produces all the answers needed in a global marketing research effort, the next step is to collect primary data specifically for the purpose of the research project.
  2. Data can be collected in several ways:
   a. ***Focus Groups.***
      1). The focus group is a popular method of doing exploratory research.
      2). The focus group is a loosely structured free-flowing discussion among a small group (8-12 people) of target customers facilitated by a professional moderator.
      3). Purposes include:
         a). To generate information to guide the quantitative research projects.
         b). To reveal new product opportunities.
         c). To test out new product concepts (to name a few).
      4). When analyzing and interpreting focus group findings, market researchers should also concentrate on the non-verbal cues as well as the verbal cues.

*****Use Review Question #3 Here; Use Discussion Question #4 Here*****

   b. ***Survey Methods for Cross-Cultural Marketing Research.*** Questionnaires are the most common method.
      1). Steps include:
         a). Design of a questionnaire.
         b). Develop a sampling plan.
         c). Physical collection of information to the questionnaires.
      2). ***Questionnaire Design*** has several procedures to help in avoiding in sloppy translation in the international area--back-translation, parallel translation, and to perform scalar equivalence.

*****Use Exhibit 6-4 Here*****

      3). ***Sampling*** has to answer the following questions:

a). Who should be surveyed? What is our target population (sampling unit)?

b). How many people should be surveyed (sample size)?

c). How should perspective respondents be chosen from the target population (sampling procedure)?

4). *Contact Method* deals with the prospective subjects of the survey. The most common choices are:

a). Mail.

b). Telephone.

c). Person-to-person interviews.

*****Use Exhibit 6-5 Here*****

5). *Collecting the Information* is done in the field. Problems that must be watched for include:

a). Non-response due to reluctance to talk.

b). The courtesy bias.

c). Biases toward yea or nay-saying.

d). Social desirability bias.

*****Use Global Perspective 6-2 "One Man's Junk Is Another Man's Treasure" Here*****

E. Market Size Assessment

1. When deciding whether or not to enter a particular country, one of the key drivers is the market potential.

2. There are four methods that can be fruitfully employed to assess the size of the market for any given product.

3. *Method of Analogy.*

   a. Pick a country that is at the same stage of economic development as the country of interest and for which the market size is known.

   b. The relationship between the demand for a product and a particular indicator (for instance, the demand for a related product) is similar in both countries.

   c. The critical issue is in finding the right comparisons.

   d. McDonald's uses a variation of this method to establish its markets.

*****Use Exhibit 6-6 Here; Use Discussion Question #2 Here*****

4. *Trade Audit.*

   a. Estimates are made on local production, import and export figures for the product of interest.

   b. While this method makes sense, the data is hard (and sometimes expensive) to find.

5. *Chain Ratio Method.*

   a. The chain ration method starts with a very rough base-number as an estimate for the market size.

    b. The base number is then systematically fine-tuned by applying a string of percentages to come up with the most meaningful estimate for the total market potential.

*****Use Discussion Question #5 Here*****

6. ***Cross-Sectional Regression Analysis.***
    a. With regression analysis, the variable of interest (market size) is related to a set of predictor variables.
    b. The predictor variables are of utmost importance to the success of this method.

*****Use Exhibit 6-7 Here*****

7. When using market size estimates, keep the following rules in mind:
    a. Whenever feasible, use several different methods that possibly rely on different data-inputs.
    b. Don't be misled by the numbers.
    c. Don't be misled by fancy methods.
    d. When many assumptions are to be made, do a sensitivity analysis by asking what-if questions.
    e. Look for interval estimates with a lower- and upper-limit rather than for point estimates.

*****Use Review Question #4 Here; Use Discussion Question #6 Here*****

F. New Market Information Technologies *(IT)*

1. Major advances in information technologies that have affected business in general and international business specifically are:
    a. ***Point-of-Sale (POS) Store Scanner Data.*** The advantage here is that far better quality of data is obtained. The information can be very detailed.
    b. ***Consumer Panel Data.*** This method is popular in some countries (Japan) where consumers enjoy being involved in the research effort.
    c. ***Single-Source Data.*** One of these methods is the people meter which can monitor in-home television viewing behavior.
2. Major developments caused by IT include:
    a. ***Shift from mass to micro marketing.***
    b. ***Continuous monitoring of brand sales/market share movements.***
        1). ***Scanning data are used by manufacturers to support marketing decisions.***
        2). ***Scanning data are used to provide merchandising support to retailers.***
3. State-of-the-art marketing research tools are being developed to track the effectiveness of newer marketing mix media vehicles such as the Internet.

*****Use Discussion Question #3 Here*****

G. Managing Global Marketing Research

1. ***Selecting a Research Agency.***
   a. Even companies with in-house expertise will often employee local research agencies to assist with multi-country research projects.
   b. The first step is to see what sort of research support services are available to conduct the research project.
   c. Factors to be considered in selecting a firm to do the work for the company would include:
      1). Subsidiary status.
      2). Expertise.
      3). Qualifications.
      4). Track record.
      5). Experience.
      6). Clients and client references.
      7). Ability to cross borders to get the job done.
      8). Cost.

*****Use Exhibit 6-9 Here*****

   d. Tips on how to use agencies more effectively would include:
      1). Use your agency creatively.
      2). Take your agency 100% into your confidence--create a partnership.
      3). Use your agency strategically.
2. ***Coordination of Multi-Country Research.***
   a. Who should do the coordinating?
   b. What degree of coordination?
   c. The degree of coordination centers around the conflicting demands of various users of marketing research--the global headquarters and local subsidiaries.
      1). Headquarters (an etic approach--emphasize universal behavioral and attitudinal traits) wants one thing.
      2). Local subsidiaries (an emic approach--focus on the peculiarities of the country) often wants something else.
   d. The key to success is coordination of needs and leave some leeway for individual country peculiarities (this is especially important when considering soft data such as lifestyles).

*****Use Global Perspective 6-3 "How Does Japanese Market Research Differ?" Here; Use Review Question #5 Here*****

REVIEW QUESTIONS

INSTRUCTOR'S NOTE: The following chapter review questions are meant to challenge the student to think about material presented in the chapter and formulate a creative answer to the review questions. Many of the answers require judgments rather than specific line-by-line quotation of facts. The answers provided are meant to provide stimulation of creative answers.

1. What are the major benefits and limitations of omnibus surveys?

The major benefits of the omnibus survey is that cost expenses of the survey are shared by the subscribers. It is a very economical way to get data on large numbers of consumers (especially if general information is what is primarily needed). However, the major disadvantage is that only a limited amount of company relevant information is obtainable through the omnibus survey format. Also, the panel (used to obtain the data) is usually not representative of the firm's target market profile.

2. What is the notion of "triangulation" in global market research?

Cross-country research often demands a comparison of indicators across countries. Different sources on a given item often produce contradictory information. Reconciliation can be achieved through triangulation. In other words, obtain information on the same item from at least three different sources and speculated on possible reasons behind these differences.

3. Discuss the major issues in running focus group discussions in an international context.

Focus groups can be used for many different purposes: to generate information to guide the quantitative research projects, to reveal new product opportunities, to test new product concepts, and so forth. Rules that should be followed are to hire a trained moderator, make sure cultural sensitivity is part of the process, make sure the group is homogeneous and able to bond, make sure the moderator is skilled in group dynamics, and make sure the moderator can recognize consensus. Lastly, analysis and interpretation on non-verbal cues is just as important as recording the verbal cues.

4. Discuss why market size estimates may differ depending on the method being used. How can such differences be reconciled?

Market size estimates in the international area are many times "guesstimates." The lack of quality data is the cause. The chapter describes four methods that can be used to approximate market size. The marketing manager is advised to use more than one measure to improve their decision making ability. The methods are the method of analogy, the trade audit, the chain ration method, and cross-sectional regression analysis.

Factors considered cause differences between these methods. An averaging, as well as a common sense approach, help to resolve differences. The watchword, however, is caution. Do not make numbers out to be more than they are. Observe where the data came from, how it was collected, the validity of the data, the recency of the data, and what the data included and excluded.

5. Contrast the emic versus the etic approach in international marketing research.

The degree of coordination of marketing research efforts centers around conflicting demands of various users of marketing research: global (or regional) headquarters and local subsidiaries. Headquarters favor standardized data collection, sampling procedures, and survey instruments. This is called an etic philosophy (emphasizes universal behavioral and attitude traits) bias. Local user groups prefer country-customized research designs that recognize peculiarities of their local environment. This approach can be described as being an emic philosophy (where attitudinal phenomena and values unique to a particular country are what is studied because the researchers feel that the uniqueness warrants study in this manner). Both approaches have merit and a combination is usually advised for accuracy.

DISCUSSION QUESTIONS

INSTRUCTOR'S NOTE: Discussion Questions are found at the end of each chapter in the text. These questions (in many cases) are too lengthy to repeat in this manual. Suggestions for answering and discussing the questions are presented in this section. Many of the questions require student opinion and judgment.

1. The answer to this question is a judgment call. Either method can produce desirable results. Factors to be considered in making the judgment between single country research and clustering might center around: 1) the number of countries involved, 2) the ability to cluster, 3) data availability, 4) amount of time to do the research, 5) agencies that might be able to do the research for the firm (such as a specialization service), and 6) cost of obtaining information versus the value of obtaining the information.

2. This question requires that the students apply the information from Exhibit 6-6 found in the chapter. Be sure to monitor the results of the mathematical exercise. If there are differences resolve these. In most cases (beyond simple math error), the differences are attributable to the consideration of different factors. Factors that are excluded from the calculation include competition and trade barriers, technological advances, and there is always the question of comparability.

3. The Internet presents a wonderful opportunity to do research. If the difficulty of specialized markets (only a few distinct groups primarily use the Internet at this point in time---though this will change in the future with wider acceptability) is overcome, the Internet will be a great data source for the future. Research has shown that the average

Internet user is willing to give information and opinions about a wide variety of subjects. In addition, based on the design of most Web pages, the interested firm will be able to tell a lot about the person who clicks on to their Web site (such as what did they look at, how long did they look, where did the inquiry come from, was there any interest in further information or inquiry about the product or service).

4. If one understands the bonding aspect that is a valuable element of the focus group technique, one sees the limitations to the videoconferencing technique except for specialized purposes. In addition, the homogeneity of the international focus group might be suspect. This does not mean that the technique might not have useful outcomes, however, the limitations and differences between domestic focus group research must be accounted for. Benefits might outweigh the disadvantages with respect to getting a multicultural outpouring. The expense might be prohibitive.

5. Before attempting to answer this question, students are encouraged to re-read the material on the chain ratio method in the text. In order to do the method, the students will have to do library research on the four countries mentioned or use the Internet to obtain information that will fit the prescribed categories of the method.

6. An excellent source of secondary information on the subject of scales is usually a text on Marketing Research. The primary concern with building scales is in what they are attempting to measure. Be careful about interpretation, use multiple measurement scales if possible, be sure to accurately describe the audience being described, use measures that will accurately measure opinions and attitudes of the survey group, and always remember that the data is opinion oriented rather than strictly factual.

STUDENT PROJECTS and INTERNET FOCUS

1. Go to the library and do research on a foreign market of your choice. Use any of the four methods mentioned in Chapter 6 (method of analogy, trade audit, chain ration method, or cross-sectional regression analysis) to make a market size assessment for a product or service of your choice. Once you have completed your assignment, evaluate your research experience. What was difficult? What additional data did you need? What was the easiest and hardest data to find? Would you be willing to make decisions regarding the market based on the data collected?

2. Using the steps outlined in the text: 1) Define the research problem, 2) Develop a research design, 3) Determine information needs, 4) Collect the data, 5) Analyze the data and interpret the results, and 6) Report and present the findings of the study, do a research project on a subject of your choice with respect to the international marketing environment or a specific country. Additional instructions can be given by your instructor. Report on your research experience. Critique your effort.

INSTRUCTOR'S NOTE: The following projects require the students to both use and understand the Internet. If students do not understand how to use the Internet, explanation should be given before these projects are undertaken. The Web sites provided were current at the time of this writing. However, since Web addresses change frequently, the instructor should re-affirm the site addresses and the content of the site before making an assignment.

3. As mentioned in the chapter, a comprehensive resource in gathering data in international marketing is the National Trade Data Bank (NTDB) found at (**http://www.stat-usa.gov**). Go to the site and report on the forms of data that can be obtained. This listing of reference areas might be useful for other reports or projects assigned in this course.

4. Another valuable on-line resource is the International Business Resources Directory maintained by the CIBER center at Michigan State University found at (**http://www.ciber.bus.msu.edu/busres.html**). Go to the site and report on the forms of data that can be obtained. This listing of reference areas might be useful for other reports or projects assigned in this course.

5. A frequently used program for computers that is useful in conducting research (especially in the international area is) is SPSS (Statistical Package for the Social Sciences). Go to the SPSS Web site at (**http://www.spss.com**) and explore the different statistical programs available that might be used for doing research as suggested in this chapter. Pick one of the packages and report on what it might be used for and how could you access it. This site can be very valuable as a reference listing for other reports and projects that might be assigned in this course.

CHAPTER 7

GLOBAL SEGMENTATION & POSITIONING

CHAPTER OBJECTIVES

1. Discuss the reasons for international market segmentation.

2. Analyze the various international market segmentation approaches.

3. Describe the bases for country segmentation.

4. List the country segmentation tools and be able to discuss each.

5. Examine the primary issues in international market segmentation.

6. Understand the managerial implications of international positioning strategies.

CHAPTER OVERVIEW

It is a corporate reality that few companies can be all things to all people. Instead of competing across the board, most companies will identify and target the most attractive market segments that they can serve effectively. Variation in customer needs is the primary motive for market segmentation.

Though there is a trend homogenization of customer needs, marketers are finding that their companies (by following policies of micromarketing) are attempting to offer more possibilities (all targeted to specific and individual needs) to the global consumer. This presents an interesting challenge.

Normally, marketers will use the marketing mix to orient product and service offerings around the specific needs of the global consumer as assessed one or more segmentation bases. Marketing programs are then developed that are in tune with the particular needs of each of the "slices of the marketing pie" that the company wants to serve.

In global marketing, market segmentation becomes especially critical given the sometimes incredibly wide divergence in cross-border consumer needs and preferences. Focus in this chapter is on motivations for international market segmentation, which segmentation criteria to use, difficulties in segmentation, tools to use, and how to position using segmentation guidelines.

CHAPTER OUTLINE

A. Reasons for International Market Segmentation

1. The goal of market segmentation is to break down the market for a product or a service into different groups of consumers which differ in their response to the firm's marketing mix program.
   a. A firm can tailor its marketing mix to each individual segment.
   b. Marketing segmentation is the logical outgrowth of the marketing concept.
2. Requirements for effective market segmentation (in either the domestic or the global environment) are that the segment be:
   a. Measurable--be easy to define and to measure.
   b. Sizable--large enough to worth going after.
   c. Accessible--easy to reach through the media.
   d. Actionable--the marketing mix program can be developed to elicit a response.
   e. Competitive intensity--the segment is not pre-empted by the firm's competition.
   f. Growth potential--should have a significant growth potential.
3. Major reasons why international marketers implement international market segmentation are:
   a. *Country Screening.* Companies usually do a preliminary screening of countries before identifying attractive market opportunities for their product or service.
      1). Primary and secondary data can be used.
      2). Different criteria will be used to screen countries, depending on the nature of the product.
   b. *Global Market Research.*
      1). Companies increasingly make an effort to design products or services that meet the needs of customers in different countries.
      2). Standardization versus adaptation must be considered.
      3). The key question is which countries to choose for the marketing effort.
         a). Group by clusters based on homogeneous characteristics and choose a prototypical member from each group.
         b). Research efforts will be concentrated on this key member initially.
   c. *Entry Decisions.*
      1). The strategic logic of many entry decisions is to launch products in countries that in some regards are highly similar to the country where the product has already been introduced.
   d. *Positioning Strategy.*
      1). Segmentation decisions are instrumental in setting the company's product positioning strategy.
      2). The company must decide on how it wants to position its products or services in the mind of the prospective target customers.
   e. *Marketing Mix Policy.*
      1). Segmentation and positioning decisions will dictate a firm's marketing mix policy.

2). One difficulty is how to balance standardization versus customization.

3). Strategies for each element of the marketing mix have to be carefully thought out.

*****Use Exhibit 7-1 Here*****

B. **International Market Segmentation Approaches**

1. Global marketers approach the segmentation process from different angles.
   a. The standard country segmentation procedure classifies prospect countries on a single dimension (e.g., per capita Gross National Product).
   b. Another approach is to classify based on multiple socio-economic, political, cultural criteria available from secondary data sources.

*****Use Exhibit 7-2 Here*****

   c. Multiple sets of variables can normally be collapsed into mobility, health, trade, lifestyle, and cosmopolitanism.

*****Use Exhibit 7-3 Here*****

2. From a marketer's perspective, the practical usefulness of macro-level segmentation is questionable.
3. An alternative method is a procedure described as:
   a. Step 1--Criteria Development--determine your cut-off criteria.
   b. Step 2--Preliminary Screening--examine which countries meet your threshold.
   c. Step 3--Microsegmentation--develop microsegments of each country.
      1). Derive microsegments in each country individually.
      2). Alternatively, you could jointly group individuals in all the prospect countries to come up with cross-border segments.

*****Use Exhibit 7-4 Here*****

4. Global marketers have three choices in terms of their target marketing strategies:
   a. Universal segment--concentrate on cross-border segments that transcend national boundaries.
   b. Diverse segments--focus on local segments that differ from country to country.
   c. Mixture of both of the above forms.

*****Use Exhibit 7-5 Here; Use Review Question #1 Here*****

C. **Bases for Country Segmentation**

1. The first step is doing international market segmentation is deciding which

criteria to use in the task.

2. Since there are many variables that can be used, (for segmentation to be meaningful) there should be a linkage between the market segments and the response variable(s) the company is interested in.

3. The different forms of variables that are most commonly used for country segmentation purposes are:

    a. *Demographics.*
       1). This information is reasonably available and accurate.
       2). Classifications are similar to those used in domestic segmentation.

*****Use Global Perspective 7-1 "The Asian Teenagers Segment: A Boon for the Nikes of the World" Here; Use Discussion Question #2 Here*****

    b. *Socio-economic Variables.*
       1). Consumption patterns for many goods and services are largely driven by the consumer wealth or the country's level of economic development in general.
       2). Five stages of economic development are:
          a). Traditional societies--economic basketcases.
          b). Pre-conditions for take-off--countries making the transition to the take-off phase.
          c). The take-off--infrastructure is mainly in place, spurring city-centered industries.
          d). The drive to maturity--country can produce a wide variety of products.
          e). High mass-consumption--countries which have a sizable middle-class with significant discretionary incomes.

*****Use Discussion Question #4 Here*****

       3). Caveats are:
          a). Monetization of transactions within a country.
          b). Gray and black sectors of the economy.
          c). Income disparities.
       4). Countries can be analyzed using the purchasing power parity (PPP) analysis or Socio-economic Strata (SES) analysis.

*****Use Exhibit 7-6 Here; Use Review Question #2 Here*****

    c. *Culture.*
       1). Culture covers a broad range of factors such as religion, language, education, et cetera.
       2). One method to classify countries according to culture is to group them into the following categories:
          a). Individualism versus collectivism (IND)--how people relate to one another.

b). Power distance (PD)--how society handles inequality among its members.

c). Uncertainty avoidance (UA)--are people threatened?

d). Masculinity-Femininity (MA)--male-female values.

*****Use Exhibit 7-7 Here*****

   d. *Political Conditions.*

      1). Countries can be grouped according to whether they are free market, mixed or centrally planned.

      2). Political risk is an important component of analysis (but is must be considered with respect to business functions).

   e. *Behavior Based Segmentation.*

      1). This form might look at such things as brand loyalty or usage rate.

*****Use Exhibits 7-8 and 7-9 Here*****

   f. *Lifestyle.*

      1). This measure looks at attitudes, opinions, and values.

      2). This form is very popular in advertising circles.

      3). Many different typologies can be developed.

*****Use Exhibit 7-10 Here*****

      4). Lifestyle segmentation has been applied to the positioning of new brands, the repositioning of existing ones, identifying new product opportunities, and the development of brand personalities.

      5). Concerns about lifestyle segmentation are:

         a). Values are too general to relate to consumption patterns or brand choice behavior within a specific product category.

         b). Value-based segmentation schemes are not always "actionable".

         c). Value segments are not stable since values typically change over time.

         d). International applicability is limited.

*****Use Review Question #3 Here; Use Discussion Question #1 Here*****

D. Country Segmentation Tools

  1. When only one segmentation variable is used to study a country, classification is quite straightforward.

  2. *Cluster Analysis.*

   a. Cluster analysis is an umbrella term that embraces a collection of statistical procedures for dividing objects into groups (clusters). The grouping is done in such a manner that members belonging to the same group are very similar to one another but quite distinct form members of other groups.

*****Use Exhibits 7-11, 7-12, and 7-13 Here*****

    b. The basic notion is to group countries together that are "similar" in value for the segmentation bases of interest.

*****Use Discussion Question #3 Here*****

3. *Regression.*
   a. This method assumes that there exists a relationship between a response variable (Y) and one or more so-called predictor variables (Xs).
   b. For each of the parameter estimates, the regression analysis will also produce a standard error.

E. Issues in International Market Segmentation

    1. *Technical Issues.*
        a. *Poor Data Quality.*
        b. *Noisy (errors) Variables.*
        c. *Presence of Outliers.*
    2. *Managerial Issues.*
        a. *Stability of Segments over Time.*
        b. *Managerial Usefulness.*

F. Positioning Strategies

    1. Once the MNC has segmented its international markets for a particular product or service, the firm needs to decide which segments to pursue and what positioning strategy to use to reach the chosen segment(s).
        a. Developing a positioning theme involves the quest for a unique selling proposition (USP).
    2. There are several choices that the marketing manager may pursue with respect to positioning:
        a. *Universal Segment/Uniform Positioning Theme.* With this option, the MNC pursues a universal segment and uses the same positioning theme to appeal to this particular segment.
        b. *Universal Segment/Different Positioning Themes.* Companies might pursue a universal target segment but adapt the positioning themes to the local markets.
        c. *Different Segment/Different Positioning Themes.* Adaptation of positioning and target is another possibility, especially for products that are marketed in developed countries and emerging markets.
    3. To determine the proper positioning theme(s), marketers need to factor in their firm's corporate culture and mission, core skills, the perception of their target

customers in the various countries (are they consistent across borders or not?), positioning themes used in the past (for existing brands), and positioning strategies used by competitors.

REVIEW QUESTIONS

INSTRUCTOR'S NOTE: The following chapter review questions are meant to challenge the student to think about material presented in the chapter and formulate a creative answer to the review questions. Many of the answers require judgments rather than specific line-by-line quotation of facts. The answers provided are meant to provide stimulation of creative answers.

1. Under what conditions should companies pursue universal market segments?

Marketers should pursue universal market segments when characteristics or segments are found that transcend national borders. Marketers appealing to universal segments have two approaches to reach their targets. One option is to adopt a largely standardized strategy. Alternatively, they might go for a country-tailored strategy that recognizes differences between various countries. The undifferentiated approach will lead to economies of scale. The country-tailored approach (a differentiated strategy) often creates more demand and is more market-oriented.

2. What are the major issues in using per capita GDP or GNP as a country segmentation criterion?

One method of segmenting countries is to use monetization of transactions within a country (a socio-economic variable). To compare measures such as per capita GNP across countries, figures based on a local currency need to be translated into a common currency. However, official exchange rates seldom reflect the purchasing power parity (PPP) of a currency. So, income figures based on GNP or GDP do not really tell one how much a given household in a given country is able to buy.

The PPP (especially in countries with wide income disparity) protects against the shortcomings of the standard "per capita income" segmentation measures. Another method is the Socio-Economic Strata analysis (SES). Under this method, income classes are created and studied.

3. Discuss the weaknesses of lifestyle based segmentation schemes. For what kind of applications would lifestyle segmentation be appropriate?

Using this method, segmentation occurs on a consumer's attitudes, opinions, and values. This is a popular method in advertising circles, however, some of these schemes can be very general and not related to a specific product category.

Lifestyle segmentation has been applied to the positioning of new brands, the repositioning of existing ones, identifying new product opportunities, and the development of brand personalities. Concerns are that: a) values are too general to relate to consumption patterns or brand choice behavior within a specific product category; b) value-based segmentation schemes are not always "actionable;" c) value segments are not stable since values typically change over time; d) their international applicability is quite limited since lifestyles vary greatly.

DISCUSSION QUESTIONS

INSTRUCTOR'S NOTE: Discussion Questions are found at the end of each chapter in the text. These questions (in many cases) are too lengthy to repeat in this manual. Suggestions for answering and discussing the questions are presented in this section. Many of the questions require student opinion and judgment.

1. This question is an extension of Review Question #3. To answer this question, should review the material found in the chapter on the subject and then formulate an opinion. To formulate that opinion consider the categories which are suggested for lifestyle segmentation (as mentioned in the text). To support the position taken, try to find evidence to support the argument. Be sure to deal with the issue of the popularity of the measure in a developed country like the United States and the lack of use in an under developed country. Consider whether individualism has a bearing on this issue (as in the case of the differences between U.S. [individualism] versus Japanese [group motivated] consumers).

2. Before answering this question, the students should re-read Global Perspective 7-1 "The Asian Teenagers Segment: A Boon for the Nikes of the World." Generally speaking, the teenage segment is like all other segments--there is some universality and some individuality (with respect to country). Age is the common denominator, however, income, freedom, education, mobility, health, work necessity and habits, and exposure to the mass media may account for significant differences between not only countries but the teenagers themselves. Try to find support arguments (or evidence) for your position.

3. This question is a project oriented question. See question instructions and directions.

4. An indication that country has reached the "high mass-consumption" stage is that it has a significant middle class with a significant discretionary income. A middle class can derive pleasures from a variety of "little things" such as bonuses, free time, home care, work place perks, vacations, education for children, parks, et cetera. The emerging nations have a growing middle class because of the increased production and productivity that is taking place in these countries. The small perks in these countries may not be much by Western standards but they are significant in the countries that are now

experiencing them. In addition, the confidence level and optimism are increasing dramatically. This usually means that purchasing will go up.

STUDENT PROJECTS and INTERNET FOCUS

1. Take a product of your choice. Then pick four international countries and describe the various market segments that might be present for your product. Try to be specific in your analysis of the segments. In addition to presenting your findings, describe where you found your data and how you made your conclusions.

2. Go to the library. Find examples of international magazines. From these magazines, photocopy (**DO NOT TEAR OUT**) examples of ads. These ads can be for familiar or unfamiliar products. Now try to identify the market segments that are the subject of the ads. What can you tell about the segments from the ads? How did you determine facts about the segment? What other segments might the ad appeal to? Are there any comparisons with this market (and its segments) to the U.S. market (and its segments) for the same product?

INSTRUCTOR'S NOTE: The following projects require the students to both use and understand the Internet. If students do not understand how to use the Internet, explanation should be given before these projects are undertaken. The Web sites provided were current at the time of this writing. However, since Web addresses change frequently, the instructor should re-affirm the site addresses and the content of the site before making an assignment.

3. Go to the following Web sites and describe what market segments are being pursued by the various companies. In addition, (if possible) describe what segmentation and/or positioning strategies are being used by the firms.

   a). Apple Computer   (**http://www.apple.com**)

   b). IBM   (**http://www.ibm.com**)

   c). Compaq   (**http://www.compaq.com**)

   d). Hewlett-Packard   (**http://www.hp.com**)

4. Go to the Advertising Research Foundation home page at (**http://www.arfsite.org**). Conduct a research search for information regarding an international product of your choice (or another product cleared by your instructor). Cite the product you studied, indicate what type of information might be available, whether the information is free or must be paid for, what can be determined about the product itself, any information on the product's competitors, the product's position relative to competition, what can be

determined about the mass media with respect to the chosen product, and whether you think that this is a good secondary resource site.

5. The world (especially in Asia) has caught *Tamagotchi* Fever. This virtual pet has swept Japan and is now beginning to spread to other markets. Bandai (makers of Tamagotchi and other toy products) has been swamped with orders. Go to their Web site at (**http://www.bandai.com**). Once there learn about the company, their other products, and Tamagotchi. Your assignment is to devise a product introduction strategy for this international product into the U.S. market. Consider steps that you would see as critical. Remember to include some form of plan for all of the marketing mix variables (product, price, promotion, and distribution). Be sure to designate which market segments would be the primary ones for your product introduction. Be sure to describe the segments and relate why that you think they would be prime prospects. How would you rate Tamagotchi's chances of success in the U.S. market?

CHAPTER 8

GLOBAL COMPETITIVE ANALYSIS

CHAPTER OBJECTIVES

1. Describe the nature of global competition.

2. Define and illustrate global strategy.

3. Define and illustrate global marketing strategy.

4. Describe the process of regionalizing global marketing strategy.

5. Analyze the primary components of competitive analysis and demonstrate its usefulness.

CHAPTER OVERVIEW

Market oriented firms, facing greater competitiveness in world markets, find it essential to assume a global perspective in designing and implementing their marketing strategies. Cost containment, rising technological costs and the dispersal of technology, a greater number of global competitors in many industries and the advent of hypercompetition in most world markets mean that the firm interested in international competition must continually refine and develop strategy. The strategies affect overall corporate goals and objectives.

Strategic planning is an essential talent of today's international marketing competitor. At the heart of successful strategic planning is the use of information technology and telecommunications to draw subsidiaries and markets closer together. In the end, a global strategy must be responsive to national needs, while at the same time, exploit opportunities on a global basis.

Strategic alignments through regional trading blocs have changed the normal competitive balances in recent years. Globally minded, proactive firms increasingly exploit their competitive position in some regions by funneling abundant resources and regionally successful marketing programs to other regions where they do not necessarily occupy a strong market position. In the future, managers must know and always be aware of the key issues that will retain competitive position.

CHAPTER OUTLINE

A. Nature of Global Competition

1. *Information Technology.*
   a. In the 1980s telecommunications grew by over 600 percent and a similar level of growth has taken place in the 1990s.
   b. *Real-Time Management.* Information that managers have about the state of operations of the firm are almost in real time. This really helps decision making.
   c. The combination of information technology, access tools and telecommunication has squeezed out huge chunks of slack from the operations of the firm which were previously slow due to the slow and circuitous nature of information flow within the firm with many holdups due to human "switches."
   d. *On-Line Communication.* This form of communication helps salespeople and problem solvers alike.
      1). Multiple design sites around the world in different time zones can now work in sync, sequentially on the same problem.
   e. *"Internet" Organization.* As information flows faster across the organization and the number of "filtering points" between the source of information and the user of the information decreases, the nature of the organization chart in the multinational firm changes dramatically.
   f. *Faster Product Diffusion.* The obvious impact of information technology is the faster dispersion of technology and the shorter product life cycles in global markets than ever before.
   g. *Global Citizenship.* English is now the language of international business.
      1). Global citizenship is no longer just a phrase.
      2). The global environment demands a different form of strategy than that of domestic marketing.

*****Use Review Question #1 Here*****

B. Global Strategy

1. *Global Industry.* These industries are defined as those where a firm's competitive position in one country is affected by its position in other countries and vice versa.
   a. The first question that faces managers is the extent of globalization of their industry.
   b. Virtually every industry has aspects that are global.
2. Four major forces that determine the globalization potential of industry are:
   a. Market Drivers.
   b. Cost Drivers.
   c. Government Drivers.
   d. Competitive Drivers.

*****Use Exhibit 8-1 Here; Use Review Question #2 Here*****

3. The differences between strategy in a multidomestic approach and a global approach are quite profound.
   a. In a multidomestic strategy, a firm manages its international activities like a portfolio.
   b. A global strategy integrates the activities of a firm on a worldwide basis to capture the linkages among countries and to treat the entire world as a single borderless market.
4. In effect, the firm which truly operationalizes a global strategy is a geocentrically oriented firm.
5. In an ethnocentric orientation, where managers operate under the dominate influence of home country practices or a polytechnic orientation where managers of individual subsidiaries operate independently of each other--the polycentric manager in practice leads to a multidomestic orientation, which prevents integration and optimization on a global basis.

*****Use Global Perspective 8-1 "Globalizing the Multidomestic Corporate Culture" Here*****

6. ***Competitive Structure.***
   a. Economies of scale remain the main feature of market competition.
      1). The theory is that the greater the economies of scale, the greater the benefits to those firms with a larger market share.
      2). As a result, many firms try to jockey for larger market shares than their competitors.
   b. A firm that builds its competitive advantage on economies of scale is known as a cost leader.
   c. Until flexible manufacturing and customized production becomes fully operational, cost leaders may be vulnerable to firms which use product differentiation to better serve the exact needs of customers.
   d. Another form of competition is niche marketing. This strategy focuses exclusively on a highly specialized segment of the market and tries to achieve a dominant position in that segment.
   e. Porter's model that portrays the multidimensional nature of competitive industry structure is described as being made of:
      1). Industry competitors.
      2). Potential entrants.
      3). The bargaining power of suppliers.
      4). The bargaining power of buyers.
      5). The threat of substitute products or services.

*****Use Exhibit 8-2 Here; Use Discussion Question #5 Here*****

7. *Hypercompetition.*
   a. Porter's model does not show change circumstances.
   b. Since all competition may be temporal, change must be accounted for.
   c. According to Schumpeter, creative destruction assumes continuous change (which is a basic assumption behind the concept of hypercompetitive strategy where the firm competes on price-quality basis vis-à-vis its competitors.
      1). The competition is based on timing and know-how.
      2). The firm creates strongholds in the markets in which it operates.
      3). The firm has a strong financial resource base on which to resist competition.
   d. Hypercompetition postulates that firms compete in the following arenas:
      1). *Cost and Quality.*

*****Use Exhibit 8-3 Here*****

      2). *Timing and Know-how.*
      3). *Strongholds.*
      4). *Financial Resources.*

*****Use Global Perspective 8-2 "Rome Could Not Be Built in a Day at Parker Pen Company" Here; Use Review Question #3 Here*****

   e. Because advantage is always fleeting, competitors constantly shift back and forth between strategies seeking to gain advantage.
      1). In essence, it is the firm which disrupts the existing status quo in the market and is able to take advantage of the disruption, that has a competitive advantage.
      2). To be able to disrupt the market, the firm must be close to the consumer and faster to respond to their needs.
   f. The two approaches to gain competitive advantage seem to be:
      1). Competitor centered.
      2). Consumer centered.
8. *Interdependency.*
   a. Recent research has shown that the number of technologies used in a variety of products in numerous industries is rising.
   b. Resource limitations may be a reason for rising interdependency.
   c. Component standardization is becoming popular.

*****Use Review Question #4 Here*****

C. Global Marketing Strategy

1. Global firms must consider whether to standardize their marketing mix with respect to world wide expansion.

*****Use Exhibit 8-4 Here; Use Review Question #5 Here*****

2. One of the fundamental requirements of a successful global marketing strategy is the need to coordinate the marketing mix and other functions (such as R & D).
3. *Benefits of Global Marketing.*
   a. Global marketing strategy can achieve one or more of four major categories of potential globalization benefits:

*****Use Global Perspective 8-3 "GM and Ford Pursue Different Benefits from Global Marketing" Here; Use Discussion Question #4 Here*****

1). *Cost Reduction.*
   a). This arises from a savings in both workforce and materials.
   b). Cost savings can also translate into increased program effectiveness by allowing more money and resources into a smaller number of more focused programs.
2). *Improved Products and Program Effectiveness.*
   a). This may be the greatest advantage of a global marketing strategy.
   b). Benefits from a multiple R & D location strategy would be:
      1]. Integration of product attributes from multiple markets.
      2]. Spreading of developmental costs.
      3]. Increase sources of product ideas.
3). *Enhanced Customer Preference.*
4). *Increased Competitive Advantage.*
   a). Firms can magnify the competitive power of their programs.
   b). Competitive intelligence increases.
4. *Limits to Global Marketing.*
   a. Diversity of local environments.
   b. Standardization versus adaptation (or any of the other derivatives).
   c. Cultural and political constraints.
   d. Critical technologies can transcend national borders.

*****Use Exhibit 8-5 Here; Use Review Question #6 Here; Use Discussion Questions #1 and 3 Here*****

D. Regionalization of Global Marketing Strategy

1. Some firms may have difficulty in organizing to be able to globalize.
2. In finding a balance between the need for greater integration and the need to exploit existing resources more effectively, many companies have begun to explore the use of regional strategies in Europe, North America, and the Pacific Rim.
   a. Regional strategies can be defined as the cross-subsidization of market share battles in pursuit of regional production, branding, and distribution advantages.
3. Two favorable effects of the formulation of regional trading blocs are:

a. The volatility of foreign exchange rates within a bloc seems to be reduced.

b. With the growing level of macroeconomic integration within regions, there is also a trend toward greater harmonization of product and industry standards, pollution and safety standards, and environmental standards.

4. To face regional forces proactively, other strategies that must be considered are:

*****Use Global Perspective 8-4 "Nike and Reebok Battling for a Global Dominance" Here*****

a. *Cross Subsidization of Markets.*
b. *Identification of Weak Market Segments.*
c. *"Lead Market" Concept.*

*****Use Review Question #7 Here; Use Discussion Question #2 Here*****

E. Competitive Analysis

1. Firms must broaden their competitive base, but must also constantly re-evaluate themselves to make sure that their current competitive position is secure.

2. SWOT analysis (Strengths, Weaknesses, Opportunities, and Threats) is useful technique for analyzing a firm's competitive position as compared to its competition.

3. A SWOT analysis looks at internal factors (Strengths or Weaknesses) and external factors (Opportunities and Threats). Positions are very important.

4. All areas of the marketing mix must be examined (internal examination).

5. Externally, look at technological changes, legislation, sociocultural changes and changes in the marketplace or competitive position.

*****Use Exhibit 8-6 Here*****

6. SWOT is just one aid and does not automatically establish priority.

7. The aim of SWOT analysis should be to isolate the key issues that will be important to the future of the firm and that subsequent marketing strategy will address.

REVIEW QUESTIONS

INSTRUCTOR'S NOTE: The following chapter review questions are meant to challenge the student to think about material presented in the chapter and formulate a creative answer to the review questions. Many of the answers require judgments rather than specific line-by-line quotation of facts. The answers provided are meant to provide stimulation of creative answers.

1. How are the developments in information technology impacting the global strategies of firms?

The development of transportation technology, including jet air transportation, cold storage containers, and large ocean carriers changed the nature of world trade in the past 50 years after the Second World War. Since the 1980s, the explosion of information technology, particularly telecommunications, has forever changed the nature of competition around the world. Geographical distance has become increasingly less relevant in designing global strategy. Areas most affected are: Real-Time management, on-line communication, Internet organization, faster product diffusion, and global citizenship.

2. What are the various factors/forces/drivers which determine the globalization potential of industries? How are global industries different from multidomestic industries?

To answer this question review the categories listed in Exhibit 8-1. Note the major categories of market globalization drivers, cost globalization drivers, government globalization drivers, and competitive globalization drivers and their associated sub-categories. Note that the difference between global industries and multidomestic industries is their nature, scope, management structure, and market thrust.

3. What do you understand by the term "hypercompetition?" What, according to hypercompetition, are the various arenas of competition?

In any given industry, firms jockey among themselves for better competitive position, given a set of customers and buyers, the threat of substitutes and the barriers to entry in that industry. A new competitor may emerge from a completely different industry given the convergence of industries. Such shifts in competition may follow a Schumpeterian view that says creative destruction assumes continuous change. This basic assumption is behind the hypercompetitive environment and strategy that says competition takes place in three arenas: 1) a firm competes on price-quality basis vis-à-vis its competitors; 2) on the basis of timing and know-how; 3) on the basis of creating strongholds in the markets it operates in (this is akin to entry barriers); 4) on the basis of financial resources to outlast one's competitors.

4. How are the concepts "interdependency" and "standardization" related? What are the implications for global strategy?

Recent research has shown that the number of technologies used in a variety of products in numerous industries is rising continuously. With resource limitations of firms circumscribing the number of distinctive competencies that a firm can be good at, firms now need to access technologies from outside the firm to be able to build a state-of-the-art product. Since most firms operating globally are subject to the limitation of lack of all required technologies, it follows that for firms to develop products that make optimal use of technologies accessed from outside, a degree of standardization of the components is required. Such component standardization would enable different firms to develop different end products using, in a large measure, the same components.

5. How is a global marketing strategy distinct form standardization?

Global marketing is not about standardizing the marketing process on a global basis. While every element of the marketing process (the marketing mix and other functions of marketing) may be a candidate for standardization, standardization is one part of a global marketing strategy and is may or may not be used by a company (depending on the mix of the product-market conditions, stage of market development, and the inclinations of the management of the multinational firm). Successful global marketing is a question of coordination.

6. What are the benefits and limitations of global marketing strategies?

Benefits of global marketing strategy fall into four categories: cost reduction, improved quality of products and programs, enhanced customer preference and increased competitive advantage. The limits to global marketing include diversity of local markets, the environments (cultural, political, and legal), the question of standardization versus adaptation (or other derivatives), and the need to have transnational technology and communication.

7. How are regional and global strategies different? What are some advantages and disadvantages of a regional strategy?

The primary difference between regional and global strategies is the degree of planning, organizational design to allow for coordination, and managerial expertise. The use of regional trading blocs considers the need to exploit existing resources more effectively and the encouragement from economic, political, and social pressures from the regional trading blocs. The advantages might be with respect to currency and exchange difficulties and the harmonization of standards. However, to make this work the trading blocs must consider cross subsidization of markets, identification of weak market segments, and the lead market concept. The inability to see "the big picture" may be the chief disadvantage. Many regional strategists forget that there are other markets to be pursued in the world environment.

DISCUSSION QUESTIONS

INSTRUCTOR'S NOTE: Discussion Questions are found at the end of each chapter in the text. These questions (in many cases) are too lengthy to repeat in this manual. Suggestions for answering and discussing the questions are presented in this section. Many of the questions require student opinion and judgment.

1. This question requires thought and consideration. A case could be made in either direction. The student should be reminded, however, to examine carefully the issue of global versus multidomestic using the suggestions and criteria suggested in the text. Please note whether planning, organization, coordination, and control are global or multidomestic. These beginning clues might be the best prescription for solution to the problem presented in this question. Try to get two groups of students to present arguments for both sides then have the class debate the answer. Lastly, the students should perceive that the food industry is very diverse and that McDonald's is not really a benchmark for the industry.

2. As in Question #1, students could make a case for any of the alternatives presented in this case. An additional decision factor might be new data that might be discovered by the students' research effort. A good technique for solution might be to assign different student groups to approach the problem as if the company fit one of the four patterns suggested. Then each group could present their findings to the class and let the class discuss the merits of their solution.

Based on the information presented in the discussion question, more weight might be given to the ethnocentric alternative (see discussion in the chapter), however, new evidence might refute this suggested alternative.

3. To answer this discussion question the student must express an opinion (they should be required to support the opinion presented). Through efforts of AACSB and other accrediting agencies, internationalism and global thinking has been mandated in business schools across the country. However, whether or not this brief flirtation with international issues (through one or two courses and some integration in core courses) has made any impact on the corporate management system remains to be seen. It would appear that progress is being made but only slowly. As companies begin to divert from multidomestic firms to global firms, an increase in international management thinking and marketing practice will certainly follow. The students should be encouraged to use their own business program as a starting point for their investigation.

4. To formulate an answer to this discussion question, the students should be encouraged to re-read the section in the chapter that deals with "Benefits of Global Marketing" and review Global Perspective 8-3 "GM and Ford Pursue Different Benefits from Global Marketing." These sections will provide data with which the student might be able to defend the statements made in this question. A useful technique for covering this material might be to have a debate. Assign both sides of the issue to different teams and ask for presentations to the class.

5. The attempt of this question is to make the students aware that not all problems faced by large multinational firms are tied directly to international competition. Many multinationals are losing market share domestically to other entities within the domestic markets besides other multinationals. Strategies need to be developed to combat this

form of competition. The best starting point for a discussion of this question would be for the students to consider the material in the chapter from Exhibit 8-1 (Market drivers) and Michael E. Porter's model as shown in Exhibit 8-2 (which describes various competitive influences that might be present in a market). For example, when does a supplier or a distributor become a competitor? By considering this information, the students should be able to respond effectively to the material and situation presented in the discussion question.

STUDENT PROJECTS and INTERNET FOCUS

1. Go to the library and research the impact of information technology on global competition. What factors (beyond those presented in the text) are having the greatest impact? Try to focus on the role of the World Wide Web and its potential impact on global competition. Report your findings to the class by means of a short discussion paper.

2. Using the information in Exhibit 8-2 (Nature of Competitive Industry Structure), find an illustration of a company or an industry where you can illustrate the various factors presented in the model from the exhibit. Be sure to document how and why you think your information fits the model. Does the model accurately describe competition in the industry or among the companies that you analyzed? What are your opinions on the Porter technique for analyzing competition? Prepare a brief report summarizing the information and conclusions you reached.

INSTRUCTOR'S NOTE: The following projects require the students to both use and understand the Internet. If students do not understand how to use the Internet, explanation should be given before these projects are undertaken. The Web sites provided were current at the time of this writing. However, since Web addresses change frequently, the instructor should re-affirm the site addresses and the content of the site before making an assignment.

3. Using the World Fact Book 1996 (formerly known as the CIA Factbook) at (**http://www.odci.gov/cia/publications/nsolo**), examine the component parts of the model presented in Exhibit 8-1 (Industry Globalization Drivers). Pick a country or region of the world and see what kind of information you can discover to answer the questions posed by the exhibit. From this data, could you build a competitive industry model that would help a company compete internationally? Whether you answer yes or no, what additional information would you need to make your model more useful? Where would you get that information? Prepare a report of your findings.

4. Take an international company of your choice and prepare a strategic business plan for the company. Be sure to include a SWOTs analysis. The length and detail depends on the preference of your instructor. Several Web sites that might be of some value in your research effort are:

a). (**http://www.sb.gov.bc.ca/smallbus/workshop/market/prepare/busplan.html**)

b). (**http://www.kciLink.com/brc/bplan/**).

5. One of the best sources for new information about competition among global firms is *Business Week* magazine. Go to the *Business Week* home page at (**http://www.businessweek.com**) and identify three firms that you perceive to be in competition with one another. Once you have done this identify what you perceive to be their primary strategy or strategies to meet their competition. Be sure to remember the discussion used in your chapter on strategy formulation and types of strategies that might be used. Describe how you diagnosed their strategy formats. If necessary, you can limit your search to only one product line. Report your findings in a written format.

CHAPTER 9

GLOBAL MARKET ENTRY STRATEGIES

CHAPTER OBJECTIVES

1. Describe the target market selection process.

2. Choose a mode for entry into a foreign market.

3. Describe the exporting process.

4. Describe the licensing process.

5. Describe the franchising process with respect to the international environment.

6. Analyze when contract manufacturing would be used.

7. Describe how joint ventures are used to build strategy.

8. Analyze why a firm would choose wholly owned subsidiaries as a method of doing international business.

9. Explain why cross-border strategic alliances are important to develop.

CHAPTER OVERVIEW

This chapter explains a smorgasbord of entry strategic choices available to the firm that wishes to expand globally. Each of these strategies have advantages and disadvantages. In fact, many firms combine several methods and create new methods of entry.

The normal method to begin expansion globally is to start conservatively and reduce risk. This is called a phased entry method. Once the perceived risk declines, the firm switches to a higher commitment mode (such as wholly-owned venture).

A wide variety of variables can affect the entry mode choice. The three major dimensions include the resource commitment the firm is willing to make, the amount of risk ("political" and "market") the firm is willing to take, and the degree of control that is desirable.

One of the more successful new forms of global expansion is the strategic alliance. These cross-border alliances depend on the strategic role and the competitive position of the business unit involved. Typical goals of a strategic alliance could be to defend, strengthen, sustain, or restructure the SBU or even the primary firm itself. All alliance firms must carefully coordinate and work together if harmony of purpose is to be achieved.

CHAPTER OUTLINE

A. Target Market Selection

1. A crucial step in developing a global expansion strategy is the selection of potential target markets.

*****Use Exhibit 9-1 Here*****

2. To identify market opportunities for a given product or service the international marketer usually starts off with a large pool of candidate countries. To narrow this list down the company undertakes preliminary screening.
3. The screening process includes:
   a. Step 1: Indicator selection and data collection.
      1). Pick a set of socio-economic and political indicators which are believed to be critical.
      2). The result is to develop an overall measure of market attractiveness.
   b. Step 2: Determine importances of country indicators.
      1). The purpose of this step is to determine weights of the different country indicators.
      2). One method is the constant-sum allocation technique.
   c. Step 3: Rate the countries in the pool on each indicator.
      1). Give countries a score on each of the indictors.
   d. Step 4: Compute overall score for each country.
      1). Sum the weighted scores.
      2). The higher the scores the more attractive the opportunity.

*****Use Exhibit 9-2 Here*****

4. When the product has already been launched in some regions, the firm can substantially reduce the subjectivity by using a variant of the screening procedure. This alternative method leverages the experience the firm gathered in its existing markets. The steps might include (the text uses a specific example for this demonstration):
   a. Collect historical data on European markets.
   b. Evaluate the MNC's post-entry performance in each of its existing European markets.

c. Derive weights for each of the country indicators.

d. Rate the Asian countries in the pool on each indicator.

e. Predict performance in prospect Asian countries.

*****Use Exhibit 9-3 Here*****

B.   Choosing the Mode of Entry

1. *Decision criteria for mode of entry.*
   a. Internal (firm-specific) criteria.
   b. External (environment-specific) criteria.
2. The major external criteria are:
   a. *Market size & growth.*
   b. *Risk.*
      1). Relates to political and economic environments.
   c. *Government regulations.*
      1). Trade barriers are major concerns.
   d. *Competitive Environment.*
   e. *Local infrastructure.*
3. Markets can be classified in five types of countries based on their respective market attractiveness:
   a. Platform countries that can be used to gather intelligence and establish a network--Singapore or Hong Kong.
   b. Emerging countries like Vietnam. Build an initial presence.
   c. Growth countries like China. Early mover advantages often push companies to build up a significant presence in order to capitalize on future market opportunities.
   d. Maturing and established countries like South Korea. These countries have established middle classes. The prime task is to look for ways to further develop the market via strategic alliances, major investments or acquisitions of local or smaller foreign players.

*****Use Exhibit 9-4 Here; Use Discussion Question #1 Here*****

4. Key internal criteria are listed as:
   a. *Company objectives.*
   b. *Need for control.*
   c. *Internal resources, assets, and capabilities.*
   d. *Flexibility.*
5. *Mode-of-Entry Choice: A Transaction Cost Explanation.*
   a. The different modes of entry can be classified according to the degree of control they offer the entrant from low-control (indirect exporting) to high control modes (wholly-owned subsidiary)
   b. The entrant faces a tradeoff between the benefits of increased control and the costs of resource commitment and risk.

1). One method is the Transaction-Cost Analysis (TCA) perspective.

2). TCA argues that the desirable governance structure will depend on the comparative transaction costs, that is, the cost of running the operation.

3). The TCA approach begins with the premise that markets are competitive. As the pressure for control increases assets may be at risk. A higher-control entry mode becomes necessary.

c. MNCs are most likely to enter with wholly owned subsidiaries when:

1). The entry involves an R&D-intensive line of business.

2). An advertising-intensive line of business.

3). When the MNC has accumulated a substantial amount of experience with foreign entries.

d. MNCs are most likely to prefer a partnership when:

1). The entry is in a highly risky country.

2). A socio-cultural distant country.

3). When there are legal restrictions on foreign ownership of assets.

C. Exporting

1. Most companies start their international operations with exporting.

*****Use Review Question #1 Here*****

2. *Indirect Exporting.*

a. Indirect exporting happens when the firm sells its products in the foreign market via an intermediary located in the firm's home country.

b. An example would be an export management company (EMC).

c. Advantages include:

1). The firm gets instant foreign market expertise.

2). Very little risk is involved.

3). No major resources have to be committed.

d. Disadvantages include:

1). No control.

2). Lack of adequate sales support.

3). Product and company image can be damaged by others.

4). Middlemen may have limited experience in handling the firm's goods.

3. *Cooperative Exporting.*

a. This is a middle ground between indirect exporting and direct exporting.

b. Piggyback exporting can be used (use someone else's distribution process).

4. *Direct Exporting.*

a. The firm sets up its own exporting department and sells its products via a middleman located in the foreign market.

b. More control is achieved.

c. Responsibility tasks can be high (risk begins to go up).

D. Licensing

1. Licensing is a contractual transaction where the firm--the licensor--offers some property assets to a foreign company--the licensee--in exchange for royalty fees.
2. ***Benefits.***
   a. Profitable.
   b. Not demanding on resources.
   c. Gets around import barriers.
   d. Gains access to markets.
   e. Lowers exposure to political or economic instabilities.
   f. Can rapidly amortize R&D expenditures.
3. ***Caveats.***
   a. Income can be small when compared to exporting.
   b. The licensee may not be fully committed to the licensor's technology or product.
   c. Sales and trademarks can be damaged.
   d. A future competitor can be built.

*****Use Global Perspective 9-1 "The Borden-Meiji Milk Saga: The Meltdown Of Lady Borden" Here*****

   e. Protection can be partially achieved by patenting and careful selection of the licensee.

*****Use Review Question #3 Here*****

E. Franchising

1. Franchising is an arrangement whereby the franchisor gives the franchisee the right to use the franchisor's business concept and product tradename in exchange for royalty payments.
   a. Master franchising gives a master franchise to a local entrepreneur who will in turn sell local franchises within a territory.
2. ***Benefits.***
   a. Companies can capitalize on a winning business formula by expanding overseas with a minimum of investment.
   b. Political risks are very limited.
   c. Profits make the franchisee motivated.
   d. Local knowledge can be secured and used.
3. ***Caveats.***
   a. The income stream is lower than through exporting or ownership.
   b. Lack of control over foreign operations.
   c. Cultural hurdles can be problems.

F. Contract Manufacturing

1. With contract manufacturing, the company arranges with a local manufacturer to manufacture parts of the product or even the entire product. The marketing of the product is still the responsibility of the international firm.
2. *Benefits.*
    a. Cost savings.
    b. Labor cost savings.
    c. Limits of political and economic exposure.
    d. Access to markets.
    e. Limits import barriers.
3. *Caveats.*
    a. Building a future competitor is a danger.
    b. Low productivity can result from low labor cost situations.
    c. Quality can suffer.
4. Foreign contractors should be screened by the following criteria:
    a. Flexible and geared toward just-in-time delivery.
    b. Able to meet quality standards and implement Total Quality Management.
    c. Solid financial footing.
    d. Able to integrate with company's business.
    e. Have contingency plans to handle sudden changes in demand.

G. Joint Ventures

1. With a joint venture, the foreign company agrees to share equity and other resources with other partners to establish a new entity in the target country.
2. Forms include:
    a. Majority.
    b. 50-50.
    c. Minority.
3. Huge infrastructure or high-tech projects that demand large amounts of expertise and money often involve multiple foreign and local partners.

*****Use Exhibit 9-5 Here*****

4. *Benefits.*
    a. The return potential can be substantial.
    b. More control can be achieved.
    c. Synergy.
5. *Caveats.*
    a. Lack of full control may still be a problem.
    b. Government restrictions.
    c. Lack of trust.
    d. Mutual conflicts.

*****Use Exhibit 9-6 Here; Use Review Question #2 Here*****

6. *Drivers Behind Successful International Joint Ventures.*
    a. *Pick the right partner.*
    b. *Establish clear objectives for the joint venture from the very beginning.*
    c. *Bridge the cultural gaps.*
    d. *Top managerial commitment and respect.*
    e. *Incremental approach works best.*

H. Wholly Owned Subsidiaries

1. Ownership can take two routes in foreign markets:
    a. Acquisitions.
    b. Greenfield operations (start from scratch).
2. *Benefits.*
    a. Full control.
    b. Full profits go to the company.
    c. Manage and control processes.
    d. Sends a commitment signal to the local market.
3. *Caveats.*
    a. Potential of full loss responsibility.
    b. Market related risks.
    c. Political and economic risks.
    d. Being a treat to the sovereignty of the country or local market. Localizing may help with this aspect.

*****Use Global Perspective 9-2 "Reebok's Entry Strategy in Russia" Here*****

4. *Acquisitions and mergers.*
    a. Provide a rapid means and access to a local market.
    b. Risks can be in the mergance of two or more corporate cultures.
5. *Greenfield operations.*
    a. Offers more flexibility than an acquisition.
    b. Encouraged by some governments.
    c. The primary disadvantage is the huge outlay of capital that is often required.

*****Use Review Question #4 Here; Use Discussion Question #2 Here*****

I. Cross-Border Strategic Alliances

1. Strategic alliances are described as being a coalition of two or more organizations to achieve strategically significant goals that are mutually beneficial.
    a. Surprisingly, many old competitive rivals choose this form of market expansion.
2. One popular form has been the Japanese *keiretsu* (uses a network of cross shareholdings, inter-company movement of personnel, R&D partnerships and regular meetings between top managers of the member companies to work together as a team, however, managers do not foreclose the option of working with outside

firms).

3. *Types of Strategic Alliances.*
   a. Can be as simple as licensing.
   b. Can be very complex--almost like a web.
   c. Normally, the alliance is based on the core product or service of the industry.
   d. Could be aligned based on resources and assets.
   e. Could be operations-based.

*****Use Exhibits 9-7 and 9-8 Here*****

4. *The Logic Behind Strategic Alliances.*
   a. *Defense.*
   b. *Catch Up.*
   c. *Remain.*
   d. *Restructure.*

*****Use Exhibit 9-9 Here; Use Discussion Question #4 Here*****

5. *Cross-Border Alliances that Succeed.*
   a. Alliances between strong and weak partners seldom work.
   b. Autonomy and flexibility.
   c. Equal ownership.
   d. Commitment and support of the top of the parent's organization.
       1). Strong managers are a key.
   e. Alliances that are related (in terms of products, markets, and/or technologies).
   f. Have similar cultures, asset sizes, and venturing experiencing levels tend to be
       be more viable.
   g. Shared vision on the goals and mutual benefits are critical.

*****Use Review Question #5 Here; Use Discussion Question #3 Here*****

REVIEW QUESTIONS

INSTRUCTOR'S NOTE: The following chapter review questions are meant to challenge the student to think about material presented in the chapter and formulate a creative answer to the review questions. Many of the answers require judgments rather than specific line-by-line quotation of facts. The answers provided are meant to provide stimulation of creative answers.

1. Why do some MNCs prefer to enter certain markets with a liaison office first?

Many companies would like to just "get their feet wet" before plunging into the foreign market arena. Opening a liaison office allows this to happen. The liaison office can not only establish a presence but become an intelligence source for the parent company. Many firms wish to evaluate risk and cultural relationships before they make a choice that will commit themselves to resource allocation and increased risk. The liaison office can perform those functions. By assessing the local environment at the local level, the company can more intelligent decisions at a later date. In addition, this office can begin the slow process of establishing networks that will be essential to later trade relationships.

2. What are the possible drawbacks of 50-50 joint ventures?

With a joint venture, the foreign company agrees to share equity and other resources with other partners to establish a new entity in the target country.

Benefits.
  a. The return potential can be substantial.
  b. More control can be achieved.
  c. Synergy.

Caveats.
  a. Lack of full control may still be a problem.
  b. Government restrictions.
  c. Lack of trust.
  d. Mutual conflicts.

3. Draw up a list of the respective pros and cons of licensing.

Licensing is a contractual transaction where the firm--the licensor--offers some property assets to a foreign company--the licensee--in exchange for royalty fees.

Benefits.
  a. Profitable.
  b. Not demanding on resources.
  c. Gets around import barriers.
  d. Gains access to markets.
  e. Lowers exposure to political or economic instabilities.
  f. Can rapidly amortize R&D expenditures.

Caveats.
  a. Income can be small when compared to exporting.
  b. The licensee may not be fully committed to the licensor's technology or product.
  c. Sales and trademarks can be damaged.
  d. A future competitor can be built.
  e. Protection can be partially achieved by patenting and careful selection of the licensee.

4. What are the respective advantages and disadvantages of greenfield operations over acquisitions?

Ownership can take two routes in foreign markets:

a. Acquisitions.

b. Greenfield operations (start from scratch).

Wholly owned subsidiaries:

Benefits.
    a. Full control.

    b. Full profits go to the company.

    c. Manage and control processes.

    d. Sends a commitment signal to the local market.

Caveats.
    a. Potential of full loss responsibility.

    b. Market related risks.

    c. Political and economic risks.

    d. Being a treat to the sovereignty of the country or local market. Localizing may help with this aspect.

Acquisitions and mergers:
    a. Provide a rapid means and access to a local market.

    b. Risks can be in the mergance of two or more corporate cultures.

Greenfield operations:
    a. Offers more flexibility than an acquisition.

    b. Encouraged by some governments.

    c. The primary disadvantage is the huge outlay of capital that is often required.

5. What mechanisms can firms use to protect themselves against ill-fated partnerships?

Strategic alliances are described as being a coalition of two or more organizations to achieve strategically significant goals that are mutually beneficial.

Cross-Border Alliances that Succeed:
    a. Alliances between strong and weak partners seldom work.

    b. Autonomy and flexibility.

    c. Equal ownership.

    d. Commitment and support of the top of the parent's organization.
        1). Strong managers are a key.

    e. Alliances that are related (in terms of products, markets, and/or technologies).

    f. Have similar cultures, asset sizes, and venturing experiencing levels tend to be be more viable.

    g. Shared vision on the goals and mutual benefits are critical.

    h. Spell out relationships in contractual form.

DISCUSSION QUESTIONS

INSTRUCTOR'S NOTE: Discussion Questions are found at the end of each chapter in the text. These questions (in many cases) are too lengthy to repeat in this manual. Suggestions for answering and discussing the questions are presented in this section. Many of the questions require student opinion and judgment.

1. Note that CPC's businesses are operated and administered with a high degree of autonomy under the company's decentralized organization. Notice how the company has expanded across Europe and has made moves into other trading regions. This expansion has followed the pattern of develop of the nations that are contained within the regions. As an example of development patterns notice that South Africa was considered (1994) only after their racial policies were changed. Students should be challenged to explore other patterns of development.

*****Use Exhibit 9-10 Here*****

2. Reviewing material in the chapter, the students should recall that acquisitions are used when the company wants rapid access to a local market. Acquisitions can also be a means to get a well-established brand name in an already established market. In the illustration cited in this question, the company might also have wanted access to a particular technology. Acquisitions can accomplish that objective.

Expansion in other markets would be viewed differently. As the objectives change or as the culture of the business environment changes, the expansion strategy changes. Students might be challenged to pick representative countries and indicate how this company might have expanded into those selected markets.

3. This question is a project question. See directions in the Discussion Question section of the chapter.

4. Students should be encouraged to research Nestle` and their chairman before making a comment on the statement included in this discussion question. It is interesting to note that not all Presidents and CEOs are thrilled at the prospect of the strategic alliance. The best way to thoroughly discuss this question (given that students have read the material in the chapter on strategic alliances) is to divide the class into two groups and have each group defend the pro and con of the issue.

STUDENT PROJECTS and INTERNET FOCUS

1. Go to the library and research the subject of joint ventures. Find a recent article from a contemporary business magazine that relates a story about a joint venture. Abstract the article and record the primary facts about the data. Be sure to name the venture partners and the primary issue of the article. Also, note whether is was a story about a successful venture or an unsuccessful venture.

2. Go to the library and find any data that you can of *The Art of War* by Sun Tzu (many other authors have interpreted this work so look for other authors of this same title). Relate the concept of strategic alliances to the principles of military warfare indicated in *The Art of War*. Find at least five principles from the writings of Sun Tzu that apply to the business concepts necessary to form a strategic alliance. Report your findings.

INSTRUCTOR'S NOTE: The following projects require the students to both use and understand the Internet. If students do not understand how to use the Internet, explanation should be given before these projects are undertaken. The Web addresses change frequently, the instructor should re-affirm the site addresses and the content of the site before making an assignment.

3. Using any of the recognized search engines (such as Yahoo at **http://www.yahoo.com** or Lycos at **http://www.lycos.com**) find information on international franchising opportunities. Once you have found a franchising opportunity, collect data and report your findings to the class. Would your chosen opportunity make a good investment? How difficult would it be to pursue the opportunity? Were you able to get all the information that you needed by using the Internet? What might be your chances of success with this opportunity?

4. Using any of the recognized search engines (such as Yahoo at **http://www.yahoo.com** or Lycos at **http://www.lycos.com**) find information about the Japanese *keiretsu* or the Korean *chaebols* as forms integrated structures. Based on the research that you performed describe the format of the structure, compare the structure to the joint venture and strategic alliance, present an example of the structure, and present your view as to your perception of the effectiveness of the structure.

5. Using the following Internet addresses determine which of the following organizations have recently engaged in franchising, joint ventures, merger, or acquisition at the international level. What information led you to your conclusion? Briefly report your findings to the class.

a. Caliber Systems   (**http://www.calibersys.com**)

b. British Telecom   (**http://www.btglobal.com**)

c. France Telecom   (**http://www.francetelecom.com**)

d. Texas Instruments   (**http://www.ti.com**)

e. Cisco Systems   (**http://www.cisco.com**)

f. Kinko's Corporate   (**http://www.kinkos.com**).

CHAPTER 10

GLOBAL SOURCING STRATEGY: R&D, MANUFACTURING, AND MARKETING INTERFACES

CHAPTER OBJECTIVES

1. Explain the extent and complexity of global sourcing strategy.

2. Identify the trends in global sourcing strategy.

3. Explain the value chain and associated functional interfaces.

4. Examine the logistics of sourcing strategy.

5. Identify the costs and consequences of global sourcing.

CHAPTER OVERVIEW

The scope of global sourcing has expanded over time. Price was all that mattered at one time with respect to sourcing. Today, however, many companies consider not only price but also quality, reliability, and technology of components and products to be procured. Those companies design their sourcing decision based on the interplay between their competitive advantages and the comparative advantages of various sourcing locations for long-term gains.

Sourcing (whether done domestically or internationally) of components and finished products around the world has dramatically increased for most multinational companies. Sourcing becomes part of the process of deciding on whether standardization or adaptation is a better global strategy.

Global sourcing strategy requires close coordination of R&D, manufacturing, and marketing activities on a global basis. Managing and coordinating these efforts is proving to be a significant challenge for today's marketing manager. Part of the reason for the challenge is that the interface between different sources and operations must be adapted to different legal, political, and cultural environments in different countries. The manager must be careful or the separation required in sourcing will damage the value chain. This damage can be costly.

In order to make the sourcing process efficient, strategy dictates that there be a conscious effort to streamline manufacturing without sacrificing flexibility. To accomplish this, the firm must develop either core components in-house or develop product design families or universal products.

Problems are still present with the global sourcing process. Such areas as life cycle, product development, impact on strategic alliances, and market entry are only a portion of the decision criteria facing the manager who chooses to pursue global sourcing.

CHAPTER OUTLINE

A. Introduction

1. A frequently used framework to describe cross-national business practices is the international product cycle theory.
   a. According to the theory, changes in inputs and product characteristics toward standardization over time determine an optimal production location at any particular phase of the product's life cycle.
   b. Three major limitations of the international product cycle theory are:
      1). The trend towards an increased pace of new product introduction and reduction in innovational lead time deprives companies of the age-old polycentric approach to global markets.
      2). Ability to preempt the product life cycle (i.e., predictable sourcing development during the product cycle) permits a shrewd company to outmaneuver competition.
      3). More active management of locational and corporate resources on a global basis gives a company a preemptive first mover advantage over competition.
2. Today, quick technological diffusion has virtually become a matter of fact.
3. Global sourcing strategy requires a close coordination among R&D, manufacturing, and marketing activities across national boundaries.
4. Differing objectives usually tend to create a "tug-of-war"-like situation among R&D, manufacturing, and marketing.

B. Extent and Complexity of Global Sourcing Strategy

1. Multinational companies who use the sourcing concept use production and distribution to supply those local markets hosting their foreign subsidiaries, and then export what remains to other foreign markets or back to their parent's home market.
2. With consideration to foreign production, the U.S. multinational companies are the most experienced in the world and sell over three times as much overseas through their subsidiaries than they export to the world.

*****Use Review Question #1 Here*****

3. Two notable changes have occurred in international trade:

a. The last thirty years have observed a secular decline in the proportion of trade between the European Community and the United States in the Triad regions, and conversely an increase in trade between the United States and Japan, and in particular, between the European Community and Japan.

b. Newly industrialized countries (NIC) in Asia have dramatically increased their trading position vis-à-vis the rest of the world.

    1). From a sourcing perspective, the United States and other multinational companies were producing a less expensive supply of components and finished products in NICs for sale in the United States and elsewhere.

    2). An increasing segment of international trade of components and finished products is strongly influenced by multinational companies' foreign production and sourcing investment activities.

*****Use Exhibit 10-1 Here*****

C. Trends in Global Sourcing Strategy

1. *Trend 1: The Decline of Exchange Rate Determination of Sourcing.*

*****Use Exhibit 10-2 Here*****

a. Since the 1970s exchange rates have fluctuated rather erratically over time.

b. Companies consider the exchange rate when determining the extent to which they can engage in foreign sourcing.

c. The exchange rate determinism of sourcing is strictly based on price factor alone.

    1). Foreign sourcing can also occur for non-cost reasons.

    2). Foreign suppliers can easily be dropped if exchange rates begin to increase.

    3). Domestic price increases have to be watched.

    4). Long-term relationships become important.

    5). Some companies are able to shift supply locations from one country to another to overcome the adverse effects of exchange rate fluctuations.

*****Use Discussion Question #5 Here*****

2. *Trend 2: New Competitive Environment Caused by Excess Worldwide Capacity.*

a. The worldwide growth in the number of manufacturers has added excess production capacity in most industries.

b. There has been a downward pressure on prices of many components and products around the world.

c. There has been a strategic shift from price and quantity to quality and reliability of products as a determinant of competitive strength.

*****Use Exhibit 10-3 Here*****

111

3. *Trend 3: Innovations in and Restructuring of International Trade Infrastructure.*
   a. The innovations and structural changes that have important influences on sourcing strategy are:
      1). The increased number of purchasing managers experienced in sourcing.
      2). Improvements made in transportation and communication.
      3). New financing options, including countertrade.
      4). Manufacturing facilities diffused throughout the world by globally minded companies.
      5). Maquiladora plants in Mexico.
4. *Trend 4: Enhanced Role of Purchasing Managers.*
   a. JIT (just-in-time) production has been increasing.
   b. JIT requires a close working relationship with suppliers.
   c. More purchasing know-how is necessary to deal with foreign suppliers.
   d. The key to achieving effective global sourcing is securing management involvement at both the top (strategic) and middle (tactical) levels.
5. *Trend 5: Trend toward Global Manufacturing.*
   a. As a global company adds another international plant to its network of existing plants, it creates the need for sourcing of components and other semi-processed goods to and from the new plant to existing plants.

*****Use Global Perspective 10-1 "Trade Follows Investment" Here; Use Review Questions #2 and #3 Here; Use Discussion Question #3 Here*****

D. Value Chain and Functional Interfaces

1. The design of global sourcing strategy is based on the interplay between a company's competitive advantages and the comparative advantages of various countries.
   a. Competitive advantage influences the decision regarding what activities and technologies a company should concentrate on.
   b. Comparative advantage affects the company's decision on where to source and market.
2. The value chain concept offers a general framework for understanding what it takes to manage the interrelated value-added activities of a company on a global basis.

*****Use Exhibit 10-4 Here*****

   a. A company is essentially made up of a collection of activities that are performed to design, manufacture, market, deliver, and support its products. This is its value chain.
3. The value chain can be divided into two major actitivities:
   a. Primary activities--inbound logistics, manufacturing, outbound logistics, sales,

and after sale activities.
   b. Support activities--such as human resource management.
4. Continuous and interactive steps in developing a global sourcing strategy along the value chain are:
   a. Identify the separable links in the company's value chain.
   b. In the context of those links, determine the location of the company's competitive advantages (considering both economies of scale and scope).
   c. Ascertain the level of transaction costs between the links in the value chain and select the lowest cost mode.
   d. Determine the comparative advantage of countries relative to each link in the value chain and to the relevant transaction costs.
   e. Develop adequate flexibility in corporate decision making and organizational design so as to permit the company to respond to changes in both its comparative advantages and the comparative advantages of countries.

*****Use Exhibit 10-5 Here; Use Review Question #5 Here*****

5. Global sourcing strategy encompasses management of:
   a. The interfaces among R&D, manufacturing, and marketing on a global basis.
   b. Logistics identifying which production units will serve which particular markets and how components will be supplied for production.

*****Use Global Perspective 10-2 "Power of Good Linkage Management" Here*****

6. *R&D/Manufacturing Interface.*
   a. Technology is broadly defined as know-how.
   b. By itself, technology will not provide a long-term advantage over competition.
   c. Manufacturing innovations are more important strategically than product innovations.
   d. To facilitate the transferability of new product innovations to manufacturing, designers should strive to make components that do not need to be re-tooled from existing processes. Interchangability is a significant advantage.
7. *Manufacturing/Marketing Interface.*
   a. Reduce this inherent conflict.
   b. Four different ways of developing global product policy are generally considered an effective means to streamline manufacturing, this lowering manufacturing cost, without sacrificing marketing flexibility:
      1). Core component standardization.
      2). Product design families.
      3). Universal product with all features.
      4). Universal product with different positioning.

*****Use Discussion Question #2 Here*****

8. *Marketing/R&D Interface.*

    a. This interface helps to establish the needs of the consumer as an important aspect of strategy and planning activities.

    b. With the example of the Japanese, the marketplace becomes a virtual R&D laboratory for Japanese companies to gain production and marketing experience as well as to perfect technology. This is done by close customer contact.

    c. The continual introduction of newer and better designed products brings a greater likelihood of market success.

*****Use Review Questions #6 and #7 Here*****

E. Logistics of Sourcing Strategy

1. Sourcing strategy includes a number of basic choices companies make in deciding how to serve foreign markets:

    a. The use of imports, assembly of production within the country to serve a foreign markets.

    b. The use of internal or external suppliers of components or finished goods.

2. Contractually, sourcing occurs as:

    a. Patents or the firm's foreign subsidiaries on an intra-firm basis (known as intra-firm sourcing).

    b. Independent suppliers on a "contractual" basis (known as outsourcing).

3. From a locational point of view, multinational companies can procure components and products either:

    a. Domestically (domestic sourcing).

    b. Abroad (offshore sourcing).

*****Use Exhibit 10-6 Here*****

4. Where to source is much less important a decision than how to source.

5. *Intra-firm sourcing.*

    a. Companies can intra-firm source and produce major components themselves (or among their subsidiaries).

    b. This is a very popular method with the Japanese and United States companies.

6. *Outsourcing.*

    a. Component procurement overseas is receiving an increasing amount of attention.

    b. The effects, however, can cause difficulties domestically for United States firms because of labor issues.

    c. Labor says that increasingly companies are becoming "hollow corporations."

    d. This method can affect a company's ability to bring about product innovations.

*****Use Global Perspective 10-3 "Offshore Sourcing and Sweatshops Overseas" Here; Use Discussion Question #4 Here*****

F. Costs and Consequences of Global Sourcing

1. *Need for Coordination.*
   a. Companies have increasingly become compelled to consider global sourcing.
   b. Competitive urgency must be considered.
   c. Competition seems to be the driving force for global sourcing.
2. *Functional Mismatch.*
   a. United States firms have drifted from manufacturing and marketing in recent years to finance functions.
   b. In a sense, production managers have taken on the role of an outside supplier even within their own firm.
   c. Outsourcing has been a direct result.

*****Use Global Perspective 10-4 "Hollow Corporations" Here; Use Review Question #4 Here; Use Discussion Question #1 Here*****

   d. Outsourcing does not always affect the competitiveness or innovativeness of a company.
3. *Long Term Consequences.*
   a. One school of thought believes that strategic alliances give firms flexible networks and that individual partner competencies bring about sourcing.
   b. Another school says that even though the above is a trend it can have bad long term effects on the firm because of the dependency it creates.
   c. *Strategic Alliances.*
      1). The advantage of this form is its structural flexibility.
      2). This is an easy option for the organization that wishes to enter into the international market rapidly.
      3). Many alliance partners have funneled out manufacturing responsibilities to partners and are therefore diminishing their own role in that area.
   d. *Dependence.*
      1). Companies that rely on independent external sources of supply of major components tend to forsake part of the most important value-creating activities to, and also become dependent on, independent operators for assurance of component quality.
      2). Uncertainty between suppliers, manufacturers, and distributors can cause problems.
   e. *Gradual loss of Design and Manufacturing Abilities.*

*****Use Review Question #8 Here*****

REVIEW QUESTIONS

INSTRUCTOR'S NOTE: The following chapter review questions are meant to challenge the student to think about material presented in the chapter and formulate a creative answer to the review questions. Many of the answers require judgments rather than specific line-by-line quotation of facts. The answers provided are meant to provide stimulation of creative answers.

1. Discuss the reasons why trade statistics do not capture the intricacies of global sourcing.

Trade statistics do not usually indicate the full nature of the intra-firm trade. In this form of trading, a multinational firm trades with one or more of its subsidiaries. Even though this might be considered exporting and importing, it is usually not carried in trade statistics in that way. This form of trading is also one of the chief reasons that the total volume of trading has increased among the Triad regions (i.e.,, the United States, the European Community, and Japan).

2. Discuss the trends in global sourcing strategy. Why is it necessary for companies to keep up with those trends?

1. *Trend 1: The Decline of Exchange Rate Determination of Sourcing.*
    a. Since the 1970s exchange rates have fluctuated rather erratically over time.
    b. Companies consider the exchange rate when determining the extent to which they can engage in foreign sourcing.
    c. The exchange rate determinism of sourcing is strictly based on price factor alone.
        1). Foreign sourcing can also occur for non-cost reasons.
        2). Foreign suppliers can easily be dropped if exchange rates begin to increase.
        3). Domestic price increases have to be watched.
        4). Long-term relationships become important.
        5). Some companies are able to shift supply locations from one country to another to overcome the adverse effects of exchange rate fluctuations.
2. *Trend 2: New Competitive Environment Caused by Excess Worldwide Capacity.*
    a. The worldwide growth in the number of manufacturers has added excess production capacity in most industries.
    b. There has been a downward pressure on prices of many components and products around the world.
    c. There has been a strategic shift from price and quantity to quality and reliability of products as a determinant of competitive strength.
3. *Trend 3: Innovations in and Restructuring of International Trade Infrastructure.*
    a. The innovations and structural changes that have important influences on

sourcing strategy are:

1). The increased number of purchasing managers experienced in sourcing.
2). Improvements made in transportation and communication.
3). New financing options, including countertrade.
4). Manufacturing facilities diffused throughout the world by globally minded companies.
5). Maquiladora plants in Mexico.

4. *Trend 4: Enhanced Role of Purchasing Managers.*
   a. JIT (just-in-time) production has been increasing.
   b. JIT requires a close working relationship with suppliers.
   c. More purchasing know-how is necessary to deal with foreign suppliers.
   d. The key to achieving effective global sourcing is securing management involvement at both the top (strategic) and middle (tactical) levels.

5. *Trend 5: Trend toward Global Manufacturing.*
   a. As a global company adds another international plant to its network of existing plants, it creates the need for sourcing of components and other semi-processed goods to and from the new plant to existing plants.

Firms that do not observe these trends will become uncompetitive and be forced into less than advantageous positions in the world marketplace.

3. Why was manufacturing ignored by U.S. multinational companies in the 1980s?

During the 1980s domestic manufacturing was ignored by many U.S. companies because acquisition mania struck. The Chief Financial Officer (CFO) became more important than the Chief Executive Officer (CEO). Even though U.S. companies continued to advance abroad, their primary concern was the bottom line profit in the United States and to some extent had a short-term stock market mentality. During this same time period, the U.S. firms clearly expanded sourcing abroad and continued to cut back on domestic manufacturing.

4. Discuss the relationships between paper entrepreneurship and hollow corporations.

Students should review Global Perspective 10-4 "Hollow Corporation" to answer this question. The intent of the question is to get students to understand that if too much sourcing takes place the corporation does not really make anything anymore. If this happens, the corporation becomes very vulnerable to dependency on foreign suppliers and sourcers. Ownership is weak, R&D becomes almost non-existent, and the firm becomes a prime candidate to fail.

5. How do multinational companies exploit the value chain on a global basis?

The design of global sourcing strategy is based on the interplay between a company's competitive advantages and the comparative advantages of various countries. The value chain concept offers a general framework for understanding what it takes to manage the interrelated value-adding activities of a company on a global basis. The set of interrelated corporate activities is called the value chain. See Global Perspective 10-2 "Power of Good Linkage Management" for additional information.

The value chain can be divided into two major activities performed by a company: 1) primary activities consisting of inbound logistics, manufacturing operations, outbound logistics, and after-sale service, and 2) support activities consisting of human resource management, technology development, and other activities that help promote primary activities. Competing companies constantly strive to create value across various activities in the value chain.

6. What are inherent difficulties in coordinating a) R&D/manufacturing, b) manufacturing/marketing, and c) marketing/R&D interfaces?

a). Product technology alone may not provide the company a long-term competitive edge over competition unless it is matched with sufficient manufacturing capabilities. Most United States companies have ignored manufacturing and only concentrated on product innovation as a strategic weapon. The firms should remember that innovation and manufacturing are intertwined.

b). The primary conflict between these two is that manufacturing seeks standardization and marketing seeks adaptation (customization) to meet individual customers demands. To offset these problems, the firm can stress 1) core component standardization, 2) product design families, 3) universal product with all features, and 4) universal product with different positioning.

c). Since R&D is normally outside the marketing manager's control, some form of interface is necessary to make sure that customer concerns and desires are not only measured but acted upon. Consumers, after all, have the final say on whether they will buy or not. Product engineers do not determine customer tastes. There must be a willingness to coordinate and cooperate. Pushing products from the top down (the traditional way of doing things) takes to much time. A short product development cycle is critical to global success.

7. What are strategic motivations for standardizing either components or products or both?

To successfully answer this question, students are referred to Review Question 6 (a) and previous chapter descriptions of the standardization versus adaptation issue. Remember that standardization usually brings economies of scale and cost efficiencies.

8. Under what conditions can a company develop its global sourcing strategy without an alliance partner?

Companies can develop global sourcing strategies without an alliance partner if they choose to use foreign subsidiaries as their suppliers. Sourcing backwards and forwards between parent and subsidiary increases the control aspect, reduces risk, prevents partnering problems, and secures lines of supply and favorable dependencies.

DISCUSSION QUESTIONS

INSTRUCTOR'S NOTE: Discussion Questions are found at the end of each chapter in the text. These questions (in many cases) are too lengthy to repeat in this manual. Suggestions for answering and discussing the questions are presented in this section. Many of the questions require student opinion and judgment.

1. In order to effectively answer this question, students are reminded to review Global Perspectives 10-3 "Offshore Sourcing and Sweatshops Overseas" and Global Perspective 10-4 "Hollow Corporations." Once this material has been read, the students should notice that just locating a manufacturing facility abroad does not necessarily mean that the firm will be "hollowed out." Hollowing out means that the firm effectively does not make anything any more (it outsources so much that it may only assemble or re-package). Company controlled foreign subsidiaries may be a move that is necessary to control costs and gain global efficiencies.

2. In the past Honda has placed emphasis on the U.S. market and keeping costs low (one result of platforming). If it intends to seriously make a move in the Japanese market, it will have to design and implement strategy that is oriented toward the Japanese market and its characteristics. If platforming is not well received in Japan, then the company should review its design methods with respect to this approach. The design conscious Japanese may require more adaptation rather than standardization.

3. One reason for the huge increase in proportion of GNP coming from the service sector is that more services are required for the increasing amount of foreign made goods. As manufacturers began to loose the manufacturing war, they turned their attention to services as an alternative. Gains have been made in manufacturing but not to the extent that foreign companies have maintained. The newly emerging Pacific Rim countries will be the competitors of the future and manufacturers from the global community must be ready to deal with those groups.

4. To answer this Discussion Question students should review material from Review Questions 6 and 7. Once this material has been reviewed, the students should be ready to construct examples of industries (as per instructions in the question) that sourcing would be appropriate. If the students need assistance with ideas, they might want to consider reviewing material found in the popular business periodicals.

5. In order to respond to the mini-case scenario presented in this Discussion Question, the students should review the material presented in the Trends in Global Sourcing

Strategy (Trend 1: The Decline of Exchange Rate Determinism of Sourcing). By reviewing this material the students should be able to get enough basic information to make a determination as to whether and how exchange rate fluctuation will affect decision making with respect to sourcing. The suggestions that students present will be opinion in nature but should be supported by facts.

STUDENT PROJECTS and INTERNET FOCUS

1. Contact a local company that (in your opinion) would probably do sourcing of some form (this could be domestic or international). Interview one of the managers about their sourcing process. Investigate how they accomplish sourcing, why they do it, and what type of gains are made because of sourcing. You may ask any other questions that might make the interview more informative. Write up your impressions of your interview experience and share the experience with the class (either in a written report and/or a verbal report).

2. Pick a global company and investigate how they have and can source globally. To understand what they have done in the past, look for data concerning relationships with other firms from which sourcing occurs. Think strategically about the firm's business, industry, and competitors. Indicate relationships that the firm might want to consider for future sourcing opportunities. Indicate how you did your discovery process. Report your findings to the class.

INSTRUCTOR'S NOTE: The following projects require the students to both use and understand the Internet. If students do not understand how to use the Internet, explanation should be given before these projects are undertaken. The Web addresses change frequently, the instructor should re-affirm the site addresses and the content of the site before making an assignment.

3. Go to the Web site entitled *Integrated Supply Chain Management* at (**http://www.ie.utoronto.ca/EIL/iscm-descr.html**) and investigate the information available on issues related to the supply chain. What can you discover about sourcing from this data? Report your findings.

4. Go to the Web site entitled *Manufacturing Information Net* at (**http://www.mfginfo.com/home.html**). At this site you will find a variety of information about manufacturing related information, different products and services. Try to get information about sourcing and companies that use this method. Report your findings.

5. An interesting site to visit is the Web site entitled *Managing Supplier Relationships.* Information about this site can be found at (**http://www.dbisna.com/dbis/purchase/vpurchas.html**). The site offers some interesting tips on managing supplier relationships. What are the tips? Which might be used to manage sourcing situations in the international arena? Report your findings.

CHAPTER 11

GLOBAL PRODUCT POLICY DECISIONS I: DEVELOPING NEW PRODUCTS FOR GLOBAL MARKETS

CHAPTER OBJECTIVES

1. Identify and analyze global product strategies.

2. Discuss the standardization versus customization alternatives.

3. Describe multinational diffusion.

4. Illustrate how to develop new products for global markets.

5. Describe NPD and culture.

CHAPTER OVERVIEW

Global product policy decisions are tremendously important for the success of a MNC's global marketing strategy. With this in mind, this chapter has as a primary focus the new product development process in a global context.

Several broad approaches include extension of the domestic strategy, adaptation of home-grown strategies, or invention by designing products that cater to the common needs of global customers. As an issue to be considered within these alternatives is whether to standardize or customize the product. This issue is not an "either-or" issue. Instead it is a "degree" issue. Proper balance is the mark of a successful global competitor. Variants (such as the modular or core-product approach) are described. Conjoint analysis can be used to help make the determination more correct.

The new product development process is explained in a step by step procedure. This process is somewhat similar to the new product development process used domestically. However, the global decision has its own set of complicating factors. Each is examined in some detail.

The customer and their individual culture must not be forgotten. The chapter closes with a discussion of culture and its relationship to product development.

CHAPTER OUTLINE

A. Introduction

1. A cornerstone of a global marketing mix program is the set of product policy decisions that multinational companies (MNCs) constantly need to formulate.
2. Blunder and success stories abound.

*****Use Global Perspective 11-1 "The Launch of 'Fruit Magix'" Here*****

3. Fostering the development of new products that satisfy or even amaze customers worldwide is the major ingredient of many global success stories.

B. Global Product Strategies

1. Companies can pursue three global strategies to penetrate foreign markets.

*****Use Exhibit 11-1 Here*****

2. ***Strategic Option 1: Product & Communication Extension: Dual Extension.***
   a. A company can choose to market a standardized product using a uniform communication strategy.
      1). Early entrants prefer this approach.
      2). Small companies with few resources prefer this form of extension.
   b. A standardized product policy coupled with a uniform communication strategy offers substantial savings coming from economies of scale.
      1). This strategy is usually product-driven rather than market-driven.
      2). This strategy can alienate foreign customers who prefer a customized product.
3. ***Strategic Option 2: Product Extension-Communications Adaptation.***
   a. Due to differences in the cultural or competitive environment, the same product often is used to offer benefits or functions that dramatically differ from those in the home market.
      1). Customized advertising is the result.
      2). Positioning themes are often used in the ad campaigns.
4. ***Strategic Option 3: Product Adaptation-Communications Extension.***
   a. Firms can adapt their product but market it using a standardized communications strategy.
      1). Local market circumstances and regulations often favor this alternative.
   b. Another reason for this strategy is the firm's expansion strategy.
      1). Brands are added as firm's buy local companies.
   c. Clever marketing ideas can be transferred from one country to another.
5. ***Strategic Option 4: Product & Communications Adaptation: Dual Adaptation.***
   a. Differences in both the cultural and physical environment across countries call

for a dual adaptation strategy.
  b. This becomes a viable option for global expansion.
6. ***Strategic Option 5: Product Invention.***
  a. Genuinely global marketers try to figure out how to create products with a global scope rather than just for a single country.
  b. This strategy focuses on opportunities and inventions.

*****Use Review Question #1 Here*****

C. Standardization Versus Customization

1. A recurrent theme in global marketing is whether companies should aim for a standardized or country-tailored product strategy.
2. Standardization means offering a uniform product worldwide.
  a. Capitalizes on commonalties among customers.
  b. Minimizes costs.
  c. These cost savings are usually passed on to customers in the form of lower prices per product.
3. Customization leverages cross-border differences in needs and wants of the firm's target customers.
  a. Changes are made to meet local conditions.
  b. This is a market-driven strategy.
4. Forces that favor a globalized product strategy are:
  a. ***Common customer needs.***

*****Use Exhibits 11-2, 11-3, and 11-4 Here*****

  b. ***Global customers.***
    1). In business-to-business marketing, the shift towards globalization means that for many companies a significant part of their business comes from MNCs that are essentially global customers. Decisions are centralized.
  c. ***Scale economies.***
    1). Savings in a variety of areas is a big reason for standardization.
    2). The result is lower prices to the consumer.
    3). Production procedures such as flexible manufacturing and just-in-time production have shifted the focus from size to timeliness.
    4). CAD/CAM allows for small batch production.
    5). There are hidden costs (such as administrative costs) associated with large size production.
  d. ***Time-to-market.***
    1). Companies must seek to shorten the cycle from invention to production to market.
    2). Centralizing efforts (such as in research) often helps.
  e. ***Europe 1992 and other regional market agreements.***
    1). Formation of single markets or market agreements helps to launch regional

or re-designed products.

5. The real question is not that of striving for standardization or customization but how to implement some form of combination globally. Degree is the real decision.

*****Use Review Questions #3 and #4 Here; Use Discussion Questions #1, #2, #3, and #4 Here*****

6. Two popular approaches are:
   a. *Modular approach.*
      1). Developing a range of products parts that can be used worldwide.
      2). These parts can be assembled into numerous configurations.

*****Use Global Perspective 11-2 "Global Takes-Off for Volvo FH" Here*****

   b. *Core-product approach.*
      1). The core-product approach starts with the design of a mostly uniform core-product and then adds attachments that might fit local needs.
      2). Savings comes from centralizing the production of the core.
      3). Easy product modification is a secret of success.

*****Use Review Question #2 Here*****

7. The balancing act between standardization and adaptation is very tricky.
8. Pitfalls can be described as:
   a. Overstandardization.
   b. Overcustomization.

D. Multinational Diffusion

1. The speed and pattern of market penetration for a given product innovation usually differs substantially between markets.

*****Use Exhibit 11-5 Here*****

2. It is not uncommon that new products that were phenomenally successful in one country turn out to be turkeys in foreign markets.
3. In general, the adoption of new products is driven by three types of factors:
   a. Individual differences.
   b. Personal influences.
   c. Product characteristics.
4. Five product characteristics are key:
   a. Relative advantage.
   b. Compatibility.
   c. Complexity.
   d. Trialability.

e. Observability.
5. Country characteristics that can be used to predict new product penetration patterns are:
   a. Communication.
   b. Homogeneous population.
   c. Time interval.
      1). Lead-countries.
      2). Lag-countries.
   d. Cosmopolitanism.
   e. Mobility.
   f. Percentage of women in the labor force.
   g. Individualism.
   h. Uncertainty avoidance.
   i. National innovativeness.

*****Use Exhibit 11-6 Here*****

E. Developing New Product for Global Markets

1. For most companies, new products are the bread-and-butter of their growth strategy. The steps are similar to that of domestic new product development and are described below.

*****Use Exhibit 11-7 Here; Use Global Perspective 11-3 "Colgate-Palmolive's Global NPD Approach" Here*****

2. *Identifying New Product Ideas.*
   a. Every new product starts with an idea.
   b. New ideas can come from:
      1). Company.
      2). Customers.
      3). Competition.
      4). Collaborators.
   c. Many MNCs create organizational structures to foster global (or regional) product development.
3. *Screening.*
   a. Once new product ideas have been identified they need to be screened.
   b. The filtering process can take the form of a formal scoring model.
   c. Regression models can be used to accomplish this task.

*****Use Exhibit 11-8 Here*****

4. *Concept Testing.*
   a. Once the merits of a new product idea have been established in the previous stage, it needs to be translated into a product concept.

b. A product concept is a fairly detailed description, verbally or sometimes even visually, of the new product or service.

c. Focus groups can be used to accomplish the concept testing phase.

d. A more sophisticated procedure to measure consumer preferences for product concepts is conjoint analysis (sometimes referred to as trade-off analysis).

   1). The starting premise of conjoint analysis is that people make trade-offs between the different product attributes when they evaluate alternatives (e.g., brands) from which they have to pick a choice.

   2). The purpose of conjoint analysis is to understand trade-offs.

   3). Steps might be to:

      a). Determine the salient attributes for the product.

      b). Consider the possible levels that each of the attributes can take.

*****Use Exhibit 11-9 Here*****

      c). Construct a product profiles by combining the various attribute levels. Each profile would represent a hypothetical product configuration.

      d). Use an experimental design to come up with a small but manageable number of product profiles.

      e). Once the profiles have been finalized you can go into the field and gather the desired information.

*****Use Exhibit 11-10 Here*****

      f). Once the preference data has been collected, analysis needs to be performed using a statistical software package. The outcome of the analysis will be a set of "utilities" that each segment (or respondent) derives from each of the attribute levels.

*****Use Exhibits 11-11 and 11-12 Here*****

5. *Test Marketing.*

a. Test marketing (primarily a Western country concept) is essentially a field experiment where the new product is marketed in a select set of cities to assess its sales potential and scores of other performance measures.

b. Reasons to run a test market include:

   1). It allows them to make fairly accurate projections of the market share, sales volume and penetration of the new product.

   2). The countries can contrast competing marketing mix strategies to decide which one is most promising in achieving the firm's objectives.

c. Shortcomings include:

   1). Time-consuming and costly.

   2). Results can be misleading.

   3). The strategic concern--it may alert your competitors.

*****Use Review Question #6 Here*****

    d. Many firms prefer to skip this stage and go directly to market simulation or immediately launch the new product.
       1). Laboratory test markets can be used.
       2). Simulation "what ifs" can be used.
       3). Sales performance in another country can be used.

*****Use Exhibit 11-13 Here*****

  6. ***Timing of Entry: Waterfall versus Sprinkler Strategies.***
    a. A key element of global product launch strategy is the entry timing decision: when should we launch the new product in the target markets?

*****Use Exhibit 11-14 Here*****

    b. Options include:
       1). The waterfall method where new products trickle down in a cascade-like manner.
          a). The typical pattern here is to introduce the product in the home country first.
          b). Next launch in advanced markets.
          c). Lastly, launch in less advanced markets.
          d). This method can be very time-consuming but is less risky.
       2). The sprinkler strategy is a simultaneous worldwide entry.
          a). Rollout occurs in one to two years.
          b). The growing prominence of universal segments and concerns about competitive pre-emption in the foreign markets are two major factors behind this expansion approach.
    c. The waterfall strategy is preferable over the sprinkler model when:
       1). The lifecycle of the product is relatively long.
       2). Nonfavorable conditions govern the foreign market.
       3). Weak competitive climate in the foreign market exists.

*****Use Review Question #5 Here; Use Discussion Questions #5 and #6 Here*****

F. Global NPD and Culture

  1. Cultural differences heavily influence the NPD process.
  2. The precise role of culture depends on the stage of the NPD process.
    a. There is a distinction between "initiation" and "implementation."
    b. Centralized versus decentralized structures change the strategy.
  3. Risk avoidance must be observed and certainly has a bearing on the NPD process.

*****Use Discussion Question #7 Here*****

REVIEW QUESTIONS

INSTRUCTOR'S NOTE: The following chapter review questions are meant to challenge the student to think about material presented in the chapter and formulate a creative answer to the review questions. Many of the answers require judgments rather than specific line-by-line quotation of facts. The answers provided are meant to provide stimulation of creative answers.

1. Under what conditions is a dual extension strategy advisable? When is product invention more appropriate?

Strategic Option 1: Product & Communication Extension: Dual Extension.
    a. A company can choose to market a standardized product using a uniform communication strategy.
        1). Early entrants prefer this approach.
        2). Small companies with few resources prefer this form of extension.
    b. A standardized product policy coupled with a uniform communication strategy offers substantial savings coming from economies of scale.
        1). This strategy is usually product-driven rather than market-driven.
        2). This strategy can alienate foreign customers who prefer a customized product.

Strategic Option 5: Product Invention.
    a. Genuinely global marketers try to figure out how to create products with a global scope rather than just for a single country.
    b. This strategy focuses on opportunities and inventions.

2. Explain the difference between the modular and core-product approaches.

Modular approach.
        1). Developing a range of products parts that can be used worldwide.
        2). These parts can be assembled into numerous configurations.
Core-product approach.
        1). The core-product approach starts with the design of a mostly uniform core-product and then adds attachments that might fit local needs.
        2). Savings comes from centralizing the production of the core.
        3). Easy product modification is a secret of success.

3. Discuss the forces that favor a globalized product design strategy.

Forces that favor a globalized product strategy are common customer needs, global customers, scale economies, time-to-market, Europe 1992 and other regional market agreements.

4. In what sense is the "standardize versus customize" question in global product design a bogus issue?

The real question is not that of striving for standardization or customization but how to implement some form of combination globally. Degree is the real concern. Issues in the chapter section indicate that degree of standardization or customization is a degree concern since most firms will have to reach a compromise between these two.

5. MNCs tend to move more and more towards a sprinkler strategy in terms of their global launch timing decisions. What forces lie behind this trend?

A key element of global product launch strategy is the entry timing decision: when should we launch the new product in the target markets?

Options include:
1). The waterfall method where new products trickle down in a cascade-like manner.
   a). The typical pattern here is to introduce the product in the home country first.
   b). Next launch in advanced markets.
   c). Lastly, launch in less advanced markets.
   d). This method can be very time-consuming but is less risky.
2). The sprinkler strategy is a simultaneous worldwide entry.
   a). Rollout occurs in one to two years.
   b). The growing prominence of universal segments and concerns about competitive pre-emption in the foreign markets are two major factors behind this expansion approach.
c. The waterfall strategy is preferable over the sprinkler model when:
   1). The lifecycle of the product is relatively long.
   2). Nonfavorable conditions govern the foreign market.
   3). Weak competitive climate in the foreign market exists.

6. What are the major dangers in using an entire country as a "test market" for new products that are to be launched globally (or regionally)?

Test marketing (primarily a Western country concept) is essentially a field experiment where the new product is marketed in a select set of cities to assess its sales potential and scores of other performance measures.

Reasons to run a test market include:
1). It allows them to make fairly accurate projections of the market share, sales volume and penetration of the new product.
2). The countries can contrast competing marketing mix strategies to decide which one is most promising in achieving the firm's objectives.

Shortcomings include:
1). Time-consuming and costly.
2). Results can be misleading.
3). The strategic concern--it may alert your competitors.

DISCUSSION QUESTIONS

INSTRUCTOR'S NOTE: Discussion Questions are found at the end of each chapter in the text. These questions (in many cases) are too lengthy to repeat in the manual. Suggestions for answering and discussing the questions are presented in this section. Many of the questions require student opinion and judgment.

1. This question requires an opinion and judgment by the student. If the student has read the material carefully in the chapter, they will probably agree with the statement. The chapter makes a case for international development of products and ideas. With more multinationals drawing their ideas from a variety of sources, the idea that the world is our innovative laboratory seems appealing. If the student chooses to disagree with this statement, they should be prepared to justify their logic.

2. To answer this question the student should review the material from the section entitled "Global Product Strategies." Strategic option #3 or #4 can be considered. However, new pricing policies might be considered. In addition, expansion and its economies of scale should perhaps be extended to the consumer. Once habits have been established or preferences built, prices might be able to go up.

3. In order to answer this question, students need to review the idea of a "global village" and the ramifications of standard approaches to that world market. Perhaps the educational material presented on this new channel are not unique to the United States. However, if a decidedly U.S. slant is given to the material then that changes the equation. Since English has become the international language programming can be held in this language. Be sure to ask students what would be advantages and disadvantages to the approach suggested in the discussion question.

4. Following the new product introduction process suggested in the chapter, the makers of the new microwave oven have some hard work set before them. Since this model is being billed as a "VIP" model several factors would have to be considered if it were to be introduced into China. The factors might be consumer income, electrification of their homes, how these ovens might be accepted culturally and traditionally, and what would

be the view of the expenditure on the part of the government. What other factors can the students think of? Be sure to let them express their opinion on the acceptability of this idea. What would it take to make this idea work?

5. The Western new product model is explained in the chapter. From the data given to the student in the discussion question, the student should see that the Japanese probably know their market very well. Remember that even though there are consumer differences, this market is much more standardized and traditional than the United States market. Segments may be much more defined and rigid. Be sure to encourage acceptability of this concept. Would it work if this strategy was tried worldwide? As the Japanese emerge into the world marketplace, will those techniques eventually be used at home?

6. The number one area that must be observed for truly new product introduction would have to be culture and how the culture of the market will accept the new product. It would certainly be advisable that numerous tests be done from a variety of models to reduce the risk of market introduction. The international marketer must remember that the foreign market is very different from the United States market.

7. This question is an "assignment" question and the students should follow the directions as stated in the question.

STUDENT PROJECTS and INTERNET FOCUS

1. Go to the library and research the product strategy of an international company. You might get your ideas from current periodicals or newspapers. You many use any of the examples cited in the chapter as a springboard from which to build your research. Be sure to give specific title and character to your strategy description. Be sure to separate what you perceive to be established product strategy and new product development. Write a brief report about your findings.

2. Think of a domestic product that you think could be introduced internationally. Using the steps as outlined in the chapter, write a plan of how to introduce the product in a market selected by you. Realizing that many of your comments may have to be general in nature, follow the steps as closely as possible and be sure to describe forms of testing and where the tests should be done. Remember to pick specific markets that you believe would be prime candidates for your product. Do a brief report on your experiences.

INSTRUCTOR'S NOTE: The following projects require the students to both use and understand the Internet. If students do not understand how to use the Internet, explanation should be given before these projects are undertaken. The Web addresses change frequently, the instructor should re-affirm the site addresses and the content of the site before making an assignment.

3. Go to Microsoft's home page at (**http://www.microsoft.com**) and determine what new products the company currently has to offer. Which of these are currently or can be marketed internationally? Pick one product and prepare a brief outline of how you believe that it can be marketed internationally.

4. Go to any of the following home Web pages, pick a product and design a product strategy for the product. Be sure to detail your strategy. Once you have done this go to the Strategic Options found at the beginning of the chapter, pick one and incorporate it into your strategy. Prepare a short report describing your strategy and the option you picked.

    a. AT&T   (**http://www.att.com**)

    b. Lotus   (**http://www.lotus.com**)

    c. Okidata   (**http://www.okidata.com**)

    d. NCR   (**http://www.ncr.com**)

5. Go to the Charles Schwab (or other investment home pages from other brokers) and determine what type of free research you can do on new products. If this proves to be too difficult go to Yahoo or other search engines and attempt the process. Once you have found a method to research new products, pick one and write about its progress in development and market acceptability.

Charles Schwab web site   (**http://www.schwab.com**)

Yahoo   (**http://www.yahoo.com**)

CHAPTER 12

GLOBAL PRODUCT POLICY DECISIONS II:
MARKETING PRODUCTS AND SERVICES

CHAPTER OBJECTIVES

1. Describe global branding strategies.

2. Analyze the process of managing multinational product lines.

3. Understand the problems associated with product piracy.

4. Describe country-of-origin effects.

5. Chart the development of global marketing of services.

CHAPTER OVERVIEW

After companies have developed product introduction strategies, they must face the tricky issues presented by branding their products in the global arena. These branding strategies (when applied to the global market) may be very different than those applied to the domestic market. Global brands is a relatively new concept, however, the case for global brands is building. Others believe that domestic branding is still the strongest policy to pursue.

Several questions should be considered in developing a global brand:

1). Which of the brands in our brand portfolio have the potential to be globalized?
2). What is the best route towards globalizing our brands?
3). Should we start by acquiring local brands, develop them into regional brands, and, ultimately, if the potential is there, into a "truly" global brand?
4). What is the best way to implement the change-over from a local to a global (or regional) brand?
5). How do we foster and sustain the consistency of our global brand image?
6). What organizational mechanisms should we as a company use to coordinate our branding strategies across markets?
7). Should coordination happen at the regional or global level?

The ultimate reward for mastering and successfully answering these questions is to develop at least a successful regional brand if not a successful strategy for a global brand.

Once the branding decision has been made other product issues must be faced. Management of the product line issues such as product assortment, line expansion, and line addition or deletion decisions must all eventually be addressed. Issues particular to the international environment (such as product piracy) are also addressed. The chapter closes with a discussion of the adaptation of services to the international environment. This sector is expected to grow in the future just as it has domestically.

CHAPTER OUTLINE

A. Global Branding Strategies

1. One of the major tasks facing international firms today is the management of their company's brand portfolio. Brands can be a firm's most valuable asset.
2. A brand can be identified as "a name, term, sign, symbol, or combination of them which is intended to identify the goods and services of one seller or group of sellers and to differentiate them from those of competitors."
3. Brand equity is tied to brand name.
   a. This includes:
      1). Brand name awareness.
      2). Perceived quality.
      3). Any other associations invoked by the brand name in the customer's mind.
   b. Issues include:
      1). How do we strike the balance between a global brand that shuns cultural barriers and one which allows for local requirements?
      2). What aspects of the brand policy can be adapted to global use? Which ones should remain flexible?
      3). Which brands are destined to become "global" mega-brands? Which ones should be kept as "local" brands?
      4). How do you condense a multitude of local brands into smaller, more manageable number of global (or regional) brands?
      5). How do you execute the changeover from a local to a global brand?
      6). How do you build up a portfolio of global mega-brands?
4. *Global brands.*
   a. A key strategic issue that appears on international marketers agenda is whether or not there should be a global brand.
   b. Questions that have to be answered are:
      1). What conditions favor launching a product with a single brand name worldwide?
      2). The same logo?
      3). The same slogan?
      4). When is more appropriate to keep brand names local?

*****Use Exhibit 12-1 Here*****

c. What is the case for global branding?
   1). Economies of scale.
   2). Development costs can be spread over large volumes.
   3). Brand awareness--global brands are more visible than local brands.
   4). Capitalize on media overlap between countries.
   5). The prestige-factor.
   6). Positioning one's self as a global brand can improve other marketing efforts.
   7). Leverage the country association.
d. Brand equity varies country by country.
e. Inter-country gaps in brand equity may be due to any of the following factors:
   1). History.
   2). Competitive climate.
   3). Marketing support.
   4). Cultural receptivity to brands.
   5). Product category penetration.

5. *Local branding.*
   a. Benefits of local branding include:
      1). Legal constraints favor local branding.
      2). Justified by cultural barriers.
      3). Local linkage proves to be powerful in countries where patriotism and buyer attitudes matter.
      4). Local names kept after an acquisition.

6. *Global or local brands?*
   a. There is no simple answer to this question.

*****Use Exhibit 12-2 Here; Use Discussion Questions #1 and #2 Here*****

   b. Many companies classify their brands in a hierarchy.

*****Use Global Perspective 12-1 "Nestle's Brand Building Strategy" Here; Use Exhibit 12-3 Here*****

   c. Even though there is a trend to global branding, local branding still is appealing.
   d. According to David Aaker, use the following checklist to analyze globalization possibilities:
      1). What is the cost of creating and maintaining awareness and associations for a local brand versus a global one?
      2). Are there significant economies of scale in the creation and running of a communication program globally?
      3). Is there value to associations of a global brand or of a brand associated with the source country?
      4). What local associations will be generated by the global name? symbol? slogan? imagery?
      5). Is it culturally and legally do-able to use the brand name, symbol, slogan

across the different countries?
6). What is the value of the awareness and associations that a regional brand might create?

*****Use Exhibit 12-4 Here; Use Review Question #1 Here*****

6. *Brand name changeover strategies.*
   a. Fade-in/fade-out strategy. The global brand name is somehow tied to an existing local brand name. After a transition period, the old name is dropped.
   b. Transparent forewarning. Alerts the consumer about a brand name change. The forewarning can be done via the communication program, in-store displays, and product packaging.
   c. Summary axing. The company simply drops the old brand name and immediately replaces it with the global name.
   d. Some considerations are:
      1). Consider the length of the transition period.
      2). The purchase cycle.
      3). Customer exposure to the communication messages.
      4). Avoid negative spillovers.
      5). Monitor the response to the name change.

*****Use Review Question #4 Here*****

7. *Private label branding ("store branding").*

*****Use Exhibit 12-5 Here*****

   a. Several factors explain the success of private labels:
      1). Improved quality of private label products.
      2). Development of premium private label brands.
      3). Shift in balance of power between retailers and manufacturers.
      4). Expansion into new product categories.
      5). Internationalization of retail chains.
      6). Economic downturns.

*****Use Review Questions #2 and #5 Here*****

   b. As a branding strategy, private labeling is especially attractive to MNCs that face well-entrenched incumbent brands in the markets they plan to enter.
8. *Umbrella (corporate) branding.*
   a. A system where a single banner brand is used worldwide, often with a sub-brand name, for almost the entire product mix of the company.
   b. The appeal seems to be:
      1). Many cultures appreciate a good corporate image.
      2). Facilitates the branding over a range of products.

3). Makes it easier to drop or add new products.

*****Use Review Question #3 Here*****

9. ***Protecting brand names.***

*****Use Exhibit 12-6 Here*****

a. Brands are vital assets to brand owners.
b. The protection of the brand name is one of the major tasks faced by the brand owner. Questions are:
   1). How should the brand be protected?
   2). Which aspects of the brand?
   3). When?
   4). Where?
   5). For what product classes?
c. The most common way of protecting a brand is to seek legal registration.
   1). The Paris Convention is the oldest form of protection. It is based on the principle of reciprocity.
d. A major stumbling block is the protection provided by developing nations.

*****Use Exhibit 12-7 Here*****

e. Other elements (such as slogans, jingles, or visual elements) besides the brand name may need to be protected.

B. Managing Multinational Product Lines

1. The product assortment is usually described on two dimensions: the width and the length of the product mix.
   a. Width refers to the collection of different product lines marketed by the firm.
   b. Length refers to the number of different items that the company sells within a given product line.
2. Four different scenarios can be considered with respect to the product mix in a host and home market:
   a. An extension of the domestic line.
   b. A subset of the home market's product line.
   c. A mixture of local and non-local product lines.
   d. A completely localized product line.

*****Use Exhibit 12-8 Here*****

3. Several factors impact the composition of a firm's international product line:
   a. Customer preferences.

*****Use Exhibit 12-9 Here*****

    b. Competitive climate.

    c. Organizational structure.

    d. History.

4. Global marketers need to decide for each market of interest which product lines should be offered and which ones are to be dropped.

    a. Market research has limits in determining this.

    b. One method that might be used to augment marketing research is a "probing-and-learning" approach. Steps would include:

        1). Start with a product line that has a minimum level of product variety.

        2). Gradually adjust the amount of product variety over time by adding new items and dropping existing ones.

        3). Analyze the incoming actual sales data and other market feedback.

        4). Make the appropriate inferences.

        5). If necessary, adjust the product line further.

    c. The essence of this procedure is to use the product line as a listening post.

5. By and large add/drop decisions should be driven by profit considerations.

6. A good start is to analyze each individual country's product portfolio on a sales turnover basis. Products can be categorized as:

    a. Core products.

    b. Niche items.

    c. Seasonal products.

    d. Filter products.

C. Product Piracy

1. Product piracy is one of the downsides that popular global marketers face.

2. Any aspect is vulnerable (the brand name, logo, the design, or the package itself).

3. Losses are from lost sales revenues and damage to the brand name by the pirated product (which is often inferior in quality).

*****Use Exhibit 12-10 Here*****

4. *Strategic options against product piracy.*

    a. Lobbying activities (such as requesting sanctions against guilty parties or countries).

        1). Most Favored Nation status might be affected.

        2). Treaties can be used to stop piracy.

    b. Legal action.

        1). Time consuming and costly.

        2). Can generate negative publicity for the multinational.

    c. Product policy options.

        1). Holograms to indicate authenticity.

        2). Make products hard to copy.

d. Communications options.
  1). Warn audiences.
  2). Anti-piracy ad campaigns.

*****Use Review Question #6 Here; Use Discussion Questions #3 and #4 Here*****

D. Country of Origin (COO) Stereotypes

  1. *Country-of-origin (COO) influences on consumers.*
    a. There is ample evidence that shows that for many products the "Made in" label matters a great deal to consumers. This is heavily used to evaluate products.
    b. Research findings with respect to this issue conclude:
      1). COO-effects are not stable, perceptions change over time.
      2). In general, consumers prefer domestic products over imports.
      3). The critical factor appears to be the place of manufacture rather than the location of the company's headquarters.
      4). Demographics make a difference.
        a). COO influences are particularly strong among the elderly, less educated, and politically conservative.
      5). Consumers are likely to use the origin of a product to cue when they are unfamiliar with the brand name carried by the product.
      6). COO-effects depend upon the product category.

*****Use Exhibit 12-11 Here*****

  2. *Strategies to cope with COO-stereotypes.*
    a. Company image stereotypes can either benefit or hurt a company's product. Research should be conducted before reviewing strategic options.
    b. Strategies can be organized around the marketing mix variables:
      1). Product policy--established brand names will reduce the COO effect.
      2). Pricing--low prices will reduce the COO effect.
      3). Distribution--respected channels will reduce the COO effect.
      4). Communication--images can be improved or the brand can be bolstered.

*****Use Discussion Questions #5 and #6 Here*****

E. Global Marketing of Services

  1. As countries grow richer, services tend to become the dominant sector of the economy.
  2. *Challenges in marketing services internationally.*
    a. *Protectionism.*
      1). Trade barriers to service marketers tend to be much more cumbersome than for their product counterparts.

*****Use Exhibit 12-12 Here*****

        2). Non-tariff barriers are problems in this area.
    b. ***Immediate face-to-face contacts with service transactions.***
        1). Since services are performed, the human element is very important.
        2). Cultural values are very important.
        3). Providing a consistent quality image globally is very difficult.
        4). Transferring know-how between branches is a challenge.
        5). A local presence is often required.
        6). Service support companies often have to follow their chief clients footsteps.
    c. ***Difficulties in measuring customer satisfaction overseas.***
  3. ***Opportunities in the global service industries.***
    a. ***Deregulation of service industries.***
    b. ***Increasing demand for premium services.***
    c. ***Increased value consciousness.***

*****Use Review Question #7 Here*****

  4. ***Global service marketing strategies.***
    a. ***Capitalize on cultural forces in the host market.***

*****Use Global Perspective 12-2 "Selling Insurance Policies in China" Here*****

    b. ***Standardize and customize.***
    c. ***Central role of information technologies (IT).***
    d. ***Add value by differentiation.***

*****Use Exhibit 12-13 Here*****

    e. ***Establish global service networks.***

*****Use Exhibit 12-14 Here; Use Discussion Question #7 Here*****

REVIEW QUESTIONS

INSTRUCTOR'S NOTE: The following chapter review questions are meant to challenge the student to think about material presented in the chapter and formulate a creative answer to the review questions. Many of the answers require judgments rather than specific line-by-line quotation of facts. The answers provided are meant to provide stimulation of creative answers.

1. For what types of product/service categories would you expect global brand names? For which ones would you anticipate localized names?

The students should be allowed to speculate on the applicability of global versus local brand names. Obviously, cultural differences are a heavy factor. One way to begin the discussion is to remind the students of David Aaker's list for analyzing global propositions:

1). What is the cost of creating and maintaining awareness and associations for a local brand versus a global one?
2). Are there significant economies of scale in the creation and running of a communication program globally?
3). Is there value to associations of a global brand or of a brand associated with the source country?
4). What local associations will be generated by the global name? symbol? slogan? imagery?
5). Is it culturally and legally do-able to use the brand name, symbol, slogan across the different countries?
6). What is the value of the awareness and associations that a regional brand might create?

2. Why is the market share of private labels much higher in Europe than in Asia?

As indicated by the question, private labels are doing better in Europe than in Asia (even though there is an increase of private label activity in Europe). The primary factor seems to be brand loyalty. Those in Asia are still very brand loyal and unwilling to try new (in this case private labels) brands as readily as the Europeans. Several factors explain the success of private labels:

1). Improved quality of private label products.
2). Development of premium private label brands.
3). Shift in balance of power between retailers and manufacturers.
4). Expansion into new product categories.
5). Internationalization of retail chains.
6). Economic downturns.

3. Explain why the strength of a global brand may vary enormously from country to country.

Global branding strength may be tied to many environmental factors including affluence of consumers, communications within the country, distribution infrastructure, the product itself, cultural adaptation of the brand, price, and history of the brand. Popularity is fleeting but can also be seen as a possibility for growth at any moment in time.

4. What factors should MNCs consider when implementing a brand-name facelift in their foreign markets?

Three broad strategic options exist for implementing a facelift. They are:

a. Fade-in/fade-out strategy. The global brand name is somehow tied to an existing local brand name. After a transition period, the old name is dropped.

b. Transparent forewarning. Alerts the consumer about a brand name change. The forewarning can be done via the communication program, in-store displays, and product packaging.

c. Summary axing. The company simply drops the old brand name and immediately replaces it with the global name.

d. Some considerations are:

   1). Consider the length of the transition period.
   2). The purchase cycle.
   3). Customer exposure to the communication messages.
   4). Avoid negative spillovers.
   5). Monitor the response to the name change.

5. Describe the key success factors behind private labels in Europe.

This question is similar to Review Question #2 and can be discussed at the same time. Key success factors according to the chapter can be listed as:

   1). Improved quality of private label products.
   2). Development of premium private label brands.
   3). Shift in balance of power between retailers and manufacturers.
   4). Expansion into new product categories.
   5). Internationalization of retail chains.
   6). Economic downturns.

6. What strategies can MNCs adopt to cope with product piracy?

The strategic options against product piracy include the following actions:

a. Lobbying activities (such as requesting sanctions against guilty parties or countries).
   1). Most Favored Nation status might be affected.
   2). Treaties can be used to stop piracy.

b. Legal action.
   1). Time consuming and costly.
   2). Can generate negative publicity for the multinational.

c. Product policy options.
   1). Holograms to indicate authenticity.
   2). Make products hard to copy.

d. Communications options.
   1). Warn audiences.
   2). Anti-piracy ad campaigns.

7. How does the marketing of global services differ from marketing tangible goods worldwide?

Several aspects make the marketing of services different from the marketing of tangible goods worldwide. These aspects are degree of protectionism, immediate face-to-face contacts within the service sector (remember services are performed), difficulties in measuring customer service satisfaction overseas, the deregulation of services, the increased demand for premium services, and the increased value that service customers are putting on excellent services. A country has to be ready for services. It is the next logical step beyond a manufacturing economy.

DISCUSSION QUESTIONS

INSTRUCTOR'S NOTE: Discussion Questions are found at the end of each chapter in the text. These questions (in many cases) are too lengthy to repeat in the manual. Suggestions for answering and discussing the questions are presented in this section. Many of the questions require student opinion and judgment.

1. As indicated by discussion in the chapter, a company makes the global branding decision depending on a variety of factors. These factors might be seen as being:

   1). Economies of scale.
   2). Development costs can be spread over large volumes.
   3). Brand awareness--global brands are more visible than local brands.
   4). Capitalize on media overlap between countries.
   5). The prestige-factor.
   6). Positioning one's self as a global brand can improve other marketing efforts.
   7). Leverage the country association.

After reviewing these factors, a company makes the decision about the global versus local brand issue.

2. Students should be encouraged to review what they perceive to be international brands and the symbols that are associated with them. Names and symbols that travel across borders are those that are culturally generic. Using Aaker's list referred to in the chapter and discussed in Review Question #1 is a good place to begin a discovery process dealing with cultural sensitivity. To repeat, Aaker's list is:

   1). What is the cost of creating and maintaining awareness and associations for a local brand versus a global one?
   2). Are there significant economies of scale in the creation and running of a communication program globally?
   3). Is there value to associations of a global brand or of a brand associated with the source country?

4). What local associations will be generated by the global name? symbol? slogan? imagery?

5). Is it culturally and legally do-able to use the brand name, symbol, slogan across the different countries?

6). What is the value of the awareness and associations that a regional brand might create?

3. This question requires that the students not only think about the issue at hand (software piracy) but also review the material in the chapter that deals with intellectual and technological property rights. Some protective measures might include:

    a. Lobbying activities (such as requesting sanctions against guilty parties or countries).
       1). Most Favored Nation status might be affected.
       2). Treaties can be used to stop piracy.
    b. Legal action.
       1). Time consuming and costly.
       2). Can generate negative publicity for the multinational.
    c. Product policy options.
       1). Holograms to indicate authenticity.
       2). Make products hard to copy.
    d. Communications options.
       1). Warn audiences.
       2). Anti-piracy ad campaigns.

4. This question is related to Discussion Question #3. The students should notice that developing nations gain short term profits from piracy but lose in terms of long term innovation development. Licensing and joint ventures would be a much acceptable way of doing business. Developing countries can ill afford to anger the developed nations with their manufacturing processes and policies. True industry development comes from playing by certain internationally accepted rules of commerce. Intellectual property protection is one of those rules. Students should the benefits of intellectual property for developed nations and see which of those benefits would transfer to the developing nation and its industry.

5. This would be a classic case of the Country-of-origin (COO) problem encountered by many developing nations. Strategies that can be used to gain acceptability might include:

Strategies can be organized around the marketing mix variables:
       1). Product policy--established brand names will reduce the COO effect.
       2). Pricing--low prices will reduce the COO effect.
       3). Distribution--respected channels will reduce the COO effect.
       4). Communication--images can be improved or the brand can be bolstered.

Students should be encouraged to think about communication changes and challenges that might be present for the product description as given by the question. What additional proactive strategies might be tried? Which segments can be targeted? Could the COO effect be diminished?

6. The Nestle Seal of Guarantee might be used for a variety of purposes. These might be freshness, a prestige seal, as a sign of quality control, as a brand booster, as a differentiation point between the label and private products, and as a way of increasing the price. Students should be encouraged to think of other uses of this and other seals of guarantee or approval.

7. Among the strategies that can be used to effectively market services worldwide include:

    a. Capitalize on cultural forces in the host market.
    b. Standardize and customize.
    c. Central role of information technologies (IT).
    d. Add value by differentiation.
    e. Establish global service networks.

Each of these strategies (separately or in concert with one another) can help the service provider market services more effectively and in a similar fashion to product marketing.

STUDENT PROJECTS and INTERNET FOCUS

1. Go to the library and research the subject of product piracy. Find an article that describes the piracy issue. In your research observe the company or group that was damaged; the offending party or country; any legal action taken; any policy action taken by the host country through political action; and, the end result of the copying or piracy case. Report your findings and make a conclusion about the your feelings about product piracy.

2. Collect (photocopy) advertisements from foreign periodicals/publications (**DO NOT TEAR OUT THIS MATERIAL FROM LIBRARY PUBLICATIONS**). Use these advertisements to formulate an opinion on Country-of-Origin effects (COO). Under what circumstances are you willing to try products from a foreign nation (list the circumstances). What would the foreign company have to do to get your business. Use your ads to illustrate your thought process. Write a descriptive report about your thoughts and experiences with this issue.

INSTRUCTOR'S NOTE: The following projects require the students to both use and understand the Internet. If students do not understand how to use the Internet, explanation should be given before these projects are undertaken. The Web addresses change frequently, the instructor should re-affirm the site address and the content of the site before making an assignment.

3. Among the newest global brands are the video game companies. Go to the following four Web sites and investigate the new products offered by these leading game makers. What strategies can you suggest for the companies to protect their products from piracy? Do the companies make any statements themselves about intellectual property on their Web sites?

a). Sega   **(http://www.segaoa.com)**
b). Sony   **(http://www.sony.com)**
c). Nintendo   **(http://www.nintendo.com)**
d). Atari   **(http://www.atari.com)**

4. Go to the Mercedes-Benz site at **(http://www.usa.mercedes-benz.com)** and investigate the company's branding strategy. Notice that they have just begun new plants in the United States. In addition, they have recently purchased significant publicity space in 1997s high profile summer movies. What comments can you make about this strategy for brand acceptance? Write a report on your conclusions about the branding strategies of Mercedes-Benz.

5. Go to the following Web sites and determine how these service companies might proceed with global expansion. After reading the material in your text, what advice could you give to these entities about global expansion?

a). Arthur Andersen   **(http://www.ArthurAndersen.com)**
b). Andersen Consulting   **(http://www.ac.com)**
c). Royal Insurance   **(http://www.royal-usa.com)**
d). GE Information Services   **(http://www.geis.com)**.

CHAPTER 13

GLOBAL PRICING

CHAPTER OBJECTIVES

1. List and explain the drivers of foreign market pricing.

2. Explain the concept of price escalation.

3. Track pricing in inflationary environments.

4. Explain currency fluctuations.

5. Define transfer pricing.

6. Explain the concept of dumping as applied to the international environment.

7. Describe the process of coordinating prices.

8. Define and explain countertrade.

CHAPTER OVERVIEW

Global pricing is one of the most critical and complex issues that global firms face. Price is the only marketing mix variable that creates revenues, all other elements entail costs. Though price is one the firm's most important variables, it often works at cross-purposes with other variables within the firm. Interests and objectives are often clash.

Many mistakes are often made in the international environment with respect to pricing policies and practices. Two common mistakes are pricing the product too high or pricing it too low. Pricing too high forces many customers to avoid using or trying the product and, therefore, limits market expansion. Pricing too low causes the appearance of "dumping" or other unsavory pricing practices. Predatory pricing is often a cause for competitive concern. In addition, customers might see the low priced product as being a signal for low quality.

Multinationals also face the challenge of how to coordinate their pricing policy across different countries. A lack of coordination will create "gray markets." These markets (through unauthorized channels) are a constant source of concern for legitimate distributors. The chapter outlines global pricing strategies that provide examples of the wide range of choices available to international managers. One strategy that receives special attention is countertrade. This method tends to bind businesses together and helps price coordination attempts.

CHAPTER OUTLINE

A. Drivers of Foreign Market Pricing

    1. Even within the same geographic area, wide cross-border price differences are quite common.

*****Use Exhibit 13-1 Here*****

    2. The main drivers of foreign market pricing can be an extensive list (as shown in the succeeding sections).

    3. *Company goals.*

       a. When developing a pricing strategy for its global markets, the firm needs to decide what it wants to accomplish with its strategy.

       b. Examples of goals include maximizing current profits and projecting a premium image.

       c. According to research, important pricing objectives are listed as:

          1). To achieve a satisfactory return on investment.

          2). To maintain market share.

          3). To meet a specified profit goal.

       d. Company goals vary from country (and market) to country and change over time.

    4. *Company costs.*

       a. Costs set the floor. The company wants to set at least a price that will cover all costs needed to make and sell its products.

       b. Cost differentials between countries can lead to wide price gaps.

       c. Company costs include variable and fixed costs.

       d. Export pricing policies differ depending on the way costs are treated.

          1). Cost-plus pricing is one method. This approach adds international costs and a mark-up to the domestic manufacturing costs.

          2). Dynamic incremental pricing is an alternative method. This strategy arrives at a price after removing domestic fixed costs.

       e. When demand is highly price sensitive, the company needs to consider how it can reduce costs from a global perspective.

    5. *Customer demand.*

       a. Whereas costs set a floor, consumers' perceived value attached to the product will set a ceiling to the price.

       b. Demand conditions (like other factors) change from country to country.

       c. Countries with low per-capita incomes are price-sensitive.

          1). One way of dealing with this issue is to go for the mass-market by adjusting the product (such as by downsizing or lowering the product quality).

*****Use Exhibit 13-2 Here; Use Discussion Question #2 Here*****

        2). Another method is to charge a higher price (similar to what might be charged in Western countries) but to a higher income market.
    d. Generally speaking, a market consists of a quality-sensitive and price sensitive market segment.
    e. Price sensitivities change over time.
6. ***Competition.***
    a. Differences in the competitive situation across countries will usually lead to cross-border price differentials.

*****Use Exhibit 13-3 Here*****

    b. The competitive situation may vary for a number of reasons:
        1). The number of competitors typically varies from country to country.
        2). The nature of the competition will differ.
        3). Smuggling and counterfeit products are problems in many markets.
        4). A company's competitive situation may very well change as it goes from market to market.
        5). The rules of competition often change from market to market and country to country.

*****Use Review Question #2 Here*****

7. ***Distribution channels.***
    a. The pressure exercised by channels can take many forms:
        1). Trade margins and the length of channels will vary.
        2). The balance of power between manufacturers and their distributors are factors.
        3). Large scale retailers have increasing power.
    b. Large cross-country price gaps open up arbitrage opportunities that lead to parallel imports from low-price countries to high-price ones.
        1). Pre-emption of cross-border bargain hunting is often times a strong motivation behind a company's pricing practices.
8. ***Government policies.***
    a. These policies can have a direct or indirect influence on pricing.
    b. Sales taxes would be examples of direct influences.
    c. Indirect influences may come from government's role in increasing inflation.

B. Managing Price Escalation

1. Exporting involves more steps and substantially higher risks than domestic marketing.

a. To cover the incremental costs involved in international marketing, the final foreign retail price will often be much higher than the domestic retail price.

b. This higher price phenomenon is called price escalation.

c. Issues are:

1). Will the foreign customer pay the higher price?

2). Will the price make the product less competitive?

2. Ways to deal with price escalation include:

a. Find ways to cut the export price.

b. Position the product as a (super) premium brand.

3. Ways to lower the export price include:

a. Rearrange the distribution channel.

1). Shorten the channel.

2). Work towards channel cost efficiencies.

b. Eliminate costly features (or make them optional).

c. Downsize the product.

d. Assemble or manufacture the product in foreign markets.

e. Adapt the product to escape tariffs or tax levies.

*****Use Review Question #1 Here; Use Discussion Questions #1 and #6 Here*****

C. Pricing in Inflationary Environments

1. High inflation rates are often coupled with highly volatile exchange rate movements.

2. Several ways to safeguard against inflation include:

a. Modify components, ingredients, parts and/or packaging materials.

b. Source materials from low-cost suppliers.

c. Shorten credit terms.

d. Include escalator clauses in long-term contracts.

e. Quote prices in a stable currency.

f. Pursue rapid inventory turnovers.

g. Draw lessons from other countries.

*****Use Global Perspective 13-1 "Selling Burgers in Hyper-inflationary Environments" Here*****

3. To combat hyper-inflation governments occasionally impose price controls (usually coupled with a wage freeze).

a. One consequence of price controls is that goods are diverted to the black market.

4. Companies faced with price controls can consider several action courses:

a. Adapt the product line.

b. Shift target segments or markets.

c. Launch new products or variants of existing products.

d. Negotiate with the government.

e. Predict incidence of price controls.
f. Leave the country (a drastic alternative).

D. Global Pricing and Currency Movements

1. Due to the interplay of a variety of economic and political factors, exchange rates continuously float up- or downward.
2. Given the sometimes dramatic exchange rate movements, setting prices in a floating exchange rate world poses a tremendous challenge.

*****Use Exhibit 13-4 Here*****

3. *Currency gain/loss pass through.*
   a. Two major issues:
      1). How much of a exchange rate gain (loss) should be passed through to our customers?
      2). In what currency should we quote our prices?

*****Use Exhibit 13-5 Here*****

   b. When considering pass through, generally speaking, the appropriate action will depend on three factors:
      1). Customers' price sensitivity.
      2). The impact of the dollar appreciation on the firm's cost structure.
      3). The amount of competition in the export market.
   c. When exporters lower mark-ups (destination specific adjustments) in response to exchange rate movements, this is referred to as pricing-to-market (PTM).
      1). PTM behaviors differ across source countries.

*****Use Exhibit 13-6 Here; Use Review Question #3 Here; Use Discussion Question #4 Here*****

   d. Playing the pricing-to-market game carries certain risks.
      1). Frequent adjustments distresses channel members and customers.
   e. Some choose to market in a special form of PTM called local-currency price stability (LCPS) where mark-ups are adjusted to stabilize prices in the buyer's currency.
4. *Currency quotation.*
   a. Which currency to use in the international business transaction?
   b. Most would prefer their own domestic currency.
   c. There is always a risk when dealing in a foreign currency.

E. Transfer Pricing

1. *Determinants of transfer pricing.*
   a. Sales transactions between related entities of the same company are called transfer pricing.
   b. Transfer pricing decisions are balanced against a variety of stakeholders:
      1). Parent company.
      2). Local country managers.
      3). Host government(s).
      4). Domestic government.
      5). Joint venture partner(s).
   c. Key drivers are:
      1). Market conditions in the foreign country.
      2). Competition in the foreign country.
      3). Reasonable profit for foreign affiliate.
      4). U.S. federal income taxes.
      5). Economic conditions in the foreign country.
      6). Import restrictions.
      7). Customs duties.
      8). Price controls.
      9). Taxation in the foreign country.
      10). Exchange controls.
   d. Generally speaking, MNCs should consider the following criteria when making transfer pricing decisions:
      1). Tax regimes.
      2). Local market conditions.
      3). Market imperfections.
      4). Joint venture partner.
      5). Morale of local country managers.

*****Use Review Question #4 Here*****

2. *Setting transfer prices.*
   a. There are two broad transfer pricing strategies:
      1). Market-based transfer pricing--uses the market or "arms length pricing."
      2). Nonmarket-based transfer pricing.
   b. Problems occur with the market-based approach in that it is difficult to find an appropriate benchmark on which to build prices.
   c. The nonmarket-based pricing approach can be:
      1). Cost-based.
      2). Negotiated pricing.
3. *Minimizing the risk of transfer pricing tax audits.*
   a. Many MNCs try to shift tax burdens from high- to low-tax environments.
   b. Most experts prefer to set transfer prices as close as possible to the Basic Arm's Length Standard (BALS). Methods include:

1). Comparable/uncontrollable price.
2). Resale price.
3). Cost plus.
4. To minimize the risk of tax audits, consider the following questions:
   a. Do comparable/uncontrolled transactions exist?
   b. Where is the most value added? Parent? Subsidiary?
   c. Are combined profits of parent and subsidiary shared in proportion to contributions?
   d. Does the transfer price meet the benchmark set by the tax authorities?
   e. Does the MNC have the information to justify the transfer prices used?

*****Use Exhibit 13-7 Here*****

F. Global Pricing and Anti-Dumping Regulation

1. Dumping occurs with imports are being sold at an "unfair" price.
   a. To protect local producers against the encroachment of low-priced imports, governments may levy countervailing duties or fines.
   b. Penetration pricing may trigger anti-dumping actions.
   c. The increase in anti-dumping actions can be referred to as protectionism.
2. There are several reasons to explain the growing popularity of anti-dumping litigation.
   a. The removal of traditional trade barriers (tariffs and quotas) has encouraged countries to switch to non-tariff barriers such as anti-dumping to protect their local industries.
   b. There are more plaintiffs than defendants. There are usually no penalties for frivolous complaints.
   c. Plaintiffs have "home court" advantage.
   d. Anti-dumping action is used to foster voluntary export restraints (VER).
   e. The concept of a "fair-price" is murky.
      1). The United States defines dumping to occur when imports are sold below the home-country price (price discrimination) or when the import price is than the "constructed value" or average cost of production (pricing below cost).

*****Use Discussion Question #5 Here*****

3. Global companies should monitor changes in anti-dumping legislation and closely track anti-dumping cases in their particular industry.
4. To minimize risk exposure to anti-dumping actions, exports might pursue any of the following marketing strategies:
   a. Trading-up.
   b. Service enhancement.
   c. Distribution and communication:
      1). The establishment of communication channels with local competitors.

2). Entering into cooperative agreements with them (strategic alliances).

3). Reallocation of the firm's marketing efforts from vulnerable products to less sensitive products.

*****Use Review Question #5 Here*****

G. Price Coordination

1. When developing a global pricing strategy, one of the most difficult problems is how much coordination should exist between prices charged in different countries.
2. In deciding how much coordination, several considerations matter:
   a. Nature of customers.
   b. Nature of channels.
   c. Nature of competition.
   d. Market integration.
   e. Internal organization.
   f. Government regulation.
3. *Aligning pan-regional prices.*
   a. Some degree of price coordination is almost a necessity.
   b. Simon and Kucher propose a three-step procedure to align prices in the Pan-European market.
      1). Step 1: Determine optimal price for each country.
      2). Step 2: Find out whether parallel imports ("gray markets") are likely to occur at these prices.
         a). Strategies to cope with parallel imports are:
            1]. Product differentiation.
            2]. Intelligence systems to measure exposure to gray markets.
            3]. Creating negative perceptions in the mind of the end-user about parallel imports.
      3). Set a pricing corridor.

*****Use Exhibit 13-8 Here*****

4. *Implementing price coordination.*
   a. Four alternatives are:
      1). Economic measures.
      2). Centralization.
      3). Formalization.
      4). Informal coordination.
   b. Choice is a matter of the complexity of the environment.
      1). When the environment is fairly stable and the various markets are highly similar, centralization is usually preferable.
      2). Highly complex environments require a more decentralized approach.

H. Countertrade

1. Countertrade is an umbrella term used to describe unconventional trade-financing transactions that involve some form of non-cash compensation.

2. *Forms of countertrade.*
    a. Simple barter. One product is swapped for another.
    b. Clearing agreement. Two governments agree to import a set number of goods from one another.
    c. Switch trading. In this deals (with a third party), rights to surplus credits are sold to specialized traders at a discount. The third party uses the credits to buy goods from the deficit country.

3. Payment flow methods:
    a. Buy-back (compensation). Typically, (especially in technology) the seller sells equipment and agrees to buy-back the finished product.
    b. Counterpurchase. Each party agrees to buy from the other.
    c. Offset. The seller agrees to "offset" the purchase price by sourcing from the importer's country.

4. *Motives behind countertrade.*
    a. Gain access to new or difficult markets.
    b. Overcome exchange rate controls or lack of hard currency.
    c. Overcome low country credit worthiness.
    d. Increase sales volume.
    e. Generate long-term customer goodwill.

*****Use Review Question #6 Here*****

5. *Shortcomings of countertrade.*
    a. No "in-house" use for goods offered by customers.
    b. Timely and costly negotiations.
    c. Uncertainty and lack of information on future prices.
    d. Transaction costs.

6. Advice for those considering countertrade:
    a. Always evaluate the pros and cons of countertrade against other options.
    b. Minimize the ratio of compensation goods to cash.
    c. Strive for goods that can be used in-house.
    d. Assess the relative merits of relying on middlemen versus an in-house staff.
    e. Check whether the goods are subject to any import restrictions.
    f. Assess the quality of the goods.

*****Use Discussion Question #3 Here*****

REVIEW QUESTIONS

INSTRUCTOR'S NOTE: The following chapter review questions are meant to challenge the student to think about material presented in the chapter and formulate a creative answer to the review questions. Many of the answers require judgments rather than specific line-by-line quotation of facts. The answers provided are meant to provide stimulation of creative answers.

1. What mechanisms can exporters use to curtail the risks of price escalation in foreign markets?

Ways to lower the export price include:
- a. Rearrange the distribution channel.
  - 1). Shorten the channel.
  - 2). Work towards channel cost efficiencies.
- b. Eliminate costly features (or make them optional).
- c. Downsize the product.
- d. Assemble or manufacture the product in foreign markets.
- e. Adapt the product to escape tariffs or tax levies.

2. How does competition in the foreign market affect your global pricing decisions?

Differences in the competitive situation across countries will usually lead to cross-border price differentials. The competitive situation may vary for a number of reasons:
- 1). The number of competitors typically varies from country to country.
- 2). The nature of the competition will differ.
- 3). Smuggling and counterfeit products are problems in many markets.
- 4). A company's competitive situation may very well change as it goes from market to market.
- 5). The rules of competition often change from market to market and country to country.

3. One recent study quoted in Chapter 13 reports that there was much more pass-through by German carmakers than their Japanese counterparts in the U.S. carmarket when both currencies depreciated against the U.S. dollar. What might explain these different responses?

Due to the interplay of a variety of economic and political factors, exchange rates continuously float up- or downward. Given the sometimes dramatic exchange rate movements, setting prices in a floating exchange rate world poses a tremendous challenge.

Two major issues:
- 1). How much of a exchange rate gain (loss) should be passed through to our customers?

2). In what currency should we quote our prices?

When formulating an answer consider the points below:
When considering pass through, generally speaking, the appropriate action will depend on three factors:

       1). Customers' price sensitivity.
       2). The impact of the dollar appreciation on the firm's cost structure.
       3). The amount of competition in the export market.

4. Should MNCs always try to minimize their transfer in high corporate tax countries? Why (or why not)?

The answer to this question is opinion-oriented and should consider a variety of factors. Students should review the material in the chapter and consider the list presented below before making a judgment. Be sure to justify the opinion expressed in the judgment.

Transfer pricing decisions are balanced against a variety of stakeholders:

       1). Parent company.
       2). Local country managers.
       3). Host government(s).
       4). Domestic government.
       5). Joint venture partner(s).

Key drivers are:

       1). Market conditions in the foreign country.
       2). Competition in the foreign country.
       3). Reasonable profit for foreign affiliate.
       4). U.S. federal income taxes.
       5). Economic conditions in the foreign country.
       6). Import restrictions.
       7). Customs duties.
       8). Price controls.
       9). Taxation in the foreign country.
      10). Exchange controls.

Generally speaking, MNCs should consider the following criteria when making transfer pricing decisions:

       1). Tax regimes.
       2). Local market conditions.
       3). Market imperfections.
       4). Joint venture partner.
       5). Morale of local country managers.

5. What measures might exporters consider to hedge themselves against anti-dumping accusations?

To minimize risk exposure to anti-dumping actions, exports might pursue any of the following marketing strategies:

    a. Trading-up.
    b. Service enhancement.
    c. Distribution and communication:
        1). The establishment of communication channels with local competitors.
        2). Entering into cooperative agreements with them (strategic alliances).
        3). Reallocation of the firm's marketing efforts from vulnerable products to less sensitive products.

6. Explain why countertrade is often viewed as a necessary evil.

Motives behind countertrade.

    a. Gain access to new or difficult markets.
    b. Overcome exchange rate controls or lack of hard currency.
    c. Overcome low country credit worthiness.
    d. Increase sales volume.
    e. Generate long-term customer goodwill.

DISCUSSION QUESTIONS

INSTRUCTOR'S NOTE: Discussion Questions are found at the end of each chapter in the text. These questions (in many cases) are too lengthy to repeat in the manual. Suggestions for answering and discussing the questions are presented in this section. Many of the questions require student opinion and judgment.

1. From the chapter, the students should recall the strategic options available to lower the export price to markets that might have trouble paying the higher price. These options are:

Ways to lower the export price include:

    a. Rearrange the distribution channel.
        1). Shorten the channel.
        2). Work towards channel cost efficiencies.
    b. Eliminate costly features (or make them optional).
    c. Downsize the product.
    d. Assemble or manufacture the product in foreign markets.
    e. Adapt the product to escape tariffs or tax levies.

2. The following question requires the student to calculate using the methods presented in the chapter. The instructor may make any suggestions that seem reasonable to make the example realistic. It is suggested that the student re-read the material from the "Customer Demand" section and review Exhibit 13-2 before beginning the work. If

students have not had basic accounting or economics, the instructor might choose to skip this question.

3. To answer this question, students should review the section in the chapter that deals with countertrade. The answer to the stated Discussion Question will require an opinion. The students should be reminded to justify their opinion. Some factors that might be considered in formulating that opinion are:

Advice for those considering countertrade:
  a. Always evaluate the pros and cons of countertrade against other options.
  b. Minimize the ratio of compensation goods to cash.
  c. Strive for goods that can be used in-house.
  d. Assess the relative merits of relying on middlemen versus an in-house staff.
  e. Check whether the goods are subject to any import restrictions.
  f. Assess the quality of the goods.

4. This question is similar to Review Question #3. Students should be encouraged to review the sections of the chapter that deal with currency before attempting to formulate an opinion on this issue. General comments about the role of currency fluctuation and pricing would also be in order when formulating an answer to this question. Some factors that might be part of the consideration of the student when establishing their creative answer might be:

1). Customers' price sensitivity.
2). The impact of the dollar appreciation on the firm's cost structure.
3). The amount of competition in the export market.

5. To answer this question, students should review the section in the chapter devoted to dumping. In addition to the material provided by the chapter, students should be encouraged to think of other ways domestic producers can play the "anti-dumping" game. Some factors to consider are:

  a. The removal of traditional trade barriers (tariffs and quotas) has encouraged countries to switch to non-tariff barriers such as anti-dumping to protect their local industries.
  b. There are more plaintiffs than defendants. There are usually no penalties for frivolous complaints.
  c. Plaintiffs have "home court" advantage.
  d. Anti-dumping action is used to foster voluntary export restraints (VER).
  e. The concept of a "fair-price" is murky.
      1). The United States defines dumping to occur when imports are sold below the home-country price (price discrimination) or when the import price is than the "constructed value" or average cost of production (pricing below cost).

6. Many firms have to consider how to market their premium brands in markets where the average consumer could not afford the product or brand. The hope is that over time the product will be able to re-coup lost revenues either by gaining market share or eventually by raising its price. Some strategies that can be used by firms in situations as shown by this question are:

Ways to deal with price escalation include:
    a. Find ways to cut the export price.
    b. Position the product as a (super) premium brand.

Ways to lower the export price include:
    a. Rearrange the distribution channel.
       1). Shorten the channel.
       2). Work towards channel cost efficiencies.
    b. Eliminate costly features (or make them optional).
    c. Downsize the product.
    d. Assemble or manufacture the product in foreign markets.
    e. Adapt the product to escape tariffs or tax levies.

STUDENT PROJECTS and INTERNET FOCUS

1. The chapter lists six (6) drivers of foreign market pricing. Go to the library and find an example of one of the drivers in action. Explain from your research how the driver impacts foreign market pricing. Explain the process you went through to obtain your data. Give a report to the class on your findings.

2. Since you will be entering a career in business shortly, it will be necessary for you to formulate opinions on pricing issues. Take any of the issues presented in the chapter (such as dumping or countertrade) and formulate an opinion (which might eventually become your managerial policy) on the issue. From your research about the subject, show how you formed your opinion and justify and be able to defend your opinion. Write a short report about your experience and your opinion.

INSTRUCTOR'S NOTE: The following projects require the students to both use and understand the Internet. If students do not understand how to use the Internet, explanation should be given before these projects are undertaken. The Web addresses change frequently, the instructor should re-affirm the site address and the content of the site before making an assignment.

3. Go to the Web site for the GATT Agreement at (**gopher.//cyfer.esusda.gov/11/ace/hot.topic.links/gatt**). Examine issues that relate to international pricing. Pick one that relates to the subjects cover in this chapter and report your findings to the class. Note: if this site is no longer operative, GATT can be researched using other search engines.

4. Go to one of the standard search engines such as Yahoo (**http://www.yahoo.com**) or Lycos (**http://www.lycos.com**) and research the subject of dumping. Find an article about dumping. Report your findings to the class. Explain your feelings about the dumping issue.

5. Go to any of the following sites and review procedures, policies, or ideas on international pricing. Report your findings.

a. Enron   (**http://www.ENRON.com**)
b. Canon USA   (**http://www.usa.canon.com**)
c. GTE   (**http://www.gte.com**)
d. MCI   (**http://www.MCI.com**)
e. Subaru   (**http://www.subaru.com**).

CHAPTER 14

COMMUNICATING WITH THE WORLD CONSUMER

CHAPTER OBJECTIVES

1. Describe the constraints on global communication strategies.

2. Identify message strategy.

3. Analyze global media decisions.

4. Review the process for making advertising agency selections.

5. Describe the process for coordinating international advertising.

6. Explain other communication forms available for the marketing manager.

CHAPTER OVERVIEW

Because of cultural environment differences, promotional strategies in the international marketplace often misfire. To be successful, multinational companies must be creative in their adaptation and customization of communication strategies.

This chapter gives the reader an overview of major decisions that must be made if communication and promotion strategy is to be successful. Some of the decisions are creating advertising campaigns, setting and allocating the budget, selecting media vehicles to carry the campaign, choosing advertising agencies, coordinating cross-country advertising programs. Many elements of the organization must interact to make the communication/promotion strategy successful. If this is done successfully, the rewards can be great.

One issue that is of particular importance is to what degree the multinational organization should push for pan-regional or even global advertising campaigns. Several arguments support the standardization of these campaigns. They are identified in the chapter as being: 1) cost savings, 2) a coherent brand image, 3) similarity of target groups, and 4) transplanting of creative ideas. However, there are also counterarguments. These include: 1) cultural differences, 2) different markets having different degree in market maturity, 3) role of advertising regulations, and 4) variations in the media-environment.

After all is said and done, the trend seems to be toward pan-regional (or even globalized) campaigns. Reasons for this trend are explored. The last word of advice for the international advertiser is to be willing to change and be willing to adopt new technology (such as the Internet) into future promotional endeavors.

CHAPTER OUTLINE

A. Introduction

1. Promotional strategies in the global marketplace easily misfire.
2. The steps in developing a promotional plan in international marketing are by and large similar to the sequence in domestic marketing:
   a. Select target audience and positioning theme.
   b. Set specific campaign objectives (strategic and operational).
   c. Determine the promotional budget.
   d. Develop a message strategy.
   e. Decide on a media strategy.
   f. Monitor and assess campaign effectiveness.

*****Use Exhibit 14-1 Here*****

B. Constraints on Global Communication Strategies

1. *Language barriers.*
   a. Language is one of the most formidable barriers that international advertisers need to surmount.
   b. Three forms of translation errors are commonly made.
      1). Pure carelessness.
      2). Words that have multiple meanings.
      3). Mistakes made because of local slang or idioms.

*****Use Exhibit 14-2 Here*****

   c. Solutions to the language can be summarized as being:
      1). Involve local advertising agencies.
      2). Don't translate into the local language. Use the English slogan worldwide.
      3). Use voice-overs to incorporate local slang.
2. *Cultural barriers.*
   a. Cultural barriers pose the biggest stumbling block in international advertising.
   b. One aid is to use Hofstede's model that classifies national cultures based on their value scheme (see Chapter 4 for more details). Five dimensions are:
      1). Power distance.
      2). Uncertainty avoidance.

3). Individualism.
4). Masculinity.
5). Long-termism.
c. The idea is that campaigns should reflect the cultural value systems of the target audience.
d. General examples of Hofstede's model in usage are that:
1). Ads that position products or services as status symbols are most likely to

be

effective in countries with large power distance.
2). Campaigns that center around hard-sell approaches are advisable for cultures with high uncertainty avoidance.
3). Performance, success, and competition (generally thought to be strong masculine traits) should be featured in messages in highly "masculine" societies.
4). Cultures with a long-term orientation are driven by future values (such as thrift and perseverance).
5). Also, remember value systems change overtime.

3. *Local attitudes towards advertising.*
a. Consumer feelings about advertising differ dramatically from country to country.

*****Use Exhibit 14-3 Here*****

b. The differing attitudes towards advertising partly explain the relative importance of advertising in shaping brand loyalty.
c. Advertising turns out to be more critical than quality, trust or value.

*****Use Exhibit 14-4 Here; Use Discussion Question #3 Here*****

4. *Media infrastructure.*
a. Markets vary in infrastructure development (number of media choices available).
b. Quality, rates, and variety may not be consistent. Promises to run ads may not mean much in certain countries.
5. *Advertising regulations.*
a. A major roadblock that global advertisers face is the bewildering set of advertising regulations advertisers need to cope with in foreign markets.
b. Many countries have self-regulation of their advertising industry (while others mandate regulation). Reasons for self-regulation include:
1). Protection of consumers against misleading or offensive advertising.
2). Protection of legitimate advertisers against false claims or accusations made by competitors.
3). Prevents more government imposed regulation or control of the advertising industry.
c. Examples of regulation include:

1). *Advertising of "vice products" and pharmaceuticals.*
2). *Comparative advertising.*
3). *Content of advertising messages.*
4). *Advertising towards children.*

6. How should marketers cope with advertising regulations? Possible actions include:
   a. Keep track of regulations and pending legislation.
   b. Lobbying activities.
   c. Challenge regulations in court.
   d. Adapt marketing mix strategy.

*****Use Global Perspective 14-1 "Do's and Don'ts for Advertisers in Vietnam" Here; Use Review Questions #1, #2, and #3 Here; Use Discussion Question #1 Here*****

C. Setting the Global Advertising Budget

1. One of the delicate decisions that marketers face when planning their communication strategy centers around the "money" issue:
   a. How much should we spend?
   b. How should we allocate our resources across our different markets?

*****Use Exhibit 14-5 Here*****

2. Companies rely on different types of budgeting rules:
   a. *Percentage of sales.*
      1). Sets the overall ad budget as a percent of sales.
      2). The base is either past or expected sales revenues.
      3). The advantage is simplicity.
      4). The downside is faulty reasoning--advertising generates sales not the reverse.
      5). This is not a good method for newly entered markets.
   b. *Competitive parity.*
      1). Use your competitors' spending as a benchmark by simply matching their spending amounts.
      2). Rationale--the competitor's collective wisdom signals the "optimal" spending amount.
      3). Shortcomings:
         a). Competitor's spending might be faulty.
         b). New entrants should spend more than established competitors.
   c. *Objective-and-task.*
      1). This is the most popular method.
      2). Promotional efforts are treated as a means to achieve the advertiser's stated objectives.
      3). Steps:
         a). Spell out the goals of the communication strategy.

b). Determine the tasks that are needed to achieve the desired objectives.

c). The planned budget is then the overall costs that the completion of these tasks will amount to.

d). Experimentation helps to refine the method.

3. Part of the budgeting process is also the allocation of resources across the different countries.

a. Bottom-up planning--each country subsidiary independently determines how much should be spent within its market and then requests the desired resources from headquarters.

b. Top-down planning--the opposite approach.

c. Regional angle--regions review needed resources and submit requests to headquarters.

*****Use Exhibit 14-6 Here; Use Discussion Question #5 Here*****

D. Message Strategy

1. *The "standardization" versus "adaptation" debate.*
   a. One of the toughest issues faced is the choice of a theme.
   b. Theme standardization is an issue that must be resolved.
      1). Truly global campaigns are quite uncommon.

*****Use Global Perspective 14-2 "'Let's Make Things Better'--Philip's First Global Image Advertising Campaign" Here*****

2. *Merits of standardization.* Major reasons include:
   a. *Scale economics.*
   b. *Consistent image.*
   c. *Global consumer segments.*
   d. *Creative talent.*
   e. *Cross-fertilization.*
   f. Time pressure.
   g. Pressure to cooperate.

*****Use Exhibit 14-7 Here*****

h. Organizational structure must be considered.

*****Use Review Question #5 Here*****

3. *Barriers to standardization.*
   a. *Cultural differences.*

*****Use Global Perspective 14-3 "Blue Diamond--A Winning Message in the

U.S. Does Not Travel" Here; Use Exhibit 14-8 Here***

    b. *Advertising regulations.*
    c. *Market maturity.*
    d. *"Not-invented-here" (NIH) syndrome.*

*****Use Review Question #4 Here*****

    4. *Approaches to creating advertising copy.*
      a. *Export advertising.* Here the creative strategy is highly centralized.
        1). Universal copy is developed for all markets.
        2). The same positioning theme is used.
        3). Benefits include:
          a). The same brand image and identify worldwide.
          b). No confusion to customers.
          c). Substantial savings.
          d). Strict control over the planning and execution of your global communication strategy.

*****Use Exhibit 14-9 Here*****

      b. *Prototype (pattern) advertising.* Guidelines are given to the local affiliates concerning the execution of the advertising.
        1). Guidelines can be in the form of manuals or tapes.
      c. *Concept cooperation advertising.* Guidelines usually center around the positioning theme to be used in the ads rather than the execution.
        1). Execution left to local offices.

*****Use Discussion Question #4 Here*****

E. Global Media Decisions

    1. Another task that international marketers need to confront is the choice of the media in each of the countries where the company is doing business.
    2. Issues to be considered include:
      a. *Media infrastructure.*
        1). Choices of media can be wide or narrow.
        2). Choices may be different from the home country choices.
        3). There may be many government controls.
        4). Local adaptation is a key.

*****Use Exhibit 14-10 Here*****

      b. *Media Limitations.*
        1). Media availability.

*****Use Exhibit 14-11 Here*****

       2). Media costs.

*****Use Exhibit 14-12 Here*****

       3). The overall quality of the media.
          a). Political orientation of the media must be considered in many countries.
   3. *Recent developments in the international media landscape.* Trends include:
     a. *Growing commercialization and deregulation of mass media.*
     b. *Shift from radio & print to TV advertising.*
     c. *Rise of global media.*
       1). This trend is increasing because of the unavailability of local media.
       2). Good for global or regional campaigns.
       3). Major barrier is the cultural issue.
       4). Satellite channels will increase in the future. These will become more customized.

*****Use Review Question #6 Here*****

     d. *Growing importance of multimedia advertising tools.*
       1). Internet skills and usage will increase.
     e. *Improved monitoring.*
       1). Monitoring includes the company's messages as well as those of the competition.
     f. *Improved TV-viewership measurement.*

*****Use Exhibit 14-13 Here*****

F. Choosing An Advertising Agency

   1. In selecting an agency, the international marketer has several options:
     a. Work with the agency that handles the advertising in the firm's home market.
     b. Pick a purely local agency in the foreign market.
     c. Choose the local office of a large international agency.
     d. Select an international network of ad agencies that spans the globe.
   2. When screening ad agencies, the following set of criteria can be used:
     a. *Market coverage.* Does the agency cover all relevant markets?
     b. *Quality of coverage.* What are the core skills of the agency?
     c. *Expertise with developing a central international campaign.*
     d. *Scope and quality of support services.* Most agencies are not just hired for their creative skills and media buying.
     e. *Desirable image ("global" versus "local").*
     f. *Size of the agency.*

g. ***Conflicting accounts.*** Does the agency already work for one of our competitors?

G. Coordinating International Advertising

1. Global or pan-regional advertising approaches require a great deal of coordination across and communication among the various subsidiaries.
2. Mechanisms that facilitate coordination include:
   a. ***Monetary incentives (cooperative advertising).***
      1). Efforts can vary.
      2). There may be little consistency in the message conveyed.
   b. ***Advertising manuals.***
   c. ***Feedback via the Internet.***

*****Use Review Question #7 Here*****

   d. ***Lead-country concept.***
      1. The details of the campaign are summarized in a "bundle" which is sent to the various subsidiaries.
   e. ***Global or pan-regional meetings.***

*****Use Exhibit 14-14 Here; Use Review Question #8 Here*****

   1. Guidelines to implement a global or pan-regional advertising approach include:
      a). Top management must be dedicated to going global.
      b). A third party (e.g., ad agency) can help to sell key managers the benefits of a global advertising approach.
      c). A global brief based on cross-border consumer research can help persuade managers to think in terms of global consumers.
      d). Find product champions and give them a charter for the success of the global marketing program.
      e). Convince local staff that they have an opportunity in developing a global campaign.
      f). Get local managers on the global marketing team, have them do the job themselves.

H. Other Forms of Communication

1. ***Sales Promotions.***
   a. Sales promotions refer to a collection of short-term incentive tools that lead to quicker and/or larger sales of a particular product by consumers or the trade.
   b. For the majority of MNCs, the sales promotion policy is a local affair.
   c. Factors that help to explain the character of sales promotion include:
      1). ***Economic development.***

2). *Market maturity.*
3). *Cultural perceptions.*
4). *Trade structure.*
5). *Government regulations.*
   d. An international sales promotion coordinator will often be helpful.

*****Use Discussion Question #2 Here*****

2. *Event sponsorships.*
   a. Ideally, the sponsored event should reinforce the brand image that the company is trying to promote.
   b. Major risks include:
      1). Organizers may let non-sponsors in.
      2). Too many sponsorships may be sold.
      3). Lack of adequate protection of the sponsorship.
   c. Measurement of effectiveness is very hard.
3. *Trade shows.*
   a. This form is a vital form of promotion and communication.
   b. Trade shows account for almost one-fifth of most communication/promotion budgets.
   c. Trade shows are especially valuable for new products.
4. Since advertising is only one element of a global communications effort, many firms are now pursuing what might be called an integrated marketing communications (IMC) program. The goal of this program is to coordinate all the communications efforts of the firm.

REVIEW QUESTIONS

INSTRUCTOR'S NOTE: The following chapter review questions are meant to challenge the student to think about material presented in the chapter and formulate a creative answer to the review questions. Many of the answers require judgments rather than specific line-by-line quotation of facts. The answers provided are meant to provide stimulation of creative answers.

1. Most luxury products appeal to global segments. Does that mean that global advertising campaigns are most appropriate for such kind of products?

This question will require a judgment on the part of the student. Before formulating an opinion, the student might consider that most luxury product buyers are more cosmopolitan in their makeup and will receive their information from a variety of sources. One of these sources will be from advertising. However, depending on the size of the luxury market, advertising may or may not be justified. To support their conclusions on this issue, the students might want to review the first major section in this chapter.

2. Discuss the major challenges faced by international advertisers.

To answer this question, the students should review each of the subjects listed below. These major constraints (challenges) require special attention. Each may be discussed in detail or the students may be assigned individual areas for special study. Additional information is found in the first section of the chapter. Major issues of concern are:

Language Barriers.
Cultural Barriers.
Local Attitudes toward Advertising.
Media Infrastructure.
Advertising Regulations.

3. Spell out the steps that international advertisers should consider to cope with advertising regulations in their foreign markets.

How should marketers cope with advertising regulations? Possible actions include:
    a. Keep track of regulations and pending legislation.
    b. Lobbying activities.
    c. Challenge regulations in court.
    d. Adapt marketing mix strategy.

4. What factors entice international advertisers to localize their advertising campaigns in foreign markets?

Several factors entice international advertisers to localize their advertising as opposed to using a standardization policy. The barriers to standardization (promote localization) include:
a. Cultural differences.
b. Advertising regulations.
c. Market maturity.
d. "Not-invented-here" (NIH) syndrome

5. What are the major reasons for standardizing an international advertising program?

Major reasons include:
    a. Scale economics.
    b. Consistent image.
    c. Global consumer segments.
    d. Creative talent.
    e. Cross-fertilization.
    f. Time pressure.

g. Pressure to cooperate.

h. Organizational structure must be considered.

6. What will be the impact of satellite TV on international advertising?

The largest anticipated impact will be that more localized advertising campaigns will be able to be directed from centralized headquarters (often located in countries with advanced media, communication, and satellite connections). It is thought that the more channel alternatives that are available, the more localization can occur. However, at present this format is still in the development and early growth phases in most countries.

7. What do you see as the major drawbacks of the Internet as a communication tool from the perspective of an international advertiser?

Students should be encouraged to give their views about the Internet. They should remember that since this concept began in the United States it has spread to the developed world, however, it is still in a less-than-developed state in many parts of the world. To be able to use the Internet (and all of its information avenues), advanced computer technologies and communication outlets must be available to the consumer. This infrastructure is still lacking in many markets. Press students for their ideas on this issue.

8. What mechanisms should MNCs contemplate to coordinate their advertising efforts across different countries?

Mechanisms that facilitate coordination include:
   a. Monetary incentives (cooperative advertising).
   b. Advertising manuals.
   c. Feedback via the Internet.
   d. Lead-country concept.
   e. Global or pan-regional meetings.

DISCUSSION QUESTIONS

INSTRUCTOR'S NOTE: Discussion Questions are found at the end of each chapter in the text. These questions (in many cases) are too lengthy to repeat in the manual. Suggestions for answering and discussing the questions are presented in this section. Many of the questions require student opinion and judgment.

1. The students should see that there are many ways to communicate and promote besides normal advertising. One method (used by alcohol manufacturers in the United States) is to be proactive and offer to do safe drinking, no drinking and driving, etc. types of public service messages. Other methods might be to sponsor events that fall outside the boundaries of the legislation. What other methods can the students think of?

See the section on Advertising Regulation for additional ideas.

2. Push and pull alternatives are too different ways of accomplishing advertising objectives. Differences in local trade structure, the balance of power between manufacturers and the trade members, and the makeup of the market itself will often dictate which of these forms is used. Lastly, the marketer must consider the differences in the distributors' inventory space and/or costs as a factor in determining which of these methods will be effective.

3. Differing attitudes toward advertising partly explain the relative importance of advertising in shaping brand loyalty. Findings from a survey done by the advertising agency DMB&B showed that advertising is the prime factor that consumers in China use to choose a brand leader. Advertising turns out to be more critical than quality, trust or value. China, however, is clearly an exception. In other countries like France and Italy, advertising plays much less of a role in determining brand images. Exhibit 14-4 points out these rankings. Students should be encouraged to discuss all the ramifications of the data presented in the exhibit.

4. This question is a project assignment. Students should follow directions and respond to the questions after they have finished the assignment.

5. This question is a project assignment that requires the students to use their research, computer, and Internet skills. After the students have followed the directions, they should respond to the comparison questions that have been formulated by this question.

STUDENT PROJECTS and INTERNET FOCUS

1. Find a local advertising agency. After receiving permission for an interview, ask the agency representative questions about international advertising. These questions can revolve around impressions about international advertising, difficulties, experience, foreign firms seeking to advertise in the United States, or United States firms seeking to advertise in foreign countries. The student should be sure to formulate questions prior to the interview so the interview will be organized. Report the findings of the interview to the class or the instructor.

2. Watch five (5) television ads for products that you believe either are or could be considered international products. Take a country of your choice. Comment on how these ads might have to adapted to fit the local markets in your chosen country. What cultural factors would be most important. After having read the chapter, are there any advertising or governmental regulations that might impact your products and the copy for the advertising that you propose? Report on your findings to the class or the instructor.

INSTRUCTOR'S NOTE: The following projects require the students to both use and understand the Internet. If students do not understand how to use the Internet, explanation should be given before these projects are undertaken. The Web addresses change frequently, the instructor should re-affirm the site addresses and the content of the site before making an assignment.

3. Go to the Web address for *Advertising Age* at (**http://www.adage.com**). Find a recent article about international advertising. Download its contents. Write a short report that abstracts the article. Report your findings on the content of the article to the class or instructor.

4. Go to the Web address for *Advertising Age* at (**http://www.adage.com**). Find the last report available about award winning international commercials (these may be from any of the media forms--note that these awards occur at different times of the year). After examining the commercials and their reported content, comment on why you think they might have won (or been designated as being award winning). Was there anything that the commercials had in common? Did the commercials seem to be standardized or adapted? If many commercials are listed, you pick a sampling for purposes of your report. Report the results of your findings to the class or to your instructor.

5. Go to the Advertising Research Foundation's home page at (**http://www.arfsite.org**). Examine what type of information might be available to the advertiser that wishes to study international advertising or advertising in other countries. Comment on the number of areas that you find. Pick one of the areas, go to it, and report on the type of data (in more detail than the original request above) that is present. Do you believe that this site can be a valuable site for those wishing to pursue international advertising?

CHAPTER 15

SALES MANAGEMENT

CHAPTER OBJECTIVES

1. Describe market entry options and salesforce strategy available to the international marketing manager.

2. Evaluate the cultural considerations relevant to the sales management process.

3. Describe the impact of culture on sales management and personal selling.

4. Evaluate expatriates and their impact and function with respect to the sales management process.

CHAPTER OVERVIEW

No matter how global a company becomes, its salesforce remains the front line for the company. However, most sales activities occur at the local level and must reflect local situations to be successful. One of the critical components of a coherent international marketing and distribution strategy is an effective salesforce management concept and process.

Since most sales activities occur at the local level, cultural differences influence the process on a day-to-day basis. These differences make standardization of the sales management process (in all global markets) extremely difficult. Because of this problem, many firms rely on merchant distributors at home or sales agents in the foreign market (who have intimate local knowledge of the market) to participate (if not control) the sales process. However, these relationships are constantly changing as the size of the company and its sales force grows.

Sales force objectives and strategy must be formulated and adapted to local market conditions. Because of the hands-on necessity, many sales managers have to become expatriates and move abroad. Expatriate managers not only become a driving force in helping the company localize its strategy but they function as a bridge between headquarters and local operations.

The difficulties faced by the new breed of expatriate managers is discussed. Cross-cultural training is critical, especially, since failure in the foreign marketplace can do great damage at home and abroad. Firms must also be willing to reward expatriates if they expect domestic managers to be interested in foreign positions.

CHAPTER OUTLINE

A. Introduction

1. No matter what job the salesperson within the organization, the salesperson is the front line for the company.

*****Use Global Perspective 15-1 "Direct Marketing: Car Sales Door-to-Door--- Why the Big Three Have Difficulty Cracking into the Japanese Market" Here*****

2. International sales management can be broken into two categories:
   a. International strategy considerations.
      1). Issues which analyze more than one country's assets, strengths, and situations, or which deal directly with cross-border coordination.
   b. Intercultural considerations.
      1). Issues which focus on the culture of the foreign country and its impact on operations within that country.

*****Use Exhibit 15-1 Here; Use Review Question #1 Here; Use Discussion Question #1 Here*****

B. Market Entry Options and Salesforce Strategy

1. The first step in the salesforce management process is to set salesforce objectives and strategy.
   a. These steps include determining the goals and purposes of the salesforce and the structure that will best meet those goals.
2. The question of how to enter the market is central to the marketing effort.
   a. This decision affects salesforce management.
   b. This decision will determine how large the salesforce will need to be, and will influence how much training it will require.
      1). Composition will be dictated.

*****Use Review Question #2 Here*****

3. Entry method can also be called degree of integration.
   a. Forward integration refers to greater ownership and control of the distribution channel.
   b. Forward integration is preferred when:
      1). The operation is large enough to spread out the overhead costs of owning and maintaining infrastructure and training and supervising employees.

2). An inability to enforce contractual obligations on outside intermediaries or some other need for greater control of the sales process requires a strong presence in the host country.

3). Sales of a service usually require a presence in the country earlier than would otherwise be considered.

*****Use Exhibit 15-2 Here; Use Review Question #3 Here*****

4. Selling through an Export Management Company (EMC) or an Export Trading Company (ETC) is considered a "low-involvement" approach to international sales.
   a. EMCs may act as an agent distributor performing marketing services for the exporter client by developing foreign business and making contacts.
   b. EMCs may alternatively act as a merchant distributor who purchases products from the domestic exporter, takes title, sells the product in its own name, and consequently assumes all trading risks.
   c. The EMC is mainly used to test the international arena.
6. ETCs are usually large conglomerates which import, export, countertrade, invest, and manufacture in the global area.
   a. The ETC can purchase products, act as a distributor abroad, or offer services.
   b. In Japan, the ETC is known as "sogoshosha."
   c. The ETC uses their vast size to benefit from economies of scale in shipping and distribution.
7. Another alternative is licensing. Here, the company licenses its product or technology abroad and allows the contracting foreign company to coordinate the production and foreign distribution of the product.
8. Limited involvement approaches to international market entry simplify sales management decisions but do not move the company closer to the foreign markets.
9. Mid-level involvement approaches to foreign sales are those approaches in which the company controls some portion of the distribution process.
   a. This step usually requires that the company consider using expatriates.
10. High involvement approaches are those in which the company substantially controls the foreign distribution channels.

*****Use Discussion Questions #2, #3, and #4 Here*****

11. *Role of foreign governments.*
    a. Rules and practices must be considered.
    b. There may be limits on how many foreign firms are allowed to sell in the market.
    c. Immigration services may limit the number of foreign managers that can legally work in the market.

*****Use Review Question #4 Here*****

C. Cultural Considerations

1. *Personal selling.*
   a. There is little international selling. The sales task tends to take place on a national level.
   b. The analysis of international personal selling is a study of how differences in culture impact the forms, rules, and norms of personal selling within each country.
      1). Personal selling is primarily a personal activity.
      2). Each country has their own norms for selling behavior.
2. *Cultural Generalization.*
   a. Each country must be viewed as a separate entity and generalizations must be be carefully controlled or mistakes will be made.
   b. Hofstede's scale is a beginning point for understanding cultural differences.

*****Use Exhibit 15-3 Here*****

3. **Corporate culture.**
   a. Companies have their own distinct cultures.
   b. Culture can be observed by company practices.
   c. Values of local employees interact with this process.
4. **Myers-Briggs type indicator.**
   a. This indicator is based on four personal dimensions:
      1). Extrovert versus introvert.
      2). Sensing versus intuitive.
      3). Thinking versus feeling.
      4). Judging versus perceiving.
   b. These differences in style can be considered when two cultures interact.
   c. When the cultural norms and cognitive styles of cultures are more clearly understood, it will help reduce misconceptions and miscommunications.

*****Use Exhibit 15-4 Here*****

D. Impact of Culture on Sales Management and Personal Selling Processes

1. In general, human resource practices of multinational corporations closely follow the local practices of the country in which they operate.
2. However, these practices also depend on the strategy desired, the culture of the company, and even the country from which the company originated.

*****Use Global Perspective 15-2 " TGI Friday's, Inc." Here*****

3. Salesforce management consists of the following six steps:
   a. *Salesforce objectives.*
      1). This depends on having already determined the larger, strategic objectives

of the company.

    2). This determines what the role of the salesforce will be.

    3). This approach is very similar to what is used domestically. The objectives are also very similar.

b. *Salesforce strategy.*

    1). Salesforce strategy addresses the issues of structure, size, and compensation of the salesforce.

    2). The structure determines the physical positioning and responsibilities of each salesperson. Alternatives are:

        a). Territorial salesforce.

        b). Product salesforce.

        c). Customer salesforce.

    3). The size of the salesforce depends on the sales structure.

    4). Salesforce compensation is the chief form of motivation for salespeople.

        a). Companies do not pay equally in all countries.

        b). Pay expectations differs between countries.

c. *Recruiting and selecting.*

    1). To successful recruit and train, the company must know what it wants and expects from its salespeople.

    2). The first decision is whether the company will recruit locally or not.

    3). If the company expects to send employees abroad, it must make sure that there will be a culture match.

    4). Talent expectations based on domestic standards sometimes creates difficulties.

    5). The employer must consider the strong influences of tribal, religious, or other group relations within a country.

    6). Joining in a joint venture effort or acquiring a local company can often speed up the process or recruiting and training.

d. *Training.*

    1). Most training takes place in the country where the salespeople reside.

    2). Training (in addition to facts) must include information about the culture.

    3). Global companies may train at the regional level.

e. *Supervising.*

    1). Supervising the salesforce means directing and motivating the salesforce to fulfill the company's objectives and it means providing the resources which allow them to do so.

    2). Support of activities is very important in the international environment.

    3). *Motivation and compensation.*

*****Use Review Question #5 Here*****

    4). *Management style.* This is the approach taken in supervising the employees.

        a). The best approach is to be culturally sensitive.

    5). *Ethical perceptions.*

a). The culture, as well as the personality of the salesperson, influences the salesperson's beliefs about the ethics of common selling practices and the need for company policies to guide those practices.

b). Most salespeople want direction with regard to ethical issues and dilemmas.

   f. *Evaluating.*

      1). This process requires that the salespeople justify their efforts and provide the company with information about their successes, failures, expenses, and time.

      2). The evaluation process is an important motivation tool.

      3). Evaluations can be quantitative or qualitative in nature.

      4). The process is of little value without proper feedback and correction suggestions.

E. Expatriates

1. Most companies with a salesforce abroad will, at the very least, send a few expatriates abroad as operations begin in a new country.

   a. Expatriates are home country personnel sent overseas to manage local operations in the foreign market.

   b. There is a trend for less reliance on expatriates. Reasons include:

      1). Increased international perspective of MNCs.

      2). Increasing competence of foreign managers.

      3). Relatively increasing competitive disadvantage of the cost of maintaining domestic managers abroad.

2. *Advantages of expatriates.*

   a. *Better communication.*

      1). They understand the home office better, its politics, and its priorities.

      2). Familiar with products being sold.

   b. *Development of talent.*

      1). These managers can use their international skills at a later point.

      2). They learn home office skills as well as foreign management skills.

*****Use Review Question #6 Here*****

3. *Difficulties of sending expatriates abroad.*

   a. *Cultural cross-training.*

      1). The difficulties of cultural misunderstandings can be large.

      2). Not all cultural information can be taught quickly or correctly.

      3). Languages present problems.

      4). High cost of training.

      5). Training becomes difficult once the manager leaves the domestic environment.

      6). The more they learn, the more they realize that they know nothing. They will always be a product of their home culture.

7). Social problems may exclude them at critical times.
  b. *Motivation.*
    1). Policies and incentives have to carefully designed to motivate expatriates to succeed abroad.
    2). Fight the "out of sight, out of mind" fear that promotions will skip them.
  c. *Compensation.*
    1). Compensation packages may include many items not included in the domestic manager's compensation package.
    2). A majority of expatriates say they are unhappy with their compensation package.

*****Use Exhibit 15-5 Here*****

    3). Higher compensation (or hardship) packages is often a source of problems with local managers.
    4). The higher package may make the manager unwilling to return home.
    5). Family life is often affected.
  d. *Family discord.*
    1). Two career families are reluctant to move abroad.
    2). English and a different life style are often factors the families consider.
    3). Safety and happiness are always issues.
    4). This is the primary reason employees request to return home early.

*****Use Global Perspective 15-3 "Screening Candidates for Expatriation" Here*****

  e. *The return of the expatriate--repatriation.*
    1). Return from abroad may cause career damage.
    2). Salaries may be lowered.
    3). The employee may have changed, have adopted different values, and not be part of the home office network or culture anymore.
    4). The effect of returning home can be dampened by:
      a). Post-arrival training.
      b). A repatriation center to help employees reform their objectives with the company
      c). Spouse adjustment assistance.
      d). Pre-return training.
      e). Increased contact with the home office while abroad.
      f). Setting up a sponsor or partner back in the home office.
4. *Generalizations about when expatriates are good/bad.*
  a. Expatriates are especially important in complex operating environments.
  b. Good when political risk is high.
  c. Good when a great cultural distance separates the home office from the local market.
  d. Bad when there is great competition in the local environment and local officials

can be of great value.
  e. Local officials can often provide very valuable custom strategies.

*****Use Review Question #7 Here*****

REVIEW QUESTIONS

INSTRUCTOR'S NOTE: The following chapter review questions are meant to challenge the student to think about material presented in the chapter and formulate a creative answer to the review questions. Many of the answers require judgments rather than specific line-by-line quotation of facts. The answers provided are meant to provide stimulation of creative answers.

1. In what ways does international sales management differ from domestic sales management?

Though there are many similarities between domestic and foreign salesforce management there are differences. Some of these differences that may be used to generate a class discussion are: salesforce skill, whether to use expatriates or locals, communication distance and problems, motivation, cultural sensitivity, organizational culture versus local culture, compensation and rewards, expectations and evaluations. There are other differences. The aforementioned areas should provide ample topics for discussion.

2. Discuss why mode of entry and sales management are closely related.

In international sales, the form of entry has even greater implications in international sales than at the domestic level. The form of entry will determine how large the salesforce will need to be, and will influence how much training it will need. It will also influence whether the salesforce is predominately local foreign citizens or whether it is primarily expatriates. It influences many of the "downstream" operations and options.

3. For what type of business does a company employ a traveling global salesforce?

This form of forward integration would be necessary for the firm that desires a great deal of control of the product and channel from beginning to end. Reasons for using the "global approach" might be:

  1). The operation is large enough to spread out the overhead costs of owning and maintaining infrastructure and training and supervising employees.
  2). An inability to enforce contractual obligations on outside intermediaries or some other need for greater control of the sales process requires a strong presence in the host country.
  3). Sales of a service usually require a presence in the country earlier than would otherwise be considered.

4. How might a foreign government affect a company's salesforce management?

Many host country governments design regulations which protect local firms from international competition and insure that local citizens benefit from the experience in management positions at international companies. Local immigration services may even monitor if not restrict the flow of foreign managers at their domestic company locations.

In addition, if a company sets up a complete sales and distribution subsidiary, it may be expected to build a local infrastructure or support local politicians or take part in local training initiatives.

5. Why is it generally considered difficult to adopt a U.S.-style commission based salesforce management in such countries as Japan and Mexico?

Commissions reinforce the negative image of the salesperson benefiting from the sale, with no regard for the purchaser's well-being. Under certain circumstances, large salary discrepancies between employees are not acceptable. In a "collectivist" culture country like Japan, it may not be acceptable that one person should earn substantially more than another in the same position. In countries like Mexico, bribery and ethical behavior might also be considered when examining the compensation issues.

6. Discuss why expatriate managers are important to a parent company despite the enormous cost of sending them overseas.

Advantages of expatriates.
  a. Better communication.
    1). They understand the home office better, its politics, and its priorities.
    2). Familiar with products being sold.
  b. Development of talent.
    1). These managers can use their international skills at a later point.
    2). They learn home office skills as well as foreign management skills.

7. Suppose you are developing a cultural training program for employees to be sent to overseas posts. What courses would you include in your two-week program? And why?

This question calls for a judgment on the part of the student. The student should arrive at that judgment after considering the expatriate and cultural issues described in this chapter. To begin a discussion of the areas that should be included in the two week course, the student should consider language, cultural sensitivity, local customs, local market conditions, how to live in the country, how adapt the family to the environment, objectives of the company in the foreign environment, how to survive everyday tasks, their role in the management of the foreign subsidiary or company, and the expectations of the parent company. Others can be added.

DISCUSSION QUESTIONS

INSTRUCTOR'S NOTE: Discussion Questions are found at the end of each chapter in the text. These questions (in many cases) are too lengthy to repeat in the manual. Suggestions for answering and discussing the questions are presented in this section. Many of the questions require student opinion and judgment.

1. This question requires the student to take a stance on the issue presented in the scenario. As is indicated, either position could be maintained and supported. The underlying issue is one of standardization versus adaptation (with an overlay of infrastructure). Since either position can be taken, students should be sure to state specifically which alternative they favor and provide supporting reasons for their choice. Their opinions can be based on material from this chapter.

2. Piggybacking is a unique concept. As mentioned in the short question description, piggybacking works best when both parties have something to gain from the partnership, when consumers might logically consider both products or services at the same time, when elements of the marketing mix can be shared (such as promotion or distribution), when the class of consumers is somewhat similar (don't piggyback luxury goods with convenience goods), when organizational and management structures are similar, and when overall corporate objectives are somewhat similar. The joint venture criteria might also be considered. Inappropriateness may be discussed by beginning to look at the opposite of the statements listed above. Students should be encouraged to expand the concepts mentioned above.

3. The material discussed in this question is somewhat a result of the desire on the part of manufacturers to expand rapidly. When this becomes an objective, the manufacturer is willing to turn over greater portions of the marketing effort to distributors (especially large retailers). This then becomes a process of losing control. When retailers decide to make their own choices on how to promote or sell the products, the manufacturer should not be surprised or dismayed. The alternative is to communicate and attempt to understand both of the philosophies of promotion. In this way common agreement might be reached. The problem of store brands is another issue. In many instances, the manufacturer of the branded product is also the manufacturer of the store brand. Complaint would not seem to be justified. If complaints still exist, the best solution would again be one of communication. In this way both parties can understand each other's objectives and reach a common agreement on the best way to market so that both parties prosper and are able to successfully compete against their competition.

4. In order to answer this question on incremental sales strategies, the student should review the material in the chapter that deals with entry methods. Since most MNCs are

interested in expansion (but also there is a desire to reduce risk), the incremental advancement method would seem to be a cautious attempt at growth. Students should be asked for their opinions and the students should be asked to use an example to support their feelings on this issue.

STUDENT PROJECTS and INTERNET FOCUS

1. Pretend that you are a company wishing to market products in the United States for the first time. You may choose any product group that you wish for your example. Write a short report to the executives of your firm telling them what they might need to know about the culture of the United States before they enter this market. You may limit your comments to particular market segments if you desire, however, the intent of the question is to have you tell general information about this market (which would be foreign to the company).

2. You have been offered a job in a foreign market environment (you may choose any market in the foreign arena). As a future expatriate, what would you like to know about the country, its culture, your job, and security for your family. Draw up a list of prospective questions for your employer. Discuss these in class.

INSTRUCTOR'S NOTE: The following projects require the students to both use and understand the Internet. If students do not understand how to use the Internet, explanation should be given before these projects are undertaken. The Web addresses change frequently, the instructor should re-affirm the site addresses and the content of the site before making an assignment.

3. Pick a country of your choice. Your assignment is to do research on that country and its markets so you can develop a cultural "must know" list for your company. Your list will be used to acquaint your company's managers with facts before they enter the country and attempt to sell in its markets (if you need to make certain assumptions because of the nature of your product or service, you may do so). Using the Yahoo (**http://www.yahoo.com**) or Lycos (**http://www.lycos.com**) search engines, find the cultural data that will help you to design your list. Report your findings to the class or your instructor.

4. One of the more interesting magazines to review about current trends in American culture is *American Demographics* magazine. Go to (**http://www.marketingtools.com**) search the site, locate the aforementioned magazine, and research contemporary trends that might help the sales force from a Japanese, German, and Russian company do business and find markets in the United States. You specialize your search in any way that you choose. Be creative. Report your findings.

5. Take the following four firms and identify what you perceive to be their corporate culture from information provided on their Web sites. Once you have identified their culture be sure to designate why you think your identification is correct and how did your assessment.

a. Honda   (**http://www.honda.com**)
b. UPS   (**http://www.ups.com**)
c. Toshiba America Information Systems   (**http://www.computers.toshiba.com**)
d. Oracle Corporation   (**http://www.oracle.com**).

CHAPTER 16

GLOBAL LOGISTICS AND DISTRIBUTION

CHAPTER OBJECTIVES

1. Define global logistics.

2. Describe how to manage global logistics.

3. Describe and identify free trade zones.

4. Explain the Maquiladora Operation.

5. Review the U.S. Special Import Tariff Provision.

6. Examine global retailing concepts.

CHAPTER OVERVIEW

Global logistics and distribution have played a critical role in the growth and development of world trade and in the integration of manufacturing on a worldwide scale. In fact, the level of world trade in goods and services, depends to a significant degree on the availability of economical and reliable international transportation services. Choosing the right channel of distribution significantly improves the chances of a ventures success in the international market.

In addition to the question of distribution opportunities, today's company must also be familiar with outsourcing opportunities. The issues that concern the international logistics manager (transportation, warehousing, inventorying, and the connection of these activities to corporate strategy) are discussed. Logistics management is closely linked to manufacturing actitivities.

Various governments, including the United States, have developed free trade zones, export processing zones, and other special economic zones designed chiefly to increase domestic employment and exports from the zone. Various tax and other cost benefits available in the zones attract both domestic and foreign firms to set up warehousing and manufacturing operations.

Lastly, the chapter discusses global retailing. In the past, retailing was largely a localized activity. However, today retailing is becoming global on a daily basis. Information technology makes it increasingly possible for large retailers to know what they are selling in hundreds of stores around the world. Given this intimate knowledge of customers around the world, those retailers that have acquired these skills have begun to overtake the channel leadership role from manufacturers.

CHAPTER OUTLINE

A. Introduction

1. Global logistics and distribution have played a critical role in the growth and development of world trade and in the integration of manufacturing on a worldwide scale.
   a. Using the appropriate distribution channels in international markets increases the chances of success dramatically.
2. The concept of business logistics is not new.
   a. Magee published material on the subject in 1960.
   b. It is estimated that over 50 percent of product cost is material related.

3. As firms start operating on a global basis, logistics managers need to manage shipping of raw materials, components, and supplies among various manufacturing sites at the most economical and reliable rates.

B. Definition of Global Logistics

1. Global logistics is defined as the design and management of a system that directs and controls the flows of materials into, through and out of the firm across national boundaries to achieve its corporate objectives at a minimum total cost.
   a. Global logistics, like domestic logistics, encompasses materials management and

   physical distribution.

*****Use Exhibit 16-1 Here; Use Review Question #1 Here*****

2. Materials management refers to the inflow of raw materials, parts and supplies in and through the firm.
3. Physical distribution refers to the movement of the firm's finished products to its customers, consisting of transportation, warehousing, inventory, customer service/order entry, and administration.
   a. These functions can be affected by tradition, culture, economic infrastructure, laws, and topography.
   b. Geographical expanse shifts the orientation of the functions.

*****Use Global Perspective 16-1 "Regional Variations in Physical Distribution Costs in Europe" Here*****

C. Managing Global Logistics

1. Logistic management is inextricably tied with international trade and multinational manufacturing and sourcing of raw materials, components, and supplies.
2. A variety of factors contribute to the increased complexity and cost of global logistics as compared to domestic logistics.
   a. *Distance.* A longer distance generally suggests a higher cost.

*****Use Discussion Question #1 Here*****

   b. *Exchange rate fluctuation.*
   c. *Foreign intermediaries.* Negotiating border crossings can be a difficult task. Building local connections can be very important to long-term success.

*****Use Review Question #2 Here*****

3. *Modes of transportation.*
   a. Three factors need to considered in this area:
      1). The value-to-volume ratio.
      2). Perishability.
      3). Cost of transportation.
   b. *Ocean shipping.* Three options are:
      1). Liner service.
      2). Bulk shipping.
      3). Irregular runs.
   c. *Air freight.* This area has seen rapid growth over the past 30 years. High value goods are more likely to be shipped by air (especially if they have a high value-to-volume ratio).
   d. *Intermodal transportation.* The choices here are all land based (truck, barge, or railroad).
4. Managing shipments so that they arrive in time at the desired destination is critical in modern-day logistic management. Delays can occur for any number of reasons.
5. Distance (the big cost determinant) increases transportation costs, requires longer term commitment to forecasts and longer lead times.
   a. Trade barriers impact this area.
   b. Regional trading blocs are trying to reduce these barriers.

*****Use Global Perspective 16-2 "Redesigning Logistics in the Emergence of the European Union" Here*****

6. *Warehousing and inventory management.*
   a. Traditional logistics strategy involves anticipatory demand management based on forecasting and inventory speculation.

b. In the past tracking was a significant problem.

c. Increased use of advanced information technology is changing the tracking problem.

d. Most firms are now able to use just-in-time management.

e. *Hedging against inflation or exchange rate fluctuations.*

    1). Inventory can be used as a hedge.

    2). Holding inventory may be better than holding cash.

    3). Some countries charge a tax on stored goods.

f. *Benefiting from tax differences.*

7. *Logistic integration and rationalization.*

a. Logistic integration refers to coordinating production and distribution across geographic boundaries.

b. Rationalization refers to reducing resources to achieve more efficient and cost-effective operations.

c. Integration is still constrained by cultural and legal differences between regional groups.

*****Use Global Perspective 16-3 "Cabotage" Here*****

8. *Intra-company versus inter-company (third party) logistic management.*

a. There is a trend toward decentralization.

b. Supply chain management firms are beginning to help in the logistics function.

*****Use Global Perspective 16-4 "IBM International Trade Management Services (ITMS) Here; Use Discussion Question #5 Here*****

c. The trend toward third party logistics may be a result of concentrating on core competencies.

    1). Core competencies refer to the mix of skills and resources that a firm possesses which enable it to produce one set of goods and/or services in a much more effective manner than another.

    2). Many logistic companies are now providing tailored logistic solutions in international markets for their clients.

    3). For smaller firms, however, third party logistics completely may not be a cost effective alternative because of the relatively lower volumes over which the logistic provider can spread his volumes.

*****Use Review Question #3 Here*****

D. Free Trade Zones

1. A free trade zone (FTZ) is an area that is located within a nation but is considered outside of the Customs territory of the nation.

a. Legally, goods remain in the zone and are counted as international commerce.

They are either held or exported.

*****Use Exhibit 16-2 Here*****

      b. No taxes are levied until the goods are brought into the country's Customs territory.
2. Operationally, an FTZ provides an opportunity to take advantage of a variety of efficiencies and economies in the manufacture and marketing of their products.
      a. Goods can be aged (wine).
      b. Repackaged.
      c. Sorted and labeled.
      d. Tested.
      e. Repaired.
      f. Reprocessed or fabricated.
      g. Assembled.
3. Governments have also established export processing zones and special economic areas.

*****Use Global Perspective 16-5 "Japan's Foreign Access Zone to Increase Imports Rather Than Exports" Here; Use Review Question #4 Here; Use Discussion Question #3 Here*****

E. Maquiladora Operation

1. The Maquiladora industry, also known as the in-bond or twin-plant program, is essentially a special Mexican version of a free trade zone.
      a. Mexico allows duty-free imports of machinery and equipment for manufacturing as well as components for further processing and assembly as long as at least 80% of the plant's output is exported.
      b. Foreign ownership is allowed.
2. Low wage rates make the program very attractive. Many labor intensive manufacturing concerns have moved to Mexico to take advantage of this opportunity.

F. U.S. Special Import Tariff Provisions

1. The maquiladoras in Mexico are not just encouraged and stimulated by Mexico.
      a. U.S. tariff provisions have also encouraged the development of these industries.
2. Duty importation into the U.S. from these programs have also stimulated growth.
3. The effect is to be able to gain entry into the U.S. market with no real penalty for manufacturing abroad.
4. NAFTA provisions will continue this trend.

*****Use Review Question #5 Here*****

G. Global Retailing

1. Retailers have grown into some the world's largest international businesses.
2. ***Push versus pull.***
    a. At the heart of global retailing is the change in the way consumers receive goods and services.
    b. The old system of top-down stimulation (push) is now giving way to bottom-up (pull) merchandising, promotion, and stimulation.
    c. There has been a real shift in power to the retailer.
3. ***On-time retail information management.*** Consequences are:
    a. ***Reduced inventory.***
    b. ***Market information at the retail level.*** This helps to extract better deals from the manufacturers.
4. Distribution is becoming more concentrated while manufacturing is becoming more
    splintered.
5. Distributors have more bargaining power.

*****Use Review Question #6 Here*****

6. ***Real differences across the world.***
    a. The density of retail and wholesale establishments in different countries varies greatly.
    b. Changes in the amount of goods demanded and the advancement of facilities is part of the reason for expansion.
    c. Not all countries have retail facilities like the United States.

*****Use Global Perspective 16-6 "Foreign Retailers Follow Toys 'R' Us to Japan" Here; Use Review Question #7 Here; Use Discussion Questions #2 and #4 Here*****

    d. Changes in rules, hours of operation, and management structure must be observed.

REVIEW QUESTIONS

INSTRUCTOR'S NOTE: The following chapter review questions are meant to challenge the student to think about material presented in the chapter and formulate a creative answer to the review questions. Many of the answers require judgments rather than specific line-by-line quotation of facts. The answers provided are meant to provide stimulation of creative answers.

1. **Define the term global logistics. Enumerate and describe the various operations encompassed by it.**

Global logistics is defined as the design and management of a system that directs and controls the flows of materials into, through and out of the firm across national boundaries to achieve its corporate objectives at a minimum total cost. Global logistics, like domestic logistics, encompasses materials management and physical distribution.

2. **What are the factors that contribute to the increased complexity and cost of global logistics as compared to domestic logistics?**

A variety of factors contribute to the increased complexity and cost of global logistics as compared to domestic logistics:
   a. *Distance.* A longer distance generally suggests a higher cost.
   b. *Exchange rate fluctuation.*
   c. *Foreign intermediaries.* Negotiating border crossings can be a difficult task. Building local connections can be very important to long-term success.

3. **What role do third-party logistics companies play in international trade? What are the advantages of using these companies over internalizing the logistics activities?**

The trend toward third party logistics may be a result of concentrating on core competencies.
   1). Core competencies refer to the mix of skills and resources that a firm possesses which enable it to produce one set of goods and/or services in a much more effective manner than another.
   2). Many logistic companies are now providing tailored logistic solutions in international markets for their clients.
   3). For smaller firms, however, third party logistics completely may not be a cost effective alternative because of the relatively lower volumes over which the logistic provider can spread his volumes.

4. **Describe the role of free trade zones (FTZs) in global logistics.**

A free trade zone (FTZ) is an area that is located within a nation but is considered outside of the Customs territory of the nation. Legally, goods remain in the zone and are counted as international commerce. They are either held or exported.

No taxes are levied until the goods are brought into the country's Customs territory. Operationally, an FTZ provides an opportunity to take advantage of a variety of efficiencies and economies in the manufacture and marketing of their products. Some of the advantages are that the goods can be:
   a. Aged (wine).
   b. Repackaged.

c. Sorted and labeled.

d. Tested.

e. Repaired.

f. Reprocessed or fabricated.

g. Assembled.

5. What are the reasons for the dramatic increase in cross-border trade between the U. S. and Mexico?

As outlined below, the primary reasons are the Maquiladora industry, special trade zones, and NAFTA.

The Maquiladora industry, also known as the in-bond or twin-plant program, is essentially a special Mexican version of a free trade zone.

a. Mexico allows duty-free imports of machinery and equipment for manufacturing as well as components for further processing and assembly as long as at least 80% of the plant's output is exported.

b. Foreign ownership is allowed.

Low wage rates make the program very attractive. Many labor intensive manufacturing concerns have moved to Mexico to take advantage of this opportunity.

The maquiladoras in Mexico are not just encouraged and stimulated by Mexico.

a. U.S. tariff provisions have also encouraged the development of these industries.

Duty importation into the U.S. from these programs have also stimulated growth. The effect is to be able to gain entry into the U.S. market with no real penalty for manufacturing abroad. NAFTA provisions will continue this trend.

6. How is information technology affecting global retailing?

There are many effects (students should be encouraged to be creative here and expand the discussion beyond the material found in the chapter). Some of the more significant effects are:

On-time retail information management. Consequences are:

a. *Reduced inventory.*

b. *Market information at the retail level.* This helps to extract better deals from the manufacturers.

Distribution is becoming more concentrated while manufacturing is becoming more splintered. Distributors have more bargaining power.

7. The U.S. and Japan have similar income and purchasing power levels. Yet, there are significant differences in the retail structures between the two countries.

Describe some of the reasons for these differences.

Though the income levels may be similar there are other great differences between the United States and Japanese retail patterns. Some of these differences that may be used to begin and generate a discussion are:

Cultural differences.
Land space.
Attitudes about consumption.
Number of small merchants.
Distribution structures.
Arrangements between manufacturers and retailers.
Bargaining power of retailers.
Attitudes toward foreign businesses.
Ability to save rather than spend.

DISCUSSION QUESTIONS

INSTRUCTOR'S NOTE: Discussion Questions are found at the end of each chapter in the text. These questions (in many cases) are too lengthy to repeat in the manual. Suggestions for answering and discussing the questions are presented in this section. Many of the questions require student opinion and judgment.

1. This question asks students to make a judgment and present an opinion. In order to accumulate a background sufficient to make a judgment, it is recommended that the student carefully review material in this chapter, the Global Perspectives, and information from previous chapters relevant to NAFTA and coordination between international partners. In addition, it is recommended that the students review the bibliographies contained at the end of the chapter and others. Carefully review the definition and concept of logistics to make the judgment.

2. This question asks the students to assume the role of a member of a management team of a large retail chain which has a moderate presence in the catalog business. To answer the questions presented by this problem situation, the student should review the material from the chapter that is relevant to coordination of logistics. It is also recommended that the students carefully review the concept of outsourcing in light of infrastructure problems that might be caused by starting a catalog business in a foreign market. Further, the student might wish to specify a particular market to use as an example since the difference between an underdeveloped and developed country might be significant.

3. The concept of the free trade zone is still a very active concept. The students should review the overview of this material in the chapter. At this point the students should be able to make a stronger argument for investing in resources in a free trade zone than in waiting for trade barriers to be reduced on a global basis. The Global Perspective on the

Maquiladora Operation is also a useful reference to prepare material to answer this question. The students should also consider how that free trade zone operations might be converted if trade barriers were reduced. Could the same plants become normal manufacturing or distribution entities?

4. This question asks students to forecast the future for global expansion in the retailing world. In order to accomplish this task, the students should review the material from the chapter on global expansion, global retailing, entry methods, and logistical problems. In addition, the Global Perspective boxes might also provide useful insight in formulating a forecast of the direction of retailing in the future. Some additional considerations are found in the answer blank to Review Question #7. Each of these factors might be incorporated into an answer.

5. The large logistics companies are an attractive alternative for the company that wants to reduce costs and approach a market with a minimum of resource expenditure and commitment. The primary problem with the "turnkey" operation is that the power of the logistical support provider grows and the manufacturer does not develop the network contacts or support mechanisms necessary to implement long-term strategy. Students should consider this dilemma when formulating an answer. It might also be useful to cite examples of pro and con arguments with respect to material in this question. Global Perspective 16-4 might also be interesting to review.

STUDENT PROJECTS and INTERNET FOCUS

1. Pretend that you are the U.S. manufacturer of: a) an automobile, b) a computer, c) a pair of jeans, and d) cut flowers. Select the best way to transport your merchandise to: a) Europe, b) Canada, and c) Japan. Once you have selected the optimal transportation form, give the reasons why you selected the method.

2. Go to the library and research the Maquiladora Operation in Mexico. Find an article that describes the Maquiladora Operation and report on your findings by abstracting the article and presenting the material to the class or to the instructor.

INSTRUCTOR'S NOTE: The following projects require the students to both use and understand the Internet. If students do not understand how to use the Internet, explanation should be given before these projects are undertaken. The Web addresses change frequently, the instructor should re-affirm the site addresses and the content of the site before making an assignment.

3. Go to the NAFTA Watch Bulletin line at (**http://www.aescon.com/naftam/index.html**). This site has various articles on NAFTA and international trade in general. Look for an article on logistics and international distribution. Abstract the article and report your findings.

4. Go to the Web site entitled Why is Mexico a Big Emerging Market? at (**http://www.stat-usa.gov/bems/bemsmex/html**). Find information on the Maquiladora Operation in Mexico. Report your findings.

5. Go to the Web site entitled International Logistics at (**http://www.commerce2000.com/logistics/woklcou.html**). Examine the wealth of information available on this site. Examples of information that can be obtained is information on roads, ships, ports, rail facilities, agencies that regulate and aid transportation and logistical endeavors, and much much more. If you were a logistical planner seeking to go abroad with your company's products, what could you use from this site? Draw a profile of the material that might be useful to you. You may assume a specific products or service and assume that the product or service might be going to a specific country if it makes your research any easier. Report your findings to the class or to your instructor.

CHAPTER 17

EXPORT AND IMPORT MANAGEMENT

CHAPTER OBJECTIVES

1. Demonstrate how companies can organize for exports.

2. Describe the indirect channels of distribution.

3. Explain direct export marketing.

4. Investigate the linkage between foreign direct investment and exports.

5. Explain the mechanics of exporting.

6. Examine the role of the government in promoting exports.

7. Review the concept of managing imports.

8. Explain the mechanics of importing.

9. Identify and explain gray markets.

CHAPTER OVERVIEW

The United States was the largest importer and exporter in the world in 1995. Importing and exporting are not only components of international trade and competition but are part of government growth objectives and policy as well. Therefore, the control of importing and exporting is not always just in the hands of those engaged in commerce.

The numerous procedures (from locating customers to shipping and receiving payment) involved in exporting are discussed in the chapter. These procedures are contrasted (and some times parallel) to those of the importing cycle. Differing methods of payment are of interest not only to the exporter but to the importer as well. After investigating the payment methods available, the exporter may need to make foreign exchange hedging transactions. Research has found that because of the strategic importance of exports and imports, the United States government is now taking a more active role in promoting exports of American firms as they bid for the big ticket items in the emerging markets of the world's economy.

As shown through many examples in the chapter, the importer is the obverse of the exporter. Unlike the exporter who faces a payment risk, the importer's risk is associated with delivery schedules and product quality. Foreign exchange risk is common to both imports and exports. The importer must also deal with the constantly changing import restriction environment that is within the control of the Federal government.

Finally, the chapter discusses an interesting concept called gray marketing. The gray marketers are unauthorized distributors taking advantage of price differences that exist among various countries due to currency exchange rate fluctuations, different market demand conditions, and price discrimination. As will be shown, companies marketing well known brands consider gray marketers to be a serious issue that should be confronted proactively as well as reactively.

CHAPTER OUTLINE

A. Introduction

1. Since 1945 world exports have expanded steadily ahead of the growth rate of the economic output.
2. Another trend is that there has been an increase in intermediate processing (value is added to the product by another source before final disposition or consumption).
3. Developing countries are no longer just exporting raw resources. At present, 60 percent of developing countries' exports are manufactured goods.

*****Use Exhibit 17-1 Here*****

4. Service exports are also growing.

B. Organizing for Exports

1. For a firm beginning exports for the first time, the first step is to use available secondary data to research potential markets.
   a. This could be in the form of databases.
   b. There is a need to understand the cultural differences on the part of the market to be entered.
2. The identification of an appropriate overseas market and an appropriate segment involves grouping by the following criteria:
   a. Socioeconomic characteristics like demographic, economic, geographic, and climatic characteristics.
   b. Political and legal variables.
   c. Consumer variables such as lifestyle, preferences, culture, taste, purchase behavior, and purchase frequency.
   d. Financial variables.

*****Use Review Question #1 Here*****

3. Data for grouping along macro-economic criteria are available from international agencies such as the World Bank.
4. ***Export market segments.***
   a. The grouping of countries and of regions among countries enables the firm to link various geographical areas into one homogeneous market segment which which the firm can cater to in meeting its export objectives.
   b. The next task is to develop a product strategy for the selected export markets.
   c. The marketer would look at country level and regional level.
   d. Products that can be standardized may satisfy basic needs that do not vary with climate, economic conditions, or culture.
      1). This form of product is easiest to sell logistically.

*****Use Review Question #2 Here*****

   e. Where it is not possible to sell a standardized product one must be adapted.
      1). Brand names may need to be altered.

*****Use Discussion Question #1 Here*****

C. **Indirect Channels of Distribution**

1. Indirect exporting involves the use of independent U.S. middlemen to market the firm's products overseas.
   a. These export representatives assume responsibility for marketing the firm's products through their network of foreign distributors and their own sales force.
      1). This form is especially useful when cost is a factor.
   b. Types include:
      1). ***The combination export manager (CEM).***
         a). Acts as the export department to a small exporter or to a large producer with small overseas sales.
         b). Operates on a commission basis.
         c). Credit support is essential.
         d). This form is diminishing in numbers and usage because of increased involvement in global marketing.
      2). ***The export merchant.***
         a). This person buys and sells on their own account and assumes all the responsibilities of exporting a product.
         b). Manufacturers are not in control. The export merchant is.
      3). ***The export broker.***
         a). This person brings together an overseas buyer and a U.S. manufacturer for the purpose of an export sale and earns a commission for establishing a contact which results in a sale.

4). An export commission house can place an order on behalf of a client and provides a finder function.

5). **A trading company** is a foreign organization engaged in exporting and importing. They buy and sell on their own account.

*****Use Exhibit 17-2 Here; Use Discussion Question #2 Here*****

6). *Piggyback exporting* refers to the practice where U.S. firms that have an established export department assume, under a cooperative agreement, the responsibility of exporting the products of other U.S. companies.

D. Direct Export Marketing

1. Direct export occurs when a manufacturer or exporter sells directly to an importer or buyer located in a foreign market.
   a. The simplest form is the export manager with some clerical help.
      1). This manager sells and directs the activities of the export process.
   b. As export activities grow, most firms create a separate export department which is largely self-contained and operates independently of domestic operations.
   c. An extension is to form an export sales subsidiary to export separate from the other operations of the firm.
      1). The major difference is that it is a legal entity and can offer tax advantages.
   d. The foreign sales branch is not a separate legal entity. This branch handles all sales, distribution, and promotional work throughout a designated market area and sells primarily to wholesalers and dealers.

*****Use Exhibit 17-3 Here; Use Review Question #3 Here*****

E. Linkage Between Foreign Direct Investment and Exports

1. Subsidiaries often export to their parent companies in foreign markets.
2. Many countries which have large potential markets for multinationals use that potential to lure the multinationals into their country. The precondition to the MNC is that a percentage must be exported.
3. These trends suggest that foreign direct investment and exports are getting interlinked and can no longer be thought of as discrete activities.

F. Mechanics of Exporting

1. To the uninitiated, the mechanics of exporting can seem to be cumbersome and full of meaningless paperwork that appears to be of no real value to anyone.
   a. The government forms are used to compile trade statistics.
   b. These statistics are barometers of economic health and are treated seriously by financial analysts.

*****Use Exhibit 17-4 Here*****

2. *Legality of exports.*
   a. Exporting starts with the search for a buyer abroad and the research that is required to locate a potential market and a buyer and the process of closing a sale.
   b. To consummate the sale certain events must occur.
      1). The first set of things that an exporter needs to make sure the sale can be concluded is to verify the legality of the transaction. This is especially important in developing nations.
         a). Currency conversion must be reviewed. Permission to convert is often necessary.
         b). Verify that no security violations occur with the sale of the product.
         c). Obtain licenses.
            1]. Export license.
            2]. General license.
            3]. Validated license.

*****Use Exhibit 17-5 Here*****

3. *Export transactions.*
   a. The logistics of the export transaction is the second pillar of an export transaction. Parts are:
      1). The terms of sale (including f.o.b./c.i.f. payment mode and schedule, dispute settlement mechanism, and service requirements.
      2). Monitoring the transportation and delivery of the goods to the assigned party (the Customs receipt).
      3). Shipping and obtaining the Bill of Lading.
         a). A bill of lading is a contract between the exporter and the shipper indicating that the shipper has accepted responsibility for the goods and will provide transportation in return for payment. Forms include:
            1]. A straight bill of lading.
            2]. A shipper's order bill of lading.
         b). A commercial invoice is a bill for the goods stating basic information about the transaction, including a description of the merchandise, total cost of the goods sold, addresses of the buyer and seller, and delivery and payment. This invoice proves ownership.
         c). Other documentation may be required.
      4). Freight forwarders can be used in complicated documentation cases since one of their primary responsibilities is handling export documentation.
4. *Terms of shipment and sale.*
   a. INCOTERMS is an acronym for International Commercial Terms. These terms help to make sure there no misunderstanding with respect to sale and receipt of products.

*****Use Exhibit 17-6 Here; Use Review Question #5 Here*****

       1). These terms also have importance in the pricing and costing areas.

5. ***Payment terms.***
   a. The financing and payments constitutes the third set of things to do with regard to an export transaction.
   b. The terms of payment between buyer and seller are a matter of negotiation and depend on a variety of factors. These factors include:
      1). The amount of the sale transaction.
      2). The availability of foreign exchange in the buyer's country.
      3). The exchange control laws in the buyer's country.
      4). The risks associated with the type of merchandise to be shipped.
      5). The usual practice in the trade.
      6). Market conditions.

*****Use Exhibit 17-7 Here*****

6. When negotiating payment terms with an importer, an exporter must be guided by the risks associated with the importer and the importer's country. Risks include:
   a. Credit risk--the risk that the importer will not pay or fail to pay on the agreed terms.
   b. Exchange risk--exists when the sale is in the importer's currency and that currency depreciates in terms of the dollar leaving the exporter with a lesser amount in their currency.
   c. Transfer risk--refers to the chances that payment will not be made due to the importer's inability to obtain U.S. dollars and transfer them to the exporter.
   d. Political risk--the risks associated with war, confiscation of the importer's business, et cetera.
7. If the sale is in cash, there is virtually no risk.
8. Credit letters can be considered.
   a. An unconfirmed letter of credit exposes the exporter to the creditworthiness of the buyer's bank in the foreign country because a U.S. bank is not guaranteeing payment.
   b. A sight draft excludes banks from the process and has less guarantees.
   c. An open account sale is truly one of trust in the buyer's ability to pay.

*****Use Review Question #4 Here; Use Discussion Question #3 Here*****

9. Associated with the payment and shipment terms is insurance. The insurance policy, stipulations, and liability should be understood by all.
10. ***Currency hedging.***
    a. The fourth task of an exporter is to arrange a foreign exchange cover transaction with the banker or through the firm's treasury in case there is a foreign exchange risk in the export transaction.
    b. Currency hedging--currency options and currency futures enables the exporter

to lock in the dollar value of the export transaction up to a year in the future.

G. Role of the Government in Promoting Exports

1. Export promotion activities generally comprise:
   a. Export service programs.
   b. Market development programs.
2. Government expenditures on export promotion seem to make sense.
   a. The government tries to get more firms to export.
   b. The government tries to get firms to overcome the perception of risk in the international area and take the plunge.
3. The United States presented a National Export Strategy in 1993.
4. *Export-import bank (the Exim bank).* Promotes exports.
   a. Helps companies get financing for exports.
   b. The bank also works with capital expansion, infrastructure projects, and trade loans.

*****Use Global Perspective 17-1 "Government Agencies Provide Export Assistance and Counter Tied Aid" Here*****

5. Though critics don't like U.S. government involvement in export trade, the United States support of exports is among the lowest of the industrialized nations.

*****Use Exhibit 17-8 Here*****

6. *U.S. tariff concessions.*
   a. *Free trade zone.* Lets businesses store, process, assemble, and display goods from abroad without paying tariff.
   b. *Foreign sales corporation.* A foreign corporation not located in a free trade zone that is allowed to earn some exempt and non-taxable income on its exports from the United States.
   c. *American export trading company.* Legislation encourages the formulation of trading companies for the purpose of exporting.
7. *Export regulations.*
   a. The Trade Act of 1974--bars Exim bank from giving credit to most communist countries.
   b. Foreign Corrupt Practices Act of 1977 prohibits influencing overseas officials.
   c. Antitrust laws.
   d. Foreign government laws that affect exports.
   e. Taxes on exports to stimulate domestic consumption first.

*****Use Review Question #6 Here*****

H. Managing Imports--The Other Side Of The Coin

1. Importing is vastly easier than exporting because of the advantages of doing business in your own home country.
2. Importing any good is predicated upon the existence of a situation where the domestic production of the good in question is not sufficient to satisfy demand.
   a. Not much research has been done on importer behavior.
   b. The buy-grid model can be used.
      1). Straight buys.
      2). Modified rebuys.
      3). New tasks.

*****Use Exhibit 17-9 Here*****

3. There are still problems with a systematic approach to vendor identification and evaluation.

I. Mechanics Of Importing

1. An import transaction is like looking at an export decision from the other side of the transaction. Steps can include:
   a. Finding a bank.
   b. Establishing a letter of credit.
   c. Deciding on a mode of transfer of goods.
   d. Compliance with national laws of the importing country and the exporting country.
   e. Making allowances for foreign exchange fluctuations.
   f. Fixing liability for payment of import duties and other costs.
2. Differences between the importing and exporting decision include:
   a. A difference in risk profile.
   b. The facility of being able to pay in the domestic currency.
   c. Because of the U.S. dollar, it is easier for a U.S. firm to import.

*****Use Review Question #7 Here*****

3. *Entry of imports into the United States.*
   a. *Import documents and delivery.* All of the export documents must now be submitted in the importing country.
   b. Custom' regulations must be considered.
   c. Delivery can be at a variety of times.
   d. *Import duties.* Forms can include:
      1). Ad valorem duty--a percentage of the value of the merchandise.
      2). A specific duty--specified amount per unit of weight or other quantity.
      3). A compound duty--combines other duties.
      4). Antidumping duties--used to balance the tables between goods.
      5). Countervailing duties--counter the effects of subsidies.

6). Duty drawbacks--refund 99 percent of all ordinary duties.

7). Direct identification drawback--refund of duties paid on imported merchandise.

8). Substitution drawback--refund of duties paid on designated import merchandise.

*****Use Discussion Question #4 Here*****

J. Gray Markets

1. Gray market channels refer to the legal export/import transaction involving genuine products into a country by intermediaries other than the authorized distributors.

   a. From the importer's side, this is also called parallel imports.

   b. Since the merchandise is obtained from an unauthorized source, competition and pricing is often affected (especially since the unauthorized distributor usually sells the merchandise below market prices).

2. *Why gray markets develop?*

   a. Three conditions are necessary for gray markets to develop:

      1). The products must be available in other markets.

      2). Trade barriers such as tariffs, transportation costs, and legal restrictions must be low enough for parallel importers to move the products from one market to another.

      3). Price differentials among various markets must be great enough to provide the basic motivation for gray marketers.

*****Use Review Question #8 Here*****

   b. Price differences are the result of:

      1). *Currency fluctuations.*

      2). *Differences in market demand.*

      3). *Segmentation strategy.*

3. A key question for the exporter of branded products is whether gray markets will cause a global strategy to become less desirable.

*****Use Exhibits 17-10 (a) and 17-10 (b) Here; Use Discussion Question #5 Here*****

REVIEW QUESTIONS

INSTRUCTOR'S NOTE: The following chapter review questions are meant to challenge the student to think about material presented in the chapter and formulate a creative answer to the review questions. Many of the answers require judgments rather than specific line-by-line quotation of facts. The answers provided are meant to provide stimulation of creative answers.

1. How does a prospective exporter choose an export market?

The identification of an appropriate overseas market and an appropriate segment involves grouping by the following criteria:

    a. Socioeconomic characteristics like demographic, economic, geographic, and climatic characteristics.

    b. Political and legal variables.

    c. Consumer variables such as lifestyle, preferences, culture, taste, purchase behavior, and purchase frequency.

    d. Financial variables.

2. What are the factors that influence the decision of the exporter to use a standardized product strategy across countries and regions?

Products that can be standardized may satisfy basic needs that do not vary with climate, economic conditions, or culture. In addition, finding appropriate geographic and psychographic segment similarity would be beneficial for segmentation. Of course, export objectives must also be similar for the standardized strategy attempt. The firm should be able to gain efficiencies in manufacturing and promotional costs. The standardized product is the easiest to sell logistically. The firm must look for similar infrastructure to make the scheme work efficiently.

3. What are the direct and indirect channels of distribution available to exporters? Under what conditions would the use of each be the most appropriate?

The students should be encouraged to summarize the material found in the chapter. Some useful hints for beginning the discussion are listed below.

Indirect exporting involves the use of independent U.S. middlemen to market the firm's products overseas. These export representatives assume responsibility for marketing the firm's products through their network of foreign distributors and their own sales force.

Types include:

    1). *The combination export manager (CEM).*

        a). Acts as the export department to a small exporter or to a large producer with small overseas sales.

        b). Operates on a commission basis.

        c). Credit support is essential.

        d). This form is diminishing in numbers and usage because of increased involvement in global marketing.

    2). *The export merchant.*

a). This person buys and sells on their own account and assumes all the responsibilities of exporting a product.

b). Manufacturers are not in control. The export merchant is.

3). ***The export broker.***

a). This person brings together an overseas buyer and a U.S. manufacturer for the purpose of an export sale and earns a commission for establishing a contact which results in a sale.

4). An export commission house can place an order on behalf of a client and provides a finder function.

5). **A trading company** is a foreign organization engaged in exporting and importing. They buy and sell on their own account.

6). ***Piggyback exporting*** refers to the practice where U.S. firms that have an established export department assume, under a cooperative agreement, the responsibility of exporting the products of other U.S. companies.

Direct export occurs when a manufacturer or exporter sells directly to an importer or buyer located in a foreign market.

a. The simplest form is the export manager with some clerical help.

1). This manager sells and directs the activities of the export process.

b. As export activities grow, most firms create a separate export department which is largely self-contained and operates independently of domestic operations.

c. An extension is to form an export sales subsidiary to export separate from the other operations of the firm.

1). The major difference is that it is a legal entity and can offer tax advantages.

d. The foreign sales branch is not a separate legal entity. This branch handles all sales, distribution, and promotional work throughout a designated market area and sells primarily to wholesalers and dealers.

4. Terms of payment are an extremely important facet of export transactions. Describe the various terms of payments in increasing order of risk.

The terms of payment are outlined in Exhibit 17-7 and should be reviewed by the student when attempting to answer this question. Briefly, the major forms are summarized below (be sure to see Exhibit 17-7 for detail and more variations of the terms):

If the sale is in cash, there is virtually no risk.

Credit letters can be considered.

a. An unconfirmed letter of credit exposes the exporter to the creditworthiness of the buyer's bank in the foreign country because a U.S. bank is not guaranteeing payment.

b. A sight draft excludes banks from the process and has less guarantees.

c. An open account sale is truly one of trust in the buyer's ability to pay.

5. Describe the various terms of shipment and sale.

The terms of shipment and sale are summarized in Exhibit 17-6 and should be reviewed by the students before they attempt to answer this question.

6. What is the role of government (home country) in export activities? Explain in context of U.S. exporters.

Generally, it is believed that governments can perform several roles with respect to export activities. They can do promotion to stimulate exportation, they can develop export strategies, they can aid in the financing of exports, and they can pass legislation that either reduces tariffs or supports exporting activities with constraints against anti-competitive situations. Some of these ideas are summarized below.

Export promotion activities generally comprise:
    a. Export service programs.
    b. Market development programs.

Government expenditures on export promotion seem to make sense.
    a. The government tries to get more firms to export.
    b. The government tries to get firms to overcome the perception of risk in the international area and take the plunge.

Export-import bank (the Exim bank). Promotes exports.
    a. Helps companies get financing for exports.
    b. The bank also works with capital expansion, infrastructure projects, and trade loans.

U.S. tariff concessions.
    a. *Free trade zone.* Lets businesses store, process, assemble, and display goods from abroad without paying tariff.
    b. *Foreign sales corporation.* A foreign corporation not located in a free trade zone that is allowed to earn some exempt and non-taxable income on its exports from the United States.
    c. *American export trading company.* Legislation encourages the formulation of trading companies for the purpose of exporting.

Export regulations.
    a. The Trade Act of 1974--bars Exim bank from giving credit to most communist countries.
    b. Foreign Corrupt Practices Act of 1977 prohibits influencing overseas officials.
    c. Antitrust laws.
    d. Foreign government laws that affect exports.

e. Taxes on exports to stimulate domestic consumption first.

7. Managing imports in the U.S. is by and large more easy and less risky than managing exports. Give reasons why this is true.

Differences between the importing and exporting decision include:
   a. A difference in risk profile.
   b. The facility is able to pay in the domestic currency.
   c. Because of the U.S. dollar, it is easier for a U.S. firm to import.

8. What are gray markets? What are the factors that led to the development of gray markets?

Gray market channels refer to the legal export/import transaction involving genuine products into a country by intermediaries other than the authorized distributors.
   a. From the importer's side, this is also called parallel imports.
   b. Since the merchandise is obtained from an unauthorized source, competition and pricing is often affected (especially since the unauthorized distributor usually sells the merchandise below market prices).

Three conditions are necessary for gray markets to develop:
   1). The products must be available in other markets.
   2). Trade barriers such as tariffs, transportation costs, and legal restrictions must be low enough for parallel importers to move the products from one market to another.
   3). Price differentials among various markets must be great enough to provide the basic motivation for gray marketers.

DISCUSSION QUESTIONS

INSTRUCTOR'S NOTE: Discussion Questions are found at the end of each chapter in the text. These questions (in many cases) are too lengthy to repeat in the manual. Suggestions for answering and discussing the questions are presented in this section. Many of the questions require student opinion and judgment.

1. This question asks the students to consider how to obtain secondary information about the exportation process. Students can recommend library research, chamber of commerce help, international trade mission investigation (using resources of those countries for which the marketing effort will be designed), and information from the Internet. The students should be encouraged to design a plan that would accomplish the goals of successful exportation and answer the questions presented by this question. The instructor might review the steps with the class and then assign Student Project question #1 so the students can get some real hands-on experience with the export process.

2. In order to answer this question the students will find it necessary to do some research on the history of the trading company and review the format used by Japan. Trading companies have had a checkered past but have certainly influenced country policy and world economic events. The Japanese have (according to some) perfected the model. Students should be encouraged to review the reasons for using the trading company (see data in the chapter) and then formulate an opinion.

3. This question asks the student to make a judgment relevant to the material on terms of payment and terms of shipment from the chapter. To make this judgment the student should carefully review the lists provided by Exhibits 17-6 and 17-7. From the alternatives presented the student can make a selection given the parameters provided by the question. Realize that there will be differences of opinion and answers in this question. Each student should be requested to submit reasons for their selection and then critique their peers selections.

4. Most students seem to come down on the side of the anti-dumping group. One is never sure why this is other than it may be because of their lack of experience with the concept. The most useful way to develop a learning experience with this question is to assign research and then debate to teams within the class. By presenting both sides, students seem to be able to then formulate a more enriched and defensible position. Remember, however, that either position can be defended. In fact, politics has a great deal to do with which position is currently in vogue.

5. To answer this question the student is encouraged to re-read the material from the chapter on the subject and then respond to the question directions. Remember to review the situations that encourage gray markets (as listed by the chapter). Can the students think of ways to respond given the situations that would be present in the case scenario presented? How do consumers react to gray markets? Sincerely, given the current state of business knowledge on the part of the students, do they really believe that gray markets are bad or do they perceive them to be just "good deals" for the consumer? The answers to these questions (in addition to those suggested within the question) should make for an interesting discussion in this area.

STUDENT PROJECTS and INTERNET FOCUS

1. Review the advertisements in your local newspaper. Identify products that you perceive to be deals that "are too good to be true." These deals are probably examples of potential gray markets (flea markets are also common places for the gray marketer). Compare these "great deal" products against the same products sold by authorized dealers. Look at prices, interview the sellers, and then make a determination about the gray market. Report your findings to the class or to your instructor.

2. Find a local company that exports products. Interview an officer with the company and investigate the process. Be sure to research how the export process began and the

advantages or disadvantages that the company has experienced. Please remember that you are a representative of your university or college and do not waste the time of the person you are interviewing. Prepare your questions in advance and be professional in your interview. Report your findings about exporting to your class or instructor.

INSTRUCTOR'S NOTE: The following projects require the students to both use and understand the Internet. If students do not understand how to use the Internet, explanation should be given before these projects are undertaken. The Web addresses change frequently, the instructor should re-affirm the site addresses and the content of the site before making an assignment.

3. A great contemporary research site is CNN news found at (**http://www.cnn.com**). Go to this site and research the field of exporting and/or importing. Find a contemporary story. Abstract the material and report your findings to the class.

4. Go to the United States Government Resources home page at (**http://www.iridium.ntte.edu/gov.res.html**) or The Federal Web Locator at (**http://www.law.vill.edu/Fed-Agency**) and find information on the Exim Bank as described in your chapter. Once you have discovered how to access the information on the Exim Bank, do a short report on a subject of your choice from the list of data that you have observed.

5. Go to the Web site for the World Trade Center at (**http://www.unicc.org/untpdc/incubator/wtca/welcome.html**). Observe the Trade Points being hosted by the World Trade Centers Association. Do a short report on the activities of the trade center and how an exporter or an importer might use this service.

CHAPTER 18

ORGANIZING GLOBAL MARKETING EFFORTS

CHAPTER OBJECTIVES

1. Identify the key criteria in global organizational design.

2. List and explain organizational design options.

3. Discuss global teamwork and associated concepts.

4. Explain the lifecycle of organizational structures.

5. Probe the question "to centralize or to decentralize?" and formulate an opinion.

6. Discuss the process of controlling global marketing efforts.

CHAPTER OVERVIEW

As a last chapter, the issues of structure and control mechanisms for the MNC that shape a truly global organization are reviewed. Each of the structural form alternatives are identified and explained. However, the decision is not simple. The organization must do much more than just pick "the right" organizational configuration and control systems if the organization is going to be successful and competitive. Such question choices as whether to centralize or decentralize, to seek local responsiveness or global integration, and choose between center and periphery operations must be addressed. The choice is not easy and many choose incorrectly.

The chapter will also address some environmental changes that affect the organization and its structure. Change requires flexibility and an attitude for sensitivity and adaptation.

In conclusion the authors offer several pertinent pieces of advice:

a. Learn the need for business asymmetry.
b. Democracy is a must.
c. Importance of a shared vision.
d. The need for a good mix of specialists of three types--country, functional, and business.
e. Moving unit headquarters abroad seldom solves the organization's problems.

CHAPTER OUTLINE

A. Key Criteria in Global Organizational Design

1. As with most other global managerial issues there is no magic formula that prescribes the "ideal" organizational setup under a given set of circumstances.
2. *Environmental factors.* These factors include:
   a. *Competitive environment.*
      1). Global competitive pressures force MNCs to implement structures that facilitate quick decision-making and alertness.
      2). In industries where competition is highly localized, a decentralized structure where most of the decision-making is made at the country-level is often appropriate.
   b. *Rate of environmental change.*
      1). Drastic environmental change is a way-of-life in scores of industries.
      2). Businesses that are subject to rapid change require an organizational design that facilitates continuous scanning of the firm's global environment and swift responsiveness to opportunities or threats posed by that environment.
   c. *Regional trading blocs.*
      1). Companies that operate within a regional trading bloc usually integrate to some extent their marketing efforts across the affiliates within the block area.
   d. *Nature of customers.*
      1). The customer based has a large influence on organizational design.
      2). Companies want global reach but also want to "stay close" to their customers.

*****Use Review Question #2 Here*****

3. *Firm specific factors.*
   a. *Strategic importance of international business.*
      1). Typically, when overseas sales account for a very small fraction of the company's overall sales revenues, simple organizational structures can easily handle the firm's global activities.
      2). As the firm grows so will its organizational structure.
   b. *Product diversity.*
      1). Companies with substantial product diversity tend to go for a global product division configuration.
   c. *Company heritage.*
      1). Differences in organizational structures within the same industry can also be explained via corporate culture.
      2). Revamping an organization to make the structure more responsive to new environmental realities can be a daunting challenge.

d. *Quality of managerial skills.*
   1). Decentralization is a problem when local managerial talent is missing.

B. Organizational Design Options

1. The principle designs that firms can adopt to organize their global activities are:
   a. *International division.* Under this design, the company basically has two entities:
      1). The domestic division which is responsible for the firm's domestic activities.
      2). The international division which is in charge of the company's international division.
   b. *Product based structure.*
      1). Organized along the company's various product divisions.
   c. *Geographic structure.*
      1). The company configures along geographic areas such as countries, regions, or some combination of the two.
   d. *Matrix organization.*
      1). The company integrates two approaches (such as product and geographic boundaries).
      2). There is a dual chain of command.
   e. *Networked organization.* (Comments to follow).
2. *International division structure.*
   a. Most companies begin with an export department.
   b. This is usually followed by an international division.
   c. International opportunities are scanned.
   d. This option is suitable for companies that have a product line that is not too diverse and that does not require a large amount of adaptation to local country needs. This also works for companies that are still primarily domestic producers.
3. *Global product division structure.*
   a. This option centers around the different product lines or strategic business units of the company. Each SBU is managed separately.
   b. This option is popular among high-tech companies with highly complex products or MNCs with a very different product portfolio.

*****Use Exhibit 18-1 Here; Use Global Perspective 18-1 "Whirlpool's Global Business Units" Here*****

   c. Benefits include:
      1). Large degree of flexibility in terms of cross-country resource allocation and strategic planning.
      2). Economies of scale in production.
      3). Competitive cost position improvement.
      4). Facilitates the development of a global strategic focus to cope with

challenges posed by global players.

    d. Shortcomings include:

        1). Lack of communication and coordination can lead to needless duplication of tasks.

        2). Can distract from local market needs.

        3). Can scatter company resources--fragmentation.

4. *Geographic structure.*

    a. Area structures are especially appealing to companies that market closely related product lines with very similar end-users and applications around the world.

*****Use Exhibit 18-2 Here*****

    b. *Country-based subsidiaries.*

        1). By setting up country affiliates, the MNC can stay in close touch with the local market conditions.

        2). Handicaps include:

            a). Too costly.

            b). Coordination cumbersome.

            c). Leads to a "not-invented-here" bias.

    c. *New role of country managers.*

        1). Most believe that this is a declining form of organization.

        2). Forces that are leading to a decline include:

            a). Threats by global competitors that must be dealt with globally.

            b). Global customers.

            c). Regional trading blocs.

        3). Factors that still point to the usefulness of this form of manager includes:

            a). Nurturing links with local governments.

            b). Local competitor consideration.

            c). Strong local brands.

            d). Innovative ideas that come from the local environment.

        4). To strike a balance, country managers must fit one of these profiles:

            a). Trader--entrepreneurial spirit.

            b). Builder--develops local markets.

            c). Cabinet member--team player.

            d). Ambassador--in charge of large or strategic markets. Good at government relations.

            e). Representative--like Ambassador but in large markets.

    d. *Regional structures.* Regional headquarters. A compromise format.

        1). Roles for regional headquarters:

            a). Scouting.

            b). Strategic stimulation.

            c). Signaling commitment.

            d). Coordination.

            e). Pooling resources.

*****Use Review Question #3 Here*****

5. *Matrix structure.*
   a. Using one structure can often be a disaster.
   b. The matrix structure combines forms and recognizes the multi-dimensional nature of global strategic decision-making.
   c. There is a dual chain of command.
   d. Structures could even be three dimensional.

*****Use Exhibit 18-3 Here*****

   e. Advantages include:
      1). Reflect complexities--local and global competitors, customers, and distributors.
      2). Fosters team spirit and cooperation.
   f. Disadvantages include:
      1). Reporting and profit responsibilities are confusing and conflict oriented.
      2). Bureaucratic bloat.
6. *The global network solution.*
   a. The network model is an attempt to reconcile the tension between two opposing forces--the need for local responsiveness and the wish to be an integrated whole.
   b. This form is a mindset rather than a real structure (in the truest sense of the term). Another term used to describe this form is transnational.
   c. Advocates of this model believe that MNCs should develop processes and linkages that allow each unit to tap into a global knowledge pool.

*****Use Exhibit 18-4 Here*****

   d. An international teaming concept can be used to form the network.

*****Use Global Perspective 18-2 "3M's European Business Centers" Here*****

   e. The network concept can center around three concepts:
      1). A set of basic assumptions about people.
      2). Assumptions about managerial policies.
      3). Assumptions about certain expectations.

*****Use Exhibit 18-5 Here; Use Review Question #1 Here*****

C. **Global Team-Work**

1. MNCs increasingly rely on international team-work to coordinate their global or pan-regional strategies or operations.

2. Four stages of development include:
   a. Launch the international team.
   b. A team mission statement.
   c. What will happen later--the maintenance step.
   d. Transfer learning throughout the organization (including to other teams).

*****Use Exhibit 18-6 Here*****

3. Teams are created for several reasons:
   a. Coordinate global strategy development and implementation efforts.
   b. Building ties to headquarters and local subsidiaries.
   c. Communication and technology transfer. Skills can include:
      1). Advocacy skills.
      2). Catalytic skills.
      3). Integrative skills.

*****Use Exhibit 18-7 Here*****

D. Life Cycle of Organizational Structures

1. A drastic change in the MNC's environment or internal circumstances sometimes requires a re-thinking of the ideal way to organize the firm's global operations.

*****Use Global Perspective 18-3 "The Revamping of Royal Dutch Shell" Here;
Use Exhibit 18-9 Here*****

2. A popular way of expressing the global mindset is to create a relationship between organizational structure, foreign product diversity, and the geographic divisions.

*****Use Exhibit 18-8 Here*****

3. Stages include:
   a. Recognize the complexity of the MNC's environment.
   b. Introduce communication channels and decision-making platforms to facilitate more flexibility.
   c. Develop a corporate culture that fosters collaborative thinking and decision-making.

*****Use Review Question #4 Here*****

E. To Centralize or Decentralize?

1. With decentralized organizations, the national operating companies are highly autonomous. Each local unit represents a profit center.
2. Under centralized operations, most decision-making is consolidated at corporate

218

headquarters.

*****Use Exhibit 18-10 Here*****

3. A solution is being offered as a middle ground. The concept is called federalism. Companies following this model share these characteristics:
   a. Non-centralization.
   b. Negotianalism.
   c. Constitutionalism.
   d. Territoriality.
   e. Balance of power.
   f. Autonomy.

*****Use Exhibit 18-11 Here; Use Review Question #5 Here*****

F. Controlling Global Marketing Efforts

1. *Formal ("bureaucratic") control systems.* Three building blocks include:
   a. *Establishing standards.*
      1). These standards should be driven by the company's corporate goals.
      2). Types include behavior and outcome-based.
      3). Ideally, standards are developed via a "bottom-up" and "top-down" planning process of listening, reflecting, dialoguing, and debating between headquarters and the local units.
   b. *Evaluating performance.*
      1). The actual performance is compared against the established standards.
      2). Though it is necessary to reward managers for their contribution, the contribution is hard to gauge.
   c. *Analyzing and correcting deviations.*
      1). Analyze the causes behind deviations and correct.
      2). Reward systems are necessary for managers. However, due process is also important. Due process has five features:
         a). The head office should be familiar with the subsidiaries' local situation.
         b). There should be a two-way communication in global strategy-making decision processes.
         c). The head office is relatively consistent in making decisions across local units.
         d). The local units can legitimately challenge headquarters' strategic views and decisions.
         e). The subsidiary units get explanations for final strategic decisions.
2. *Informal control methods.*
   a. *Corporate culture.* Forms can be classed as:
      1). Clan-based--they embody a long socialization process, strong and powerful norms, and a defined set of internalized controls.
      2). Market cultures--(the opposite) norms are loose or absent, socialization

processes are limited, and control systems are purely based on performance measures.

3). Corporate values have properties.
    a). Clarity.
    b). Continuity.
    c). Consistency.

*****Use Exhibit 18-12 Here*****

b. ***Human resource development.*** Critical in three regards:
    1). Training programs can help managers worldwide in understanding the MNC's mission and vision and their part in pursuing them.
    2). Such programs can speed up the transfer of new values when changes in the company's environment dictate a "new" corporate mentality.
    3). They can also prove fruitful in allowing managers from all over the world to share their best practices and success stories.

REVIEW QUESTIONS

INSTRUCTOR'S NOTE: The following chapter review questions are meant to challenge the student to think about material presented in the chapter and formulate a creative answer to the review questions. Many of the answers require judgments rather than specific line-by-line quotation of facts. The answers provided are meant to provide stimulation of creative answers.

1. How does a global networked organization differ from the matrix structure?

To correctly answer this question, students should re-read the material in the chapter and find information to support their conclusions. Facts that should be considered when making their assessment of the differences are shown below.

The matrix structure:
    a. Using one structure can often be a disaster.
    b. The matrix structure combines forms and recognizes the multi-dimensional nature of global strategic decision-making.
    c. There is a dual chain of command.
    d. Structures could even be three dimensional.
    e. Advantages include:
        1). Reflect complexities--local and global competitors, customers, and distributors.
        2). Fosters team spirit and cooperation.
    f. Disadvantages include:
        1). Reporting and profit responsibilities are confusing and conflict oriented.
        2). Bureaucratic bloat.

The global network solution:
   a. The network model is an attempt to reconcile the tension between two opposing forces--the need for local responsiveness and the wish to be an integrated whole.
   b. This form is a mindset rather than a real structure (in the truest sense of the term). Another term used to describe this form is transnational.
   c. Advocates of this model believe that MNCs should develop processes and linkages that allow each unit to tap into a global knowledge pool.
   d. An international teaming concept can be used to form the network.
   e. The network concept can center around three concepts:
      1). A set of basic assumptions about people.
      2). Assumptions about managerial policies.
      3). Assumptions about certain expectations.

2. Describe how external environmental drivers influence the organizational design decision.

Students should review the material in the chapter on external drivers so a conclusion can be reached about this question. Some facts that might be considered in formulating that answer are listed below.

Environmental factors. These factors include:
   a. Competitive environment.
      1). Global competitive pressures force MNCs to implement structures that facilitate quick decision-making and alertness.
      2). In industries where competition is highly localized, a decentralized structure where most of the decision-making is made at the country-level is often appropriate.
   b. Rate of environmental change.
      1). Drastic environmental change is a way-of-life in scores of industries.
      2). Businesses that are subject to rapid change require an organizational design that facilitates continuous scanning of the firm's global environment and swift responsiveness to opportunities or threats posed by that environment.
   c. Regional trading blocs.
      1). Companies that operate within a regional trading bloc usually integrate to some extent their marketing efforts across the affiliates within the block area.
   d. Nature of customers.
      1). The customer based has a large influence on organizational design.
      2). Companies want global reach but also want to "stay close" to their customers.

3. What are the pros and cons of a regional organization structure?

A variety of organizational structures are described in this chapter. To analyze the regional organizational structure, students should review the material in the chapter and consider the information listed below when formulating answer.

Regional structures:

Regional headquarters. A compromise format.
   1). Roles for regional headquarters:
     a). Scouting.
     b). Strategic stimulation.
     c). Signaling commitment.
     d). Coordination.
     e). Pooling resources.

The intent behind most regional headquarters is to address two concerns: lack of responsiveness of HQ to local market conditions and parochialism among local country managers.

4. What mechanisms can companies use to foster a global corporate culture?

In order to answer this question, the student will need to consider several pieces of information from the chapter. Consider the material on teams, communication, and common thinking. This material is briefly summarized below.

Teams are created for several reasons:
   a. Coordinate global strategy development and implementation efforts.
   b. Building ties to headquarters and local subsidiaries.
   c. Communication and technology transfer. Skills can include:
     1). Advocacy skills.
     2). Catalytic skills.
     3). Integrative skills.

To create the multinational corporate culture consider the following stages of organizational design:

   a. Recognize the complexity of the MNC's environment.
   b. Introduce communication channels and decision-making platforms to facilitate more flexibility.
   c. Develop a corporate culture that fosters collaborative thinking and decision-making.

5. What does it take for a MNC to be a "multi-local multinational?"

There can be a variety of creative suggestions to answer this question. To answer, the student must consider the sum of the material in the chapter. This form would really can for a multi-level hybrid of most existing models. To begin a discussion, the instructor might ask the students if the concept (indicated below) of federalism might be a way to consider this format (when reviewing centralized versus decentralized forms)?

The concept of so called federalism says companies following this model share these characteristics:
    a. Non-centralization.
    b. Negotianalism.
    c. Constitutionalism.
    d. Territoriality.
    e. Balance of power.
    f. Autonomy.

STUDENT PROJECTS and INTERNET FOCUS

1. Go to the library or a local stock broker and obtain an original or copy of a multinational firm's corporate annual report. This document (in addition to giving many financial details about the firm's performance over the last year) will normally give some indication of the organizational structure of the firm. Once you have the document, classify the firm using the organizational schemes suggested in the chapter. Be sure to document why you think the firm falls into the category you have selected. If you believe the firm is using a combination or hybrid form, be sure to explain the form and why you think it is being used. Report your findings to the class or the instructor.

2. Go to the library. Use current periodicals or literature to examine matrix organizations. Find an example of a matrix organization and explain its organizational concept as best as is possible. What do you see as the strengths and weaknesses of the method. Report your findings to the class or to the instructor.

INSTRUCTOR'S NOTE: The following projects require the students to both use and understand the Internet. If students do not understand how to use the Internet, explanation should be given before these projects are undertaken. The Web addresses change frequently, the instructor should re-affirm the site addresses and the content of the site before making an assignment.

3. Go to the home page for the journal entitled *Studies in Cultures, Organization, and Societies*. Find an article on organizational change or design, abstract the article, and report the findings (if this search cannot be accomplished, use on of the search engines mentioned in other projects from previous chapters [Yahoo or Lycos] to accomplish the same task). The Web site for the above journal is **(http://www.ucalgary.ca/~cancomm/studies.html)**.

4. Several noted Washington decision makers have expressed comments on how organizational structure might be transformed to meet the challenges of the next century.

The comments are carried in The National Performance Review. Go to this government site, explore the material, and develop an opinion about the changes that might be coming in the next century with respect to organizational structure and design. The site is located at (**http://www.npr.gov/NPR/Reports/tosint.html**).

5. Take the following organizations, go to their Web sites, and make a determination about their organizational format and design. You may use the classification in the chapter or may use creative combinations to describe your observations. If you cannot find adequate data on their Web sites you might also do traditional library research to give your answers. Be sure to document your opinion as to why you selected a particular organizational format for the organizations.

    a. Siemens   (**http://www.siemens.com**)

    b. IBM   (**http://www.ibm.com**)

    c. Toyota Motors   (**http://www.toyota.com**)

    d. Raytheon   (**http://www.raytheon.com**)

    e. U.S. Robotics   (**http://www.ust.com**).

Case-Chapter Grid

CASE	Chapters in which to be used
1. Starbucks Coffee: Expansion in Asia	**4**, **8**, 16
2. Gap, Inc.	4, **5**, **8**, 10, **16**
3. SEGA: The Way the West was Won	9, **10**, **14**, 16, 17
4. Procter & Gamble: Facelle Division Facial Tissue	**6**, **7**, 12, **13**, 14
5. Waste Management International, Inc.: Strategy for Asia	**2**, **8**, 18
6. Baxter International—Renal Division: Market Opportunities in Latin America	**2**, **8**, **9**
7. Tilting Windmills: Sanex Tries to Conquer Europe	**8**, **12**
8. Club Med: The Party is Over	**6**, **7**, **8**
9. Ford Motor Company and Die Development	9, **10**, **11**
10. Pharma Swede: Gastirup	**13**
11. Anheuser-Busch International, Inc.	**2**, 3, **4**, **9**, **14**, 17
12. Toys "R" Us Goes to Japan	4, **5**, **9**, 15, **16**

Bold numbers suggest the primary chapters in which cases may be used.

Teaching Notes:

Starbucks Coffee: Expansion in Asia

Introduction:

Many Singaporeans view Starbucks as a young and trendy American coffee shop. Therefore, it would be to Starbucks greatest advantage to market the brand as a sophisticated and trendy coffee. Starbucks should continue to set up additional stores in shopping districts where tourists and locals shop. Furthermore, other potential store locations include hotels and the financial district area. Setting up a Starbucks in a hotel will service tourists, as well as the local people. Many locals frequent the restaurants and coffee shops within the various hotels. Finally, Starbucks could open a store in the financial district. This will allow Starbucks to be exposed to the high volume of pedestrian traffic.

Though Starbucks has plans to eventually open a roasting plant in Japan to reduce costs, we recommend that Starbucks look into a plant in Singapore instead of Japan. Singapore is at the crossroads of international shipping and air routes. They would then have a roasting plant in Asia that could supply the coffee beans for Starbucks' retail stores in those countries. With their plans to expand into Malaysia and Thailand, Singapore is an ideal country to set up a roasting plant because Malaysia, Thailand and Singapore are linked together with roads and rails for easy transportation. Also, Singapore would be a more cost efficient country to set up a plant relative to Japan because of lower fixed costs.

As with any new company, Starbucks must market itself effectively in Singapore to be successful. Starbucks has already received free press coverage due to its recent entry, as well as through competitors' reactions. In addition, Starbucks will need to rely on customers' word-of-mouth to get it's name out there. Furthermore, they should concentrate on in-store promotions to lure the tourists, shoppers and other pedestrians into the stores and keep them coming back. A promotion like a frequent buyer card might be effective in drawing in repeat customers. Such a promotion will reward those loyal users, and further increase their consumption of Starbucks coffee.

Finally, Starbucks should continue to form joint ventures with well-established companies in Asia. This will give Starbucks additional resources to work with, as well as further build its brand equity. In order to insure its success in Singapore, Starbucks must plan its next step carefully. It is important to take into account the obstacles that the company will face as it enters this competitive environment. At the same time, Starbucks' success lies in its ability to build a strong presence for itself in Asia.

Discussion Questions:

1. How does Starbucks create brand equity?

Starbucks has created a strong brand equity for itself in several ways. First, the company revolutionized the whole concept of specialty gourmet coffeehouses in the U.S. Starbucks is seen as the pioneer of such coffeehouses that allow customers to sit down, socialize and chat over a nice cup of coffee. Starbucks' stores project a warm, upbeat people-oriented style. Also, they have a grass-roots and back-to-nature feel. In doing so, they present more of an overall experience with the coffee and an atmosphere to soak up the image Starbucks has project out to its customers. In addition, Starbucks is able to maintain a consistent brand image throughout its 1,000 plus retail stores by keeping store decor and designs similar throughout all its retail outlets. The stores offer an environment in which customers can relax and socialize, as well as one in which customers on the run can pick up a quick cup of coffee and leave. Starbucks' appreciation for the natural goodness of coffee and the artistry grabs the customer even before the aroma does. In addition, the creative packaging design seeks to attract consumers of all languages and cultures. All this has contributed in building the customer's perception of Starbucks as a premium retailer of specialty coffee.

2. Why enter the Asian market? Why enter Singapore?

With a profitable business in North America, Starbucks is seeking international expansion in hopes of increasing its profits as well as further building its brand name. The company choose to enter Asia over Europe because they felt offered more potential. First, consumers' disposable income is increasing as their countries' economies are growing rapidly. This means that consumers have more money to spend on luxury items, such as specialty coffee. Also, there is also an increased amount of coffee consumption in that part of the world. For instance, Japan is the third largest market for coffee consumption in the world. Finally, the Asian market is also more receptive to Western lifestyles and trends. Starbucks is already being perceived as another American icon like McDonald's.

After Japan, Singapore seemed like the most appropriate market to enter. Singapore consumes 10,000 cups of coffee in a day. 1 This makes the market potential in Singapore an extremely attractive one. Singaporeans are also very susceptible to Western ideals and trends. They seem to adopt American pop culture with open arms, and therefore love American products. Singapore is also an ideal country because of its location. Singapore has the second most active port in the world, the crossroads of international shipping and air routes. Also access to Malaysia and Thailand from Singapore is very easy with roads and rail linking the three. Singapore has also lots of shopping centers for tourists and locals, with cafes and restaurants lining the area for tired shoppers to rest their feet, cool off and put their bags down to sip some coffee.

Starbucks will look into the European market once it has established itself in the Asian market.

---

1 "Barista, Give Me a Kopi Baba." The Straits Times, Nov. 24, 1996.

3. Who is the target market?

Starbucks targets the middle to upper income segment with an emphasis on the gourmet coffee lovers and the socialites of this generation. In Singapore, they target the middle income consumers. The population in Singapore has 90% under the age of 35. They need to target that segment since they are the generation with the disposable income and will set the trend for generations to come. This segment of the population is also very receptive to Western ideas and trends. They will be the ones who are drinking coffees and hanging out with friends.

4. Is Starbucks facing cannibalization?

As seen in the United States, there is a Starbucks retail store on every corner of the block. For instance, Seattle, Washington , the coffee capitol of the world, has about 300 coffee cafes in about the same area size as Singapore. Though overall sales are not affected by store cannibalization, sales growth has been affected. In hopes of saturating the market by opening store after store, sales growth at existing stores have turned sluggish.

5. Who are some of Starbucks joint venture partners?

Starbucks has teamed up with a couple of the most well-known companies in setting up joint ventures. The list includes Pepsi-Cola, Dreyer's Grand Ice Cream, Redhook Ale Brewery, Capitol Records, Westin Hotels & Resorts, United Airlines and Barnes & Noble. With Pepsi-Cola, they developed a bottle version of the popular Frappuccino beverage to be distributed in vending machines and retail merchants. Starbucks' joint venture with Dreyer's has yielded a line of premium coffee-flavored ice cream. Double Black Stout, a coffee laced beer brewed by Redhook Ale Brewery, is another product that Starbucks has introduced through its alliances. Capitol Records has customized music CD for sale at Starbucks outlets. Starbucks is also the exclusive distributor of coffee in Westin Hotels & Resorts and United Airlines. Aside from airports and hotels, Barnes & Noble, a national superstore of books, also serves Starbucks' coffee in most of their bookstores.

Additionally, Starbucks is looking to other channels of distribution. A recent joint venture with Intel Corp. has led the company to develop a cyber cafe site for the internet. This will allow internet surfers access to the Internet through their cybercafe site. Starbucks has also started to manufacture a brand of coffee beans to be sold in supermarkets. The blend is specifically manufactured for the Meije Stores in 10 Midwestern market, and is called Navigator. Finally, an agreement with Price Costco will allow Starbucks to sell a coffee blend called Meridien in its warehouses. All of these joint ventures has put the Starbucks name everywhere. Starbucks has created a name for itself in the premium coffee market and has extended it to its coffee-loving customers.

Similarly, Starbucks is also entering into joint ventures as they further expand abroad. BonStar Pte. Ltd., has entered an agreement to help Starbucks set up outlets in Singapore. In Japan, Starbucks' alliance partner is SAZABY Inc., a Japanese retailer and restaurateur.

6. Is Starbucks a socially responsible company?

Starbucks is very involved with various community programs. It is the first company in history to implement a code of conduct for the growers of coffee beans in the coffee growing countries. The living conditions in these countries are often very brutal and poor. Starbucks has done tremendous charity work to help the people in these countries raise their standard of living with adequate working and living conditions. They have also donated money to CARE, a non-profit organization, to help develop these coffee growing countries. For instance, when the first Starbucks store opened in Singapore, BonStar donated all proceeds from sales that day to the National Kidney Foundation (NKF), and also invited VIP guests for a two-day open house before the official store opening to raise more money for NKF. Also, they have a partnership with the National Council of Social Service to donate coffee to two homes for the elderly.

Starbucks also treat their employees with respect, offering even its part-time employees health benefits and stock options. These are very progressive personnel policies that keep their best people on board. Through all its efforts, Starbucks has received tremendous positive consumer press for its charity work and community involvement. Evidence of this is shown when Starbucks received the 1996 International Humanitarian Award from CARE.

7. How does Starbucks market themselves?

Starbucks does virtually no media advertising and very little promotion. In 1995, the company spent under $3 million on measurable media and still did tremendously well. Instead, through its joint ventures, Starbucks' name appears on the advertisements of its partners. For example, United Airlines has repeatedly advertised that Starbucks is the exclusive coffee that is served on all of its flights. In addition, Starbucks relies on word-of-mouth from its customers. Through this, they hope that existing customers will spread the good word about Starbucks. Starbucks has managed to turn coffee from a pedestrian beverage into a premium product with attitude.

8. What are some substitutes?

There are many substitutes for coffee. Among those include soda, water, fruit drinks and other pedestrian beverages. The major substitute for coffee is tea because tea and coffee are synonymous with each other. They are perfect together and divided only by their tastes. In Asian, tea is the traditional drink. Most members of the older generations drink tea because coffee is too bitter and heavy for the stomach. It would be very difficult to convert this segment of the population into coffee drinkers. Will this be a factor for Starbucks when they enter this market? Well, it will because tea is already part of the tradition and has been around for centuries in these countries. There is already a culture in the art for drinking tea and growing it as well. Starbucks will need to target the younger generation, who will be more receptive to this new trend of coffee-drinking. This generation is also very much in tune to American pop culture, and would most likely sit in a cafe with friends relaxing and sipping gourmet coffee.

9. How did they come up with the name Starbucks?

Starbucks was founded in Seattle, the coffee capital of the world, by three coffee aficionados. They named the shop Starbucks after a coffee-loving first mate in *Moby Dick*, a novel by Herman Melville. It is a very unique name, and fits the image that Starbucks has created for itself.

Teaching Notes:

Gap, Inc.

Since it was founded in 1969, the company has experienced a phenomenal growth and has already become the second largest selling brand in the world. Such a rapid growth usually comes with a growth pain of having to shift management attention from how to grow to how to manage the existing stores in various parts of the world with differing cultures, laws and competition. The instructor relates Gap, Inc.'s experience to McDonald's global expansion.

A rapid expansion of stores is highly correlated with the sales growth. While the case does not show Gap, Inc.'s profitability, students should be reminded that sales and profitability do not necessarily improve in tandem. However, the case amply shows the complexity of managing Gap stores in different countries with different sets of market demands and requirements. Students are encouraged to explore how to implement some sort of operational consolidation while accepting the different needs and conditions of the markets around the world (integration vs. customization issues). Some of the illustrative discussion questions are presented below.

Discussion Questions

1. As mentioned in the case, Gap, Inc., conducts sourcing from 700 different sources both domestically and abroad. What would be some of the advantages for this type of sourcing strategy? What would be the disadvantages?

The most important advantage from conducting sourcing from so many different manufacturers is that Gap Inc. operation would not be affected if any single supplier fails to commit. Another important advantage is that sourcing from a foreign country usually requires business to be conducted in that country's currency, and by sourcing from many different countries, exchange rate fluctuation from any particular country would not affect Gap Inc.'s operation. In Gap's current situation, the only country that might cause trouble if the economy turns bad is Hong Kong. Disadvantages of sourcing from so many different sources is that Gap Inc. probably cannot take advantage of cheaper prices which can be achieved by mass procuring from a few manufacturers. In addition, Gap Inc. probably would not achieve the level of friendly relationships with the manufacturers that would result if Gap mass procured. Having a more friendly relationship with a supplier bring advantages, which might include bargaining power and reliability of source.

2. How can Gap Inc. benefit from the freeports in the UK?

Gap Inc. does not manufacture products in the UK. The company imports finished products and sells them. As mentioned in the case, Gap must pay a 14 percent duty for finished apparel items, plus a 17.5 percent value-added tax. Gap could locate its store in freeports and store merchandise there without paying any duty or tax until it needed to bring in the merchandise to sell. This way, any extra merchandise would not incur duty or tax charge.

3. As discussed in the case, the North American Free Trade Agreement has benefited many US companies by reducing tariffs on NAFTA country goods traded between each other. How has this actually benefited Gap Inc.? In the future?

Gap Inc. sends all its manufactured products through the US parent company and from there to the local branches of the Gap stores in Canada. Because the Canadian Gap stores import all their products from the US, NAFTA saves them the traditionally high cost of import taxes. Now the Canadian subsidiaries of Gap are not at the usual disadvantage of having to pay import taxes and can be much more competitive with Canadian national companies. With the addition of Mexico as part of the agreement, Gap Inc. could possibly open subsidiaries south of the US. The country of Mexico has many large cities in which the Gap could now open more stores and smaller cities in which they could produce more of their raw materials. This will consequently create new avenues for expansion into Central and South America.

4. Now that more and more US companies are moving into Canadian apparel markets, Gap Inc. is facing more and more competition from apparel manufacturing companies from its own country. How can it maintain its Canadian market share?

With the new arrival of US-based companies like The Limited, Gap must continue with its present style of innovation and expansion. The innovation comes with presenting to the public new variations on the original Gap store. This gives the consumer a fresh new look at a company that was already highly regarded. Canada's new Banana Republic and GapKids stores provide this new change to keep consumer coming back. The expansion part of the plan will come when Gap Inc. continues to open its different stores across Canada.

5. In Canada there is a recent trend of consumers abandoning their name brands and buying cheaper garments to save money. What can Gap Inc. do to take advantage of this new development?

During the past year, Gap Inc. has opened yet a new type of store across the US. Old Navy stores consist of Gap style clothing for more cost conscious consumers. Presently, there are no international versions of this new store, but as the Canadian market seems obviously ripe for such a venture, Gap Inc. will no doubt expand into Canada and from there into other markets as well.

6.   What steps should Gap Inc. take to combat "knock off" items?

Knock off artists and their products are a problem that every successful manufacturer should be ready to face. As consumers become increasingly price conscious, those products pose a major threat to Gap Inc.'s market share. Gap Inc.'s executives should keep one thing in mind when considering the alternatives: competing on the basis of price, especially in the international market, is not their forte. Attempting to undercut their imitator's price is an impractical and temporary solution. Gap Inc. should therefore focus on product positioning and distinctive advertising. Ad campaigns should continue to focus on the company's blend of California style and image of quality. Advertisements should also reinforce the notion that there is no real substitute. Additionally, Gap Inc. should position it's product lines as trend setting, and introduce new products on a regular basis. Keeping one step ahead of these knock off artists is the only way to survive in the long run.

Teaching Notes:

Sega: How the West Was Won

Immediately after the Korean War, David Rosen, an American, founded an entertainment business in Japan, importing arcade games from the United States. In 1965, he founded SEGA Enterprises by merging his import business with another American-owned business in Japan, Service Games (SEGA is an acronym from <u>SE</u>rvice <u>GA</u>mes). SEGA expanded fast in Japan by becoming an integrated entertainment business that covered all aspects of electronic entertainment, including coin-operated game machines, arcade centers, exclusive distribution of jukeboxes, among others. To cope with rapid product changes needed in the fast-moving game industry, SEGA subcontracts most component production and concentrate mainly on assembly.

In 1986, SEGA of America was established to launch its video games in the United States. With introduction of a line of extremely successful video game systems and software titles in the United States, SEGA propelled itself to becoming the world's second largest video game producer.

SEGA offers a successful amalgam of U.S.- and Japanese style business practices. Japanese strengths lie in tightly knit production and subcontracting arrangements (known as *keiretsu*) and tight control of distribution channels. U.S. strengths come from strong promotional activities creating brand equity. Have students discuss these issues and come to realize that good business practices can be adopted from around the world.

This case also provides an interesting scenario for competitor analysis in a rapidly changing market environment. It could also be interesting for the instructor to raise the issue regarding the "scope" of this industry. To conduct competitor analysis, should it be confined to the video game industry, or should it be expanded to include other forms of entertainment?

Discussion Questions

1. Is SEGA's aim for diversity in the market going to overextend its capabilities?

No, SEGA Enterprises Ltd. is expanding its market in the right direction. Instead of being content with consumer products, SEGA is utilizing its capacities to the fullest, pushing the market to the next level. It seems rather appropriate considering their motto is, "WELCOME TO THE NEXT LEVEL."

2. Who is SEGA's market in the US?

SEGA's market is mainly males age 10-27. One reason is the popularity of sports software. Forty percent of all video software sales in 1994 were sports games. Currently, SEGA offers a better system to run sports games, hence, more people buy them.

3. How are SEGA and Nintendo different?

Nintendo has a slight edge with graphics and sound quality, but SEGA has the speed and software that propels them to the lead. In addition, SEGA has a more appealing image to the market.

4. Who are SEGA's new competitors?

The new competitors are Sony, Atari, Pentium PC, and any PC maker using quad speed CD ROM.

5. What games are popular and what will be popular?

Popular SEGA consumer games are "Sonic the Hedgehog,' 'NFL '95," "World Series Baseball," but with the introduction of the Saturn 64, a definite seller will be "Virtua Fighter 2."

6. What is the general direction SEGA is leaning towards?

SEGA is pushing toward entertainment by combining multimedia, live action, and the "gamer' to create a whole new level of video entertainment.

7. What was the first worldwide hit produced by SEGA?

In 1966, David Rosen designed "Periscope." For Ks time, R was an innovative, cutting edge game that utilized sound effects and better graphics. Today we would call it an antique.

8. Does SEGA rate its games for violence?

Yes, SEGA games are rated, but it's image allows SEGA to have an irreverent attitude towards ratings. SEGA targets consumers in the late teens and early twenties, which means their irreverence does not affect them.

9. Will SEGA pass Nintendo in Japan?

SEGA will not pass Nintendo in the consumer products area, but yes, on the overall. Through the strategy of diversification, SEGA's Amusement Centers (video game theme parks) seem to offer 'gamers" a whole new experience.

10. Does SEGA have plans to become a player on the Information Superhighway?

Yes, this is an area that truly excites SEGA executives because most everyone feels that, after people taste multimedia with live video feed, there will be no turning back.

(1) BUSINESS SEGMENT INFORMATION

The Company and its subsidiaries operate principally in the following three lines of business: consumer products sales division, amusement center operations division and amusement machine sales division.
Sales of the Company and consolidated subsidiaries (the "Companies") for the years ended March 31, 1993 (unaudited) and 1994, classified by lines of business, are summarized as follows:

	Millions of yen (unaudited) Year ended March 31, 1993 Lines of business			
	Consumer product sales division	Amusement center operations division	Amusement machine sales division	Total
Net sales to outside customers	¥298,899	¥58,946	¥58,389	¥416,234
Cost of sales and operating expenses	257,559	49,398	41,883	348,840
	¥41,340	¥9,548	¥16,506	¥67,394

	Millions of yen Year ended March 31, 1994 Lines of business			
	Consumer product sales division	Amusement center operations division	Amusement machine sales division	Total
Net sales to outside customers	¥301,145	¥61,968	¥53,427	¥416,540
Cost of sales and operating expenses	291,214	53,069	42,323	386,606
	¥9,931	¥8,899	¥11,104	¥29,934

2) GEOGRAPHICAL SEGMENT INFORMATION

Sales of the Companies for the years ended March 31, 1993 (unaudited) and 1994, classified by geographical segments (sales within Japan and outside Japan), are summarized as follows:

	Millions of yen (unaudited) Year ended March 31, 1993				
	Within Japan	Outside Japan	Total	Elimination	Consolidated Total
Net sales to:					
Outside customers	¥181,134	¥235,100	¥416,234	¥—	¥416,234
Inter-segment sales/transfers	165,803	7,330	173,133	(173,133)	—
	¥346,937	¥242,430	¥589,367	¥(173,133)	¥416,234

	Millions of yen Year ended March 31, 1994				
	Within Japan	Outside Japan	Total	Elimination	Consolidated Total
Net sales to:					
Outside customers	¥181,320	¥235,200	¥416,540	¥—	¥416,540
Inter-segment sales/transfers	172,712	20,292	193,004	(193,004)	—
	¥354,032	¥255,512	¥609,544	¥(193,004)	¥416,540

3) OVERSEAS SALES INFORMATION

Overseas sales of the Companies for the years ended March 31, 1993 and 1994 aggregated ¥291,611 million and ¥289,931 million, respectively, which accounted for 70.1% and 69.6% of consolidated net sales for the respective years.

CONSOLIDATED STATEMENTS OF INCOME AND RETAINED EARNINGS
Sega Enterprises, Ltd., and Subsidiaries
For the years ended March 31, 1993 and 1994

	Millions of yen		Thousands of US dollars (Note 3)
	1993	1994	1994
Net Sales	¥416,234	¥416,540	¥4,038,197
Cost of Sales	267,664	300,802	2,916,161
Gross profit	148,570	115,738	1,122,036
Selling, General and Administrative Expenses	81,176	85,804	831,837
Operating income	67,394	29,934	290,199
Other Income/(Expenses):			
Interest and dividend income	3,879	2,823	27,368
Gain (loss) on sales of marketable securities and short-term investment	(188)	699	6,777
Interest expense	(4,545)	(4,205)	(40,766)
Loss on valuation of marketable securities and short-term investment	(292)	--	--
Loss on sale or disposal of property and equipment	(342)	(261)	(2,530)
Loss on valuation of investment securities	(299)	(64)	(620)
Foreign exchange losses	(482)	(962)	(9,326)
Amoritization of discounts on bonds	(1,515)	(2,087)	(20,233)
Bond issue expenses	(687)	--	--
Loss on settlement of litigation	(2,821)	--	--
Amoritization of excess investment costs over net assets of consolidated subsidiaries acquired	(462)	(556)	(5,390)
Other, net	(465)	1,384	13,416
Total other income/(expenses)	(8,219)	(3,229)	(31,304)
Income before income taxes	59,175	26,705	258,895
Income Taxes:			
Current	34,566	25,488	247,096
Current refunds	--	(2,733)	(26,495)
Deferred [Note 2.(4)]	(3,502)	2,956	28,658
	31,064	25,711	249,259
	28,111	994	9,636
Adjustments on Foreign Currency Statements Translation	2,646	10,221	99,089
Net income	30,757	11,215	108,725
Retained Earnings:			
Balance at beginning of year	39,890	70,330	681,823
Increase due to recognition of deferred tax on timing differences from eliminating intercompany profits in consolidation [Note 2.(4)]	2,217	--	--
Cash dividends paid	(1,903)	(2,961)	(28,706)
Transfer to legal reserve	(197)	(307)	(2,976)
Bonuses to directors and statutory auditors	(68)	(108)	(1,047)
Adjustments on foreign currency statements translation	(366)	(564)	(5,468)
Balance at end of year	¥70,330	¥77,605	¥752,351

	Yen		US dollars (Note 3)
Per Share:			
Net income	¥317.0	¥112.4	$ 1.09
Cash dividends	25.0	38.0	0.37

The accompanying notes are an integral part of these statements.

	Millions of yen		Thousands of US dollars (Note 3)
	1993	1994	1994
LIABILITIES AND SHAREHOLDERS' EQUITY			
Current Liabilities:			
Short-term bank loans	¥24,877	¥46,478	$ 450,587
Current portion of long-term debt	1,168	--	--
Notes and accounts payable			
Trade	56,170	52,067	504,770
Other	2,639	3,731	36,171
	58,809	55,798	540,941
Accrued expenses	15,888	16,746	162,346
Income taxes payable	23,658	9,830	95,298
Other current liabilities	1,720	1,267	12,282
Total current liabilities	126,120	130,119	1,261,454
Long-Term Liabilities:			
Long-term debt	99,751	70,333	681,852
Accrued employees' retirement benefits	803	747	7,242
Accrued retirement benefits for directors and Statutory auditors	151	191	1,852
Other	535	617	5,981
Total long-term disabilities	101,240	71,888	696,927
Adjustments on Foreign Currency Statements Translation	5,357	1,611	15,618
Shareholders' Equity			
Common stock			
Authorized -- 200,000,000 shares at March 31, 1993 and 1994. Issued par value ¥50 per share - 80,884,944 shares and 100,488,673 shares at March 31, 1993 and 1994, respectively	24,437	38,839	376,529
Additional paid-in capital	23,983	38,385	372,128
Legal reserve	498	806	7,814
Retained earnings	70,330	77,605	752,351
Total shareholders' equity	119,248	155,635	1,508,822
Total liabilities and shareholders' equity			

CONSOLIDATED BALANCE SHEETS
Sega Enterprises, Ltd., and Subsidiaries
March 31, 1993 and 1994

	Millions of yen		Thousands of US dollars (Note 3)
	1993	1994	1994
ASSETS			
Current Assets:			
Cash	¥24,043	¥24,929	$ 241,677
Time deposits	68,304	70,562	684,072
Marketable securities and short-term investments	19,725	7,686	74,513
Notes and accounts receivable:			
Trade	54,606	45,383	439,971
Nonconsolidated subsidiaries and affiliates	1,698	2,583	25,041
Other	9,198	5,307	51,450
	65,502	53,273	516,462
Less allowance for doubtful accounts	(1,521)	(1,344)	(13,030)
	63,981	51,929	503,432
Inventories	62,497	79,326	769,035
Prepaid expenses	7,400	8,293	80,397
Deferred tax - current [Note 2.(4)]	6,698	3,585	34,755
Other current assets	1,476	1,111	10,771
Total current assets	254,124	247,421	2,398,652
Investments and Advances:			
Investments in securities	4,270	4,632	44,095
Investments in unconsolidated subsidiaries and affiliates	7,370	7,608	73,757
Other investments	2,218	2,310	22,395
Total investments and advances	13,858	14,550	141,057
Property and Equipment:			
Amusement machines and facilities	36,517	46,044	446,379
Buildings and structures	21,761	32,722	317,227
Machinery and equipment	14,221	20,194	195,774
	72,499	98,960	959,380
Less accumulated depreciation	(34,029)	(48,831)	(473,398)
	38,470	50,129	485,982
Land	9,639	10,318	100,029
Construction in progress	3,247	1,757	17,033
Total property and equipment	51,356	62,204	603,044
Fixed Leasehold Deposits	16,998	20,461	198,362
Deferred Changes and Intangible Assets	9,580	7,760	75,230
Excess Investment Cost Over Net Assets of Consolidated Subsidiaries Acquired	6,049	6,857	66,476
Total assets	¥ 351,965	¥ 359,253	$3,482,821

The accompanying notes are an integral part of these statements.

Teaching Notes:

Procter & Gamble: Facelle Division of Facial Tissue

Synopsis

Early in March 1992, Randall Beard was reviewing performance of the brands of facial tissue that Procter & Gamble had acquired in August 1991. Although Procter & Gamble had global brands in some categories of paper products (e.g., Pampers, the leading disposable diaper), the Facelle acquisition in Canada was P&G's first step outside the U.S. in the tissue/towel business. For that reason, senior management would be closely watching the progress of the Facelle brands of facial tissue, paper towels, and bathroom tissue.

As Associate Advertising Manager for Tissue, Towel, and Facial Products, Randall Beard reported directly to Barbara Fraser, Vice President and General Manager of the Paper Products business in Canada. Together, the two would be responsible for several major decisions about tissue brands, including positioning, product formulations, and promotion. For his forthcoming meeting with Fraser, Beard wanted to have a set of definite recommendations on the future of the brands.

Case Background

Procter & Gamble originated in 1837, when William Procter and James Gamble, two immigrant soap and candle makers, formed a partnership in Cincinnati, Ohio. The partnership rapidly flourished, gaining a name as a principled manufacturer of high quality consumer goods sold at competitive prices. By 1992, P&G was a multinational company with annual sales of almost $30 billion (U.S.), profits exceeding $1.8 billion (U.S.), and a long-standing reputation for quality products, high integrity, strong marketing, and conservative management.

As Procter & Gamble grew, it increasingly focused on international markets. In 1992, P&G's brands were sold in more than 140 countries around the world. Major areas and representative brands included laundry and cleaning products (e.g., Tide, Cheer, Mr. Clean), paper products (Pampers, Luvs, Always, Bounty, Charmin), health care (Pepto-Bismol, Metamucil), oral care (Crest, Scope), food and beverage (Jif, Crisco), bar soaps (Ivory, Zest) and cosmetics (Oil of Olay, Max Factor, Cover Girl). Many of these brands were leaders in their categories.

In Canada, P&G operated as Procter & Gamble Inc., with 1992 sales expected to exceed S1.7 billion, and earnings before taxes of over $100 million. P&G Inc. operated as four divisions, of which Paper Products was one, organized on a category basis within each division (e.g. Tissue/Towel/Facial within Paper Products).

Procter & Gamble first entered the consumer paper market in 1957 with its acquisition of Charmin Paper Company,, a regional paper company with a strong presence in the north central U.S. In the early 1960s, P&G launched Bounty towels using new technologies which allowed it to deliver softness, strength and absorbency. P&G subsequently expanded the brand to national distribution in 1972. Finally, P&G entered the facial tissue market in the early 1970's by launching the Puffs brand.

P&G built Charmin, Bounty and Puffs with similar strategies. First, proprietary technology was used to deliver products with superior performance at a competitive price. Second, consumers were offered "value-added" products which delivered additional benefits (e.g., Puffs Plus with lotion, Charmin Free with no inks, dyes or perfumes). Third, the brands were supported with successful advertising themes and consistently high media weights. Finally, P&G achieved competitive costs among premium brands by using Total Quality Methods to improve the papermaking process.

By 1991, P&G was sufficiently satisfied with its U.S. successes in Charmin, Bounty and Puffs that it was ready to take its first step in expanding the business. Early in 1991, an attractive acquisition opportunity developed for P&G in Canada. Canadian Pacific Forest Product Company, a large diversified paper company, was prepared to sell Facelle Paper Products, its tissue division. Facelle was a medium-sized manufacturer and marketer of tissue, towel, and sanitary products, headquartered in Toronto. In 1990, Facelle reported an operating profit of $13.4 million on sales of $170.5 million.

The Consumer Paper Business in Canada

The Canadian consumer paper market in 1992 was about 25 million cases. Of the 25 million cases, bathroom tissue accounted for 13 million, paper towels seven million, and facial tissue five million. Tissue products were inexpensive (usually less than $2.00 per package), they were widely used (in more than 95% of Canadian households), and they were frequently purchased (on average, once every two weeks). Brand switching was common. The challenge for manufacturers was to differentiate their products enough on performance to build loyalty.

Traditional retail food stores typically carried a full line of paper products and featured them frequently. In recent years, however, mass merchandiser and drug chains had expanded their paper business substantially, focusing almost exclusively on price deals to attract customers to their stores. Recently, "club stores," with their emphasis on everyday low pricing, further squeezed retail and manufacturer margins.

The paper business in Canada had a few very large national manufacturers and a few smaller regional players. Therefore, the industry was characterized by high capital and fixed costs. Manufacturers marketed broad product lines in an attempt to compete in all segments of the market and utilize as much capacity as possible.

The Facial Tissue Market in Canada

The size of the facial tissue market in 1991 was 4,894,000 cases shipped, up 7% over 1990 sales. Market shares of the major producers will be highlighted in the following paragraphs.

Facelle brands. Shipments of the Facelle brands of facial tissue in 1991 were only 587,000 cases, or 84% of the 1990 results. Two brands, Royale and Florelle, accounted for most of Facelle's sales. Until recently, the Royale brand had been the only 3-ply tissue on the market, and it enjoyed a brand image as the traditional, strong, premium quality facial tissue. Its market share increased very slightly during 1991. Florelle was a 2-ply tissue that had received little promotional attention. Not surprisingly, it had low awareness, trial and image. It had lost about one-third of its market share in 1991, and was down to 5.8% at the beginning of 1992.

Kimberly-Clark. The Kleenex brand had enjoyed a very good year in 1991, gaining 2.5 share points to reach 39.5% of units shipped in the Canadian market. There were several Kleenex product initiatives during 1991 which affected the brand's sales results such as the new 300-tissue family size (2-ply), 2-ply Kleenex 150's, and Kleenex Ultra, a 3-ply tissue which contained a silicone-based lotion.

Scott. Scott's major brand, Scotties, fell from a share of 18.9% in 1990 to 15.9% in 1991. The main reason for the decline was the loss of trade support relative to Kleenex 150s. Scott relaunched the brand in September 1991 with a new positioning strategy. They also launched a 300-tissue family size of Scotties. Scott's secondary brand, White Swan (sold only in 150s), maintained a 7.1% share in 1991.

Irving. Next to the aggressive developments in the Kleenex brand, the most significant competitive event in the facial tissue business in 1991 was the entry of Irving into the facial tissue market with it's new Majesta brand. Majesta was packaged in an attractive format, and its feature pricing averaged 15-20% below Kleenex. It achieved a 4.2% national share in 1991.

All others. Overall, the other brands in the Canadian marketplace retained 98% of their cumulative market share in 1991.

Advertising

Advertising expenditures in the facial tissue category had historically been low averaging nearly $3.0 million over the last five years with television accounting for 47% of spending.

Regarding the competition's advertising strategies, Randall Beard believed that Kimberly-Clark had established a contemporary image for the Kleenex brand, but not a strong image for either softness or tissue strength. Until the past year, when all Scotties' advertising was focused on the recycled paper relaunch, Scotties had consistently advertised softness. Royale had historically focused on the superior cold care afforded by the softness and strength of the 3-ply tissue

By Procter & Gamble standards, advertising in the facial tissue category had not been strong. Not only were expenditures low, but only a small proportion of that spending was on brand equity. Furthermore, campaigns in the industry had tended to be of short duration, while

P&G's extensive research on consumer advertising indicated that to be effective, advertising had to be sustained.

Consumer Promotion and Pricing

While consumer promotions for facial tissues were relatively rare, price features were commonplace. There was always at least one brand on feature at any sizable food or drug retailer. In fact, the vast majority of facial tissues sold at retail during 1991 were feature-priced.

Issues for the Facelle Brands

In planning, the future of Facelle brands, several problems had to be confronted. But first, Randall Beard reviewed a summary of the research which P&G had obtained in the seven months since acquiring the Facelle business.

The Royale brand

Image. Royale's long-term premium positioning, based upon its historically unique 3-ply product design and its softness claim, had built the leading brand image in the product category. Royale enjoyed an image advantage for strength and thickness versus all other competition, but an image weakness for package design. It was also seen as less fashionable than Kleenex and Scotties. Although Royale enjoyed a very favorable brand image, knowledge about the brand was not as high as Beard would have expected.

Product Usage. Although half of the households had used Royale sometime in the last year, only 13% claimed that it was their usual brand. Research indicated that it was used as a part-time brand that was bought on feature or for cold care and usually purchased by older consumers and smaller households.

Pricing vs. Kleenex. In the past four months average feature price for Kleenex had been $0.69, and for Royale $0.73. During this period, 80% of the Royale sold at retail had been on feature.

The Florelle Brand

In 1991, 80% of facial tissue units sold were standard 2-ply tissue, the segment in which Facelle was represented by the Florelle brand. Only 3% of those surveyed claimed that Florelle was their usual brand. The obvious alternatives were to drop the Florelle brand, rejuvenate it with support, or continue it as an unsupported price brand.

The Softness Issue

A key success factor in the successful development of the Puffs brand in the U.S. was the effort that P&G invested in making the tissue softer. Data from P&G's experience in the U.S. market indicated that consumer preferred a strong tissue, but had a stronger preference for a soft tissue. Relative tissue strength depended on the conditions of the test, especially whether the tissue was wet or dry. Proctor and Gamble believed that dry strength was much less important than wet strength.

Commenting on the test data, Randall Beard said, "This just reinforces what I have been told about Facelle's strategy prior to the acquisition. They choose to maximize strength - particularly dry strength - but that approach cost them severely on the softness dimension."

In mid-1991, a blind paired comparison test was conducted with Royale and Kleenex Ultra. Kleenex Ultra was rated significantly better on softness (9.1 vs. 7.4) and only 27% of the participants choose Royale as their preferred brand.

Beard was convinced that P&G needed to upgrade the softness of the Facelle products. By adding eucalyptus fibre and sacrificing some tissue strength, their softness could be significantly improved without the need for a major capital expenditure. In the long run, investments in process improvement could produce further softness enhancements, but the so-called -Eucalyptus Upgrade" could be done in a few months for a modest investment. Accordingly, P&G carried out a pilot project to produce enough of the upgraded products for consumer acceptance testing. Early in 1992, testing was done on the upgraded product, in both 2-ply and 3-ply form, as well as the current Royale, Florelle, Kleenex (Regular and Ultra), Scotties, and White Swan. Participants in Facelle's testing were female heads of households whose first language was English. There were eight groups of participants, one for each brand. Group sizes ranged from 259 to 280 individuals. Overall ratings of the brands were found to be a function of consumer impressions of a tissue's softness and its thickness.

Randall Beard had to make a decision about what brand name would be used on it. Two apparent alternatives were Florelle (as an upgrade of the existing brand) and Royale (as a line extension). Another possibility would be to introduce the new product under the Puffs label that had been so successfully launched in the U.S. some twenty years earlier.

Conclusion

Using the Puffs label in Canada would be a step toward making Puffs a North American brand, an alternative which would certainly have the blessing of the U.S. parent. However, the primary responsibility for the decision rested with Randall Beard and Barbara Fraser, and the choice had to be made soon if product, packaging and advertising and merchandising programs were to be ready for the fall cold season.

Case Discussion Questions and Answers

1. Quite a bit of research was conducted on the tissue market in Canada. What were the results of this research regarding consumers perceptions of Royale and Facelle?

Consumers perceive Royale as a premium quality 3-ply brand of tissue, relatively expensive and especially known for its strength. The weaknesses include it's lack of softness and it's use as a product primarily used for colds.

Florelle was a 2-ply tissue that had received little promotional attention resulting in low awareness, trial and image. Consumers perceive Facelle as a low cost tissue. There are many weakness such as its lack of softness, low image due to a lack of advertising, and overall low ratings on performance.

2. What are the possible alternatives for the Florelle brand of tissue? What recommendations would you make and why?

According to research, Florelle has few strengths other than its low price. Options for a product that does not have a competitive advantage include: (1) a growth strategy such as Market Penetration which emphasizes growth through more effective marketing of the product in existing markets, or (2) consolidation strategies such as Retrenchment where an organization continues to offer the same product but focuses on the strongest target markets or (3) Divestment where a company sells a product line.

Through **Market Penetration**, P&G could try to focus additional advertising strategies on current customers to try to increase product sales. The advantage of this strategy would be that it might be possible to reach more price sensitive consumers. The disadvantage is that it will cost additional money and the overall gain would not likely be significant.

Through **Divestment**, P&G would eliminate the tissue from its product line. This is an option if the brand is unprofitable. However, if the brand is making some contribution to the profit margin, there seems little reason to eliminate it.

Through **Retrenchment,** P&G would continue to offer the product focusing all its marketing efforts on price sensitive consumers. This strategy seems to offer the most potential financial reward to the company since there are a small amount of "value oriented" consumers.

3. What are the possible alternatives for the Royale brand of tissue? What recommendations would you make and why?

Research for the Royale brand of tissue suggest several competitive strengths such as a premium image which commands higher prices and it's thickness and strength compared to the competition. Based on these results, several growth strategies may be considered including: (1) Market Penetration which emphasizes growth through more effective marketing of the product in existing markets, or (2) Product Development which continues to market to the same customers but does so through changes in the set of product offered.

Through **Market Penetration,** P&G could continue to offer Royale as a 3-ply brand which would capitalize on the competitive strengths of tissue durability, strong image and use for illness. Increased advertising and promotion could increase the market share of this product.

Through **Product Development,** P&G could continue to offer the premium 3-ply brand but use the "Eucalyptus Upgrade" to increase the softness. This alternative would give the brand both of the two most important attributes desired by consumers; strength and softness. Additional advertising would need to be created to tell consumers about the new improvement.

4. Should Randall Beard recommend that the facial tissue be introduced as Puffs into the Canadian market? Why or why not?

Advantages: Puffs has a strong brand appeal in the U.S. and through some of the advertising, Puffs was already know to many Canadians. This strategy also has the support of the parent company, P&G. Puffs positioning strategy focuses on softness, a positioning which is different from Royale (strength) or Florelle (low price). Thus the introduction of Puffs would be less likely to result in cannibalization among the brands.

Disadvantages: It is expensive to build a brand name within a new market such as Canada. There would be many issues related to this to plan for. Royale and Florelle are existing brands in Canada, though each with specific problems.

Teaching Notes:

Waste Management International plc: Strategy for Asia

Synopsis:

Waste Management international Pic (Wml) aims to be the world leader in offering comprehensive environmental services to industry, government, and, residential customers. Faced with a recession in Europe in late 1993, WMI is considering how to expand in the Asian marketplace. The case provides details on the Hong Kong Chemical Waste Treatment Center, one of the most advanced facilities of its kind in the region to date. The project at the time is nearing completion. Greg Feutril, senior VP for Asia, needs to develop a strategic plan for the Asian Region.

Uses:

The case deals with global strategy issues. Although the case was originally developed for a global marketing class, it can be fruitfully employed in a more general global business class. Given the emphasis on global strategy issues, it fits in the modules such as "Opportunity Analysis" or "Global versus Local Strategy".

The case is also a neat illustration of doing business with government authorities (at the local and/or federal level). Hence, it could also serve as a vehicle to highlight marketing-to-government issues.

Objectives:

1. To explore the strategic options in the Asian marketplace for a global competitor in a h highly complex industry.

2. To illustrate the notion of "global know-how, local presence" as the underlying theme of a successful global strategy.

3. To highlight the issues in doing business with government authorities.

4. To illustrate the process of assessing market opportunities.

Assignment Questions:

1. What are the key competitive advantages of WMI?

2. What are the major differences between the European and Asian marketplace?

3.	How would you assess WMI's expansion strategy ("global know-how, local presence")? Would you describe it as a global strategy? If not, do you feel it should be global?

4.	What Asian markets are key for further expansion?

Teaching Plan:

A good opening question is to ask the students whether or not they would invest in WMI (or the parent company, WMX Technologies). Most students realize the importance of environmental services (witness the presence of specialized mutual funds that exclusively target companies in this sector). Economic growth puts pressure on the environment. Environmental awareness and concerns are increasing among governments and the public at large. These pressures lead towards more stringent regulation creating a need for the kinds of services that WMI provides.

Some students might be concerned about the strategic path WMI is taking. The company, though large, and so far quite successful, appears to be somewhat conservative and risk averse. Criteria for investment (stable political and economic climate, currency convertibility) are fairly stringent. Students might debate whether this is the right attitude for a company of WMI's caliber (students' comments will probably reflect their own risk attitude).

After focusing on these issues, a discussion of WMI's strategy appears appropriate. It is important to point out the differences between Europe and Asia (and hence the need for a regional rather than "global" strategy). WMI summarizes its strategy with the catch-phrase (used in their print advertising and on the cover of their annual reports): "Local Presence. Global Know-How" (is this just a variation on the Greens' bumper sticker "Think Global. Act Local"?). Most students will probably largely agree with the ingredients of WMI's strategy (given the nature of the company and the environmental conditions). Instructors may ask the class to think about the kind of companies where this strategy might (not) be appropriate. What are the risks? Potential drawbacks?

Finally, the class should explore opportunities in the various Asian markets (based on the information provided in **Exhibit 8).** Most of these markets are very appealing. Despite the fact that WMI has deep pockets, it will still need to establish priorities (the bucks may be there, but not necessarily other resources such as human assets). Students can rank the markets on various criteria. Key is the environmental regulation climate (and the enforcement policies). Though regulations are in place in most of these countries, there is still some gradation in terms of enforcement and coverage.

Towards the end of the case, the instructor could show the accompanying videotape (approximately 15 minutes) prepared by the case-writer.

Discussion:

1. <u>What are the key competitive advantages of Waste Management International?</u>

WMX Technologies, the parent company of WMI, is a family of companies that provides a full range of environmental services (see **Exhibits 5** and **6** in the case):

- · integrated solid waste services
- · trash-to-energy and co-generation facilities
- · maintenance services for water and waste water treatment facilities
- · a broad range of air pollution control technologies

Competitors can provide some of these services, but at this stage, none of them is able to offer the entire spectrum. WMX Technologies (and thus WMI) is therefore in a unique position to offer integrated solutions. A case in point is the Hong Kong project (described in the case), where WMI takes care of solid and hazardous waste, operates a landfill and an incineration plant with trash-to-energy facilities, as well as a waste water treatment operation.

Consequently, WMI might be preferred by local governments over their competitors as the authorities only need to deal with one company instead of having to shop at a multitude of companies, offering different (possibly incompatible) technologies. This situation is likely to change in the future as several competitors consolidate their activities via M&As and/or strategic alliances.

Pricing can be an issue for smaller projects. However, the capability to provide certain services is still the key selection criterion for many projects. WMI is not only a full range supplier, but has a reputation for being a first class provider of leading edge environmental technology. Many governments or commercial customers want to have the very best for their money. Given WMI's reputation as a leader (and pioneer) in the environmental services business, the company is well-placed to win contracts.

Even when pricing becomes an issue, WMI has the advantage that it can cross-subsidize different activities. If, for instance, chemical waste treatment and waste water treatment services are needed, WMI can cite a more competitive price for one service to compete against a low cost supplier and ask a higher price for the other service where competition is less fierce.

Another big asset of WMI is that they have acquired an excellent skill to pick the right local partners in Asian markets and to develop close connections with local government authorities. WMI offers advice on how to come up with a solid environmental policy. The company also assists governments in enhancing public awareness on green issues. Fostering government relationships is a time-consuming process. However, tight connections are likely to favor WMI when governments invite bids.

2. What are the key differences between the European and Asian marketplace?

The major difference is the wide gap in terms of economic development between Asia and Western Europe. Western Europe is still far ahead in economic development, despite the high growth rate of the Asian tigers (countries such as South Korea, Singapore, Hong Kong, Taiwan) and cubs (Indonesia, Malaysia, Thailand). The awareness of environmental issues is also much more developed in Europe than in Asia (although this is changing tremendously).

One can summarize the situation via the notion of the International Product Life Cycle. Whereas Europe is in an advanced stage (as far as environmental services go), Asia is still in the early/growth phase, as far as the environment goes. In Europe, environmental services and regulations are well established. In most Asian countries, however, regulations are still in the infancy stage.

From WMI's perspective, this gap between Europe and Asia also demands a drastically different strategic approach. In Europe, many environmental service providers already exist. Hence, WMI could rely on an acquisition strategy to expand their business. Acquisitions are the easiest and least expensive way to expand. On the other hand, in Asia, WMI basically has to start from scratch.

3. How do you assess WMI's expansion strategy? Would you describe it as a global strategy? If not, should it be global?

WMI's expansion strategy drastically differs in Asia from the approach taken in Europe for the reasons stated above (Question 2). In Asia, the company prefers partnerships whereas in Europe, the emphasis is on acquisitions.

Even within regions, each project tends to be very localized. WMI aims to establish partnerships with local partners. It also makes a deliberate attempt to hire local employees, and run its operations with local managers. Further, WMI tries to project a local identity in terms of brand names and logos to be responsive to local cultures. Countries widely differ in terms of their social structures and cultures. These environmental differences favor a customized country-by-country approach. The "local presence" strand of WMI's strategy creates enormous challenges. In some countries, local talent is scarce, forcing WMI to train their recruits. One issue that the company apparently faced (e.g., in Hong Kong) was high turnover. Given WMI's reputation in the industry, competitors are eager to hire WMI's employees away. This forced WMI to improve their incentive package.

Despite the need for a customized approach, there are also payoffs from a global perspective. This goes back to WMI's competitive advantage: the skills and international expertise of the member companies. A lot of the expertise and knowledge gained in Europe can be leveraged on in Asia. This basically refers to the notion of cross-fertilization. So, whereas WMI's presence is very local, the company capitalizes on its global know-how.

4. What Asian markets are key for further expansion?

Several criteria need to be met. A strict regulatory environment needs to be in place. The country also needs to be politically stable. The convertibility of the local currency is another must (this would exclude mainland China). Students can debate these criteria. Overall, WMI (and its parent company, WMX Technology) appears to be fairly conservative (especially, with regard to the last criterion). Looking to the countries surveyed in the case, one can make the following observations:

India:

There is a tremendous need for environmental services. The economy continues to grow at a steady rate. Demand for waste treatment equipment is expected to grow from $100m in '91 to $245m by '95. Massive projects need to be developed such as land-fills and specialized waste facilities. Because of the lack of infrastructure, only large financially sound companies will be able to cope. The Indian government is beginning to establish environmental regulations but enforcement is rare. The rupee has recently become convertible.

India provides major opportunities. The political environment is relatively unstable. The economic infrastructure is still very poor. Though a viable market, expansion should probably occur at a slow pace.

Indonesia:

Indonesia has experienced rapid economic growth. The downside of this growth is the negative impact on the environment. The government has issued more environmental legislation. This legislation boosts demand for the kinds of services that WMI offers. The government is fairly stable and the economy is expected to continue to g row.

WMI already has some presence in Indonesia with a partner (Bimantara). Given the environmental conditions, WMI should definitely pursue further opportunities in Indonesia.

Malaysia:

Malaysia's consistent growth, stable political conditions and environmental reforms make it an attractive market for companies such as WMI. In those regards, the country is very similar to Indonesia, one of the other tiger cubs.

Philippines:

Just as in many other countries in the region, there is a strong need for environmental services in the Philippines. The economy is not as solid as elsewhere in the area. The overall political situation has improved but is still quite unstable (e.g., unrest in Muslim populated areas). Government agencies are attempting to establish guidelines for environmental controls but enforcement is weak. Infrastructure is also lacking.

Given that other markets are more appealing, WMI should take a wait-and-see attitude. At this time, entry into the Philippines appears premature.

Singapore:

Environmental awareness is well established in Singapore. Economically and politically, Singapore is very stable. The Ministry of Environment is very active in improving environmental conditions via regulations (banning of chewing gum; heavy fines for not flushing public toilets). The infrastructure is solid.

Singapore is a prime opportunity. A quick move in Singapore seems desirable. The Singapore government prefers investments from leading edge companies with a well-established reputation. This desire on the part of Singapore would favor WMI.

Taiwan:

Taiwan's environment is suffering due to a dramatic increase in population density coupled with industrialization. The Environmental Protection Administration has created a number of regulations and enforcement procedures to deal with waste problems. The EPA has also developed a "Green Plan" under which 23 incinerators are to be built, 722 collection and disposal vehicles will be purchased, 60 landfills will be constructed, and one compost site will be developed. The economic and political climate in Taiwan is strong.

Bidding for contracts under the Green Plan umbrella should be top priority.

Thailand.

The opportunities in the environmental services business seem huge. Pollution is the price Thailand had to pay for its economic expansion. Regulation is in place. However, there is little coordination among the various agencies. Enforcement is another issue.

Compared to other opportunities in the region, Thailand should probably get low priority.

South Korea:

The Korean government has set up the Environmental Management Corporation to construct and operate waste treatment plants. The EMC is apparently highly interested in US technologies. On the other hand, environmental law enforcement is weak.

The economic and political environment is superb. Korea appears to offer appealing opportunities to WMI.

In all these target markets, environmental awareness (coupled with regulations) is improving. Most of these countries experienced (and still are experiencing) tremendous economic growth. The downside has been a noticeable deterioration of the environment. The responsiveness of local governments differs however. In some countries, legislation is still in an early stage. Enforcement ranges from very strict (e.g., Singapore, Indonesia) to very loose (e.g., Thailand, India). WMI should probably concentrate its resources on those markets where enforcement is stringent.

At the same time, it should not ignore the other countries. As is described in the case, WMI takes a long-term perspective to exploit market opportunities. WMI may start to build up an organization, develop strategic plans, and scout around for prospective partners long before any opportunities materialize. For instance, though the Chinese currency, the yuan, is not yet convertible, WMI has begun to set up an organization in mainland China.

Epilogue:

WMI's expansion strategy in Asia is in full gear now. The company started up the Hong Kong chemical waste treatment facility in '93. WMI was also awarded a contract to construct a landfill (45 million cubic meter capacity) in Hong Kong.

In Indonesia, a chemical waste treatment plant in Bogor (60 km from Jakarta) was opened in May of '94. The processing capacity is 5000 tons.

WMI has also been selected by the Thai government to form a joint venture company to construct a chemical waste treatment network.

Plans are also underway for activities in Malaysia, Taiwan, and Singapore. WMI is also exploring opportunities in China.

Students familiar with the environmental situation in Central and Eastern Europe might wonder whether WMI has any plans for that region. Though the demand for environmental services is huge (most of the region is a showcase for Dante's Inferno as far as the environment goes), the time to enter these markets is not right. Most of these countries simply do not have the capital available. Even if they do, environmental demands rank low on their priority list.

A videotape for the case study is available. The tape contains an 18-minute interview with Michael Rogan, Vice-President Product Development at WMX Technologies and a commercial spot shown on CNN International. The commercial centers on the Hong Kong project.

Teaching Notes:

Baxter International--Renal Division: Strategy for Latin America

Case Synopsis:

The Renal Division of Baxter International plans to expand their presence in the Latin American region. More specifically, Vernon Loucks, Baxter's CEO, has four countries in mind: Brazil, Colombia, Mexico, and, Venezuela. These countries, as well as other emerging markets, offer a tremendous opportunity for "continuous ambulatory peritoneal dialysis" (CAPD), a treatment for kidney disease, pioneered by Baxter. This technology seems to be much more cost-effective than hemodialysis (HD).

Baxter faces several challenges. The company must decide how to allocate their resources across these different markets. In the United States (and other developed markets) Baxter stands out with its devotion to customer service. It is not clear to what degree this amount of customer service can be replicated in emerging markets, such as the ones under consideration in the case study. Also, Baxter needs to reflect on how to handle the threat posed by patent infringement and counterfeiting, rampant in several countries in this region.

Teaching Objectives:

The case is suited to illustrate the following problem areas in a global marketing course:

1. *Market Opportunity Analysis.* To perform an analysis of market opportunities and to decide how a company's resources should be allocated over its different target markets.

2. *Marketing in Emerging Markets.* To examine the complexities and challenges of marketing in "emerging markets" (the Latin American region in this case).

3. *Health Care Marketing.* The case is also useful to illustrate the peculiarities of health care marketing in a global setting.

4. *Patent infringement and Counterfeiting.* A major stumbling block for many marketers in emerging markets are the phenomena of patent infringement and counterfeiting (especially for health care companies). The case forces students to reflect on these issues and to come up with possible solutions to handle such problems.

Assignment Questions:

1. From Baxter's perspective, what are the key differences between emerging markets like the countries in the Latin American region and developed countries like the US?

2. Is this the right time for Baxter to focus its expansion efforts on the Latin American region?

3. Should Baxter's renal division focus on CAPD or HD?

4. How should Baxter allocate its resources across the four target markets (Brazil, Colombia, Mexico, and, Venezuela)?

5. Do you feel Baxter will be able to duplicate the kind of customer service that it provides in developed markets?

6. How would you address the issue of patent infringement?

Analysis:

1) From Baxter's perspective, what are the key differences between emerging markets, like the countries in the Latin American region, and developed countries, like the USA?

It is important to realize that there are enormous differences "within" the Latin American region itself. So, it can be very misleading to simply lump together countries in this continent. With that caveat in mind, there are several observations that can be drawn. First, the economic and political situation in many of these countries is far less stable than in the USA. Venezuela's economy collapsed in 1994. Early 1995, Mexico's economy went on the respirator when the Mexican peso collapsed against the US dollar. This volatility means that doing business in this region is not for the faint-hearted. Getting paid by the government can be a problem. Likewise, profit repatriation can be a problem.

Spending on healthcare is far less in this region than in most developed countries. This forces health care companies like Baxter to reflect on low-cost strategies. For instance, the product lines offered in emerging countries are typically less expensive, older technologies.

2) **Is this the right time for Baxter to focus its expansion efforts on the Latin American region? Should Baxter "give gas" or "apply the brakes"?**

It is important to realize that Baxter's renal division currently has already a strong foothold in Latin America. A cursory glance at case exhibits 10 and 11 shows that Baxter dominates the dialysis markets in all four countries.

In the past, most Latin American countries went through a lot of economic turmoil. However, in recent years, a number of significant steps have been taken throughout the region to address the major economic problems. Economic reforms are implemented to keep down inflation. Several countries in the region are privatizing state-owned industries. Markets are opened up to foreign investors. Significant efforts have been made to stabilize local currencies. Scores of indicators point towards a better business environment.

Baxter also has a product (CAPD) that matches the needs of these countries. CAPD is a cost-effective treatment for renal dialysis. Virtually all Latin American governments are under cost-containment pressures with regard to their public budgets. In addition to being cost effective, CAPD is mobile. Since a large proportion of the population is rural, Baxter's CAPD products would open up dialysis treatment to many more patients.

Yet, there are significant challenges. As discussed above, spending power is pretty low in most of these countries. Local economies are still on an unstable footing. There are also the threats posed by patent infringement and product counterfeiting.

3) **Should Baxter's renal division focus on CAPD or HD in the Latin American region?**

The usage of CAPD (as a percentage of dialysis treatment) varies widely. In fact, in Mexico, CAPD is already well-entrenched, representing more than 90% of the dialysis-patient population. Some countries, like the United States, made substantial investments in hemodialysis centers. Because of that, physicians tend to prescribe that form of treatment. Reimbursement of physicians is another major influence in the penetration of CAPD versus HD. Where governments or reimbursing agencies realize that incenting the doctor towards PD can save money, that is where the highest levels of utilization occur. In countries where the reimbursement structure presents an even playing field, PD rates are fairly high. However, in Japan for instance, PD penetration is low because the reimbursement schema makes it more appealing for the phrenologist to treat a patient on hemodialysis.

The cost advantages of PD-therapy make the treatment attractive to both the private and public sector. In Latin America, peritoneal dialysis will offer a special benefit to the less affluent population. Dialysis patients living outside the major urban centers currently receive less than adequate treatment. This is primarily due to their limited financial resources and geographical remoteness. The absence of medical resources such as hospitals and doctors reinforces the case for CAPD. Dialysis treatment would become affordable and practical to that segment of the local population.

However, distribution will be an issue for Baxter when trying to penetrate this market. Distribution of PD solutions to the patient's door and excellent customer service are Baxter's key success factors in the U.S. It is questionable whether the same level of customer service can be replicated in the target countries.

4) How should Baxter allocate its resources across the four target markets (Brazil, Colombia, Mexico, and, Venezuela)?

The resource allocation decision is driven by a number of factors. If Baxter desires to focus on CAPD, the focus could be on those countries with the largest CAPD population -- primarily Mexico (percentage -wise) and Brazil (in absolute numbers). Mexico has a couple of other advantages: member of NAFTA (meaning that it presumably offers more patent protection than some of the other countries), close to the U.S., and a local manufacturing presence (though this also applies to Brazil).

Baxter might also consider putting its resources in those countries with the highest growth potential. One could use as a proxy for growth potential the percentage of patients that are on CAPD. The lower this percentage, the higher the growth potential. Countries with the lowest proportion include Brazil and Colombia. Arguing against Brazil is geographical remoteness. Other factors brought up by the students include:

- Buying power. A possible indicator here is per capita GNP. This factor would favor Venezuela.

- Economic and political stability. Unfortunately, none of these countries do well on this dimension.

- Presence of local manufacturing facilities. Venezuela is the only country where Baxter does not have a plant.

- Health care expenditures, either on a "per capita" basis or as a "percentage of GNP". Either measure would favor Venezuela.

A summary market assessment of the four target markets is given in the Table below:

Criterion	Brazil	Columbia	Mexico	Venezuela
Penetration CAPD (as % of total dialysis)	Low	Low	High	Medium
CAPD Patient Population	High	Low	High	Low
Per Capita GNP	Medium	Low	Medium	High
Local Manufacturing	Yes	Yes	Yes	No
Health Expenditures ($ per capita)	Medium	Low	Medium	High

Students could be prompted for percentages to indicate their investment priorities. Most allocation schemes will probably put Mexico and Brazil on top. Personally, I would put Venezuela next and at the bottom Colombia.

Baxter also must decide where to target growth: urban or rural areas. If the urban centers are chosen, Baxter will most likely face competition. However, this competition would most likely come from other multinational health care providers, the same companies that Baxter faces elsewhere. The urban areas have relatively well developed health care systems. Baxter should be accustomed to competing in this type of environment.

The rural areas offer tremendous opportunities for Baxter. This segment of the population is undeserved as far as health care goes. Given the cost-effectiveness and mobility offered by CAPD, there is a definite match between these markets and Baxter's product portfolio. If Baxter chooses to target this sector, it must resolve the logistics problems it will encounter to distribute and serve this segment.

5)   Do you feel Baxter will be able to duplicate the customer service that it provides in developed countries?

Dedicated customer service gave Baxter's renal division a distinct competitive advantage in most developed countries. Baxter hopes to replicate this type of service in emerging markets. Success is not guaranteed though. Distribution is expected to be one area that will prove to be difficult for Baxter. The local infrastructure in many of these countries is most likely not conducive to support the routine deliveries that are crucial to the success of PD treatments in markets like the U.S.

If Baxter plans to obtain growth by providing PD-treatment in Latin America's rural areas, it must develop innovative distribution and servicing schemes. As stated in the case, much of the rural population is serviced by roaming medical teams that are sponsored by the government. Treatments from these teams are limited to examinations and vaccinations. Thus, it is probably not feasible that these teams distribute Baxter's PD products to these remote areas. Moreover, visits by these teams are too infrequent to function in a distributive capacity.

Even if Baxter is able to duplicate the kind of patient services offered in the U.S., it is not clear whether patients (or local governments) are willing to pay for these services. Offering such services costs money. Customers (in particular, payers--governments, patients, and/or private insurers) could be much more price sensitive than in developed markets. Before investing resources in value-added services, Baxter needs to figure out to what degree local customers are willing to pay a premium.

6)   How would you address the issue of patent infringement?

In most of these countries (with the possible exception of Mexico), patents do not enjoy the type of protection offered in the U.S. The legal system is usually not watertight. Hence, companies like Baxter are very vulnerable to patent infringement. The issue is serious. Sales are lost. Counterfeit products of shoddy quality could also damage Baxter's corporate image.

There are several possible strategies that Baxter might consider to combat patent infringement and counterfeiting:

- *LegalAction.* Where possible, legal action could be used to attack patent violators. Such efforts are both time consuming and costly. Needless to say, a positive outcome is never guaranteed.

- *Lobbying.* Baxter could also exercise pressure by lobbying local governments for tougher legislation (or enforcement of existing laws). Alternatively, the company could lobby the U.S. government to impose sanctions against countries where counterfeiting is rampant.

- *Product Development.* Continuous product innovation (including service aspects) is another option to cope with product piracy. Again, this is a fairly expensive strategy. Baxter also runs the risk that new customers prefer cheaper, copy-cat products to the stream of product innovations.

- *Collaborating with Counterfeiters.* Baxter might consider collaborating with local manufacturers that produce counterfeit goods. Several options exist ranging from licensing to subcontracting all the way to acquisition. This option is especially appealing if the local manufacturers are highly cost-efficient (which is usually the case). It may not be a smart move if Baxter's existing plants have a lot of excess capacity.

260

Local Manufacturing. Finally, Baxter could also protect its patents by establishing a local manufacturing presence. As a quid-pro-quo, many governments will provide patent protection (or at least promise it) if the company manufactures the product locally.

Epilogue:

The most dramatic change is that Baxter experiences much more competitive pressure than it used to. Until recently, Baxter was the sole supplier of CAPD equipment in many of the Latin American countries. Not surprisingly, most local governments were not very happy about that situation (especially when they are the payer for Baxter's products and services). To loosen these ties, several governments (e.g., Mexico's and Venezuela's) now split up the business whenever there is more than one qualified bidder.

A two-part videotape is available from the European Case Clearing House. The first part (about 3 1/2 minutes) is a product demo on CAPD. The second part is a taped interview (about 13 1/2 minutes) with Bill Hicks, Marketing Director Intercontinental Region of Baxter international's Renal Division.

Teaching Notes:

Tilting Windmills: Sanex Tries to Conquer Europe

Introduction:

Following a costly failure in the LTK market, the chairman of Sara Lee/DE has charged the principal character in the case, Mr. Martin Munoz, with the responsibility for rolling out Sanex, a dermo-protective liquid soap product, throughout Europe. Martin, previously confident that executing the same strategy that he successfully implemented in launching the product in Spain was the best way to go, is having second thoughts. He is now flying back to Spain after his meeting with the chairman and presidents of the country subsidiaries during which he was officially appointed project coordinator for Sanex. But he cannot help thinking about the negative results of market research in the Netherlands, France, and Denmark, despite which the launching of Sanex in these markets was successful. What if these early market signals were premature or were a fluke? What should he do -- should he stick with his original plan to pursue a pan-European strategy based on what he did in Spain, or should he shift to a multi-domestic, or "localized" strategy as he rolls out Sanex in other European countries? And what corrective action should be taken in the UK market?

Case background and structure:

To familiarize students with the issues Mr. Munoz is confronting, we first provide a brief historical overview of Sara Lee/DE, which is a part of Sara Lee corporation, a U.S.-based multinational corporation. We discuss the intended corporate grand strategy of growth through acquisition, which is how Douwe Egberts was acquired by Sara Lee and subsequently named Sara Lee/DE, and how this corporate entity also pursued growth via acquisition. We provide a brief overview of Sara Lee/DE's structure, with special emphasis on the Household and Personal Care (HPC) division and the various products it offers. We next discuss the Spanish HPC market and reintroduce Mr. Martin Munoz, the senior manager of Cruz Verde-Legrain (CVL) in Spain, which was acquired by Sara Lee/DE in the early 1980s.

We review the key role that Mr. Munoz played in helping CVL diversify out of insecticides, its primary business, whose performance was subjected to seasonal fluctuations. Under his leadership, CVL sought to buffer itself from erratic annual performance by diversifying into other product areas where it might be able to draw from its expertise in developing products for "protection". We discuss the "fishing expedition" Mr. Munoz went on, utilizing the services of a marketing research firm to conduct focus group interviews of consumers to surface new product ideas. We reveal that almost by chance, the idea of a dermo-protector product that would provide features of cosmetic-type liquid soaps and pharmaceutical-type liquid soaps emerged from this process.

We then provide a summary analysis of liquid soap market segments and discuss how CVL created a functional new product that filled a "gap" in the market by combining characteristics of the pure medicinal liquid soap and the pure cosmetic liquid soap. The pure medicinal products were perceived to be for use only when people were sick (e.g., when they had a skin rash). On the other hand, the cosmetic products were generally perceived to take care of things only superficially and not in depth. That is, they were perceived more as creating a sense of fresh and dirt-free skin (through perfumes) than as a real dirt-cleansing soap. The product that CVL developed under the brand name Sanex nicely filled the void between these two extremes. It is more medicinal than a typical cosmetic soap and more cosmetic than a typical medicinal soap. Against all odds, Martin pushed to introduce Sanex, which was a name that connoted the Unique Selling Point of *healthy skin* and was previously registered by CVL for a discontinued product.

We then discuss product diffusion and extension efforts undertaken by Mr. Munoz and various country managers. Building from the success of the product in Spain, the chairman of Sara Lee/DE, CVL's parent, decided to launch Sanex in other European countries. We point out that Sara Lee/DE's policy has been to run its acquisitions as autonomous operations. The case highlights the experiences of its subsidiaries in the Netherlands, France, Denmark, and the UK. Market research results for the Netherlands, France, and Denmark were all negative for a variety of reasons. Though the country managers of these subsidiaries had the right to modify the product packaging, marketing strategies, and so forth, they elected to launch the product as it was, with minor changes in promotion. We reveal how Martin tried to overcome their initial concerns -- by thoughtfully sending them numerous product samples and encouraging them to have their wives, friends, and others use the product. He believed, and rightfully so, that those who used the product would respond favorably and ask for more!

We then discuss one of the difficult challenges that Martin could not overcome -- the extremely negative reactions of the manager of the UK subsidiary and his subsequent lack of co-operation. This person refused to adopt Martin's proposed strategies, changed the product name from Sanex to Sante, and launched the product using different marketing strategies. Though Sanex was successful on the continent, Sante was a costly failure in the UK. This poor performance result has prompted Sara Lee/DE's chairman to take swift and decisive action.

We finally come to the dilemma that Martin is struggling with. It is now August, 1993, and he is flying, back to Spain, having been charged by Sara Lee/DE's chairman and members of the board with the responsibility to roll out Sanex across Europe "as is" with the same product, packaging, positioning, and strategies he employed to achieve success in Spain. In reviewing what has transpired, Martin is having second thoughts about pursuing his "pan-European" strategy, and is wondering if he isn't acting like the fictitious Don Quixote, foolishly attacking windmills.

a. Immediate Issues, Basic Issues and Key Points or Highlights:

The **immediate** issue in this case pertains to whether or not Mr. Martin Munoz should press forward with a pan-European strategy for Sanex, based on the business, marketing, manufacturing and other supportive functional strategies he successfully formulated and implemented in launching the product in Spain. Does this imply that Sanex will be able to succeed "as is" in other European countries with absolutely no change in these various strategies? Or is Mr. Martin Munoz, the principal character in the case, foolishly attempting to "tilt windmills" like the fictitious Don Quixote by pushing for the implementation of a "pan-European" marketing strategy for Sanex? Students preparing this case are asked to analyze the factors that may enhance or impede the success of launching Sanex as a Euro brand based upon the successfully executed Spanish strategies, and to advise Mr. Martin Munoz, the principal character in the case as to what they think he should do.

This case also provides opportunities for students to examine and discuss several other **basic** and **key** Marketing and International Business issues. How much attention should be paid to marketing research results, especially when one is launching a new product concept that the consumer heretofore has not seen and/or may not understand? On what basis should one contest negative market research findings and "go with the gut" reaction? Third, under what circumstances and for what types of products is a pan-European marketing strategy likely to be appropriate and effective? What national "cultural" differences or circumstances might warrant modifications in strategy? That is, under what conditions should modifications be made -- and to what degree -- and in what areas (e.g., label, packaging, advertising and promotion) as products are rolled out in Europe? What are the consequent implications, therefore, for "value chain" management? One that comes to mind pertains to R&D, manufacturing, marketing and distribution in a centralized or decentralized manner. And politically, how can one "co-opt" those who may be potential adversaries and overcome negative reactions at the country-level when attempting to diffuse a product that was proven to be successful in another country. After all, many would argue that in general, there are distinctive differences in attitudes and preferences between "southern" Europeans and "northern" Europeans.

For advanced-level elective courses, there is the potential for the discussion of other contemporary basic and key issues such as types of business strategies, organizational design, corporate governance, and also, characteristics of the "learning organization". For example, regarding the latter, how can Sara Lee/DE capitalize on the learnings from the Sanex experience and diffuse them throughout the corporation? Such learnings include creating(, a new brand within a company that Historically grew by acquiring existing brands, and the processes involved in making that brand successful in one market after another, oftentimes against conventional thinking. Another leaning pertains to an issue discussed above: an objective assessment of the value of marketing research when introducing novel product concepts which require "educating" the consumer, and appropriately managing the tension between unconvincing market research with intuition or a "gut feel" for the success of a product. The issues discussed have implications for changes in Sara Lee/DE's "corporate culture", or the basic assumptions underlying- its shared values pertaining to introducing and launching new brands and brand extensions in the multinational European environment.

b. Level of Analysis and Potential Use of the Case:

Conceivably, this case could be used for a wide range of audiences. Although the intended audience is MBA or Executive MBA students, for whom we developed the case and to whom we have successfully taught the case, it could also be used in advanced undergraduate courses in marketing or international business or at another level in management education workshops or marketing seminars.

c. Suggested Student Assignment:

Below is a list of questions that can be assigned to students as they prepare for a case session:

1. Why was Sanex successful in Spain? Provide a thorough analysis of those factors that were critical to the launching of this product in the Spanish market.

2. Is the "Spanish theme" or set of strategies developed by Martin and his management team applicable to or generalizable to other countries?

3. With respect to marketing products within Europe, does it matter whether product or its strategies are localized or not?

4. Under what circumstances should one question the results of market research, especially when such research generates the same negative results in different markets?

d.   Suggested Additional Readings or References:

1. Bartlett, C. A., and Ghoshal, S. (*1992*). *Transnational management: Text, cases, and readings in cross-border management.* Homewood, IL USA: Richard D. Irwin, Inc.
2. Daniels, J.D., and Radebaugh, L.H. (1994). *International business: Environments and operations.* Wokingham England: Addison-Wesley Publishing Company.
3. Dawar, N., & Parker, P. (1994). Marketing universals: Consumers' use of brand name, price, physical appearance, and retailer reputation as signals of product quality. *Journal of Marketing, 58:* 81-95.
4. Garvin, D.A. (1993). Building a learning organization *Harvard Business Review,* 71, 4: 78-9 1.
5. Hoecklin, L. (1995). *Managing cultural differences: Strategies for competitive advantage.* Wokingham, England: Addison-Wesley Publishing Company.
6. Hofstede, G. (1980). Motivation, leadership, and organization: Do American theories apply abroad? *Organizational Dynamics* (Summer): 42-63.
7. Hofstede, G. (1 99 *1). Cultures and organizations.* London: McGraw-Hill.
8. Jain, S.C. (1989). Standardization of international marketing strategy: Some research hypotheses. Journal of Marketing, 53: 70-79.

9. Leeflang, P.S.H., and van Raaij, W.F. (1995). The changing consumer in the European Union: A "meta-analysis". *International Journal of Research in Marketing, 12:* 373-387.

10. Tse, D.K., Vertinsky, I, and Wehrung, D.A. (1988). Does culture matter? A cross-cultural study of executives' choice, decisiveness, and risk adjustment in international marketing. *Journal of Marketing, 52:* 81-95.

11. Usunier, J. C. (1 993). *International marketing. A cultural approach.* London: Prentice-Hall.

e.   Possible Discussion Questions:

In teaching this case in class, we have found that the four questions listed above that we suggest should be assigned to students as preparation for the case are quite effective in initiating discussion. However, depending on whether the case is taught in a core or an advanced elective course, and the type of course taught (e.g., Marketing or International Business), the instructor may want to consider the following additional discussion questions:

1. Discuss Sara Lee/DE's and Martin's motivation for developing Sanex as a Euro brand.

2. Much as been written about national and corporate cultures. What are the similarities and differences of European countries along cultural dimensions and consequently, what are the implications for pursuing a pan-European (global) strategy versus a "localized" marketing strategy?

3. By the end of the case, Martin Munoz is faced with a predicament. He believed that a global strategy (standardized product sold the same way everywhere) building from his experiences with Sanex in Spain was the only way to succeed, but now he is having doubts. Using Bartlett and Ghoshal's typology, compare and contrast the merits and downsides of the various strategic approaches to doing business across borders that they identify.

4. What are the key learnings that Sara Lee/DE should capture from the Sanex experience?

f. Potential Uses of the Case:

This case could be used to introduce and discuss concepts that generally are covered in a core introductory Marketing or International Business course. It addition, the immediate, basic, and key issues embedded in the case could serve as the basis for the discussion of advanced topics such as formulating/implementing business, marketing, and other functional strategies within MNCs operating in the European environment, the utility of market research when introducing new concepts in this environment, national vs. corporate cultures, and generating/transferring leamings. These topics might generally be covered in an elective course in Strategic Marketing or Managing the Transnational Corporation at the latter stages of a MBA program, or, perhaps, for management education seminars or workshops.

g. Analysis

In this section, we provide answers to the four questions that we proposed as the suggested student assignments and possible discussion questions.

1. Why was Sanex successful in Spain? Provide a through analysis of those factors that were critical to the launching of this product in the Spanish markets.

There are many reasons for Sanex's success in Spain. A "short list" of Key Success Factors that we generated includes the following:

- 'Fishing Expedition' for new product ideas launched under the direction of Martin Munoz
- Identification of the 'gap" between cosmetics-type liquid soaps and pharmaceutical-type liquid soaps derived from consumers through semistructured focus group interviews, and subsequent exploitation of this "gap" (see the two figures below)
- Good rational positioning of Sanex: *healthy skin!*
- Good planning (save in production and spend on marketing, advertising and promotion
- Choice of very creative advertising agency: Casadevall & Pedreno Appropriate marketing mix (pricing, advertisement copies, packaging) all geared toward accomplishing very specific marketing objectives
- 'They know what they are up to'
- Good brand name: Sanex has "health" connotations
- Go for it' and 'just do it' attitude of CVL's leader, Martin Munoz
- Quick realization of success
- Risky but quick extensions and consolidations (some extensions might have not worked, but nevertheless increased the exposure in a short time for the concept)
- Consistent strategy

2. Is the "Spanish theme" developed by Martin and his management team applicable to or generalizable to other countries?

As this case and other examples demonstrate, with a good product, it is possible *to organize the business activities around products* in place of the usual system of having, it *organized around countries*. There are two essential ingredients for making this happen. First, is the unequivocal and vociferous support of the top management for such products. Second, is the realization that it is not the *globalability of the product* that matters but the *globalability of the concept therein* that matters. Key points the instructor may want to bring up include:

- The need for such a product is physical and rational and not emotional
- EU countries are more or less the same with respect to the need for this product (sports lovers, travelers, etc.)
- Intelligent neglect of Marketing Research results and use of free sampling (the experience attributes of Sanex can only be gauged by putting the product to actual use, since it is especially at the top of the line)
- 'Ready to bear the cross' attitude of Martin
- 'No compromise on product positioning or on associated strategies'
- Recognition and strong support by SL/DE's chairman and the board
- 'No compromise on product positioning or on associated strategies'
- Good balance between controlling the autonomy of countries and product integrity ('no explicit authority, but tacit force by Martin')
- Dearth of in-house products at SL/DE

3. With respect to marketing products within Europe, does it matter whether a product or its strategies are localized or not?

1.) This is a hypothetical question for which a great diversity in responses is expected. Among the additional readings we suggested above, there are six in particular which will help the students gain a solid understanding of the pros and cons regarding this issue. The instructor may want to consider assigning one or more of these readings, depending on the level of the audience and whether the course is a core or advanced elective.

1. Dawar, N., & Parker, P. (1994). Marketing universals: Consumers' use of brand name, price, physical appearance, and retailer reputation as signals of product quality. *Journal of Marketing, 58:* 81-95.
2. Tse, D.K., Vertinsky, 1, and Wehrung, D.A. (1988). Does culture matter? A cross-cultural study of executives' choice, decisiveness, and risk adjustment in international marketing. *Journal of Marketing, 52:* 81-95.
3. Jain, S.C. (1989). Standardization of international marketing strategy: Some research hypotheses. Journal of Marketing, 53: 70-79.
4. Leeflang, P.S.H., and van Raaij, W.F. (1995). The changing consumer in the European Union: A "meta-analysis". *International Journal of Research in Marketing, 12:* 3 73 -3 87.
5. Hofstede, G. (1980). Motivation, leadership, and organization: Do American theories apply abroad? *Organizational Dynamics* (Summer): 42-63.
6. Hofstede, G. (199 1). *Cultures and organizations.* London: McGraw-1-Ell.

Readings # 1, 2 and 4 in general support that localization is not necessary; reading # 3 splits the decisions into what-to-localize and what-not-to-localize. Reading # 5 is the pioneering paper that tries to measure the cultural differences across countries, and reading, # 6, which is a book by the same author, provides a panoramic view of research findings on this topic. The final conclusion is: Nobody knows for sure. A good deal of time can be spent discussing the facts brought out by Martin in the last page of the case regarding increasing homogeneity among the people in the developed countries and the influence of EU.

2.)   In our opinion, most of the studies try to measure and talk about the differences between geographically distanced markets (such as the USA and Europe, or Europe vs. the Gulf countries, or Europe/USA vs. Asian countries such as China, India or Japan, etc.), and not about the economically homogeneous European countries this case is dealing with. Hence, this question may not be relevant at all for this case.

Having said that, one should bear in mind that the LTK never considers itself a part of the European continent. Its people distance themselves as Anglo-Saxons from those who reside on the European continent.

3.)   It depends on the product. A product with a very clear message and positioning need not be localized; such products basically appeal to the fundamental buying rationale of consumers, "do I get good value for my money." (Other examples: private labels which are making inroads in almost all of the developed countries).

4.)   Maybe it matters. Had the Dutch or Danish fine-tuned their marketing strategies to suit their respective consumers, Sanex might have done even better than what it is doing now. The fact it did not do well with such 'localizing' changes in the UK may be due to something else.

5.)   Sometimes though it looks anti-cultural for a specific country -- just do not localize, and there is a good chance that the product will get accepted and may become a part of the culture. After all, culture is a product of such forceful changes that had happened in the past. However, you need to support the product through strong Share Of Voice, very catchy advertising copies, strong distributor support, consistently good quality and reasonable pricing. Any halfhearted attempt would result in market failures.

4.   **Under what circumstances should one question the results of market research, especially when such research generates the same negative results in different markets?**

The effectiveness of traditional market research studies is not reliable in the case of break-through products such as Sanex. But the question is: Who knows for sure whether a newly developed product is a break-through or a flop? In the absence of help from any theoretical and/or scientific framework, the good old 'gut feel' plays a major role here. This is a limitation to market research studies, and in fact, a limitation to any scientific analysis of consumers' purchasing behavior.

Other examples:

- Pringle potato chips from P & G (failure in spite of excellent support in terms of advertising, distribution, etc.),

- *New Coke* (a spectacular failure in spite of the most expensive and very renowned market research and test marketing),

- *Sony Walkman* (turned out to be a superb success story in spite of all the warnings from market research studies),

- *Baking Soda tooth-paste* from Arm & Hammer (captured 7% market share in the first year in the US tooth-paste market- P & G mocked it in the initial years, but later introduced its own baking soda version),

- *Ultra detergent* (a success story from P & G which exceeded its own expectations and which caught Unilever, its strongest competitor, completely by surprise),

- The *video-telephone* (remains a failure from the 1960s in spite of three introductions and the many advancements that have been made),

- The *calculator* (market research showed that engineers would not like it; eventually it grew out of its use with students and others),

- *Multimedia* (is the Internet all hype or not?)

- *Post-it note pads* (became a great success in spite of poor predictions by everybody including the company 3M except the inventor).

The students should be stimulated to come up with their own analogies (perhaps they could be asked a week before the discussion to do some library research and come up with some interesting and relevant information on other such products which will add more richness to the discussion).

The instructor could then draw the students to many conclusions:

1. Consumer behavior is, after all, *random* (because they themselves could not predict what they would do given a situation ... as is true for many of us), especially with respect to adopting something *totally new*.

2. It may be that there is something missing in all these traditional market research studies, and there should be another way of eliciting correct responses (e.g., opinions, attitudes, preferences) from consumers regarding totally new products.

3. It may be that every case has its own explanation for its unexpected success or failure and the results therefore may not be generalizable.

4. It may be that some new products ride at margin, and it all depends on whether a sound marketing support could pull it off.

5. Organizational flexibility exhibited by SL/DE in the crucial moment as a key success factor (KSF)

6. Commitment from Top management as a KSF

7. What. is New and who knows before hand?

8. **Subtle points** students should be able to get out of the case:

   Taking the Bath & Shower gel as introduced in Spain:

   · In the hands of the Dutch: it was split into one for body and one for hair. The Dutch maintain that healthy skin does not imply healthy scalp.

   · In the hands of the French: Got split into one for leisurely bath and one for quick shower.

Responses to Possible Discussion Questions:

1. What are possible reasons for Sara Lee/DE's and Martin's motivation for developing Sanex as a Euro brand.

There are many potential answers to this question. Contemporary texts on International Business (e.g., Bartlett & Ghoshal, Daniels & Radebaugh, Usunier) identify many driving forces for international expansion. These include expanding sales, market-seeking behavior, acquiring resources, securing key supplies, accessing low-cost factors, and diversifying sources of sales and supplies. Of course, other motivational factors are possible, including the egos of senior managers fueled by the desire to crush the competition! Undergirding much of this is Sara Lee's desire to shift from near total dependence on growth through acquisitions to "inventing" brands in-house. And Sanex is among the first of their successes, on which, of course, they would like to capitalize.

2.   **Much as been written about national and corporate cultures. What are the similarities and differences of European countries along cultural dimensions and consequently, what are the implications for pursuing a pan-European (global) strategy versus a "localized" marketing strategy?**

Students should be directed to the article and book authored by Hofstede for a cogent response to this question. Based on data he gathered in a large multinational corporation, Hofstede has identified four "cultural dimensions", some of which he maps out in the earlier (1980) article. The instructor could facilitate a discussion on the differences between European countries along the dimensions of Power Distance, Uncertainty Avoidance, Individualism, and Masculinity and what are the consequent implications for how to "do business" across borders in Europe. The question remains are these differences meaningful when it comes to a product like Sanex? Not likely, for reasons we mention elsewhere in this teaching note.

3.   **By the end of the case, Martin Munoz is faced with a predicament. He believed that a global strategy (standardized product. sold the same way everywhere) building from his experiences with Sanex in Spain was the only way to succeed, but now he is having doubts. Using Bartlett and Ghoshal's typology, compare and contrast the merits and downsides of the various strategic approaches to doing business across borders that they identify.**

Building from their seminal research which is elaborated in their earlier (1989) book, *Managing Across Borders: The Transnational Solution,* Bartlett and Ghosiah identify four evolving "mentalities" with respect to conducting international business (pp. 11-14). The first is the *International mentality* whereby MNC managers tend to think of the company's foreign operations as "outposts" which are intended to support the parent company in various ways. The second is the *Multinational mentality* whereby managers begin to recognize and emphasize the differences among national markets and operating environments. Here, companies tend to be more flexible with respect to foreign operations by modifying their products, strategies, and management practices country by country. The third is the *Global mentality,* where managers assume that national tastes and preferences are more similar than different, or where the differences can be minimized, if not erased by providing consumers with standardized products with adequate cost and quality advantages over comparable domestic products. The fourth mentality is that which Bartlett and Ghoshal describe as the *Transnational mentality*, whereby companies endeavor to become more responsive to local needs while retaining their global efficiency. Bartlett and Ghoshal point out that in such companies, key activities and resources are neither centralized in the parent company nor decentralized so that each subsidiary can carry out its own tasks in its own local markets. In their words:

In contrast to the global model, the Transnational mentality recognizes the importance of flexible and responsive country-level operations -- hence the return of national into the terminology. And compared to the multinational approach, it provides for linking and coordinating those operations to retain competitive effectiveness and economic efficiency -as indicated by the prefix trans. The resulting need for intensive organization-wide co-ordination and shared decision-making implies that this is a much more sophisticated and subtle approach to MNC management.

Applying this typology, International Business students could be asked to trace the history of Sara Lee Corporation with respect to its international operations, identify where it is today (Multinational mentality whereby wholly-owned subsidiaries are largely autonomous), and building from the material above, they could be asked to discuss the advantages and disadvantages of this orientation.

4. What are the key learnings that Sara Lee/DE should capture from the Sanex experience?

There are many key learnings that can be derived from the SL/DE experience. Many of these are in the form of the key success factors for launching Sanex in Spain, which have been listed above. The basic identification of a "gap" in the market that could be filled by CVL which was seeking, to diversify into other products outside of the insecticides business is a learning. How to building a brand within a large MNC which heretofore grew through acquiring existing brands is a learning. Using novel advertising and promotion to educate consumers and create awareness is a learning, and most certainly, overcoming the liabilities of consistently negative marketing research in several countries is a learning. The instructor can add another perspective here, which is not evident in the case. Martin Munoz had a close relationship with Sara Lee/DE's chairman, and did not hesitate to use that relationship to his advantage when it came to seeking resources for Sanex, developing product extensions, and promoting the product in other European countries.

For advanced-level courses or electives, students could be assigned the recent article by David Garvin in *Harvard Business Review,* which is referenced in the Suggested Readings above. Garvin identifies several characteristics of the "learning organization" which he defines as *an organization skilled at creating, acquiring, and transferring knowledge, and at modifying its behavior to reflect new knowledge and insights.* (HBS, Vol. 74., No. 4, p. 80). In his view, learning organizations are characterized by;

1. systematic problem solving
2. experimentation
3. learning from past experience
4. learning from others
5. transferring knowledge

Students could be asked to evaluate the extent to which Sara Lee/DE has become a learning organization according to these criteria. Indications are the SL/DE is making progress, but has a considerable distance to travel yet. Where has the company made progress, considering the material in the case?

Example 1: The Danish manager was able to overrule marketing research because he 'had learned' from his previous experience in a somewhat similar situation. Marketing research results were negative, but there was a good "gut feel" for the toothpaste product.

Example 2: For the Dutch, it was a sheer coincidence that the Marketing Director happened to have formerly worked for CVL. He put his foot down to overrule the market research results. Think about the situation -what would have happened if the Marketing director were someone else? Sanex might not have been introduced in the Dutch market; Sara Lee/DE's chairman would have had less faith in it; Martin could not have forced his thinking on the French.

h.   Suggested Teaching Approach:

There are a variety of innovative approaches an instructor can employ in discussing this case in class. Regardless, we strongly recommend that the case be prepared the evening prior to class, and if teams are used, that each team be assigned the question of what would they do if they were Martin Munoz? Would they pursue a pan-European (or "global") strategy, a multi-domestic strategy, or another strategic course of action and why? Other questions could be assigned, depending on the course objectives (for example, stand-alone case for a core or elective Marketing course or a core International Business course, or an advanced elective in Transnational Management) and number of teams. At a bare minimum, we recommend that students reconsider the questions they originally assigned for homework.

In addition, we have utilized the aforementioned team approach with another variation, which is to form new teams comprised of individuals who have been assigned various questions for class discussion, whether those identified above, or the additional questions which appear below. These questions could be assigned to teams who are then instructed to go to "break-out" rooms to discuss them among themselves prior to reporting back to a plenary session.

Additional Questions for Consideration for Team Break-Outs:

1.   As a well-established company that has grown through acquisition, is it worthwhile to pioneer in new brand development or not -- what are the pros and cons?

2.   What is the best course of action--To do market research or to keep 'trying' new products in the market? What factors or conditions warrant consideration as you answer this question (e.g., type of product and the type of organization, cultural values)

3.   Can a good positioning overrule all other factors ?

Part of the answer should be: 'it need not' as long as fine tuning the other factors does not spoil the positioning. For example, the French, who had favored a better packaging as a result of their market research, should not be given credit .. and it was not ... If given credit, the fancier packaging might have spoiled the ability to effectively communicate the health message which was central to the Sanex concept.

4. At what point was Martin very likely to give up the fight with respect to his pan-European strategy?

   Think about this in the context of organizational dis-efficiency: There exists a priest (an organization) between God (the product) and the people (the consumers). People may like to approach God, but the Priest sometimes may be in a position not to allow it, and he won't. And, it needs a product champion in those instances to throw out the priest.

5. Is Sara Lee/DE a learning organization? (Material discussed above could referenced in responses to this question). What can be done to enhance its ability to capitalize on its learnings from this experience?

6. Should Sara Lee/DE "Europeanize" Sanex or not? Argue for or against each point.

7. Comment on Sara Lee/DE's governance structure. In your opinion, what are the advantages or disadvantages of full autonomy/ full freedom versus partial or full centralization? Or are there any other options to consider from a different perspective.

Another method we have used is role-playing whereby class members are assigned the role of Mr. Martin Munoz, Presidents of Sara Lee/DE country subsidiaries, and the chairman of Sara Lee/DE, and perhaps as "external consultants".

An interesting variation of the role-playing method is assigning the case to teams as a "consulting assignment." There are two ways we have tried this. One is having teams serve as external consultants to Martin, who has commissioned them to provide them with an objective "check" on his thinking after he has returned to Spain by evaluating all meaningful alternatives and offering specific recommendations.

A second way we have tried is instructing one team to re-visit the meeting that Martin has just had with the chairman of Sara Lee/DE and country presidents. The team is asked to simulate the role of "external consultants" and present its analysis to the instructor, who is simulating the role of chairman of Sara Lee/DE, and to members of the class, who would be simulating the role of country presidents, including Mr. Munoz. In this manner, the chairman is asking for an external "objective opinion" regarding the situation.

Regardless of either of the two ways we have ran this simulation, we require the following-. The presenting team and teams assigned the case as a write-up would be asked to prepare the case according to the following outline:

1 . a situation analysis--the marketing consulting team's view of the key problems in the case [SUBJECT HEADING: Situation Analysis],

2. a listing of alternatives available with associated costs and benefits (may also be summarized in the Appendix) [SUBJECT HEADING: -Alternative Courses of Managerial Action],

3. The consulting team's specific recommendations or proposed actions, and the rationale/justification for taking the action--both <u>content</u>, or details of <u>what</u> they are recommending, and <u>process</u>, or <u>how</u> their recommendations should be implemented, [SUBJECT HEADING: <u>Recommendations and Implementation Plan</u>] , and

4. a sketch of how the organization might measure whether the proposed action has had the intended impact, should the chairman decide to implement the consulting team's recommendations. [SUBJECT HEADING: <u>Effectiveness Measures</u>].

Then the consulting team would be allowed forty-five minutes to present the case, with appropriate time allotted for questions and answers. They are evaluated by the instructor as well as their classmates with respect to content issues (identification of correct problems in the case, incorporation of course material in their analysis, etc.), organization/style (was the presentation well-organized and professionally delivered, were visual aids clear and did they add value to the presentation, etc.) and "thinking on their feet" which is a measure of how thorough the team conducted its analysis and thought of the critical issues from a variety of perspectives, and how well they justified/defended their recommendations considering other courses of managerial action that could be pursued. The instructor collects the class evaluations and compares them to his or her own, and later prepares written feedback for the presenting consulting team to which is appended the class evaluations. But once Q&A is over, then there is a plenary discussion of the case, with other members of the class asked to share their analysis, alternatives they considered, recommendations, implementation plan, and effectiveness measures.

What we suggest that may help facilitate the analysis of the case in class regardless of teaching approach used is utilization of a matrix on the whiteboard with the case issues on one axis and the fundamental issues noted above as the second axis.

i. Audio-Visual Support:

As of the date of submission of this case, we are awaiting a compilation of television advertisements from Sara Lee/DE. This compilation includes the three highly-regarded award-winning- segments regarding Sanex which were discussed in the case. The videos are extremely helpful in enabling students to visualize the Sanex concept, as the advertisements nicely fulfill the four Advertising and Promotion objectives outlined in the case. Once we have received this material and final approval from Sara Lee/DE, we will investigate ways to make it available to instructors. It is possible that some instructors may already have video segments that they have made when these ads were aired on television.

j. Proposed Session Plans:

The case could be handled in a 2 to 3 hour class session, the design of which is contingent upon method employed. A generic plan is as follows:

0 - 30 minutes	Overview of discussion, introduction of SL/DE, Martin Munoz, the fast-changing BPC market, and his role and ideas leading to the successful launching of Sanex in Spain.
30 - 60 minutes	Discussion of driving and constraining forces regarding globalizing a brand.
60 - 120 minutes	Formation of teams to evaluate the merits and deficiencies of attempting to pursue developing a Euro-brand ("globalisation") versus a country-specific "localization" strategy for the Sanex product.
120 - 170 minutes	Plenary discussion to consider the alternatives Martin Munoz can consider, given his current predicament.
170 - 180 minutes	De-briefing--review of the course of action Martin chose and the results to date. Conclusions, wrap-up.

If the consulting team approach is used, the suggested 2.5 hour format is as follows:

0 - 45 minutes	Team presentation.
45 - 75 minutes	Direct questioning of the consulting teams analysis and recommendations.
75 - 85 minutes	Class written evaluations, brief hallway feedback from instructor to consulting team
85 - 150 minutes or beyond	Other consulting teams asked to compare/contrast their analysis and recommendations to those of the presenting team. Plenary discussion facilitated by the instructor.

k. Postscript: The Status of Sanex as of 1995:

- Roger was dismissed, not necessarily because of the Sanex issue.
- The new President in the UK, in consultation with Martin, analyzed the causes for the failure. He agreed with Martin on the necessity of maintaining the integrity of the product in all aspects of the strategy. Hence Sanex was relaunched in March 1995 with the Spanish theme (i.e., same name Sanex, same advertising message as was done in Spain, etc.).
- Within 8 months, Sanex captured about 4.7% of market share in the UK, as per the Nielsen reports. By the BPC standard, capturing 4.7% within 8 months is a tremendous success. In short, Martin was right !
- The earlier positive signals in the Danish and the French markets did prove to be correct, very correct indeed! In Denmark, Sanex achieved a market share which is greater than that in its home base Spain.
- Sanex was not launched in Germany, since SL/DE had equivalent products which were similar.
- In Greece, it did succeed- however a different name was adopted because the name Sanex was already in use for some other product.
  Martin was moved (promoted) to Sara Lee/DE headquarters.
- However, in spite of the success of Sanex and Martin's uncompromising stand on maintaining the integrity of the concept, Martin didn't stay long in his new position at Sara Lee/DE headquarters. He moved back to Spain. It is interesting to note that this reverse-move somewhat coincided with the change in top management at Sara Lee/DE. In fact, the CEO who had been backing Martin and Sanex all long, left the company. Hence, it is not c clear whether it is Martin's lack of managerial capability (in controlling the different countries) or the change in top management that resulted in Martin's return to Spain. However, as of year-end 1995, Martin was still affiliated with SL/DE.
- Sanex was tried in a few Asian markets and the USA, where it did not succeed as expected. Reasons offered by the company are many: "the USA market has to be educated a lot in terms of the need for 'healthy' gels," and, "the Asian markets are not that developed (matured) to feel the 'gap' between the medical and the cosmetic extremes" etc. We understand that relaunches are in the offing.

Teaching Notes:

Club Med: The Party is Over

Synopsis

Club Mediterranee, a corporation in the all-inclusive resort market, has found that customers' preferences have changed. As stated in the case, vacationers are no longer willing to spend large amounts of money for vacations which include many activities that the vacationers are not using as much as they had in the past. This change in preference poses a problem for the company because Club Med's competition has not been able to customize travel packages for each customer at prices that vacationers feel more comfortable with.

Students are encouraged to come up with alternative solutions to the following discussion questions. One suggested solution is provided.

Discussion Questions:

1. Given Club Med's current problems, do you feel the company could have avoided its pricing scheme problems through different expansion plans?

No. A major part of Club Med's product is location. The only solution to the location problem would be to close down a resort when negative external factors occur. This would be out of the question because there may be instances where, for example, the Mexican peso may just take time to appreciate and the Mexican government may be able to help contribute in maintaining the Club Med facilities. In other words, these problems may not necessarily be permanent problems. The key is in distinguishing which problems are temporary and which problems are permanent.

Club Med's decision to be a global company helps build its strong brand equity. It if was to shut down locations too often, it could damage its image as a whole. If Club Med can decrease the rate at which it expands, it can redirect its energy into satisfying the customer and increase its sales.

2. Why is Club Med unable to offer competitive prices?

Club Med cannot afford to cut back on its prices because of some external factors. This includes the loss of money that it was counting on from the Mexican government and the money Club Med needs to maintain its Tahitian resorts until the negative publicity dies down. With all of these additional expenditures, lowering the price to the customer may not leave Club Med with substantial profits.

3. Given Club Med's current problems, do you think that "the Club" will be able to survive by keeping its current pricing strategy or doe you think a new strategy should be implemented?

Club Med will be able to maintain its current sales for the time being. However, if it wants to boost sales, the company will have to take action and rethink its present strategies. Club Med should analyze carefully what it is that the customer wants, because in essence this is what the company's products/services are aimed at.

Club Med should target its packages to the individuals just like its competitors are doing. The loss in income for "the Club" may be offset by gains in other locations. Additionally, it may be able to redirect the amount of help that each resort has if it finds that the clients for that specific week are not interested in and did not sigh up for specific activities. This is not to say that Club Med has to redesign completely its way of doing things, but maybe a slight strategic restructuring is in order.

Club Med can have certain activities that are grouped together that the individual can sign up for, prior to coming to the resort. A vacationer can pick any activity in that group to participate in during that week. If a client wishes to gain access to an activity in which he/she did not prepay for, he/she can sign up during his/her stay for an additional charge. To help monitor each client during his/her stay, an identification badge could be assigned to him/her that he/she can wear around his/her neck. Each badge would have codes that allow him/her to gain access to the activities. This would enable the customer to make the Club Med experience an affordable on.

4. How can Club Med continue to differentiate itself in order to sustain its competitive advantage against its competitors who seem to be imitating its service concepts?

Club Med was one of the first companies to enter the all-inclusive resort market. It has been able to create a global brand image unlike that of its competitors. Its larger competitors are located only in certain regions while Club Med has locations worldwide. Club Med has a strong presence in the all inclusive resort market as a result of this. Although Club Med has this advantage, it finds itself experiencing flat sales. What in essence needs to be done is that "the Club" should restructure its definition of "all-inclusive". This should not, however, be to the point where clients feel that the Club Med image has been negatively affected. Instead of terming "all-inclusive" as paying one large sum for everything that the resort has to offer and finding that the customer is unhappy because they are paying for services that they are not using, the company may define it slightly differently. "All-inclusive" may encompass all the services within a package that the client has chosen prior to arriving at the resort. In this way, it can keep up with the dynamic changes in the industry, keep the customer happy, and still maintain high levels of profitability.

Teaching Notes:

Ford Motor Company and Die Development

Ever since the competitive juggernaut of Japanese companies was attributed chiefly to their famed just-in-time operations based on their *Keiretsu* relationships, many U.S. companies have adopted this closely knit supply relationship. In the late 1980s, Ford Motor Company began to rearrange its supplier system to a keiretsu structure patterned after the Toyota system of managing component procurement and product development.

What is keiretsu?

In Japan, a keiretsu not only exists across industries (e.g., the Mitsui Group), but also exists within non-financial industries (e.g., the Toyota Group in the automobile industry). The keiretsu arrangement within a non-financial industry is often called *kigyo keiretsu* (enterprise group). Kigyo keiretsu consists of a non-financial principal company and a set of affiliated companies tied by ownership, management interlockings, and/or credit policy to the principal company. In a way, kigyo keiretsu constitutes a vertically, yet loosely, integrated manufacturing network.

Toyota Motor (Toyota hereafter) has a vertically integrated group of affiliates. The Toyota Group consists of Toyota as the principal company, ten or so first-tier suppliers, and a myriad of second- and third-tier suppliers beneath them. What is rarely discussed about the Toyota Group is the way supplier affiliates were formed. Although Toyota itself is an integrated automobile company, performing all automobile development and assembly, there is a point in every aspect of productive activity beyond which diseconomies of scale set in. Toyota spun off various activities when diseconomies set in. As a result, Toyota formed a consortium of specialized affiliates. Toyota's spin-off policy has solved the following two major problems.

1. Functional specialization is made possible for technical as well as cost efficiency.
2. Such resource bottlenecks as limited plant size and labor are reduced as spun-off affiliates have been relocated in Japan and abroad.

This spin-off based integration contrasts sharply with the one observed at Ford that are based mostly on takeovers and strategic alliances. It is no wonder Toyota's affiliates are intimately linked to the principal company through interlockings of personnel and mutual trust as employees at the principal company have been spun off and assigned to affiliates.

In addition, loyalty of affiliates to the principal company is further reinforced by the just-in-time manufacturing system. The just-in-time manufacturing system often extends beyond a group of closely related firms that used to be part of the principal company through socialization and compensation according to length of service and other nonperformance criteria. Toyota's supply chain system is said to *represent functional relationships which help reduce transactional uncertainty and opportunism among members, thus assuring mutual trust and efficiency.*

Keiretsu-ization at Ford

This case focused on what is considered to be the third most crucial technology in automobile manufacturing business after engines and transmissions, and explores how Ford's product development ability has been affected. Although this upstream aspect of product development is rarely discussed in a marketing course, it has significant and immediate implications to marketers who need to be concerned about time-to-market and product quality as well as customer satisfaction.

Today, Ford's supply chain looks very much like Toyota's; some pundits even concluded that Ford's keiretsu is more Japanese than Toyota's. In this case, Ford's close working relationship with Ogihara is highlighted. Ogihara is a Japanese company and one of the largest and most technologically advanced die manufacturers in the world. Dies are essentially molds that are used to stamp various parts of car panels. They are initially designed and manufactured with the aid of computers out of the clay model and subsequently fine-tuned by trained technicians. Die development capability directly affects the automaker's design capability upstream. And the quality of dies determines the fits and finish of the car downstream.

Ford relies on Ogihara for the two high ends of its line, namely Lincoln and Jaguar models, making dies for its mass production models such as Taurus and Escort. Incidentally, Toyota's die procurement contrasts sharply with Ford's. Toyota develops dies for its high-end Lexus models and contracts out die development and manufacturing to its first-tier suppliers for mass production cars such as Corolla and Tercel. This operational difference despite the two companies' similar keiretsu structures should be noted.

Ford has benefited immensely from Ogihara's die-making expertise in terms of quality improvement and shortened product development cycle. Bill Cunningham, vice president of marketing operations, is extremely delighted with Ford's relationship with Ogihara as customer inputs have been incorporated swiftly into new auto designs and the fits and finish of Ford cars has improved dramatically. On the other hand, Bob May, vice president of corporate procurement, is somewhat cautious about the company's long-term dependency on Ogihara and potential loss of in-house die development expertise and subsequently in-house automobile design capability, which he fears could reduce one of the company's crucial core competencies over time.

While there is no clear cut answer to the issues described in the case, it illustrates a gap in the views on sources of competitive advantage between marketers and those in charge of product development and corporate procurement. In the short- to intermediate-run, Ford could enjoy lower cost and faster product development cycle, but in the long run, as Bob May fears, Ford would become increasingly dependent on Ogihara for new product design and product development. Could Ford expect to be working in tandem with Ogihara the way Toyota is with its first-tier suppliers? The instructor may share with students how Toyota and Ford keiretsu developed over time (explained earlier).

Teaching Notes:

PHARMA SWEDE

Synopsis

This case is based on an European Pharmaceutical company that wishes to remain anonymous, hereafter, referred to as Pharma Swede. With the approach of "1992" and the completion of Europe's single market, the management of Pharma Swede is faced with a serious pricing dilemma in Italy where the company's main product-Gastiros-is priced far lower than in other European markets. In concert with the free movement of goods and services anticipated in the near future, Gastiros could become subject to a large parallel trade from Italy to higher priced countries in Europe. The management of Pharma Swede must choose one of four options to avert substantial losses.

Teaching Objectives

Pharma Swede can be used for a variety of objectives:

1. To examine developments reshaping the European pharmaceutical industry;

2. To demonstrate different pricing strategies (e.g. skimming vs. penetration) in international/global marketing;

3. To provide an understanding of the growing influence of governments on one important aspect of marketing practice, pricing;

4. To highlight the potential impact of post-1992 developments on parallel trade in Europe;

5. To exercise decision-making in a complex setting of several stakeholders with conflicting objectives.

Depending on the instructor's own plan, one or more of the above objectives may be emphasized in the assignment and class discussion.

Discussion Questions

1. What are the relevant trends in Pharma Swede's environment which may affect its future performance?

2. How was Gastiros priced in Europe? What explains the wide price range across the continent?

3. In retrospect, was the Italian management's decision on the price of Gastiros a wise one? Why or why not?

4. What might be the impact of "1992" on Gastric in Europe? What are the threats and opportunities?

5. Evaluate the options Pharma Swede management is considering to deal with Gastirup's pricing discrepencies in Europe. For each option, who are the stakeholders and how might they react or be affected?

6. As Bjorn Larsson, what would you recommend t the company president? Why?

Analysis

1. What are the relevant trends in Pharma Swede's environment which may affect its future performance?

The instructor may want to begin by discussing some of characteristics of the pharmaceutical industry in general, followed by a review of the industry in Europe. Thus, one might ask the participants to look at the main classes of drugs-ethical and over-the-counter-and the types of pharmaceutical companies-generic and research-based. Research-based pharmaceutical companies, for example, must invest substantial sums in basic and applied research--upwards of 15% of sales--to maintain a stream of new and innovative products. On the other hand, by waiting for drugs from the research-based companies to go off patent, generic drug companies are spared the costs of research, registration and initial marketing. Nonetheless, generic players may not project the same corporate image as companies which conduct their own research. Nor do they have the same profit margins enjoyed by the research firms, as generic drugs tend to be considered as a commodity and be mainly price-oriented.

As a research-based drug company, Pharma Swede will be affected by the following trends in Europe:

Aging Population

Since ulcers occur most frequently among middle-aged individuals, especially men, sales of ulcer remedies could expect to benefit from Europe's aging population with a growing segment in this bracket. The impact of aging on other Pharma Swede products is less clear.

Rising R&D and Marketing Costs

Developing new products is becoming an expensive undertaking in the pharmaceutical industry. Pharma Swede's options are: to remain a research-led company which will continue to spend significant sums on research; or, to find other ways of competing such as through generics or by licensing as with Gastirup's OROS. Being a medium-sized firm in the industry makes the former option increasingly difficult for Pharma Swede.

One might argue then, that if Pharma Swede marketed only generic drugs, albeit in conjunction with the OROS and other unique drug delivery system, its R&D costs could be significantly less. Furthermore, one might add that, because governments are placing an increased emphasis on cost
containment, it could be an excellent time for Pharma Swede to distance itself from research-based drugs and become more of a generic player. But, to compete in the, generic category, a
company needs low-cost production, which may be difficult for a medium-sized player in the industry. As a result, through a growing sector, generics alone do not necessarily offer Pharma Swede a profitable business.

Generics

Once ethical drugs come off patent, price becomes the predominate purchase criterion. However, one may emphasize, if a novel method of *administration* were developed for a generic drug, a premium price could still be possible. Gastirup is an excellent example; although ranitdine is a generic drug, the oral osmotic therapeutic system is a novel method of administration, allowing Pharma Swede a healthy gross margin on its sales.

Governments

Given the case focus on pricing, the instructor may want to discuss in detail how governments have come to play such a significant role in the pricing of pharmaceuticals. In brief, because European governments have paid, on average, two-thirds of their countries' health care costs, they have consequently been in a strong position to influence pharmaceutical manufacturers' pricing practices. The instructor may want to discuss some of the criteria used by government health agencies to judge a drug's treatment value and, likewise, its final price. Among these criteria are doctors' services, hospitalization, days of illness, patient compliance, and quality of life.

Doctors' Services: Reduced patient contact translates into lower health care costs borne by the government.

Hospitalization: Where hospitals are a leading indicator in health care costs, even a small change in the number of hospital admissions and/or length of stay has a considerable impact on costs.

Days of Illness: A reduction in the number of absences from work translates into a gain in economic activity. Studies indicate that one of the benefits of OROS is a decrease in the number of days off work.

Patient Compliance: Using the OROS system allows more simplified therapeutic regimes, fewer dosage errors, and encourages the patient to take medication as instructed--important steps to improving patient compliance.

Quality of Life: Several studies were specially designed to examine the effects of OROS on the subjective well-being of patients, their objective life circumstances, and their treatment preference. It is one factor that may be emphasized by drug companies in their discussion with health authorities.

2. How was Gastirup priced in Europe? What explains the wide price range?

As a backdrop to answering this question, the instructor may want to ask the class to discuss why there are such big price differences to begin with in the Gastiros/Gastirup product across Europe. Historically, pricing within the EEC was left to country management when dealing with local government authorities. In turn, these authorities acted independently of other local authorities in Europe. These factors combined have resulted in a 148% difference between the top and bottom prices for Gastirup.

Here, the teacher may ask how the price differentials could be justified. Possible answers (besides "whatever price one can get away with") include the high cost of new product development, which might not be possible if all public authorities insisted on the lowest price. Another justification is that different competitive situations in different markets require different prices. Also, one may add that prices also reflect a number of other factors including the influence of local authorities, local management objectives and their respective bargaining strategies.

Some might see Gastirup's premium price as too high when compared with those of traditional ulcer preparations. Having reviewed the criteria for judging a drug's treatment value and, given Gastirup's competitive advantages over other ranitidine-containing remedies, the class should appreciate some of the arguments for its premium price. These advantages include, potential for a reduction in doctors' services, reduced hospitalization, fewer days of illness, improved patient compliance, and an improved quality of life.

3. In retrospect, was the Italian management's decision on the low price of Gastiros a wise one?

Students might argue, that the Italian management of Pharrna Swede gave up its pricing negotiations with Italian officials too easily. In fact, one could point out, the drug's early success had led management to believe that the government was planning to admit Gastiros to the positive list. Why then did the management not wait longer, or press for a higher price, when Italian health care authorities continued to receive requests from patients and doctors? Had Pharrna Swede Italy waited, and been granted reimbursement at the price of $31/pack, its potential profits would have been significantly more than at the final price of $24/pack.

Some could also argue that, if Pharma Swede in Stockholm had helped its Italian subsidiary with the types of cost-benefit analyses performed at the headquarters, the Italian branch might have been better prepared to convince the Italian authorities that Gastiros was worth a premium. On the other hand, the Italian management may have believed they could earn higher profits with a penetration pricing at the lower price for greater volumes. If this were so, then the market share and sales level thus far tend to support Italian management's strategy. (In 1983, at $3.70 per tablet, sales reached $6 million, or 2% of the market, By 1989, at a price of $2.40 per tablet, sales reached $27 million, or 7% of the market.)

4. What might be the impact of "1992" on Gastirup in Europe?

In answering the financial aspects of this question, students should be able to use the case data to reconstruct Gastirup's cost/price structure (summarized in TN Exhibits 1 and 2).

It should be noted that for every tablet sold at current prices in Italy, a total of $1.00 is contributed to corporate profitability, $0.30 of it in Italy (TN Exhibit 1) and $0.70 of it in Sweden (TN Exhibit 2). These figures are *unit contributions* and should not be confused with profits (determined after all fixed costs are deducted).

To see the potential impact of price changes in the EEC, one may examine three possible, *though not necessarily likely*, scenarios:

1. Because of parallel trade or otherwise, all retail prices in the EEC drop to the Italian level of $2.40 per tablet--the lowest price on the continent.

2. Because of management actions or otherwise, Gastiros' retail prices across the EEC are harmonized at around $4.29 per tablet--the current average price in the EEC.

3. Through effective management action or other factors, all retail prices in the EEC are raised to the level in Denmark, or $5.96 per tablet (the highest in Europe).

Though scenarios 1 and 3 are not necessarily likely to happen, by examining their impact on corporate contribution, the students can appreciate the high stakes involved. The financial impact of these scenarios is shown in TN Exhibit 3. Beyond these possible scenarios, opening up trade in pharmaceuticals poses several risks to Pharma Swede. Among these are:

◆ **Problems with local authorities in high-priced countries.** How might Pharma Swede, look if became widely known that consumers and/or governments in high-priced countries such as Germany and Denmark were subsidizing low-priced countries such as Italy? Or, worse, what if the high-priced countries felt they were being "robbed blind" by the Swedish pharmaceutical company?

◆ **Uncontrolled parallel trade as a result of price differences.** Will Pharma Swede lower its prices in high-priced countries to reduce parallel importing? Will it withdraw products from low-priced countries to remove the temptation? If so, how does an ethical drug company counter claims of unethical behavior by withholding product from the Italian consumer?

◆ **Potential for confusion with doctors and channels of distribution as a result of parallel imports in high priced countries.**

5. Evaluate the options Pharma Swede management is considering to deal with Gastirup's pricing discrepancies in Europe. For each option, who are the stakeholders and how might they react or be affected?

The options being considered by Pharma Swede management are:

   1. Remove Gastirup from Italy.

   2. Remove Gastirup from the Italian reimbursement scheme.

   3. Appeal to the European Commission.

   4. Wait and see.

An overview of possible reactions among Pharma Swede's many stakeholders is given in TN Exhibit 4. The teacher may encourage the students to come up with other ways of dealing with the pricing problem beyond the four alternatives being considered by the management.

6. As Bjorn Larsson, what would you recommend to the company president? Why?

In deciding what to recommend, students must consider Larsson's position as advisor to the company president; his objective is to protect the corporate-wide interests of Gastirup. The stakes at the corporate level, and thus for Larsson, should be evident after reviewing the numbers in Question 4. Larsson could easily be less sympathetic to country management, although he will need to take local interests into consideration. He will probably recommend removing Gastirup from the reimbursement scheme; if not, he might favor appealing to the European Commission. But, it would be unlikely for Larssson to suggest that Pharma Swede remove Gastirup from Italy altogether. The potential losses for this action and the and the likely negative reaction of the Italian subsidiary would be, the reasons why Larsson would not recommend the "removal" option.

Epilogue

As of late 1990, the company management was seriously considering appealing to the European Commission to consider Italian price regulations as barriers to free trade.

Exhibit 1

Gastirup Cost/ Price Structure
$ per Tablet

		Actual
	Retail price in Italy	2.40
Less:	Pharmacy's margin	0.72
	Wholesale price	1.68
Less:	Wholesale margin (based on ex-factory price and retail margin)	0.18
	Ex-factory	1.50
Less:	Transfer price (paid to parent)	1.00
Less:	Other variable costs (Italy)	0.20
	Unit contribution (Italy)	0.30

PHARMA SWEDE Teaching Note

Exhibit 2

Gastirup Contribution Margin (Parent)
per tablet

	Transfer price	1.00
Less.	Variable costs including licensing fees	0.30
	Unit contribution (parent)	0.70
Add:	Unit contribution (Italy)	0.30
	Unit contribution (corporate)	1.00

Exhibit 3

Gastirup Pricing Scenarios
per tablet

		Scenario 1 (Actual Italy) Denmark)	Scenario 2 (1) EEC Average	Scenario 3 (Actual
	Retail Price	2.40	4.29	5.96
Less:	Trade Margins (2)	0.90	1.60	2.24
	Ex-factory price	1.50	2.69	3.72
Less:	Variable Costs (3)			
	Packaging, etc.	0.20	0.20	0.20
	Manufacturing & Licensing (parent)	0.30	0.30	0.30
	Corporate contribution	1.00	2.19	3.22
	Level of contribution relative to current situation in Europe	46%	100%	147%

1 Scenario 2 corresponds to the current (1990) average EEC price of $4.29 per tablet (see case
Exhibit 9).

2 Assumes same % as in Italy or 37.5% of retail price.

3 Assumes same variable cost as in the case for Italy.

EXHIBIT 4
POSSIBLE REACTIONS TO PHARMA SWEDE OPTIONS

Stakeholder	Remove Gastirup from Italy	Remove from Reimbursement Scheme	Appeal to European Commision	Wait and See
Management in Sweden	• Loss in sales/profits • Counter to policy of marketing company products in all European countries	• Loss in sales/profits • May want to repeat in other low-priced countries	• Opportunity to settle once and for all • Lengthy process • No previous experience	• No guarantees • Potential long term profit erosion across Europe
Management in Italy	• Loss in sales/profits • Resentment of HQ decision	• Loss in sales/profits • Resentment of HQ decision	• Potential harm to rapport with Italian officials • Possibility of higher prices	• Potential for increased prices/profits • Gastiros remains in Italy
Management in high-priced countries	• Relieved of threat of parallel imports • Continued sales/profits • Happy and silent	• Relieved of threat of parallel imports • Continued sales/profits	• Outcome may support or undermine high prices • Parallel imports unresolved	• Possible loss of sales/profits to parallel trade
Italian authorities	• Unhappy to lose a drug • Possible retaliation	• Likely to favor shifting cost to patients • Possible backfire as in Denmark	• Possible retaliation	• EEC pressure on Italy
EEC regulators	• Possibly uninvolved		• Opportunity to assert growing influence	• Possible increase in Italian prices and subsidiary profits
Medical profession	• Italy: loss of company goodwill • Potential for backlash in other products	• Italy: loss of company goodwill • Potential for backlash in other products	• Possibly uninvolved	• Possibly uninvolved/status quo
Patients	• Possible consumer backlash • Damage to company image	• Possible consumer backlash • Damage to company image	• Possibly uninvolved	

293

Teaching Notes:
Anheuser-Busch International, Inc.

Anheuser-Busch, the world's largest brewer, has tremendous opportunities for growth in the international market. Of particular interest in the markets in Latin America, ranging from Mexico all the way to Brazil. Major countries in Latin America, such as Mexico, Brazil, Argentina, and Chile, are experiencing a rising income level. Although per capita beer consumption in Latin American countries is much lower than it is in the United States, beer consumption is growing as their income grows. Latin American markets seem to be a natural market expansion path for Anheuser-Busch International (ABI).

In the United States, Budweiser is a moderately priced beer marketed to a mass market. However, Budweiser is relatively new in Latin America and most rural areas do not sell Budweiser. Budweiser has been positioned as a premium beer and sold in a niche market in Latin America where prices are two to three times higher than local beers. The delivered cost of exporting to Latin American markets has limited volume potential, and ABI did not have control over pricing by local wholesalers and retailers. ABI is contemplating on targeting Latin America's younger population that is the fastest growing and is the largest segment of the market. A younger population is often less price sensitive and more concerned with image and how others perceive them.

Strategic alliance issues: ABI recently began exploring Mexico and other Latin American markets through strategic alliances with major local breweries. ABI formed production, distribution, and overall marketing alliances with them. Local production will allow ABI brands to compete with local beers sold in each country. In Mexico, ABI invested in Grupo Modelo, the country's largest brewer. The agreement calls for an exchange program for executives in key areas (such as accounting, marketing, and operations) between the two companies. The agreement also gives Modelo distribution rights to Budweiser within Mexico. In Brazil, ABI invested in a new Antarctica subsidiary, which will allow both companies to build distribution. ABI also signed a licensing agreement with Antarctica to allow the latter to brew Budweiser in Brazil. The latter agreement is a joint venture which is 51% owned and controlled by ABI.

It would be interesting if the instructor asks students to do some background check on Grupo Modelo in Mexico and Antarctica in Brazil and see whether they would be appropriate partners for ABI to work with. In fact, while Modelo is a very aggressive and profitable brewer in Mexico, Antarctica seems to lag behind Kaiser and other brewers in Brazil in terms of product innovativeness and marketing skills. Antarctica is better known for its Antarctica brand guarana drink (non-alcoholic beverage just like Coca Cola).

Exporting vs. local production: Other agreements in place for ABI include distribution and marketing rights within brewers in Costa Rica, Honduras, Guatemala, and El Salvador. ABI has to consider not only the exchange rates which could make American products more expensive, but also the current economic conditions that exist in Mexico today, and what it means for consumers in Mexico, i.e., loss of purchasing power, higher inflation, and unemployment. There is a wide spread concern that the Mexican peso depreciation might be repeated in other Latin American countries.

Growth in beer consumption is leveling off in the United States while costs are climbing. This is one reason why ABI should continue exploiting Latin American markets despite the recent depreciation of the peso against the U.S. dollar. In the short run, ABI faces unfavorable conditions and may need to accept a lower profit margin to stay at its current level of exports to Mexico. By producing locally, ABI can take advantage of lower labor cost and shorten the channels of distribution. Also, reduction of transportation cost, insurance, tariffs, and other expenses paid by the importer from across the border would contribute to keeping prices under control.

Product positioning and advertising: ABI executives believe that a mass market appeal using American imagery, television, and sponsorships of sporting events would attract the younger population and would lead to an increase in sales and market share. With the combined efforts of producing locally in Mexico and Brazil, with a marketing campaign focusing on the younger population, ABI would expect to see an increase in sales, lower costs, and lower prices for Budweiser.

The instructor may raise an issue of taste differences between Budweiser beers and local beers in Mexico and Brazil. While Mexican beers taste somewhat like an American beer, beers in other parts of Latin America seem to be more European with stronger tastes. A major hurdle for ABI to overcome is a sentiment shared by many Latin Americans that Budweiser beers taste as if they were watered down; they argue why they have to pay more for less.

This raises a major positioning issue to be discussed in class. ABI was originally going to use advertising aimed at Hispanics living in the United States. However, now the company believes in localizing, rather than standardizing, the message. It will allow local advertising agencies to select the appropriate message and conduct their own media planning. The product is basically standardized, with the same basic product being marketed to all countries.

Further discussion: In Mexico, for example, it might be a good opportunity for ABI to exercise its option to purchase the remaining interest in Modelo giving ABI a 35% minority interest there. If both companies agree, the agreement for Modelo could be written to set aside a portion of its production capacity to brew Budweiser locally. In return for the licensing agreement, ABI might have to lower its profit margin and give Modelo a percentage of net sales for brewing ABI brand beers since Budweiser would be competing locally with Corona which Modelo produces. A percentage of net sales would give Modelo an incentive to produce and sell Budweiser in Mexico.

This licensing agreement to produce Budweiser at the Modelo Plant would allow ABI to maintain its market share by reducing the price of Budweiser in Mexico. In 1994, the peso was exchanging for 3.36 pesos for one U.S. dollar. One year later, the peso was exchanging for 6.79 pesos for one U.S. dollar, about twofold devaluation of the peso. Ask the students if such a strategy is appropriate. Why and why not?

Teaching Notes:

Toys "R" Us in Japan

Toys "R" Us is a 1000-store chain of large scale toy outlets which dominates toy retailing in the United States, and since 1986, has expanded overseas with essentially the same marketing formula (later to be adapted locally). In 1991, Toys "R" Us entered Japan as a joint venture with McDonald's Japan owning 20% of the Toys "R" Japan.

One of Toys "R" Us' major attribute is its selection in toys, and bikes, and games, and everything else. Toys "R" Us currently has 23% toy market share of a $13.8 billion US retail market, $3.174 million; which has been consistently growing. As of January 1994, they were operating 581 stores in the United States, and 234 stores internationally with consolidated net sales of nearly $8 billion as of the year ending in 1993.

Toys "R" Us's success is driven by its low expense structure, which consists of having a self-service atmosphere. The process of purchasing a toy is highly involved, and in the past has required little product knowledge. Most of the information needed by buyers is printed on the packaging, for example age. Toys "R" Us uses this to their advantage; their store structure is based on selection, which is the best in the industry. They pride themselves on having all the latest in toys and plenty of them.

Part of Toys "R" Us's competitive advantage is EDLP (every day low pricing). They can afford to have this kind of pricing strategy due to their procurement process. Toys "R" Us purchases direct from the manufacturer, therefore cutting out the middleman and their added costs. They also buy in bulk and save on unit costs. Toys "R" Us's goal is to have the best selection, a plentiful supply, and EDLP.

Over the last several years, Toys "R" Us has grown at a tremendous rate of 30% plus per year and their cost structure has consistently been reduced due to the reinvestment in technology that increases its productivity. Some of their investment includes automated state-of-the-art distribution facilities and automated systems.

Toys "R" Us is a good case to study because it brings out many different aspects of international marketing. It addresses the issues of Triad World View, since competition around the world is so intense, a company must introduce itself in different markets at a faster pace than ever before. American companies often try to introduce themselves in Europe and Japan before going to other nations. This is exactly how Toys "R" Us went about its expansion.

Toys "R" Us strategy in Japan was initially no different from its strategy in many other countries. However, this case also serves to point out that Japan may not necessarily be considered a homogeneous and tightly knit country that many companies assume it is. Particularly when it comes to retailing, each local community in Japan may handle its business differently especially when dealing with foreign companies like Toys "R" Us.

The following issues may be discussed in class.

Strengths and Weaknesses of Toys "R" Us's Strategy

Toys "R" Us had several factors in its favor. To begin with, its size was something in the toy market to be reckoned with. Toys "R" Us had established itself firmly in the Unite States and had significant capital accumulated before it ventured overseas. Its size gave it an economy of scale advantage. It could afford to price aggressively because it purchased directly from manufacturers in the millions, therefore Toys "R" Us enjoys large manufacturer discounts. Its size also made it an attractive shopping experience because Toys "R" Us offered varieties currently unmatched.

Its biggest weakness was that it went overseas with the idea to standardize the entire toy retail industry. This might be considered tunnel vision. It did not account for the barriers that are inevitable when establishing a business in a foreign country. Japan is a perfect example of the legal barriers that Toys "R" Us encountered. In this country, Toys "R" Us is still going through various legal hurdles and local oppositions to the specifics of its operations such as open hours and days. Although Japan's Large-Scale Retail Store Law has been amended making it easier for large retailers to open stores in Japan, Toys "R" Us's strategy assumed that it could open nearly 100 stores by 2001. It proved to be a difficult task to accomplish.

Simple geographical limitations were also barriers. Toys "R" Us needs an average of 45,000 sq. feet in space in order to set up a store. This kind of size was not easily available nor easily accessible to customers in Japan. Promotional costs went up drastically to encourage customers to spend up to two hours to visit Toys "R" stores. One more recent weakness that Toys "R" Us faces is leveling margins and it is still dealing with the 1991-1996 recession in Japan. Toys "R" Us has realized that customers are demanding more specialization and customer service. This could potentially force Toys "R" Us to alter its traditional way of doing business. This point should be explored in class.

Adapting Toys "R" Us's Marketing Strategies

The initial intent was to enter Japan with the same "formula" as it had been operating with in the United States. This was standardization. The company assumed that what worked in the United States would work anywhere. This was soon proven wrong. Its first ventures in Europe offered the company a taste of the many barriers it would encounter along the way during expansion. Toys "R" Us faced geographical limitations when trying to find warehouse space. In other countries it faced governmental limitations when it tried to set up the company, retaining 100% ownership. Many countries did not condone this and forced Toys "R" Us to alter its company structure. Such was the case in Japan.

Toys "R" Us began to realize that being big in Japan did not necessarily mean being better. It had to adapt its business to the local needs of its clientele. This has led Toys "R" Us to train its sales force to make them more knowledgeable about the products, thus better service. Currently, various stores are propping up offering different specialized toys such as educational ones. This is a new kind of market Toys "R" Us is not willing to lose out on.

Wal-Mart Operations in Brazil

The following case, Wal-Mart Operations in Brazil, is available to students on the text web page at http://www.wiley.com/college/kotabe.

The text of the entire case and accompanying instructor's notes are included in this section of the Instructor's Manual.

Professor Masaaki Kotabe of The University of Texas at Austin Graduate School of Business and Kleber G. de Godoy and Moacir Salzstein of Fundação Getúlio Vargas, São Paulo, Brazil, *prepared this case as the basis for class discussion rather than to illustrate either effective or ineffective management of a situation described, 1997.*
Copyright @ 1997 by Masaaki Kotabe

Introduction

In September 1994, Brazil was experiencing a new thrust in its economy. After several years of hyperinflation, the "Real Plan," implemented in March, 1994, an economic stabilization program that indexed the Brazilian currency to the U.S. dollar, began to reduce inflation to reasonable levels. In February 1994, a monthly inflation rate was 40%, whereas by September it was a relatively low 3%. Lower inflation rates would help improve the purchasing power, particularly of the lower socioeconomic segment of the population.

The optimistic scenario encouraged many foreign companies to make new investments in Brazil. If Brazil is the leading economy in Latin America, with a population of more than 150 million, why not invest there, now that a better business horizon lies ahead in this continental country? Wal-Mart Stores, the world leader in retailing, announced on May 9, 1994 that it had decided to invest heavily in Brazil, through a partnership with Lojas Americanas, Brazil's leading department store chain.

Wal-Mart Stores would own 60% of Wal-Mart do Brasil, whereas Lojas Americanas would retain the remaining 40%. The North-American "giant" was known to provoke a market revolution in every country it decided to enter. Wal-Mart not only announced the decision to enter the market with Supercenters (stores with 20,000 m^2 of area and more than 50,000 different items) and Sam's Club stores (a buyers' club, founded in 1976 in the U.S.).

Brazilian competitors had good reasons to be concerned. Wal-Mart was known also to be a leading company for its low operational costs and logistics. Another concern was that the partnership with Lojas Americanas could leverage Wal-Mart businesses in Brazil. Lojas Americanas has been owned by Banco Garantia, an aggressive and very profitable investment bank, since 1989. Only after Banco Garantia assumed Lojas Americanas' management did it achieve the number one position in department store sales. Banco Garantia also has the control of Companhia Cervejaria Brahma, the leading brewer in Brazil and the fifth largest in the world.

Wal-Mart Operations

Sam Walton opened a small store in Newport, Arkansas, in 1945, as a franchisee of variety stores owned by Ben Franklin. Six years later, Walton decided to open his own stores with the name Walton's Five and Dime, referring in the name to the coins that could have value to the customers.

In 1962 the first Wal-Mart Discount Store was opened, but Sam Walton was already known as a very sensitive and clever retailing businessman. Wal-Mart expanded very rapidly. By 1970, when Walton decided to go public in order to accelerate the expansion, as many as 30 Wal-Mart stores had been spread out in Arkansas, Missouri, and Oklahoma.

The fast and consistent Wal-Mart expansion, which enabled the company to achieve the number one position in retailing by surpassing Sears, Roebuck, made his founder and main shareholder, Sam Walton, a legend in the industry. He was the ultimate practitioner of what is now called "Management By Walking Around" (MBWA), namely, to go to every store, observe the customers and talk to them to find out what they desired and what kind of complaint they might have.

Sam Walton's most famous paradigms, present in his biography "Made in America" are:

- Be different
- Be close to the customer; be the first one to notice the changes in consumer habits
- Simplicity reduces costs
- Reinvest all the profits
- If you want your staff to take care of the customers, take care of your staff first

By the end of 1995, there were 2,799 Wal-Mart units around the world, with 2,562 located in the U.S., 134 in Canada, 83 in Mexico, 11 in Puerto Rico, 5 in Brazil and 4 in Argentina.

Wal-Mart operates with five different divisions: Wal-Mart Stores, Wal-Mart Supercenters, Sam's Club, McLane's Company and Wal-Mart International.

Wal-Mart Stores is the division accounting for 55% of total company revenues (US$93.6 billion in 1995, and US$100 billion in 1996). Wal-Mart Supercenters generates 10% of total company revenues and is the fastest growing division. In the U.S., there are three different "Supercenters" : Wal-Mart Supercenters, Hypermart USAs and Bud's Warehouse Outlets. "Supercenters" are stores with more than 10,000 m^2 of area and a minimum of 40,000 items. Sam's Club is the division responsible for 25% of revenues. The first Sam's Club - a "buyers' club", namely, a store where the consumer pays an annual fee to have access - was opened in 1976. By the end of 1995, there were already more than 400 Sam's Clubs in the U.S. McLane's Company is Wal-Mart's distribution company. Wal-Mart acquired this company, a leading distribution company, in 1990. In 1995, McLane's represented 6% of Wal-Mart total revenues. McLane's has 14 distribution centers in the U.S. and caters not only to Wal-Mart needs but also to other 25,000 retailing stores in the U.S. Wal-Mart International, the fifth division, will be described in details later.

The closest Wal-Mart competitor in the U.S. in terms of revenues is K-Mart with total sales of US$43 billion in 1995. Wal-Mart has special characteristics and qualities that enabled the company to be a leading retailer giant: namely, the company

- operates with low operational costs, due to efficient logistics, an advanced information technology systems and scale economies.

- has a high level of employee involvement; the company has been sharing profits with its employees since 1974.

- has low prices; Wal-Mart famous slogan, "Everyday Low Prices", is accepted by the customer as absolutely true.

- has high bargaining power vis-à-vis its suppliers, which permits the above mentioned low price policy

- is spread out throughout the U.S.; it is present in all 50 states. Most of the stores are located in small and medium towns, which has been one of the major corporate strategies.

In the second half of the 1980's, Wal-Mart began its international expansion. The company expected that all its strengths and retailing knowledge could leverage operations abroad as well as the efficient logistics and communication systems. Also, the company considered that with a prospective of market globalization, the brand, "Wal-Mart," could be a competitive advantage in many countries where it would operate. The company also decided that the entry strategy in each country should be through a partnership with local companies.

Mexico was the first country in which Wal-Mart initiated its international expansion. The first store was opened in 1991. The local partner was Cifra, a Mexican retailing leader. Despite a tremendous initial hype, Wal-Mart has now 25% less sales than predicted five years ago.

It is undeniable that Wal-Mart has had some difficulties in adapting to and understanding Mexican culture and consumer habits. For example, Mexican consumers prefer to buy Mexican food and other goods rather than American products. Wal-Mart insisted on prioritizing imported goods from the U.S. for a long time. Another problem in Mexico is related with the Mexican habit of buying food in small stores rather than in supermarkets. Wal-Mart has been trying to change this habit without much success.

In Canada, Wal-Mart preferred to acquire a local chain - Woolco - instead of having a local partner. Coincidence or not, Canada is the most successful Wal-Mart operation abroad. Nevertheless, out of the 134 stores in Canada, 122 were originally Woolco stores.

Entry in Argentina was also different from the original strategy: Wal-Mart entered alone in 1994, with four stores, two Supercenters and two Sam's Club, all of them in the Buenos Aires area. Similar to the Brazilian situation (to be described later), competitors in Argentina reacted very quickly, opening new stores and neutralizing Wal-Mart's promotions and discounts. As a result, Wal-Mart had two years in sequence with losses in Argentina.

The greatest failure happened in Hong Kong, where Wal-Mart entered with three home appliance stores in partnership with local retailing companies. The poor results caused the decision to leave the Hong Kong market by closing those three stores.

Since 1991, when the first store was opened in Mexico, Wal-Mart International Division has kept losing money, which is, to say the least, concerning. Its total 1995 sales reached US$4 billion.

Although the results do not justify an aggressive expansion plan, Wal-Mart still intends to expand globally. In 1996, the first store was opened in China. One more time, Wal-Mart decided to enter alone in China instead of having a local partner.

So far, the greatest challenge is to tackle the following issue: Is it possible to transform a typical American company in a global economy without changing its corporate culture? According to David Glass, Wal-Mart president, everything that is done in Arkansas or Kansas can also be done in Brazil or China.

Brazil Entry Decision

In 1982, one event took place that would link Wal-Mart to the Brazilian market. Sam Walton answered a letter in which a Brazilian company - Grupo Garantia - was prospecting a possible partner for its retail business in the domestic market. This letter represented the beginning of a long business relationship. But it was only twelve years later, more precisely in September, 1994, that the official communiqué was announced: Wal-Mart had decided and was ready to enter the Brazilian market. The entry mode would be in association with Lojas

Americanas, which is controlled by Grupo Garantia. Wal-Mart would own 60% of the partnership and Lojas Americanas the remainder 40%.

Grupo Garantia has a very aggressive strategy in all businesses in which it participates and has made Lojas Americanas the leading department store in Brazil.

The bombastic announcement, which made Brazilian supermarket operators and wholesalers "shudder," included an initial investment of US$ 120 million, to construct and initiate an operation of 5 stores - 3 Sam's Clubs and 2 Supercenters - in a record short time. The first stores would be located in Brazil's largest city - São Paulo and also its outskirts.

Supermarket and Wholesale Industry in Brazil

The supermarket sector in Brazil accounted, in 1995, for about 6.6% of GNP, with consolidated sales of US$ 43.7 billion. The ranking, which considers only companies with a minimum of 24 checkout lanes, includes 360 different organizations, operating a total of 3,743 stores.

The five largest supermarket chains, in terms of sales volume, are Carrefour (US$ 4.68 billion), Pão-de-Açúcar (US$ 3.17 billion), Casas Sendas (US$ 1.32 billion), Bompreço (US$ 1.18 billion) and Paes Mendonça (US$ 876 million). The general profile of Wal-Mart's five main Brazilian competitors is presented in **Exhibit 1**.

Supermarkets in Brazil

- Consolidated sales in 1996: US$ 43.7 billion
- 6.6% of Brasil GNP
- 3,473 stores (biggest 360 companies)
- Ranking: 1- Carrefour   US$ 4.68 billion
            2- Pão-de-Açúcar   US$ 3.17
            3- Casas Sendas   US$ 1.32
            4- Bompreço   US$ 1.18
            5- Paes Mendonça   US$ 876 million

- Exhibit 1 -

Contrary to a trend in countries like Germany, where only 5 companies dominate 70% of the market, or France, with 65%, the trend in Brazil shows a declining concentration. The 20 largest companies had generated 64% of the total sales of the 300 largest companies in 1987. This percentage fell to 57.6% in 1995.

During the last five years since 1990 (see **Exhibit 2**), sales have grown by 25.3% for the largest 300 companies, while the 20 largest companies grew only by 15%. The explanation is simple: facing problems such as high inflation, economic plans and changing government rules, the largest companies initiated a restructuring process that compromised their performance during this period. But the adjustment was worthwhile, because they exhibited a consistent sales growth rate over the five year period.

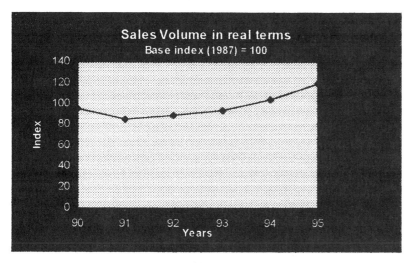

- Exhibit 2 -

Another indicator confirming the favorable results of restructuring was that they were able to increase sales even with a significantly reduced number of stores. Besides restructuring, another important factor contributing to a favorable performance was the consumers' increased purchasing power as a result of reduced inflation under the "Real Plan."

The economy of supermarket and wholesaler sector in Brazil is concentrated in the Southeast region (see **Exhibit 3a** and **3b**), the richest and most developed part of the country, with São Paulo State being located in this region.

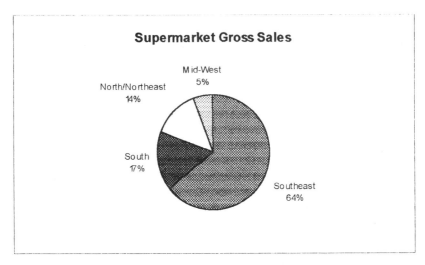

- Exhibit 3a -

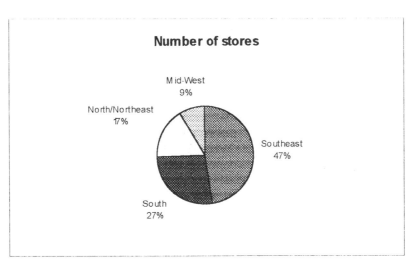

- Exhibit 3b -

The main competitor for Wal-Mart in Brazil is Carrefour, a famous French supermarket chain, which entered the Brazilian market in 1974. Today, the chain is responsible for the operation of 39 stores spread over the country, and is fully adapted to Brazilian culture and consumption habits, therefore not being perceived by customers as a foreign company. As a matter of fact, Carrefour is known as the lowest price retailer by people of all social classes. With a decentralized management style, it encourages initiative and creativity among store managers and employees. Using an effective advertising campaign, with constant presence in most important domestic media (TV, newspapers, radio and outdoors), the company made its annual campaign known as *Carrefour Birthday Month*.

Makro, a Dutch company, in a partnership with a local group, is the leading wholesale outlet with total sales of around US$ 800 million. Established in Brazil in 1972, it has more than 25 stores spread across several states, including the Northeast region with the highest consumer purchasing power in the nation. Makro has registered about 1.3 million customers, mainly owners of small businesses, constituting about 80% of the total clientele base. The other 20% of its customer base consists of individual customers. To become a Makro customer, people need to apply for association, but do not have to pay any fee. One of its main strategy components is to sell products from third parties under its own brand. These products have no associated promotional expenses and can be sold at competitive prices.

A recent research study conducted by CBPA (a Brazilian market research company) shows that price continues to be a major determinant of the consumer's preference of a store chain. But the same survey shows other interesting results: a significant part of consumers surveyed mentioned quality of products as being more important than price, and certain features such as services and store cleanliness as equally important.

Strategy for Brazil

The intention of Wal-Mart was to achieve the number one retailer position in the Brazilian retail market in a very short period of time. In order to achieve this ambitious goal, Bentonville headquarters planned a logistics and communication infrastructure capable of supporting no less than 80 stores in the Brazilian market.

To rapidly achieve the number one position, a fast expansion strategy was planned by executives of Wal-Mart International. The store location strategy was developed, targeting at the most populous areas with high consumer purchasing power. The São Paulo State satisfied those characteristics. The headquarters' intention was to export its expertise and practices in the form of an extensive set of operational manuals that proved successful in the U.S., including product assortment and internal space utilization as well as its product mix.

Market Entry

Wal-Mart began its operation in Brazil in an absolutely fantastic way. The five stores were opened in a few months and, through a very aggressive pricing strategy, attracted thousands of enthusiastic consumers ready to empty the shelves.

Inside the stores, consumers found a large variety of products that has never been offered by any other retailer in Brazil. Especially in the Supercenters, with a mix of 50,000 different products, from domestic apparels to golf club sets, including a complete lline of food products.

Another attraction was employees' disposition to help consumers, trying to do everything to get every customer who entered the stores to come back home with their purchase needs fully satisfied. It is important to mention that executives of Brazilian operation had successfully recruited a well motivated team, which facilitated the training activities and organizational learning.

To locate near its main competitors, Wal-Mart Supercenter and Sam's Club are both located in Osasco, a suburb of São Paulo, in front of a Carrefour unit across the street and near two Pão-de-Açúcar stores. After all, Osasco Supercenter broke the sales record in Wal-Mart's history, selling US$ 1 million a day, twice the sales volume of Extra, another major competitor, located not far from there.

During its initial periods of operation in the Brazilian market, Wal-Mart had captured a very favorable image from consumers and, subsequently, had painted a dark picture for its competitors' future.

Wal-Mart executives certainly would wish the golden times could last forever. But reality has been a bit different. They were not prepared for such a sensational success in a short period: the crowded stores' positive signal soon showed its negative side --- long lines at the check-out lanes.

Customers impressed by low prices and extensive product lines, besides special offers, who had to travel several miles to reach the stores, were in for a surprise. In case the products that customers were looking for had been sold out a few moments earlier, there was no provision as to when a new stock would arrive in the store. A badly planned product turnover? The fact is that they were facing an average stockout rate of 40%, while its stockout rate in the U.S. stores is no higher than 5%. Maybe this stockout rate has occurred due to various problems with suppliers, whom Wal-Mart executives expected to be capable of working in a just-in-time delivery environment.

But the worst situation had yet to occur --- seemingly false advertising of products, which were not available in the store shelves as had been announced. It made customers angry.

Managers' behavior was another source of headache. Since performance was measured based on sales volume, many products had their prices set below cost by managers as a way to increase sales and obtain a high performance evaluation, independently of the net loss this practice would bring to the bottom line results.

Every customer appreciates low prices. However, when the prices were lowered much too deeply, important suppliers such as Nestlé, Gradiente (electronics) and Brastemp (refrigerators and air-conditioners) were not satisfied at all to see their products being sold in Wal-Mart stores at prices below their production costs, and launched a dumping accusation against the American company.

Trying to bring its Brazilian operation back on track, Wal-Mart headquarters resorted to a hasty solution for a management turnaround with some local executives dismissed and head managers switched between Brazilian and Argentine units, and more recently, even store managers switched between two units in Brazil. Wal-Mart advertising in Brazil also has been inconsistent (See **Exhibit 4**). Wal-Mart chose a local advertising agency - Norton, currently the 13th ranked Brazilian advertising agency in the industry. However, Norton professionals, according to a former executive for Wal-Mart, had very little autonomy to determine the appropriate advertising as well as the right media. Wal-Mart invests not more than 2% of the revenues in advertising in Brazil.

Insert Exhibit 4 here

The customers, once very happy and satisfied to cross São Paulo traffic lights despite a constant traffic jam to shop in one of the Wal-Mart stores, are now becoming almost a rare view along both Supercenters and Sam's Club empty corridors. The vast parking lots in front of the stores, most of the time with just a dozen or so cars, are a worrisome picture.

Exhibit 4

310

In the mean time, Wal-Mart's competitors began to work harder to recover their lost time. Not only did they answer Wal-Mart's inroads with many promotions and lower prices to recover their lost customer base, but they also accelerated their own expansion. Just to mention one case, Carrefour opened as many as five stores in 1996.

On the other hand, Wal-Mart planned expansion, considering 8 new stores to be opened during 1997, was significantly modified. Now, only 10 Supercenters are planned to be constructed in the next two years. It is a much slower and conservative pace than initially announced. Despite the initial success, Wal-Mart International has consistently posted a net cumulative loss, considering Supercenter and Sam's Club together, of around US$ 32 million by 1996.

****

For further research, consult the following web pages:

Wal-MartHome Page **(http://www.wal-mart.com/home/home.shtm)**
Wal-Mart International Divivsion **(http://www.wal-mart.com/stores/interdiv.shtm)**
MERCOSUR and Beyond **(http://lanic.utexas.edu/cswht.kotabe.html)**

Case Notes

for

Wal-Mart Operations in Brazil

Wal-Mart, a very successful American mass merchandiser, offers a classic example of foreign entry that has gone awry. São Paulo is the largest city in South America and the São Paulo state's GDP is larger than that of the whole country of Mexico. It is a geographically concentrated and promises to offer a potentially lucrative market.

The problems that Wal-Mart has experienced in Brazil may be grouped into four categories: 1) cultural differences, 2) management, 3) advertising and 4) logistics and distribution. The following background information adds to the case discussion.

Cultural Differences: No company that decided to operate globally could ignore socio-cultural differences across countries. Wal-Mart had all the opportunities to deal with cultural issues without many problems. When Lojas Americanas was chosen to be the local partner, many people thought that the Brazilian department store leader could help Wal-Mart not only with logistics and marketing, but also as an advisor and consultant on Brazilian consumer habits.

It is important to mention that Wal-Mart had already had socio-cultural problems in Mexico. With this experience behind, Wal-Mart should not have caused the same mistakes in Brazil. First of all, Wal-Mart chose wrong store locations, especially for its "Supercenters". Brazilian usually go to a supermarket once a month to make so-called "monthly purchase" instead of once a week as in the United States. Osasco and Santo André, the two towns where Wal-Mart installed the first two Supercenters, are located in the outskirts of São Paulo. Both are medium-size towns, with 600,000 inhabitants each, the first west of São Paulo and the second south of São Paulo. The distance between these two cities and São Paulo downtown is almost the same - approximately 10 miles.

The average *paulistano* (São Paulo resident) would drive 10 miles to go shopping. Because of São Paulo's unbelievably bad traffic jam, it would take an easy two hours one way by car. At first, the very low prices at Wal-Mart really motivated this "trip". This motivation simply disappeared after a few weeks. Osasco and Santo André population would never justify the installation of Supercenters as the first stores in Brazil. Should Wal-Mart have intended to "test" the Brazilian market, Curitiba, for example, could have been a better test market (Curitiba, Campinas and Belo Horizonte are known as preferred Brazilian test markets). This was clearly a decision made without the influence and/or opinion from executives of Lojas Americanas who knew the traffic situation.

Another error was Wal-Mart's entry via Supercenters and Sam's Club. The idea of a "buyers club" has been successful in the United States, although some analysts consider that this model is clearly declining and may not last more than ten years.

Nevertheless, Sam's Club is an innovation for the Brazilian market that, with some effort, could convince Brazilian consumers to adopt this new type of shopping. It would have been much easier for Wal-Mart to concentrate all the efforts on the Supercenters implementations than on Sam's Club. Brazilian consumers disapproved the annual fee to be paid at Sam's Club. Besides this, the stores offer only 3,500 items, compared to more than

50,000 items present at the Supercenters and at competitors' stores such as Carrefour and Pão de Açúcar.

Another problem was the fact that prices in Sam's Club stores were higher than in Supercenters in the first two months. This consolidated the image of a "not-so-cheap" store, especially if we consider Sam's Club having wholesale prices.

Sam's Club could obviously be compared to Makro, a well-known wholesale store whose main characteristic is the low price and reasonable availability of products. Wal-Mart seems not to have been concerned about this competitor and did not try to offer a better option than Makro did. It should be noted that Makro offers in each of its 22 stores an average of 25,000 items.

The product portfolio in Supercenters comprises some nonsense. Wal-Mart, showing complete ignorance of Brazilian habits, offered products such as golf equipment, vacuum cleaners for garden leaves and food grinders, all popular in the United States but absolutely useless in Brazil. On the other hand, areas dedicated to food at Supercenters in Brazil are similar to those in the United States, namely, 25%. However, food represents 60% of sales in supermarkets in Brazil. Would it be so difficult to figure out that this is Brazilian reality?

Management: The main problem can be defined as a lack of "management by walking around". Curiously, Sam Walton, Wal-Mart's founder, was the person who practiced this concept, always traveling either by plane or truck to the furthest stores, just to understand and know better the customers. If Wal-Mart executives walked around they would probably have chosen better places to install the Supercenters and the product mix in the stores would also have been different.

This management problem is closely related to very low synergy with Lojas Americanas expertise. It seems quite strange that a company that intends to operate globally loses the opportunity to learn from a local partner.

Although some degree of centralized management is desired, the present Brazilian Wal-Mart subsidiary has little autonomy. Just as a comparison, Carrefour in Brazil has complete autonomy from the parent company in Paris, and has enjoyed an outstanding performance in Brazil. Wal-Mart acts as though everything that works well in the United States could be exported to the rest of the world and also work well.

As a matter of fact, Wal-Mart is not the first example of a company with difficulties to operate in foreign countries. As a good example, Procter & Gamble committed a serious of mistakes in its international operations such as in Japan and Brazil. In Brazil, P&G made money six years after its entry in 1988. During this period, P&G had five different regional presidents. Nevertheless, P&G was willing to recognize its mistakes; now its Brazilian operation is doing reasonably well.

Advertising: In Wal-Mart's case, the lack of advertising was a problem. For a company that can spend US$120 million to establish itself in Brazil, it is very strange that advertising has been so poor, almost nonexistent. In the first weeks after the two Supercenters opened, some advertising was present on TV and in newspapers. Absolutely nothing on the radio. Brazilian housewives have the habit to listen to the radio during the day, while cooking and/or cleaning the house. Carrefour, Pão de Açúcar and other supermarkets realized this Brazilian habit and invested heavily in radio advertising. Even in TV and newspaper ads, Wal-Mart advertising in Brazil has been disappointing. To become a very well known "brand", Wal-Mart, new in Brazil, should invest heavily in advertising.

Wal-Mart chose a local advertising agency - Norton, currently top 13 in Brazilian agencies ranking. The choice of this Brazilian company has been considered acceptable by many. However, Norton professionals, according to one former Brazilian executive responsible for Wal-Mart, had very little autonomy to determine appropriate advertising as well as appropriate media. Wal-Mart allocated not more than 2% of its revenues to advertising. It is quite difficult to find a current Wal-Mart advertising in newspaper.

Logistics and distribution: Despite Wal-Mart's reputation in this area of expertise, it has not been effective in its Brazilian operations. We consider that Wal-Mart failed when the company ignored its Brazilian suppliers. Unfortunately, Brazilian suppliers are years behind compared to American counterparts in logistics technology. Thus, modern computerized systems that control inventories, deliveries and invoices could not be utilized in Brazil. Wal-Mart could not operate with large distribution centers to which suppliers could deliver products.

Whose fault is it? Wal-Mart or Brazilian suppliers? Mainly Wal-Mart. Since Brazilian logistical systems are not modern and far from the state-of-the-art, Wal-Mart should have adapted its mode of operations.

Finally, Wal-Mart overestimated the Brazilian market for supermarkets. Although the country's total supermarket revenues reach US$45 billion, 80 stores may unlikely be installed in 10 years, mainly considering the size of each store. Just as a comparison, Carrefour installed 39 stores in 22 years.

Video-Case Grid

Video Clip	Chapters for use
1. Consumers Across Borders in Europe	7
2. Automobile Competition in the Emerging Markets	8
3. Baby Bells offering Cable TV in the United Kingdom	9
4. NAFTA and its Sourcing Implications	10
5. Sara Lee Corporation: Building Brands Worldwide	12
6. Bartering Pepsi for Vodka and Tankers	13
7. Hypermarkets in Japan	16
8. The Chinese Auto Market	2, 4, 5, 7, 9
9. Foreign Car Makers in Japan	2, 4, 7, 9, 15, 16
10. Interview with Campbell Soup's Chairman, Mr. David Johnson	9, 11, 12, 14, 18

Consumers Across Borders in Europe

The European integration, which formed the European Union, is a political and economic success in the making. Now, not only products, but also people travel freely throughout the European Union. There is no denying that such a regional unification will enhance the gradual homogenization of product standards, industrial regulations, commercial codes, and fiscal and monetary policies in the long run (as well as a common currency in the making). These factors will promote regional integration of corporate activities, such as standardizing products (or components) and services across national boundaries similar to the situation in the United States.

However, the video clip clearly shows that culture, taste, and lifestyle differences tend to remain as diverse as they have been across national borders in the European Union. Furthermore, as a result of the political and economic unification movement forced onto them, people of different nationalities may even try to emphasize their national heritage and cultural differences more than ever before. Such nationalistic needs may even create a more complex cultural diversity in an era of homogenization.

Pre-Viewing Assignment

Review the purpose, advantages and disadvantages of the European Union. Identify the major countries that are involved in the Union.

Post-Viewing Questions

1. From the consumer's standpoint, what are some of the immediate advantages of the European Union?

Some of the advantages to consumers include (1) more products available to them on store shelves, (2) monetary incentives based on differences in currency between countries.

2. How can tastes vary in Europe?

The video clip uses chocolate as an example indicating preferences. Milk chocolate is popular in Britain, but not in France. The French like dark chocolate, whereas the Germans prefer chocolate with hazelnuts. The alternative seems to be to use products that lack a national identity such as Snickers.

3. What seems to be the most popular language for business, advertising and communication, and computers?

English

Automobile Competition in the Emerging Markets

Japan remains one of the toughest markets for foreign automakers since there are eight domestic car makers vying for the top market share, led by Toyota, Nissan, Honda, Mazda, and Mitsubishi. Among foreign imports, Mercedes-Benz, BMW, Ford, Chrysler, among others, have also established their niches in the already congested auto market in Japan.

Now attracted to the growing Asian markets, many U.S., European, and Japanese automakers are hastily expanding their operations in those emerging markets through wholly owned subsidiaries and joint ventures with local partners. Despite economic and political uncertainties, China remains the single most attractive market with virtually unlimited demand potential for automobiles.

Pre-Viewing Assignment

Examine the auto industry potential in Chile by researching the number of imports.

Post-Viewing Questions

1. How have Japanese automakers slashed costs in recent years?

By moving production off shore. They have been hurt by a recession in their home market and increasing prices abroad. The market of the future is Asia.

2. What percentage of Mitsubishi auto production is off shore?

Approximately two-thirds. They have led the sales race in Southeast Asia for three years. It is the world's biggest potential market.

3. Why is Asia the biggest potential market for automobiles?

Asia is a lucrative target market for several reasons including: (1) the large population, (2) it is currently in the growth stage of the Product Life Cycle, (3) consumers are demanding inexpensive cars, and finally (4) for the company who is first in this market, there will be lots of profits.

4. What American firm has a joint venture in auto production with China?

Chrysler- Jeep.

Baby Bells offering cable TV in the United Kingdom

A relaxed regulatory climate in the British telecom market has opened up opportunities for American local phone companies such as NYNEX, US West and Southwestern Bell. These so-called Baby Bells are heavily investing in the cable TV industry in Britain. Why? Their ultimate goal is to gain a foothold in the British telecom market. They plan to offer telephony services such as local phone, teleconferencing and video-text services along with the entertainment.

The Baby Bells' strategy is to compete with British Telecom (BT) by offering cheaper phone service and innovations that BT cannot provide. BT is barred for several years from entering the cable TV market in Britain. With less than 12 % of British homes and businesses hooked up to cable, the Baby Bells will have to wait for at least a decade before their operations will start making profits. Part of the pay-off will also be the expertise that the Baby Bells hope to gain in the new businesses and can then apply back to their homebase once regulations in the United States ease.

Pre-Viewing Assignments

By looking for information about NYNEX, U.S. West, or Southwestern Bell on the world wide web, research U.S. firms expansion into England.

Post-Viewing Questions

1. Why has NYNEX expanded into cable TV in Britain?

The company has expanded to Britain so they could provide telephone service, teleconferencing services, and technical services. The overall objective is to get into competition with British Telecom.

2. What are the American companies focus in England?

Their objectives include providing cheaper phone services for the U.K. , but then to also export those services back to the United States after gaining the expertise.

NAFTA and its Sourcing Implications

The North American Free Trade Area (NAFTA) is the free trade agreement among Canada, the United States, and Mexico. It promises to eliminate all tariffs on industrial products traded between Canada, Mexico and the United States by the end of year 2003. A freer trading region will result. As comparative advantage theory predicts, competitive industries will benefit from freer access to the neighboring markets across national boundaries, while uncompetitive industries will experience an inevitable gradual decline.

This video clip presents both views: an argument for and an argument against NAFTA, based upon the creation/loss and relocation of jobs in the NAFTA member countries. While both arguments have merit, history has shown that a freer and larger market economy promotes healthy competition among companies. As shown in the video, NAFTA prompts many companies, including Wal-Mart, Microsoft, and U.S. automakers, to develop more efficient and technologically advanced procurement, production, and/or logistics operations.

For example, Wal-Mart in Mexico clearly benefited from NAFTA. However, you should also be warned that the larger, integrated economy does not necessarily mean stable exchange rates. The Mexican peso plummeted in value against the U.S. dollar in December 1994.

Pre-Viewing Assignment

Review the purpose, advantages and disadvantages of NAFTA. Which industries should benefit from the treaty and why?

Post -Viewing Questions

1. How many Wal-marts and Sam's Clubs are now in Mexico? What percentage of their merchandise do they import?

Wal-mart currently has three stores in Mexico and Sam's Club has 15 stores. Approximately 40% of the merchandise that the stores carry is imported.

2. How has Microsoft (Mexico) benefited from NAFTA?

The treaty has opened a window for a proposed law to protect copy rights and increase the fines for any violations of these copy rights.

3. How has NAFTA benefited car manufacturers in Mexico?

The treaty has caused a reduction in tariffs from 20% to 10% on cars, it has caused a increase in exports of these cars, and it has helped to open doors for Mexican auto parts manufacturers.

Sara Lee Corporation: Building Brands Worldwide

Back in the early 1980s, Sara Lee started its overseas expansion. Today, the company markets over one hundred well-known consumer brands across the globe. Non-U.S. businesses now generate 40 % of Sara Lee's sales ($18 billion in 1995). Twelve of the largest brands - including Hanes (underwear), Douwe Egberts (coffee), Sara Lee (bakery products), and Playtex (apparel) - have annual sales of more than $250 million. Brands like Dim (hosiery), Zwitsal (baby-care), and Kiwi (shoecare) are sold in 118 countries.

Sara Lee pursues global opportunities through five strategies:

♦ Build brands in new distribution channels and new ways. In many product lines, the firm uses hybrid channels. Apparel products, for instance, are distributed via department stores, catalogs and mass merchandisers.
♦ Achieve low-cost production worldwide. In most of its businesses, Sara Lee has the scale to maintain a low cost position.
♦ Make acquisitions that are strategic and complementary to Sara Lee's core positions.
♦ Concentrate investments on high-margin, value-added products.
♦ Focus on developing economies, especially in Asia and South America, with rapid growth and a high desire for U. S. brands.

Pre-Viewing Assignment

Go to a secondary resource or the worldwide web page and research the Sara Lee Corporation. Research their domestic and international strategies.

Post-Viewing Questions

1. How much of Sara Lee's sales are outside the United States?

Approximately 40% of sales are outside the domestic U.S.

2. What are two of the problems that Sara Lee has experienced in their overseas expansion?

Sara Lee has discovered that many of the different markets or countries (1) do not have broad distribution standards which can lead to problems in shipping/receiving products, and (2) have different tastes in products than U.S. consumers.

3. How has Sara Lee adapted it's advertising to the European markets?

Their Platex hosiery ads in France are more revealing and racy than those shown in the U.S.

4. Kiwi Shoe Polish rules in how many world markets?

In 118 countries world-wide.

Bartering Pepsi for Vodka and Tankers

In countries that do not have the resources to pay for their imports or with a non-convertible currency, firms often times must look for alternative ways to repatriate their revenues. Countertrade is one mechanism that companies rely on to escape the hard currency crunch faced by their customers in many developing countries.

One of the most eye-catching barter deals in recent years was a transaction that Pepsi set up in the former Soviet Union to exchange Pepsi concentrated syrup for ocean freighters and tankers. For years, Pepsi traded concentrated syrup for Stolichnaya vodka. The Pepsi/ship barter deal was expected to generate $3 billion over a ten-year period. While selling Pepsi for other beverages such as vodka is not that unusual, getting involved in the shipping brokerage business to sell Pepsi certainly is.

Pre-Viewing Assignment

Investigate and define counter trade.

Post-Viewing Questions

1. What has Pepsi traded it's syrup for in Russia?

Ocean freighters, tankers, and vodka.

2. How much money is Pepsi expected to gain over 10 years with the Pepsi/ ship barter?

$3 billion.

Hypermarkets in Japan

Japan experienced six years of recession, characterized as the "Burst of the Bubble Economy" caused primarily by a decline in overinflated land prices, from 1990 to 1996. This long recession triggered price deflation across Japan. Furthermore, during the same time period, the Japanese yen appreciated drastically relative to the U.S. and other major currencies, making foreign imports cheaper in Japan.

Until recently, the Japanese distribution system was characterized as having stable relationships between manufacturers and their distributors. In a way, the channel was in large part controlled by large Japanese manufacturing companies such as Toyota, Panasonic, and Kao. The reduction in consumer demand and the rapid increase in less expensive imports from abroad made Japanese consumers very price-sensitive. Price discounters, such as large discount stores and hypermarkets, have suddenly become popular among the budget-weary Japanese consumers in recent years.

Procter & Gamble in Japan (P&G Japan), albeit an American company, manufactures almost all the products locally for the Japanese market, and has been affected by price deflation the same way Japanese companies have.

Pre-Viewing Assignment

Review distribution relationships in Japan such as Keiretsu and special relationships between manufacturers and distributors. As an alternative, review the advantages and disadvantages of hypermarkets.

Post-Viewing Questions

1. Why are Japanese consumers turning to foreign products?

Simply, because price deflation of the yen appreciating against the U.S. dollar, consumers are buying the cheaper foreign products.

2. What has been a major change in the shopping habits of a Japanese housewife?

The housewife is now buying at hypermarkets where prices are cheaper and there is a wide selection of products to choose from.

The Chinese Auto Market

For some time, marketers have realized that no two countries or economic systems are alike. The challenge of the 21st century will be how to position a particular company's products in an emerging foreign market, such as China.

China offers huge growth potential in the next decade. With one billion consumers, they are the fastest growing economy in the world. With respect to auto manufacturers, the market is just beginning to emerge. At present, only one in seven hundred people own an auto as most still use bikes or carts. However, world auto makers are betting that this will change.

Chrysler, through Bejin-Jeep, makes 50,000 cars per year and expects to double that amount in five years. They currently own 43% of the joint venture and believe that profitability is just over the horizon. At present, though, quality is a chief concern.

Other auto manufacturers such as VW also have a significant presence in the country. However, China will not let in just any company. The companies that enter the Chinese market must be willing to share technology, build components in China, and create joint venture opportunities. China's main objective is to develop a national family car. However, along with cars must come roads and at present, roads have not been built to accommodate auto traffic.

Pre-Viewing Assignment

Research the Chinese market and determine how many auto manufactures currently sell in China?

Post-Viewing Questions

1. Describe the current auto market in China.

The current market contains over one billion potential customers and only one in seven hundred have a car. China would like to create a national family car and the Chinese are trying to attract auto makers to address all of these unmet needs.

2. What does China need from foreign car makers?

Technology, venture capital, manufacturing knowledge and experience, component parts, and opportunities for joint ventures.

3. Who is the leading auto maker in China at the present?

VW.

Foreign Car Makers in Japan

What does it take to be a successful auto manufacturer in Japan? United States firms are now trying to learn.

They have been successful to some extent in 1994. For example, 1) Ford sales are up by 20%, 2) GM's successful European Opel is doubling sales every month and expects 28,000 units to be sold.

The primary sales advantages to the Japanese consumer seem to be safety features and an inexpensive price for the value.

However, the U.S. should perhaps take a lesson from the German car makers if they want to be successful in Japan. The Germans, instead of asking for access into the Japanese market as the U.S. car makers did, spent the money and time to develop their own sales, distribution, and dealer networks.

Most analysts believe that the Germans responded in the only way to ever really have staying power in the Japanese car market.

Pre-Viewing Assignment

Do secondary research on the Japanese car market and it's potential .

Post-Viewing Questions

1. To what extent has GM been successful in Japan?

GM's Opel is doubling sales every month and expects to sell 28,000 units in 1994.

2. Why are Japanese consumers buying foreign cars?

Safety features and inexpensive price for the value.

3. What methods have German auto makers used to penetrate the Japanese market?

The Germans spent the money and time to develop their own sales, distribution, and dealer networks.

Interview With Campbell Soup's Chairman, Mr. David Johnson

Though several topics were covered in this interview with Campbell Soup's Chairman, Mr. David Johnson, his primary message was one of global expansion by acquisition of brand extensions.

Campbell Soup is currently restructuring. While expanding in Europe, they are reducing their workforce in the United States by 1%.

The restructuring in Europe includes the purchase of soup and food giant ERASCO. The German firm is the leading producer of soup in Germany. Campbell plans to capitalize on the fact that Germans eat six times as much soup as U.S. consumers. Campbell will keep the ERASCO products and will use line extensions of Campbell products. This should be a successful way to increase Campbell share of the European market.

Pre-Viewing Assignment

Go to the library or use the internet to investigate Campbell Soup's activities in Europe.

Post-Viewing Questions

1. How does Campbell Soup plan to expand in Europe?

They recently purchased German soup giant ERASCO. They will offer these products plus line extensions of Campbell Soup's products.

2. Describe the German soup market.

Germans eat six times as much soup as U.S. consumers. ERASCO is the leading producer of soup in Germany and has three times the market share of their nearest competitor.

Test Bank

GLOBAL MARKETING MANAGEMENT

Test Bank
Contents

Introduction

Welcome to the Test Bank for Kotabe and Helsen's <u>Global Marketing Management</u> text. This test bank was designed with the student and instructor in mind. All the questions contained in this bank are drawn directly from the master text. Therefore, the instructor will never have to try and explain where the questions on a test came from. Careful attention has been paid to the selection of each and every question.

Each chapter in the Test Bank contains three sections. Multiple choice, true/false and short answer, and essay questions. Each question is formatted with the question number, the question itself, suggested answers, the correct answer, a difficulty scale, a type of knowledge tested scale, and the page(s) where the question and answer may be found in the master text. For each chapter in the master text, the questions in the Test Bank begin at the first of the chapter and follow a logical sequence to the end of the chapter. If questions are drawn from exhibits in the chapter, a special designation has been made to alert the instructor.

The instructor will notice the scales used at the end of each question. The scales are intended to aid the instructor in determining (a) the degree of difficulty of the question and answer and (b) the type of knowledge tested. The degree of difficulty scale appears as:

a (1) indicating low degree of difficulty,

a (2) indicating a moderate degree of difficulty,

or a (3) indicating a high degree of difficulty.

As an illustration of the type of questions that might fall in these categories consider the following: type (1) questions are generally very easy, do not require detailed knowledge or comprehension and have rather obvious answers; type (2) questions are not as obvious, require moderate comprehension, demonstrate a clear understanding of material in the text, and have answers that may in some instances may be similar without being the same; type (3) questions are the most difficult, require a complete understanding of the concept involved, demonstrate that the student has read and studied the material, and has been able to synthesize the material to respond to detailed or creative material. There is a mixture of all of these types in each of the major question areas.

The type of knowledge tested scale indicates whether the question is factual in nature (F) or application oriented (A). Factual material (F) is related directly to citations from the text. Application questions (A) are related to examples, creative situations, or unique application to material found in the chapter. To repeat, all questions in this Test Bank are drawn directly from the material contained in the chapter. All questions and answers have been verified.

Before giving students examinations from the material contained in this Test Bank, they should be encouraged to read and question the material in the master text. They should also understand that a best answer will always be available to a question. Careful reading of the question to determine differences between potential answers would be prudent.

The instructor is encouraged to review this Test Bank before giving an exam review so students can be helped to concentrate on areas that will appear on the examination. The instructor is also encouraged to develop original questions (especially in the discussion or essay format) so the exam can be customized to the particular instructor's class and style.

If the instructor chooses to use the associated Instructor's Resource Guide for this text, they will find a correlation between order and sequence of the questions in the Test Bank and the order of the chapter summaries in the Instructor's Resource Guide. In addition, many of the essay (discussion) questions follow the discussion format used in the master text and Instructor's Resource Guide to solidify the learning experience for the student.

Good luck with your course preparation, instruction, and examination of your students. It is the author's hope that this manual will help with your effort.

Chapter 1

Multiple Choice

1. One of the chief political and economic events that has shaped the nature of global competition is:

    a) global warming.
    b) the demise of the Soviet Union.
    c) the aging of generation of X.
    d) the rise of prices in the stock market.
    e) cooperation in space exploration.

Answer: (b) Difficulty: (1) Knowledge: (F) Page: 3

2. Because of changing global competitive situations, there have been great changes in where the world's top 100 largest companies are located. Which of the following countries has the largest percentage of top 100 companies according to *Fortune's* 500 criteria in 1995?

    a) Britain.
    b) France.
    c) German.
    d) United States.
    e) Japan.

Answer: (e) Difficulty: (2) Knowledge: (F) Page: 3

3. The term, "_____," epitomizes both the competitive pressure and the expanding market opportunities around the world.

    a) marketing
    b) segmentation
    c) global
    d) capitalism
    e) nationalism.

Answer: (c) Difficulty: (2) Knowledge: (F) Page: 3

4. When Weyerhaeuser, a forest products company headquartered in Seattle, began exporting newspaper rolls to Japan, it had to meet the exacting quality standard Japanese newspaper publishers demanded. This is an example of company applying itself to the term _____.

a) global
b) competition
c) monopoly
d) dual marketing
e) capitalism.

Answer: (a) Difficulty: (2) Knowledge: (A) Page: 4

5. When a country's per capita income is below $5,000, much of the income is spent on:

a) taxes
b) cars
c) electronic appliances
d) food and other necessity items
e) bribes.

Answer: (d) Difficulty: (1) Knowledge: (F) Page: 4

6. When a person's income exceeds $10,000 people tend to enjoy similar educational levels, academic and cultural backgrounds, lifestyles, and:

a) investment strategies
b) occupations
c) access to information
d) ability to own a computer
e) desire to own their own business.

Answer: (c) Difficulty: (3) Knowledge: (F) Page: 4

7. In the popular press, the trade deficits have often been portrayed as a declining competitiveness of the United States. This assumes that:

a) Deficits are the fault of producers of goods.
b) U.S. companies engaged only in exports and imports.
c) Canada was different from the United States is their approach to trade deficits.
d) Competition in the international marketplace is not important to producers as long as domestic markets are covered.
e) The United States will always be more competitive that Europe.

Answer: (b) Difficulty: (3) Knowledge: (F) Page: 6

8. _____ consists of exports and imports between a country and the rest of the world.

   a) Global reach
   b) Competition
   c) International trade
   d) International business
   e) International investment.

Answer: (c) Difficulty: (2) Knowledge: (F) Page: 6

9. _____ consists of exports and imports between a country and the rest of the world and foreign production.

   a) Global reach
   b) Competition
   c) International trade
   d) International business
   e) International investment.

Answer: (d) Difficulty: (3) Knowledge: (F) Page: 6

10. Which of the following is not a method that U.S. companies normally can use to market their products internationally?

   a) Indirectly export products through exporting middlemen.
   b) Directly export products to international markets.
   c) Invest in foreign production and manufacture abroad.
   d) Use gray marketers to distribute goods and services.
   e) Contract out manufacturing in a foreign country.

Answer: (d) Difficulty: (3) Knowledge: (A) Page: 6

11. The extensive international penetration of U.S. and other companies has been referred to as _____.

   a) Subsidization
   b) International trade
   c) International business
   d) Gray markets
   e) Global reach.

Answer: (e) Difficulty: (2) Knowledge: (F) Page: 6

12. Since the mid-1960s U.S.-owned subsidiaries located around the world have produced and sold _____ times the value of all U.S. exports. This ration of foreign manufacture to international trade has remained largely unchanged.

a) three
b) four
c) five
d) two
e) six.

Answer: (a) Difficulty: (3) Knowledge: (F) Page: 6

13. Experienced companies tend to manufacture overseas much more than they export. European-owned subsidiaries operating in the United States sold _____ times as much as the U.S. imports from Europe.

a) three
b) four
c) five
d) two
e) six.

Answer: (c) Difficulty: (3) Knowledge: (F) Page: 6

14. Texas Instruments has a large semiconductor manufacturing plant in Japan, marketing its semiconductor chips not only in Japan but also exports them from Japan to the United States and elsewhere. This is an example of:

a) cross-competition
b) line-filling
c) intra-firm trade
d) contra trade
e) trade between competitors.

Answer: (c) Difficulty: (2) Knowledge: (A) Page: 7

15. _____ is essentially a creative corporate activity involving the planning and execution of the conception, pricing, promotion, and distribution of ideas, products, and services in an exchange that not only satisfy customers' present needs but also anticipate and create their future needs at a profit.

 a) Selling
 b) Business administration
 c) Management
 d) Marketing
 e) Production

Answer: (d) Difficulty: (1) Knowledge: (F) Page: 8

16. Marketing strategy requires a close attention to both _____.

 a) customers and competitors.
 b) customers and land value.
 c) costs and control.
 d) competitors and control.
 e) demand and inventory.

Answer: (a) Difficulty: (2) Knowledge: (F) Page: 8

17. After Dell computer successfully marketed products in the United States, it decided to market its products in Europe and Japan. This strategy would be characterized as a:

 a) supply driven strategy.
 b) predictable pattern of foreign expansion.
 c) strategy of skipping middlemen.
 d) gray market expansion.
 e) an unusual expansion attempt.

Answer: (b) Difficulty: (1) Knowledge: (A) Page: 8

18. Companies generally develop different marketing strategies depending on the degree of experience and:

 a) the cost of capital in international markets.
 b) the span of control of management.
 c) their consumer concept.
 d) the nature of operations in international markets.
 e) the corporate focus.

Answer: (d) Difficulty: (2) Knowledge: (A) Page: 9

19. Five types of marketing have led to the evolution of global marketing are domestic marketing, export marketing, international marketing, _____, and global marketing.

   a) trade marketing
   b) consumer marketing
   c) gray marketing
   d) expansion marketing
   e) multinational marketing

Answer: (e) Difficulty: (1) Knowledge: (F) Page: 9

20. Responding to changes in the market and competitive environments by moving forward in a _____ manner waits for others to formulate strategy before making decisions.

   a) proactive
   b) deductive
   c) constructive
   d) reactive
   e) participative

Answer: (d) Difficulty: (2) Knowledge: (A) Page: 9

21. Responding to changes in the market and competitive environments by moving forward in a _____ manner anticipates changes and then formulates strategies.
   a) proactive
   b) deductive
   c) constructive
   d) reactive
   e) participative

Answer: (a) Difficulty: (2) Knowledge: (A) Page: 9

22. There are five identifiable stages in the evolution of marketing across national boundaries. The first stage is:
   a) global marketing
   b) international marketing
   c) export marketing
   d) indirect marketing
   e) domestic marketing.

Answer: (e) Difficulty: (1) Knowledge: (F) Page: 9

23. When a company focuses solely on its domestic market, this strategy is characterized as one employing:

    a) global marketing
    b) international marketing
    c) domestic marketing
    d) indirect marketing
    e) direct marketing.

Answer: (c) Difficulty: (1) Knowledge: (F) Page: 9

24. Domestic marketing strategy is characterized as a strategy that is developed based on information about domestic customer needs and wants, economic, technological, and political environments at home, and _____.

    a) industry trends
    b) customer habits
    c) geography
    d) culture
    e) taxes.

Answer: (a) Difficulty: (2) Knowledge: (F) Page: 9

25. Domestic marketers tend to be _____ and pay little attention to changes taking place in the global marketplace.

    a) polycentric
    b) ethnocentric
    c) regiocentric
    d) geocentric
    e) egocentric

Answer: (b) Difficulty: (3) Knowledge: (F) Page: 11

26. The ethnocentric product is made:

    a) in each country
    b) regionally
    c) globally
    d) at headquarters
    e) jointly with mutual consultation.

Answer: (d) Difficulty: (3) Knowledge: (A) Page: 10

27. U.S. automobile and consumer electronics manufacturers in the 1960s and 1970s are examples of a:

    a) regiocentric orientation
    b) polycentric orientation
    c) ethnocentric orientation
    d) geocentric orientation
    e) egocentric orientation.

Answer: (c) Difficulty: (3) Knowledge: (A) Page: 11

28. The _____ stage begins with unsolicited orders from foreign customers.

    a) export marketing
    b) domestic marketing
    c) indirect marketing
    d) international marketing
    e) multinational marketing

Answer: (a) Difficulty: (2) Knowledge: (F) Page: 11

29. Some companies progress from export marketing to a more involved stage of internationalization once:

    a) managers can speak a foreign language
    b) management is willing to commit adequate resources to export activities.
    c) the companies stock increases
    d) the metric system becomes standard
    e) new management has been hired.

Answer: (b) Difficulty: (2) Knowledge: (A) Page: 11

30. Export marketers still tend to take an _____ approach to foreign markets.

    a) geocentric
    b) polycentric
    c) ethnocentric
    d) dualcentric
    e) regiocentric

Answer: (c) Difficulty: (1) Knowledge: (F) Page: 12

31. Once export marketing becomes an integral part of the company's marketing activity, it will begin to seek new directions for growth and expansion. This stage is called

_____.

a) exporting
b) international marketing
c) multinational marketing
d) global marketing
e) direct marketing.

Answer: (b) Difficulty: (1) Knowledge: (F) Page: 12

32. A unique feature of international marketing is its _____ orientation with emphasis on product and promotional adaptation in foreign markets.

a) geocentric
b) regiocentric
c) ethnocentric
d) polycentric
e) egocentric

Answer: (d) Difficulty: (2) Knowledge: (F) Page: 12

33. As a company's market share in a number of countries reach a certain point, it becomes important for the company to defend its position vis-à-vis local competition. This is an example of _____ orientation.

a) geocentric
b) regiocentric
c) ethnocentric
d) egocentric
e) polycentric

Answer: (e) Difficulty: (3) Knowledge: (A) Page: 12

34. In a polycentric orientation, marketers begin to _____ products to local conditions.

    a) standardize
    b) regulate
    c) adapt
    d) centralize
    e) subsidize

Answer: (c) Difficulty: (1) Knowledge: (A) Page: 12

35. If international marketing is taken to the extreme, a company may establish an independent foreign subsidiary in each and every foreign market and have each of the subsidiaries operate independently of each other without any measurable headquarters control. This special case is called:

    a) multinational marketing
    b) export marketing
    c) international marketing
    d) multi-domestic marketing
    e) resource-based marketing.

Answer: (d) Difficulty: (3) Knowledge: (F) Page: 12

36. When management of the company comes to realize the benefit of economies of scale in product development, manufacturing, and marketing by consolidating some of its activities on a regional basis, the company is ready to move into the _____ stage of marketing.

    a) multinational
    b) customization
    c) global
    d) international
    e) polycentric

Answer: (a) Difficulty: (1) Knowledge: (F) Page: 13

37. If a company were to standardize its product groups within a region (for instance, Western Europe), the company would be characterized as taking a _____ orientation to its planning activities.

   a) ethnocentric
   b) polycentric
   c) geocentric
   d) regiocentric
   e) concentric

Answer: (d) Difficulty: (1) Knowledge: (A) Page: 13

38. General Motors has a regional subsidiary, Opel headquartered in Germany, to market both GM and Opel cars with a strong European distinction. This would be an example of _____ marketing.

   a) domestic
   b) global
   c) export
   d) international
   e) multinational

Answer: (e) Difficulty: (2) Knowledge: (A) Page: 13

39. Global marketing strategy realizes that _____ leads to higher costs.

   a) operational fragmentation
   b) standardization
   c) production ISO standards
   d) market promotion
   e) high technology robots

Answer: (a) Difficulty: (3) Knowledge: (F) Page: 13

40. Global marketing is characterized as having a _____ orientation.

   a) ethnocentric
   b) concentric
   c) polycentric
   d) regiocentric
   e) geocentric

Answer: (e) Difficulty: (1) Knowledge: (F) Page: 10

41. Black & Decker, a U.S. hand tool manufacturer, adopted a(n) _____ perspective by standardizing and streamlining components such as motors and rotors while maintaining a wide range of product lines, and created a universal image for its products.

a) international marketing
b) global marketing
c) multinational marketing
d) export marketing
e) concentric marketing

Answer: (b) Difficulty: (2) Knowledge: (A) Page: 14

42. If the objective of a company is to emphasize reduction of cost inefficiencies and duplication of efforts among their national and regional subsidiaries, they will likely choose _____ as a strategy.

a) multinational marketing
b) international marketing
c) global marketing
d) export marketing
e) concentric marketing

Answer: (c) Difficulty: (3) Knowledge: (F) Page: 13

43. The emergence of global customers leads firms to choose a _____ orientation towards their marketing efforts.

a) concentric
b) regiocentric
c) polycentric
d) ethnocentric
e) geocentric

Answer: (e) Difficulty: (3) Knowledge: (A) Page: 13

Appendix to Chapter 1

44. Comparative advantage theory was first presented by:

    a) Milton Friedman
    b) John Stuart Mill
    c) John Maynard
    d) David Ricardo
    e) Adam Smith.

Answer: (d) Difficulty: (3) Knowledge: (F) Page: 17

45. _____ theory states that a country can gain from engaging in trade even if it has an absolute advantage or disadvantage.

    a) constructive advantage
    b) comparative advantage
    c) concentric advantage
    d) supply and demand
    e) relative cost advantage

Answer: (b) Difficulty: (2) Knowledge: (F) Page: 17

46. Even if the United States is more efficient in the production of everything than China, both countries will benefit from trade between them by specializing in what each country can produce relatively more efficiently. This statement is an example of which economic theory?

    a) Relative cost advantage
    b) Supply and demand
    c) Concentric advantage
    d) Comparative advantage
    e) Constructive advantage

Answer: (d) Difficulty: (3) Knowledge: (A) Page: 17

47. The _____ argument says that two countries cannot engage in trade if one country has an _____ over the other country. Note: the phrase will fit in both blanks.

    a) Supply and demand advantage
    b) Concentric advantage
    c) Absolute advantage
    d) Comparative advantage
    e) Constructive advantage

Answer: (c) Difficulty: (3) Knowledge: (F) Page: 17

48. _____ theory suggests that a country should find those product categories in which it has an advantage and seek to specialize in those areas.

   a) Concentric advantage
   b) Absolute advantage
   c) Comparative advantage
   d) Constructive advantage
   e) Conglomerate advantage

Answer: (c) Difficulty: (2) Knowledge: (A) Page: 18

49. The term that describes a price of one good in terms of another is called:

   a) comparative advantage
   b) inventory assessment
   c) factor endowment theory
   d) commodity terms of trade
   e) principle of efficiency.

Answer: (d) Difficulty: (2) Knowledge: (F) Page: 18

50. An actual exchange rate between two countries is affected by consumer demands and _____ in the two countries.

   a) money supply situations
   b) political alliances
   c) the deficit
   d) the Federal Reserve
   e) the factor formula

Answer: (a) Difficulty: (3) Knowledge: (F) Page: 19

51. Which of the following is a principle of international trade?

   a) Japanese workers are more productive than any other workers in the world.
   b) Countries benefit from international trade.
   c) Manufacturers must be forced into international trade.
   d) Specialization is bad for international trade.
   e) Exchange rates are determined by the World Bank.

Answer: (b) Difficulty: (1) Knowledge: (A) Page: 19

52. Which of the following is a principle of international trade?

    a) German workers will not work without Union representation.
    b) International trade hurts many countries since it is basically unfair to developing nations.
    c) International trade increases worldwide production by specialization.
    d) Exchange rates are determined by the Hague.
    e) Bribery drives up prices in world trade.

Answer: (c) Difficulty: (1) Knowledge: (A) Page: 19

53. Which of the following is a principle of international trade?

    a) United States workers rebel against productivity programs.
    b) Outsourcing must be used to succeed in international trade.
    c) The United Nations will settle all trade disputes.
    d) Exchange rates are determined primarily by traded goods.
    e) Gray markets make third world countries more efficient.

Answer: (d) Difficulty: (1) Knowledge: (A) Page: 19

54. In general, a capital-abundant country (such as the United States) tends to specialize in capital-intensive industry and export capital-intensive products, and import labor-intensive products. This statement is an illustration of the _____ of comparative advantage.

    a) commodity terms of trade theory
    b) supply and demand theory
    c) diminishing returns theory
    d) factor-sourcing theory
    e) factor endowment theory

Answer: (e) Difficulty: (3) Knowledge: (A) Page: 19

55. In general, a labor-abundant country (such as China) tends to specialize in labor-intensive industry and export labor-intensive products, and imports capital-intensive products. This statement is an illustration of the _____ of comparative advantage.
    a) commodity terms of trade theory
    b) supply and demand theory
    c) factor-sourcing theory
    d) factor endowment theory
    e) relative advantage theory

Answer: (d) Difficulty: (3) Knowledge: (A) Page: 19

56. To encourage improved standards of living among workers, governments should encourage investment in _____ industries.

a) high value added per worker
b) capital intensive
c) labor intensive
d) skill-intensive
e) strength-intensive

Answer: (d) Difficulty (3) Knowledge: (A) Page: 20

57. Suppose that you are a strategic planner for Nike. You observe that shoe manufacturing is extremely labor-intensive, while shoe designing is becoming increasingly skill-intensive. If you advise to open a manufacturing-assembly plant in Vietnam, your decision is an illustration of _____ thinking.

a) relative advantage
b) absolute advantage
c) comparative advantage
d) production advantage
e) exploitation advantage

Answer: (c) Difficulty: (2) Knowledge: (A) Page: 19

58. When a company such as Nike has product designing and development and special material development conducted in the United States and has manufacturing operations in labor-abundant countries like China, the company is using _____ strategy.

a) relative advantage
b) absolute advantage
c) production advantage
d) comparative advantage
e) geometric advantage

Answer: (d) Difficulty: (1) Knowledge: (A) Page: 19

59. When a company such as Nike wishes to pursue a comparative advantage strategy, it would have product designing and development and special material development conducted in the United States and _____ operations conducted in labor-abundant countries like China or Brazil.

    a) manufacturing
    b) custom painting
    c) testing
    d) inventory
    e) promotion

Answer: (a) Difficulty: (1) Knowledge: (A) Page: 19

60. The comparative advantage theory is useful in explaining _____ between countries that have very different factor endowments.

    a) cost advantages
    b) resource allocations
    c) promotional expenses
    d) intra-industry trade
    e) inter-industry trade

Answer: (e) Difficulty: (1) Knowledge: (F) Page: 20

61. An example of _____ competition is when BMW exports its sports cars to Japan, while Honda exports its competing models to Germany.
    a) inter-industry
    b) between-industry
    c) intra-industry
    d) superficial
    e) conglomerate

Answer: (c) Difficulty: (3) Knowledge: (A) Page: 20

62. The _____ addresses the following questions: Why and how does competition tend to evolve over time and across national boundaries in the same industry? How does a company develop its marketing strategy in the presence of competitors at home and abroad?
    a) international banking theory
    b) international product life cycle theory
    c) the product adoption process
    d) production curves
    e) supply and demand theory

Answer: (b) Difficulty: (1) Knowledge: (F) Page: 20

63. A large domestic market such as in the United States makes it possible for U.S. companies to enjoy _____ in mass production and mass marketing, enabling them to become lower cost producers than their competition in foreign countries.

    a) monopoly power
    b) preference similarity
    c) economies of scale
    d) competitive advantage
    e) duopoly power

Answer: (c) Difficulty: (2) Knowledge: (F) Page: 20

64. When Nestle`, a Swiss food company, enjoys economies of scale by considering European, U.S., and Japanese markets together as its primary market it is using the _____ argument.

    a) economies of scale
    b) market expansion
    c) market contraction
    d) technology power
    e) economies of scope

Answer: (e) Difficulty: (3) Knowledge: (A) Page: 20

65. Technological innovation can provide an innovative company a competitive advantage, or _____ over its competitors both at home and abroad.

    a) monopoly power
    b) preference similarity
    c) technological gap
    d) economies of scope
    e) life cycle advantage

Answer: (c) Difficulty: (1) Knowledge: (F) Page: 20

66. Preference similarity explains why:

   a) monopoly power
   b) low cost producers can still enjoy economies of scale
   c) profits are at an all time high in the industrialized world
   d) intra-industry trade has grown tremendously among the industrialized countries with similar income levels
   e) comparative advantage theory works best in third world countries.

Answer: (d) Difficulty: (2) Knowledge: (F) Page: 20

67. One of the key underlying assumptions in the international product cycle theory is that:
   a) "What goes around, comes around."
   b) "Necessity is the mother of invention."
   c) "If it ain't broke, don't fix it."
   d) "You get what you pay for."
   e) "If something can go wrong, it usually will."

Answer: (b) Difficulty: (2) Knowledge: (A) Page: 21

68. The following statement characterizes which country's orientation to introducing products to their mass market: Developed and introduced many products that were labor- and time-saving or responded to high-income consumer needs (such as microwave ovens).
   a) Japan
   b) Germany
   c) England
   d) United States
   e) Mexico

Answer: (d) Difficulty: (1) Knowledge: (A) Page: 21

69. The following statement characterizes which country's orientation to introducing products to their mass market: Innovate on material- and capital-saving products and processes to meet their local consumer's needs and lifestyle orientation (such as small and no-frill automobiles and recyclable products).

   a) Japan
   b) Western Europe
   c) Canada
   d) Mexico
   e) United States

Answer: (b) Difficulty: (2) Knowledge: (A) Page: 21

70. The following statement characterizes which country's orientation to introducing products to their mass market: Developing and marketing products that not only conserve material and capital but also space to address their consumer's acute concern about space limitation.

a) Japan
b) Western Europe
c) Mexico
d) Canada
e) United States

Answer: (a) Difficulty: (1) Knowledge: (A) Page: 21

71. With respect to the international product cycle, which stage's orientation is primarily domestic in nature?

a) Growth
b) Maturity
c) Saturation
d) Introduction
e) Decline

Answer: (d) Difficulty: (1) Knowledge: (F) Page: 21

72. In the _____ stage of the international product cycle, U.S. companies typically increase exports to Europe and Japan as those foreign markets expand.

a) introduction
b) saturation
c) growth
d) maturity
e) decline

Answer: (c) Difficulty: (1) Knowledge: (F) Page: 21

73. In the _____ stage of the international product cycle, U.S. companies which have carved out market share in Europe and Japan by exporting decide to make a direct investment in production in those markets to protect their market position there.

   a) introduction
   b) saturation
   c) growth
   d) decline
   e) maturity

Answer: (e) Difficulty: (2) Knowledge: (F) Page: 21

74. In the _____ stage of the international product cycle, the United States eventually begins to import what was once a U.S. innovation.

   a) introduction
   b) saturation
   c) growth
   d) decline
   e) maturity

Answer: (d) Difficulty: (2) Knowledge: (A) Page: 21

75. One way to maintain competitive advantage with respect to product innovation is to have a(n) _____.

   a) dominant design
   b) quick response team
   c) "invisible hand"
   d) production orientation
   e) consumer fashion sense

Answer: (a) Difficulty: (2) Knowledge: (F) Page: 23

True/False   Short Answer

1. From 1970 to 1995, the United States share of the top 100 companies in the world declined from 64 to 24.

Answer: (True) Difficulty: (1) Knowledge: (F) Page: 2

2. The decade in which live today is much less competitive in terms of world trade than it

   was 20 years ago when the Soviet Union was a world force.

Answer: (False) Difficulty: (2) Knowledge: (F) Page: 2

3. The establishment of the European Union has changed the market environments around the world.

Answer: (True) Difficulty: (1) Knowledge: (F) Page: 3

4. Japan, which enjoys one of the highest per capita income levels in the world, has been the most important single market for foreign, as well as for domestic companies, for years.

Answer: (False) Difficulty: (2) Knowledge: (F) Page: 5

5. International trade is a broader concept than international business because it includes international trade and foreign production.

Answer: (False) Difficulty: (2) Knowledge: (F) Page: 6

6. An example of intra-firm trade would be when Honda's U.S. plant ships parts back to Japan to be placed in cars which are then sold in Japan and the United States.

Answer: (True) Difficulty: (3) Knowledge: (A) Page: 7

7. For the United States, about 30% of U.S. exports is attributed to U.S. parent companies transferring products and components to their affiliates overseas, and about 40% of U.S. imports is accounted for by foreign affiliates exporting to their U.S. parent companies. These transactions are called
_____ transactions.

Answer: (Intra-firm transactions) Difficulty: (3) Knowledge: (A) Page: 8

8. In many cases, U.S. companies have won the battle of discovering and filing customer needs initially only to be defeated in the competitive war by losing the markets they pioneered.

Answer: (True) Difficulty: (1) Knowledge: (A) Page: 8

9. The text described four broad orientations that explained and characterized product planning and marketing mix decisions in the evolution of global marketing. The orientation that is characterized as being one where product development is determined primarily by the needs of the home country customers is called the _____ orientation.

Answer: (ethnocentric) Difficulty: (2) Knowledge: (F) Page: 10

10. The text described four broad orientations that explained and characterized product planning and marketing mix decisions in the evolution of global marketing. The orientation that is characterized as being one where product development is standardized within a region, but not across is called the _____ orientation.

Answer: (regiocentric) Difficulty: (2) Knowledge: (F) Page: 10

11. Operational fragmentation leads to higher costs.

Answer: (True) Difficulty: (1) Knowledge: (F) Page: 13

Appendix to Chapter 1

12. John Stuart Mill developed the comparative advantage theory 180 years ago.

Answer: (False) Difficulty: (3) Knowledge: (F) Page: 17

13. If a country has an absolute advantage (with respect to trade) over another country, there is no reason to trade.

Answer: (False) Difficulty: (2) Knowledge: (F) Page: 17

14. Assume that the United States can make computers better than any other country. Also assume that China can make rubber shoes better than any other country. Then in this example it may be said that the United States has a _____ advantage in making desks and China has a _____ advantage in making rubber shoes. Note: one term can be used in both blanks.

Answer: (comparative) Difficulty: (3) Knowledge: (A) Page: 18

15. One rule of the _____ theory of comparative advantage is that that a capital-abundant country (e.g., the United States) tends to specialize in capital-intensive industry and export capital-intensive products (personal computers) and import labor-intensive products (desks).

Answer: (factor endowment) Difficulty: (3) Knowledge: (A) Page: 19

Essay

1. Explain the primary differences between international marketing and global marketing.

Answer:

Global marketing is a more advanced phase of international marketing. Once export marketing becomes an integral part of a company's marketing activity, it begins to seek growth and expansion through international marketing. The emphasis is polycentric (emphasis on product and promotional adaptation in foreign markets--wherever necessary). In global marketing, fragmentation caused by international marketing is overcome.

Global marketing refers to marketing activities by companies that emphasize:

1). Reduction of cost inefficiencies and duplication of efforts among their national and regional subsidiaries.
2). Opportunities for the transfer of products, brands, and other ideas across subsidiaries.
3). Emergence of global customers.
4). Improved linkages among national marketing infrastructures leading to the development of a global marketing infrastructure.

Difficulty: (2) Knowledge: (F) Page: 2, 12

2. Explain the differences between international trade and international business. How does the United States typically participate in international business?

Answer:

International trade consists of exports and imports. If a nations imports exceed their exports, then the nation would record a trade deficit. If the opposite were the case, then the country would record a trade surplus.

International business is a broader concept and includes international trade and foreign production. U.S. companies typically market their products in three ways. First, they can export their products from the United States, which is recorded as a U.S. export. Second, they can invest in their foreign production on their own and manufacture those products abroad for sale there. This transaction does not show up as a U.S. export, however. And third, they can contract out manufacturing in whole or part to a company in a foreign country either by way of licensing of joint venture agreement. While it is not widely known, foreign production constitutes a much larger portion of international business than international trade.

Difficulty: (2) Knowledge: (A) Page: 6

3. Explain intra-firm trade. Give an example to illustrate your answer.

Answer:

International trade and foreign production are increasingly managed on a global basis. Furthermore, international trade and foreign production are also intertwined in a complex manner. Intra-firm trade demonstrates that a company can export from their home base, manufacture their products in various foreign countries both for local sale and for further exporting to the rest of the world, and even export back to their respective home countries. In other words, multinational companies using the concept to intra-firm trade are managing international trade flow within themselves.

An example would be Texas Instruments. Texas Instruments has a large semiconductor manufacturing plant in Japan, marketing its semiconductor chips not only in Japan but also exports them from Japan to the United States and elsewhere.

Difficulty: (1) Knowledge: (A) Page: 7

Appendix to Chapter 1

4. Explain the general and associated concepts of comparative advantage theory.

Answer:

The following facts may be used to construct an answer to the above question:

Countries trade with one another for fundamentally the same reasons that individuals trade with one another--mutual benefit. Comparative advantage theory is a arithmetic demonstration made by the English economist, David Ricardo, almost 180 years ago.
   a. The idea was that a country can gain from engaging in trade even if it has an *absolute* advantage or disadvantage.
   b. Examine what trading partners can produce *relatively* more efficiently.

When one looks at products produced in the United States and China it would seem that trade might be prohibited because the United States has an *absolute advantage* in most trade areas. However, upon close inspection, one observes that trade can take place because of the concept of *comparative advantage.*

 a. This suggests that the two trading partners should specialize.

 b. *Commodity terms of trade* (a price of one good in terms of another) must be agreed upon.

In reality, trading members rarely trade one good for another. Instead, they use foreign exchange. Actual exchange rate will be affected by consumer demands. They are also determined by the money supply situations in the affected countries.

General *principles of international trade* include:

 a. Countries benefit from international trade.

 b. International trade increases worldwide production by specialization.

 c. Exchange rates are determined primarily by traded goods.

The *factor endowment theory* indicates that:

 a. A capital-abundant country tends to specialize in capital-intensive industry and export capital-intensive products and import labor-intensive products.

 b. A labor-abundant country tends to specialize in labor-intensive industry and export labor-intensive products and import capital-intensive products.

 c. Be careful of assuming that labor productivity alone shows industry competitiveness.

The comparative advantage theory is useful in explaining *inter-industry* trade between countries that have very different factor endowments.

 a. It suggests efficient allocation of limited resources across national boundaries by specialization and trade.

 b. It does not explain trade where there is no competition.

 c. It also fails to explain trade between countries with similar factor endowments.

 d. *Intra-industry* competition cannot be explained by comparative advantage theory.

Difficulty: (3) Knowledge: (A) Page: 17, 18

5. Explain the international product cycle theory. Be sure to describe the stages that a a product might pass through.

Answer:

Facts that might be considered in formulating an answer to this question are listed below.

International product cycle theory suggests that new products are developed primarily to address the needs of the local consumers, only to be demanded by foreign consumers who have similar needs with a similar purchasing power. Intra-industry competition is addressed in the international product cycle theory. As an explanation of international business behavior, international product cycle theory has limited explanatory power. It does, however, describe initial expansion in the international market.

To set the stage for the development of the international product cycle theory speculations must be made:
  a. A large domestic market (such as in the United States) makes it possible for domestic firms to enjoy *economies of scale*.
  b. Low cost producers can engage in international trade.
  c. *Economies of scope* allows the firms to extend there advantages beyond the domestic market into foreign ones.

  d. Technological innovation can provide an innovative company a competitive advantage, or *technological gap*, over its competitors both at home and abroad. The firms may temporarily have *monopoly power*.
  e. It is generally the per-capita income level that determines consumers' *preference similarity*, or consumption patterns, irrespective of nationality.

The stages of the international product cycle theory include:
  a. The *introductory stage* where a company innovates on a new product to meet domestic consumers' needs in the domestic market.
  b. The *growth stage* has product standards emerging and mass production becomes feasible.
  c. In the *maturity stage,* many companies vie for market share and prices fall and product differentiation occurs.
  d. In the *decline stage*, companies in developing countries also begin producing the product and marketing it.

Difficulty: (3) Knowledge: (F) Page: 20, 21, 22

Chapter 2

Multiple Choice

1. In no other time in history have countries been more economically interdependent than they are today. This can be seen by the fact that annual trade in goods and services totaled _____ in 1995.

    a. $100 billion
    b. $500 billion
    c. $1 trillion
    d. $5 trillion
    e. $9 trillion

Answer: (e) Difficulty: (2) Knowledge: (F) Page: 25

2. Examples of the ten Big Emerging Markets (BEMs) include all of the following EXCEPT:

    a. Russia.
    b. China.
    c. India.
    d. Mexico.
    e. Poland.

Answer: (a) Difficulty: (3) Knowledge: (F) Page: 26

3. Because of its market and economy's rise to prominence in the next decade, _____ may be a big trade headache for the United States. This country's trade surplus already toped $39 billion in 1995.

    a. Japan
    b. Russia
    c. Mexico
    d. China
    e. Canada

Answer: (d) Difficulty: (2) Knowledge: (F) Page: 26

4. When trade statistics are examined, which of the following countries tops the total trade list (in 1995) with the United States?

   a. Japan
   b. Canada
   c. Mexico
   d. China
   e. United Kingdom

Answer: (b) Difficulty: (2) Knowledge: (F) Page: 26

5. Remembering research that you have read, which of the following countries joins the United States, Japan, and Singapore as the world's top four economies with respect to global competitiveness?

   a. Mexico
   b. Russia
   c. Germany
   d. Hong Kong
   e. Taiwan

Answer: (d) Difficulty: (2) Knowledge: (A) Page: 26

6. _____ refers to investment in foreign countries that are withdrawable at short notice (such as investment in foreign stocks and bonds).

   a. Direct investment
   b. Economic investment
   c. Portfolio investment
   d. Demand investment
   e. Global investment

Answer: (c) Difficulty: (1) Knowledge: (F) Page: 28

7. An example of portfolio investment (or indirect investment) in foreign markets is:

   a. cars.
   b. computers.
   c. stocks and bonds.
   d. buildings.
   e. manufacturing facilities.

Answer: (c) Difficulty: (2) Knowledge: (A) Page: 28

8. Trading in foreign currencies has an effect on world trade. For example, a rise in the value of the local currency due to daily flows vis-à-vis other currencies makes exports:

   a. less expensive.
   b. more expensive.
   c. come under government control.
   d. parallel with imports.
   e. be banned.

Answer: (b) Difficulty: (1) Knowledge: (A) Page: 29

9. About _____ of what Americans consume is produced in America.

   a. 50%
   b. 60%
   c. 70%
   d. 75%
   e. 90%

Answer: (e) Difficulty: (2) Knowledge: (F) Page: 30

10. The dominant feature of the global economy is that the share of world output from the _____ is rising in a sustained manner, and it has been estimated to overtake the share of the current rich industrial nations before the year 2000.

    a. developing nations
    b. Western European nations
    c. Slavic nations
    d. African nations
    e. South American nations

Answer: (a) Difficulty: (1) Knowledge: (A) Page: 30

11. Differences in nations manifest themselves in the type of economic systems that are found in the different countries. One way to visualize these differences is to look at the method of resource allocation and control and _____ in an economy.

   a. the number of automobiles
   b. the number of roads
   c. the type of property ownership
   d. the type of government
   e. the type of currency

Answer: (c) Difficulty: (3) Knowledge: (A) Page: 30

12. With respect to analyzing the type of economic systems, the method of resource allocation and control refers to where the national economy lies in the continuum between:

   a. a socialist and capitalist economy.
   b. a market economy and a command economy.
   c. a market economy and a service economy.
   d. a communist economy and a service economy.
   e. supply and demand allocation.

Answer: (b) Difficulty: (3) Knowledge: (A) Page: 30

13. In a _____, the supply and demand of goods and services determine the price; the role of the government is minimal.

   a. command economy
   b. complex economy
   c. communistic economy
   d. market economy
   e. gray market economy

Answer: (d) Difficulty: (2) Knowledge: (F) Page: 30

14. In a market economy, the supply and demand of goods and services:

   a. are unknown.
   b. determine the price.
   c. create barriers to efficiency.
   d. are tightly controlled by the government.
   e. are strictly monitored by the government.

Answer: (b) Difficulty: (1) Knowledge: (A) Page: 30

15. In a _____, the government determines the supply and the prices and, therefore, the demand.

   a. complex economy
   b. democratic economy
   c. market economy
   d. command economy
   e. service economy

Answer: (d) Difficulty: (2) Knowledge: (F) Page: 30

16. In a command economy, the government:

   a. is not an economic force.
   b. stays out of business relations.
   c. determines the supply but allows the market to determine the prices.
   d. cannot control demand.
   e. determines the supply and the prices and, therefore, the demand.

Answer: (e) Difficulty: (1) Knowledge: (A) Page: 30

17. With respect to forms of economic environment, the United States is most accurately described as:

   a. market-private.
   b. market-mixed.
   c. market-public.
   d. command-private.
   e. command-public.

Answer: (a) Difficulty: (2) Knowledge: (A) Page: 30

18. With respect to forms of economic environment, countries such as North Korea and Cuba would most accurately be described as being:

   a. market-private.
   b. market-mixed.
   c. market-public.
   d. command-private.
   e. command-public.

Answer: (e) Difficulty: (3) Knowledge: (A) Page: 30

19. With respect to forms of economic environment, China would be most accurately be described as being:

   a. market-private.
   b. market-mixed.
   c. market-public.
   d. command-mixed.
   e. command-public.

Answer: (d) Difficulty: (3) Knowledge: (A) Page: 31

20. The Japanese economy is characterized by _____----groups of firms bound together by strong, informal ties, and interlocking ownership.

   a. gangster groups
   b. financial cartels
   c. keiretsus
   d. cabals
   e. franchises

Answer: (c) Difficulty: (1) Knowledge: (A) Page: 31

21. Which of the following countries is known for having strong industrial and policy (as promoted by their Ministry of Industrial Trade and Industry and Ministry of Finance)?

   a. United States
   b. Japan
   c. Australia
   d. United Kingdom
   e. France

Answer: (b) Difficulty: (2) Knowledge: (A) Page: 31

22. The International Trade Organization (ITO) because of difficulty with charter approval by the United States eventually became:

   a. General Agreements of Tariffs and Trade (GATT).
   b. North American Free Trade Agreement (NAFTA).
   c. the European Union.
   d. World Trade Organization (WTO).
   e. International Monetary Fund (IMF).

Answer: (a) Difficulty: (2) Knowledge: (F) Page: 32

23. The main operating principle of the General Agreements of Tariffs and Trade (GATT) is the concept of:

a. a world bank.
b. Most Favored Nation status (MFN).
c. the world court.
d. the World Trade Organization (WTO).
e. the world currency being the dollar.

Answer: (b) Difficulty: (3) Knowledge: (F) Page: 32

24. When GATT was successful in lowering tariff barriers to world trade, many nations created:

a. cartels.
b. keiretsus.
c. joint ventures.
d. nontariff barriers.
e. boycotts.

Answer: (d) Difficulty: (1) Knowledge: (F) Page: 34

25. With respect to the GATT accords, developed nations have moved from manufacturing-based economies to services- and knowledge-based economies. The big challenge is to bring _____ within the purview of international agreement.

a. automobiles
b. computers
c. advertising
d. intellectual property
e. religion

Answer: (d) Difficulty: (2) Knowledge: (A) Page: 34

26. Developed nations are attempting to bring intellectual property within the purview of the GATT agreements. An example of intellectual property that might apply is:

a. automobiles.
b. a computer.
c. advertising.
d. religion.
e. recorded music.

27. Each GATT round is named after the country in which the round was held. The latest round has been named the:

a. Peru round.
b. Cuba round.
c. France round.
d. Uruguay round.
e. Bolivia round.

28. Perhaps the most important accomplishment of the latest GATT round was the establishment of:

a. the World Trade Organization (WTO).
b. the North American Free Trade Agreement (NAFTA).
c. the World Bank.
d. the International Monetary Fund (IMF).
e. the World Court.

29. The _____ is the new legal and institutional foundation for a multilateral trading system.

a. the World Trade Organization (WTO).
b. the North American Free Trade Agreement (NAFTA).
c. the World Bank.
d. the International Monetary Fund (IMF).
e. the World Court.

30. A new legal and institutional foundation oversees the contractual obligations determining how governments frame and implement domestic trade legislation and regulations. This best describes the function of:

a. the World Bank.
b. the North American Free Trade Agreement (NAFTA).
c. the World Trade Organization (WTO).
d. the International Monetary Fund (IMF).
e. the World Court.

Answer: (c) Difficulty: (2) Knowledge: (A) Page: 34

31. The World Trade Organization (WTO) is the platform on which trade relations among countries evolve through collective debate, negotiation, and:

    a. argument.
    b. adjudication.
    c. force.
    d. power.
    e. barter.

Answer: (b) Difficulty: (2) Knowledge: (F) Page: 34

32. One of the primary differences between GATT and WTO is that WTO is:

    a. service based.
    b. funded by the United Nations.
    c. for the advanced countries only.
    d. does not accept communistic countries or governments.
    e. a permanent institution with its own secretariat.

Answer: (e) Difficulty: (3) Knowledge: (F) Page: 35

33. GATT is a part of (lives within):

    a. the World Bank.
    b. the North American Free Trade Agreement (NAFTA).
    c. the World Trade Organization (WTO).
    d. the International Monetary Fund (IMF).
    e. the World Court.

Answer: (c) Difficulty: (1) Knowledge: (A) Page: 35

34. One of the differences between WTO and GATT is that WTO's dispute settlement mechanism is:

    a. inferior.
    b. faster and more automatic.
    c. very limited.
    d. controlled by the World Bank.
    e. controlled by the negotiation section of the United Nations.

Answer: (b) Difficulty: (2) Knowledge: (F) Page: 35

35. Which of the major countries has not "signed-on" with WTO's attempt to bring global trading of financial services (such as banking, insurance, and securities) under WTO's rules?

   a. United Kingdom
   b. France
   c. Germany
   d. United States
   e. Japan

Answer: (d) Difficulty: (3) Knowledge: (A) Page: 35, 36

36. The United States has not supported and refused to "sign-on" with the WTO's attempt to bring global trading of financial services (such as banking, insurance, and securities) under WTO's rules. What was the United States major objection?

   a. Too many countries have not signed.
   b. Too many countries have signed.
   c. The measure does not go far enough in organizing global trading of financial services.
   d. The measure goes too far in organizing global trading of financial services.
   e. The measure is illegal and restrains trade.

Answer: (c) Difficulty: (3) Knowledge: (A) Page: 36

37. _____ refers to the investment by firms in one nation to create productive facilities in another nation.

   a. Franchising
   b. A joint venture
   c. Domestic investment
   d. Global investment
   e. Foreign direct investment

Answer: (e) Difficulty: (1) Knowledge: (F) Page: 37

38. Inflow of foreign direct investment goes from the developed nations into the developing nations. The largest percent (60%) of foreign direct investment goes to:
   a. South America
   b. Africa
   c. Asia
   d. Southern Europe
   e. The Middle East

Answer: (c) Difficulty: (2) Knowledge: (F) Page: 37

39. The United States began to invest overseas in 1945. The name of the plan that spurred this movement was called the:

    a. Eisenhower Plan.
    b. Reconstruction Plan.
    c. McArthur Plan.
    d. Pan-European Plan.
    e. Marshall Plan.

Answer: (e) Difficulty: (3) Knowledge: (F) Page: 37

40. After 1985 the United States began to curtail its foreign investment abroad. One of the chief reasons for this was:

    a. the depreciation of the yen.
    b. the depreciation of the dollar.
    c. the fall of the stock market.
    d. growing dependency on foreign oil.
    e. the fall of the Soviet Union.

Answer: (b) Difficulty: (2) Knowledge: (A) Page: 38

41. Part of the reason for a surge in investment in the United States in the late 1980s was the:

    a. end of the Gulf War.
    b. end of the Cold War.
    c. fall in the value of the yen.
    d. fall in the value of the German mark.
    e. fall in the value of the dollar.

Answer: (e) Difficulty: (1) Knowledge: (F) Page: 38

42. Traditionally, which of the following countries have been the leaders in investment in the United States?

    a. Canada
    b. United Kingdom
    c. Japan
    d. Netherlands
    e. Germany

Answer: (b) Difficulty: (3) Knowledge: (F) Page: 38

43. The new leader of foreign investment in the United States is recognized to be:

    a. Canada.
    b. United Kingdom.
    c. Japan.
    d. Netherlands.
    e. Germany.

Answer: (c) Difficulty: (1) Knowledge: (F) Page: 38

44. As far as the balance of payments position is concerned, the United States has run a persistent deficit on the current account since:

    a. the end of the Gulf War.
    b. since the first oil shock in 1973.
    c. since the end of the Viet Nam War.
    d. since the first Japanese automobile was imported.
    e. since the fall of the Soviet Union.

Answer: (b) Difficulty: (2) Knowledge: (F) Page: 39

45. There is a growing feeling that conventional measures of the trade deficit may not be an accurate reflection of a country's transactions with the rest of the world. One of the reasons for this doubt is:

    a. a wholly owned foreign subsidiary's transactions may not be accurately reflected.
    b. many countries use double entry accounting.
    c. records are not kept accurately.
    d. many countries will not release records.
    e. government records are not to be trusted.

Answer: (a) Difficulty: (2) Knowledge: (A) Page: 40

46. With respect to intellectual property rights, an example of an information-related product is:

    a. computer hardware.
    b. an automobile.
    c. computer software.
    d. jewelry.
    e. a new drilling bit.

Answer: (c) Difficulty: (1) Knowledge: (A) Page: 42

47. With respect to electronically represented intellectual property, the to control may be to control not the copies of the firm's information product but instead a relationship with the customers. An example of this relationship would be a(n):

a. insurance.
b. service.
c. hard drive.
d. subscription or membership.
e. restriction.

Answer: (d) Difficulty: (2) Knowledge: (A) Page: 43

48. One hurdle that used to protect information from being acquired easily was that it was unfungible. Unfungible means:

a. information contained viruses.
b. information was expensive.
c. information could only be processed with proper equipment.
d. information was not for the uninformed.
e. it was difficult to replace one item with another.

Answer: (e) Difficulty: (3) Knowledge: (A) Page: 43

49. One way around having your intellectual property copied (such as software) because of easy access is to sell:

a. demos.
b. to new markets.
c. to governments.
d. upgrades or ancillary products.
e. only to a chosen few.

Answer: (d) Difficulty: (1) Knowledge: (A) Page: 43

50. An evolving trend in international economic activity is the formation of:

a. multinational advertising agencies.
b. multinational insurance agencies.
c. multinational trading blocs.
d. multinational purchasing agencies.
e. multinational courts.

Answer: (c) Difficulty: (2) Knowledge: (F) Page: 44

51. The universal reason for forming trading blocs is to:

    a. bypass tariff restrictions.
    b. bypass legal restrictions.
    c. bypass government controls.
    d. ensure the economic growth and benefit of the participating countries.
    e. make competition suffer.

Answer: (d) Difficulty: (2) Knowledge: (A) Page: 44

52. Which of the following is an example of an international trading bloc?

    a. World Trade Organization.
    b. GATT.
    c. The World Court in the Hague.
    d. NAFTA.
    e. ECOMCOM.

Answer: (d) Difficulty: (1) Knowledge: (F) Page: 44

53. Before the formation of a trading bloc, many governments agree to cooperate informally by participating jointly in projects that create:

    a. banking systems.
    b. economic supply and demand structures.
    c. economic infrastructure (such as dams).
    d. work-relief projects.
    e. Food-for-Peace programs.

Answer: (c) Difficulty: (2) Knowledge: (A) Page: 45

54. A _____ is a formal agreement among two or more countries to reduce or eliminate customs duties and nontariff trade barriers among partner countries.

    a. Trade Union
    b. regional cooperative
    c. Customs Union
    d. Common Market
    e. Free Trade Area

Answer: (e) Difficulty: (3) Knowledge: (F) Page: 45

55. An example of a Free Trade Area would be:

    a. the European Union.
    b. the Soviet Union.
    c. the United Kingdom.
    d. NAFTA.
    e. the United Nations.

Answer: (d) Difficulty: (1) Knowledge: (A) Page: 45

56. A free trade area has the weakness of not necessarily being free of:

    a. government control.
    b. trade barriers.
    c. angry consumers.
    d. poor roads and infrastructure.
    e. high taxes on citizen's income.

Answer: (b) Difficulty: (2) Knowledge: (A) Page: 46

57. When members of a free trade area add common external tariffs to the provisions of the free trade agreement, the free trade area becomes a:

    a. cartel.
    b. common market.
    c. monetary union.
    d. political union.
    e. customs union.

Answer: (e) Difficulty: (2) Knowledge: (F) Page: 46

58. One difference between a customs union and a free trade area is that the customs union:

    a. adds external tariffs to nonmember countries.
    b. adds higher taxes to its consumers.
    c. refuses to import from nonmember nations.
    d. demands that a common currency be used among members.
    e. requires that member countries align themselves politically.

Answer: (a) Difficulty: (2) Knowledge: (A) Page: 46

59. A _____ eliminates all tariffs and barriers to trade among members, adopts a common set of external tariffs on nonmembers, and removes all restrictions on the flow of capital and labor among member nations.

   a. cartel.
   b. common market.
   c. monetary union.
   d. political union.
   e. customs union.

Answer: (b) Difficulty: (2) Knowledge: (A) Page: 47

60. The primary difference between a common market and a customs union is that the common market:

   a. adopts a common set of external tariffs on nonmembers.
   b. eliminates all tariffs.
   c. eliminates all trade barriers.
   d. removes all restrictions on the flow of capital and labor among member nations.
   e. the number of countries involved.

Answer: (d) Difficulty: (3) Knowledge: (A) Page: 47

61. The effect of a monetary union is that members:

   a. can buy goods from one another.
   b. refuse to buy goods from nonmembers.
   c. switch to a common currency and a central bank.
   d. give up all sovereignty.
   e. no longer recognize national boundaries.

Answer: (c) Difficulty: (3) Knowledge: (A) Page: 47

62. When the European Union switches to a monetary union the new common currency will be called:

   a. the pound.
   b. the franc.
   c. the mark.
   d. the Euro-dollar.
   e. European Currency Unit (ECU).

Answer: (e) Difficulty: (1) Knowledge: (F) Page: 47

63. The last step of the possible integration forms is the:

    a. cartel.
    b. common market.
    c. monetary union.
    d. political union.
    e. customs union.

Answer: (d) Difficulty: (2) Knowledge: (F) Page: 47

64. The principle goal of a political union is that it:

    a. can buy goods from one another.
    b. can refuse to buy goods from nonmembers.
    c. can switch to a common currency and a central bank.
    d. gives up all sovereignty among individual members.
    e. no longer recognizes national boundaries.

Answer: (d) Difficulty: (3) Knowledge: (A) Page: 47

65. Researchers have reported that multinationals have not been as great a threat to countries' national sovereignty because multinationals have yet to solve the problem of:

    a. demand.
    b. size.
    c. war.
    d. religious conflict.
    e. language differences.

Answer: (b) Difficulty: (3) Knowledge: (F) Page: 49

True/False   Short Answer

1. Today, countries have become economically independent.

Answer: (False) Difficulty: (1) Knowledge: (F) Page: 25

2. The biggest trade headache for the United States in the future is predicted to be with Japan.

Answer: (False) Difficulty: (2) Knowledge: (F) Page: 26

3. The biggest trade headache for the United States in the future is predicted to be with
_____.

Answer: (China) Difficulty: (3) Knowledge: (F) Page: 26

4. According to the World Economic Forum's global competitiveness report in 1995, the world's top four economies were the United States, Japan, Singapore, and Hong Kong.

Answer: (True) Difficulty: (2) Knowledge: (F) Page: 26

5. According to the World Economic Forum's global competitiveness report in 1995, the world's top four economies were the United States, Japan, Singapore, and
_____.

Answer: (Hong Kong) Difficulty: (3) Knowledge: (F) Page: 26

6. The number one country (with respect to world trade) that accounts for the most trade dollars with the United States is Canada.

Answer: (True) Difficulty: (2) Knowledge: (F) Page: 26

7. The number one country (with respect to world trade) that accounts for the most trade dollars with the United States is Japan.

Answer: (False) Difficulty: (3) Knowledge: (F) Page: 26

8. The number one country (with respect to world trade) that accounts for the most trade dollars with the United States is _____.

Answer: (Canada) Difficulty: (3) Knowledge: (F) Page: 26

9. _____ is investing in manufacturing and service facilities in a foreign country.

Answer: (Foreign direct investment) Difficulty: (1) Knowledge: (A) Page: 28

10. Foreign direct investment can be thought of as an alternative to exports.

Answer: (True) Difficulty: (1) Knowledge: (A) Page: 28

11. Toyota Motors of Japan makes more cars in the United States than it imports from Japan.

Answer: (True) Difficulty: (1) Knowledge: (F) Page: 28

12. _____ investment refers to investment in foreign countries that are withdrawable on short notice (such as investment in foreign stocks or bonds).

Answer: (Portfolio) Difficulty: (2) Knowledge: (F) Page: 28

13. A rising currency value usually does not deter foreign investment in the country in which the rise occurs.

Answer: (False) Difficulty: (2) Knowledge: (A) Page: 29

14. The United States continues to be one of the nations that remains relatively insulated from the global economy.

Answer: (True) Difficulty: (2) Knowledge: (A) Page: 29

15. In a pure command economy, the supply and demand of goods and services determine the price.

Answer: (False) Difficulty: (1) Knowledge: (A) Page: 30

16. The United States would be an example of a market-private economy.

Answer: (True) Difficulty: (2) Knowledge: (A) Page: 30

17. An example of a command-public economy would be Canada.

Answer: (False) Difficulty: (2) Knowledge: (A) Page: 30

18. North Korea and Cuba would be examples of a command-public economy.

Answer: (True) Difficulty: (2) Knowledge: (A) Page: 30

19. Groups that are bound together by strong, informal ties and interlocking ownership are called _____.

Answer: (Keiretsus) Difficulty: (3) Knowledge: (F) Page: 31

20. There appears to be a highly positive relationship between the number of telephone lines per hundred people and the Gross Domestic Product (GDP) of a

nation.

Answer: (True) Difficulty: (2) Knowledge: (F) Page: 31

21. The GATT accords and the WTO are basically the same thing.

Answer: (False) Difficulty: (1) Knowledge: (A) Page: 34, 37

22. WTO is trying to absorb GATT.

Answer: (True) Difficulty: (2) Knowledge: (A) Page: 37

23. _____ refers to the investment by firms in one nation to create productive facilities in another nation.

Answer: (Foreign direct investment) Difficulty: (3) Knowledge: (F) Page: 37

24. The number one foreign investor in the United States is Japan.

Answer: (True) Difficulty: (1) Knowledge: (F) Page: 38

25. When members of a free trade area add common external tariffs to the provisions of a free trade agreement then the free trade area becomes a _____.

Answer: (customs union) Difficulty: (2) Knowledge: (F) Page: 46

Essay

1. The world marketplace is shrinking and changing. One of the vehicles that has been instrumental in this change is the GATT accords. Explain what GATT is and how it has affected international business.

Answer:

The General Agreements of Tariffs and Trade (GATT) provides a forum for multilateral discussion among countries to reduce trade barriers. Nations met periodically to review the status of world trade and to negotiate mutually agreeable reductions in trade barriers.

The main operating principle of GATT was the concept of Most Favored Nation. The MFN status meant that any country which was a member state to a GATT agreement and which extended a reduction in tariff to another nation would have to automatically extended the same benefit to all members of GATT. However, there is no enforcement mechanism. Trade barriers were lowered but services were largely unaffected.

Difficulty: (1) Knowledge: (A) Page: 32, 33

2. To improve on GATT the WTO was established. Explain what the WTO is, how it is different from GATT, and what specific functions the WTO is expected to perform.

Answer:

The World Trade Organization (the WTO) is different from GATT in that it has statutory powers with authority to adjudicate trade disputes among nations. The WTO is the new legal and institutional foundation for a multilateral trading system. It provides the contractual obligations determining how governments frame and implement domestic trade legislation and regulations.

WTO is not just an extension of GATT. The GATT was a multilateral agreement with no institutional foundations. WTO is a permanent institution with its own secretariat. WTO is legally binding. The WTO dispute settlement mechanism, is faster, more automatic and therefore much less susceptible to blockages than the old GATT system.

Difficulty: (2) Knowledge: (A) Page: 34, 35, 36

3. Explain what foreign direct investment is and how trade patterns have changed over the past decade. Be sure to comment on how the U.S. has participated in foreign direct investment and been affected by this form of investment.

Answer:

Foreign direct investment refers to the investment by firms in one nation to create productive facilities in another nation. In the latter twentieth century, the U.S. has always been in the forefront of investing in other countries (much like Britain in the nineteenth century).

As shown in Exhibit 2-5, the United States continues to invest in Europe (as it has in the past). New investment is occurring in increasing amounts in Asian countries. This is expected to continue into the future.

Historically, investment in the United States had been modest. However, the 20th century brought a sharp increase in outside investment (especially since the 1980s). Reasons have been attributed to the fall in the price of the dollar (as measured against other currencies) and because of a persistent trade deficit the government has increased pressure on trading partners to invest in the country through a variety of channels. The United States is predicted to be a prime investment for several years to come. The top three investors in the United States at present are Japan, the United Kingdom, and the Netherlands.

Difficulty: (1) Knowledge: (F) Page: 37-40

4. Some of the greatest challenges in trade in the next century will come in the area information technology and intellectual property. Describe these challenges, the mechanisms that are in place to protect one's intellectual property, and how trade in general will be affected.

Answer:

With advent of the information age, firms are faced with new situations. Not only is it easy for individuals to make duplicates of many works or to re-use their content in new works, but the physical manifestation of content is almost irrelevant. The United States, in an attempt to protect intellectual property rights, has insisted that intellectual property rights be dealt with in GATT and WTO. Technology based protection of electronic information through hardware, software, or a combination thereof in the form of encryption and digital signatures have been suggested as a means of circumventing the problem of unauthorized copying.

Controlling copying is a difficult problem. The solution may be in not controlling the copies but instead controlling the relationship with the customers through subscriptions or membership. There are other larger questions or hurdles to be overcome. One is the rise of a truly efficient market for information. Second, is the role of and attempts by governments to regulate international commerce.

Difficulty: (2) Knowledge: (A) Page: 42, 43

5. It has been suggested that cooperative inter-relationships between countries (regional groupings) can be classified into five broad categories. Briefly summarize and describe each of these categories and indicate differences that may be present.

Answer:

  a. *Free Trade Area.* This form has a higher level of integration than a loosely formed regional cooperation and is a formal agreement among two or more countries to reduce or eliminate customs duties and non-tariff barriers among partner countries.
     1). NAFTA is an illustration.
     2). The free trade area is not free of all trade barriers.
  b. *Customs Union.* When members of a free trade area add common external tariffs to the provisions of the free trade agreement then the free trade area becomes the customs union (ASEAN is an example).
  c. *Common Market.* A common market eliminates all tariffs and barriers to trade among members of the common market, adopts a set of external tariffs on non-members, and removes all restrictions on the flow of capital and

380

labor among member nations.

d. ***Monetary Union.*** In this form member nations move to a common currency and a central bank.

1). The European Union is attempting to achieve this step (slowly).

e. ***Political Union.*** In this phase new nations are created. Integration is achieved on a voluntary basis. A loose political union normally comes first (such as the British Commonwealth).

Difficulty: (3) Knowledge: (F) Page: 44-48

Chapter 3

Multiple Choice

1. Each country has its own currency. Through this currency the country expresses the value of its:

   a. land.
   b. products.
   c. government.
   d. central bank.
   e. labor.

Answer: (b) Difficulty: (1) Knowledge: (F) Page: 54

2. For international trade settlements, the various currencies of the world must be exchanged from one to another. This is accomplished through:

   a. foreign exchange markets.
   b. commodities trading.
   c. stock markets.
   d. the World Bank.
   e. central banking.

Answer: (a) Difficulty: (2) Knowledge: (A) Page: 54

3. Following World War II, the United States agreed to exchange the dollar at:

   a. 1 for 5 German marks.
   b. 1 for 3 British pounds.
   c. $35 per ounce of gold.
   d. $15 per ounce of gold.
   e. 1 for 100 Mexican pesos.

Answer: (c) Difficulty: (2) Knowledge: (F) Page: 54

4. After World War II when the U.S. stabilized its dollar, countries could deal in dollars without being constrained by currency fluctuations. Thus, the dollar became the _____ in world trade.

    a. most valuable money
    b. gold standard
    c. inflation protector
    d. common denominator
    e. money that was hoarded

Answer: (d) Difficulty: (3) Knowledge: (A) Page: 54

5. Today, as the value of the dollar climbs, the effect is that U.S. exports:

    a. become more inexpensive.
    b. become more demanded.
    c. become less productive because of labor wages.
    d. become the primary goods used for barter.
    e. become more expensive.

Answer: (e) Difficulty: (2) Knowledge: (F) Page: 54

6. Under the _____, the major nations of the world issued paper money backed by gold.

    a. silver standard
    b. gold standard
    c. monetary agreement system
    d. World Bank concept
    e. Paris, France agreement

Answer: (b) Difficulty: (1) Knowledge: (F) Page: 55

7. Which of the following is NOT a feature of the gold standard?

    a. Establishment of a fixed system of fixed exchange rates between participating countries.
    b. Stable exchange rates.
    c. Limitations were placed on the rate of growth in a country's money supply.
    d. All money must be backed by gold.
    e. Gold must be shared since some countries did not have any mining resources.

Answer: (e) Difficulty: (2) Knowledge: (A) Page: 55

8. If a monetary system declares that all money must be backed by gold, the system would best be described as being:

   a. a gold standard.
   b. a silver standard.
   c. a free-floating exchange system.
   d. a government controlled system.
   e. a dollar-enhanced system.

Answer: (a) Difficulty: (1) Knowledge: (F) Page: 55

9. One of the problems with returning to the gold standard after World War I was:

   a. the gold supply was no longer growing and could not keep pace with the needs of commerce.
   b. almost all gold was held by the United States, Russia, and the United Kingdom.
   c. gold had become to abundant and had lost its value.
   d. paper money was more important than gold.
   e. agreements prohibited certain countries from having gold.

Answer: (a) Difficulty: (2) Knowledge: (A) Page: 55

10. The gold standard (after World War I) limited a nation's:

   a. ability to have banks.
   b. ability to have an independent monetary policy.
   c. ability to repay war debts.
   d. ability to invest in agriculture.
   e. ability to pay government workers.

Answer: (b) Difficulty: (2) Knowledge: (F) Page: 55

11. One of the major contributing factors that lead to the Great Depression was:

   a. the auto assembly line.
   b. labor unions.
   c. the silver standard.
   d. the gold standard.
   e. the League of Nations.

Answer: (d) Difficulty: (2) Knowledge: (A) Page: 55

12. Prior to World War I, the dominant world currency was the:

a. dollar.
b. British rupee.
c. British pound sterling.
d. German mark.
e. Spanish peso.

Answer: (c) Difficulty: (2) Knowledge: (F) Page: 55

13. What event forced the United States to abandon the gold standard in 1933?

a. World War I.
b. The rise of communism in Russia.
c. Labor unions and strikes.
d. Bread lines in Washington D.C.
e. The Great Depression.

Answer: (e) Difficulty: (1) Knowledge: (F) Page: 56

14. One of the results of the Great Depression (with respect to monetary and international policy) was that the United States adopted a policy of:

a. one job for every man.
b. adhering to the gold standard.
c. adhering to the silver standard.
d. isolationism and protectionism.
e. expansion into depressed areas to take advantage of competitive weakness.

Answer: (d) Difficulty: (3) Knowledge: (F) Page: 56

15. The Bretton Woods Conference followed:

a. World War I.
b. World War II.
c. the Korean War.
d. the Viet Nam War.
e. the Gulf War.

Answer: (b) Difficulty: (2) Knowledge: (F) Page: 56

16. Negotiations to establish the postwar (World War II) international monetary system took place at:

   a. Bretton Woods, NH.
   b. New York, NY at the United Nations.
   c. the Postdam conference.
   d. the Malta conference.
   e. in London, England on VE day.

Answer: (a) Difficulty: (2) Knowledge: (F) Page: 56

17. Which of the following was <u>NOT</u> a recommendation of the Bretton Woods conference following World War II?

   a. Each nation should be at liberty to use macroeconomic policies for full employment.
   b. Recognizing that free-floating exchange rates could not work.
   c. Recommending that the gold standard be scrapped.
   d. Avoid trading with communistic countries who were against capitalistic standards and therefore opposed to stabilized monetary policy.
   e. Avoid the extremes of both permanently fixed and floating rates.

Answer: (d) Difficulty: (2) Knowledge (A) Page: 56

18. In order to avoid both the rigidity of a fixed exchange rate system and at the same time the chaos of freely floating exchange rates, the Bretton Woods conference provided for an adjustable:

   a. stock market.
   b. banking system.
   c. peg (par values in terms of gold but little convertibility).
   d. bond market.
   e. monitoring system.

Answer: (c) Difficulty: (3) Knowledge: (A) Page: 56

19. Under the Bretton Woods peg system, a country experiencing a balance-of-payments deficit, would:

   a. sell its currency on the open market.
   b. defend its currency by using its foreign currency reserves.
   c. add tariffs to protect itself.
   d. add nontariff barriers to protect itself.
   e. would not allow any additional foreign investment until it gained control of its monetary system.

Answer: (b) Difficulty: (3) Knowledge: (A) Page: 57

20. Under the Bretton Woods peg system, a country experiencing a balance-of-payments surplus, would:

   a. sell its currency on the open market.
   b. defend its currency by using its foreign currency reserves.
   c. add tariffs to protect itself.
   d. add nontariff barriers to protect itself.
   e. would not allow any additional foreign investment until it gained control of its monetary system.

Answer: (a) Difficulty: (3) Knowledge: (A) Page: 57

21. What was the name of the organization established at Bretton Woods to oversee the newly agreed upon postwar monetary system?

   a. The World Bank.
   b. The International Monetary Fund (IMF).
   c. GATT.
   d. NAFTA.
   e. The International Bank for Reconstruction and Development.

Answer: (b) Difficulty: (1) Knowledge: (F) Page: 57

22. One of the functions of the International Monetary Fund (IMF) was to monitor problems that a country might experience in maintaining equilibrium in its balance of payments. By agreement, countries would need permission from the IMF to alter their peg if the initial par value was to be adjusted by more than:

   a. 5%.
   b. 7%.
   c. 10%.
   d. 15%.
   e. a country did not need permission to alter their peg.

Answer: (c) Difficulty: (3) Knowledge: (F) Page: 57

23. The _____ is a specialized agency within the United Nations that was established to promote international monetary cooperation and to facilitate the expansion of trade.

   a. International Monetary Fund
   b. World Bank
   c. NASDAQ
   d. New York Stock Exchange
   e. International Credit Bureau

Answer: (a) Difficulty: (1) Knowledge: (F) Page: 57

24. All of the following are purposes of the International Monetary Fund (IMF) EXCEPT:

   a. To promote international monetary cooperation through a permanent institution.
   b. To facilitate the expansion and balanced growth of international trade.
   c. To develop a world currency by 2010.
   d. To promote exchange stability.
   e. To give confidence to members by making the general resources of the fund temporarily available to them under adequate safeguards.

Answer: (c) Difficulty: (2) Knowledge: (A) Page: 57, 58

25. To expand services for countries in monetary difficulties, the IMF created:

    a. Euro-checks.
    b. Euro-dollars.
    c. ever expanding credit with no payback dates.
    d. Special Drawing Rights (SRDs).
    e. a world factoring system.

Answer: (d) Difficulty: (3) Knowledge: (A) Page: 58

26. The original purpose of the World Bank was to:

    a. to provide a place where any country could cash a check.
    b. to provide a place where members could meet and discuss problems.
    c. to provide an organization to oversee a new world order.
    d. to provide a central place to provide an international interest rate.
    e. to provide a place and system for financing postwar reconstruction and development.

Answer: (e) Difficulty: (2) Knowledge: (F) Page: 58

27. The world financial community has come to recognize in recent years that real financial stability can only be achieved in _____ and not through imposed pegged exchange rates and official intervention.

    a. stable economic and financial conditions
    b. financial control by the United Nations
    c. financial control by the World Court
    d. financial control by the United States Federal Reserve
    e. creating a world currency

Answer: (a) Difficulty: (2) Knowledge: (A) Page: 59

28. According to research, the effect of floating exchange rates were supposed to facilitate balance of payments adjustments. What has really happened?

    a. Balance of payments has stabilized.
    b. Balance of payments has remained unchanged.
    c. Balance of payments have increasingly become more imbalanced.
    d. Balance of payments are now controlled by the United Nations for all major countries.
    e. Balance of payments is no longer a serious world problem.

Answer: (c) Difficulty: (3) Knowledge: (A) Page: 60

29. All of the following were supposed to be benefits of floating exchange rates EXCEPT:

    a. Facilitation of balance of payments adjustments.
    b. The adoption of world currency.
    c. A curtailing of currency speculation.
    d. Market forces would determine the correct foreign exchange rate balance.
    e. Preservation of autonomy in economic and monetary policy.

Answer: (b) Difficulty: (2) Knowledge: (A) Page: 60

30. _____ float is the closet approximation to perfect competiton, because there is no government intervention and because billions of units of currency are being traded by buyers and sellers.

    a. Managed (clean)
    b. Managed (dirty)
    c. Free (dirty)
    d. Free (clean)
    e. Vertical

Answer: (d) Difficulty: (1) Knowledge: (F) Page: 60

31. _____ float allows for a limited amount of government intervention to soften sudden swings in the value of a currency.

    a. Free (dirty)
    b. Free (clean)
    c. Restricted
    d. Profit
    e. Managed

Answer: (e) Difficulty: (2) Knowledge: (F) Page: 60

32. Consider the following example: In 1988, Mexico allowed a gradual slide in the value of the peso in order to retain investor confidence, as well as to avoid rapid inflation and other negative effects of sudden devaluations. This would be an example of which form of float?
    a. Free (dirty)
    b. Free (clean)
    c. Restricted
    d. Managed
    e. Profit

Answer: (d) Difficulty: (2) Knowledge: (A) Page: 60

33. Today, the global economy is increasingly dominated by three major currency blocs. They are:

    a. the U.S. dollar, the French franc, and the Japanese yen.
    b. the U.S. dollar, the Spanish peso, and the Japanese yen.
    c. the U.S. dollar, the British pound, and the Japanese yen.
    d. the U.S. dollar, the British pound, and the German mark.
    e. the U.S. dollar, the German mark, and the Japanese yen.

Answer: (e) Difficulty: (2) Knowledge: (F) Page: 62

34. _____ refers to the exchange of one country's money for that of another country.

    a. Conversion
    b. Factoring
    c. Foreign exchange
    d. Free float
    e. Managed float

Answer: (c) Difficulty: (1) Knowledge: (F) Page: 62

35. One of the most fundamental determinates of the exchange rate is _____ whereby the exchange rate between the currencies of two countries is in equilibrium when it equates the prices of a basket of goods and services in both countries.

    a. free float
    b. free float (dirty)
    c. managed float
    d. purchasing power parity (PPP)
    e. absolute cost advantage

Answer: (d) Difficulty: (2) Knowledge: (F) Page: 62

36. Each year the *Economist* publishes a purchasing power parity (PPP) study based on McDonald's Big Mac hamburger that is sold all over the world. This index shows whether currencies are at their "correct" exchange rate. The index is called:
    a. the Big Mac Index.
    b. the Purchasing Power Parity (PPP) Index.
    c. the *Economist* Purchasing Index.
    d. the Parity Index.
    e. the Exchange/Inflation Rate Index.

Answer: (a) Difficulty: (2) Knowledge: (F) Page: 63

37. Actual exchange rates can be very different from the expected rates forecasted by economists. Many interrelated factors influence the value of a floating currency. The three most important fundamental factors are the nation's balance of payments situation, world political events, and:

    a. the world inflation rate.
    b. the country's currency value.
    c. the nation's inflation rate relative to its trading partners.
    d. the tax structure of the nation.
    e. the supply of gold that the nation holds.

Answer: (c) Difficulty: (3) Knowledge: (A) Page: 63

38. Factors that might influence foreign exchange rates with respect to political factors would include election year or leadership change and:

    a. money supply.
    b. balance of payments.
    c. exchange rate control as imposed by a government.
    d. size of the military.
    e. amount of armed conflict in the world.

Answer: (c) Difficulty: (3) Knowledge: (A) Page: 65, Exhibit 3-3

39. If payment on a transaction is to be made immediately, the purchaser has no choice other than to buy foreign exchange on:

    a. the spot market.
    b. the forward market.
    c. a hedge.
    d. a future date invoice.
    e. an exchange rate pass-through.

Answer: (a) Difficulty: (2) Knowledge: (F) Page: 67

40. If payment for goods is to be made at some future date, the purchaser has the option of buying foreign exchange on the _____ for delivery at some future date.

   a. black market
   b. gray market
   c. forward market
   d. exchange rate pass-through market
   e. commodities market

Answer: (c) Difficulty: (1) Knowledge: (F) Page: 67

41. When buyer locks in an exchange rate and avoids the risk of currency fluctuations, it is called:

   a. the spot market.
   b. the gray market.
   c. vertical purchasing.
   d. hedging.
   e. factoring.

Answer: (d) Difficulty: (2) Knowledge: (A) Page: 67

42. Protecting oneself against potential loss is called:

   a. hedging.
   b. factoring.
   c. risk analysis.
   d. portfolio reduction strategy.
   e. devaluing.

Answer: (a) Difficulty: (1) Knowledge: (F) Page: 67

43. By custom, when quoting the value of a foreign currency, it is expressed in how many units of that currency it takes to buy:

   a. one unit of that currency.
   b. one British pound.
   c. one dollar.
   d. one Swiss franc.
   e. one Japanese yen.

Answer: (c) Difficulty: (1) Knowledge: (F) Page: 68

44. The extent to which a foreign company changes dollar prices of its products in the U.S. market as a result of exchange rate fluctuations is called:

    a. hedging.
    b. exchange rate pass-through.
    c. a target exchange rate.
    d. factoring.
    e. inflation-proofing.

Answer: (b) Difficulty: (2) Knowledge: (F) Page: 70, 71

45. The _____ of a nation summarizes all the transactions that have taken place between its residents and the residents of other countries over a specified time period (usually a month, quarter or a year).

    a. target exchange rate
    b. portfolio acquisition
    c. balance of payments
    d. debt accumulation
    e. exchange inflation

Answer: (c) Difficulty: (1) Knowledge: (F) Page: 71

46. With respect to a balance of payments between nations calculation, transactions are recorded in three categories. These are the current account, the capital account, and:
    a. goods inventory.
    b. cost of goods sold.
    c. manufacturer's inventory.
    d. capital goods.
    e. official reserves.

Answer: (e) Difficulty: (3) Knowledge: (F) Page: 71

47. With respect to balance of payments calculation, when a German tourist visits the United States and spends money on meals and lodging, it is a(n) _____ to the U.S. trade in services balance.
    a. debit
    b. credit
    c. convertible
    d. exchange interest factor
    e. non-entity

Answer: (b) Difficulty: (1) Knowledge: (A) Page: 71

48. Balance of payments between nations is based on which of the following principles of accounting?

   a. Debit only.
   b. Credit only.
   c. Factor analysis.
   d. First in, last out.
   e. Double entry accounting.

Answer: (e) Difficulty: (2) Knowledge: (F) Page: 71

49. Double entry accounting, with respect to calculation of balance of payments calculation, means:

   a. the balance of payments statement must always balance.
   b. the balance of payments statement will always favor the larger nation.
   c. the balance of payments statement will always favor the smaller nation.
   d. the balance of payments statement will never be in complete balance.
   e. the balance of payments statement will rarely be accurate.

Answer: (a) Difficulty: (2) Knowledge: (F) Page: 71

50. The government entity which prepares the balance of payments statement in the United States is:

   a. the Federal Reserve.
   b. the Internal Revenue Service.
   c. the Customs Department.
   d. the Department of Commerce.
   e. the National Industrial Policy Board.

Answer: (d) Difficulty: (2) Knowledge: (F) Page: 75

51. The balance of payments in goods account or _____ shows trade in currently produced goods as well as unilateral transfers of merchandise.

   a. current account balance
   b. capital account
   c. trade balance
   d. direct investments
   e. portfolio investment

Answer: (c) Difficulty: (2) Knowledge: (F) Page: 75

52. The balance of payments in _____ shows trade shows trade in currently produced goods and services, as well as unilateral transfers of merchandise.

   a. current account balance
   b. capital account
   c. trade balance
   d. direct investments
   e. portfolio investment

Answer: (a) Difficulty: (1) Knowledge: (F) Page: 75

53. The balance of payments in _____ summarizes financial transactions with respect to short and long term accounts.

   a. current account balance
   b. capital account
   c. trade balance
   d. direct investments
   e. portfolio investment

Answer: (b) Difficulty: (2) Knowledge: (F) Page: 75

54. _____ are those investments in enterprises or properties that are effectively controlled by residents of another country.

   a. Current account balance
   b. Capital account
   c. Trade balance
   d. Direct investments
   e. Portfolio investment

Answer: (d) Difficulty: (1) Knowledge: (F) Page: 75

55. _____ includes all long-term investments that do not give the investors effective control over the investment. Such transactions typically involve the purchase of stocks or bonds of foreign investors for investment.

   a. Current account balance
   b. Capital account
   c. Trade balance
   d. Direct investments
   e. Portfolio investment

Answer: (e) Difficulty: (2) Knowledge: (F) Page: 75

56. Everyone knows that the United States regularly runs a deficit in merchandise trade. In which of the following categories does the United States regularly run a surplus?

    a. Services
    b. Automobiles
    c. China
    d. Fashion footwear
    e. Machine tools (such as a drill press)

Answer: (a) Difficulty: (2) Knowledge: (A) Page: 77

57. According to the theory of international trade and balance of payments, a surplus or deficit in a country's basic balance should be:

    a. always weighted toward the deficit side.
    b. always weighted toward the surplus side.
    c. self correcting.
    d. continually out of balance.
    e. only brought into balance by government tariff action.

Answer: (c) Difficulty: (3) Knowledge: (A) Page: 77

58. The mechanisms (according to the theory of international trade and balance of payments) for producing self-correction in out-of-balance accounts is accomplished through:

    a. internal market adjustments.
    b. external market adjustments.
    c. internal and external market adjustments.
    d. governmental control.
    e. governmental tariff and nontariff barriers.

Answer: (c) Difficulty: (2) Knowledge: (A) Page: 77

59. With respect to self-correction in out-of-balance balance of payments accounts, _____ refers to the movement of prices and incomes in a country.

    a. internal market adjustments.
    b. external market adjustments.
    c. internal and external market adjustments.
    d. governmental control.
    e. governmental tariff and nontariff barriers.

Answer: (a) Difficulty: (1) Knowledge: (F) Page: 77

60. With respect to self-correction in out-of-balance balance of payments accounts,
_____ refers to exchange rates or a nation's currency and
its value with respect to the currencies of other nations.

    a. internal market adjustments.
    b. external market adjustments.
    c. internal and external market adjustments.
    d. governmental control.
    e. governmental tariff and nontariff barriers.

Answer: (b) Difficulty: (1) Knowledge: (F) Page: 78

True/False   Short Answer

1. All international transactions must take place within the context of an international
   government control system.

Answer: (False) Difficulty: (2) Knowledge: (A) Page: 54

2. All international transactions must take place within the context of an international
   monetary system.

Answer: (True) Difficulty: (1) Knowledge: (A) Page: 54

3. The absence of a universal currency means we must have a system that allows for
   the transfer of purchase power between countries with different national currencies.

Answer: (True) Difficulty: (1) Knowledge: (F) Page: 54

4. One reason that commerce is able to work as well as it does is that the world
   economic order has accepted the dollar as the universal currency.

Answer: (False) Difficulty: (2) Knowledge: (A) Page: 54

5. In order to have international trade settlements, the various currencies of the world
   must be exchanged from one to another. This accomplished through _____
   markets.

Answer: (foreign exchange) Difficulty: (3) Knowledge: (F) Page: 54

6. After World War II, the dollar became the common denominator in world trade.

Answer: (True) Difficulty: (2) Knowledge: (F) Page: 54

7. Because of its use in international commerce, the dollar has remained strong throughout the 1980s and 1990s.

Answer: (False) Difficulty: (2) Knowledge: (F) Page: 54

8. The gold standard means that gold could be surrendered to the monetary authorities of two trading nations in return for local currency at its respective value.

Answer: (True) Difficulty: (1) Knowledge: (F) Page: 55

9. The gold standard's main difficulty was that it did not establish a system of fixed exchange rates between participating countries.

Answer: (False) Difficulty: (2) Knowledge: (F) Page: 55

10. The gold standard failed after World War I because the world's gold supply could not keep up with the demands of commerce.

Answer: (True) Difficulty: (1) Knowledge: (F) Page: 55

11. One of the chief causes (with respect to international monetary policy) of the Great Depression was the use of the _____.

Answer: (Gold Standard) Difficulty: (2) Knowledge: (F) Page: 55

12. The dominant currency prior to World War I was the _____.

Answer: (British pound sterling) Difficulty: (3) Knowledge: (F) Page: 55

13. The United States was forced to abandon the Gold Standard because of the Great Depression.

Answer: (True) Difficulty: (1) Knowledge: (F) Page: 56

14. Following World War II, negotiations to establish the postwar international monetary system took place at the _____ conference.

Answer: (Bretton Woods, NH) Difficulty: (3) Knowledge: (F) Page: 56

15. The Bretton Woods conference (following World War II) effectively killed a return to the gold standard.

Answer: (True) Difficulty: (2) Knowledge: (F) Page: 56

16. In order to avoid both the rigidity of a fixed exchange rate system and the chaos of freely floating exchange rates, the Bretton Woods Agreement provided for an adjustable _____.

Answer: (peg) Difficulty: (3) Knowledge: (F) Page: 56

17. The International Monetary Fund (IMF) was established to oversee the newly agreed upon monetary system proposed at Bretton Woods.

Answer: (True) Difficulty: (2) Knowledge: (F) Page: 57

18. President Nixon suspended the convertibility of the dollar to gold on August 15, 1971.

Answer: (True) Difficulty: (2) Knowledge: (F) Page: 57

19. The International Monetary Fund is a specialized agency within the United States Federal Reserve.

Answer: (False) Difficulty: (2) Knowledge: (F) Page: 57

20. The reason for a creating a World Bank was to aid countries in financing their imports.

Answer: (False) Difficulty: (2) Knowledge: (A) Page: 58

21. One of the advantages of a floating exchange rate is that floating exchange rates are supposed to facilitate balance of payments adjustments.

Answer: (True) Difficulty: (1) Knowledge: (F) Page: 60

22. One of the valuable consequences of floating exchange rates is that they have facilitated balance of payments adjustments without governmental controls.

Answer: (False) Difficulty: (2) Knowledge: (A) Page: 60

23. _____ float is the closest approximation to perfect competiton.

Answer: (Free or clean) Difficulty: (2) Knowledge: (F) Page: 60

24. _____ float allows for a limited amount of government intervention to soften sudden swings in the value of a currency.

Answer: (Managed) Difficulty: (3) Knowledge: (F) Page: 60

25. One of the most fundamental determinates of the exchange rate is purchasing power parity.

Answer: (True) Difficulty: (2) Knowledge: (F) Page: 62

26. The *Economist* publishes a ppp study every year based on McDonald's Big Mac hamburger. This index is called the Big Mac Index.

Answer: (True) Difficulty: (2) Knowledge: (F) Page: 63

27. If a seller requests payment now, the international purchaser has no choice but to buy foreign exchange on the _____ market.

Answer: (spot) Difficulty: (3) Knowledge: (F) Page: 67

28. If a seller will accept payment in the future for goods purchased now, the international

purchaser can have the option of buying foreign exchange on the _____ market.

Answer: (forward) Difficulty: (3) Knowledge: (F) Page: 67

29. Balance of payments in international trade is based on the principle of _____ accounting.

Answer: (double entry) Difficulty: (3) Knowledge: (F) Page: 71

30. Under a system of double entry accounting, balance between credits and debits often does not occur.

Answer: (False) Difficulty: (2) Knowledge: (A) Page: 71

Essay

1. Explain the primary roles played by the International Monetary Fund and the World Bank.

Answer:

The International Monetary Fund (IMF) was created at Bretton Woods to oversee the newly created monetary system. The IMF was a specialized agency within the United Nations established to promote international monetary cooperation and to facilitate the expansion of trade, and in turn to contribute to increased employment and improved conditions in all member countries.

Another creation of the Bretton Woods conference was the International Bank for Reconstruction and Development, known as the World Bank. The World Bank (as different from the IMF) was initially intended for the financing of postwar reconstruction and development and later for infrastructure building projects in the developing world. More recently, the Bank has begun to participate actively with the IMF to resolve debt problems of the developing world and may also play a major role in bringing a market economy to the former members of the Eastern bloc.

Difficulty: (2) Knowledge: (F) Page: 56-59

2. Explain the concept of managed float.

Answer:

A managed float allows for a limited amount of government intervention to soften sudden swings in value of a currency. If a nation's currency enters into a rapid ascent or decline, that nation's central bank may wish to sell or buy that currency on the open market in a countervailing movement to offset the prevailing market tendency. This is for the purpose of maintaining an orderly, less volatile foreign exchange market.

Difficulty: (1) Knowledge: (A) Page: 60

3. Explain how knowledge of the spot and forward exchange rate market helps international marketers to be successful in the global arena.

Answer:

If payment on a transaction is to be made immediately, the purchaser has no choice other than to buy foreign exchange on the spot (or current) market, for immediate delivery. However, if payment is to be made at some future date, the purchaser has the option of buying foreign exchange on the spot market or on the forward market, for delivery at some future date. The advantage of the forward market is that the buyer can lock in an exchange rate and avoid the risk of currency fluctuations; this is called hedging, or protecting oneself against potential loss.

Difficulty: (2) Knowledge: (A) Page: 67, 68

4. Explain what exchange rate pass-through is and what difficulties might be incurred with its successful application.

Answer:

The extent to which a foreign company changes dollar prices of its products in the U.S. market as a result of exchange rate fluctuations is called exchange rate pass-through. It is usually less than perfect because it requires an estimate of the average increase with respect to dollar prices (with respect to the currency of the trading country or company).

Difficulty: (3) Knowledge: (F) Page: 68, 71

5. List and briefly describe the four types of balance of payments measures.

Answer:

a. The balance of payments in goods account (trade balance, for short) shows trade in currently produced goods as well as unilateral transfers (private gifts) of merchandise.

b. The balance of payments in current account (current account balance) shows trade in currently produced goods and services, as well as unilateral transfers (private gifts and foreign aid) of merchandise.

c. The balance of payments in capital account (capital account) summarizes financial transactions and is divided into two sections, short and long capital accounts.

d. Subaccounts include direct investments and portfolio investment. Direct investments are those investments in enterprises or properties that are effectively controlled by residents of another country. Portfolio investment includes all long term investments that do not give the investors effective control over the investments.

Difficulty: (3) Knowledge: (F) Page: 75-77

Chapter 4

Multiple Choice

1. From a global marketing perspective, the cultural environment matters for two main reasons. First, cultural forces are a major factor in shaping a company's global marketing mix program. The second reason is:

   a. cultural analysis expensive.
   b. cultural analysis often pinpoints market opportunities.
   c. cultural analysis is difficult.
   d. accurate cultural analysis is next to impossible.
   e. cultural analysis is required by many host governments.

Answer: (b) Difficulty: (2) Knowledge: (F) Page: 81, 82

2. From a global marketing perspective, the cultural environment matters. The most important reason is that cultural forces are major factors in shaping a company's global:

   a. sales territories.
   b. vision.
   c. competitive response.
   d. marketing mix program.
   e. global ethics program.

Answer: (d) Difficulty: (2) Knowledge: (F) Page: 81

3. Companies that ignore cultural needs often:

   a. loose permission to export.
   b. loose permission to import.
   c. have more lawsuits.
   d. loose more salespeople.
   e. loose a competitive edge.

Answer: (e) Difficulty: (1) Knowledge: (A) Page: 82

4. Since China has 300 million children, they are often treated as:

   a. little emperors and empresses.
   b. outcasts.
   c. a source for hard labor.
   d. a tax burden.
   e. food liability.

Answer: (a) Difficulty: (1) Knowledge: (F) Page: 82

5. One reason Chinese parents treat their children as little "emperors and empresses" is that:

   a. they have no choice since it is mandated by Chinese law.
   b. China has a one child per couple (without penalties) birth control policy.
   c. advertising has influenced parents.
   d. children are cared for by Grandparents.
   e. China pays parents to have children.

Answer: (b) Difficulty: (2) Knowledge: (A) Page: 82

6. Children in China impact consumption patterns in all of the following ways EXCEPT:

   a. spending power.
   b. special nature of one child families.
   c. pester power.
   d. change agents.
   e. legacy due to inherited wealth.

Answer: (e) Difficulty: (3) Knowledge: (A) Page: 82

7. Within a given culture, consumption processes can be described via a sequence of stages. All of the following describe those stages EXCEPT:

   a. Access.
   b. Buying Behavior.
   c. Racial heritage.
   d. Consumption characteristics.
   e. Disposal.

Answer: (c) Difficulty: (3) Knowledge: (F) Page: 82

8. Asking the question "Does the consumer have physical and/or economic access to the product/service?" is an indication of which stage of consumption processes (as influenced by culture)?

   a. Buying behavior.
   b. Consumption characteristics.
   c. Disposal.
   d. Access.
   e. Acceleration.

Answer: (d) Difficulty: (2) Knowledge: (F) Page: 82

9. Asking the question "How is the decision to buy made by the consumers in the foreign market?" is an indication of which stage of consumption processes (as influenced by culture)?

   a. Buying behavior.
   b. Consumption characteristics.
   c. Disposal.
   d. Access.
   e. Acceleration.

Answer: (a) Difficulty: (2) Knowledge: (F) Page: 82

10. A vital ingredient in the attractiveness of U.S.-style fast food is that it:

   a. is cheap.
   b. is fast.
   c. caters to the family.
   d. it is American.
   e. it is usually spicy.

Answer: (c) Difficulty: (3) Knowledge: (A) Page: 83

11. One of the fears of any country that imports American fast food is that it might:

   a. be importing American values as well.
   b. be importing contaminated products.
   c. not make money.
   d. damage religious values.
   e. cause a revolution.

Answer: (a) Difficulty: (2) Knowledge: (A) Page: 83

12. _____ is a learned, shared, compelling, interrelated set of symbols whose meanings provide a set of orientations for members of society.

   a. Social class
   b. Reference groups
   c. Culture
   d. Material life
   e. Social interaction

Answer: (c) Difficulty: (2) Knowledge: (F) Page: 84

13. All of the following are unique features of culture EXCEPT:

   a. it is learned.
   b. it is inherited genetically.
   c. elements are interrelated with one another.
   d. culture is shared.
   e. culture is compelling.

Answer: (b) Difficulty: (3) Knowledge: (F) Page: 84

14. A culture can be defined by national borders (especially when the country is isolated by natural barriers. An example would be:

   a. the United States.
   b. Canada.
   c. Mexico.
   d. Japan.
   e. Germany.

Answer: (d) Difficulty: (2) Knowledge: (A) Page: 85

15. Below is a list of elements from culture that matter to international marketers. Pick the item that is likely to matter the least in doing business with a foreign culture.

   a. Material life.
   b. Political party affiliation.
   c. Language.
   d. Religion.
   e. Education.

Answer: (b) Difficulty: (3) Knowledge: (F) Page: 85

16. _____ primarily refers to the technologies that used to produce, distribute, and consume goods and services within society.

    a. Material life.
    b. Political party affiliation.
    c. Language.
    d. Values.
    e. Education.

Answer: (a) Difficulty: (1) Knowledge: (F) Page: 85

17. Selling different sizes of soft drinks in foreign cultures is an example of which component of culture?

    a. Material life.
    b. Social interaction.
    c. Language.
    d. Values.
    e. Education.

Answer: (a) Difficulty: (1) Knowledge: (A) Page: 85

18. Poor transportation and distribution infrastructure in many developing countries would be examples of:

    a. investment requirements.
    b. technology gaps tied to material life.
    c. governmental corruption that must be dealt with.
    d. government ineptitude.
    e. different value systems.

Answer: (b) Difficulty: (2) Knowledge: (A) Page: 85

19. _____ is often described as the most important element that sets human beings apart from animals.

    a. Materialism
    b. Destruction
    c. Life styles
    d. Language
    e. Computer skills

Answer: (d) Difficulty: (2) Knowledge: (F) Page: 86

20. As a communication medium, language has two components: spoken language and
_____ language.

   a. business
   b. slang
   c. signal
   d. silent
   e. electronic

Answer: (d) Difficulty: (3) Knowledge: (F) Page: 86

21. _____ refers to the complex of nonverbal communication
mechanisms that people use to get a message across.

   a. Spoken language
   b. Slang language
   c. Silent language
   d. Harmonious language
   e. Electronic language

Answer: (c) Difficulty: (2) Knowledge: (F) Page: 86

22. Gestures, grimaces, body language, and eye contact would all be illustrations of:

   a. spoken language.
   b. power language.
   c. social language.
   d. harmonious language.
   e. silent language.

Answer: (e) Difficulty: (2) Knowledge: (F) Page: 86

23. Careless translation of advertising slogans or product labels leads to:

   a. language blunders.
   b. high cost.
   c. government regulation.
   d. imprisonment of offending parties.
   e. preference of domestic products.

Answer: (a) Difficulty: (2) Knowledge: (F) Page: 87

24. _____ refers to the manner in which members of society relate to one another.

   a. Materialism
   b. Social interaction
   c. Buying behavior
   d. Value systems
   e. Cultural homogeneity

Answer: (b) Difficulty: (2) Knowledge: (F) Page: 87

25. Probably the most critical expression of social interactions is the concept of:

   a. silent language.
   b. gestures.
   c. kinship.
   d. reference groups.
   e. cultural homogeneity.

Answer: (c) Difficulty: (3) Knowledge: (F) Page: 87

26. A Los Angeles radio contest targeting Hispanic families offered two tickets to Disneyland. The contest failed because the station forgot about the effect of _____ on the Hispanic culture.

   a. cultural homogeneity
   b. nuclear family
   c. reference groups
   d. social class
   e. extended family

Answer: (e) Difficulty: (3) Knowledge: (A) Page: 88

27. _____ refer(s) to the set of people to which an individual looks for guidance in values and attitudes.

   a. Cultural homogeneity
   b. Reference groups
   c. Social class
   d. The extended family
   e. The nuclear family

Answer: (c) Difficulty: (2) Knowledge: (F) Page: 88

28. Membership groups are those groups that:

    a. require dues.
    b. exclude people.
    c. are exclusive.
    d. people belong.
    e. people would like to be a part of.

Answer: (d) Difficulty: (1) Knowledge: (F) Page: 88

29. _____ refers to a community's set of beliefs that relate to a reality that cannot be verified empirically.

    a. Vision
    b. Customs
    c. Taboos
    d. Religion
    e. Culture

Answer: (d) Difficulty: (2) Knowledge: (F) Page: 88

30. Religious _____ often force companies to adapt their marketing mix program.

    a. visions
    b. taboos
    c. culture
    d. leaders
    e. books

Answer: (b) Difficulty: (2) Knowledge: (F) Page: 89

31. An example of a religious taboo that might affect a company's marketing mix is:

    a. failing to say rosary.
    b. going uncovered into a church.
    c. excluding pork and/or beef from menu options in a restaurant.
    d. offering to sell food on Saturday.
    e. not closing the restaurant before dark.

Answer: (c) Difficulty: (2) Knowledge: (A) Page: 89

32. All of the following would be issues to consider when marketing in an Islamic framework EXCEPT:

   a. have less formal product warranties.
   b. avoid direct use of credit as a marketing tool.
   c. "excessive profits" should be turned over to stockholders.
   d. do not manufacture products that contain pork.
   e. take into account prayer timings.

Answer: (c) Difficulty: (3) Knowledge: (A) Page: 90, 91

33. Taking prayer timings into account when designing a company's marketing mix would be an essential in which of the following cultural environments?

   a. Baptist.
   b. Catholic.
   c. Islamic.
   d. Atheist.
   e. Lutheran.

Answer: (c) Difficulty: (1) Knowledge: (A) Page: 91

34. If your company were to employ male salespeople and they needed to get access to female shoppers, which of the following countries would this become the most difficult?

   a. United States.
   b. Japan.
   c. China.
   d. Saudi Arabia.
   e. Israel.

Answer: (d) Difficulty: (2) Knowledge: (A) Page: 92

35. In which of the following countries or cities would it be important to honor feng shui ("Wind and Water") when designing corporate headquarters?

   a. Viet Nam.
   b. Japan.
   c. Thailand.
   d. Hong Kong.
   e. Sidney.

Answer: (d) Difficulty: (3) Knowledge: (A) Page: 92

36. _____ drive(s) the holiday calendar in many countries.

   a. Culture
   b. Religion
   c. Government tax assessors.
   d. Reference groups.
   e. Family units.

Answer: (b) Difficulty: (1) Knowledge: (F) Page: 92

37. In which of the following countries would it be very difficult to conduct marketing research involving women or their preferences?

   a. Japan.
   b. Korea.
   c. Jordan.
   d. Greece.
   e. France.

Answer: (c) Difficulty: (2) Knowledge: (A) Page: 93

38. In which of the following countries would an ad campaign emphasizing more that shaving is good have difficulty be accepted?

   a. United States.
   b. Russia.
   c. Japan.
   d. Norway.
   e. Iran.

Answer: (e) Difficulty: (3) Knowledge: (F) Page: 93

39. Two facets of education matter to international marketers. They are the _____ of education.

   a. cost and location
   b. level and quality
   c. cost and quantity
   d. cost and availability
   e. level and cost

Answer: (b) Difficulty: (3) Knowledge: (F) Page: 94

40. With respect to education, which of the following societies or countries emphasize the sciences and engineering more that the others mentioned?

 a. Far eastern.
 b. Western.
 c. European.
 d. South American.
 e. Nordic.

Answer: (a) Difficulty: (2) Knowledge: (F) Page: 95

41. _____ shape(s) people's norms and standards. In addition, people's attitudes towards objects and behavioral codes are also influenced.

 a. Value systems
 b. Cultural philosophy
 c. Reference groups
 d. Family extension
 e. Government involvement

Answer: (a) Difficulty: (2) Knowledge: (F) Page: 95

42. One example of a value system in action is a person's attitude toward time. _____ people tend to do one thing at a time.

 a. Polychronic
 b. Monochronic
 c. Mesochronic
 d. Olichronic
 e. Dualchronic

Answer: (b) Difficulty: (3) Knowledge: (F) Page: 95

43. One example of a value system in action is a person's attitude toward time. _____ people tend to do several things at one time and usually less organized.
 a. Polychronic
 b. Monochronic
 c. Mesochronic
 d. Olichronic
 e. Dualchronic

Answer: (a) Difficulty: (3) Knowledge: (F) Page: 95

44. "Time is money" would be a phrase used by people that would be described as being _____ people with respect to their attitude toward time.

    a. polychronic
    b. monochronic
    c. mesochronic
    d. olichronic
    e. dualchronic

Answer: (b) Difficulty: (3) Knowledge: (A) Page: 95

45. Societies that are resistant towards change are usually _____ to adopt new products.

    a. more willing
    b. excited
    c. ambivalent
    d. less willing
    e. somewhat willing

Answer: (c) Difficulty: (2) Knowledge: (A) Page: 95

46. All of the following are guidelines to overcome resistance to change by cultures hostile toward changes, EXCEPT:

    a. Identify roadblocks toward change.
    b. Attack those leaders that are highly resistant. By overcoming a few, many can be influenced.
    c. Determine which cultural hurdles can be met.
    d. Test and demonstrate the innovation's effectiveness in the host culture.
    e. Seek out those values that can be used to back up the proposed innovation.

Answer: (b) Difficulty: (3) Knowledge: (F) Page: 96

47. _____ toward foreign cultures will drive a product's positioning and design decisions.

    a. Government attitudes
    b. Mass media attitudes
    c. Critic's attitudes
    d. Senior citizen's
    e. Local attitudes

Answer: (e) Difficulty: (3) Knowledge: (F) Page: 96

48. "What is left unsaid is as important as what is said" would be an example of what form of culture?

   a. Agrarian.
   b. Low context
   c. Intellectual.
   d. High context.
   e. Northern European.

Answer: (d) Difficulty: (2) Knowledge: (A) Page: 97

49. _____ cultures put emphasis of the written or spoken word.

   a. Agrarian.
   b. Low context
   c. Intellectual.
   d. High context.
   e. European.

Answer: (b) Difficulty: (2) Knowledge: (A) Page: 97

50. Research indicates that there is a faster rate of adoption of new products in _____ cultures than in other forms.

   a. native
   b. low context
   c. intellectual
   d. older cultures
   e. high context

Answer: (e) Difficulty: (3) Knowledge: (F) Page: 97

51. A _____ culture has people who share the same beliefs, speak the the same language, and practice the same religion.

   a. heterophilous
   b. native
   c. monophilous
   d. homophilous
   e. bi-cultural group

Answer: (d) Difficulty: (2) Knowledge: (F) Page: 97

52. Which of the following countries matches characteristics of a homophilous culture?

   a. United States
   b. Russia
   c. South Africa
   d. India
   e. Japan

Answer: (e) Difficulty: (3) Knowledge: (F) Page: 97

53. If a culture has a fair amount of difference in its religions, languages, and beliefs, it is called a _____ culture.

   a. heterophilous
   b. native
   c. monophilous
   d. homophilous
   e. bi-cultural group

Answer: (a) Difficulty: (2) Knowledge: (F) Page: 97

54. Pick the country from the list below that most exhibits characteristics of a heterophilous culture.

   a. Japan
   b. United States
   c. South Korea
   d. Norway
   e. North Korea

Answer: (b) Difficulty: (3) Knowledge: (A) Page: 97

55. Making a separate television commercial for each major city or province in a country would be a strategy that might be pursued in a country that had a _____ culture.

   a. heterophilous
   b. native
   c. monophilous
   d. homophilous
   e. bi-cultural group

56. Which of the following is <u>NOT</u> one of Hofstede's cultural classification dimensions?

    a. power distance
    b. uncertainty avoidance
    c. individualism
    d. romanticism
    e. masculinity

57. With respect to Hofstede's cultural classification scheme, _____ refers to the degree of inequality which people of a country view acceptable.

    a. power distance
    b. uncertainty avoidance
    c. individualism
    d. masculinity
    e. long-termism

58. An example of a high power distance country would be:

    a. Germany
    b. Britain
    c. United States
    d. Canada
    e. Mexico

59. With respect to Hofstede's cultural classification scheme, _____ refers to the extent to which people in a given culture prefer structured situations with clear rules over unstructured ones.

    a. power distance
    b. uncertainty avoidance
    c. individualism
    d. masculinity
    e. long-termism

Answer: (b) Difficulty: (2) Knowledge: (F) Page: 98

60. An example of a high uncertainty avoidance country would be:

    a. Germany
    b. Britain
    c. United States
    d. Canada
    e. Japan

Answer: (e) Difficulty: (3) Knowledge: (A) Page: 98

61. With respect to Hofstede's cultural classification scheme, _____ refers to the extent to which people in a given culture prefer to act as individuals rather than group members.

    a. power distance
    b. uncertainty avoidance
    c. individualism
    d. masculinity
    e. long-termism

Answer: (c) Difficulty: (1) Knowledge: (F) Page: 98

62. With respect to Hofstede's cultural classification scheme, _____ refers to the extent to which people in a given culture label their society male or female based on value characteristics of the two genders.

    a. power distance
    b. uncertainty avoidance
    c. individualism
    d. masculinity
    e. long-termism

Answer: (d) Difficulty: (1) Knowledge: (F) Page: 98

63. An example of a high "feminine culture" based on important values would be:

    a. Germany
    b. Britain
    c. United States
    d. Indonesia
    e. Japan

Answer: (d) Difficulty: (3) Knowledge: (A) Page: 98

64. With respect to Hofstede's cultural classification scheme, _____ refers to the extent to which people in a given culture label their as having their focus on the future or the present.

    a. power distance
    b. uncertainty avoidance
    c. individualism
    d. masculinity
    e. long-termism

Answer: (e) Difficulty: (1) Knowledge: (F) Page: 98, 99

65. An example of a short-term focus country (with respect to long-termism) would be:

    a. Hong Kong
    b. Britain
    c. China
    d. Thailand
    e. Japan

Answer: (b) Difficulty: (2) Knowledge: (A) Page: 99

66. _____ refers to people's unconscious tendency to resort to their own cultural experience and value systems to interpret a given business situation.

    a. Cultural morals
    b. Cultural ethics
    c. Self-reference criterion
    d. Monocultural
    e. Global culture

Answer: (c) Difficulty: (2) Knowledge: (F) Page: 101

67. Ethnocentrism is the belief that one's own culture is:

    a. superior to another culture.
    b. inferior to another culture.
    c. more racial pure than another culture.
    d. exports more than another culture.
    e. has a more rich and colorful history than any other country in the world.

Answer: (a) Difficulty: (3) Knowledge: (F) Page: 102

68. All of the following are stages encountered in most negotiation processes <u>EXCEPT</u>:

   a. nontask surroundings
   b. task costs
   c. task-related information exchange
   d. persuasion
   e. concessions and agreement

Answer: (b) Difficulty: (2) Knowledge: (F) Page: 104

69. With respect to the negotiation process and its four recognized stages, American negotiators tend to make concessions:

   a. at the beginning of the process.
   b. during the course of the process.
   c. at the end of the process.
   d. only in a follow-up meeting.
   e. only in rare cases because of the use of the business contract.

Answer: (b) Difficulty: (2) Knowledge: (A) Page: 105

70. _____ is a measure of a party's current knowledge of his counterpart's culture and ability to use that knowledge competently.

   a. Cultural adiaphoria
   b. Cultural ethnocentrism
   c. Cultural familiarity
   d. Debate style
   e. Cultural quantification

Answer: (c) Difficulty: (2) Knowledge: (F) Page: 106

71. All of the following are possible negotiation strategies that could be selected when undertaking a negotiation <u>EXCEPT</u>:

   a. employ industrial security experts for the purpose of spying or gathering intelligence.
   b. employ an agent or advisor.
   c. involve a mediator.
   d. adapt to the counterpart's negotiation script.
   e. embrace the counterpart's script.

Answer: (a) Difficulty: (1) Knowledge: (F) Page: 106, 107

True/False   Short Answer

1. Within a given culture, consumption processes can be described via a sequence of four stages: access, buying behavior, cost analysis, and disposal.

Answer: (False) Difficulty: (2) Knowledge: (F) Page: 82

2. A vital ingredient in the attractiveness of U.S.-style fast food (when sold abroad) is that it caters to the family.

Answer: (True) Difficulty: (1) Knowledge: (A) Page: 83

3. _____ is a learned, shared, compelling, interrelated set of symbols whose meanings provide a set of orientations for members of society.

Answer: (Culture) Difficulty: (2) Knowledge: (F) Page: 84

4. Culture can be biologically transmitted via the genes.

Answer: (False) Difficulty: (1) Knowledge: (F) Page: 84

5. Cultures may be defined by national borders.

Answer: (True) Difficulty: (1) Knowledge: (F) Page: 85

6. An example of a culture that can be defined by a national border would be Japan.

Answer: (True) Difficulty: (2) Knowledge: (A) Page: 85

7. _____ primarily refers to the technologies that are used to produce, distribute, and consume goods and services within a society.

Answer: (Material Life) Difficulty: (3) Knowledge: (F) Page: 85

8. _____ is often described as the most important element that sets human beings apart from animals.

Answer: (Language) Difficulty: (3) Knowledge: (F) Page: 86

9. Silent language refers to the thoughts that humans have within their minds.

Answer: (False) Difficulty: (2) Knowledge: (A) Page: 86

10. Gestures, grimaces, body language, and eye contact are all examples of _____ language.

Answer: (silent) Difficulty: (3) Knowledge: (A) Page: 86

11. Probably the most crucial expression of social interactions is the concept of kinship.

Answer: (True) Difficulty: (2) Knowledge: (F) Page: 87

12. _____ groups are those groups of which one would like to be a part.

Answer: (Anticipatory) Difficulty: (3) Knowledge: (F) Page: 88

13. _____ refers to a community's set of beliefs that relate to a reality that cannot be verified empirically.

Answer: (Religion) Difficulty: (2) Knowledge: (F) Page: 88

14. The two facets of education that matter the most to the business planner are the level and the quality of education.

Answer: (True) Difficulty: (1) Knowledge: (F) Page: 94

15. Monochronic people tend to do one thing at a time.

Answer: (True) Difficulty: (2) Knowledge: (F) Page: 95

16. Because of its affluence, the United States is a typical example of a high-context culture.

Answer: (False) Difficulty: (2) Knowledge: (A) Page: 97

17. Examples of homophilous cultures would be South Korean, Japan, and Norway.

Answer: (True) Difficulty: (2) Knowledge: (A) Page: 97

18. An example of a high power distance country would be the United States.

Answer: (False) Difficulty: (2) Knowledge: (A) Page: 98

Essay

1. Within a given culture, consumption processes can be described via a sequence of four stages. List and describe each stage. Your description can use the form of indicating questions that might be asked at each stage.

Answer:

a. Access: Does the consumer have physical and/or economic access to the product/service?

b. Buying Behavior: How is the decision to buy made by the consumers in the foreign market?

c. Consumption Characteristics: What factors drive the consumption patterns?

d. Disposal: How do consumers dispose of the product (in terms of resale, recycling, etc.)?

Difficulty: (2) Knowledge: (F) Page: 82, Exhibit 4-1 on page 85

2. Language is one of the cultural elements that affect the way marketers do business in foreign markets. Explain how language can complicate the task of the global marketer. In addition, identify the differences between spoken and silent language.

Answer:

The huge diversity of languages creates a headache to multinational companies. Language is often described as a mirror of a culture. Differences exist across and within borders. Countries with many languages (such as India) present unique problems.

Even within the same language, meanings and expressions vary a great deal between countries that share the language (for example: the United States and Britain). Language blunders are most often seen on product labels and in advertising slogans.

Spoken language uses vocal sounds or written symbols to communicate. Silent language refers to the complex of nonverbal communication mechanisms (such as gestures, grimaces, body language, eye contact, and conversation distance) that people use to get a message across.

Difficulty: (1) Knowledge: (F) Page: 86, 87

3. Social interactions are extremely important in the process of international marketing. One aspect of the social interaction process is the role of the reference group. Explain this importance and identify the chief forms of reference groups.

Answer:

An important form of social interaction is an individual's reference group. Reference groups are the set of people to which an individual looks to for guidance in his/her values and attitudes. As such, reference groups have an enormous impact on people's consumption behavior patterns. Knowledge on reference group patterns can provide an input in formulating product positioning strategies and devising advertising campaigns. Group conformity pressure must also be considered.

Reference group forms include:

a. Membership group--those groups to which people belong.

b. Anticipatory group--groupings of which one would like to be a part.

c. Dissociative group--groups with which individuals do not want to be associated.

Difficulty: (2) Knowledge: (F) Page: 88

4. Explain and comment on high- and low-context cultures. Give examples of each.

Answer:

For additional information see Exhibit 4-7. To begin a discussion of this area note that cultural complexity refers to the way messages are communicated within a society. High-context cultures (such as Japan) rely heavily on contextual cues (what is left unsaid is often as important as what is said). While low-context cultures (such as the United States) put more emphasis on the written or spoken word (what is meant is what is said).

Typical examples of high-context societies are Confucian cultures (China, Korea, Japan) and Latin America.

Typical examples of low-context cultures are the United States, Scandinavia, and Germany.

Difficulty: (2) Knowledge: (F and A) Page: 96, 97

5. List the primary components of Hofstede's classification scheme for classifying cultures. Define each component. Comment on the effect that these various elements might play on marketing products internationally.

Answer:
Hofstede's scheme is presented as having five components:

a. Power distance--refers to the degree of inequality among people that is viewed as being equitable.
b. Uncertainty avoidance--the extent to which people in a given culture prefer structured situations with clear rules over unstructured ones.
c. Individualism--describes the degree to which people prefer to act as individuals rather than group members ("me" versus "we" societies).
d. Masculinity--considers the importance of "male" values as opposed to "female" values.
e. Long-termism--the difference between societies that have a long-term orientation versus a short-term orientation.

Exhibit 4-5 portrays how different countries score on the various dimensions mentioned above. One must be cautious with applying these schemes to global buyer behavior. It is important to bear in mind that the five dimensions and the respective country scores that were derived in Hofstede's work were not determined in a consumption context. Questions have been raised about the validity of the measure.

Difficulty: (3) Knowledge: (F and A) Page: 98-101 and Exhibits 4-5(a) and 4-5(b)

Chapter 5

Multiple Choice

1. National politics affect business environments directly, through changes in policies, regulations, and:

   a. political parties.
   b. penalties.
   c. laws.
   d. taxes.
   e. tariffs.

Answer: (c) Difficulty: (2) Knowledge: (F) Page: 112

2. The government in each country determines which industries will receive:

   a. protection in the country and which will face open competition.
   b. benefits.
   c. penalties.
   d. monopolies.
   e. special protection from the armed services.

Answer: (a) Difficulty: (2) Knowledge: (A) Page: 112

3. When marketing executives do business across national boundaries, where do they primarily face regulations and laws?

   a. at home
   b. in the foreign country
   c. both at home and in the foreign country
   d. at the World Court in the Hague
   e. at the United Nations (which controls the oversight of international business)

Answer: (c) Difficulty: (3) Knowledge: (F) Page: 112

4. A(n) _____ country refers to a country the parent company is based in and operates from.

   a. origin
   b. domestic
   c. host
   d. home
   e. plural

Answer: (d) Difficulty: (1) Knowledge: (F) Page: 112

5. A(n) _____ country refers to a country in which foreign companies are allowed to do business in accordance with its government policies and within its laws.

   a. foreign trade zone
   b. domestic
   c. origin
   d. home
   e. host

Answer: (e) Difficulty: (1) Knowledge: (F) Page: 112

6. What type of political events are executives most concerned within host countries?

   a. major political upheavals
   b. day-to-day low-key events that produce a fairly significant change in policy
   c. property seizures
   d. terrorist strikes
   e. labor strikes

Answer: (b) Difficulty: (2) Knowledge: (A) Page: 112, 113

7. When China finally opened its doors to foreign direct investment, the first companies to invest have stood the most to gain. An example of one such company that invested early in China would be:

   a. Baskin-Robbins
   b. Chrysler
   c. Sears
   d. J.C. Penny's
   e. Microsoft

Answer: (b) Difficulty: (3) Knowledge: (A) Page: 113

8. How would China's current policy toward joint ventures in the automobile field best be described?

   a. excellent
   b. non-existent
   c. marginal, with more strict rules
   d. active encouragement
   e. China still has no joint ventures in automobiles

Answer: (c) Difficulty: (3) Knowledge: (A) Page: 113

9. One way to characterize the nature of government is by its _____, ranging from communism and socialism to capitalism.

   a. wealth standards
   b. view towards government control
   c. popular support of business
   d. socioeconomic ideology
   e. populist ideology and attention to the gold standard

Answer: (d) Difficulty: (2) Knowledge: (F) Page: 113

10. _____ refers to an economic system in which free enterprise is permitted and encouraged along with private ownership.

   a. Socialism
   b. Communism
   c. Fascism
   d. Capitalism
   e. Planned economics

Answer: (d) Difficulty: (1) Knowledge: (F) Page: 114

11. _____ if unfettered, may result in excessive production and excessive consumption, thereby causing social problems of great magnitude.

   a. Socialism
   b. Communism
   c. Protected economies
   d. Monopolies
   e. Capitalism

Answer: (e) Difficulty: (1) Knowledge: (F) Page: 114

12. _____ is generally considered to be a system that falls in the middle between largely independent systems and controlled economic systems.

a. Socialism
b. Communism
c. Neo-facism
d. Capitalism
e. Monarchies

Answer: (a) Difficulty: (1) Knowledge: (F) Page: 114

13. An example of a country that is classed as a single-party dominant country is:

a. the United States.
b. Great Britain.
c. India.
d. Israel.
e. Mexico.

Answer: (e) Difficulty: (2) Knowledge: (A) Page: 114

14. An example of the dual-party system in operation is found in:

a. Mexico
b. Britain
c. Italy
d. Israel
e. Japan

Answer: (b) Difficulty: (2) Knowledge: (F) Page: 114, 115

15. Lack of political stability and continuity is usually a characteristic of which of the following systems?

a. single party
b. dual party
c. multiple party
d. bi-cameral system
e. communist

Answer: (c) Difficulty: (1) Knowledge: (F) Page: 115

16. Governments often decide to block trade. All of the following are reasons <u>EXCEPT</u>:

    a. national security
    b. protect the stock market
    c. desire to remain independent
    d. developing new industries
    e. protecting declining industries

Answer: (b) Difficulty: (2) Knowledge: (A) Page: 115

17. An example of a country that actively protects its domestic business interests with a clear national industrial policy is:

    a. the United States.
    b. Britain.
    c. Japan.
    d. Russia.
    e. Australia.

Answer: (c) Difficulty: (3) Knowledge: (A) Page: 116

18. One method used by governments to support export activities is:

    a. to encourage tourism abroad.
    b. to use government loans.
    c. to watch for tax loopholes.
    d. to monitor bribery.
    e. to do away with artificial subsidies.

Answer: (b) Difficulty: (1) Knowledge: (F) Page: 116

19. In the United States, the _____ has a national network of district offices in every state, offering export promotion assistance to local businesses.

    a. Ministry of International Trade and Industry (MITI)
    b. EXIM Bank
    c. National Industrial Council (NIC)
    d. International Trade Administration (ITA)
    e. United Nations, Division of Commerce

Answer: (d) Difficulty: (3) Knowledge: (F) Page: 116

20. An example of an objective of any state government wishing to support businesses that will be exporting or relocating to the United States (specifically, within their state) is:

a. job creation.
b. increasing the defense industry in their state.
c. in gaining control of multinational corporations.
d. in accumulating wealth.
e. employing "street people."

Answer: (a) Difficulty: (2) Knowledge: (A) Page: 116

21. With respect to the involvement of state governments in the encouragement of international businesses investing in the state, investment missions are often headed by:

a. the Secretary of State.
b. the President of the United States.
c. the Governor of the State.
d. wealthy bankers in the state.
e. wealthy retailers in the state.

Answer: (c) Difficulty: (1) Knowledge: (F) Page: 118

22. An example of a direct government subsidy by the United States to meet foreign competition would be:

a. Microsoft.
b. COMCON.
c. The Tennessee Valley Authority.
d. BART in California.
e. SEMATECH (Semiconductor Manufacturing Technology).

Answer: (e) Difficulty: (2) Knowledge: (A) Page: 118

23. The ultimate government involvement in trade is when the government:

a. gives tax breaks to businesses.
b. itself is the customer.
c. prevents competition.
d. controls the foreign competiton with tariffs.
e. allows domestic businesses to bribe in foreign countries so they can remain competitive.

Answer: (b) Difficulty: (2) Knowledge: (F) Page: 118

24. The United States government accounts for _____ of the total U.S. consumption.

a. a tenth
b. a third
c. a fourth
d. a half
e. nearly sixty percent

Answer: (c) Difficulty: (3) Knowledge: (F) Page: 119

25. With respect to foreign competition bidding for government contracts, the _____ gives a bidding edge to domestic suppliers.

a. Anti-foreign Business Act (ABA)
b. Buy Domestic Act
c. Foreign Corrupt Practices Act
d. Robinson-Patman Act
e. Buy American Act

Answer: (e) Difficulty: (2) Knowledge: (F) Page: 119

26. Trade controls can be broken into two categories---economic trade controls and:

a. covert trade controls.
b. political trade controls.
c. geophysical trade controls.
d. maritime trade controls.
e. most favored nation trade controls.

Answer: (b) Difficulty: (2) Knowledge: (F) Page: 119

27. An example of an economic trade control would be a trade restraint instituted to:

   a. protect local jobs.
   b. embargo goods.
   c. sanction trading in certain goods.
   d. refrain from trading with communist Cuba.
   e. freeze the assets of Iraq.

Answer: (a) Difficulty: (1) Knowledge: (A) Page: 119

28. Weapons that might be used as economic trade controls to protect locally produced goods against imports would be:

   a. embargoes.
   b. sanctions.
   c. asset freezes.
   d. tariffs and nontariff barriers.
   e. confiscation.

Answer: (d) Difficulty: (3) Knowledge: (F) Page: 119

29. _____ are country-based political trade controls.

   a. Tariffs
   b. Nontariff barriers
   c. Taxing imports.
   d. Taxing exports.
   e. Embargoes and sanctions

Answer: (e) Difficulty: (2) Knowledge: (F) Page: 119

30. A(n) _____ restricts all trade with a nation for political reasons.

   a. tariff
   b. sanction
   c. asset freeze
   d. embargo
   e. confiscation

Answer: (d) Difficulty: (1) Knowledge: (F) Page: 119

31. All of the following are considered forms of tariffs <u>EXCEPT</u>:

   a. direction based.
   b. purpose based.
   c. time length.
   d. import restraint.
   e. quotas.

Answer: (e) Difficulty: (2) Knowledge: (F) Page: 120

32. All of the following are considered forms of nontariff barriers <u>EXCEPT</u>:

   a. government participation in trade.
   b. customs and entry procedures.
   c. product requirements.
   d. countervailing duties.
   e. quotas.

Answer: (d) Difficulty: (3) Knowledge: (F) Page: 120

33. An example of a product-based trade control would be the:

   a. quota.
   b. countervailing duty.
   c. export license requirement.
   d. ownership control.
   e. asset freezing.

Answer: (c) Difficulty: (2) Knowledge: (F) Page: 121

34. Trade laws that harm other countries are likely to invoke _____.

   a. war.
   b. retaliation.
   c. domestication attempts.
   d. covert action.
   e. United Nations sanction.

Answer: (b) Difficulty: (1) Knowledge: (A) Page: 121

35. Which of the following countries have very few restrictions on foreign ownership of corporations within their borders (domestic businesses)?

    a. United States.
    b. Russia.
    c. Japan.
    d. Iraq.
    e. Saudi Arabia.

Answer: (a) Difficulty: (1) Knowledge: (A) Page: 122

36. Profit remittances and differential taxation and interest rates are illustrations of which of the following types of control?

    a. ownership control
    b. incentive control
    c. industry control
    d. financial control
    e. political control

Answer: (d) Difficulty: (2) Knowledge: (F) Page: 123

37. Some companies use such tactics such as currency swaps, parallel loans, and countertrade to offset government attempts to control:

    a. dividends.
    b. profits.
    c. inventory.
    d. ownership.
    e. investment accounts.

Answer: (b) Difficulty: (3) Knowledge: (F) Page: 123

38. All of the following are examples of interest groups that might pressure a country's government to enact laws that harm foreign interests EXCEPT:

    a. the public at large.
    b. lobbyists for businesses.
    c. sponsors of advertising that goes abroad.
    d. the churches.
    e. personal interests of members of the government.

Answer: (c) Difficulty: (1) Knowledge: (F) Page: 124

39. A(n) _____ represents an outburst of anger expressed by an interest group to protest a foreign country's activities that do not agree with the value system of the interest group.

    a. embargoes.
    b. sanction.
    c. asset freeze.
    d. boycott.
    e. confiscation.

Answer: (d) Difficulty: (2) Knowledge: (F) Page: 126

40. All of the following are examples of political factors in a country that must be recognized and understood by a firm seeking to market in that country EXCEPT:

    a. political stability.
    b. the makeup and nature of all political parties (no matter how small).
    c. the predominant ideology toward business.
    d. the roles institutions have in the country.
    e. international links to other countries' legal and ideological structures.

Answer: (b) Difficulty: (2) Knowledge: (F) Page: 126

41. The types of risk that are generally associated with operating in a foreign country are risks associated with changes in company ownership, operations, and:

    a. transfers of employees.
    b. transfers of goods and money.
    c. distribution channels.
    d. factory locations.
    e. promotion sources (such as ad agencies).

Answer: (b) Difficulty: (2) Knowledge: (A) Page: 126

42. With respect to risks that are generally associated with operating in a foreign country, changes in ownership structure are usually due to dramatic:

    a. rises in the interest rate.
    b. changes in the population rate.
    c. political changes (such as wars).
    d. city elections (where the mayor changes).
    e. stock market upheavals (where the CEO changes).

Answer: (c) Difficulty: (3) Knowledge: (F) Page: 127

43. _____ refers to a foreign government's takeover of company goods, land, or other assets, with compensation that tends to fall short of their market value.

    a. Expropriation
    b. Confiscation
    c. Nationalization
    d. Retaliation
    e. Boycott

Answer: (a) Difficulty: (2) Knowledge: (F) Page: 127

44. _____ is an outright takeover of assets by a host government without compensation.

    a. Expropriation
    b. Confiscation
    c. Nationalization
    d. Retaliation
    e. Boycott

Answer: (b) Difficulty: (2) Knowledge: (F) Page: 127

45. _____ refers to a foreign government's takeover for the purpose of making the industry a government-run industry (some level of compensation may be received).

    a. Expropriation
    b. Confiscation
    c. Nationalization
    d. Retaliation
    e. Boycott

Answer: (c) Difficulty: (2) Knowledge: (F) Page: 127, 128

46. To overcome the problems of expropriation, confiscation, and even nationalization many companies are now adopting a policy of _____ where the company gradually turns over management and operational responsibilities as well as ownership to local companies over time.
    a. retaliation
    b. boycott
    c. sanction
    d. domestication
    e. profit sharing

Answer: (d) Difficulty: (1) Knowledge: (F) Page: 128

47. When countries are evaluated by potential political, financial, and economic risk factors, which of the following countries has the LOWEST risk appraisal?

   a. Switzerland
   b. Mexico
   c. Japan
   d. United States
   e. Argentina

Answer: (a) Difficulty: (3) Knowledge: (F) Page: 129

48. When countries are evaluated by potential political, financial, and economic risk factors, which of the following countries has the HIGHEST (most risky) risk appraisal?

   a. Switzerland
   b. Mexico
   c. Japan
   d. United States
   e. Argentina

Answer: (e) Difficulty: (2) Knowledge: (F) Page: 129

49. Recently the Russian subsidiary of PepsiCo needed to import bottling equipment from the United States. However, the Russian government did not allow the company to exchange rubles for dollars, so it exported Russian vodka to the United States to earn enough dollars to import the needed equipment. This would be an example of _____.

   a. retaliation.
   b. countertrade.
   c. sanction.
   d. domestication.
   e. profit sharing.

Answer: (b) Difficulty: (2) Knowledge: (A) Page: 130

50. _____ is an economic policy coordination group made up of political leaders from Canada, England, France, Germany, Italy, Japan, and the United States.

    a. The NATO alliance
    b. The Western bloc
    c. UNESCO
    d. The G-7 (Group of Seven)
    e. The Western Cabal

Answer: (d) Difficulty: (2) Knowledge: (F) Page: 131

51. All of the following are members of the G-7 (Group of Seven) <u>EXCEPT</u>:

    a. Canada
    b. Australia
    c. Germany
    d. United States
    e. Italy

Answer: (b) Difficulty: (2) Knowledge: (F) Page: 131

52. _____ was founded in 1949 to stop the flow of Western technology to the Soviet Union. Australia, Japan, and the NATO countries (except Ireland) are members.

    a. The NATO alliance
    b. The Western bloc
    c. UNESCO
    d. The G-7 (Group of Seven)
    e. COCOM (The Coordinating Committee for Multilateral Controls)

Answer: (e) Difficulty: (2) Knowledge: (F) Page: 131

53. _____ may be defined as that body of rules or laws that is binding on states and other international persons in their mutual relations.

    a. Legal systems
    b. International law (or law of nations)
    c. Local law
    d. Napoleonic code law
    e. Civil law

Answer: (b) Difficulty: (1) Knowledge: (A) Page: 132

54. International law represents _____ among countries.

   a. very loose arrangements
   b. contractually binding agreements
   c. gentlemen's agreements
   d. almost no control of law
   e. the best and most recognized legal standards

Answer: (c) Difficulty: (2) Knowledge: (A) Page: 132

55. International law comes from customs, national and international court decisions, and:

   a. tradition
   b. joint ventures
   c. strategic alliances
   d. cabals
   e. international treaties

Answer: (e) Difficulty: (1) Knowledge: (F) Page: 133

56. Customs are usages or practices that have become so firmly accepted that they become rules of law. An example of the above would be:

   a. countries claiming sovereignty over space exploration.
   b. countries claiming sovereignty over the moon.
   c. countries claiming sovereignty over the resources in their offshore continental shelves.
   d. countries claiming that foreign religions will not be allowed in their country.
   e. countries claiming that they own lands that were theirs as described in history.

Answer: (c) Difficulty: (3) Knowledge: (A) Page: 133

57. Foreign subsidiaries and expatriate employees live within the legal bounds of:

   a. their home countries only.
   b. their host countries only.
   c. both their home and host countries in most cases.
   d. the United Nations International Court of Justice.
   e. the World Court at the Hague, Belgium.

Answer: (c) Difficulty: (2) Knowledge: (A) Page: 133

58. _____ systems base the interpretation of law on prior court rulings (that is, legal precedents and customs of time).

    a. Common law
    b. Code law
    c. Written law
    d. Islamic law
    e. Napoleonic law

Answer: (a) Difficulty: (1) Page: 135

59. A country that follows common law as its primary system is:

    a. France.
    b. the United States.
    c. Iraq.
    d. Egypt.
    e. Quebec, Canada

Answer: (b) Difficulty: (1) Knowledge: (A) Page: 135

60. _____ systems rely on statutes and codes for the interpretation of the law. There is very little interpretation in this form of law.

    a. Common law
    b. Code (written) law
    c. United Nation's law
    d. Germanic Confederation law
    e. Spanish Constitutional law

Answer: (b) Difficulty: (1) Knowledge: (A) Page: 135

61. The law system that holds that law was established by God and a "natural law" embodies all justice is represented by:

    a. Common law.
    b. Code (written) law.
    c. Islamic law.
    d. Germanic Confederation law.
    e. Napoleonic law.

Answer: (c) Difficulty: (2) Knowledge: (F) Page: 135

62. Civil laws regulating business contracts and transactions are usually called:

   a. business law.
   b. code law.
   c. confederation law.
   d. commercial law.
   e. contract law.

Answer: (d) Difficulty: (1) Knowledge: (F) Page: 135

63. All of the following countries believe that most disputes can be solved outside the litigation system EXCEPT:

   a. Brazil.
   b. Japan.
   c. China.
   d. United States.
   e. Taiwan.

Answer: (d) Difficulty: (1) Knowledge: (A) Page: 136

64. The _____ (based in Geneva, Switzerland) has instituted a set of process standards that has been subscribed to by the European Union.

   a. International Standards Organization
   b. International Production Standards Organization
   c. Quality Council
   d. Demming Committee
   e. Baldridge Foundation

Answer: (a) Difficulty: (2) Knowledge: (F) Page: 137

65. _____ refers to ideas that are translated into tangible products, writings, and so on, and that are protected by the state for a limited period of time from unauthorized commercial exploitation.

   a. A copyright
   b. A trademark
   c. A trade secret
   d. Intellectual property
   e. A patent

Answer: (d) Difficulty: (2) Knowledge: (F) Page: 138

66. Which of the following countries follows the rule of "first-to-invent" with respect to patent awards?

   a. United States
   b. Japan
   c. Britain
   d. Germany
   e. Canada

Answer: (a) Difficulty: (3) Knowledge: (F) Page: 138

67. The international treaty (convention) established in 1883 that explains international protection rights of intellectual property (such as how long one has to file for property protection in foreign countries) is called:

   a. the Berne Convention.
   b. the London Convention.
   c. the Paris Convention.
   d. the New York Convention.
   e. the Rome Convention.

Answer: (c) Difficulty: (3) Knowledge: (F) Page: 140

68. The _____ specifically forbade every contract, combination, or conspiracy to restrain free and open trade.

   a. Sherman Act
   b. Clayton Act
   c. Federal Trade Commission Act
   d. Foreign Corrupt Practices Act
   e. Export Trading Company Act

Answer: (a) Difficulty: (3) Knowledge: (F) Page: 142

69. The _____ strengthened the U.S. antitrust arsenal by prohibiting trade practices that were not covered by in previous legislation. It outlawed exclusive dealing and price discrimination.

   a. Sherman Act
   b. Clayton Act
   c. Federal Trade Commission Act
   d. Foreign Corrupt Practices Act
   e. Export Trading Company Act

Answer: (b) Difficulty: (2) Knowledge: (F) Page: 142

70. The _____ empowered a commission to enjoin unfair methods of competition in commerce.

    a. Sherman Act
    b. Clayton Act
    c. Federal Trade Commission Act
    d. Foreign Corrupt Practices Act
    e. Export Trading Company Act

Answer: (c) Difficulty: (2) Knowledge: (F) Page: 142

71. The _____ encourages firms to join forces to improve their export performance by exempting them from antitrust laws. This act was patterned after similar legislation in Japan and Germany.

    a. Sherman Act
    b. Clayton Act
    c. Federal Trade Commission Act
    d. Foreign Corrupt Practices Act
    e. Export Trading Company Act

Answer: (d) Difficulty: (1) Knowledge: (F) Page: 142

72. The _____ was designed to prohibit the payment of any money or anything of value to foreign official, foreign political party, or any candidate for for foreign political office for purposes of obtaining, retaining, or directing business.

    a. Sherman Act
    b. Clayton Act
    c. Federal Trade Commission Act
    d. Foreign Corrupt Practices Act
    e. Export Trading Company Act

Answer: (e) Difficulty: (1) Knowledge: (F) Page: 142

True/False   Short Answer

1. A _____ country refers to a country the parent company is based in and operates from.

Answer: (home) Difficulty: (1) Knowledge: (F) Page: 112

2. A _____ country is a country in which foreign companies are allowed to do business in accordance with its government's policies and its laws.

Answer: (host) Difficulty: (2) Knowledge: (F) Page: 112

3. Under strict socialism, the government owns and manages all businesses and no private ownership is allowed.

Answer: (False) Difficulty: (2) Knowledge: (F) Page: 113

4. _____ refers to an economic system in which free enterprise is permitted and encouraged along with private ownership.

Answer: (Capitalism) Difficulty: (1) Knowledge: (F) Page: 114

5. There are only a few countries that still exist that could be classed as examples of true and extreme communism. Russia and Cuba would be among those examples.

Answer: (False) Difficulty: (2) Knowledge: (A) Page: 114

6. One of the problems with a multiple party governmental system is a lack of political stability and continuity.

Answer: (True) Difficulty: (1) Knowledge: (F) Page: 115

7. Chief among the reasons for a government wanting to block or restrict trade is national security, protection of developing new industries, and protecting patents and intellectual property.

Answer: (False) Difficulty: (3) Knowledge: (A) Page: 115

8. In the United States, the organization that seeks to help firms considering exports to other countries is the International Trade Administration (ITA).

Answer: (True) Difficulty: (2) Knowledge: (F) Page: 116

9. Within the United States, Tennessee is considered an export-active state.

Answer: (True) Difficulty: (2) Knowledge: (A) Page: 118

10. The United States government is the largest single consuming entity in the United States.

Answer: (True) Difficulty: (1) Knowledge: (F) Page: 118, 119

11. _____ restrict all trade with a nation for political purposes.

Answer: (Embargoes) Difficulty: (3) Knowledge: (F) Page: 119

12. Export license requirements are supply-based trade controls.

Answer: (False) Difficulty: (2) Knowledge: (F) Page: 121

13. When political groups tried to stop purchases of an abortion pill (RU 486, developed by Hoechst AG in Germany), this was an example of an expropriation policy.

Answer: (False) Difficulty: (2) Knowledge: (A) Page: 126, 127

14. _____ by a government is an outright takeover of a business's assets without compensation.

Answer: (Confiscation) Difficulty: (3) Knowledge: (F) Page: 127

15. A _____ policy by a host government means that the foreign company doing business within the country's borders must gradually turn over management and operational responsibilities as well as ownership to local companies over time.

Answer: (domestication) Difficulty: (3) Knowledge: (F) Page: 128

16. The Group of 7 (or G-7) is made up of France, Germany, Italy, England, Canada, Japan, and the United States.

Answer: (True) Difficulty: (2) Knowledge: (F) Page: 131

17. The rule and form of law in the United States (with the exception of Louisiana) is _____ law.

Answer: (common law) Difficulty: (2) Knowledge: (F) Page: 135

18. With respect to types of law used within their borders, the majority of the world's governments rely on some form of code law system.

Answer: (True) Difficulty: (2) Knowledge: (F) Page: 135

Essay

1. List and briefly characterize the three chief reasons why governments often want to block or restrict trade.

Answer:

a. National security--in this case reasons are that the government wants to retain the ability to produce goods necessary to remain independent (e.g., self-sufficiency) and, in general, the government does not want to encourage exportation of goods, services, information, or intellectual property that will help enemies or unfriendly nations.

b. Developing new industries--in this case the government wants to nurture developing industries and infrastructures and provide strength to protect a developing market.

c. Protecting declining industries--as some industries grow old or uncompetitive, most governments are sensitive to problems associated with decline (such as unemployment or erosion of a tax base) and they attempt to protect the industry in the hopes that political stability will be achieved.

Difficulty: (2) Knowledge: (F) Page: 115

2. What are the two primary types of trade controls? Give a description and an example of each major type.

Answer:

Trade controls can be either economic or political.

Economic trade controls are those trade restrictions that are instituted for primarily economic reasons, such as to protect local jobs or industries.

Examples of economic trade controls are tariffs and nontariff barriers. Tariff barriers can be directional (import or export tariffs), purpose oriented (protected tariffs or revenue tariffs), time length (tariff surcharge or a countervailing duty), import restraints (such as special duties), tariff rates (such as ad valorem duties), and production, distribution, and consumption oriented (such as excises). *For more detail, see Exhibit 5-1 page 120.*

Nontariff barriers can involve government participation in trade (such as a subsidy), customs and entry procedures (such as licenses or permits), product requirements (such as product standards), quotas, financial controls (such as credit restrictions), and other policies.

Political trade controls are those trade restraints that are instituted for national interests or for international political reasons. Examples would be embargoes and sanctions. Embargoes restrict all trade with a nation for political purposes. Sanctions are more narrowly defined trade restrictions and are sometimes punitive in nature.

Difficulty: (3) Knowledge: (F) Page: 119, 120, and Exhibit 5-1

3. How do the macroeconomic and fiscal policies of a host country affect a foreign company's operations?

Answer:

A host country is a country in which foreign companies are allowed to do business in accordance with its government policies and within its laws. Therefore, international marketing executives should be concerned about the host government's policies and their possible changes in the future as well as their home government's political climate.

Companies can face hostility, uncertain economic climates, devaluation of currency, confiscation of assets, and labor controls in foreign countries. Political upheavals are the primary source of these difficulties. International marketers must understand the fluidity of political climate in the host country if successful business ventures are to be accomplished.

Difficulty: (1) Knowledge: (A) Page: 112, 113

4. International law is derived from three sources. Identify, compare and contrast the sources.

International law is derived from three sources--customs, international treaties, and national and international court decisions. Customs are usages or practices which have become so firmly accepted that they become rules of law. Custom-based laws develop slowly. Treaties and international contracts represent formal agreements among nations or firms which set down rules and obligations to govern their mutual relationships. While treaties and contracts are only binding on those who are members of them, if a great number of treaties or contracts share similar stipulations, these may take on the character of a customer-based law or a general rule. When these rulings offer an unusually useful insight into the settlement of international cases, or when they develop into a series of interpretations consistent with other nation's courts, then national rulings may be accepted as international laws. Arbitration may be called for.

Difficulty: (2) Knowledge: (F) Page: 132, 133

5. Describe the various types of local legal systems. Describe how these differences might affect a company that wishes to conduct international business.

Answer:

There are three types of local legal systems from which most others are built. Common law systems are those which base the interpretation of law on prior court rulings. Code (written) law systems rely on statutes and codes for the interpretation of the law. Islamic law systems rely on some interpretation of the Koran and the words of Mohammed.

These systems primarily affect international business when the legal system differs between countries. Culture, customs, and interpretation of the law and rulings would all come into play. This is especially true when religious law (such as Islamic Law) is being used to govern contracts.

Difficulty: (2) Knowledge: (A) Page: 133, 135

Chapter 6

Multiple Choice

1. In the late 1970s Proctor & Gamble launched Pampers diapers in Japan. The product was not as successful as projected because the company failed to provide thin diapers for the Japanese mother (thin diapers were needed because of storage space constraints in the average Japanese home). Which of the following phrases best indicates the kind of problem that P & G failed to address?

    a. "Let the buyer beware."
    b. "You get what you pay for."
    c. "Test, test, test."
    d. "Don't put all you eggs in one basket."
    e. "Location, location, location."

Answer: (c) Difficulty: (2) Knowledge: (A) Page: 151

2. Proctor & Gamble stumbled into a cultural minefield in Japan by showing a Camay commercial that featured a man walking into the bathroom while his wife was taking a bath. Which of the following phrases best indicates the kind of problem that P & G failed to address?

    a. "Let the buyer beware."
    b. "Test, test, test."
    c. "Always study bathing or swimming."
    d. "The male is king of his castle."
    e. "Always pamper a lady."

Answer: (b) Difficulty: (2) Knowledge: (A) Page: 151, 152

3. Marketing research assists the global marketing manager by making better decisions that recognize cross-country similarities and differences and by:

    a. gaining support from local subsidiaries for proposed marketing decisions.
    b. fulfilling legal obligations to host governments.
    c. utilizing all the staff in the marketing department.
    d. following proper marketing procedure.
    e. providing all the information necessary to construct an intelligent commercial.

Answer: (a) Difficulty: (3) Knowledge: (F) Page: 152

4. All of the following are steps to be followed to conduct global market research EXCEPT:

   a. define the research problem(s).
   b. develop software to integrate with the Internet databases.
   c. determine information needs.
   d. collect the data.
   e. analyze the data and interpret the results.

Answer: (b) Difficulty: (1) Knowledge: (F) Page: 152

5. The first step in conducting global market research is usually characterized as being to:

   a. determine the information needs.
   b. determine the information sources.
   c. hire research workers.
   d. define the research problem(s).
   e. check all secondary sources for previous research in the area.

Answer: (d) Difficulty: (2) Knowledge: (F) Page: 152

6. All of the following are major challenges that a global marketing researcher might face EXCEPT:

   a. argument over budget expenditures between international markets.
   b. complexity of research design due to environmental differences.
   c. lack and inaccuracy of secondary data.
   d. time and cost requirements to collect primary data.
   e. coordination of multicountry research efforts.

Answer: (a) Difficulty: (3) Knowledge: (F) Page: 152

7. A diary kept by a physician for 2 weeks, a questionnaire completed by a patient, and telephone interviews of ex-patients would all be examples of the _____ in a research study.

   a. research problem
   b. research hypothesis in practice
   c. secondary data research process
   d. primary data research process
   e. sampling procedure

Answer: (d) Difficulty: (2) Knowledge: (A) Page: 153

8. In marketing research, once the problem has been identified it is translated into:

   a. a secondary research search.
   b. a primary research search.
   c. specific research questions.
   d. a sampling process.
   e. a choice of scales to be used in measurement.

Answer: (c) Difficulty: (3) Knowledge: (F) Page: 153

9. In global marketing research, the marketing research problem formulation is often hindered by the _____ where person's habit is to fall back on their own cultural norms and values.

   a. gender bias
   b. culture bias
   c. proximity effect
   d. global distance factor
   e. self-reference criterion

Answer: (e) Difficulty: (2) Knowledge: (F) Page: 154

10. In a multicountry research process, the _____ makes a meeting-of-the-minds between headquarters and local people an immensely formidable task.

    a. gender bias
    b. culture bias
    c. proximity effect
    d. global distance factor
    e. self-reference criterion

Answer: (e) Difficulty: (2) Knowledge: (F) Page: 154

11. A major difficulty in formulating the research problem in the global marketing research effort is the unfamiliarity with the _____.

    a. foreign mass media.
    b. laws governing marketing research.
    c. foreign environment.
    d. domestic environment's attitude toward foreign research.
    e. people who will actually conduct the research.

Answer: (c) Difficulty: (3) Knowledge: (A) Page: 154

12. In a foreign market, the _____ survey is probably the most economical way to gather preliminary information on target markets.

   a. upper-middle class
   b. omnibus
   c. environmental
   d. demographic specific
   e. local distributor

Answer: (b) Difficulty: (3) Knowledge: (F) Page: 154

13. Even though omnibus surveys can be very valuable in gathering marketing research information in the foreign market, a major disadvantage is that:

   a. it is usually culturally biased.
   b. it is very expensive.
   c. clients cannot incorporate their own questions in the survey.
   d. the survey does not usually contain many consumer-related questions.
   e. only a limited amount of company-relevant information is obtainable.

Answer: (e) Difficulty: (3) Knowledge: (A) Page: 154

14. If a foreign marketing researcher were to design a survey that covered three key cities in a target country, conducted 1,000 convenience (a random gathering procedure) sample interviews, and asked general questions about purchasing habits of products, likes and dislikes, and preferences that might be of interest to ten of the researcher's clients, the type of survey would probably be a(n):

   a. secondary survey.
   b. omnibus survey.
   c. randomized block survey.
   d. restricted movement survey.
   e. mobile matrix survey.

Answer: (b) Difficulty: (2) Knowledge: (A) Page: 154, 155

15. When market researchers find information that might be useful in their exploration process to already be available (usually collected for some other purpose by other data gathers), this type of information is called:

a. public information.
b. primary data.
c. unrestricted information.
d. secondary data.
e. used information.

Answer: (d) Difficulty: (1) Knowledge: (F) Page: 154

16. When data is collected specifically for the purpose of the research study, it is called:

a. public information.
b. primary data.
c. unrestricted information.
d. secondary data.
e. used information.

Answer: (b) Difficulty: (1) Knowledge: (F) Page: 154

17. Since accurate secondary data is difficult to obtain in many foreign markets, a recommended starting place is to use a computerized service such as:

a. Microsoft's foreign data banks.
b. Lexis/Nexis.
c. the CIA fact book.
d. National Geographic's Info-Net.
e. the University of Texas's Fiber-Net service.

Answer: (b) Difficulty: (3) Knowledge: (A) Page: 155

18. One of the most widely recognized and comprehensive international business sources that may be used and accessed via the Internet is the:

a. Microsoft's foreign data banks.
b. the CIA fact book.
c. National Geographic's Info-Net.
d. the University of Texas's Fiber-Net service.
e. the U.S. Department of Commerce's National Trade Data Bank (NTDB).

Answer: (d) Difficulty: (1) Knowledge: (F) Page: 155

19. Many countries have a network of government-sponsored commercial delegations that provide valuable information to firms that desire to do business in that country. One of the most noteworthy of these is found in _____ and is called _____.

    a. Britain; Britannia Net.
    b. Canada; Canada First.
    c. Japan; Japan External Trade Organization (JETRO).
    d. the United States; Buy American.
    e. Mexico; the Mexican Organization of Commercial Enterprise (MOCE).

Answer: (c) Difficulty: (3) Knowledge: (A) Page: 156

20. A recent form of secondary data sources is the syndicated datasets sold by market research companies like A. C. Nielsen and Information Resources, Inc. One of the ways that these firms acquire data in foreign markets and most developed countries (especially in the retail environment) is to use:

    a. observation.
    b. telephone interviews.
    c. direct mail.
    d. expert opinion.
    e. optical scanners tied to cash registers.

Answer: (e) Difficulty: (2) Knowledge: (F) Page: 157

21. All of the following are major sources of problems for the market researcher wishing to use secondary data obtained either about or from foreign markets EXCEPT:

    a. government control of data for taxing purposes.
    b. accuracy of data.
    c. age of data.
    d. reliability of data over time.
    e. comparability of data.

Answer: (a) Difficulty: (1) Knowledge: (F) Page: 157, 158

22. Accuracy of data in foreign markets may be suspect. This is especially true if it neglects to record significant commercial and non-commercial activity. One example of data that is often not recorded (though it might be significant) is:

    a. trade across national borders.
    b. trade by mail.
    c. smuggling activities.
    d. trade carried by package shippers such as FedEx or UPS.
    e. trade with foreign banks.

Answer: (c) Difficulty: (2) Knowledge: (F) Page: 157

23. With respect to comparing data over time, one way to handle contradictory information would be to _____ data. Obtain information on the same item from at least _____ sources and speculate on possible reasons behind these differences.

    a. duplicate; two
    b. triangulate; three
    c. multiply; ten
    d. duplicate; five
    e. extrapolate; five

Answer: (b) Difficulty: (2) Knowledge: (A) Page: 158

24. Comparability might also be hindered by the lack of _____.
    This refers to the degree to which similar activities or products in different countries fulfill similar functions.

    a. conceptual equivalence.
    b. functional factors.
    c. functional equivalence.
    d. lumping of data.
    e. comparison equivalence.

Answer: (c) Difficulty: (2) Knowledge: (F) Page: 158

25. The concept of "equal rights" for women in Muslim societies is unfamiliar. This would be an example of which of the following possible hindrances for marketing research efforts based on comparability of data.

a. conceptual equivalence
b. functional factors
c. functional equivalence
d. lumping of data
e. comparison equivalence

Answer: (a) Difficulty: (3) Knowledge: (A) Page: 158

26. To avoid the difficulty of "lumping of data" of encountered in conducting international marketing research, all of the following questions should be asked EXCEPT:

a. When were the data collected?
b. How were the data collected?
c. How much did it cost to collect the data?
d. Have the variables been redefined over time?
e. Who collected the data?

Answer: (c) Difficulty: (2) Knowledge: (F) Page: 159

27. If a marketing researcher asks "who collected the data?" they would probably be trying to overcome one of the major difficulties of collecting data in the international marketplace. Which of the following best describes the effect that the researcher is trying to overcome?

a. conceptual equivalence
b. functional factors
c. functional equivalence
d. lumping of data
e. comparison equivalence

Answer: (d) Difficulty: (3) Knowledge: (A) Page: 158, 159

28. Primary research can be collected in several ways. One method that is excellent to use when doing exploratory research is:

    a. mail surveys.
    b. telephone surveys.
    c. mall intercept.
    d. home interviews.
    e. focus groups.

Answer: (e) Difficulty: (2) Knowledge: (F) Page: 159

29. As a research technique, a _____ is a loosely structured free-flowing discussion among a small group of target customers facilitated by a professional moderator.

    a. mall intercept
    b. contra-group design
    c. Delphi-group
    d. focus group
    e. probe panel

Answer: (d) Difficulty: (2) Knowledge: (F) Page: 159

30. All of the following are typical uses of the focus group research technique EXCEPT:

    a. to generate information to guide the quantitative research projects.
    b. to obtain data on unproductive or problem employees.
    c. to reveal new product opportunities.
    d. to test out new product concepts.
    e. to test out new ad images.

Answer: (b) Difficulty: (2) Knowledge: (A) Page: 159

31. Getting focus groups to work in certain societies (because of their view to group dynamics and proper decorum) is difficult. Which of the following countries would be most difficult for successful focus groups?

    a. Japan
    b. United States
    c. Canada
    d. Britain
    e. Germany

Answer: (a) Difficulty: (1) Knowledge: (A) Page: 160

32. Consensus-claiming behavior would be the cause of focus group difficulties in which of the following countries?

    a. United States
    b. Canada
    c. Britain
    d. France
    e. Japan

Answer: (e) Difficulty: (2) Knowledge: (A) Page: 160

33. When analyzing and interpreting focus group findings, market researchers should also concentrate on _____.

    a. income expected as an honorarium.
    b. nonverbal cues (such as gestures).
    c. race bias.
    d. language correctness.
    e. intellect above experience.

Answer: (b) Difficulty: (3) Knowledge: (F) Page: 160

34. Once a marketing researcher has completed designing a questionnaire, they are ready to:

    a. collect data.
    b. analyze data.
    c. choose a writing format.
    d. choose a dissemination format.
    e. develop a sampling plan to collect the data.

Answer: (e) Difficulty: (2) Knowledge: (F) Page: 161

35. By far the most popular instrument to gather primary data is the:

    a. mall intercept.
    b. casual observation.
    c. questionnaire.
    d. optical scanner.
    e. eye tracking camera used in psychology.

Answer: (c) Difficulty: (1) Knowledge: (F) Page: 161

36. The astute marketing researcher must be aware of the need for conceptual and functional equivalence in designing questionnaires for the international market. In addition, it also necessary to fulfill two additional criteria. They are:

a. time and cost evaluation.
b. translation and scalar equivalence.
c. translation and polar equivalence.
d. religious and bias equivalence.
e. polar and scalar equivalence.

Answer: (b) Difficulty: (3) Knowledge: (F) Page: 161

37. Two procedures that can overcome problems with sloppy questionnaire translation in conducting international marketing research is to provide for:

a. polar and psychographic translation.
b. lifestyle and psychographic translation.
c. back-translation and parallel translation.
d. forward-translation and parallel translation.
e. lifestyle and parallel translation.

Answer: (c) Difficulty: (3) Knowledge: (F) Page: 161

38. _____ translation involves using multiple interpreters who translate the same questionnaire independently.

a. Polar
b. Parallel
c. Back
d. Forward
e. Lifestyle

Answer: (b) Difficulty: (2) Knowledge: (F) Page: 161

39. To make findings of cross-country market research projects meaningful, it is paramount to pursue _____ (where scores from subjects of different countries should have the same meaning and interpretation).
a. time evaluation
b. scalar equivalence
c. polar equivalence
d. bias equivalence
e. focus equivalence

Answer: (b) Difficulty: (2) Knowledge: (F) Page: 161

40. The purpose of _____ is to get scores from subjects of different countries to have the same meaning and interpretation.

   a. time evaluation
   b. scalar equivalence
   c. polar equivalence
   d. bias equivalence
   e. focus equivalence

Answer: (b) Difficulty: (2) Knowledge: (F) Page: 161

41. Though the "seven-point" scale to determine agreement or disagreement is common in the United States, France uses a _____ scale.

   a. eleven
   b. ten
   c. twenty
   d. five
   e. fifteen

Answer: (c) Difficulty: (3) Knowledge: (F) Page: 161

42. With respect to asking scaled questions to determine the degree of agreement or disagreement, in illiterate societies scaled questions often use:

   a. numbers (such as 1-10).
   b. letters (such as a-z).
   c. use symbols (such stars).
   d. use degrees of smiling or funny faces (from happy to sad).
   e. use number of animals (ownership demonstrated by one through seven goats or cows).

Answer: (d) Difficulty: (2) Knowledge: (A) Page: 161, 162

43. With respect to conducting marketing research in countries that are unfamiliar with survey research, it is advisable to avoid:

   a. references to the government.
   b. lengthy questionnaires or open-ended questions.
   c. references to religion.
   d. questioning females.
   e. any scaled questions.

Answer: (b) Difficulty: (3) Knowledge: (F) Page: 163

44. _____ is the only foolproof way to debug the questionnaire and spot embarrassing mistakes.

    a. Pretesting
    b. Posttesting
    c. Using approved software
    d. Using standard questionnaire formats
    e. Having a linguist read the questionnaire

Answer: (a) Difficulty: (1) Knowledge: (F) Page: 163

45. To collect data, the researcher has to draw a _____ from the target population.

    a. group item
    b. reference list
    c. sample
    d. quota
    e. portion

Answer: (c) Difficulty: (1) Knowledge: (F) Page: 163

46. All of the following items are covered in a sampling plan EXCEPT:

    a. Who should be surveyed?
    b. How much will the survey cost?
    c. What is our target population?
    d. How many people should be surveyed?
    e. How should prospective respondents be chosen from the target population?

Answer: (b) Difficulty: (3) Knowledge: (F) Page: 163

47. Which of the following questions is most associated with the term "sampling unit?"

    a. Who should be cannot be considered as a valid respondent?
    b. How much will the survey cost?
    c. What is our target population?
    d. How many people should be surveyed?
    e. How should prospective respondents be chosen from the target population?

Answer: (c) Difficulty: (2) Knowledge: (F) Page: 163

48. Which of the following questions is most associated with the term "sample size?"

    a. Who should be cannot be considered as a valid respondent?
    b. How much will the survey cost?
    c. What is our target population?
    d. How many people should be surveyed?
    e. How should prospective respondents be chosen from the target population?

Answer: (d) Difficulty: (2) Knowledge: (F) Page: 163

49. Which of the following questions is most associated with the term "sampling procedure?"

    a. Who should be cannot be considered as a valid respondent?
    b. How much will the survey cost?
    c. What is our target population?
    d. How many people should be surveyed?
    e. How should prospective respondents be chosen from the target population?

Answer: (e) Difficulty: (3) Knowledge: (F) Page: 163

50. With respect to approved sampling theory, heterogeneous cultures (e.g., India) demand _____ samples than homogeneous cultures (e.g. South Korea).

    a. bigger
    b. smaller
    c. less stratified
    d. more randomized
    e. less randomized

Answer: (a) Difficulty: (1) Knowledge: (A) Page: 163

51. When preparing a sampling plan, the researcher needs to decide how to contact prospective subjects for the survey. The most common choices are:

    a. mail, telephone, and Internet.
    b. mail, telephone, and optical scan.
    c. mail, telephone, and personal interview.
    d. observation, personal interview, and experimentation on a person-by-person basis.
    e. observation, telephone, and personal interview.

Answer: (c) Difficulty: (2) Knowledge: (F) Page: 164

52. Once collection of data in a research project begins, there can be many problems with collection. A very common problem in the international arena is nonresponse due to:

a. a reluctance to be photographed.
b. a reluctance to talking with strangers.
c. a reluctance to talking with officials or official pollsters.
d. a fear of government reprisals.
e. a fear of cultural conflict.

Answer: (b) Difficulty: (2) Knowledge: (F) Page: 165

53. When conducting research several biases may be present. The _____ bias is present when the respondent feels a desire to be polite toward the other person.

a. yea-or nay-saying
b. social desirability
c. gender
d. tradition
e. courtesy

Answer: (e) Difficulty: (1) Knowledge: (F) Page: 165

54. The courtesy bias with respect to marketing research responses is fairly common in:

a. the United States.
b. France.
c. Germany.
d. Asia and the Middle East.
e. Mexico.

Answer: (d) Difficulty: (2) Knowledge: (A) Page: 165

55. In some countries, responses to questionnaires may reflect a _____ bias where the subject attempts to reflect a certain social status in their response.

a. yea-or nay-saying
b. social desirability
c. gender
d. tradition
e. courtesy

Answer: (b) Difficulty: (1) Knowledge: (F) Page: 165

56. All of the following are methods that can be fruitfully employed to assess the size of the market for any given product <u>EXCEPT</u>:

a. analogy method.
b. Latin square.
c. trade audit.
d. chain ratio method.
e. cross-sectional regression analysis.

Answer: (b) Difficulty: (3) Knowledge: (F) Page: 166

57. The procedure for the _____ of assessing market size is to pick a country that is at the same stage of economic development as the country of interest and for which the market size is known. This country then becomes an indicator for the market size of the country that is under question.

a. analogy method.
b. Latin square.
c. trade audit.
d. chain ratio method.
e. cross-sectional regression analysis.

Answer: (a) Difficulty: (2) Knowledge: (F) Page: 167

58. Suppose that a consumer electronics company wants to estimate the market size for VCRs in Poland but does not have much information about that market. Instead, it chooses Hungary (a country for which it does have information) and uses it as an indicator for the market in Poland. This method of determining market size most resembles which of the following methods?

a. analogy method
b. Latin square
c. trade audit
d. chain ratio method
e. cross-sectional regression analysis

Answer: (a) Difficulty: (2) Knowledge: (A) Page: 167

59. One common problem with using the analogy method of determining market size is:

a. cost.
b. language problems.
c. consumption patterns are different due to a cultural difference.
d. different monetary units.
e. there be more men than women in one of the cultures.

Answer: (c) Difficulty: (2) Knowledge: (F) Page: 168

60. An alternative way to derive market size estimates is based on local production and import and export figures for the product of interest. This method is best described as being a(the):

a. analogy method
b. Latin square
c. trade audit
d. chain ratio method
e. cross-sectional regression analysis

Answer: (c) Difficulty: (2) Knowledge: (F) Page: 168

61. The _____ method of assessing market size begins with a rough base-number as an estimate for the market size (such as the entire population for the country) and systematically fine-tunes by applying a string of percentages (such as birth rate) to come up with the most meaningful estimate possible.

a. analogy method
b. Latin square
c. trade audit
d. chain ratio method
e. cross-sectional regression analysis

Answer: (d) Difficulty: (2) Knowledge: (F) Page: 169

62. If a company wishing to sell baby monitors (to help with infants that have trouble breathing) wanted to estimate the size of their potential market in a developing country for which little data was available, they could get the population size, examine the number of births per year, focus on cities that had the highest birthrates, and contact hospitals that had the most problems with SID (sudden infant death syndrome). This logic most closely approximates which of the following methods listed below?

a. analogy method
b. Latin square
c. trade audit
d. chain ratio method
e. cross-sectional regression analysis

Answer: (d) Difficulty: (2) Knowledge: (A) Page: 169

63. One method for determining market size estimates takes the variable of interest (such as market size) and relates it to a set of predictor variables (indicators closely related to demand). This method would be best described as being which of the following?

a. analogy method
b. Latin square
c. trade audit
d. chain ratio method
e. cross-sectional regression analysis

Answer: (e) Difficulty: (3) Knowledge: (F) Page: 170

64. If a researcher were to take ten Central and Eastern European countries where per capita income and automobile ownership by per capita were known, trying to find the overall picture of market size for the market could probably be done by using which of the following methods?

a. analogy method
b. Latin square
c. trade audit
d. chain ratio method
e. cross-sectional regression analysis

Answer: (e) Difficulty: (3) Knowledge: (A) Page: 170, 171

470

65. When using market size estimates, it is always a good idea to keep all the following rules in mind <u>EXCEPT</u>:

   a. Use several different methods if possible.
   b. Always use the least expensive method.
   c. Don't be misled by the numbers.
   d. Don't be misled by fancy methods.
   e. Ask "what-if" questions when many assumptions must be made.

Answer: (b) Difficulty: (2) Knowledge: (F) Page: 172

66. The emergence of _____ data, coupled with rapid developments in computer hardware and software has led to a revolution in market research.

   a. the Internet
   b. scanner
   c. cost efficient
   d. mail-in rebate
   e. direct-feedback

Answer: (b) Difficulty: (3) Knowledge: (F) Page: 172

67. Scanning technology has spurred several sorts of databases that are very important to the marketing researcher. The major one listed below is:

   a. Point-of-attack strategy data.
   b. Inventory control data.
   c. Point-of-Sale store scanner data.
   d. Voting block patterns.
   e. Tele-Us recorders in retail stores.

Answer: (c) Difficulty: (1) Knowledge: (F) Page: 173

68. Innovations in marketing decision support systems have spurred several major developments in the marketing area. One of most dramatic has been:

   a. the shift from mass to micro marketing.
   b. the shift from a demand to a supply economy.
   c. the fact that everyone now has a personal computer.
   d. the overcrowding of the Internet.
   e. home shopping on the Internet.

Answer: (a) Difficulty: (2) Knowledge: (A) Page: 174

69. One of the reasons that Japan has been able to launch thousands of new products rather successfully is that tracking information can be done by _____ rather than by store audit.

a. database assessment
b. electronic promotion
c. the Internet
d. scanning
e. computer modeling

Answer: (d) Difficulty: (2) Knowledge: (A) Page: 174

70. In many situations companies are now having to rely on local market agencies to conduct market research for their firms. This is usually necessary in which of the following countries?
a. Mexico
b. United States
c. China
d. Netherlands
e. Britain

Answer: (c) Difficulty: (3) Knowledge: (A) Page: 175

71. With respect to standardization of research results, even when dealing with cross-country marketing research which of the following entities usually desires standardization of data collection, sampling procedures, and survey instruments?
a. the local government
b. the local research agency
c. the local subsidiary
d. the home office
e. the home research agency

Answer: (d) Difficulty: (1) Knowledge: (F) Page: 178

72. Some marketing managers believe that the "scientific method" of doing marketing research for new products does not really reflect consumer attitudes. Which of the following is not a reason cited as being why the "scientific method" has shortcomings?

a. indifference of respondents
b. absence of responsibility
c. conservative attitudes
d. vanity
e. egotism.

Answer: (e) Difficulty: (3) Knowledge: (F) Page: 179

True/False   Short Answer

1. "Test, test, test" is a maxim that marketers can never forget.

Answer: (True) Difficulty: (1) Knowledge: (F) Page: 151

2. Procedures and methods that are followed to conduct global marketing research are very different from those used to conduct domestic research.

Answer: (False) Difficulty: (1) Knowledge: (F) Page: 152

3. The first step in the marketing research process is described as being to

_____.

Answer: (define the research problem) Difficulty: (2) Knowledge: (F) Page: 152

4. Any research effort starts off with a precise definition of who the marketer wants to research.

Answer: (False) Difficulty: (2) Knowledge: (F) Page: 153

5. Today researchers have found that sophisticated analytical tools will compensate for inaccuracies in problem definition.

Answer: (False) Difficulty: (1) Knowledge: (F) Page: 153

6. The _____ is a person's habit to fall back on their own cultural norms and values when making decision or in reviewing problem decisions.

Answer: (self-reference criterion) Difficulty: (3) Knowledge: (F) Page: 154

7. To gain familiarity with a foreign environment, one can undertake an omnibus survey.

Answer: (True) Difficulty: (2) Knowledge: (F) Page: 154

8. _____ data are collected specifically for the purpose of the research study.

Answer: (Primary) Difficulty: (2) Knowledge: (F) Page: 154

9. If a company were to go to JETRO (the Japanese External Trade Organization) for data on exporting to Japan, they would be engaging in a _____ data search.

Answer: (secondary) Difficulty: (3) Knowledge: (A) Page: 156

10. A. C. Nielsen now sells syndicated databases to help firms with their research efforts.

Answer: (True) Difficulty: (1) Knowledge: (F) Page: 157

11. The purpose for which data is collected can affect the accuracy of the data.

Answer: (True) Difficulty: (2) Knowledge: (F) Page: 157

12. With respect to comparability of data, _____ equivalence refers to the degree to which similar activities or products in different countries fulfill similar functions.

Answer: (functional) Difficulty: (2) Knowledge: (F) Page: 158

13. The concept of "equal rights" for women in Muslim countries would be an example of difficulties with economic equivalence.

Answer: (False) Difficulty: (3) Knowledge: (A) Page: 158

14. A _____ is a loosely structured free-flowing discussion among a small group of target customers facilitated by a professional moderator.

Answer: (focus group) Difficulty: (2) Knowledge: (F) Page: 159

15. One of the procedures used in practice to avoid sloppy translation of questionnaires is forward-translation.

Answer: (False) Difficulty: (2) Knowledge: (F) Page: 161

16. Using the "Funny Faces Scale" would be one way to overcome literacy problems among third world countries in answering marketing research questionnaires.

Answer: (True) Difficulty: (1) Knowledge: (A) Page: 162

17. In Russia, limited experience with brands could result in low ratings because the consumer only prefers those brands with which they are familiar. This would be an example of ipsatizing response bias.

Answer: (False) Difficulty: (3) Knowledge: (A) Page: 165

18. There are various methods for estimating market size. The _____ method starts by picking a country that is at the same stage of economic development as the country of interest and for which the market size is known.

Answer: (analogy) Difficulty: (3) Knowledge: (F) Page: 167

Essay

1. List the stages of the marketing research process. What do most think is the most important step?

Answer:

a. Define the research problems(s).

b. Develop a research design.

c. Determine information needs.

d. Collect the data (secondary and primary).

e. Analyze the data and interpret the results.

f. Report and present the findings of the study.

Most believe that the first step, that of defining the research problem(s), is the most important step because it sets the stage and focus for all that follows.

Difficulty: (2) Knowledge: (F) Page: 152

2. Discuss the function, purpose, limitations, and benefits of omnibus surveys.

Answer:

Omnibus surveys are conducted by research agencies at regular intervals. The survey generally contains a wide variety of consumer-related questions. The surveys are usually administered to a very large sample of consumers (sometimes a panel). Marketers can then use these general comments to better design specific surveys.

The major benefits of the omnibus survey is that cost expenses of the survey are shared by the subscribers. It is a very economical way to get data on large numbers of consumers (especially if general information is what is primarily needed). However, the major disadvantage is that only a limited amount of company relevant information is obtainable through the omnibus survey format. Also, the panel (used to obtain the data) is usually not representative of the firm's target market profile.

Difficulty: (2) Knowledge: (F) Page: 154

3. What are the generally accepted problems associated with collecting and using secondary data research?

Answer:

a. Accuracy of data--the accuracy of secondary data is often questionable for various reasons. The definition used for certain indicators often differs across countries. The quality of information may also be compromised by the mechanisms that were used to collect them. The purpose for which the data were collected could affect the data's accuracy.

b. Age of data--data may be outdated. Many countries collect data on a much less frequent basis than developed countries.

c. Reliability over time--historical trends are hard to accumulate in the international environment. Sudden changes can often jeopardize data accumulation.

d. Comparability of data--comparison of cross-country indicators can be a very real problem in international marketing research. One method to overcome this is to triangulate data.

Different sources on a given item often produce contradictory information. Reconciliation can be achieved through triangulation. In other words, obtain information on the same item from at least three different sources and speculated on possible reasons behind these differences.

It is also wise to consider functional or conceptual equivalence of data and data accumulation.

e. Lumping of data--many times lumping compromises the accuracy of data. Categories often conflict from one country to another.

Difficulty: (3) Knowledge: (F) Page: 157-159

4. Discuss the major issues that a marketing researcher would want to consider for focus group discussions in an international market environment.

Answer:

Focus groups can be used for many different purposes: to generate information to guide the quantitative research projects, to reveal new product opportunities, to test new product concepts, and so forth. Rules that should be followed are to hire a trained moderator, make sure cultural sensitivity is part of the process, make sure the group is homogeneous and able to bond, make sure the moderator is skilled in group dynamics, and make sure the moderator can recognize consensus. Lastly, analysis and interpretation on non-verbal cues is just as important as recording the verbal cues.

Difficulty: (2) Knowledge: (A) Page: 159-161

5. List the four primary methods of estimating market size. Discuss why market size estimates may differ depending on the method being used. How can such differences be reconciled? Which method do you think is the best? Explain your reasoning.

Answer:

a. analogy method--the method starts by picking a country that is at the same stage of economic development as the country of interest and for which the market size is known.

b. trade audit--derive market estimates based on local production and import and export figures for the product of interest.

c. chain-ratio method-- method of assessing market size begins with a rough base-number as an estimate for the market size (such as the entire population for the country) and systematically fine-tunes by applying a string of percentages (such as birth rate) to come up with the most meaningful estimate possible.

d. cross-sectional regression analysis-- this method for determining market size estimates takes the variable of interest (such as market size) and relates it to a set of predictor variables (indicators closely related to demand).

Market size estimates in the international area are many times "guesstimates." The lack of quality data is the cause. The chapter describes four methods that can be used to approximate market size. The marketing manager is advised to use more than one measure to improve their decision making ability. The methods are the method of analogy, the trade audit, the chain ration method, and cross-sectional regression analysis. Factors considered cause differences between these methods. An averaging, as well as a common sense approach, help to resolve differences. The watchword, however, is caution. Do not make numbers out to be more than they are. Observe where the data came from, how it was collected, the validity of the data, the recency of the data, and what the data included and excluded.

Students may choose whichever method they prefer to as a "best" method. They should, however, be required to justify their answer.

Difficulty: (3) Knowledge: (F and A) Page: 166-172

Chapter 7

Multiple Choice

1. The primary motivation for market segmentation is:

   a. profit.
   b. government mandate.
   c. variation in customer needs.
   d. quality control.
   e. accountability.

   Answer: (c) Difficulty: (1) Knowledge: (F) Page: 183

2. The goal of market segmentation is to break down the market for a product or a service into different groups of consumers so the firm can:

   a. tailor its marketing mix to each individual segment.
   b. make the sales job easier.
   c. offer a customized product to every consumer.
   d. offer a standard product to every consumer.
   e. make more money.

   Answer: (a) Difficulty: (2) Knowledge: (A) Page: 184

3. Market segmentation is a logical outgrowth of:

   a. the demand function.
   b. the supply function.
   c. efficiency in inventory control.
   d. the marketing concept.
   e. the product life cycle.

   Answer: (d) Difficulty: (2) Knowledge: (F) Page: 184

4. Which of the following is NOT a property that segments ideally should possess?

   a. Measurable.
   b. Sizable.
   c. Defensible.
   d. Accessible.
   e. Actionable.

Answer: (c) Difficulty: (3) Knowledge: (F) Page: 184

5. With respect to properties that an international market segment should ideally possess, the _____ property is easily met for target country when the researcher examines socioeconomic variables (such as per capita income).

   a. measurable
   b. sizable
   c. defensible
   d. accessible
   e. actionable

Answer: (a) Difficulty: (2) Knowledge: (F) Page: 184

6. With respect to properties that an international market segment should ideally possess, the _____ property is important when the target country has differences in the quality of the media infrastructure (such as the absence of commercial television).

   a. measurable.
   b. sizable.
   c. defensible.
   d. accessible.
   e. actionable.

Answer: (d) Difficulty: (2) Knowledge: (F) Page: 184

7. With respect to properties that an international market segment should ideally possess, the _____ property is important (when for market segmentation to be meaningful) when effective marketing programs involving the 4 Ps can be developed to evoke the desired response from the target segment.

   a. measurable
   b. sizable
   c. defensible
   d. accessible
   e. actionable

Answer: (e) Difficulty: (2) Knowledge: (F) Page: 184

8. Which of the following would be major reason why international marketers implement international market segmentation?

    a. Promotion strategy.
    b. Demand problems.
    c. Cost efficiency.
    d. Positioning strategy.
    e. Government mandate.

Answer: (d) Difficulty: (3) Knowledge: (A) Page: 184, 185

9. All of the following are reasons for international marketers to implement international market segmentation EXCEPT:

    a. country screening.
    b. government mandate.
    c. global market research.
    d. positioning strategy.
    e. entry decisions.

Answer: (b) Difficulty: (3) Knowledge: (F) Page: 185, 186

10. When market analysts examine indicators and classify countries into consideration piles (based on some criteria) that are doing _____.

    a. country screening.
    b. government research.
    c. global market research.
    d. positioning strategy.
    e. country quadrant positioning.

Answer: (a) Difficulty: (2) Knowledge: (A) Page: 186

11. Given the sheer number of countries in which many companies operate, doing marketing research in each one of them is often inefficient. One approach to reduce this problem is narrow the list of those countries that might be examined by grouping prospective markets into _____ countries.

    a. financial categories for
    b. clusters of homogeneous
    c. clusters of heterogeneous
    d. dissimilar qualifiers for
    e. statistical tracts for

Answer: (b) Difficulty: (3) Knowledge: (F) Page: 185

12. Cadbury-Schweppes was confident about launching Schweppes tonic water in Brazil, given that the beverage had done well in culturally similar countries such as Mexico. This would be an example of which of the following reasons why international marketers implement international market segmentation?

a. country screening.
b. government mandate.
c. global market research.
d. positioning strategy.
e. entry decisions.

Answer: (e) Difficulty: (2) Knowledge: (A) Page: 186

13. Cathay Pacific (a Hong Kong based airline carrier) recently wanted to increase services to its Asian customers. It added a wide variety of Asian meals and entertainment and introduced a new advertising slogan "The Heart of Asia." This would be an example of which of the following reasons why international marketers implement international market segmentation?

a. country screening.
b. government mandate.
c. global market research.
d. positioning strategy.
e. entry decisions.

Answer: (d) Difficulty: (2) Knowledge: (A) Page: 186

14. A persistent problem faced by international marketers is how to strike the balance between standardization and customization. Using international marketing segmentation to shed some light on this issue would be an example of which of the following reasons why international marketers implement international market segmentation?

a. country screening.
b. marketing mix policy.
c. global market research.
d. positioning strategy.
e. entry decisions.

Answer: (b) Difficulty: (2) Knowledge: (F) Page: 186

15. Which of the following ARE NOT characteristics suggested by analysts for classifying countries into distinct segments?

   a. Health.
   b. Trade.
   c. Lifestyle.
   d. Automobile consumption and infrastructure.
   e. Cosmopolitanism.

Answer: (d) Difficulty: (3) Knowledge: (F) Page: 188

16. From a marketer's perspective, the practical usefulness of macro-level segments is questionable. To address this shortcoming of the standard country segmentation approach the following steps can be considered. Which of the steps below would be INCONSISTENT with the suggested procedure?

   a. Criteria development.
   b. Determine cut-off criteria.
   c. Preliminary screening to see if the thresholds for criteria can be met.
   d. Develop macrosegments.
   e. Develop microsegments.

Answer: (d) Difficulty: (1) Knowledge: (A) Page: 189, 190

17. When marketers use a(n) _____ segment, they concentrate on cross-border segments that transcend national boundaries.

   a. diverse
   b. universal
   c. combination
   d. customized
   e. international

Answer: (b) Difficulty: (2) Knowledge: (F) Page: 191

18. When Nokia used a global campaign to promote their new product that combined phone, fax, e-mail, and Internet functions with the slogan "Everything. Everywhere," they were appealing to a(n) _____ segment.
   a. diverse
   b. universal
   c. combination
   d. customized
   e. international

Answer: (b) Difficulty: (2) Knowledge: (A) Page: 191

19. When marketers use a(n) _____ segment, they focus on local segments that differ from country to country.

   a. diverse
   b. universal
   c. combination
   d. customized
   e. international

Answer: (a) Difficulty: (1) Knowledge: (F) Page: 191

20. When Canon (a camera manufacturer) sold its AE-1 camera to young replacement buyers in Japan and upscale first-time camera(35 mm single-lens reflex) buyers, they were probably pursuing a(n) _____ segment policy.

   a. diverse
   b. universal
   c. combination
   d. customized
   e. international

Answer: (a) Difficulty: (2) Knowledge: (A) Page: 191

21. A typical example of a universal consumer segment is the _____ segment.

   a. global motorcycle
   b. global insurance
   c. global teenager
   d. global female
   e. global urban male

Answer: (c) Difficulty: (3) Knowledge: (A) Page: 191

22. The first step in doing international market segmentation is deciding which:

   a. criteria to use in the task.
   b. criteria to fund.
   c. how many customers must be evaluated.
   d. how best to spend research funds.
   e. evaluating demand.

Answer: (a) Difficulty: (3) Knowledge: (F) Page: 192

23. All of the following are bases for country segmentation <u>EXCEPT</u>:

   a. demographics.
   b. socioeconomic variables.
   c. culture.
   d. political conditions.
   e. views toward ownership.

Answer: (e) Difficulty: (2) Knowledge: (F) Page: 192

24. Which of the following bases would probably be in use if a researcher were examing population size, age structure, urbanization degree, and ethnic composition?

   a. demographics.
   b. socioeconomic variables.
   c. culture.
   d. political conditions.
   e. views toward ownership.

Answer: (a) Difficulty: (2) Knowledge: (F) Page: 192

25. Consumption patterns for many goods and services are largely driven by:

   a. government subsidy.
   b. the consumer wealth.
   c. local taxes.
   d. dual demand.
   e. degree of substitutes.

Answer: (b) Difficulty: (2) Knowledge: (F) Page: 193

26. A well known income-based schema considers five stages of economic development. All of the following are part of that schema <u>EXCEPT</u>:

   a. traditional societies.
   b. preconditions for take-off.
   c. the take-off.
   d. adolescence.
   e. the drive to maturity.

Answer: (d) Difficulty: (2) Knowledge: (F) Page: 193, 194

27. With respect to a well known income-based schema that considers stages of economic development, a(n) _____ are viewed as economic basket cases that remain in a quagmire of relentless poverty.

   a. traditional societies
   b. preconditions for take-off (societies)
   c. the take-off (societies)
   d. adolescence (societies)
   e. the drive to maturity (societies)

Answer: (a) Difficulty: (1) Knowledge: (F) Page: 194

28. Because of advances in agriculture, countries like the Philippines, Viet Nam, and Romania have advanced to the income-based schema stage of:

   a. traditional societies
   b. preconditions for take-off (societies)
   c. the take-off (societies)
   d. adolescence (societies)
   e. the drive to maturity (societies)

Answer: (b) Difficulty: (2) Knowledge: (A) Page: 194

29. In the _____, modernization (because of city-centered industries) leads to rapid development in all sectors of the country's economy.

   a. traditional societies
   b. preconditions for take-off (societies)
   c. the take-off (societies)
   d. adolescence (societies)
   e. the drive to maturity (societies)

Answer: (c) Difficulty: (2) Knowledge: (F) Page: 194

30. Under the income-based schema for considering economic development, most of the ASEAN countries, such as Thailand, Malaysia, and Indonesia, are considered:

   a. traditional societies.
   b. preconditions for take-off (societies).
   c. the take-off (societies).
   d. adolescence (societies).
   e. the drive to maturity (societies).

Answer: (c) Difficulty: (2) Knowledge: (A) Page: 194

31. When countries are able to produce a wide variety of products, they generally have entered which of the following stages of the income-based schema for economic development?

   a. traditional societies.
   b. preconditions for take-off (societies).
   c. the take-off (societies).
   d. adolescence (societies).
   e. the drive to maturity (societies).

Answer: (e) Difficulty: (3) Knowledge: (F) Page: 194

32. Most Central European countries (like Hungary, Poland, and the Czech Republic) would be considered in the _____ stage of the income-based schema for classifying stages of economic development.
   a. traditional societies
   b. preconditions for take-off (societies)
   c. the take-off (societies)
   d. high mass-consumption (societies)
   e. the drive to maturity (societies)

Answer: (e) Difficulty: (2) Knowledge: (A) Page: 194

33. When a country has a sizable middle class with significant discretionary incomes, it probably has reached which of the following stages of the income-based schema for classifying stages of economic development.
   a. traditional societies
   b. preconditions for take-off (societies)
   c. the take-off (societies)
   d. high mass-consumption (societies)
   e. the drive to maturity (societies)

Answer: (d) Difficulty: (2) Knowledge: (F) Page: 194

34. Many consumer-goods marketers view _____ as one of the key criteria in segmenting countries.

   a. per-household expenditures
   b. per-capita income
   c. per-capita divorce rates
   d. per-capita capital expenditures
   e. the national demand curve

Answer: (b) Difficulty: (3) Knowledge: (F) Page: 194

35. All of the following are shortcomings of standard "per-capita income" segmentation processes EXCEPT:

   a. monetization of transactions within a country.
   b. not knowing how much a household can buy.
   c. gray and black sectors of the economy being accounted for.
   d. income disparities.
   e. a huge middle class.

Answer: (e) Difficulty: (2) Knowledge: (F) Page: 194, 195

36. Religion, language, and education are examples of which base for segmenting international markets?

   a. demographics.
   b. socioeconomic variables.
   c. culture.
   d. political conditions.
   e. views toward ownership.

Answer: (c) Difficulty: (1) Knowledge: (F) Page: 196

37. Aesthetic preferences of a society clearly have ramifications for product design and the creative aspects of an advertising campaign. Aesthetic preferences of the society would be an example of which base for segmenting an international market?
   a. demographics.
   b. socioeconomic variables.
   c. culture.
   d. political conditions.
   e. views toward ownership.

Answer: (c) Difficulty: (2) Knowledge: (F) Page: 196

38. According to a noted Dutch researcher, countries can be classified along four cultural dimensions. All of the following are illustrations of those dimensions EXCEPT:

   a. individualism versus collectivism.
   b. leadership versus followership.
   c. power distance.
   d. uncertainty avoidance.
   e. masculinity-femininity.

Answer: (b) Difficulty: (3) Knowledge: (F) Page: 196

39. Within the classifications of countries based on cultural dimensions suggested by a Dutch researcher, _____ refers to how members of a given culture relate one to another.

   a. individualism
   b. collectivism
   c. power distance
   d. uncertainty avoidance
   e. masculinity-femininity

Answer: (a) Difficulty: (2) Knowledge: (F) Page: 196

40. In countries where collectivism (within a culture) is high, the _____ is the major focus.

   a. individual
   b. female
   c. male
   d. group
   e. self-concept

Answer: (d) Difficulty: (2) Knowledge: (A) Page: 196

41. Within the classifications of countries based on cultural dimensions suggested by a Dutch researcher, _____ refers to how a society handles inequalities among its members.

   a. individualism
   b. collectivism
   c. power distance
   d. uncertainty avoidance
   e. masculinity-femininity

Answer: (c) Difficulty: (3) Knowledge: (F) Page: 196

42. Within the classifications of countries based on cultural dimensions suggested by a Dutch researcher, _____ refers to whether people tend to feel threatened by uncertainties and ambiguities.

   a. individualism
   b. collectivism
   c. power distance
   d. uncertainty avoidance
   e. masculinity-femininity

Answer: (d) Difficulty: (2) Knowledge: (F) Page: 196

43. Within the classifications of countries based on cultural dimensions suggested by a Dutch researcher, people from high _____ societies tend to be quite risk- averse and dogmatic.

   a. individualism
   b. collectivism
   c. power distance
   d. uncertainty avoidance
   e. masculinity-femininity

Answer: (d) Difficulty: (3) Knowledge: (A) Page: 196

44. Values traditionally regarded as _____ (e.g., competitiveness, ambition, making money, performance) are held in high respect in so-called _____ societies.
   a. individualism
   b. collectivism
   c. power distance
   d. uncertainty avoidance
   e. masculine

Answer: (e) Difficulty: (1) Knowledge: (F) Page: 196

45. Values traditionally regarded as _____ are "quality of life," solidarity, nurturing warm personal relationships dominate in low MA-societies.
   a. individualism
   b. collectivism
   c. power distance
   d. uncertainty avoidance
   e. feminine

Answer: (e) Difficulty: (1) Knowledge: (A) Page: 196

46. Within the classifications of countries based on cultural dimensions suggested by a Dutch researcher, consider which of the following countries would belong in a cluster where power distance was small, uncertainty avoidance was medium, individualism was medium-high, and masculinity was high.

a. Denmark
b. Sweden
c. Great Britain
d. Finland
e. Norway

Answer: (c) Difficulty: (3) Knowledge: (A) Page: 197

47. Within the classifications of countries based on cultural dimensions suggested by a Dutch researcher, consider which of the following countries would NOT belong in a cluster where power distance was small, uncertainty avoidance was low, individualism was high, and masculinity was low.

a. Denmark
b. Sweden
c. Great Britain
d. Finland
e. Norway

Answer: (c) Difficulty: (3) Knowledge: (A) Page: 197

48. Within the classifications of countries based on cultural dimensions suggested by a Dutch researcher, consider which of the following countries would NOT belong in a cluster where power distance was small, uncertainty avoidance was low, individualism was high, and masculinity was low. All but one of these countries have relatively weak resistance to new products, strong consumer desire for novelty and variety, and a high consumer regard for "environmentally friendly" marketers and socially conscious firms.

a. Denmark
b. Sweden
c. Great Britain
d. Finland
e. Norway

Answer: (c) Difficulty: (2) Knowledge: (A) Page: 197

49. When Singapore's government imposed a total ban on the sale and consumption of chewing gum in a drive to clean up the city, Wrigley (the chewing gum manufacturer was adversely affected). Which of the following segmentation bases would this situation best fall under?

a. demographics.
b. socioeconomic variables.
c. culture.
d. political conditions.
e. views toward ownership.

Answer: (d) Difficulty: (1) Knowledge: (A) Page: 198

50. Examples of _____ segmentation include degree of brand/supplier loyalty, usage rate (based on per-capital consumption), and product penetration.

a. demographics
b. socioeconomic variables
c. culture
d. political conditions
e. behavior-based

Answer: (e) Difficulty: (2) Knowledge: (F) Page: 198

51. Examples of _____ segmentation include attitudes, opinions, and values.
a. demographics
b. socioeconomic variables
c. culture
d. lifestyle
e. behavior-based

Answer: (d) Difficulty: (2) Knowledge: (F) Page: 198

52. Of all the segmentation base forms listed, which is the most popular within advertising circles?

a. demographics
b. socioeconomic variables
c. culture
d. lifestyle
e. behavior-based

Answer: (d) Difficulty: (3) Knowledge: (F) Page: 198

53. If a research firm created a list types (segments) named "Traditionalists, Homebody, Rationalist, Pleasurist, Striver, and Trendsetter," from which segmentation base listed would they most likely come from?

   a. demographics
   b. socioeconomic variables
   c. lifestyle
   d. culture
   e. behavior-based

Answer: (c) Difficulty: (2) Knowledge: (F) Page: 199

54. _____ segmentation has been applied for the positioning of new brands, the repositioning of existing ones, identifying new product opportunities, and the development of brand personalities.

   a. demographics
   b. socioeconomic variables
   c. lifestyle
   d. culture
   e. behavior-based

Answer: (c) Difficulty: (3) Knowledge: (A) Page: 200

55. Lifestyle segmentation has been applied for all the following EXCEPT:

   a. positioning of new brands.
   b. the repositioning of existing ones.
   c. parasite brands.
   d. identifying new product opportunities.
   e. the development of brand personalities.

Answer: (c) Difficulty: (2) Knowledge: (F) Page: 200

56. All of the following EXCEPT "_____" has been raised as a concern about using lifestyle segmentation.

   a. values are too general to relate to consumption patterns.
   b. values are too personal to be revealed in research efforts.
   c. value-based segmentation schemes are not always "actionable."
   d. value segments are not stable.
   e. international applicability is quite limited.

Answer: (b) Difficulty: (3) Knowledge: (F) Page: 200

57. With respect to comparing country segmentation (classifying countries into groups), when only one segmentation tool is used the researcher could:

a. simply compute the mean or median and split the countries into two groups.
b. simply compute chi-square and look for differences.
c. use cluster analysis.
d. use correlation analysis.
e. use nonparametric statistics.

Answer: (a) Difficulty: (2) Knowledge: (F) Page: 201

58. _____ is an umbrella term that embraces a collection of statistical procedures for dividing objects into groups.

a. The mean
b. The median
c. Cluster analysis
d. Correlation analysis
e. Regression analysis

Answer: (c) Difficulty: (2) Knowledge: (F) Page: 201

59. If the researcher uses _____ to study relationships between countries, they assume that there exists a relationship between a response variable (Y) and one or more so-called predictor variables (X).

a. the mean
b. the median
c. cluster analysis
d. Latin square design analysis
e. regression analysis

Answer: (e) Difficulty: (3) Knowledge: (F) Page: 203

60. Data in the European market was gathered on the penetration of microwave ovens. The data collected consisted of three potential segmentation variables (income, participation of women in the labor force, and per-capita consumption of frozen foods). Which of the following methods would probably be used to obtain a picture of the segments for microwave usage?

a. the mean
b. the median
c. random block design analysis
d. Latin square design analysis
e. regression analysis

Answer: (e) Difficulty: (3) Knowledge: (F) Page: 203

61. Which of the following is <u>NOT</u> one of the technical issues faced by researchers as they attempt to segment markets in the international environment?

a. poor data quality
b. missing information
c. libelous information
d. "noisy" variables
e. the presence of "outliners"

Answer: (c) Difficulty: (3) Knowledge: (F) Page: 205

62. All of the following are problems encountered when collecting data in the international market <u>EXCEPT</u>:

a. libelous information.
b. some pieces of information are missing.
c. outdated information.
d. unreliable information.
e. inaccurate information.

Answer: (a) Difficulty: (1) Knowledge: (F) Page: 205

63. Data for many of the variables (used in international marketing research) that are collected may suffer from _____ because of reporting errors, sampling mistakes, and other data collection problems.

 a. quality
 b. noise
 c. outlining
 d. misreporting
 e. fabricated

Answer: (b) Difficulty: (2) Knowledge: (F) Page: 205

64. _____ refers to datapoints that deviate from the general pattern followed by the bulk of the data.

 a. Quality
 b. Noise
 c. Outliners
 d. Misreporting
 e. Fabricated

Answer: (c) Difficulty: (3) Knowledge: (F) Page: 206

65. When collecting data in the international market, managerial issues can become a a problem. Which of the following would be ONE of those problems?

 a. The presence of outliners.
 b. Correlation difficulties.
 c. Fabrication of data.
 d. Noisy variables.
 e. The stability of segments over time.

Answer: (e) Difficulty: (2) Knowledge: (F) Page: 206

66. When collecting data in the international market, managerial issues can become a a problem. Which of the following would be ONE of those problems?

 a. The presence of outliners.
 b. Correlation difficulties.
 c. Fabrication of data.
 d. Noisy variables.
 e. The managerial usefulness of country segmentation.

Answer: (e) Difficulty: (1) Knowledge: (F) Page: 206

67. In the international market segmentation game, developing a positioning theme involves the quest for a:

   a. large segment.
   b. profitable segment.
   c. unique selling proposition (USP).
   d. strong manager.
   e. a friendly host government.

Answer: (c) Difficulty: (2) Knowledge: (F) Page: 206

68. Within the arena of positioning strategy, the battle is for:

   a. the mind of your target customer.
   b. the high ground.
   c. the new territory.
   d. the competition's heartland.
   e. the best market share.

Answer: (a) Difficulty: (2) Knowledge: (A) Page: 206

69. When considering positioning themes for low-margin products, the _____ positioning strategy is only viable when the cross-border segment that is chosen represents a sizable group of consumers.

   a. uniform segment
   b. different segment
   c. universal position
   d. variable
   e. standard

Answer: (a) Difficulty: (2) Knowledge: (F) Page: 207

70. An example of the uniform segment/positioning strategy would be:

   a. the global car buyer.
   b. the global insurance buyer.
   c. the international female
   d. the international male.
   e. the global teenager.

Answer: (e) Difficulty: (2) Knowledge: (A) Page: 207

71. A global theme of "Here Today. Here Tomorrow" aimed at the global financial decision maker would be an example of which of the following positioning themes?

    a. uniform segment/positioning strategy
    b. different segment strategy
    c. universal demand
    d. variable
    e. standard

Answer: (a) Difficulty: (2) Knowlege: (F) Page: 207

72. Reasons to adapt positioning themes include all the following EXCEPT:
    a. cultural differences.
    b. legal restraints.
    c. money problems.
    d. competitive factors.
    e. competitive themes.

Answer: (c) Difficulty: (1) Knowledge: (F) Page: 208

73. When Ford Escort sells itself as a mainstream passenger car in the United States and Europe and as a luxury/premium car in India, this would be an example of which of the following strategies with respect to positioning and target markets?

    a. Universal segment/different positioning themes
    b. Universal segment/uniform positioning themes
    c. Different segment/uniform positioning theme
    d. Universal segment/different positioning theme
    e. Different segment/different positioning theme

Answer: (e) Difficulty: (2) Knowledge: (A) Page: 208

74. Many firms position a brand that is mainstream in its home market as a premium brand in their overseas markets, thereby targeting a narrower segment that is willing to pay a premium for imports. This strategy is best described as being:

    a. Universal segment/different positioning themes
    b. Universal segment/uniform positioning themes
    c. Different segment/uniform positioning theme
    d. Universal segment/different positioning theme
    e. Different segment/different positioning theme

Answer: (e) Difficulty: (2) Knowledge: (A) Page: 208

75. Examples of brands that mainstream in their home markets but are perceived as premium in the overseas markets are Heineken, Levi's, and Budweiser. To capitalize on this perception, these companies are seen as following which of the strategies listed below?

a. Universal segment/different positioning themes
b. Universal segment/uniform positioning themes
c. Different segment/uniform positioning theme
d. Universal segment/different positioning theme
e. Different segment/different positioning theme

Answer: (e) Difficulty: (2) Knowledge: (A) Page: 208

True/False   Short Answer

1. Variation in customer needs is the primary motive for market segmentation.

Answer: (True) Difficulty: (1) Knowledge: (F) Page: 183

2. The goal of market segmentation is to ensure profit for all product categories and promote customization to meet customer needs.

Answer: (False) Difficulty: (2) Knowledge: (F) Page: 184

3. The requirements for effective market segmentation in the domestic environment are significantly different than those of the international environment.

Answer: (False) Difficulty: (1) Knowledge: (F) Page: 184

4. The size of segments (in the international environment) based on cultural or lifestyle indicators are typically easy to gauge and to factor into overall planning.

Answer: (False) Difficulty: (2) Knowledge: (F) Page: 184

5. When Cadbury-Schweppes introduced tonic water successfully in Brazil, it was at least partially because of its success in introducing the product in similar countries such as Mexico. With respect to successful segmentation strategies, this example would be an illustration of a positioning strategy.

Answer: (False) Difficulty: (3) Knowledge: (A) Page: 186

6. Environmental changes or shifting consumer preferences often force a firm to rethink its positioning strategy.

Answer: (True) Difficulty: (1) Knowledge: (F) Page: 186

7. In the past, marketers have almost always chosen the strategy of standardization over the strategy of customization.

Answer: (False) Difficulty: (2) Knowledge: (A) Page: 186

8. Nokia's global campaign slogan "Everything. Everywhere." would be an example of a strategy that seeks to appeal to the _____ segment.

Answer: (universal or global) Difficulty: (3) Knowledge: (A) Page: 191

9. The first step in doing international market segmentation is deciding how much budget to allocate to the segmentation process.

Answer: (False) Difficulty: (1) Knowledge: (F) Page: 192

10. _____ variables are among the most popular segmentation criteria.

Answer: (Demographic) Difficulty: (2) Knowledge: (F) Page: 192

11. Two thirds of Asia's population is under 30, with about 250 million people between the ages of 12 and 24. This huge segment will be a great market in the future.

Answer: (True) Difficulty: (1) Knowledge: (F) Page: 193

12. A _____ society is one where there is a relentless quagmire of economic poverty, low productivity, and illiteracy.

Answer: (traditional) Difficulty: (2) Knowledge: (F) Page: 194

13. A society (or stage in the economic schema based on income) that has a sizable middle class with significant discretionary income is described as being one that has high _____.

Answer: (mass-consumption) Difficulty: (3) Knowledge: (F) Page: 194

14. _____ refers to how a society handles inequalities among its members.

Answer: (Power distance) Difficulty: (3) Knowledge: (F) Page: 196

15. One of the problems with using lifestyle variables in forming market segments is that values are too general to relate to consumption patterns or brand choice behavior within a specific product category.

Answer: (True) Difficulty: (2) Knowledge: (F) Page: 200

Essay

1. The requirements for effective market segmentation in a domestic marketing context also apply in international market segmentation. List and briefly describe the properties that these segments should ideally possess.

Answer:

a. Measurable--the segments should be easy to define and measure. This criterion is easily met for "objective" country traits such as socioeconomic variables (e.g., per capita income).

b. Sizable--the segments should be large enough to be worth going after. Some small segments become more attractive if they are lumped across borders.

c. Accessible--the segments should be easy to reach via the media. Quality in media infrastructure must be analyzed.

d. Actionable--for market segmentation to be meaningful, it is important that effective marketing programs (the four Ps) can be developed to evoke the desired response from the target segment.

e. Competitive intensity--preferably, the segments are not preempted by the firm's competition.

f. Growth potential--segments should hopefully have a significant growth potential. Typically, there is a trade off between competitive intensity and growth prospects.

Difficulty: (2) Knowledge: (F) Page: 184

2. Discuss the major reasons why international marketers implement international market segmentation.

Answer:

There are five primary reasons why international marketers implement international market segmentation. They are:

a. Country screening--companies usually do a preliminary screening of countries before identifying attractive market opportunities for their product or service. For preliminary screening, market analysts rely on a few indicators for which information can usually be easily identified. Different criteria is used for each product category.

b. Global market research--country segmentation plays a role in global market research. Companies increasingly make an effort to design products or services that meet the needs of customers in different countries. In order to pursue a policy of standardization, companies need segmentation information to do market research to make sure that the proper ingredients are in the marketing mix.

c. Entry decisions--when a product does well in one country, it is hoped that it will do well in other similar countries. Market segmentation can help to identify the significant characteristics that transcend borders and markets.

d. Positioning strategy--segmentation decisions are instrumental in setting the company's product positioning strategy. Once the firm has selected the target segments, management needs to develop a positioning strategy to embrace the chosen segments. Basically, the company has to decide on how it wants to position its product or services in the mind of the prospective target customers.

e. Marketing mix policy--country segmentation decisions will guide the global marketer's mix decisions. The mix decisions are especially important when deciding between a standardization and customization policy.

Difficulty: (3) Knowledge: (F) Page: 184-186

3. Comment on when marketers should pursue universal market segments versus diverse segments.

Answer:

Marketers should pursue universal market segments when characteristics or segments are found that transcend national borders. Marketers appealing to universal segments have two approaches to reach their targets. One option is to adopt a largely standardized strategy. Alternatively, they might go for a country-tailored strategy that recognizes differences between various countries. The undifferentiated approach will lead to economies of scale. The country-tailored approach (a differentiated strategy) often creates more demand and is more market-oriented.

Difficulty: (1) Knowledge: (F) Page: 191

4. Socioeconomic variables are among the most important bases to be considered when segmenting markets. Comment on the major issues that might be faced when making the decision on whether to use per capita GDP or GNP as a country segmentation criterion.

Answer:

One method of segmenting countries is to use monetization of transactions within a country (a socio-economic variable). To compare measures such as per capita GNP across countries, figures based on a local currency need to be translated into a common currency. However, official exchange rates seldom reflect the purchasing power parity (PPP) of a currency. So, income figures based on GNP or GDP do not really tell one how much a given household in a given country is able to buy.

The PPP (especially in countries with wide income disparity) protects against the shortcomings of the standard "per capita income" segmentation measures. Another method is the Socio-Economic Strata analysis (SES). Under this method, income classes are created and studied.

Difficulty: (3) Knowledge: (A) Page: 193-195

5. For many years researchers and academics believed that lifestyle segmentation (which was often a very successful technique in a home country's domestic market) was a valid segmentation technique. However, recently doubts have been raised. Discuss the weaknesses of lifestyle based segmentation schemes. Think of applications when lifestyle segmentation might be the most appropriate?

Answer:

Using this method, segmentation occurs on a consumer's attitudes, opinions, and values. This is a popular method in advertising circles, however, some of these schemes can be very general and not related to a specific product category.

Lifestyle segmentation has been applied to the positioning of new brands, the repositioning of existing ones, identifying new product opportunities, and the development of brand personalities. Concerns are that: a) values are too general to relate to consumption patterns or brand choice behavior within a specific product category; b) value-based segmentation schemes are not always "actionable;" c) value segments are not stable since values typically change over time; d) their international applicability is quite limited since lifestyles vary greatly.

Difficulty: (2) Knowledge: (F) Page: 199, 200

Chapter 8

Multiple Choice

1. More than 10 million Japanese traveling abroad every year are exposed to larger-sized homes and much lower consumer prices abroad. Such information access creates demand that would not have existed before and it restricts the power of governments to influence consumer choice. This would be an example of:

   a. stable demand structure in the international marketplace.
   b. the explosion of information technology that has changed global competition.
   c. a growing travel industry.
   d. how the Japanese are changing global competition.
   e. how the government's of the world distrust the mass media.

   Answer: (b) Difficulty: (3) Knowledge: (A) Page: 211

2. Geographical boundaries and distance have become less of a constraint in designing strategies for the global market because of:

   a. a stable demand structure in the international marketplace.
   b. a growing travel industry.
   c. the revived role of the United Nations.
   d. the explosion of information technology that has changed global competition.
   e. the expanding role of government in international trade.

   Answer: (d) Difficulty: (2) Knowledge: (A) Page: 211, 212

3. Since the 1980s, the explosion of _____, has forever changed the nature of competition around the world. Geographical distance has become increasingly less relevant in designing global strategy.

   a. new product designs
   b. genetic breakthroughs
   c. information technology
   d. fuel efficient automobiles
   e. interest in the stock market

   Answer: (c) Difficulty: (2) Knowledge: (F) Page: 212

4. In 1996, the total value of physical exports of the United States, Germany, and Japan combined amounted to $1.05 trillion a year; however, in one week London's international electronic transactions in the form of foreign exchange, securities, funds transfer, and credit card transactions amounted to that much. These latter transactions would be an example of a _____.

   a. Gross Domestic Product.
   b. Gross National Product.
   c. Gross Information Product.
   d. Information Dialog.
   e. Gross Financial Transactions.

Answer: (c) Difficulty: (3) Knowledge: (A) Page: 212

5. The chief executive officer of a firm can know the previous day's sales down to a penny because of the increased capacity of information technology. This leads to:

   a. lags.
   b. real-time management.
   c. cyclical trends.
   d. confusion in strategic planning.
   e. is very costly given the benefit.

Answer: (b) Difficulty: (2) Knowledge: (A) Page: 212

7. Top retailers such as Wal-Mart and Toys "R" Us get information from their stores around the world every two hours via telecommunications. This would be an example of _____ in action.

   a. productivity management
   b. trend management
   c. a very costly procedure
   d. management by objectives
   e. real-time management

Answer: (e) Difficulty: (2) Knowledge: (A) Page: 212

8. Ordering and purchasing components, which was once a cumbersome, time-consuming process, is now done by _____, reducing the time involved in such transactions from weeks to days and eliminating a considerable amount of paperwork.

   a. Electronic Data Systems (EDS)
   b. Purchasing International Network (PIN)
   c. Electronic Data Interchange (EDI)
   d. Global Buying Network (GBN)
   e. Internet Buying Network (IBN)

Answer: (c) Difficulty: (3) Knowledge: (F) Page: 212, 213

9. Field representatives using laptop computers, faxes, and satellite uplinks to communicate with the field and the home office are all examples of:

   a. internet buying.
   b. intranet buying.
   c. extranet data exchange.
   d. on-line communication.
   e. nonpersonal communication.

Answer: (d) Difficulty: (2) Knowledge: (F) Page: 213

10. An increasing number of multinational firms have begun to use internal Web servers on the Internet to facilitate communications and transactions among employees, suppliers, independent contractors, and distributors. This would be an example of which of the following organizational forms?

   a. vertical
   b. horizontal
   c. matrix
   d. consensus
   e. Internet

Answer: (e) Difficulty: (1) Knowledge: (A) Page: 213

11. All of the following are the effects of the increased use of information technology on global competition EXCEPT:

  a. real-time management.
  b. on-line communication.
  c. "Internet" organization.
  d. faster product diffusion.
  e. more fashion product life cycles.

Answer: (e) Difficulty: (2) Knowledge: (F) Page: 212-214

12. A contributing factor in the globalization of markets is the spread of _____ as the international language of international business.

  a. computer dialog.
  b. English
  c. accounting
  d. compressed speech
  e. Spanish

Answer: (b) Difficulty: (1) Knowledge: (F) Page: 214

13. The global environment demands a form of strategy that encompasses numerous boundaries and tastes, and that integrates a firm's operations:

  a. across the national borders.
  b. with competitors.
  c. large trading blocs.
  d. with communist and capitalist countries alike.
  e. with standard United Nation's business practice.

Answer: (a) Difficulty: (2) Knowledge: (F) Page: 214

14. A global strategy dictates that a modern firm be _____ in its orientation to the world and its markets.

  a. ethnocentric
  b. polycentric
  c. geocentric
  d. regiocentric
  e. duocentric

Answer: (c) Difficulty: (3) Knowledge: (F) Page: 214

15. The acid test of a well-managed company is being able to conceive, develop, and implement an effective _____ strategy.

    a. ethnocentric
    b. polycentric
    c. global
    d. regiocentric
    e. duocentric

Answer: (c) Difficulty: (2) Knowledge: (F) Page: 215

16. Which of the following would NOT be one of the factors that has persuaded many multinational firms to pursue true global strategies?

    a. global industry.
    b. competitive structure.
    c. hypercompetition.
    d. interdependency.
    e. supply and demand.

Answer: (e) Difficulty: (2) Knowledge: (F) Page: 215-225

17. _____ are defined as those industries where a firm's competitive position in one country is affected by its position in other countries, and vice versa.

    a. Interdependent industries
    b. Global industries
    c. Transcontinental industries
    d. Hypercompetitive industries
    e. Multidomestic industries

Answer: (b) Difficulty: (1) Knowledge: (F) Page: 215

18. General Motors was able to keep afloat during the late 1980s and early 1990s because of the strength of its European operations (as opposed to its American operations). This would be an example of a firm that see itself as being in a:

    a. Interdependent industry.
    b. Global industry.
    c. Transcontinental industry.
    d. Supercompetitive industry.
    e. Multidomestic industry.

Answer: (b) Difficulty: (1) Knowledge: (A) Page: 215

19. Which of the following are <u>NOT</u> one of the four major forces that determines the globalization potential of an industry?

a. market drivers.
b. cost drivers.
c. government drivers.
d. demand drivers.
e. competitive drivers.

Answer: (d) Difficulty: (2) Knowledge: (F) Page: 215, 216

20. In a _____ strategy, a firm manages its international activities like a portfolio.

a. interdependent strategy
b. global strategy
c. transcontinental strategy
d. supercompetitive strategy
e. multidomestic strategy

Answer: (e) Difficulty: (3) Knowledge: (F) Page: 215

21. In a _____ strategy, a firm integrates the activities of a firm on a worldwide basis to capture the linkages among countries and to treat the entire world as a single, borderless market.

a. interdependent strategy
b. global strategy
c. transcontinental strategy
d. supercompetitive strategy
e. multidomestic strategy

Answer: (b) Difficulty: (1) Knowledge: (F) Page: 215

22. With respect to industry globalization drivers, _____ depend on the nature of customer behavior and the structure of channels of distribution.

a. cost drivers
b. competitive drivers
c. quality drivers
d. government drivers
e. market drivers

Answer: (e) Difficulty: (2) Knowledge: (F) Page: 216

23. All of the following are examples of market drivers EXCEPT:

    a. common customer needs.
    b. global customers and channels.
    c. transferable marketing.
    d. experience curves.
    e. lead countries.

Answer: (d) Difficulty: (3) Knowledge: (F) Page: 216

24. Which of the following would be considered a market driver with respect to industry globalization drivers?

    a. favorable logistics.
    b. steep experience curves.
    c. global economics of scale and scope.
    d. global sourcing efficiencies.
    e. transferable marketing.

Answer: (e) Difficulty: (3) Knowledge: (F) Page: 216

25. Lead countries represent countries where innovations in particular industries are prone to take place. All of the following are examples of lead countries EXCEPT:

    a. the United States in computer software.
    b. Japan in consumer electronics.
    c. Germany for industrial control equipment.
    d. France for fashion clothing and perfume.
    e. Hong Kong for computer hardware.

Answer: (e) Difficulty: (1) Knowledge: (A) Page: 216

26. _____ depend on the economics of the business. These drivers particularly affect production location decisions.

    a. cost drivers
    b. competitive drivers
    c. quality drivers
    d. government drivers
    e. market drivers

Answer: (a) Difficulty: (2) Knowledge: (F) Page: 216

27. All of the following are examples of cost drivers EXCEPT:

   a. favorable logistics.
   b. steep experience curves.
   c. global economics of scale and scope.
   d. global sourcing efficiencies.
   e. transferable marketing.

Answer: (e) Difficulty: (3) Knowledge: (F) Page: 216

28. Which of the following would be considered a cost driver with respect to industry globalization drivers?

   a. common customer needs.
   b. global customers and channels.
   c. transferable marketing.
   d. steep experience curves.
   e. lead countries.

Answer: (d) Difficulty: (3) Knowledge: (F) Page: 216

29. Differences in country costs, high product development costs, and fast-changing technology would all be examples of what kind of industry globalization drivers?

   a. cost drivers
   b. competitive drivers
   c. quality drivers
   d. government drivers
   e. market drivers

Answer: (a) Difficulty: (2) Knowledge: (F) Page: 217

30. _____ are rules set by national governments that can affect the use of global strategic decision-making.

   a. cost drivers
   b. competitive drivers
   c. quality drivers
   d. government drivers
   e. market drivers

Answer: (d) Difficulty: (1) Knowledge: (F) Page: 217

31. All of the following might be considered as being government globalization drivers EXCEPT:

    a. favorable trade policies.
    b. compatible technical standards.
    c. common market regulations.
    d. competitors from different continents and countries.
    e. government-owned competitors.

Answer: (d) Difficulty: (2) Knowledge: (F) Page: 217

32. Which of the following would be considered a government globalization driver with respect to industry globalization drivers?

    a. high imports and exports.
    b. compatible technical standards.
    c. competitors from different continents and countries.
    d. interdependent countries.
    e. globalized competitors.

Answer: (b) Difficulty: (3) Knowledge: (F) Page: 217

33. Import tariffs and quotas, nontariff barriers, export subsidies, and local content requirements are all examples of which kind of industry globalization driver?

    a. cost drivers
    b. competitive drivers
    c. quality drivers
    d. government drivers
    e. market drivers

Answer: (d) Difficulty: (1) Knowledge: (F) Page: 217

34. _____ raise the globalization potential of their industry and spur the need for a response on the global strategy level.

    a. cost drivers
    b. competitive drivers
    c. quality drivers
    d. government drivers
    e. market drivers

Answer: (b) Difficulty: (3) Knowledge: (F) Page: 217

35. Which of the following would be considered a competitive globalization driver with respect to industry globalization drivers?

    a. favorable trade policies.
    b. compatible technical standards.
    c. common market regulations.
    d. competitors from different continents and countries.
    e. government-owned competitors.

Answer: (d) Difficulty: (2) Knowledge: (F) Page: 217

36. All of the following might be considered as being competitive globalization drivers EXCEPT:

    a. high imports and exports.
    b. compatible technical standards.
    c. competitors from different continents and countries.
    d. interdependent countries.
    e. globalized competitors.

Answer: (b) Difficulty: (3) Knowledge: (F) Page: 217

37. In effect, the firm that truly operationalizes a global strategy is a _____ oriented firm.

    a. ethnocentric
    b. polycentric
    c. geocentric
    d. regiocentric
    e. duocentric

Answer: (c) Difficulty: (3) Knowledge: (F) Page: 218

38. If a firm considers the whole world as its arena of operation, and its managers maintain equidistance from all markets and do not permit any intrinsic national preferences to influence decisions concerning the global firm, the would be _____ in their orientation.
    a. ethnocentric
    b. polycentric
    c. geocentric
    d. regiocentric
    e. duocentric

Answer: (c) Difficulty: (2) Knowledge: (F) Page: 218

39. If a firm operates where managers operate under the dominant influence of home country practices, the firm would be characterized as being _____ in their orientation.

    a. ethnocentric
    b. polycentric
    c. geocentric
    d. regiocentric
    e. duocentric

Answer: (a) Difficulty: (1) Knowledge: (F) Page: 218

40. If a firm has an orientation where managers of individual subsidiaries operate independently of each other, the firm is characterized as being _____ in their orientation.

    a. ethnocentric
    b. polycentric
    c. geocentric
    d. regiocentric
    e. duocentric

Answer: (b) Difficulty: (2) Knowledge: (F) Page: 218

41. The _____ manager in practice leads to a multidomestic approach, which prevents integration and optimization on a global basis.

    a. ethnocentric
    b. polycentric
    c. geocentric
    d. regiocentric
    e. duocentric

Answer: (b) Difficulty: (2) Knowledge: (F) Page: 218

42. When Unilever used a highly decentralized orientation, with individual operating companies, each with their own identity, linked by a common corporate culture and some common services (such as research, finance, and management development), they would be classed as being _____ in their orientation.

    a. ethnocentric
    b. polycentric
    c. geocentric
    d. regiocentric
    e. duocentric

Answer: (b) Difficulty: (2) Knowledge: (A) Page: 218

43. With respect to market competition, economies of scale still remain the main feature. The theory is that the greater the economies of scale, the greater the benefits to those firms with a larger:

    a. market mix.
    b. market share.
    c. position.
    d. stock portfolio.
    e. employee base.

Answer: (b) Difficulty: (3) Knowledge: (F) Page: 218

44. Once a high level of economies of scale is achieved, it provides the firm with strong barriers against:
    a. new entrants to the market.
    b. the bargaining power of suppliers.
    c. the bargaining power of buyers.
    d. the threat of substitute products or services.
    e. rivalry among existing firms.

Answer: (a) Difficulty: (2) Knowlege: (F) Page: 219

45. The firm that builds its competitive advantage on economies of scale is known as a(n):
    a. product differentiator.
    b. cost leader.
    c. price leader.
    d. innovator.
    e. niche leader.

Answer: (b) Difficulty: (2) Knowledge: (A) Page: 219

46. Firms using a(n) _____ strategy focus exclusively on a highly specialized segment of the market and try to achieve a dominant position in that segment.

    a. product differentiator
    b. cost leader
    c. price leader
    d. innovator
    e. niche

Answer: (e) Difficulty: (2) Knowledge: (F) Page: 219

47. Mercedes-Benz of Germany and Volvo of Sweden are examples of companies using a(n) _____ strategy to achieve success.

    a. product differentiation
    b. cost leader
    c. price leader
    d. innovator
    e. niche

Answer: (a) Difficulty: (2) Knowledge: (A) Page: 219

48. Porsche and Saab maintain their competitive strengths in the high-power sports car enthusiast category by following a(n) _____ strategy.

    a. product differentiation
    b. cost leader
    c. price leader
    d. innovator
    e. niche

Answer: (e) Difficulty: (3) Knowledge: (A) Page: 219

49. _____ determine the rivalry among existing firms.

    a. New entrants to the market
    b. The bargaining power of suppliers
    c. The bargaining power of buyers
    d. The threat of substitute products or services
    e. Industry competitors

Answer: (e) Difficulty: (2) Knowlege: (F) Page: 219

50. _____ can be deterred by strong entry barriers.

a. Potential new entrants to the market
b. The bargaining power of suppliers
c. The bargaining power of buyers
d. The threat of substitute products or services
e. Existing rivals or competitors

Answer: (a) Difficulty: (2) Knowlege: (F) Page: 219

51. The strength of Intel as a dominant producer of microprocessors would be an example of _____ in the PC industry.

a. strength of potential new entrants to the market
b. the bargaining power of suppliers
c. the bargaining power of buyers
d. the threat of substitute products or services
e. existing rivals or competitors

Answer: (b) Difficulty: (2) Knowlege: (A) Page: 219

52. Nestle` has centralized its procurement decision at its headquarters to take advantage of its consolidated bargaining power over cocoa producers around the world. This would be an example of:

a. the strength of potential new entrants to the market.
b. the bargaining power of suppliers.
c. the bargaining power of buyers.
d. the threat of substitute products or services.
e. existing rivals or competitors.

Answer: (c) Difficulty: (2) Knowlege: (A) Page: 220

53. OPEC learned in the late 1970s that it could not raise oil prices artificially high without driving buyers to sources such as alcohol and natural gas. This would be an example of:

a. the strength of potential new entrants to the market.
b. the bargaining power of suppliers.
c. the bargaining power of buyers.
d. the threat of substitute products or services.
e. existing rivals or competitors.

54. The Schumpeterian view of creative destruction assumes continuous change. This is a basic assumption behind the concept of _____ strategy, where the firm's focus is on disrupting the market.

    a. product differentiation
    b. cost leader
    c. price leader
    d. innovator
    e. hypercompetition

55. In a _____ environment, a firm competes on the basis of price-quality, timing and know-how, creating strongholds in the markets in which it operates, and financial resources to outlast one's competitors.

    a. product differentiation
    b. cost leader
    c. price leader
    d. innovator
    e. hypercompetition

56. All of the following are means by which a firm in a hypercompetition environment competes EXCEPT:
    a. price-quality.
    b. timing and know-how.
    c. creating entry barriers.
    d. establishing new corporate cultures based on Asian philosophy.
    e. using financial resources to outlast one's competition.

57. Sony is an excellent example of how to be a first-mover (with the introduction of Trinitron color television, Betamax videorecorders, the Walkman, and an 8-mm videorecorder) using which of the following strategies?
    a. price-quality.
    b. timing and know-how.
    c. creating entry barriers.
    d. establishing new corporate cultures based on Asian philosophy.
    e. using financial resources to outlast one's competition.

Answer: (b) Difficulty: (3) Knowledge: (A) Page: 222

58. One of the problem with using financial resources alone to compete globally is that:

    a. only status quo may be achieved if competitors match expenditures.
    b. the firm may go broke.
    c. the international governments may punish the company.
    d. the international image may be damaged.
    e. no one likes a bully.

Answer: (a) Difficulty: (1) Knowledge: (F) Page: 223

59. Parker Pen company is a classic example of a firm whose global strategy was doomed to failure because:

    a. they failed to appreciate the results of marketing research.
    b. they tried to enter every viable segment and became over extended.
    c. they had image problems.
    d. they had a poor international product.
    e. the had bad managers.

Answer: (b) Difficulty: (3) Knowledge: (A) Page: 224

60. In essence, _____ goes to firms that disrupt the existing status quo in the market and take advantage of the disruption.

    a. profit
    b. inventory control
    c. patents
    d. competitive advantage
    e. international awards

Answer: (d) Difficulty: (2) Knowledge: (F) Page: 224

61. _____ is defined as the organization-wide generation, dissemination, and responsiveness to the intelligence from customers and the market.

    a. Customer-orientation
    b. Service-orientation
    c. Market-orientation
    d. International-orientation
    e. Product-orientation

Answer: (c) Difficulty: (3) Knowledge: (F) Page: 224

62. There are two primary approaches for gaining competitive advantage. One of these methods is the _____ approach that involves a comparison with the competitor on costs, prices, technology, market share, profitability, and other related activities.

   a. customer-centered
   b. market-centered
   c. competitor-centered
   d. service-centered
   e. quality-centered

Answer: (c) Difficulty: (1) Knowledge: (F) Page: 224

63. One of the disadvantages for following an approach of being customer-centered is that the firm may fail to:

   a. innovate because customers might not want rapid change.
   b. price their products effectively.
   c. provide services.
   d. provide product guarantees.
   e. provide for adequate sales support.

Answer: (a) Difficulty: (1) Knowledge: (A) Page: 225

64. Research findings indicate that _____ (the degree of R & D expenditure a firm incurs as a proportion of sales) is a primary determinate of cross-border firms integration.
   a. product intensity
   b. technology intensity
   c. service intensity
   d. quality intensity
   e. communication intensity

Answer: (b) Difficulty: (2) Knowledge: (F) Page: 225

65. Which of the following are benefits of global marketing?

   a. better advertising.
   b. cost reduction.
   c. high profit.
   d. ethics enhancement.
   e. leadership strength.

Answer: (b) Difficulty: (2) Knowledge: (F) Page: 226

66. All of the following are benefits of global marketing EXCEPT:

a. cost reduction.
b. improved quality of products and programs.
c. enhanced customer preference.
d. better advertising.
e. increased competitive advantage.

Answer: (d) Difficulty: (2) Knowledge: (F) Page: 226

67. Which of the following are ways that cost reduction can be achieved by following a program of global marketing?

a. standardized packaging.
b. customized products.
c. using old products from one market for another.
d. hiring more workers.
e. eliminating warranties.

Answer: (a) Difficulty: (3) Knowledge: (F) Page: 227

68. By using a _____ global marketing strategy, a smaller firm can compete against a larger competitor in a more effective manner.

a. focused
b. expensive
c. standard
d. ethnocentric
e. domestic

Answer: (a) Difficulty: (1) Knowledge: (F) Page: 229

69. One of the chief barriers or limits to global marketing is the:

a. lack of respect for foreigners.
b. the diversity of local environments.
c. the amount of poor people in the world.
d. the desire for affluent markets.
e. government control of markets.

Answer: (b) Difficulty: (2) Knowledge: (F) Page: 229

70. One particularly useful technique in analyzing a firm's competitive position relative to its competitors is referred to as SWOT. SWOT stands for:

   a. Strengths, Weaknesses, Organization, Total value.
   b. Strengths, Weaknesses, Operations, Tangible costs.
   c. Strengths, Weaknesses, Opportunities, Total costs.
   d. Strengths, Weaknesses, Opportunities, Total revenues.
   e. Strengths, Weaknesses, Opportunities, Threats.

Answer: (e) Difficulty: (1) Knowledge: (F) Page: 236

71. _____ factors can be looked at as strengths or weaknesses.

   a. External factors
   b. Company factors
   c. Global factors
   d. Internal factors
   e. Service factors

Answer: (d) Difficulty: (1) Knowledge: (F) Page: 236

72. _____ factors can be looked at as opportunities or threats.

   a. External factors
   b. Company factors
   c. Global factors
   d. Internal factors
   e. Service factors

Answer: (a) Difficulty: (1) Knowledge: (F) Page: 236

True/False   Short Answer

1. On a competitive map, financial, trading, and industrial activities across national boundaries have rendered political borders increasingly irrelevant.

Answer: (True) Difficulty: (1) Knowledge: (F) Page: 211

2. Information access creates demand that would not have existed before and it restricts the power of governments to influence consumer choice.

Answer: (True) Difficulty: (1) Knowledge: (F) Page: 211

3. Despite the information explosion of the last several years, geographic boundaries and distance are still a sizable constraint in designing strategies for the global market.

Answer: (False) Difficulty: (2) Knowledge: (F) Page: 212

4. Because of the complexity of international competition and markets, real-time management is not practical for the modern executive seeking new competitive weapons with which to compete.

Answer: (False) Difficulty: (2) Knowledge: (F) Page: 212, 213

5. In a multidomestic strategy, a firm manages its international activities like a portfolio.

Answer: (True) Difficulty: (2) Knowledge: (F) Page: 215

6. _____ drivers depend on the nature of customer behavior and the structure of channels of distribution.

Answer: (Market) Difficulty: (3) Knowledge: (F) Page: 216

7. Some common market drivers are global economies of scale and scope and a steep experience curve.

Answer: (False) Difficulty: (2) Knowledge: (A) Page: 216

8. Cost drivers depend on the _____ of the business.

Answer: (economics or financial aspects) Difficulty: (3) Knowledge: (F) Page: 216

9. Favorable trade policies, compatible technical standards, and common marketing regulations are examples of _____ globalization drivers.

Answer: (government or political) Difficulty: (2) Knowledge: (A) Page: 217

10. _____ drivers raise the globalization potential of their industry and spur the need for a response on the global strategy levels.

Answer: (Competitive) Difficulty: (2) Knowledge: (F) Page: 217

11. High exports and imports, competitors from different continents and countries, and interdependent are all examples of _____ globalization drivers.

Answer: (competitive) Difficulty: (2) Knowledge: (A) Page: 217

12. Unilever is an example of a highly decentralized company that has switched from being a multidomestic company and culture to one where globalism is emphasized.

Answer: (True) Difficulty: (1) Knowledge: (A) Page: 217

13. _____ competitors determine the rivalry among existing firms.

Answer: (Industry) Difficulty: (2) Knowledge: (F) Page: 219

14. Potential entrants may change the rule of competition but can be deterred through _____.

Answer: (entry barriers) Difficulty: (3) Knowledge: (F) Page: 219

15. Intel is an example of how the bargaining power of _____ can change the structure of industries.

Answer: (suppliers) Difficulty: (2) Knowledge: (A) Page: 219

16. The basic premise of hypercompetition is the Schumpeterian view that the secret to success is coordination of competition by negotiation, cooperation, and alliance.

Answer: (False) Difficulty: (2) Knowledge: (F) Page: 221

17. In essence, competitive advantage goes to firms that disrupt the existing status quo in the market and take advantage of the disruption.

Answer: (True) Difficulty: (2) Knowledge: (F) Page: 224

18. SWOT stands for _____.

Answer: (Strengths, Weaknesses, Opportunities, and Threats) Difficulty: (1) Knowledge: (F) Page: 236

Essay

1. Identify and briefly discuss the various factors/forces/drivers which determine the globalization of potential industries. Indicate common examples of each.

Answer:

a. Market globalization drivers--these drivers depend on the nature of customer behavior and the structure of channels of distribution. Some common examples are:

    1). Common customer needs.
    2). Global customers and channels.
    3). Transferable marketing.
    4). Lead countries.

b. Cost globalization drivers--these drivers depend on economics of the business. These drivers particularly affect production location decisions, as well as global market participation and global product development decisions. Some of the cost drivers are:

    1). Global economies of scale and scope.
    2). Steep experience curves.
    3). Global sourcing efficiencies.
    4). Favorable logistics.
    5). Differences in country costs.
    6). High product development costs.
    7). Fast-changing technology.

c. Government globalization drivers--rules set by national governments can affect the use of global strategic decision-making. Some of these rules and policies include:
    1). Favorable trade policies.
    2). Compatible technical standards.
    3). Common marketing regulations.
    4). Government-owned competitors.
    5). Government-owned customers.

d. Competitive globalization drivers--raise the globalization potential of their industry and spur the need for a response on the global strategy level. The common competitive drivers include:
    1). High exports and imports.
    2). Competitors from different continents and countries.
    3). Interdependent countries.
    4). Globalized competitors.

Difficulty: (3) Knowledge: (F) Page: 215-217

2. What does the term "hypercompetition" mean? What are the various arenas of competition covered by this concept?

Answer:

In any given industry, firms jockey among themselves for better competitive position, given a set of customers and buyers, the threat of substitutes and the barriers to entry in that industry. A new competitor may emerge from a completely different industry given the convergence of industries. Such shifts in competition may follow a Schumpeterian view that says creative destruction assumes continuous change. This basic assumption is behind the hypercompetitive environment and strategy that says competition takes place in three arenas: 1) a firm competes on price-quality basis vis-à-vis its competitors; 2) on the basis of timing and know-how; 3) on the basis of creating strongholds in the markets it operates in (this is akin to entry barriers); 4) on the basis of financial resources to outlast one's competitors.

Difficulty: (2) Knowledge: (F) Page: 220-225

3. Relate the concepts of interdependency and standardization to one another. Indicate the strategic implications of the terms.

Answer:

Recent research has shown that the number of technologies used in a variety of products in numerous industries is rising continuously. With resource limitations of firms circumscribing the number of distinctive competencies that a firm can be good at, firms now need to access technologies from outside the firm to be able to build a state-of-the-art product. Since most firms operating globally are subject to the limitation of lack of all required technologies, it follows that for firms to develop products that make optimal use of technologies accessed from outside, a degree of standardization of the components is required. Such component standardization would enable different firms to develop different end products using, in a large measure, the same components.

Difficulty: (1) Knowledge: (F) Page: 225

4. Characterize global marketing strategy. Indicate how it is a separate and distinct form of strategy.

Answer:

Global marketing is not about standardizing the marketing process on a global basis. While every element of the marketing process (the marketing mix and other functions of marketing) may be a candidate for standardization, standardization is one part of a global marketing strategy and is may or may not be used by a company (depending on the mix of the product-market conditions, stage of market development, and the inclinations of the management of the multinational firm). Successful global marketing is a question of coordination.

Difficulty: (1) Knowledge: (A) Page: 226

5. Describe the benefits and limitations of global marketing strategy.

Answer:

Benefits of global marketing strategy fall into four categories: cost reduction, improved quality of products and programs, enhanced customer preference and increased competitive advantage. The limits to global marketing include diversity of local markets, the environments (cultural, political, and legal), the question of standardization versus adaptation (or other derivatives), and the need to have transnational technology and communication.

Difficulty: (2) Knowledge: (F) Page: 226-231

Chapter 9

Multiple Choice

1. All of the following are entry decisions that must be made by management before entering an international market <u>EXCEPT</u>:

   a. decide on the target budget.
   b. decide on the target product/market.
   c. decide on the goals of the target markets.
   d. decide on the mode of entry.
   e. decide on the time of entry.

Answer: (a) Difficulty: (2) Knowledge: (F) Page: 242

2. When marketers are making the decision to enter an international market or not, the first step is generally to:

   a. decide on the target budget.
   b. decide on the target product/market.
   c. decide on the goals of the target markets.
   d. decide on the mode of entry.
   e. decide on the time of entry.

Answer: (b) Difficulty: (1) Knowledge: (F) Page: 242

3. When marketers are making the decision to enter an international market or not, the final step in the decision process is generally to:

   a. decide on a control system to monitor the performance of the entered market.
   b. decide on the target product/market.
   c. decide on the goals of the target markets.
   d. decide on the mode of entry.
   e. decide on the time of entry.

Answer: (a) Difficulty: (1) Knowledge: (F) Page: 242

4. Which of the following most accurately describes the first step in the market entry decision process?

    a. Decide on the goals of the target markets.
    b. Decide on the mode of entry.
    c. Decide on the time of entry.
    d. Decide on the target product/market.
    e. Decide on the marketing mix plan.

Answer: (d) Difficulty: (2) Knowledge: (F) Page: 242

5. Which of the following is a step in the market entry decision process?

    a. Forecast a corporate budget.
    b. Conduct a marketing audit.
    c. Decide on a mode of entry.
    d. Review transportation strengths.
    e. Analyze domestic demand.

Answer: (c) Difficulty: (3) Knowlege: (A) Page: 242

6. To identify market opportunities for a given product or service, the international marketer usually starts off with a large pool of candidate countries. To narrow down this pool, the company will typically do a(n) _____.

    a. internal audit.
    b. external audit.
    c. cross-border budget.
    d. preliminary screen.
    e. econometric analysis.

Answer: (d) Difficulty: (2) Knowledge: (F) Page: 242

7. The goals of a preliminary screen to determine market opportunities are to minimize mistakes of ignoring countries that offer viable opportunities for the product and:

    a. offending local governments.
    b. offending local cultures.
    c. offending local merchants.
    d. violating local advertising laws.
    e. wasting time on countries that offer little or no potential.

Answer: (e) Difficulty: (2) Knowledge: (F) Page: 242

8. The four-step procedure that can be employed for the initial screening process includes all of the following EXCEPT:

   a. indicator and data selection.
   b. analyze parallel strengths and weaknesses of the market.
   c. determine the importances of country indicators.
   d. rate the countries in the pool on each indicator.
   e. compute overall scores for each country.

Answer: (b) Difficulty: (1) Knowledge: (F) Page: 242, 244

9. When Nestle` sees prospects in countries with population an buying power growth and McDonald's starts with countries that are similar to the United States in lifestyle, they are following which of the following steps of the initial screening process for market entry?

   a. indicator and data selection.
   b. analyze parallel strengths and weaknesses of the market.
   c. determine the importances of country indicators.
   d. rate the countries in the pool on each indicator.
   e. compute overall scores for each country.

Answer: (a) Difficulty: (2) Knowledge: (A) Page: 242

10. One common method for determining the importances of country indicators (by determining the importance of weights of each of the country indicators) is to follow the _____ technique where the researcher assigns one hundred points across the set of indicators according to their importance in achieving the company's goals.

   a. Latin-square
   b. Random-block design
   c. multiplied summation
   d. constant-sum
   e. chi-Rho

Answer: (d) Difficulty: (3) Knowledge: (F) Page: 244

11. All of the following would be typical indicators that could be used (through a weighting procedure) to evaluate country or market strength or opportunity EXCEPT:

a. per-capital income.
b. population.
c. number of radios.
d. competition.
e. political risk.

Answer: (c) Difficulty: (2) Knowledge: (A) Page: 244

12. Wrigley, the U.S. chewing gum manufacturer, has not been interested in most Latin American markets because many of the local governments imposed ownership restrictions. This would be an example of _____ in markets.

a. finding opportunities
b. "weeding out"
c. cross-fertilization
d. demand conflict
e. unfairness

Answer: (b) Difficulty: (2) Knowledge: (A) Page: 244

13. One method of assessing whether a company should enter a foreign market or not is use an opportunity matrix. To use such a matrix, the marketer should assess high, moderate, and low opportunities as measured on business and political risk and _____ scales or cells.

a. demand
b. financial constraints
c. market opportunities
d. market sensitivity
e. distance from home market

Answer: (c) Difficulty: (3) Knowledge: (A) Page: 246, Exhibit 9-3

14. All of the following are major external criteria for making a decision as to a mode of entry into a foreign market <u>EXCEPT</u>:

a. company leadership.
b. market size and growth.
c. risk.
d. government regulations.
e. local infrastructure.

Answer: (a) Difficulty: (2) Knowledge: (F) Page: 246, 247

15. In many instances, the key determinant of entry choice decisions is the:

a. risk.
b. local infrastructure.
c. flexibility.
d. internal resources and assets.
e. market size and growth potential.

Answer: (e) Difficulty: (2) Knowledge: (F) Page: 246

16. If a company is concerned with political risk in a country, they can use a _____. This concept functions as a low-cost listening post to gather market intelligence and establish contacts with potential distributors.

a. joint venture.
b. export management company.
c. liaison office.
d. contract exporter.
e. licensor.

Answer: (c) Difficulty: (3) Knowledge: (F) Page: 247

17. The _____ of a market refers to the country's distribution system, transportation network, and communication system.

a. demographic environment
b. infrastructure
c. logistical
d. physical distribution
e. physical infrastructure

Answer: (e) Difficulty: (2) Knowledge: (F) Page: 247

18. Markets can be classified in five types of countries based on their respective market attractiveness. All of the following are part of the classification scheme EXCEPT:

   a. platform countries.
   b. emerging countries.
   c. boot-strap countries.
   d. growth countries.
   e. maturing countries.

Answer: (c) Difficulty: (1) Knowledge: (F) Page: 247

19. Markets can be classified in five types of countries based on their respective market attractiveness. Which of the following of those types can be used to gather intelligence and establish a network?

   a. platform countries.
   b. emerging countries.
   c. established countries.
   d. growth countries.
   e. maturing countries.

Answer: (a) Difficulty: (1) Knowledge: (F) Page: 247

20. Markets can be classified in five types of countries based on their respective market attractiveness. Hong Kong and Singapore would fall into which of the types listed below (where the purpose would be to gather intelligence and establish a network)?

   a. platform countries.
   b. emerging countries.
   c. established countries.
   d. growth countries.
   e. maturing countries.

Answer: (a) Difficulty: (3) Knowledge: (A) Page: 247

21. Markets can be classified in five types of countries based on their respective market attractiveness. Which of the following of those types can be used to build up an initial presence (such as through a liaison office)?

a. platform countries.
b. emerging countries.
c. established countries.
d. growth countries.
e. maturing countries.

Answer: (b) Difficulty: (2) Knowledge: (F) Page: 247

22. Markets can be classified in five types of countries based on their respective market attractiveness. Viet Nam and the Philippines would fall into which of the types listed below (where the purpose would be to build up an initial presence such as through a liaison office)?

a. platform countries.
b. emerging countries.
c. established countries.
d. growth countries.
e. maturing countries.

Answer: (b) Difficulty: (3) Knowledge: (A) Page: 247

23. Markets can be classified in five types of countries based on their respective market attractiveness. Which of the following countries would most likely be listed as a maturing market?

a. Hong Kong.
b. Burma.
c. India.
d. Taiwan.
e. Japan.

Answer: (d) Difficulty: (3) Knowledge: (A) Page: 247, 248

24. Markets can be classified in five types of countries based on their respective market attractiveness. Which of the following countries would most likely be listed as an established market?
    a. Hong Kong.
    b. Burma.
    c. India.
    d. Taiwan.
    e. Japan.

Answer: (e) Difficulty: (2) Knowledge: (A) Page: 247, 248

25. Companies with tight resources (human and/or financial) or limited assets are constrained to _____ commitment entry modes such as exporting and licensing.
    a. low
    b. moderate
    c. basic
    d. medium
    e. high

Answer: (a) Difficulty: (1) Knowledge: (F) Page: 249

26. _____ perspective argues that the desirable governance structure (high- versus low-control mode) will depend on the comparative transaction costs (the costs of running an operation).

    a. Demand-delivery
    b. Just-in-time management
    c. Management-by-objectives
    d. Quantity-cost allocation
    e. Transaction-cost analysis

Answer: (e) Difficulty: (2) Knowledge: (F) Page: 250

27. From a Transaction-cost analysis perspective, market failure typically happens when transaction-specific assets become _____ and therefore more high-control situations are needed.
    a. optional
    b. valuable
    c. expendable
    d. less-valuable
    e. lost

28. An empirical study of entry decisions found that MNCs were most likely to enter with wholly owned subsidiaries when all <u>BUT</u> _____ existed.

   a. the entry involved an R & D intensive line of business.
   b. the entry involved an advertising-intensive line of business.
   c. the entry involved a high brand-equity line of business.
   d. the MNC had only marginal intelligence on the market.
   e. the MNC had accumulated a substantial amount of experience with foreign entries.

Answer: (d) Difficulty: (1) Knowledge: (F) Page: 250

29. An empirical study found that MNCs were more likely to prefer a partnership when entering a market when _____ existed.

   a. the entry involved an R & D intensive line of business.
   b. the entry involved an advertising-intensive line of business.
   c. the entry involved a high brand-equity line of business.
   d. the entry was in a sociocultural distant country.
   e. the MNC had accumulated a substantial amount of experience with foreign entries.

Answer: (d) Difficulty: (2) Knowledge: (A) Page: 250

30. Most companies start their international expansion with _____.

   a. exporting.
   b. importing.
   c. licensing.
   d. joint ventures.
   e. strategic alliances.

Answer: (a) Difficulty: (1) Knowledge: (F) Page: 250

31. Companies that plan to engage in exporting have a choice between indirect, _____, and direct exporting.

   a. licensing
   b. parallel
   c. cooperative
   d. venture
   e. summation

Answer: (c) Difficulty: (2) Knowledge: (F) Page: 251

32. _____ exporting means that the firm uses a middleman based in its home market to do the exporting.

   a. Licensing
   b. Parallel
   c. Cooperative
   d. Venture
   e. Indirect

Answer: (e) Difficulty: (2) Knowledge: (A) Page: 251

33. _____ exporting means that the firm enters into an agreement with another firm (local or foreign) where the partner will use its distribution network to sell the exporter's goods.
   a. Licensing
   b. Parallel
   c. Cooperative
   d. Venture
   e. Indirect

Answer: (c) Difficulty: (2) Knowledge: (F) Page: 251

34. _____ exporting means that the company sets up its own export organization within the company and relies on a middleman based in a foreign market (foreign distributor).
   a. Licensing
   b. Parallel
   c. Cooperative
   d. Direct
   e. Indirect

Answer: (d) Difficulty: (1) Knowledge: (F) Page: 251

35. _____ exporting offers several advantages. Chief among these are the firm gets instant foreign market expertise, very little risk is involved, and no major resource commitments are required.

   a. Licensing
   b. Parallel
   c. Cooperative
   d. Direct
   e. Indirect

Answer: (e) Difficulty: (2) Knowledge: (A) Page: 251

36. _____ has disadvantages. Chief among these are that the company has little or no control over the way their product is marketed in a foreign country, lack of adequate sales support (among other support variables) can lead to poor sales, and bad decisions made by an intermediary can damage the corporate image.
   a. Licensing
   b. Parallel
   c. Cooperative
   d. Direct
   e. Indirect

Answer: (e) Difficulty: (2) Knowledge: (A) Page: 251

37. One of the most popular forms of cooperative exporting is _____.
   With this method, the company uses the overseas distribution network of another company (local or foreign) for selling its goods in the foreign market.

   a. parallel exporting.
   b. venture exporting.
   c. piggyback exporting.
   d. make-or-buy exporting.
   e. foreign export management exporting.

Answer: (c) Difficulty: (1) Knowledge: (A) Page: 251

38. One of the main advantages of direct exporting over indirect exporting is that the exporter has more:
   a. leverage.
   b. risk.
   c. control over its operations.
   d. budget.
   e. leadership.

Answer: (c) Difficulty: (1) Knowledge: (F) Page: 252

39. _____ is a contractual strategy where the firm offers some proprietary assets to a foreign company in exchange for royalty fees.

   a. Licensing
   b. Parallel exporting
   c. Cooperative exporting
   d. Direct exporting
   e. Indirect exporting

Answer: (a) Difficulty: (2) Knowledge: (F) Page: 252

40. The Oriental Land Company in Japan owns Tokyo Disneyland. This would be an example of an international _____ agreement between the Oriental Land Company (owner) and Disneyland (receives royalties).

    a. licensing
    b. parallel exporting
    c. cooperative exporting
    d. direct exporting
    e. indirect exporting

Answer: (a) Difficulty: (1) Knowledge: (A) Page: 252

41. Benefits of licensing include:

    a. not very demanding on company resources.
    b. always protected against copying or technical theft.
    c. always a strong partner relationship.
    d. low profits, therefore, low taxes.
    e. licensee is always enthusiastic.

Answer: (a) Difficulty: (2) Knowledge: (F) Page: 252, 253

42. Nurturing a future competitor is the biggest danger in _____.

    a. licensing
    b. parallel exporting
    c. cooperative exporting
    d. direct exporting
    e. indirect exporting

Answer: (a) Difficulty: (2) Knowledge: (A) Page: 253

43. One of the most popular entry modes in the international marketplace for service firms is:

    a. licensing.
    b. franchising.
    c. cooperative exporting.
    d. direct exporting.
    e. indirect exporting.

Answer: (b) Difficulty: (2) Knowledge: (F) Page: 254

44. One of the most popular franchise plans used in international marketing is _____ where the franchisor gives the franchise to a local entrepreneur who in turn sells local franchises within a territory.

  a. sales franchise
  b. master franchise
  c. strategic franchise
  d. cross-country franchise
  e. border-territory franchise

Answer: (b) Difficulty: (3) Knowledge: (A) Page: 254

45. All of the following are felt to be difficulties of disadvantages of franchises in the international marketplace EXCEPT:

  a. the income stream is not as great as with direct investment.
  b. lack of control over the franchisees.
  c. lack of control over franchise operations.
  d. cultural hurdles.
  e. government payoffs are necessary in many instances.

Answer: (e) Difficulty: (1) Knowledge: (F) Page: 255

46. In _____, the company arranges with a local manufacturer to manufacture parts of the product or even the entire product. The marketing of the product, however, is still the responsibility of the international firm.

  a. licensing
  b. franchising
  c. cooperative exporting
  d. contract manufacturing
  e. indirect exporting

Answer: (d) Difficulty: (2) Knowledge: (F) Page: 255

47. _____ are(is) the prime motivation behind contract manufacturing.

  a. Advertising cooperation
  b. Leadership
  c. Cost savings
  d. Profit expansion
  e. Desire to be part of a cartel

48. Like licensing and franchising, nurturing a future competitor is one of the biggest dangers in _____.

    a. contract manufacturing.
    b. parallel exporting.
    c. cooperative exporting.
    d. using an export management company.
    e. indirect exporting.

Answer: (a) Difficulty: (2) Knowledge: (A) Page: 255

49. When screening a foreign subcontractor, the ideal candidate should meet all the following EXCEPT:

    a. have no local partners.
    b. be flexible and geared to Just-In-Time delivery.
    c. able to meet quality standards and implement Total Quality Management.
    d. have a solid financial base.
    e. have a contingency plan to handle sudden changes in demand.

Answer: (a) Difficulty: (1) Knowledge: (A) Page: 256

50. With a _____, the foreign company agrees to share equity and other resources with other partners to establish a new entity in the target country.

    a. contract manufacturing agreement
    b. parallel exporting agreement
    c. cooperative exporting agreement
    d. export management company
    e. joint venture

Answer: (e) Difficulty: (2) Knowledge: (F) Page: 256

51. A major advantage of joint ventures, as compared to lesser forms of resource commitment such as licensing, is:

    a. the return potential.
    b. infrastructure enhancement.
    c. expansion of stockholders.
    d. division of leadership.
    e. an increase in ethical standards.

Answer: (a) Difficulty: (2) Knowledge: (F) Page: 256

52. All of the following are considered benefits of forming joint ventures <u>EXCEPT</u>:

    a. greater return potential.
    b. shared profits instead of shared royalties.
    c. more control over operations.
    d. increased cost controls.
    e. synergies.

Answer: (d) Difficulty: (3) Knowledge: (F) Page: 256

53. With respect to joint ventures, the _____ argument is illustrated by not only shared capital and risk but possible contributions brought in by the local partner in land, raw materials, expertise on the local environment, and access to local distribution networks.

    a. demand
    b. parallel management
    c. consensus management
    d. domestication
    e. synergy

Answer: (e) Difficulty: (2) Knowledge: (F) Page: 256, 257

54. Lack of trust and mutual conflicts can often turn _____ into partnerships doomed to failure.
    a. contract manufacturing agreements
    b. parallel exporting agreements
    c. cooperative exporting agreements
    d. export management companies
    e. joint ventures

Answer: (e) Difficulty: (2) Knowledge: (F) Page: 257

55. One of the problems with joint ventures is _____ between partners. An example would be when one partner wants to stress high quality and the other wants to stress high quantity.

    a. conflicting purchasing arrangements
    b. conflicting process objectives
    c. sharing
    d. budgets
    e. staffing

Answer: (b) Difficulty: (3) Knowledge: (A) Page: 257

56. One of the problems with joint ventures is _____ between partners. An example would be when one partner wants to stress reduction of political and economic controls on decision-making and the other partner wants to accept technology and capital but precludes foreign authority infringement on sovereignty and ideology.

    a. conflicting purchasing objectives
    b. conflicting process objectives
    c. control objectives
    d. budget objectives
    e. staffing objectives

Answer: (c) Difficulty: (3) Knowledge: (A) Page: 257

57. There are no magic ingredients to foster the stability of joint ventures, however, all of the following are good guidelines EXCEPT:

    a. pick a partner with which control can be maintained.
    b. pick the right partner.
    c. establish clear objectives from the beginning.
    d. bridge cultural gaps.
    e. get top management commitment and respect.

Answer: (a) Difficulty: (2) Knowledge: (F) Page: 258, 259

58. _____ come about when multinational companies prefer to enter new markets with 100 percent ownership.

    a. Contract manufacturing agreements
    b. Parallel exporting agreements
    c. Cooperative exporting agreements
    d. Wholly owned subsidiaries
    e. Joint ventures

Answer: (d) Difficulty: (2) Knowledge: (F) Page: 259

59. When a multinational company chooses to invest in foreign markets with wholly owned subsidiaries, these subsidiaries may be acquisitions or _____ operations.

   a. joint venture
   b. strategic alliance
   c. greenfield
   d. franchise
   e. piggyback

Answer: (c) Difficulty: (2) Knowledge: (F) Page: 259

60. A _____ operation (with respect to wholly owned subsidiaries) is one which is started from scratch.

   a. joint venture
   b. strategic alliance
   c. greenfield
   d. franchise
   e. piggyback

Answer: (c) Difficulty: (2) Knowledge: (F) Page: 259

61. Wholly owned subsidiaries give MNCs _____ of their operations.

   a. almost no control
   b. partial control
   c. moderate control
   d. full control
   e. strategic control only

Answer: (d) Difficulty: (1) Knowledge: (A) Page: 259

62. Advantages of wholly owned subsidiaries include all of the following EXCEPT:

   a. full control.
   b. control of profits.
   c. own processes.
   d. control government relationships.
   e. can often be set quicker that other forms of investment.

Answer: (d) Difficulty: (2) Knowledge: (F) Page: 259

63. One of the chief disadvantages of a wholly owned subsidiary is that:

    a. it is often perceived of as a threat to cultural or economic sovereignty.
    b. relatively low profits.
    c. distant supply lines.
    d. more expensive labor.
    e. inability to exploit local media for promotion.

Answer: (a) Difficulty: (1) Knowledge: (A) Page: 260

64. One way to address hostility to foreign acquisitions in the host country is by
    _____ the firm's presence in the foreign market by hiring local managers,
    sourcing locally, and developing local brands.

    a. regionalizing
    b. localizing
    c. socializing
    d. acculturating
    e. emphasizing the self-reference criterion (SRC)

Answer: (b) Difficulty: (3) Knowledge: (A) Page: 260

65. When Reebok Russia (a wholly owned subsidiary of Reebok) donated $50,000
    worth of products to highly visible outlets such as schools, orphanages, and the
    Russian Olympic team, they were attempting to emphasize a _____
    policy.
    a. regionalizing
    b. localizing
    c. socializing
    d. acculturating
    e. emphasizing the self-reference criterion (SRC)

Answer: (b) Difficulty: (2) Knowledge: (A) Page: 260

66. The chief reason that some firms choose acquisitions (or mergers) to enter a foreign
    market is that they can:

    a. receive greater tax relief.
    b. receive greater profits.
    c. reduce debt.
    d. increase stock price.
    e. enter the market more quickly.

Answer: (e) Difficulty: (2) Knowledge: (F) Page: 261

67. One of the chief reasons that some firms choose greenfield operations as a means to enter foreign markets is that can often:

a. receive greater tax relief.
b. receive greater profits.
c. reduce debt.
d. increase stock price.
e. enter the market more quickly.

Answer: (a) Difficulty: (2) Knowledge: (F) Page: 262

68. _____ are described as a coalition of two or more organizations to achieve strategically significant goals that are mutually beneficial.

a. Joint ventures
b. Strategic alliances
c. Greenfield operations
d. Franchises
e. Piggyback arrangements

Answer: (b) Difficulty: (2) Knowledge: (F) Page: 262

69. One reason for the increase in the number of strategic alliances has been the observed success of the Japanese _____.

a. chaebols.
b. electronics cartels.
c. keiretsus.
d. cabals.
e. syndicates.

Answer: (c) Difficulty: (1) Knowledge: (A) Page: 262

70. All of the following are illustrations of the four generic reasons for forming strategic alliances EXCEPT:

a. Offense.
b. Defense.
c. Catch-up.
d. Remain.
e. Restructure.

Answer: (a) Difficulty: (2) Knowledge: (F) Page: 264, 265

71. The underlying goal of _____ in creating a strategic alliance is to sustain the firm's leadership position by learning new skills, getting access to new markets, and developing new technologies.

    a. offense
    b. defense
    c. catch-up
    d. remain
    e. restructure

Answer: (b) Difficulty: (2) Knowledge: (F) Page: 265

72. When Nestle` and General Mills launched Cereal Partners Worldwide to attack Kellogg-dominated global cereal market, this was an example of which of the following strategies with respect to strategic alliances?

    a. Offense.
    b. Defense.
    c. Catch-up.
    d. Remain.
    e. Restructure.

Answer: (c) Difficulty: (2) Knowledge: (A) Page: 265

73. The strategic alliance strategy of _____ might be enacted when the firm has an established leadership position but that only plays a peripheral role in the company's business portfolio.

    a. offense
    b. defense
    c. catch-up
    d. remain
    e. restructure

Answer: (d) Difficulty: (3) Knowledge: (F) Page: 265

74. When a firm uses a strategic alliance as a vehicle to rejuvenate a business that is not core and in which it has no leadership position, it is probably using a _____ strategy.

    a. offense
    b. defense
    c. catch-up
    d. remain
    e. restructure

Answer: (e) Difficulty: (1) Knowledge: (F) Page: 265

75. Research has shown that to achieve an enduring alliance between partners all of the following must exist EXCEPT:

    a. strong government support.
    b. partnership between equals works best.
    c. autonomy.
    d. flexibility.
    e. equal ownership.

Answer: (a) Difficulty: (1) Knowledge: (A) Page: 266

True/False   Short Answer

1. The first step in the process of entering a foreign market is to decide on the

   _____.

Answer: (target product/market) Difficulty: (2) Knowledge: (F) Page: 242

2. Preliminary screening is an accepted method of reducing the number of candidates for market entry.

Answer: (True) Difficulty: (1) Knowledge: (F) Page: 242

3. As example of a preliminary screening process in assessing international market opportunities, Colgate-Palmolive uses assessments of whether people bath regularly or not as a critical factor in deciding whether to enter a market or not.

Answer: (False) Difficulty: (2) Knowledge: (A) Page: 242

4. As an example of a preliminary screening process in assessing international market opportunities, McDonald's starts with countries that are similar to the United States in lifestyle.

Answer: (True) Difficulty: (1) Knowledge: (A) Page: 242

5. In many instances, the key determinant of entry choice decisions is the size of the market.

Answer: (True) Difficulty: (1) Knowledge: (F) Page: 246

6. _____ countries (with respect to market attractiveness) can be used to gather intelligence and establish a network.

Answer: (Platform) Difficulty: (3) Knowledge: (F) Page: 247

7. An example of a platform country is India.

Answer: (False) Difficulty: (2) Knowledge: (A) Page: 247, 248

8. The major goal in an emerging country is to build up an initial presence via a _____ office.

Answer: (liaison) Difficulty: (3) Knowledge: (F) Page 247

9. An example of an emerging country (with respect to market attractiveness) is the Philippines.

Answer: (True) Difficulty: (2) Knowledge: (A) Page: 247

10. When going abroad most companies start their international expansion with _____.

Answer: (exporting) Difficulty: (1) Knowledge: (F) Page: 250

11. Piggyback exporting is when two different transportation modes (such as truck and rail) are combined.

Answer: (False) Difficulty: (2) Knowledge: (A) Page: 251

12. Under _____ exporting, a firm sets up its own export department and sells its products via a middlemen located in the foreign market.

Answer: (direct) Difficulty: (2) Knowledge: (F) Page: 252

13. In a master franchise, the franchisor gives a master franchise to a local entrepreneur, who will, in turn, sell local franchises within a territory.

Answer: (True) Difficulty: (1) Knowledge: (F) Page: 254

14. Synergy is one of the benefits of contract manufacturing.

Answer: (False) Difficulty: (2) Knowledge: (F) Page: 256

15. Strategic alliances between strong and weak partners often work because of the synergy and learning that can take place between mentor and subordinate.

Answer: (False) Difficulty: (2) Knowledge: (F) Page: 266

Essay

1. List the steps in global market entry decision process. Which of the steps is probably the most important in the overall success of the foreign venture. Justify your answer.

Answer:

Steps are: (1) decide on the target product/market; (2) decide on the goals of the target markets; (3) decide on the mode of entry; (4) decide on the time of entry; (5) decide on a marketing mix plan; and, (6) decide on a control system to monitor the performance in the entered market.

Most research indicates that the first step (deciding on the target product/market) is probably the most important and where many mistakes are made.

Students should cover the material in the preliminary screening process to justify their answer. If another answer is chosen, the instructor must judge the validity and quality of the choice and the justification.

Difficulty: (2) Knowledge: (F) Page: 242, 242-246

2. Explain what is meant by the concept of a liaison office and why some firms prefer to use this technique to enter markets.

Answer:

Many companies would like to just "get their feet wet" before plunging into the foreign market arena. Opening a liaison office allows this to happen. The liaison office can not only establish a presence but become an intelligence source for the parent company. Many firms wish to evaluate risk and cultural relationships before they make a choice that will commit themselves to resource allocation and increased risk. The liaison office can perform those functions. By assessing the local environment at the local level, the company can more intelligent decisions at a later date. In addition, this office can begin the slow process of establishing networks that will be essential to later trade relationships.

Difficulty: (1) Knowledge: (F) Page: 247, 250-252

3. Briefly, explain the concept of licensing in a foreign market. In addition, cite the benefits and drawbacks of licensing. Be specific in your responses.

Answer:

Licensing is a contractual transaction where the firm--the licensor--offers some property assets to a foreign company--the licensee--in exchange for royalty fees.

Benefits.
  a. Profitable.
  b. Not demanding on resources.
  c. Gets around import barriers.
  d. Gains access to markets.
  e. Lowers exposure to political or economic instabilities.
  f. Can rapidly amortize R&D expenditures.

Caveats.
  a. Income can be small when compared to exporting.
  b. The licensee may not be fully committed to the licensor's technology or product.
  c. Sales and trademarks can be damaged.
  d. A future competitor can be built.
  e. Protection can be partially achieved by patenting and careful selection of the licensee.

Difficulty: (3) Knowledge: (F) Page: 252-254

4. Briefly, explain the concept of the joint venture. Additionally, give the benefits and drawbacks of entering into a joint venture.

Answer:

With a joint venture, the foreign company agrees to share equity and other resources with other partners to establish a new entity in the target country.

Benefits.
    a. The return potential can be substantial.
    b. More control can be achieved.
    c. Synergy.

Caveats.
    a. Lack of full control may still be a problem.
    b. Government restrictions.
    c. Lack of trust.
    d. Mutual conflicts.

Difficulty: (2) Knowledge: (F) Page: 256-258

5. Provide an assessment of strategic alliances. What are they used for, what are the characteristics of those the generally succeed, and what are the general types? Be sure to be specific in your answers.

Answer:

Strategic alliances are described as being a coalition of two or more organizations to achieve strategically significant goals that are mutually beneficial.

Cross-Border Alliances that Succeed have the following characteristics:
    a. Alliances between strong and weak partners seldom work.
    b. Autonomy and flexibility.
    c. Equal ownership.
    d. Commitment and support of the top of the parent's organization.
        1). Strong managers are a key.
    e. Alliances that are related (in terms of products, markets, and/or technologies).
    f. Have similar cultures, asset sizes, and venturing experiencing levels tend to be be more viable.
    g. Shared vision on the goals and mutual benefits are critical.
    h. Spell out relationships in contractual form.

General types include:

    a. Defense--companies create alliances for their core businesses to defend their leadership position.
    b. Catch-up--firms may also shape strategic alliances to catch up (especially when they don't have a leadership position).
    c. Remain--this might occur for business divisions where the firm has established a leadership position but that only plays a peripheral role in the company's business portfolio.
    d. Restructure--use the alliance to restructure a business that is not core and in which it has no leadership position.

Difficulty: (3) Knowledge: (F) Page: 262-266

Chapter 10

Multiple Choice

1. Global competition suggests a(n) _____ for most products, and no longer permits companies a polycentric, country-by-country approach to international business.

   a. service gap
   b. drastically shortened life cycle
   c. failure of portfolio analysis
   d. kinked demand curve
   e. quality problem

Answer: (b) Difficulty: (3) Knowledge: (A) Page: 271

2. According to the _____ theory, changes in inputs and product characteristics toward standardization over time determine an optimal production location at any particular phase of the product's life cycle.

   a. product life cycle
   b. break-even analysis
   c. portfolio analysis
   d. mini-max
   e. hypercompetition

Answer: (a) Difficulty: (1) Knowledge: (F) Page: 271, 272

3. All of the following are major limitations to the international product cycle theory <u>EXCEPT</u>:

   a. the increased pace of new product introduction limits a firms options.
   b. companies are deprived of the age-old polycentric approach because of speed of innovations.
   c. demands are even more unpredictable than they were a few short years ago.
   d. preempting (by sourcing) the product life cycle allows a shrewd company to outmaneuver competition.
   e. more active management of local and corporate resources on a global basis gives a company a preemptive first-mover advantage over competition.

Answer: (c) Difficulty: (3) Knowledge: (F) Page: 272

4. When Sony first introduced transistorized solid-state color TVs in the United States (even before they introduced them in Japan) and then used that market to spring board to the rest of the world, this was an example of _____ advantage as well as economies of scale advantages.

   a. first-to-strike
   b. position
   c. leader
   d. prime locator
   e. first-mover

Answer: (e) Difficulty: (2) Knowledge: (A) Page: 272

5. Even though the British company EMI developed CAT scanners in 1972, they failed to export them to the United States because of a slow and deliberate policy of following dictates of the _____ theory. This caused them to arrive late and loose the giant U.S. markets to other more aggressive competitors.

   a. product life cycle
   b. break-even analysis
   c. portfolio analysis
   d. mini-max
   e. hypercompetition

Answer: (a) Difficulty: (1) Knowledge: (A) Page: 272

6. Without established _____ plans, distribution, and service networks, it is extremely difficult to exploit both emerging technology and potential markets around the world simultaneously.

   a. advertising
   b. inventory
   c. warranty
   d. sourcing
   e. labor

Answer: (d) Difficulty: (2) Knowledge: (F) Page: 272

7. Global _____ strategy is logistical management of the interfaces of R & D, manufacturing, and marketing activities on a global basis.

   a. production
   b. inventory
   c. warranty
   d. sourcing
   e. labor

Answer: (d) Difficulty: (2) Knowledge: (A) Page: 272

8. If marketing wants repeated product modification and proliferation for the sake of satisfying the ever-changing customer needs and manufacturing wants lowering of costs through standardization, then the organization has a "tug-of-war"-like situation because of:

   a. failure of leadership.
   b. differing objectives.
   c. poor strategy.
   d. no vision.
   e. international competition.

Answer: (b) Difficulty: (2) Knowledge: (A) Page: 273

9. One way manufacturing can meet marketing's desire for repeated product modification for the sake of ever-changing customer needs is use _____ which provide for flexibility without appreciably raising costs.

   a. consultants
   b. movable plant locations
   c. flexible machine tools
   d. CAD/CAM facilities
   e. turn-key information systems

Answer: (d) Difficulty: (2) Knowledge: (F) Page: 273

10. U.S. multinational companies sell more than _____ times as much overseas through their subsidiaries than they export to the world. This ratio has remained stable since the mid-1960s.

    a. one to one
    b. two to one
    c. three to one
    d. four to one
    e. five to one

Answer: (c) Difficulty: (2) Knowledge: (F) Page: 274

11. The most important Triad region (with respect to trading) in the marketing of goods and services through the world is made up of which of the following countries?

    a. United States, Canada, and Mexico.
    b. United States, Britain, and Canada.
    c. United States, Mexico, and South America.
    d. United States, European Community, and Japan.
    e. United States, Japan, and China.

Answer: (d) Difficulty: (2) Knowledge: (F) Page: 274

12. Peter Drucker once said that _____ would remain the darkest continent of business--the least exploited area of business for competitive advantage.

    a. marketing
    b. information systems
    c. sourcing and logistics
    d. inventory control
    e. marketing services

Answer: (c) Difficulty: (1) Knowledge: (F) Page: 275

13. All of the following are recognized trends in global sourcing EXCEPT:

    a. the decline of exchange rate determinism in sourcing.
    b. the failure of industrialized producers to respect third world producers.
    c. new competitive environments caused by excess worldwide capacity.
    d. innovations in and restructuring of international trade infrastructure.
    e. enhanced role of purchasing managers.

Answer: (b) Difficulty: (3) Knowledge: (F) Page: 275-280

14. If the dollar _____, U.S. companies find it easy to procure components and products from abroad.

a. depreciates
b. remains stable
c. appreciates
d. floats
e. is valued

Answer: (c) Difficulty: (2) Knowledge: (F) Page: 275

15. If the dollar _____, U.S. companies find it difficult and costly to procure components and products from abroad.

a. depreciates
b. remains stable
c. appreciates
d. floats
e. is valued

Answer: (a) Difficulty: (2) Knowledge: (F) Page: 275

16. In a recent study it was determined that exchange rate determinism (the appreciation and depreciation of the dollar with respect to whether global sourcing is pursued) and fluctuations have _____ impact on the nature of sourcing strategy for crucial components.

a. a huge
b. a moderate
c. little
d. absolutely no
e. positive

Answer: (c) Difficulty: (3) Knowledge: (A) Page: 275

17. All of the following are reasons that foreign sourcing is not influenced by exchange rate determinism <u>EXCEPT</u>:

    a. it takes time to establish relationships and networks and these with not be broken because of short-term exchange rate fluctuations.
    b. many governments will not allow cancellation of sourcing relationships.
    c. domestic suppliers change prices themselves.
    d. relationships are developed with all forms of suppliers (even if they are not subsidiaries.
    e. some companies can shift locations between countries because of their own flexibility.

Answer: (b) Difficulty: (3) Knowledge: (F) Page: 275

18. Strategic non-cost factors that might be considered in sourcing are quality, flexibility, technology, global rationalization, and:

    a. leadership.
    b. attitude.
    c. dependability.
    d. service.
    e. promotion adaptation.

Answer: (c) Difficulty: (2) Knowledge: (F) Page: 278, Exhibit 10-2

19. Because of the expansion in the number of producers in the world environment there has been a shift from price and quantity to _____ as a determinant of competitive strength.

    a. quantity and service
    b. timing and technology
    c. technology and information
    d. quality and information
    e. quality and reliability

Answer: (e) Difficulty: (2) Knowledge: (F) Page: 279

560

20. According to a recent survey, all of the following are important reasons for increased sourcing from abroad <u>EXCEPT</u>:

    a. better product and component quality.
    b. government tax breaks.
    c. lower price.
    d. unavailability of the item in the United States.
    e. more advanced technology abroad.

Answer: (b) Difficulty: (2) Knowledge: (F) Page: 279

21. Advances in structural elements of international trade have made it easier for companies to employ sourcing for strategic purposes. The most important influences on sourcing strategy are the increased number of purchasing managers experienced in sourcing, improvements made in transportation and communication, and:
    a. new financing options.
    b. relaxing of tariff barriers.
    c. relaxing of nontariff barriers.
    d. relaxation of labor laws.
    e. guaranteed service by producers.

Answer: (a) Difficulty: (2) Knowledge: (F) Page: 279

22. Advances in structural elements of international trade have made it easier for companies to employ sourcing for strategic purposes. All of the following are the most important influences on sourcing strategy <u>EXCEPT</u>:
    a. the increased number of purchasing managers experienced in sourcing.
    b. improvements made in transportation and communication.
    c. new financing options.
    d. relaxing of tariff barriers.
    e. Maquiladora plants on the Mexican side of the border with the United States.

Answer: (d) Difficulty: (2) Knowledge: (F) Page: 279

23. A Maquiladora plant is one where:

    a. child labor is exploited.
    b. cheap and shoddy goods are made.
    c. free-trade zone manufacturing takes place in Mexico.
    d. Mexican goods can be shipped to Mexican provinces without taxes being levied.
    e. U.S. workers can work without paying U.S. taxes or Social Security.

Answer: (c) Difficulty: (2) Knowledge: (A) Page: 279

24. A _____ plant is the Mexican version of free-trade-zone manufacturing facilities (mostly located close to the U.S. border) that provides a unique form of sourcing options to manufacturers operating in the United States.

 a. free trade
 b. Maquiladora
 c. chaebol
 d. blanco
 e. spinoza

Answer: (b) Difficulty: (2) Knowledge: (F) Page: 279

25. JIT production requires close working relationships with component suppliers, and places an enourmous amount of responsibility on:

 a. CEOs.
 b. line managers.
 c. inventory managers.
 d. service specialists.
 e. purchasing managers.

Answer: (e) Difficulty: (2) Knowledge: (F) Page: 280

26. Sourcing directly from foreign suppliers requires greater purchasing know-how and is _____ than other alternatives that use middlemen.

 a. more secure
 b. riskier
 c. slower
 d. more steady
 e. requires less service

Answer: (b) Difficulty: (1) Knowledge: (F) Page: 280

27. The key to achieving effective global sourcing is:

 a. being at the right place at the right time.
 b. being able to speak the language of your supplier.
 c. in not having unrealistic profit expectations.
 d. securing management involvement at the top (strategic) and middle (tactical) levels.
 e. in having a guaranteed return policy.

Answer: (d) Difficulty: (1) Knowledge: (F) Page: 280

28. In the late 1980s, statistical trends clearly show that U.S. companies have increased sourcing from abroad, despite:

    a. the hostilities in many third world countries.
    b. the appreciation of the U.S. dollar.
    c. the depreciation of the U.S. dollar.
    d. decreasing productivity in domestic plants.
    e. decreasing productivity in foreign plants.

Answer: (c) Difficulty: (3) Knowledge: (A) Page: 280

29. The design of global sourcing strategy is based on the interplay between a company's:

    a. supply and demand curves.
    b. competitive advantages and the comparative advantages of various countries.
    c. inventory and purchasing activities.
    d. control of domestic and foreign markets.
    e. control of domestic and foreign plants.

Answer: (b) Difficulty: (3) Knowledge: (A) Page: 281

30. _____ influences the decision regarding what activities and technologies a company should concentrate its investment and managerial resources in (in relation to its competitors in the industry).
    a. Relative advantage
    b. Absolute cost advantage
    c. Comparative advantage
    d. Competitive advantage
    e. Sourcing advantage

Answer: (d) Difficulty: (2) Knowledge: (F) Page: 281

31. _____ affects the company's decision on where to source and market, based on lower cost of labor and other resources in one country relative to another.

    a. Relative advantage
    b. Absolute cost advantage
    c. Comparative advantage
    d. Competitive advantage
    e. Sourcing advantage

Answer: (c) Difficulty: (2) Knowledge: (F) Page: 281

32. _____ offers a general framework for understanding what it takes to manage the interrelated value-adding activities of a company on a global basis.

   a. Relative advantage
   b. Absolute cost advantage
   c. Comparative advantage
   d. Competitive advantage
   e. The value chain concept

Answer: (e) Difficulty: (2) Knowledge: (F) Page: 281

33. The value chain can be divided into two major activities. They are best described as being:

   a. primary and secondary activities.
   b. operational and support activities.
   c. primary and support activities.
   d. customer and non-customer issues.
   e. domestic and foreign activities.

Answer: (c) Difficulty: (2) Knowledge: (F) Page: 282

34. Within the value chain concept, _____ activities are best described as being inbound logistics, manufacturing operations, outbound logistics, and after-sale service.

   a. primary
   b. secondary
   c. support
   d. ancillary
   e. programmed

Answer: (a) Difficulty: (1) Knowledge: (F) Page: 282

35. Within the value chain concept, _____ activities are best described as primarily being human resource management and technology development.

   a. primary
   b. secondary
   c. support
   d. ancillary
   e. programmed

Answer: (c) Difficulty: (1) Knowledge: (F) Page: 282

36. The _____ that a company creates is measured ultimately by the price buyers are willing to pay for its products.

   a. products
   b. value
   c. image
   d. focus
   e. concepts

Answer: (b) Difficulty: (1) Knowledge: (F) Page: 282

37. _____ is a useful concept that provides an assessment of the activities that a company performs to design, manufacture, market, deliver, and support its products in the marketplace.
   a. Relative advantage
   b. Absolute cost advantage
   c. Comparative advantage
   d. Competitive advantage
   e. The value chain concept

Answer: (e) Difficulty: (2) Knowledge: (F) Page: 282

38. All of the following are continuous and interactive steps involved in developing a global sourcing strategy along the value chain EXCEPT:

   a. identify the separable links in the company's value chain.
   b. identify the weak links in the company's value chain.
   c. determine the location of the company's competitive advantages.
   d. ascertain the level of transaction costs.
   e. determine the comparative advantages of countries relative to each link in the value chain and the transaction costs.

Answer: (b) Difficulty: (3) Knowledge: (F) Page: 282, 283

39. Most researchers agree that the three most important interrelated activities in the value chain are:
   a. R&D, inventory control, and service.
   b. R&D, manufacturing, and marketing.
   c. manufacturing, purchasing, and management of information.
   d. manufacturing, purchasing, and marketing.
   e. management, finance, and marketing.

40. Global sourcing strategy encompasses management of _____
    and logistics of identifying which production units will serve which particular
    markets and how components will be supplied for production.

    a. information
    b. services
    c. linkages between supply and demand
    d. linkages between purchasing and inventory control
    e. interfaces among R&D, manufacturing, and marketing on a global basis

41. Technology is broadly defined as _____.
    a. new products.
    b. creative ideas.
    c. entrepreneurs.
    d. know-how.
    e. creative thoughts and solutions.

42. Technology can be classified on the nature of know-how composed. Two groups
    emerge. Know-how composed of product technology and _____.

    a. service technology.
    b. process technology.
    c. marketing.
    d. management.
    e. operations research.

43. Technology can be classified on the nature of know-how composed. One of the
    groups that might fall under this classification is _____ which is the
    set of ideas involved in the manufacture of the product or the steps to combine new
    materials to produce a finished product.

    a. service technology
    b. product technology
    c. process technology
    d. marketing technology
    e. operations research technology

Answer: (c) Difficulty: (2) Knowledge: (F) Page: 283

44. Technology can be classified on the nature of know-how composed. One of the groups that might fall under this classification is _____ where the set of ideas embodied in the product are considered.

    a. service technology
    b. product technology
    c. process technology
    d. marketing technology
    e. operations research technology

Answer: (b) Difficulty: (2) Knowledge: (F) Page: 283

45. It is widely known that good linkage between R&D, manufacturing, and marketing is increasingly necessary to compete in the international marketplace. All of the following are benefits of linkage EXCEPT:

    a. a powerful linkage develops the requisite personal/business relationships between the primary linkage groups.
    b. a powerful linkage is necessary to ensure that issues are on top of the table at beginning of a project.
    c. a powerful linkage allows for speed.
    d. a powerful linkage usually doubles profit.
    e. a powerful linkage develops a high sense of urgency.

Answer: (d) Difficulty: (3) Knowledge: (A) Page: 284

46. Ignoring manufacturing as a strategic weapon, many U.S. companies have historically emphasized _____.

    a. cost efficiencies.
    b. quality imperatives.
    c. product promotion.
    d. public relations and image enhancement.
    e. product innovations.

Answer: (e) Difficulty: (2) Knowledge: (F) Page: 285

47. Because of intense international competition, most firms now recognize that manufacturing and product innovations are _____ and must work together as a unit.

   a. cost inefficient
   b. labor intensive
   c. creatively incompatible
   d. intertwined
   e. separate and sometimes unequal

Answer: (d) Difficulty: (1) Knowledge: (F) Page: 285

48. Low levels of retooling requirements and _____ of components are necessary conditions for efficient sourcing strategy on a global scale.
   a. cost efficiencies
   b. interchangability
   c. coordination
   d. substitution
   e. elimination

Answer: (b) Difficulty: (1) Knowledge: (F) Page: 285

49. There is a continual conflict between manufacturing and marketing divisions. This conflict can be summarized by stating that manufacturing wants products _____ and marketing wants products _____.

   a. standardized/customized.
   b. of high quality/cheap.
   c. engineered well/fashion attractive.
   d. engineered well/quickly.
   e. standardized/cheap.

Answer: (a) Difficulty: (2) Knowledge: (F) Page: 285, 286

50. It now seems that global _____ is necessary to link manufacturing and product innovations for long-term competitive position.

   a. quality control
   b. cost containment
   c. product policy
   d. promotion policy
   e. cultural sensitivity

Answer: (c) Difficulty: (2) Knowledge: (F) Page: 286

51. Which of the following are one of the four ways of developing a global product policy to streamline manufacturing (thus lowering manufacturing cost without sacrificing marketing flexibility)?

   a. dynamic service packages.
   b. multiple source options.
   c. universal electrification of components.
   d. core component standardization.
   e. universal prices.

Answer: (d) Difficulty: (3) Knowledge: (F) Page: 286

52. If Toyota Motor Company makes a universal bumper that fits all of the models of their cars, this would be an example of which of the following global product policies?

   a. Universal promotion strategy.
   b. Universal pricing strategy.
   c. Universal product with all features.
   d. Universal product with different positioning.
   e. Core components standardization.

Answer: (e) Difficulty: (2) Knowledge: (A) Page: 286

53. All of the following are examples of global product policies EXCEPT:
   a. core component standardization.
   b. core component miniaturization.
   c. product design families.
   d. universal product with all features.
   e. universal product with different positioning.

Answer: (b) Difficulty: (2) Knowledge: (F) Page: 286

54. Seiko, a Japanese watchmaker, offers a wide range of designs and models, but they are based on only a handful of different operating mechanisms. This would be an example of which of the global product policies listed below?

   a. core component standardization.
   b. core component miniaturization.
   c. product design families.
   d. universal product with all features.
   e. universal product with different positioning.

Answer: (a) Difficulty: (2) Knowledge: (A) Page: 286

55. Electrolux, a Swedish appliance manufacturer, has adopted which of the following product policies when offer different products under four different brand names, but use the same basic designs?

a. core component standardization.
b. core component miniaturization.
c. product design families.
d. universal product with all features.
e. universal product with different positioning.

Answer: (c) Difficulty: (1) Knowledge: (A) Page: 286

56. A key to pursuing a product policy of product design families (or product design standardization) lies in:

a. good engineering.
b. quality control.
c. good die-casts.
d. standardization of components.
e. standardization of labor.

Answer: (d) Difficulty: (1) Knowledge: (F) Page: 286

57. When Canon designed its AE-1 camera and newer models, it built in a common set of features that were demanded by global customers. This would be an example of which of the following product policies?
a. core components standardization.
b. core components miniaturization.
c. product design families.
d. universal product with all features.
e. universal product with different positioning.

Answer: (d) Difficulty: (3) Knowledge: (A) Page: 286, 287

58. When a universal product is developed with different market segments in mind, it is an example of which of the following product policies?

a. core components standardization.
b. core components miniaturization.
c. product design families.
d. universal product with all features.
e. universal product with different positioning.

59. In recent years Honda has begun to market the Honda Accord around the world by positioning them differently from country to country. The car, however, is almost identical no matter which market it is sold in. This would be an example of which of the following product policy options?

   a. core components standardization.
   b. core components miniaturization.
   c. product design families.
   d. universal product with all features.
   e. universal product with different positioning.

Answer: (e) Difficulty: (2) Knowledge: (A) Page: 287

60. One of the real sources of Japanese inspiration and competitiveness is that they excel in the management of the _____ interface.
   a. production/quality
   b. marketing/R&D
   c. purchasing/marketing
   d. purchasing/outsourcing
   e. budget/manufacturing

Answer: (b) Difficulty: (3) Knowledge: (F) Page: 287

61. Research has shown that the marketplace has become a virtual _____ for Japanese companies to gain production and marketing experience, as well as to perfect technology.
   a. human laboratory
   b. marketing laboratory
   c. psychological laboratory
   d. R&D laboratory
   e. promotions laboratory

Answer: (d) Difficulty: (2) Knowledge: (A) Page: 288

62. When Japanese firms use "fuzzy" logic applications in electronics or computer products, this is an example of a strategy of:

   a. total new product innovation.
   b. taking old products and reworking them.
   c. taking an idea, improving it, and applying it to other purposes and applications.
   d. improving on cost structures.
   e. outsourcing.

Answer: (c) Difficulty: (3) Knowledge: (A) Page: 288

63. Sourcing strategy includes two basic choices. One of these is intra-firm sourcing and the other is _____.

a. exporting.
b. outsourcing.
c. vertical integration.
d. matrix manipulation.
e. horizontal integration.

Answer: (b) Difficulty: (1) Knowledge: (F) Page: 289

64. As a type of intra-firm sourcing, _____ is where a company procures major components in-house by producing them domestically.

a. domestic in-house sourcing
b. offshore subsidiary sourcing
c. domestic purchasing arrangement
d. offshore outsourcing (offshore sourcing)
e. export management company

Answer: (a) Difficulty: (2) Knowledge: (F) Page: 289

65. As a type of intra-firm sourcing, _____ is where a company procures major components from its foreign subsidiary.

a. domestic in-house sourcing
b. offshore subsidiary sourcing
c. domestic purchasing arrangement
d. offshore outsourcing (offshore sourcing)
e. export management company

Answer: (b) Difficulty: (1) Knowledge: (F) Page: 289

66. As a type of outsourcing, _____ is where a company buys major components from independent suppliers at home.

a. domestic in-house sourcing
b. offshore subsidiary sourcing
c. a domestic purchasing arrangement
d. offshore outsourcing (offshore sourcing)
e. export management company

Answer: (c) Difficulty: (2) Knowledge: (F) Page: 289

67. As a type of outsourcing, _____ is where a company buys major components from independent suppliers overseas.

   a. domestic in-house sourcing
   b. offshore subsidiary sourcing
   c. a domestic purchasing arrangement
   d. offshore outsourcing (offshore sourcing)
   e. export management company

Answer: (d) Difficulty: (1) Knowledge: (F) Page: 289

68. Companies that outsource to the extent that they adopt a "designer role" in global competition (they offer innovations in product design without investing in manufacturing process technology) have been described by some as being:

   a. vertical corporations.
   b. horizontal corporations.
   c. hollow corporations.
   d. supply and demand corporations.
   e. monopoly manufacturers.

Answer: (c) Difficulty: (3) Knowledge: (F) Page: 291

69. General Electric spent $1.4 billion in 1995 to import products sold in the U.S. under the GE label. This list included consumer electronics, color TVs, and microwave ovens. Critics of this excessive outsourcing have labeled such companies as being:

   a. vertical corporations.
   b. horizontal corporations.
   c. hollow corporations.
   d. supply and demand corporations.
   e. monopoly manufacturers.

Answer: (c) Difficulty: (3) Knowledge: (A) Page: 295

70. One way to coordinate outsourcing activities and manage the results effectively is to form:

a. vertical corporations.
b. horizontal corporations.
c. hollow corporations.
d. supply and demand corporations.
e. strategic alliances.

Answer: (e) Difficulty: (3) Knowledge: (F) Page: 294

71. The advantage of forming a strategic alliance is claimed to be its:

a. capital accumulation.
b. profit potential.
c. structural flexibility.
d. ability to move quickly.
e. superior R&D.

Answer: (c) Difficulty: (3) Knowledge: (F) Page: 296

72. The advantage of forming a strategic alliance is claimed to be its:

a. capital accumulation.
b. profit potential.
c. ability to concentrate on performing the task at which it is most efficient.
d. ability to move quickly.
e. superior R&D.

Answer: (c) Difficulty: (3) Knowledge: (F) Page: 296

73. Companies that rely on independent external sources of supply of major components tend to forsake part of the most important value-creating activities (such as quality assurance). The term that describes this phenomenon is called _____.

a. profit portfolios.
b. dependence.
c. strategic alliance.
d. joint venture.
e. independence.

Answer: (b) Difficulty: (1) Knowledge: (F) Page: 296

74. The decline of IBM in the personal computer market in recent years offers the most vivid example of the problems caused by _____.

    a. profit portfolios.
    b. dependence.
    c. strategic alliances.
    d. joint ventures.
    e. independence.

Answer: (b) Difficulty: (2) Knowledge: (A) Page: 297

75. Multinational companies that depend heavily on independent suppliers can gradually loose:

    a. design and manufacturing abilities.
    b. their dependent status.
    c. profit portfolios.
    d. labor efficiencies.
    e. union support.

Answer: (a) Difficulty: (2) Knowledge: (F) Page: 297

True/False   Short Answer

1. A frequently used framework to describe cross-national business practices is the international product portfolio cycle.

Answer: (False) Difficulty: (1) Knowledge: (F) Page: 271

2. One of the limitations of the international product life cycle is that there is a trend toward a slower pace of new product introduction and an increase in the innovational lead time.

Answer: (False) Difficulty: (3) Knowledge: (F) Page: 272

3. Sourcing allows the shrewd company to outmaneuver competition that might be following what they perceive to be predictable product life cycles.

Answer: (True) Difficulty: (2) Knowledge: (A) Page: 272

4. Sony is often cited as an example of a global strategist that has learned how to use sourcing to accelerate a product life cycle to their advantage.

Answer: (True) Difficulty: (1) Knowledge: (A) Page: 272

5. Today, quick technology diffusion is virtually assured.

Answer: (True) Difficulty: (1) Knowledge: (F) Page: 272

6. _____ is the logistical management of the interfaces of R&D, manufacturing, and marketing activities on a global basis.

Answer: (Global sourcing strategy) Difficulty: (2) Knowledge: (F) Page: 272

7. If the dollar depreciates, U.S. companies find it easy to procure components and products from abroad.

Answer: (False) Difficulty: (2) Knowledge: (F) Page: 275

8. _____ advantage influences the decisions regarding what activities and technologies a company should concentrate its investment and managerial resources in, relative to competitors in the industry.

Answer: (Competitive) Difficulty: (2) Knowledge: (F) Page: 281

9. _____ advantage affects the company's decision on where to source and market, based on the lower cost of labor and other resources in one country relative to another.

Answer: (Comparative) Difficulty: (2) Knowledge: (F) Page: 281

10. The _____ concept offers a general framework for understanding what it takes to manage the interrelated value-adding activities of a company on a global basis.

Answer: (value-chain) Difficulty: (2) Knowledge: (F) Page: 281

11. Global product policy is a generally accepted way to streamline manufacturing (thus lowering manufacturing cost) without sacrificing marketing flexibility.

Answer: (True) Difficulty: (1) Knowledge: (F) Page: 286

12. One of the key global product policy alternatives for a manufacturer to consider as a way of streamlining manufacturing processes is to pursue product customization.

Answer: (False) Difficulty: (3) Knowledge: (A) Page: 286

13. Honda Motor Co. is an example of a company that uses universal product with differing positioning when they market an almost identical Honda Accord around the world by positioning them differently from country to country.

Answer: (True) Difficulty: (1) Knowledge: (A) Page: 287

14. Two forms of outsourcing can be described as being domestic in-house sourcing and offshore subsidiary sourcing.

Answer: (False) Difficulty: (3) Knowledge: (F) Page: 289

15. A _____ corporation is one where the company no longer makes anything. Instead, it adopts a designer role and does not invest in the manufacturing process.

Answer: (hollow) Difficulty: (2) Knowledge: (F) Page: 291

Essay

1. Over the last twenty years or so, gradual yet significant changes have taken place in global sourcing strategy. Discuss the major trends that have and will affect global sourcing strategy. Be sure to list each trend separately.

Answer:

Trend 1: The Decline of Exchange Rate Determination of Sourcing.
    a. Since the 1970s exchange rates have fluctuated rather erratically over time.
    b. Companies consider the exchange rate when determining the extent to which they can engage in foreign sourcing.
    c. The exchange rate determinism of sourcing is strictly based on price factor alone.
        1). Foreign sourcing can also occur for non-cost reasons.
        2). Foreign suppliers can easily be dropped if exchange rates begin to increase.
        3). Domestic price increases have to be watched.
        4). Long-term relationships become important.
        5). Some companies are able to shift supply locations from one country to another to overcome the adverse effects of exchange rate fluctuations.

Trend 2: New Competitive Environment Caused by Excess Worldwide Capacity.
  a. The worldwide growth in the number of manufacturers has added excess production capacity in most industries.
  b. There has been a downward pressure on prices of many components and products around the world.
  c. There has been a strategic shift from price and quantity to quality and reliability of products as a determinant of competitive strength.

Trend 3: Innovations in and Restructuring of International Trade Infrastructure.
  a. The innovations and structural changes that have important influences on sourcing strategy are:
    1). The increased number of purchasing managers experienced in sourcing.
    2). Improvements made in transportation and communication.
    3). New financing options, including countertrade.
    4). Manufacturing facilities diffused throughout the world by globally minded companies.
    5). Maquiladora plants in Mexico.

Trend 4: Enhanced Role of Purchasing Managers.
  a. JIT (just-in-time) production has been increasing.
  b. JIT requires a close working relationship with suppliers.
  c. More purchasing know-how is necessary to deal with foreign suppliers.
  d. The key to achieving effective global sourcing is securing management involvement at both the top (strategic) and middle (tactical) levels.

Trend 5: Trend toward Global Manufacturing.
  a. As a global company adds another international plant to its network of existing plants, it creates the need for sourcing of components and other semi-processed goods to and from the new plant to existing plants.

Firms that do not observe these trends will become uncompetitive and be forced into less than advantageous positions in the world marketplace.

Difficulty: (3) Knowledge: (F) Page: 275-280

2. Describe the "hollow" corporation. What effect does this have on a firm's rush to join the outsourcing stampede on the 1990s?

Answer:

Students should review Global Perspective 10-4 "Hollow Corporation" to answer this question. The intent of the question is to get students to understand that if too much sourcing takes place the corporation does not really make anything anymore. If this happens, the corporation becomes very vulnerable to dependency on foreign suppliers and sourcers. Ownership is weak, R&D becomes almost non-existent, and the firm becomes a prime candidate to fail.

Difficulty: (1) Knowledge: (A) Page: 291, 295

3. Explain the value-chain concept and its component parts (to include competitive advantage and comparative advantage). How does the modern firm exploit the value-chain?

Answer:

The design of global sourcing strategy is based on the interplay between a company's competitive advantages and the comparative advantages of various countries. The value chain concept offers a general framework for understanding what it takes to manage the interrelated value-adding activities of a company on a global basis. The set of interrelated corporate activities is called the value chain. See Global Perspective 10-2 "Power of Good Linkage Management" for additional information.

The value chain can be divided into two major activities performed by a company: 1) primary activities consisting of inbound logistics, manufacturing operations, outbound logistics, and after-sale service, and 2) support activities consisting of human resource management, technology development, and other activities that help promote primary activities. Competing companies constantly strive to create value across various activities in the value chain.

Competitive advantage influences the decision regarding what activities and technologies a company should concentrate its investment and managerial resources in, relative to its competitors in the industry. Comparative advantage affects the company's decision on where to source and market, based on the lower cost of labor and other resources in one country relative to another.

Difficulty: (2) Knowledge: (F) Page: 281-285

4. Explain the difficulties that management faces in coordinating R&D, manufacturing, and marketing interfaces in the modern global environment.

Answer:

Product technology alone may not provide the company a long-term competitive edge over competition unless it is matched with sufficient manufacturing capabilities. Most United States companies have ignored manufacturing and only concentrated on product innovation as a strategic weapon. The firms should remember that innovation and manufacturing are intertwined.

The primary conflict between manufacturing and marketing is that manufacturing seeks standardization and marketing seeks adaptation (customization) to meet individual customers demands. To offset these problems, the firm can stress 1) core component standardization, 2) product design families, 3) universal product with all features, and 4) universal product with different positioning.

Since R&D is normally outside the marketing manager's control, some form of interface is necessary to make sure that customer concerns and desires are not only measured but acted upon. Consumers, after all, have the final say on whether they will buy or not. Product engineers do not determine customer tastes. There must be a willingness to coordinate and cooperate. Pushing products from the top down (the traditional way of doing things) takes to much time. A short product development cycle is critical to global success.

Difficulty: (3) Knowledge: (A) Page: 283-289

5. Describe the major forms or types of sourcing strategy.

Answer:

There are four major types of sourcing strategy as described in Exhibit 10-6. This exhibit describes how to source, where to source, and the type of sourcing. The major forms are sourcing are:

Forms of intra-firm sourcing:

a. Domestic In-house Sourcing--a company procures major components in-house by producing them domestically.

b. Offshore Subsidiary Sourcing--a company procures major components from its foreign subsidiary.

Forms of Outsourcing:

a. Domestic Purchasing Arrangement--a company buys major components from independent suppliers at home.

b. Offshore Outsourcing (Offshore Sourcing)--a company buys major components from independent suppliers overseas.

Difficulty: (2) Knowledge: (F) Page: 289

Chapter 11

Multiple Choice

1. Ikea, the Swedish furniture chain, insists that all its stores carry the basic product line with little room for adaptation to local tastes. If research of the U.S. market showed that Americans preferred larger beds than their Swedish counterparts, which of the following strategies would be advisable for Ikea?

    a. standardization.
    b. new product development.
    c. adaptation.
    d. withdraw from market.
    e. lower prices to encourage attitude change.

Answer: (c) Difficulty: (1) Knowledge: (A) Page: 301

2. When Wal-Mart went to Hong Kong, it stocked basketball court backboards (just as they did in the United States). Since most people live in tiny apartments in land-locked Hong Kong, sales were very poor. Indicate the strategy that Wal-Mart followed once research revealed the problem.

    a. standardization.
    b. new product development.
    c. adaptation.
    d. withdraw from market.
    e. lower prices to encourage attitude change.

Answer: (d) Difficulty: (3) Knowledge: (A) Page: 302

3. Even though other combination alternatives can be devised, companies generally can pursue three global product strategies to penetrate foreign markets. These strategies are to extend the home-grown product/communication strategies, adapt their strategy to the local marketplace, and:

    a. invent new products for foreign customers.
    b. concentrate on services.
    c. apply for permission to copy domestic products.
    d. concentrate on image adjustment.
    e. focus on secondary issues (such as warranties).

Answer: (a) Difficulty: (2) Knowledge: (F) Page: 302, 303

4. Even though other combination alternatives can be devised, companies generally can pursue three global product strategies to penetrate foreign markets. These strategies are to extend the home-grown product/communication strategies, invent new products for foreign customers, and:

a. adapt their strategy to the local marketplace.
b. concentrate on services.
c. apply for permission to copy domestic products.
d. concentrate on image adjustment.
e. focus on secondary issues (such as warranties).

Answer: (a) Difficulty: (2) Knowledge: (F) Page: 302, 303

5. Which of the following is NOT one of the strategic options available to the marketing planner, considering various product policies that could be devised for the international marketplace?

a. product and communication extension--dual extension.
b. communication extension--mono extension.
c. product extension--communications adaptation.
d. product adaptation--communications extension.
e. product and communications adaptation--dual adaptation.

Answer: (b) Difficulty: (3) Knowledge: (F) Page: 304

6. If a company were to follow a strategy of product and communication extension (dual extension) in a foreign market, an example of a product category that would fit this strategy would be _____.

a. soft drinks.
b. motorscooters.
c. gasoline.
d. clothing.
e. hand-powered washing machines.

Answer: (a) Difficulty: (2) Knowledge: (A) Page: 304, Exhibit 11-1

7. If a company were to follow a strategy of product adaptation-communications extension in a foreign market, an example of a product category that would fit this strategy would be _____.

   a. soft drinks.
   b. motorscooters.
   c. gasoline.
   d. clothing.
   e. hand-powered washing machines.

Answer: (c) Difficulty: (3) Knowledge: (A) Page: 304, Exhibit 11-1

8. If a company were to follow a strategy of product extension-communications adaptation in a foreign market, an example of a product category that would fit this strategy would be _____.

   a. soft drinks.
   b. motorscooters.
   c. gasoline.
   d. clothing.
   e. hand-powered washing machines.

Answer: (b) Difficulty: (3) Knowledge: (A) Page: 304, Exhibit 11-1

9. If a company were to follow a strategy of product and communications adaptation (dual adaptation) in a foreign market, an example of a product category that would fit this strategy would be _____.

   a. soft drinks.
   b. motorscooters.
   c. gasoline.
   d. clothing.
   e. hand-powered washing machines.

Answer: (d) Difficulty: (3) Knowledge: (A) Page: 304, Exhibit 11-1

10. If a company is an early entrant in the global arena and does wish to spend much in the way of resources, they will probably chose _____ as a method of entry.
   a. product and communication extension--dual extension
   b. product invention
   c. product extension--communications adaptation
   d. product adaptation--communications extension
   e. product and communications adaptation--dual adaptation

Answer: (a) Difficulty: (1) Knowledge: (F) Page: 304, Exhibit 11-1

11. As a strategy, _____ will work when the company targets a "global" segment with similar needs.
   a. product and communication extension--dual extension
   b. product invention
   c. product extension--communications adaptation
   d. product adaptation--communications extension
   e. product and communications adaptation--dual adaptation

Answer: (a) Difficulty: (2) Knowledge: (F) Page: 304

12. The biggest advantage of a product and communication extension--dual extension policy is:

   a. it is easy for management to understand.
   b. it offers substantial savings because of economies of scale.
   c. it passes most legal tests.
   d. it is service oriented.
   e. it will usually not violate cultural taboos.

Answer: (b) Difficulty: (2) Knowledge: (F) Page: 304

13. Due to differences in the cultural or competitive environment, a company may choose the _____ strategy if it wishes to keep its product economies scale intact but customize its communications.

   a. product and communication extension--dual extension
   b. product invention
   c. product extension--communications adaptation
   d. product adaptation--communications extension
   e. product and communications adaptation--dual adaptation

Answer: (c) Difficulty: (1) Knowledge: (F) Page: 305

14. When Wrigley chewing gum company markets its basic products abroad, it keeps its well-known brands but customizes promotional approaches in individual countries. Which of the following strategies best describes the strategy that Wrigley is following?

    a. product and communication extension--dual extension
    b. product invention
    c. product extension--communications adaptation
    d. product adaptation--communications extension
    e. product and communications adaptation--dual adaptation

Answer: (c) Difficulty: (1) Knowledge: (A) Page: 305

15. Many companies add brands to their portfolio via acquisitions of local companies. When the local brand is retained but incorporated into the existing communications strategy, the strategy can be described as being one of:

    a. product and communication extension--dual extension
    b. product invention
    c. product extension--communications adaptation
    d. product adaptation--communications extension
    e. product and communications adaptation--dual adaptation

Answer: (d) Difficulty: (2) Knowledge: (F) Page: 305

16. Differences in both the cultural and physical environment across countries call for a _____ strategy.

    a. product and communication extension--dual extension
    b. product invention
    c. product extension--communications adaptation
    d. product adaptation--communications extension
    e. product and communications adaptation--dual adaptation

Answer: (e) Difficulty: (1) Knowledge: (F) Page: 306

17. Because of differences in preferences in flavors and government regulations regarding the marketing of diet products, Slim-Fast normally uses which of the following strategies?

    a. product and communication extension--dual extension
    b. product invention
    c. product extension--communications adaptation
    d. product adaptation--communications extension
    e. product and communications adaptation--dual adaptation

Answer: (e) Difficulty: (2) Knowledge: (A) Page: 306

18. Genuinely global marketers try to figure out how to create products with a global scope rather than just for a single country. The mindset is to zero in on global opportunities. The strategy that best describes this approach is called:
    a. product and communication extension--dual extension
    b. product invention
    c. product extension--communications adaptation
    d. product adaptation--communications extension
    e. product and communications adaptation--dual adaptation

Answer: (b) Difficulty: (2) Knowledge: (F) Page: 306

19. Black & Decker is a good example of a company that adopts the _____ approach to global expansion. The company aims to bring out new products that cater to common needs and opportunities around the world.
    a. product and communication extension--dual extension
    b. product invention
    c. product extension--communications adaptation
    d. product adaptation--communications extension
    e. product and communications adaptation--dual adaptation

Answer: (b) Difficulty: (1) Knowledge: (A) Page: 306

20. _____ means offering a uniform product on a regional or worldwide basis (only minor alterations are made to meet local standards).

    a. Customization
    b. Standardization
    c. Proliferation
    d. Expansion
    e. Synthesizing

Answer: (b) Difficulty: (1) Knowledge: (F) Page: 307

21. The primary advantage to using a standardization approach to marketing a product in the international arena is:

    a. minimization of costs (which can be passed on to customers).
    b. more profit.
    c. less service complaints.
    d. less product returns.
    e. standard budgets.

Answer: (a) Difficulty: (2) Knowledge: (F) Page: 307

22. _____ is leveraging cross-border differences in needs and wants of the firm's target customers.

    a. Customization
    b. Standardization
    c. Proliferation
    d. Expansion
    e. Synthesizing

Answer: (a) Difficulty: (1) Knowledge: (F) Page: 307

23. Standardization of product has a _____ orientation.

    a. market-driven
    b. service-driven
    c. budget-driven
    d. promotion-driven
    e. product-driven

Answer: (e) Difficulty: (2) Knowledge: (F) Page: 307

24. Customization of product has a _____ orientation.

    a. market-driven
    b. service-driven
    c. budget-driven
    d. promotion-driven
    e. product-driven

Answer: (a) Difficulty: (2) Knowledge: (F) Page: 307

25. One of the forces that favors a globalized product strategy is:

    a. lower budgets.
    b. increased attention on quality.
    c. desire to fit in with the crowd.
    d. common customer needs.
    e. increasing problems with logistics and purchasing.

Answer: (d) Difficulty: (2) Knowledge: (F) Page: 307

26. All of the following are factors that favor a globalized product strategy EXCEPT:

    a. common customer needs.
    b. global customers.
    c. scale economies.
    d. time-to-market.
    e. rising strength of the Asian markets.

Answer: (e) Difficulty: (3) Knowledge: (F) Page: 307-310

27. During the last decade, car buyers in the Triad markets (Japan, the United States, and Europe) have increasing begun to have the same outlook and preferences in cars. Which of the following factors that favor globalization of product, would most accurately be associated with this trend?

    a. common customer needs.
    b. global customers.
    c. scale economies.
    d. time-to-market.
    e. Europe 1992 and other Regional Market Agreements.

Answer: (a) Difficulty: (2) Knowledge: (A) Page: 307-310

28. With respect to scale economies (as a factor that favors globalization of product strategy), savings are often realized because of:

    a. promotion expenditures.
    b. warranty expansion.
    c. sourcing efficiencies or lowered R&D expenditures.
    d. labor costs.
    e. vision focus.

Answer: (c) Difficulty: (2) Knowledge: (F) Page: 309

29. One attempt to combine the strengths of standardization and customization of products is to deal with both issues as functions of product design. The _____ approach consists of developing a range of product parts that can be used worldwide. The parts can be assembled into numerous product configurations.

a. core-product
b. uniform commercial code
c. die-casting
d. modular
e. PRIZM

Answer: (d) Difficulty: (2) Knowledge: (F) Page: 311

30. With respect to product design strategies, the _____ approach is very popular in the automotive industry (where a broad range of parts can be used worldwide in a variety of configurations).

a. core-product
b. uniform commercial code
c. die-casting
d. modular
e. PRIZM

Answer: (d) Difficulty: (2) Knowledge: (A) Page: 311

31. One attempt to combine the strengths of standardization and customization of products is to deal with both issues as functions of product design. The _____ approach consists of developing a mostly uniform core-product then adding attachments that match local market needs.

a. core-product
b. uniform commercial code
c. die-casting
d. modular
e. PRIZM

Answer: (a) Difficulty: (1) Knowledge: (F) Page: 311

32. With respect to product design strategies, the _____ approach is very popular with the French carmaker Renault. They use common core-products but customize them in each market (such as making stronger heaters for the Nordic market).

   a. core-product
   b. uniform commercial code
   c. die-casting
   d. modular
   e. PRIZM

Answer: (a) Difficulty: (1) Knowledge: (A) Page: 311

33. One of the pitfalls that a global marketer can run into is _____. This would occur when too much standardization stifles initiative and experimentation at the local level.

   a. overcustomization.
   b. micro-managing.
   c. technocracy.
   d. group think.
   e. overstandardization.

Answer: (e) Difficulty: (2) Knowledge: (F) Page: 311

34. One of the pitfalls that a global marketer can run into is _____. This would occur when too much adaptation to the local market occurs and the brand becomes vulnerable to losing its unique foreigness.

   a. overcustomization.
   b. micro-managing.
   c. technocracy.
   d. group think.
   e. overstandardization.

Answer: (a) Difficulty: (2) Knowledge: (F) Page: 311

35. In general, the rate of adoption of new products (in foreign markets) is driven by individual differences, personal influences, and:

   a. fashion.
   b. trends.
   c. cash on hand.
   d. product characteristics.
   e. promotion characteristics.

Answer: (d) Difficulty: (2) Knowledge: (F) Page: 312

36. When consumers are eager to try new products and new ideas, they are called _____.

   a. early adopters.
   b. early majority.
   c. late majority.
   d. laggards.
   e. experimenters.

Answer: (a) Difficulty: (1) Knowledge: (F) Page: 312

37. Word-of-Mouth testimonials is often spread by _____.

   a. early adopters.
   b. early majority.
   c. late majority.
   d. laggards.
   e. prior adopters.

Answer: (e) Difficulty: (2) Knowledge: (F) Page: 312

38. Which of the following would NOT be one of the five key product characteristics that contribute to its acceptance?

   a. low service maintenance
   b. relative advantage
   c. compatibility
   d. complexity
   e. trialability

Answer: (a) Difficulty: (3) Knowledge: (F) Page: 313

39. To what extent does the new product offer more perceived value to potential adopters than exiting alternatives, would be a question that best fits with which of the following key product characteristics acceptance categories?

    a. observability
    b. relative advantage
    c. compatibility
    d. complexity
    e. trialability

Answer: (b) Difficulty: (1) Knowledge: (A) Page: 313

40. Is the product consistent with exiting values and attitudes of the individuals in the social system, would be a question that best fits with which of the following key product characteristics acceptance categories?
    a. observability
    b. relative advantage
    c. compatibility
    d. complexity
    e. trialability

Answer: (c) Difficulty: (2) Knowledge: (A) Page: 313

41. Is the product easy to understand or use, would be a question that best fits with which of the following key product characteristics acceptance categories?

    a. observability
    b. relative advantage
    c. compatibility
    d. complexity
    e. trialability

Answer: (d) Difficulty: (3) Knowledge: (A) Page: 313

42. The adoption rate for new product in countries with a _____ population is usually faster than in countries with a highly diverse culture.

    a. heterogeneous
    b. culturally deprived
    c. culturally poor
    d. homogeneous
    e. monogamous

Answer: (d) Difficulty: (2) Knowledge: (F) Page: 313

43. The adoption rate for a new product in countries with a homogeneous population is usually faster than in countries with a highly diverse culture. Which of the following countries would probably have the fastest adoption based on the information provided above?

   a. Russia
   b. United States
   c. Japan
   d. United Kingdom
   e. Spain

Answer: (c) Difficulty: (3) Knowledge: (A) Page: 313

44. With respect to adoption rates in the international marketplace, it appears to be generally true that adoption rates are higher in _____ countries than in _____ countries.

   a. lead/lag
   b. lag/lead
   c. lead/middle adopters
   d. lag/middle adopters
   e. lead/opinion-lead

Answer: (b) Difficulty: (3) Knowledge: (F) Page: 314

45. A _____ country is where a product is first introduced.
   a. lag
   b. middle adopter
   c. lead
   d. opinionated
   e. innovative

Answer: (c) Difficulty: (1) Knowledge: (F) Page: 314

46. A _____ country is where a product is entered after initial introduction has taken place.

   a. lag
   b. middle adopter
   c. lead
   d. opinionated
   e. innovative

Answer: (a) Difficulty: (1) Knowledge: (F) Page: 314

47. _____ are people who look beyond their immediate social surroundings and are not local in their opinions.

a. Domestics
b. Gadflies
c. Dappers
d. Cosmopolitans
e. Regionalists

Answer: (d) Difficulty: (2) Knowledge: (F) Page: 314

48. All of the following are factors that affect product penetration in the European market (according to a recent survey), EXCEPT:

a. cosmopolitanism.
b. number of locals in the market.
c. mobility.
d. percentage of children in the labor force.
e. percentage of women in the labor force.

Answer: (d) Difficulty: (2) Knowledge: (A) Page: 314

49. All of the following are steps in the new product development process EXCEPT:

a. identification of new product ideas.
b. budget development.
c. screening.
d. concept testing.
e. test marketing.

Answer: (b) Difficulty: (2) Knowledge: (F) Page: 315-324

50. Which of the following are among the best sources for finding new product ideas?

a. company, customers, competition, and collaborators.
b. trade magazines, television, and the internet.
c. government statistics, demographic charts, and psychological profiles.
d. reverse engineering, industrial spying, and out-of-date patents.
e. rumors, stories, and intuition.

Answer: (a) Difficulty: (3) Knowledge: (A) Page: 315

51. Once new product ideas have been identified, the next logical step is to have the ideas _____.

    a. modeled.
    b. budgeted.
    c. screened.
    d. concept tested.
    e. test marketed.

Answer: (c) Difficulty: (2) Knowledge: (F) Page: 317

52. One common statistical method for screening new products is to use:

    a. chi-square.
    b. correlation analysis.
    c. factor analysis.
    d. regression analysis.
    e. the median of attitudes.

Answer: (d) Difficulty: (2) Knowledge: (F) Page: 317

53. A(n) _____ is a fairly detailed description, verbally or sometimes visually, of the new product or service.

    a. attitude screen
    b. product model
    c. product concept
    d. market test
    e. focus concept

Answer: (c) Difficulty: (2) Knowledge: (F) Page: 319

54. One of the most common methods for concept testing new product ideas is to use:

    a. chi-square.
    b. correlation analysis.
    c. focus groups.
    d. regression analysis.
    e. the median of attitudes.

Answer: (c) Difficulty: (3) Knowledge: (F) Page: 319

55. A sophisticated method (sometimes called trade-off analysis) for measuring consumer preferences for product concepts is called:

a. chi-square.
b. correlation analysis.
c. focus groups.
d. regression analysis.
e. conjoint analysis.

Answer: (e) Difficulty: (3) Knowledge: (F) Page: 319

56. The starting premise of _____ is that people make trade-offs between the different product attributes when they evaluate alternatives (or brands) from which they pick a choice.

a. chi-square
b. correlation analysis
c. focus groups
d. regression analysis
e. conjoint analysis

Answer: (e) Difficulty: (3) Knowledge: (A) Page: 319

57. If a consumer considered four attributes to be important in the purchase of a TV, by using _____ the researcher might be able to determine the trade-offs between the different product attributes (such as purchase price or number of channels that could be received) when the consumer evaluated the alternatives for eventual purchase.

a. chi-square
b. correlation analysis
c. focus groups
d. regression analysis
e. conjoint analysis

Answer: (e) Difficulty: (3) Knowledge: (A) Page: 319

58. A(n) _____ is essentially a field experiment where the new product is marketed in a select set of cities to assess its sales potential and scores of other performance measures.

   a. attitude screen
   b. product model
   c. product concept
   d. test market
   e. focus concept

Answer: (d) Difficulty: (2) Knowledge: (F) Page: 323

59. Testing objectives, testing marketing mixes, making projections of sales volume, and analyzing potential competitive marketing mixes are all reasons to conduct:

   a. attitude screens.
   b. product models.
   c. product concepts.
   d. test markets.
   e. focus concepts.

Answer: (d) Difficulty: (2) Knowledge: (A) Page: 323

60. One alternative to the test market is the _____.
   a. thought panel.
   b. laboratory test market.
   c. internet exposure technique.
   d. preferred patron experiment.
   e. use of break-even analysis.

Answer: (b) Difficulty: (3) Knowledge: (F) Page: 324

61. If prospective customers are contacted and shown commercials for the new product and existing brands (then asked to state attitudes and preferences of what they have seen), then the marketing research entity will probably have conducted a(n) _____ instead of a full test market.

   a. thought panel
   b. laboratory test market
   c. internet exposure technique
   d. preferred patron experiment
   e. break-even analysis

Answer: (b) Difficulty: (2) Knowledge: (A) Page: 324

62. A common technique to avoid a global test market is to make global sales projections based on product performance in a _____ market.

a. lag
b. middle adopter
c. lead
d. opinionated
e. innovative

Answer: (c) Difficulty: (1) Knowledge: (F) Page: 324

63. When Miller beer used Canada to introduce Red Dog beer, then based on its success introduced it in the larger United States market, it was following a strategy of making sales projections based on product performance in a _____ market.

a. lag
b. middle adopter
c. lead
d. opinionated
e. innovative

Answer: (c) Difficulty: (1) Knowledge: (A) Page: 324

64. Timing is a very important element in any new product launch. One of the strategies is described as being the _____ where there is a phased rollout. In this approach the product uses a trickle down approach.

a. sprinkler method
b. shotgun method
c. rifle method
d. dribble method
e. waterfall method

Answer: (e) Difficulty: (1) Knowledge: (F) Page: 325

65. Timing is a very important element in any new product launch. One of the strategies is described as being the _____. This method often involves introducing the new product in the company's home market and then is moved to other advanced markets. Finally, less advanced markets are exposed to the product.

   a. sprinkler method
   b. shotgun method
   c. rifle method
   d. dribble method
   e. waterfall method

Answer: (e) Difficulty: (2) Knowledge: (F) Page: 325

66. The prime motive for the waterfall model (in introducing new products on a global scale) is that the customization of the product for the foreign market is:
   a. impractical.
   b. very expensive.
   c. time consuming.
   d. promotionally limited.
   e. not supported by top management.

Answer: (c) Difficulty: (3) Knowledge: (F) Page: 325

67. Timing is a very important element in any new product launch. One of the strategies is described as being the _____ where there is a simultaneous introduction and normally is accomplished in one to two years.

   a. sprinkler method
   b. shotgun method
   c. rifle method
   d. dribble method
   e. waterfall method

Answer: (a) Difficulty: (1) Knowledge: (F) Page: 325

68. Microsoft's introduction of Windows 95 worldwide in August of 1995 would be an example of which of the following new product entry strategies?
   a. sprinkler method
   b. shotgun method
   c. rifle method
   d. dribble method
   e. waterfall method

Answer: (a) Difficulty: (3) Knowledge: (A) Page: 325

69. The chief reason for a company choosing the sprinkler method of new product introduction is to off-set:

   a. rising costs.
   b. unstable labor.
   c. competitive pre-emption.
   d. government control.
   e. shoddy promotions.

Answer: (c) Difficulty: (2) Knowledge: (A) Page: 325

70. The waterfall strategy of sequential entry is preferable over the sprinkler model when all of the following conditions exist EXCEPT:

   a. the lifecycle of the product is relatively long.
   b. high costs of entry are present.
   c. very weak local competitors.
   d. fast growth is anticipated.
   e. no real competitors.

Answer: (d) Difficulty: (3) Knowledge: (F) Page: 326

71. The waterfall strategy of sequential entry is preferable over the sprinkler model when:

   a. the lifecycle of the product is relatively short.
   b. there are low costs of entry into the market.
   c. there are many competitors.
   d. very weak local competitors.
   e. fast growth is anticipated.

Answer: (d) Difficulty: (3) Knowledge: (F) Page: 326

72. The sprinkler strategy of one to two entry (globally) is preferable over the waterfall model when all of the following conditions exist EXCEPT:

   a. the lifecycle of the product is relatively short.
   b. there are low costs of entry into the market.
   c. there are many competitors.
   d. very weak local competitors.
   e. fast growth is anticipated.

Answer: (d) Difficulty: (3) Knowledge: (F) Page: 326

73. The sprinkler strategy of one to two entry (globally) is preferable over the waterfall model when:

   a. the lifecycle of the product is relatively long.
   b. high costs of entry are present.
   c. very weak local competitors.
   d. fast growth is anticipated.
   e. no real competitors.

Answer: (d) Difficulty: (3) Knowledge: (F) Page: 326

74. One of the differences in the way industrialized nations introduce new products is the Japanese method of incremenatilization. This means they introduce products:

   a. in a very slow, deliberate manner.
   b. in foreign markets before they introduce the products domestically.
   c. in generational phases (the second generation is ready when competition responds to the first generation).
   d. that are only at the bottom end of the price curve.
   e. are profit sensitive.

Answer: (c) Difficulty: (2) Knowledge: (A) Page: 327

75. One of the differences in the way industrialized nations introduce new products is the Japanese method of product churning. This means they introduce products:

   a. in a very slow, deliberate manner.
   b. in foreign markets before they introduce the products domestically.
   c. in a rush with little of no market research and then gauge the market's reaction.
   d. that are only at the bottom end of the price curve.
   e. are profit sensitive.

Answer: (c) Difficulty: (2) Knowledge: (A) Page: 327

True/False   Short Answer

1. Early market entrants often choose dual extension (product and communication extension) as a strategy to enter markets with new products.

Answer: (True) Difficulty: (1) Knowledge: (F) Page: 304

2. The biggest savings to the company when following a strategy of dual extension is in economies of scale.

Answer: (True) Difficulty: (2) Knowledge: (F) Page: 304

3. Because of their universally known products, Wrigley chewing gum company can use product adaptation-communications extension strategies effectively.

Answer: (False) Difficulty: (2) Knowledge: (A) Page: 304

4. Because of their universally known products, Wrigley chewing gum company should probably choose _____ as their product entry strategy.

Answer: (product extension-communications adaptation) Difficulty: (3)
        Knowledge: (A) Page: 305

5. If a recognized company wants to change its product to meet local conditions, but retain its international communications strategy, it should retain any local brands that have been obtained and bring them under the international communications strategy.

Answer: (True) Difficulty: (2) Knowledge: (F) Page: 305

6. Differences in both the cultural and physical environment across countries call for a _____ strategy.

Answer: (dual adaptation) Difficulty: (3) Knowledge: (F) Page: 306

7. _____ means offering a uniform product on a regional or worldwide basis.

Answer: (Standardization) Difficulty: (2) Knowledge: (F) Page: 307

8. The goal of standardization is to minimize competition.

Answer: (False) Difficulty: (2) Knowledge: (F) Page: 307

9. _____ leverages cross-border differences in needs and wants of the firm's target customers.

Answer: (Customization) Difficulty: (2) Knowledge: (F) Page: 307

10. The core-product approach consists of developing a range of product parts that can be used worldwide.

Answer: (False) Difficulty: (2) Knowledge: (F) Page: 311

11. Overstandardization is a risk of the core-product approach to introducing new products in the world market.

Answer: (True) Difficulty: (1) Knowledge: (F) Page: 311

12. In general, the adoption of new products is driven by individual differences, personal influences, and product characteristics.

Answer: (True) Difficulty: (1) Knowledge: (F) Page: 312

13. With respect to categories of consumers that adopt new products, the _____ category is eager to experiment with new ideas or products.

Answer: (early adopters) Difficulty: (2) Knowledge: (F) Page: 312

14. To what extent does the new product offer more perceived value to potential adopters than existing alternatives, would be a question that would be relevant to the observability characteristic of a new product's successful adoption.

Answer: (False) Difficulty: (2) Knowledge: (F) Page: 313

15. New product ideas can come from the company, customers, competition, and collaborators.

Answer: (True) Difficulty: (1) Knowledge: (F) Page: 315

Essay

1. List the strategic options available to the firm considering global expansion in the product area. Detail the conditions that make the strategic option favorable. Be sure to detail your answer.

Answer:

Strategic Option 1: Product & Communication Extension: Dual Extension.
    a. A company can choose to market a standardized product using a uniform communication strategy.
        1). Early entrants prefer this approach.
        2). Small companies with few resources prefer this form of extension.
    b. A standardized product policy coupled with a uniform communication strategy offers substantial savings coming from economies of scale.
        1). This strategy is usually product-driven rather than market-driven.
        2). This strategy can alienate foreign customers who prefer a customized product.

Strategic Option 2: Product Extension-Communications Adaptation.
    a. Due to differences in the cultural or competitive environment, the same product often is used to offer benefits or functions that dramatically differ from those in the home market.
        1). Customized advertising is the result.
        2). Positioning themes are often used in the ad campaigns.

Strategic Option 3: Product Adaptation-Communications Extension.
    a. Firms can adapt their product but market it using a standardized communications strategy.
        1). Local market circumstances and regulations often favor this alternative.
    b. Another reason for this strategy is the firm's expansion strategy.
        1). Brands are added as firm's buy local companies.
    c. Clever marketing ideas can be transferred from one country to another.

Strategic Option 4: Product & Communications Adaptation: Dual Adaptation.
    a. Differences in both the cultural and physical environment across countries call for a dual adaptation strategy.
    b. This becomes a viable option for global expansion.

Strategic Option 5: Product Invention.
    a. Genuinely global marketers try to figure out how to create products with a global scope rather than just for a single country.
    b. This strategy focuses on opportunities and inventions.

Difficulty: (3) Knowlege: (F) Page: 304-306

2. Comment on the forces that now favor a globalized product design strategy.

Answer:

Forces that favor a globalized product strategy are common customer needs, global customers, scale economies, time-to-market, Europe 1992 and other regional market agreements.

Difficulty: (1) Knowledge: (F) Page: 307-311

3. There are strategic options that allow the firm to modify their product while keeping most of the benefits of following a uniform product policy. Explain the differences between the modular and core-product approaches.

Answer:

Modular approach.
      1). Developing a range of products parts that can be used worldwide.
      2). These parts can be assembled into numerous configurations.
Core-product approach.
      1). The core-product approach starts with the design of a mostly uniform core-product and then adds attachments that might fit local needs.
      2). Savings comes from centralizing the production of the core.
      3). Easy product modification is a secret of success.

Difficulty: (2) Knowlege: (F) Page: 311-312

4. Test marketing is considered a critical step in new product development in most Western countries. Comment on test marketing. When do you run a test market and what might be the shortcomings of test marketing?

Answer:

Test marketing (primarily a Western country concept) is essentially a field experiment where the new product is marketed in a select set of cities to assess its sales potential and scores of other performance measures.

Reasons to run a test market include:
      1). It allows them to make fairly accurate projections of the market share, sales volume and penetration of the new product.
      2). The countries can contrast competing marketing mix strategies to decide which one is most promising in achieving the firm's objectives.

Shortcomings include:
   1). Time-consuming and costly.
   2). Results can be misleading.
   3). The strategic concern--it may alert your competitors.

Difficulty: (2) Knowledge: (F) Page: 323-324

5. In marketing timing is crucial. In new product development it might be even more crucial given the risk of the venture. Explain the waterfall and sprinkler approaches to introducing a new product to the market. When is the waterfall method preferred over the sprinkler method? Be sure to be specific as to your comments on these two strategic options.

Answer:

A key element of global product launch strategy is the entry timing decision: when should we launch the new product in the target markets?

Options include:
   1). The waterfall method where new products trickle down in a cascade-like manner.
      a). The typical pattern here is to introduce the product in the home country first.
      b). Next launch in advanced markets.
      c). Lastly, launch in less advanced markets.
      d). This method can be very time-consuming but is less risky.
   2). The sprinkler strategy is a simultaneous worldwide entry.
      a). Rollout occurs in one to two years.
      b). The growing prominence of universal segments and concerns about competitive pre-emption in the foreign markets are two major factors behind this expansion approach.

The waterfall strategy is preferable over the sprinkler model when:
   1). The lifecycle of the product is relatively long.
   2). Nonfavorable conditions govern the foreign market.
   3). Weak competitive climate in the foreign market exists.

Difficulty: (3) Knowledge: (F) Page: 325-326

Chapter 12

Multiple Choice

1. What product assortment should the company launch when it first enters a new market and how should the firm expand its multinational product line over time are typical questions to be asked by:

   a. the service manager.
   b. the promotion specialist.
   c. product-line manager.
   d. the quality control coordinator.
   e. the purchasing manager.

Answer: (c) Difficulty: (1) Knowledge: (A) Page: 331

2. A _____ is a name, term, sign, symbol, or combination of them which is intended to identify the goods and services of one seller or group of sellers and to differentiate them from those of competitors.

   a. trademark
   b. patent
   c. signature
   d. brand equity
   e. brand

Answer: (e) Difficulty: (1) Knowledge: (F) Page: 332

3. Linked to the brand name is a collection of assets and liabilities called _____.

   a. the trademark.
   b. the patent.
   c. signatures.
   d. proprietary investments.
   e. brand equity.

Answer: (e) Difficulty: (2) Knowledge: (F) Page: 332

4. Brand-name awareness, perceived quality, and other associations invoked by the brand name in the customer's mind are all illustrations of the concept called
_____.

    a. proprietary investments.
    b. brand equity.
    c. brand warranty.
    d. local brand name.
    e. brand mark.

Answer: (b) Difficulty: (3) Knowledge: (F) Page: 332

5. How do we strike a balance between a global brand that shuns cultural barriers and one that allows for local requirements is an illustration of a question that needs to be asked when building up and managing _____ in a multinational setting.

    a. proprietary investments.
    b. brand equity.
    c. brand warranty.
    d. local brand name.
    e. brand mark.

Answer: (b) Difficulty: (3) Knowledge: (A) Page: 332

6. All of the following are questions that must be asked when building up and managing brand equity in a multinational setting EXCEPT:

    a. How do we strike a balance between a global brand that shuns cultural barriers and one that allows for local requirements?
    b. What aspects of service are too expensive to be included in the brand warranty?
    c. What aspects of brand policy can be adapted to global use?
    d. Which brands are destined to become "global" mega-brands?
    e. How do you execute the changeover from a local to a global brand?

Answer: (b) Difficulty: (3) Knowledge: (F) Page: 332

7. Brand awareness is sometimes measured by _____.

    a. promotional recognition.
    b. share of market.
    c. profit potential.
    d. share of mind.
    e. cultural awareness.

Answer: (d) Difficulty: (2) Knowledge: (F) Page: 333

8. Truly global brands are at present _____.

    a. relatively common.
    b. relatively common from the United States.
    c. still a rare phenomenon.
    d. dramatically increasing in Europe.
    e. outlawed in Japan.

Answer: (c) Difficulty: (3) Knowledge: (A) Page: 333

9. The most obvious reason for having a global brand would be to take advantage of:

    a. power promotions.
    b. a large labor and selling force.
    c. economies of scale.
    d. coordinated logistics.
    e. corporate vision.

Answer: (c) Difficulty: (1) Knowledge: (F) Page: 333

10. An often forgotten reason for developing a global brand is the _____ factor of having a global brand.

    a. budget
    b. service
    c. profit
    d. prestige
    e. pyramid

Answer: (d) Difficulty: (1) Knowledge: (F) Page: 333

11. According to recent research, which of the following brands has the number one position in the United States with respect to share of mind (SOM)?

    a. Disney
    b. Coca-Cola
    c. Campbell's
    d. Pepsi
    e. IBM

Answer: (b) Difficulty: (2) Knowledge: (A) Page: 334, Exhibit 12-1

12. According to recent research, which of the following brands has the number one position in the United States with respect to esteem associated with the brand name?

    a. Disney
    b. Coca-Cola
    c. Campbell's
    d. Pepsi
    e. IBM

Answer: (c) Difficulty: (3) Knowledge: (A) Page: 334, Exhibit 12-1

13. According to recent research, which of the following brands has the number one position in Europe with respect to share of mind (SOM)?

    a. BMW
    b. Coca-Cola
    c. Campbell's
    d. Sony
    e. Mercedes-Benz

Answer: (b) Difficulty: (2) Knowledge: (A) Page: 334, Exhibit 12-1

14. According to recent research, which of the following brands has the number one position in Europe with respect to esteem associated with the brand name?

    a. BMW
    b. Coca-Cola
    c. Campbell's
    d. Sony
    e. Mercedes-Benz

Answer: (d) Difficulty: (3) Knowledge: (A) Page: 334, Exhibit 12-1

15. Brand equity for global brands varies greatly from country to country. All of the following factors contribute to the variation EXCEPT:

    a. competitive climate.
    b. marketing support.
    c. cultural receptivity to brands.
    d. literacy.
    e. product category penetration.

Answer: (d) Difficulty: (2) Knowledge: (F) Page: 335

16. From which of the following countries is brand loyalty the usually the highest? Base your conclusion on the amount of risk aversion brought about by group-orientation (either high or low).

  a. Germany.
  b. France.
  c. United States.
  d. Mexico.
  e. Japan.

Answer: (e) Difficulty: (2) Knowledge: (A) Page: 335

17. _____ often justify(ies) local branding instead of global branding.

  a. Domestic pressure
  b. Government pressure
  c. Cultural barriers
  d. Common sense
  e. Religious leaders

Answer: (c) Difficulty: (2) Knowledge: (A) Page: 336

18. One reason for keeping a local brand name after an acquisition rather than incorporating the brand into a global brand is:

  a. budget concerns.
  b. the brand equity that might have been built up by the local brand.
  c. the hostility toward global brands.
  d. to make dealers feel comfortable.
  e. to make government officials feel less threatened.

Answer: (b) Difficulty: (3) Knowledge: (F) Page: 336

19. All of the following are items that might be used as a checklist for analyzing globalization propositions <u>EXCEPT</u>:

    a. What is the cost of creating and maintaining awareness and associations for local brand versus a global one?
    b. Are there significant economies of scale in the creation and running of a communication program globally?
    c. Is there value to associations of a global brand or of a brand associated with the source country?
    d. Is global branding a requirement of forming strategic alliances?
    e. What local associations will be generated by the global name?

Answer: (d) Difficulty: (2) Knowledge: (A) Page: 339

20. With respect to a brand name changeover strategy, the _____ strategy ties the new global brand name to the existing local brand name. After a transition period, the old name is dropped.

    a. transparent forewarning
    b. summary axing
    c. fade-in/fade-out
    d. pyramid focusing
    e. parallel dimension

Answer: (c) Difficulty: (1) Knowledge: (F) Page: 340

21. Euro Disney eventually becoming Disneyland Paris (where the Euro shrunk until "land" could be added in its place) is an example of which of the following brand name changeover strategies?

    a. transparent forewarning
    b. summary axing
    c. fade-in/fade-out
    d. pyramid focusing
    e. parallel dimension

Answer: (c) Difficulty: (2) Knowledge: (A) Page: 340

22. With respect to a brand name changeover strategy, the _____ strategy alerts customers about the brand name change (via communications such as in-store displays).

    a. transparent forewarning
    b. summary axing
    c. fade-in/fade-out
    d. pyramid focusing
    e. parallel dimension

Answer: (a) Difficulty: (2) Knowledge: (F) Page: 340

23. When Mars candy company took over Raider candy products and used the theme line "Now Raider becomes Twix, for it is Twix everywhere in the world," the company used the _____ strategy for changing brand names.

    a. transparent forewarning
    b. summary axing
    c. fade-in/fade-out
    d. pyramid focusing
    e. parallel dimension

Answer: (a) Difficulty: (3) Knowledge: (A) Page: 340

24. With respect to a brand name changeover strategy, the _____ strategy where the company simply drops the old brand name and immediately replaces it with the global name.
    a. transparent forewarning
    b. summary axing
    c. fade-in/fade-out
    d. pyramid focusing
    e. parallel dimension

Answer: (b) Difficulty: (2) Knowledge: (F) Page: 340

25. If a retail firm sells a product under its own store name it is called a:

    a. domestic brand.
    b. national brand.
    c. manufacturers brand.
    d. store brand or private label.
    e. service label.

Answer: (d) Difficulty: (1) Knowledge: (F) Page: 341

26. When Heinz sells its soup products to grocery store chains and allows them to put their own store names on the product, the product is being sold as a:

   a. domestic brand.
   b. national brand.
   c. manufacturers brand.
   d. store brand or private label.
   e. service label.

Answer: (d) Difficulty: (1) Knowledge: (A) Page: 341

27. In which of the following countries are store brands the <u>LEAST</u> popular because of loyalty to national or manufacturer brands?

   a. United States.
   b. United Kingdom.
   c. Japan.
   d. France.
   e. Canada.

Answer: (c) Difficulty: (3) Knowledge: (A) Page: 341

28. Which of the following is one of the primary reasons that store brands (or private labels) have become more popular and successful in recent years?

   a. Better packaging decoration.
   b. Successful domestic economic recovery.
   c. Lack of concern with quality issues.
   d. Maintenance of private labels in only a few selected areas.
   e. Development of premium private-label brands.

Answer: (e) Difficulty: (3) Knowledge: (F) Page: 341, 342, 343

29. All of the following are factors that have explained the success of private labels in recent years <u>EXCEPT</u>:

   a. better packaging decoration.
   b. improved quality of private-label products.
   c. development of premium private-label brands.
   d. expansion into new product categories.
   e. internationalization of retail chains.

Answer: (a) Difficulty: (2) Knowledge: (F) Page: 341, 342, 343

30. _____ is probably the key success factor behind the spread of store brands.

    a. Better packaging decoration.
    b. Improved quality of private-label products.
    c. Development of premium private-label brands.
    d. Expansion into new product categories.
    e. Internationalization of retail chains.

Answer: (b) Difficulty: (2) Knowledge: (A) Page: 341, 342, 343

31. As a branding strategy, _____ is especially attractive to MNCs that face well-entrenched incumbent brands in the markets they plan to enter (this overcomes the problem of shelf-space denial).

    a. domestic branding
    b. national branding
    c. manufacturers branding
    d. store branding or private labeling
    e. service labeling

Answer: (d) Difficulty: (1) Knowledge: (F) Page: 343

32. To get around the monopoly of Fuji and Konica in the film market in Japan, Kodak decided to offer _____ film to the Japanese Cooperative Union, a group of 2,500 retail stores.

    a. domestic brand
    b. national brand
    c. manufacturer's brand
    d. store brand or private label
    e. service label

Answer: (d) Difficulty: (2) Knowledge: (A) Page: 343

33. _____ is a system where a single banner brand is used worldwide, often with a sub-brand name, for almost the entire product mix of the company.

    a. Domestic branding
    b. National branding
    c. Manufacturer's branding
    d. Store branding or private labeling
    e. Umbrella (corporate) branding

Answer: (e) Difficulty: (2) Knowledge: (F) Page: 343

34. When Matsushita uses brand names like JVC and Panasonic as their banner brands, they are using a(n) _____ system.

    a. domestic branding
    b. national branding
    c. manufacturer's branding
    d. store branding or private labeling
    e. umbrella (corporate) branding

Answer: (e) Difficulty: (2) Knowledge: (A) Page: 343

35. In the minds of most consumers, umbrella branding serves as a:

    a. risk-reducing device.
    b. cost-reducing device.
    c. low-price strategy.
    d. service-reduction device.
    e. image-enhancement or prestige strategy.

Answer: (a) Difficulty: (3) Knowledge: (F) Page: 343

36. All of the following are reasons to use a banner brand EXCEPT:

    a. a good corporate image will have a strong positive impact on the evaluation of attributes of the product endorsed by the banner brand.
    b. the banner brand's logo means trust.
    c. brand building efforts are facilitated.
    d. profits are higher than using national or private brands.
    e. banner branding makes it easier to add or drop new products.

Answer: (d) Difficulty: (2) Knowledge: (F) Page: 343, 344

37. When Nokia (a leading maker of cellular phones) consolidated scores of brand names into their one _____ brand, they found that strength occurred because consumers were able equate the Nokia quality with more products.

    a. domestic brand
    b. national brand
    c. manufacturer's brand
    d. store brand or private label
    e. umbrella or banner brand

Answer: (e) Difficulty: (1) Knowledge: (A) Page: 344

38. Because of the huge investment that many companies have in their brand names (Coca-Cola's brand name is valued at $39 billion dollars), _____ of the brand name is one of the major tasks faced by the brand owner.

a. promotion
b. protection
c. patenting
d. advertising
e. servicing

Answer: (b) Difficulty: (1) Knowledge: (A) Page: 344, 345

39. The most common way of protecting a brand name is by:

a. promotion.
b. securing it through franchising.
c. legal registration.
d. government involvement.
e. gentleman's agreements.

Answer: (c) Difficulty: (1) Knowledge: (F) Page: 345

40. The oldest treaty that provides protection of a brand name is the:

a. Uniform Commercial Code.
b. Brussels Brand Name Cordex.
c. Paris Convention for the Protection of Intellectual Property.
d. Sherman Anti-Trust Act.
e. United Nations Intellectual Property Act.

Answer: (c) Difficulty: (2) Knowledge: (F) Page: 345

41. All of the following are brand areas that might need protection EXCEPT:

a. the name itself.
b. the slogan.
c. the jingle.
d. visual imagery.
e. the size of the logo.

Answer: (e) Difficulty: (1) Knowledge: (F) Page: 345, 346

42. McDonald's golden arches are part of the famous brand. Which of the following elements best describes that element of the brand that should be protected (according to the example provided)?

   a. the name itself.
   b. the slogan.
   c. the jingle.
   d. visual imagery.
   e. the size of the logo.

Answer: (d) Difficulty: (1) Knowledge: (A) Page: 345, 346

43. Most companies sell a wide assortment of products. The assortment is usually described on the dimensions of _____ of the product mix.

   a. width and scale
   b. width and timing
   c. width and ingredients
   d. width and length
   e. scale and length

Answer: (d) Difficulty: (1) Knowledge: (F) Page: 347

44. The _____ of the product assortment refers to the collection of different product lines marketed by the firm.

   a. length
   b. width
   c. horizontal scale
   d. vertical scale
   e. consistency

Answer: (b) Difficulty: (2) Knowledge: (F) Page: 347

45. The _____ of the product assortment refers to the number of items that the company sells within a given product line.

   a. length
   b. width
   c. horizontal scale
   d. vertical scale
   e. consistency

Answer: (a) Difficulty: (2) Knowledge: (F) Page: 347

46. When comparing the product mix in the company's host and home markets, all of the following are possible scenarios EXCEPT:

   a. an extension of the domestic line.
   b. an extension of a joint venture or strategic alliance.
   c. a subset of the home market's product line.
   d. a mixture of local and nonlocal product lines.
   e. a completely localized product line.

Answer: (b) Difficulty: (2) Knowledge: (F) Page: 347

47. Small firms with narrow product assortment will normally choose which of the following strategies when attempting to enter an international market?

   a. an extension of the domestic line.
   b. an extension of a joint venture or strategic alliance.
   c. a subset of the home market's product line.
   d. a mixture of local and nonlocal product lines.
   e. a completely localized product line.

Answer: (a) Difficulty: (2) Knowledge: (A) Page: 347

48. Blistex, a tiny U.S. company that makes primarily lip-care products, has a very limited range of product lines that are marketed to foreign markets. Blistex would probably choose which of the following strategies for entering foreign markets?

   a. an extension of the domestic line.
   b. an extension of a joint venture or strategic alliance.
   c. a subset of the home market's product line.
   d. a mixture of local and nonlocal product lines.
   e. a completely localized product line.

Answer: (a) Difficulty: (3) Knowledge: (A) Page: 347

49. All of the following are drivers that impact the composition of a firm's international product line EXCEPT:

   a. customer service and warranty requirements.
   b. customer preferences.
   c. competitive climate.
   d. organizational structure.
   e. history.

Answer: (a) Difficulty: (3) Knowledge: (F) Page: 347-350

50. When attempting to enter a new foreign market for the first time with a new radically different product or product line, marketing research may not provide all the answers needed by the firm. In this case, the firm might try the _____ as means of acquiring data.

   a. drop/add matrix
   b. ship and shop approach
   c. probing and learning approach
   d. seal and deal approach
   e. push down approach

Answer: (c) Difficulty: (2) Knowlege: (F) Page: 351

51. The _____ procedure uses a product line as a listening post for the new foreign market to see what product items work best.
   a. drop/add matrix
   b. ship and shop approach
   c. probing and learning approach
   d. seal and deal approach
   e. push down approach

Answer: (c) Difficulty: (2) Knowlege: (F) Page: 351

52. By and large, a company should base add/drop decisions in foreign markets on _____ considerations.
   a. service
   b. inventory
   c. profit
   d. quality
   e. logistics

Answer: (c) Difficulty: (1) Knowledge: (F) Page: 351

53. A good place to start to analyze each individual country's product portfolio on the basis of a sales turnover basis. Product lines can be categorized by all the following ways EXCEPT:

   a. core products.
   b. cultural products.
   c. niche items.
   d. seasonal products.
   e. filler products.

Answer: (b) Difficulty: (2) Knowledge: (F) Page: 351

54. With respect to product categories analyzed on the basis of sales turnover, a
_____ product is one where the item represents the bulk of the subsidiary's
sales volume.

    a. core product
    b. cultural product
    c. niche item
    d. seasonal product
    e. filler product

Answer: (a) Difficulty: (1) Knowledge: (F) Page: 351

55. With respect to product categories analyzed on the basis of sales turnover, a
_____ product is one where the product appeals to a small segment of the
population (which might grow in time).

    a. core product
    b. cultural product
    c. niche item
    d. seasonal product
    e. filler product

Answer: (c) Difficulty: (2) Knowledge: (F) Page: 351

56. With respect to product categories analyzed on the basis of sales turnover, a
_____ product is one where the product has most of its sales during limited
times during the year.

    a. core product
    b. cultural product
    c. niche item
    d. seasonal product
    e. filler product

Answer: (d) Difficulty: (1) Knowledge: (F) Page: 351

57. With respect to product categories analyzed on the basis of sales turnover, a _____ product is one where the product is only a small portion of the subsidiary's overall sales. These even might be "dead-weight" items.

a. core product
b. cultural product
c. niche item
d. seasonal product
e. filler product

Answer: (e) Difficulty: (1) Knowledge: (F) Page: 351

58. All of the following are strategic options available to international marketers to stop product piracy EXCEPT:

a. joint ventures.
b. lobbying activities.
c. legal action.
d. product policy options.
e. communication options.

Answer: (a) Difficulty: (2) Knowledge: (F) Page: 353

59. Trying to obtain sanctions against countries that tolerate product piracy would be an example of which of the following strategic options available to international marketers trying to stop product piracy?

a. joint ventures.
b. lobbying activities.
c. legal action.
d. product policy options.
e. communication options.

Answer: (b) Difficulty: (2) Knowledge: (A) Page: 353

60. Intellectual property rights violations has been a major stumbling block to China receiving most favored nation (MFN) status. This would be an example of the successful attempt of which of the following strategic options available to international marketers trying to stop product piracy?

   a. joint ventures.
   b. lobbying activities.
   c. legal action.
   d. product policy options.
   e. communication options.

Answer: (b) Difficulty: (2) Knowledge: (A) Page: 353

61. Including holograms on the product to discourage counterfeiters would be an example of which of the following strategic options available to international marketers trying to stop product piracy?

   a. joint ventures.
   b. lobbying activities.
   c. legal action.
   d. product policy options.
   e. communication options.

Answer: (d) Difficulty: (3) Knowledge: (A) Page: 353

62. When international marketers warn consumers about the ramifications of accepting or buying counterfeit merchandise, this would be an example of which of the following strategic options available to international marketers trying to stop product piracy?

   a. joint ventures.
   b. lobbying activities.
   c. legal action.
   d. product policy options.
   e. communication options.

Answer: (e) Difficulty: (1) Knowledge: (A) Page: 353

63. Holding cultural stereotypes about countries as an important source in assessing the value of a product is an example of:

    a. the country of origin effect.
    b. nationalism.
    c. racial bias.
    d. social sensitivity.
    e. xenophobia.

Answer: (a) Difficulty: (3) Knowledge: (A) Page: 354

64. The "Made In" label as an important source of assessing the value of a product is an example of:

    a. the country of origin effect.
    b. nationalism.
    c. racial bias.
    d. social sensitivity.
    e. xenophobia.

Answer: (a) Difficulty: (1) Knowledge: (A) Page: 354

65. Find the general statement about the country of origin (COO) effect listed below that is NOT true.

    a. COO effects are not stable.
    b. consumers prefer domestic products over imports.
    c. the critical factor appears to be the place of manufacture rather than the location of the company's headquarters.
    d. COO effects do not change very much over time.
    e. demographics make a difference.

Answer: (d) Difficulty: (2) Knowledge: (F) Page: 354, 355

66. All of the following statements about the country of origin effect are true EXCEPT:

    a. COO effects are not stable.
    b. consumers prefer domestic products over imports.
    c. the critical factor appears to be the place of manufacture rather than the location of the company's headquarters.
    d. COO effects do not change very much over time.
    e. demographics make a difference.

Answer: (d) Difficulty: (2) Knowledge: (F) Page: 354, 355

67. If the country of origin effect is anticipated to be negative, a company can follow all of the following strategies to offset the effect <u>EXCEPT</u>:

a. select a brand name that disguises the country of origin.
b. select a local brand name.
c. select a high prestigious price.
d. try to explain any negative government policy that might influence buyers.
e. select a relatively low price.

Answer: (d) Difficulty: (3) Knowledge: (F) Page: 357

68. One of the major challenges faced by international marketers of services is:

a. protectionism.
b. high costs.
c. patent infringement.
d. piracy.
e. low profits.

Answer: (a) Difficulty: (2) Knowledge: (F) Page: 358

69. The need for direct customer interface in providing services means that service providers must often have _____.

a. a warranty.
b. a command of the local language.
c. a local presence.
d. low profit expectation.
e. an inside government contact.

Answer: (c) Difficulty: (2) Knowledge: (F) Page: 360

70. Which of the following would your perceive to be opportunities for international service providers in the future?

a. deregulation of service industries.
b. better understanding of the pricing structure of services.
c. higher profit potential in services.
d. more employment in the service industry.
e. more lax standards and regulations with most international service providers by host governments.

Answer: (a) Difficulty: (2) Knowledge: (A) Page: 360

True/False   Short Answer

1. A _____ is a name, term, sign, symbol, or combination of them which is intended to identify the goods and services of one seller or group of sellers and to differentiate them from those of competitors.

Answer: (brand) Difficulty: (1) Knowledge: (F) Page: 332

2. Brand name awareness, perceived quality, and other associations invoked by the brand name in the customer's mind can be described as being part of brand equity.

Answer: (True) Difficulty: (1) Knowledge: (F) Page: 332

3. A good example of a global brand name is Coca-Cola.

Answer: (True) Difficulty: (1) Knowledge: (A) Page: 333

4. Research indicates there are numerous brands that qualify as truly global brands.

Answer: (False) Difficulty: (2) Knowledge: (F) Page: 333

5. One of the chief reasons for having a global brand is economies of scale.

Answer: (True) Difficulty: (2) Knowledge: (F) Page: 333

6. It is typically easier to build up awareness of a local brand than for a global brand.

Answer: (False) Difficulty: (2) Knowledge: (F) Page: 333

7. One of the reasons for pursuing a global brand as part of product policy is what might be called a prestige factor.

Answer: (True) Difficulty: (1) Knowledge: (F) Page: 333

8. The number one brand with respect to share of mind in Japan is Sony.

Answer: (True) Difficulty: (2) Knowlege: (A) Page: 334, Exhibit 12-1

9. The number one brand with respect to esteem in Japan is Rolls Royce.

Answer: (True) Difficulty: (3) Knowledge: (A) Page: 334, Exhibit 12-1

628

10. The number one brand with respect to share of mind in the world is Disney.

Answer: (False) Difficulty: (2) Knowledge: (A) Page: 334, Exhibit 12-1

11. The number one brand with respect to esteem in the world is Sony.

Answer: (True) Difficulty: (2) Knowledge: (A) Page: 334, Exhibit 12-1

12. Brand equity is usually consistent from country to country.

Answer: (False) Difficulty: (2) Knowledge: (F) Page: 335

13. Asian societies tend to be very receptive to brand loyalty.

Answer: (True) Difficulty: (2) Knowledge: (A) Page: 335

14. Normally, the less the product is used the more one will depend on brand loyalty because of the lack of information.

Answer: (False) Difficulty: (3) Knowledge: (F) Page: 335

15. With respect to brand name changeover strategies, a _____ strategy consists of somehow tying the global brand name to the local name. Eventually, the local brand is phased out.

Answer: (fade-in/fade-out) Difficulty: (3) Knowledge: (F) Page: 340

16. With respect to brand name changeover strategies, a _____ strategy consists of alerting the consumer about an impending brand name change and then changing the brand name to the global brand name.

Answer: (transparent forewarning) Difficulty: (3) Knowledge: (F) Page: 340

17. If a company simply drops the old brand name and immediately replaces it with the global name, it is called summary axing.

Answer: (True) Difficulty: (1) Knowledge: (F) Page: 340

18. _____ is a system where a single banner brand is used worldwide, often with a sub-brand name, for almost the entire product mix of the company.

Answer: (Umbrella branding) Difficulty: (3) Knowledge: (F) Page: 343

19. Core products are the items that represent the bulk of the subsidiary's sales volume.

Answer: (True) Difficulty: (1) Knowledge: (F) Page: 351

20. Country of origin effects have been shown to be unstable over time.

Answer: (False) Difficulty: (2) Knowledge: (F) Page: 354

Essay

1. Deciding to move toward global branding is a difficult decision. This must often be considered with respect to the globalization versus localization issue. What are the questions that might be useful in reaching a decision as to whether to pursue globalization over localization?

Answer:

The students should be allowed to speculate on the applicability of global versus local brand names. Obviously, cultural differences are a heavy factor. One way to begin the discussion is to remind the students of David Aaker's list for analyzing global propositions:

  1). What is the cost of creating and maintaining awareness and associations for a local brand versus a global one?
  2). Are there significant economies of scale in the creation and running of a communication program globally?
  3). Is there value to associations of a global brand or of a brand associated with the source country?
  4). What local associations will be generated by the global name? symbol? slogan? imagery?
  5). Is it culturally and legally do-able to use the brand name, symbol, slogan across the different countries?
  6). What is the value of the awareness and associations that a regional brand might create?

Difficulty: (3) Knowledge: (F) Page: 339

2. In which parts of the world are private labels popular? Why? What factors might explain this?

Answer:

Private labels are doing better in Europe than in Asia (even though there is an increase of private label activity in Asia). The primary factor seems to be brand loyalty. Those in Asia are still very brand loyal and unwilling to try new (in this case private labels) brands as readily as the Europeans. Several factors explain the success of private labels:

1). Improved quality of private label products.
2). Development of premium private label brands.
3). Shift in balance of power between retailers and manufacturers.
4). Expansion into new product categories.
5). Internationalization of retail chains.
6). Economic downturns.

Difficulty: (2) Knowledge: (A) Page: 341-343

3. When the case for a transition from a local to a global (or regional) brand name is made, the firm needs to decide on how to implement the changeover in practice. Comment on the strategies that might be available for doing this and the considerations that might steer the manager toward one of the strategies.

Answer:

Three broad strategic options exist for implementing a facelift. They are:

a. Fade-in/fade-out strategy. The global brand name is somehow tied to an existing local brand name. After a transition period, the old name is dropped.
b. Transparent forewarning. Alerts the consumer about a brand name change. The forewarning can be done via the communication program, in-store displays, and product packaging.
c. Summary axing. The company simply drops the old brand name and immediately replaces it with the global name.
d. Some considerations are:
   1). Consider the length of the transition period.
   2). The purchase cycle.
   3). Customer exposure to the communication messages.
   4). Avoid negative spillovers.
   5). Monitor the response to the name change.

Difficulty: (2) Knowlege: (F) Page: 340

4. Describe the strategies that might be used by multinational corporations to cope with the growing threat of product piracy. What are your feelings about purchasing pirated products? Give a brief illustration.

Answer:

The strategic options against product piracy include the following actions:

    a. Lobbying activities (such as requesting sanctions against guilty parties or countries).
        1). Most Favored Nation status might be affected.
        2). Treaties can be used to stop piracy.
    b. Legal action.
        1). Time consuming and costly.
        2). Can generate negative publicity for the multinational.
    c. Product policy options.
        1). Holograms to indicate authenticity.
        2). Make products hard to copy.
    d. Communications options.
        1). Warn audiences.
        2). Anti-piracy ad campaigns.

Students should express their own opinion about piracy at this point. In addition, they should provide an example. The most common example will probably be about pirated movies, CDs, or computer software.

Difficulty: (2) Knowledge: (A) Page: 351-354

5. Comment on how you perceive the marketing of services on a global basis to be different from marketing tangible goods. Think about the difficulties that might be present with marketing services.

Answer:

Several aspects make the marketing of services different from the marketing of tangible goods worldwide. These aspects are degree of protectionism, immediate face-to-face contacts within the service sector (remember services are performed), difficulties in measuring customer service satisfaction overseas, the deregulation of services, the increased demand for premium services, and the increased value that service customers are putting on excellent services. A country has to be ready for services. It is the next logical step beyond a manufacturing economy.

Difficulty: (1) Knowledge: (F) Page: 358-361

Chapter 13

Multiple Choice

1. . _____ is the only marketing mix instrument that creates revenues.

   a. Product
   b. Price
   c. Place (distribution)
   d. Promotion
   e. Service

Answer: (b) Difficulty: (1) Knowledge: (F) Page: 367

2. A(n) _____ market is one where products marketed in low-priced countries are shipped and resold by unauthorized channels in high-priced markets.

   a. black
   b. gray
   c. white
   d. demand
   e. zero

Answer: (b) Difficulty: (3) Knowledge: (A) Page: 367

3. All of the following are drivers that govern global pricing decisions <u>EXCEPT</u>:

   a. Company
   b. Customers
   c. Controls
   d. Competition
   e. Channels

Answer: (c) Difficulty: (1) Knowledge: (F) Page: 368

4. In addition to company, customers, competition, and channel drivers that influence price, _____ can a dramatic affect on the way price is used and administered.

    a. break-even analysis
    b. regression functions
    c. supply and service curves
    d. government policies
    e. business ethics

Answer: (d) Difficulty: (2) Knowledge: (F) Page: 368

5. When developing a pricing strategy for its global markets, one of the first steps that a company must go through is to decide:

    a. what the actual price should be.
    b. how high or low to price.
    c. how much money will price bring in.
    d. what it wants to accomplish with its strategy.
    e. what form of controls will regulate price.

Answer: (d) Difficulty: (3) Knowledge: (F) Page: 368

6. Maximizing current profits or projecting a premium image are examples of pricing _____.

    a. results.
    b. goals.
    c. thoughts.
    d. constructs.
    e. theories.

Answer: (b) Difficulty: (1) Knowledge: (F) Page: 368

7. According to recent research, all of the following are examples of important pricing objectives EXCEPT:

    a. drive competition out of business.
    b. to achieve a satisfactory return on investment.
    c. maintain market share.
    d. expand market share.
    e. to meet a specified profit goal.

Answer: (a) Difficulty: (2) Knowledge: (A) Page: 368

8. Levi's jeans being sold for $80 per pair in Europe versus $30 per pair in the United States is an example of:

   a. different or changing pricing goals.
   b. different service expectations.
   c. unwise buying by consumers.
   d. a monopoly versus competition.
   e. a cartel in action.

Answer: (a) Difficulty: (2) Knowledge: (A) Page: 368

9. When making pricing decisions, _____ set(s) the floor.

   a. profits
   b. costs
   c. demand
   d. supply
   e. service

Answer: (b) Difficulty: (1) Knowledge: (F) Page: 369

10. _____ costs change with sales volume.

   a. Demand
   b. Supply
   c. Derived
   d. Fixed
   e. Variable

Answer: (e) Difficulty: (1) Knowledge: (F) Page: 369

11. _____ costs do not vary with sales volume changes.

   a. Demand
   b. Supply
   c. Derived
   d. Fixed
   e. Variable

Answer: (d) Difficulty: (1) Knowledge: (F) Page: 369

12. In the international marketplace, _____ pricing adds international costs and a mark-up to the domestic manufacturing cost.

   a. dynamic incremental pricing
   b. export price
   c. import price
   d. cost-plus price
   e. target-return price

Answer: (d) Difficulty: (3) Knowledge: (F) Page: 370

13. In the international marketplace, _____ pricing arrives at a price after removing domestic fixed costs. Only variable export costs generated by the exporting effort and a portion of the overhead load should be recuperated by the pricing effort (according to this method).

   a. dynamic incremental pricing
   b. export price
   c. import price
   d. cost-plus price
   e. target-return price

Answer: (a) Difficulty: (3) Knowledge: (F) Page: 370

14. Examples of exporting-related _____ include manufacturing costs, shipping expenses, insurance, and overseas promotional costs.

   a. incremental costs
   b. demand costs
   c. fixed costs
   d. target costs
   e. service costs

Answer: (a) Difficulty: (2) Knowledge: (F) Page: 370

15. One of the risks of dynamic incremental pricing (in the case where the export list price is far below the domestic price) that _____ can be triggered in the export market.

    a. high profit potential
    b. dumping charges or accusations
    c. falling profits
    d. falling quality
    e. falling service

Answer: (b) Difficulty: (2) Knowledge: (A) Page: 370

16. When demand is highly price sensitive, the company needs to consider how it can _____ from a global perspective.

    a. raise prices
    b. lower prices
    c. lower service
    d. raise quality
    e. reduce costs

Answer: (e) Difficulty: (2) Knowledge: (F) Page: 370

17. _____ attached to the product will set the ceiling to a price.

    a. Costs
    b. Services
    c. Perceived value
    d. Discounts
    e. Quality

Answer: (c) Difficulty: (2) Knowledge: (F) Page: 370

18. _____ is a function of buying power, tastes, habits, and substitutes.

    a. Costs
    b. Derived demand
    c. Service
    d. Consumer demand
    e. Attitudes

Answer: (d) Difficulty: (2) Knowlege: (F) Page: 370

19. Countries with low per-capita income are _____ than in developed countries.

    a. promotion sensitive
    b. price sensitive
    c. need sensitive
    d. demand sensitive
    e. service sensitive

Answer: (b) Difficulty: (3) Knowledge: (F) Page: 370

20. One alternative for successful marketing to the price sensitive low per-capita income market is to produce a _____ product or lower product quality.

    a. downsized
    b. upgraded
    c. synthetic
    d. copy
    e. parallel

Answer: (a) Difficulty: (2) Knowledge: (F) Page: 370

21. If Wrigley chewing gum company were to make 3-stick rather than 5-stick packages of gum for the Philippines market, this would be an example of _____ for low per-capita income market.

    a. downsizing
    b. upgrading
    c. synthesis
    d. copying
    e. paralleling

Answer: (a) Difficulty: (2) Knowledge: (A) Page: 370

22. Standard microeconomic theory suggests that companies should exploit differences in price sensitivity by _____.

    a. product differentiation.
    b. service distinction.
    c. price discrimination.
    d. lowering quality.
    e. escalating the prestige factor.

Answer: (c) Difficulty: (2) Knowledge: (F) Page: 371

23. _____ is the percentage change in unit demand resulting from a one percentage point change in price.

   a. Price sensitivity
   b. Price demand
   c. Derived demand
   d. Marginal pricing
   e. Price elasticity

Answer: (e) Difficulty: (2) Knowledge: (F) Page: 371

24. Wide gaps in the price sensitivity between countries for the same product many times create conditions that promote _____ markets.

   a. black
   b. gray
   c. white
   d. demand
   e. zero

Answer: (b) Difficulty: (3) Knowledge: (F) Page: 371

25. Once brand loyalty has been established, price will play less of a role as a purchase criterion, and the firm may be able to institute a _____ strategy.

   a. demand-based
   b. premium pricing
   c. elastic pricing
   d. promotion-related pricing
   e. sensitivity-based

Answer: (b) Difficulty: (2) Knowledge: (F) Page: 372

26. To be able to use a _____ strategy, the firm must be able to differentiate its product from the competition.

   a. demand-based
   b. premium pricing
   c. elastic pricing
   d. promotion-related pricing
   e. sensitivity-based

Answer: (b) Difficulty: (2) Knowledge: (F) Page: 372

27. All of the following are reasons that competitive situations vary from country to country (with respect to the competitive environment) EXCEPT:

   a. the number of competitors varies from country to country.
   b. the nature of competition changes.
   c. the presence of counterfeit products.
   d. the presence of gray markets.
   e. the competitive position of a firm changes from one country to another.

Answer: (d) Difficulty: (3) Knowledge: (F) Page: 372

28. An example of nonprice competition that is faced in some markets is:

   a. retailer sales.
   b. discounts.
   c. coupons.
   d. advertising.
   e. cents-off deals.

Answer: (d) Difficulty: (2) Knowledge: (A) Page: 372

29. Large cross-country price gaps open up arbitrage opportunities that lead to _____ imports from low-price countries to high-price ones.

   a. black market
   b. white market
   c. zero market
   d. smuggled
   e. parallel

Answer: (e) Difficulty: (2) Knowledge: (F) Page: 374

30. Sales tax rates, tariffs, and price controls are all examples of _____ that
   can have a direct or indirect impact on the pricing policies of a firm in the international
   marketplace.

   a. sales volume policies
   b. price policies
   c. government policies
   d. restrictions
   e. punishments

Answer: (c) Difficulty: (2) Knowledge: (F) Page: 374

31. Huge government deficits are examples of a(n) _____ impact on pricing decisions.

    a. direct
    b. indirect
    c. artificial
    d. planned
    e. uncontrollable

Answer: (b) Difficulty: (2) Knowledge: (F) Page: 375

32. Inflation in an economy is an example of a(n) _____ impact on pricing decisions.

    a. direct
    b. indirect
    c. artificial
    d. planned
    e. uncontrollable

Answer: (b) Difficulty: (2) Knowledge: (F) Page: 375

33. To cover the incremental costs (such as shipping), the final foreign retail price will often be much higher than the domestic retail price. This phenomenon is known as _____.

    a. inflation.
    b. the price deflator.
    c. price escalation.
    d. price sensitivity.
    e. global arbitrage.

Answer: (c) Difficulty: (2) Knowledge: (F) Page: 375

34. There are two ways to deal with the price escalation phenomenon. One of these methods is to cut the export price. The other is to:

    a. change the promotion strategy.
    b. position the product as a (super) premium brand.
    c. position the product as a lower quality brand.
    d. reduce retailer margins.
    e. reduce distances that the good must be shipped.

Answer: (b) Difficulty: (3) Knowledge: (A) Page: 375

35. Which of the following would be a good option to follow if lowering the export price were the firm's objective?

    a. rearrange the distribution channel.
    b. change the promotion.
    c. change the warranty provisions.
    d. give more of the product in the package as an incentive to purchase.
    e. study the demand curve.

Answer: (a) Difficulty: (3) Knowledge: (A) Page: 375

36. All of the following are options that might be followed if the firm wished to lower its export price on a product EXCEPT:

    a. rearrange the distribution channel.
    b. eliminate costly features (or make them optional).
    c. downsize the product.
    d. expand the warranty categories to give incentive for higher quality.
    e. assemble or manufacture the product in foreign markets.

Answer: (d) Difficulty: (2) Knowledge: (F) Page: 375, 376

37. Recently, several U.S. firms decided to penetrate the Japanese consumer market through direct marketing (such as catalog or telemarketing sales). Which of the following strategies best describes this option for lowering the price of an exported product?

    a. rearrange the distribution channel.
    b. eliminate costly features (or make them optional).
    c. downsize the product.
    d. expand the warranty categories to give incentive for higher quality.
    e. assemble or manufacture the product in foreign markets.

Answer: (a) Difficulty: (2) Knowledge: (A) Page: 375, 376

38. When the U.S. levied a 10 percent tax on plus-$30,000 luxury cars, Land Rover changed the weight of Range Rover models so they could be classed as a truck and thereby avoid the luxury status, the company was attempting to follow which of the price strategies listed below for lowering the price of an exported product?

   a. rearrange the distribution channel.
   b. eliminate costly features (or make them optional).
   c. downsize the product.
   d. adapt the product to escape tariffs or tax levies.
   e. assemble or manufacture the product in foreign markets.

Answer: (d) Difficulty: (1) Knowledge: (A) Page: 376

39. LEGO, the Dutch toymaker, rather than worrying about finding ways to lower the price of its product in foreign markets has chosen (most LEGO sets are sold from $6-$235) to adopt a _____ strategy position.

   a. demand-based
   b. premium pricing
   c. elastic pricing
   d. promotion-related pricing
   e. sensitivity-based

Answer: (b) Difficulty: (1) Knowledge: (A) Page: 376

40. When McDonald's first opened their restaurants in Russia, the Big Mac meal cost 6 rubles. Three years later, the same meal cost 1,100 rubles. This would be an example of how:

   a. demand can change.
   b. how premium pricing can damage a product.
   c. price elasticity works.
   d. inflation can damage a market.
   e. service is what matter the most to the average customer.

Answer: (d) Difficulty: (1) Knowledge: (A) Page: 376

41. All of the ways listed below are ways to safeguard against inflation <u>EXCEPT</u>:

   a. modify components, ingredients, parts and/or packaging materials.
   b. source materials from low-cost suppliers.
   c. lengthen credit terms.
   d. include escalator clauses in long-term contracts.
   e. quote prices in a stable currency.

Answer: (c) Difficulty: (3) Knowledge: (F) Page: 377

42. Including escalator clauses in long-term contracts and quoting prices in a stable currency would both be ways that a firm might _____ when dealing with a foreign market or foreign distributor.

   a. safeguard against government intervention
   b. safeguard against losses
   c. safeguard against governmental confiscation
   d. safeguard against recession
   e. safeguard against inflation

Answer: (e) Difficulty: (3) Knowledge: (F) Page: 377

43. To fight inflation, some governments imposed price controls. One consequence of price controls is goods:

   a. become scarce in all markets.
   b. can be diverted to black markets.
   c. are purchased by the rich only.
   d. are removed from the market by government order.
   e. are usually impervious to price controls and are, therefore, unaffected.

Answer: (b) Difficulty: (2) Knowledge: (A) Page: 377

44. According to lessons learned in Brazil's hyperinflationary economy, McDonald's will deal with Russia's runaway inflation by using all of the following tools <u>EXCEPT</u>:

   a. emphasize cash flow management.
   b. control of raw materials.
   c. institute sales and price setting strategies.
   d. hedge for potentially substantial distortions in the exchange rate.
   e. make loans to local franchise investors to bring them past hard times.

Answer: (e) Difficulty: (2) Knowledge: (A) Page: 378

45. Firms faced with price controls can take any of the following strategies EXCEPT:

    a. shift the target segment or markets.
    b. launch new products or variants of existing products.
    c. negotiate with the government.
    d. predict the incidence of price controls.
    e. have the home government bring pressure on the host government.

Answer: (e) Difficulty: (3) Knowledge: (F) Page: 378

46. When a manufacturer of breakfast cereals for humans shifts production to a chicken feed product to overcome the effects of price controls, the firm would be following which of the strategies outlined below?

    a. adapt the product line.
    b. shift target segments or market.
    c. negotiate with the government.
    d. launch a variant of an existing product.
    e. predict the incidence of price controls.

Answer: (b) Difficulty: (2) Knowledge: (A) Page: 378

47. If a company that is threatened with price controls diversifies into product lines that are relatively free of price controls, the firm would be following which of the following strategies?

    a. adapt the product line.
    b. shift target segments or market.
    c. negotiate with the government.
    d. launch a variant of an existing product.
    e. predict the incidence of price controls.

Answer: (a) Difficulty: (2) Knowledge: (A) Page: 378

48. The most drastic reaction to government-imposed price controls is to:

    a. adapt the product line.
    b. shift target segments or market.
    c. negotiate with the government.
    d. launch a variant of an existing product.
    e. leave the country.

Answer: (e) Difficulty: (1) Knowledge: (A) Page: 379

49. One of the chief reasons for staying in a country that has government-imposed price controls to deal with hyperinflation is:

a. the government might not let you out.
b. when the danger is over you cannot get back in.
c. you gain experience for other markets with similar problems.
d. you do not want to loose face.
e. you do not want to show weakness to your competition.

Answer: (c) Difficulty: (2) Knowledge: (A) Page: 379

50. _____ reflect how much one currency is worth in terms of another currency.

a. Interest rates
b. Credit rates
c. Bond rates
d. Inflation rates
e. Exchange rates

Answer: (e) Difficulty: (2) Knowledge: (F) Page: 379

51. All of the following are exporter strategies when the domestic currency is weak EXCEPT:
a. stress price benefits.
b. engage in nonprice competition by improving quality, delivery, and aftersale service.
c. expand the product line and add more.
d. shift sourcing and manufacturing to domestic market.
e. exploit export opportunities in all markets.

Answer: (b) Difficulty: (3) Knowledge: (F) Page: 380, Exhibit 13-4

52. Which of the following are exporter strategies when the domestic currency is strong?

a. stress price benefits.
b. engage in nonprice competition by improving quality, delivery, and aftersale service.
c. expand the product line and add more.
d. shift sourcing and manufacturing to domestic market.
e. exploit export opportunities in all markets.

Answer: (b) Difficulty: (3) Knowledge: (F) Page: 380, Exhibit 13-4

53. All of the following are considered to be exporter strategies when the domestic currency is strong EXCEPT:

    a. conduct conventional cash-for-goods trade.
    b. engage in nonprice competition by improving quality, delivery, and aftersale service.
    c. improve productivity and engage in vigorous cost reduction.
    d. shift sourcing and manufacturing overseas.
    e. give priority to exports to relatively strong-currency countries.

Answer: (a) Difficulty: (3) Knowledge: (F) Page: 380, Exhibit 13-4

54. Which of the following are considered to be exporter strategies when the domestic currency is weak?

    a. conduct conventional cash-for-goods trade.
    b. engage in nonprice competition by improving quality, delivery, and aftersale service.
    c. improve productivity and engage in vigorous cost reduction.
    d. shift sourcing and manufacturing overseas.
    e. give priority to exports to relatively strong-currency countries.

Answer: (a) Difficulty: (3) Knowledge: (F) Page: 380, Exhibit 13-4

55. Two major issues confronting international marketers result from currency movement. The first of these is in which currency do we quote our prices? The second is:

    a. how much of the loss or gain (because of pass through) should be passed to consumers?
    b. how much should we invest in the local currency?
    c. how much should we invest in our own currency?
    d. what role should the central bank play in currency movement?
    e. should we trust international arbitrage as a means of settling currency value?

Answer: (a) Difficulty: (3) Knowledge: (A) Page: 380

56. A weakening of the U.S. dollar relative to the Japanese yen has the effect of:

    a. strengthening the Japanese position in the United States.
    b. strengthening the U.S. position in Japan.
    c. weakening the dollar in Europe.
    d. strengthening the yen in Europe.
    e. all positions remain unchanged.

Answer: (b) Difficulty: (2) Knowledge: (A) Page: 380

57. A strengthening of the U.S. dollar relative to the Japanese yen has the effect of:

    a. strengthening the Japanese position in the United States.
    b. strengthening the U.S. position in Japan.
    c. weakening the dollar in Europe.
    d. strengthening the yen in Europe.
    e. all positions remain unchanged.

Answer: (a) Difficulty: (2) Knowledge: (A) Page: 380

58. One of the ways that a weakening of the U.S. dollar relative to the Japanese yen may not necessarily be a benefit to a U.S. firm is that:

    a. the government may not allow the pass through.
    b. the government might erect tariff barriers.
    c. Japanese parts might become more expensive and when imported for inclusion into an exported product prices might actually rise.
    d. other currencies might be the ones actually traded.
    e. costs can be cut in other ways.

Answer: (c) Difficulty: (2) Knowledge: (A) Page: 381

59. When considering the currency pass-through phenomenon, all of the following factors give an indication as to the appropriate action EXCEPT:

    a. the customer's price sensitivity.
    b. government actions.
    c. the impact of dollar appreciation on the firm's cost structure.
    d. the impact of dollar depreciation on the firm's cost structure.
    e. the amount of competition in the export market.

Answer: (b) Difficulty: (2) Knowledge: (F) Page: 382

60. When exporters lower their mark-ups in a more price-conscious export market than in a price-sensitive market, with respect to exchange rate movements this is called _____.

a. local-currency price stability (LCPS).
b. pricing-to-market (PTM).
c. transfer pricing.
d. countertrade pricing.
e. demand mark-up pricing.

Answer: (b) Difficulty: (3) Knowledge: (F) Page: 382

61. When an exporter uses the _____ method, the effect can be negative. Frequent adjustments of prices in response to currency movements will distress local channels and customers.
a. local-currency price stability (LCPS).
b. pricing-to-market (PTM).
c. transfer pricing.
d. countertrade pricing.
e. demand mark-up pricing.

Answer: (b) Difficulty: (3) Knowledge: (F) Page: 383

62. _____ is a special form of pricing where mark-ups are adjusted to stabilize prices in the buyer's currency. This method helps to create stability in the local currency.

a. local-currency price stability (LCPS).
b. pricing-to-market (PTM).
c. transfer pricing.
d. countertrade pricing.
e. demand mark-up pricing.

Answer: (a) Difficulty: (1) Knowledge: (F) Page: 383

63. With respect to currency quotation when preparing for buying and selling transactions, buyers and sellers generally prefer to quote in:
a. a world currency.
b. the seller's currency.
c. the buyer's currency.
d. in their own currency.
e. in the dollar.

Answer: (d) Difficulty: (2) Knowledge: (A) Page: 383

64. When sales take place between related entities of the same company, _____ is often used.

    a. local-currency price stability (LCPS)
    b. pricing-to-market (PTM)
    c. transfer pricing
    d. countertrade pricing
    e. demand mark-up pricing

Answer: (c) Difficulty: (2) Knowledge: (F) Page: 383

65. Transfer pricing decisions in an international context need to balance off the interests of a broad range of stakeholders. All of the following would be examples of those stakeholders EXCEPT:

    a. the parent company.
    b. the competition.
    c. local country managers.
    d. host government(s).
    e. the domestic government.

Answer: (b) Difficulty: (2) Knowledge: (F) Page: 383

66. There are a series of key drivers behind transfer pricing decisions. The most important of these drivers is thought to be:

    a. competition in the foreign country.
    b. economic conditions in the foreign country.
    c. price controls.
    d. exchange controls.
    e. market conditions in the foreign country.

Answer: (e) Difficulty: (3) Knowledge: (F) Page: 384

67. _____ uses the market mechanism as a cue for setting transfer prices.

    a. Local-currency price stability (LCPS) pricing
    b. Pricing-to-market (PTM)
    c. Market-based pricing
    d. Countertrade pricing
    e. Nonmarket-based pricing

68. _____ (as a form of market-based pricing) basically dictates that the company charges the price that any buyer outside the company would pay (as if the transaction occurred between two unrelated entities).

    a. Local-currency price stability (LCPS) pricing
    b. Pricing-to-market (PTM)
    c. Arm's length pricing
    d. Countertrade pricing
    e. Nonmarket-based pricing

Answer: (c) Difficulty: (2) Knowledge: (F) Page: 385

69. _____ simply adds a mark-up to the cost of the goods.

    a. Demand-based pricing
    b. Negotiated pricing
    c. Cost-based pricing
    d. Markup-based pricing
    e. Target return pricing

Answer: (c) Difficulty: (2) Knowledge: (F) Page: 385

70. To conduct _____, conflicts between country affiliates are resolved through mutual discussion of the transfer pricing problems.

    a. demand-based pricing
    b. negotiated pricing
    c. cost-based pricing
    d. markup-based pricing
    e. target return pricing

Answer: (b) Difficulty: (1) Knowledge: (F) Page: 385

71. _____ occurs when imports are being sold at an "unfair" price.

    a. Price fixing
    b. Dumping
    c. Gray marketing
    d. Countertrade
    e. Predatory pricing

Answer: (b) Difficulty: (1) Knowledge: (F) Page: 386

72. Which of the following pricing policies can trigger antidumping actions?

a. Skimming pricing.
b. Penetration pricing.
c. Discount pricing.
d. Cents-off deals.
e. Everyday low pricing.

Answer: (b) Difficulty: (2) Knowledge: (F) Page: 386

73. To reduce exposure and risk of antidumping actions, the exporter can follow any of the following marketing strategies EXCEPT:

a. trading-up.
b. service enhancement.
c. distribution
d. government intervention.
e. communication.

Answer: (d) Difficulty: (1) Knowledge: (F) Page: 388

74. _____ is an umbrella term used to describe unconventional trade-financing transactions that involve some form of noncash compensation.

a. local-currency price stability (LCPS) pricing
b. pricing-to-market (PTM)
c. arm's length pricing
d. countertrade pricing
e. nonmarket-based pricing

Answer: (d) Difficulty: (2) Knowledge: (F) Page: 393

75. When Pepsi traded their cola product to the Russians in exchange for vodka and ocean tankers, they were using which of the following pricing forms?

a. local-currency price stability (LCPS) pricing
b. pricing-to-market (PTM)
c. arm's length pricing
d. countertrade pricing
e. nonmarket-based pricing

Answer: (d) Difficulty: (2) Knowledge: (A) Page: 397

True/False   Short Answer

1. In gray markets, products marketed in low-priced countries are shipped and resold by unauthorized channels in high-priced markets.

Answer: (True) Difficulty: (2) Knowledge: (F) Page: 367

2. One of the most important pricing objectives that most companies have is to avoid paying any taxes on their sales.

Answer: (False) Difficulty: (1) Knowledge: (F) Page: 368

3. Export pricing policies differ depending on the way costs are treated.

Answer: (True) Difficulty: (2) Knowledge: (F) Page: 369

4. It is often said that profits set the floor for pricing decisions.

Answer: (False) Difficulty: (3) Knowledge: (F) Page: 369

5. _____ pricing adds international costs and a mark-up to the domestic manufacturing cost.

Answer: (Cost-plus) Difficulty: (3) Knowledge: (F) Page: 370

6. In incremental pricing a price is determined after removing domestic fixed costs.

Answer: (True) Difficulty: (2) Knowledge: (F) Page: 370

7. When an international chewing gum company sells three sticks of gum in a pack (instead of the normal five sticks) in a market where poverty is rampant, this would be an example of _____ the product.

Answer: (downsizing) Difficulty: (3) Knowledge: (A) Page: 370

8. Standard microeconomic theory suggests that companies should exploit differences in price sensitivity by price discrimination.

Answer: (True) Difficulty: (2) Knowledge: (A) Page: 371

9. To cover the incremental costs of doing business in a foreign market, the final foreign retail price will often be much higher than the domestic retail price. This is called price _____.

Answer: (escalation) Difficulty: (3) Knowledge: (F) Page: 375

10. To justify higher prices and offset transfer pricing effects, Levi's jeans sells mainly to upscale boutiques in Japan and Europe.

Answer: (True) Difficulty: (1) Knowledge: (A) Page: 376

11. One of the courses of action that a company can follow when faced with price controls is to adapt the product line.

Answer: (True) Difficulty: (2) Knowledge: (F) Page: 378

12. An exporter strategy when faced with a weak domestic currency would be to engage in nonprice competition by improving quality, delivery, and aftersale service.

Answer: (False) Difficulty: (2) Knowledge: (F) Page: 380, Exhibit 13-4

13. If an exporter were to stress price benefits, the exporter would probably be facing a domestic currency that was perceived as being weak.

Answer: (True) Difficulty: (2) Knowledge: (F) Page: 380, Exhibit 13-4

14. When sales transactions occur between related entities of the same company, _____ pricing often occurs.

Answer: (transfer) Difficulty: (3) Knowledge: (F) Page: 383

15. When sales transactions occur in some form of compensation other than money (such as trading corn for whiskey), the two trading companies are engaged in

_____.

Answer: (countertrade) Difficulty: (3) Knowledge: (A) Page: 393

Essay

1. Price escalation can be a serious problem in foreign markets. To offset these difficulties marketers must be prepared to creatively meet the price escalation challenge. List the various ways that marketers might attack this problem.

Answer:

Ways to lower the export price include:
    a. Rearrange the distribution channel.
        1). Shorten the channel.
        2). Work towards channel cost efficiencies.
    b. Eliminate costly features (or make them optional).
    c. Downsize the product.
    d. Assemble or manufacture the product in foreign markets.
    e. Adapt the product to escape tariffs or tax levies.

Difficulty: (2) Knowledge: (F) Page: 375, 376

2. Setting prices in a floating exchange rate world poses unique problems. Comment on how a company might react to floating exchange rates. What considerations are probably the most important for the decision maker to consider?

Answer:

Due to the interplay of a variety of economic and political factors, exchange rates continuously float up- or downward. Given the sometimes dramatic exchange rate movements, setting prices in a floating exchange rate world poses a tremendous challenge.

Two major issues:
        1). How much of a exchange rate gain (loss) should be passed through to our customers?
        2). In what currency should we quote our prices?

When formulating an answer consider the points below:
When considering pass through, generally speaking, the appropriate action will depend on three factors:
        1). Customers' price sensitivity.
        2). The impact of the dollar appreciation on the firm's cost structure.
        3). The amount of competition in the export market.

Difficulty: (3) Knowledge: (A) Page: 379-383

3. What is transfer pricing? Comment on the stakeholders and key drivers that impact the decision maker faced with transfer pricing.

Answer:

Transfer pricing is the primary mechanism used when sales transactions take place between related entities of the same company.

The answer to this question is opinion-oriented and should consider a variety of factors. Students should review the material in the chapter and consider the list presented below before making a judgment. Be sure to justify the opinion expressed in the judgment.

Transfer pricing decisions are balanced against a variety of stakeholders:
      1). Parent company.
      2). Local country managers.
      3). Host government(s).
      4). Domestic government.
      5). Joint venture partner(s).

Key drivers are:
      1). Market conditions in the foreign country.
      2). Competition in the foreign country.
      3). Reasonable profit for foreign affiliate.
      4). U.S. federal income taxes.
      5). Economic conditions in the foreign country.
      6). Import restrictions.
      7). Customs duties.
      8). Price controls.
      9). Taxation in the foreign country.
     10). Exchange controls.

Generally speaking, MNCs should consider the following criteria when making transfer pricing decisions:
      1). Tax regimes.
      2). Local market conditions.
      3). Market imperfections.
      4). Joint venture partner.
      5). Morale of local country managers.

Difficulty: (3) Knowledge: (F) Page: 383-385

4. Antidumping measures are very popular with most the governments of industrialized nations. What measures might exporters consider to hedge themselves against antidumping procedures? Which method do think is probably the best? Justify your answer.

Answer:

To minimize risk exposure to anti-dumping actions, exports might pursue any of the following marketing strategies:
   a. Trading-up.
   b. Service enhancement.
   c. Distribution and communication:
      1). The establishment of communication channels with local competitors.
      2). Entering into cooperative agreements with them (strategic alliances).
      3). Reallocation of the firm's marketing efforts from vulnerable products to less sensitive products.

Students can pick from the above list. The instructor should carefully assess how they justified their answer.

Difficulty: (2) Knowledge: (A) Page: 386-388

5. Discuss the motives behind countertrade and the guidelines for making countertrade successful.

Answer:

Motives behind countertrade.
   a. Gain access to new or difficult markets.
   b. Overcome exchange rate controls or lack of hard currency.
   c. Overcome low country credit worthiness.
   d. Increase sales volume.
   e. Generate long-term customer goodwill.

Advice for those considering countertrade:
   a. Always evaluate the pros and cons of countertrade against other options.
   b. Minimize the ratio of compensation goods to cash.
   c. Strive for goods that can be used in-house.
   d. Assess the relative merits of relying on middlemen versus an in-house staff.
   e. Check whether the goods are subject to any import restrictions.
   f. Assess the quality of the goods.

Difficulty: (2) Knowledge: (F) Page: 393-397

Chapter 14

Multiple Choice

1. The steps in developing a promotional plan international marketing are by and large similar to the sequence in domestic marketing. All of the following are part of that sequence <u>EXCEPT</u>:

   a. Determine manufacturing tie-ins.
   b. Select target audiences and positioning theme.
   c. Determine the promotional budget.
   d. Develop a message strategy.
   e. Decide on a media strategy.

   Answer: (a) Difficulty: (1) Knowledge: (F) Page: 402

2. Which of the following would probably be the logical first step in developing a promotional plan in international marketing?

   a. Determine manufacturing tie-ins.
   b. Select target audiences and positioning theme.
   c. Determine the promotional budget.
   d. Develop a message strategy.
   e. Decide on a media strategy.

   Answer: (b) Difficulty: (1) Knowledge: (F) Page: 402

3. All international promotions are constrained by elements in the international environment. All of the following are representative of these constraints <u>EXCEPT</u>:

   a. language barriers.
   b. management barriers.
   c. cultural constraints.
   d. local attitudes toward advertising.
   e. poor media infrastructure.

   Answer: (b) Difficulty: (2) Knowledge: (F) Page: 402

4. Which of the following would be considered a constraint on international promotion?

   a. management barriers
   b. creative barriers
   c. technology barriers
   d. advertising regulations
   e. ethical barriers

Answer: (d) Difficulty: (3) Knowledge: (F) Page: 402

5. In an advertising message, the original slogan was "Body by Fisher." The translation in a foreign market was "Corpse by Fisher." This would be an example of which of the following constraints on international promotion?

   a. language barriers.
   b. advertising regulations.
   c. cultural constraints.
   d. local attitudes toward advertising.
   e. poor media infrastructure.

Answer: (a) Difficulty: (1) Knowledge: (A) Page: 402

6. All of the following are language barriers that can be identified as typical international translation errors EXCEPT:

   a. simple carelessness.
   b. idioms.
   c. local slang.
   d. multiple-meaning words.
   e. incorrect grammar.

Answer: (e) Difficulty: (3) Knowledge: (F) Page: 402-404

7. In an advertising message, the original slogan was "Body by Fisher." The translation in a foreign market was "Corpse by Fisher." This would be an example of which of the following types of translation errors?

   a. simple carelessness.
   b. idioms.
   c. local slang.
   d. multiple-meaning words.
   e. incorrect grammar.

Answer: (a) Difficulty: (2) Knowledge: (A) Page: 402-404

8. In an advertising message, the original slogan was "When I used this shirt, I felt good." The translation in a foreign market was "Until I used this shirt, I felt good." This would be an example of which of the following types of translation errors?

   a. simple carelessness.
   b. idioms.
   c. local slang.
   d. multiple-meaning words.
   e. incorrect grammar.

Answer: (a) Difficulty: (2) Knowledge: (A) Page: 402-404

9. One would expect that the Chevy Nova would not sell well in Spanish speaking countries since in Spanish "nova" means "it doesn't go." This would be an example of which of the following types of translation errors?

   a. simple carelessness.
   b. idioms.
   c. local slang.
   d. multiple-meaning words.
   e. incorrect grammar.

Answer: (d) Difficulty: (3) Knowledge: (A) Page: 402-404

10. In Spanish, five different words can be used for the word "tires" (cauchos, cubiertas, gomas, llantas, and neumaticos). Obviously, this might present problems is advertising. This would be an example of which of the following types of translation errors?

   a. simple carelessness.
   b. idioms.
   c. local slang.
   d. multiple-meaning words.
   e. incorrect grammar.

Answer: (d) Difficulty: (1) Knowledge: (A) Page: 404

11. In Britain one U.S. advertiser ran a campaign that centered around the slogan "You can use no finer napkin at your dinner table." In Britain, some people use the word "napkin" for the word "diapers." This would be an example of which of the following types of translation errors?

    a. simple carelessness.
    b. idioms.
    c. local slang.
    d. multiple-meaning words.
    e. incorrect grammar.

Answer: (c) Difficulty: (2) Knowledge: (A) Page: 404

12. Given that so many errors can occur with translation and misunderstanding of advertising in the foreign market, which of the following is probably the easiest solution to the problem?

    a. Involve ad agencies from the company's domestic environment.
    b. Involve ad agencies from the host country's environment.
    c. Check with government officials.
    d. employ foreign language specialists for all markets.
    e. Don't worry about it, the problem usually corrects itself.

Answer: (b) Difficulty: (3) Knowledge: (F) Page: 404

13. All of the following are strategies for dealing with translation problems in a foreign market EXCEPT:

    a. involve ad agencies from the host country's environment.
    b. don't translate the message for the foreign market.
    c. add foreign language subtitles.
    d. use voice-overs that use foreign slang.
    e. check with foreign officials.

Answer: (e) Difficulty: (3) Knowledge: (F) Page: 404

14. Of the barriers that face a foreign company when attempting to promote products in a foreign market, _____ are arguably the biggest stumbling block to successful advertising in the foreign market.

   a. language barriers
   b. advertising regulations
   c. cultural constraints or barriers
   d. local attitudes toward advertising
   e. poor media infrastructure

Answer: (c) Difficulty: (2) Knowledge: (F) Page: 405

15. When considering barriers that are faced by international marketers attempting to successfully advertise in foreign markets cultural constraints can pose huge difficulties. The trickiest problem within this category is usually posed by:

   a. the government.
   b. trade unions.
   c. environmental rights groups.
   d. women.
   e. the host country's religion(s).

Answer: (e) Difficulty: (3) Knowledge: (F) Page: 405

16. In Eastern Europe, lifestyle ads are apparently far less effective that informational ads. Eastern Europeans want to know the facts about the product before they buy. This would be an example of which of the following general barriers that block effective promotion in the international advertising environment?

   a. language barriers
   b. advertising regulations
   c. cultural constraints or barriers
   d. local attitudes toward advertising
   e. poor media infrastructure

Answer: (c) Difficulty: (2) Knowledge: (A) Page: 405

17. One framework that helps with studying the influence of culture on global advertising is the cultural classification scheme developed by Dutch researcher Geert Hofstede. All of the following are dimensions of a value system used in scheme <u>EXCEPT</u>:

a. power distance.
b. possessions.
c. uncertainty avoidance.
d. individualism.
e. masculinity.

Answer: (b) Difficulty: (2) Knowledge: (F) Page: 405

18. One framework that helps with studying the influence of culture on global advertising is the cultural classification scheme developed by Dutch researcher Geert Hofstede. One dimension refers to the degree of inequality that is seen as acceptable within the country. This dimension would best be described as:

a. power distance.
b. long-termism.
c. uncertainty avoidance.
d. individualism.
e. masculinity.

Answer: (a) Difficulty: (2) Knowledge: (F) Page: 405

19. One framework that helps with studying the influence of culture on global advertising is the cultural classification scheme developed by Dutch researcher Geert Hofstede. One dimension refers to the extent that people within the culture prefer structured situations with clear cut rules and little ambiguity. This dimension would best be described as:

a. power distance.
b. long-termism.
c. uncertainty avoidance.
d. individualism.
e. masculinity.

Answer: (c) Difficulty: (2) Knowledge: (F) Page: 405

20. If ads in a foreign country stress performance, success, and completion, they would probably be focusing on which of the following cultural classification schemes as way to reach a segment of the population where this dimension was high or important.

  a. power distance.
  b. long-termism.
  c. uncertainty avoidance.
  d. individualism.
  e. masculinity.

Answer: (e) Difficulty: (2) Knowledge: (A) Page: 405

21. If a company presented an ad with such future-directed values as thrift, perseverance, longevity to an audience in Japan, it would probably be directing its efforts toward which of the following cultural classification schemes?

  a. power distance.
  b. long-termism.
  c. uncertainty avoidance.
  d. individualism.
  e. masculinity.

Answer: (b) Difficulty: (2) Knowledge: (A) Page: 405

22. According to research into local attitudes toward advertising, only one of the countries listed below says that advertising is an important factor in judging and choosing a brand leader. Which country is it?

  a. Italy.
  b. Spain.
  c. United Kingdom.
  d. France.
  e. China.

Answer: (e) Difficulty: (3) Knowledge: (A) Page: 406, 408, Exhibit 14-4

23. A major roadblock that global advertisers face is the bewildering set of advertising regulations in foreign markets. All of the following are examples of advertising regulations or primary regulation categories EXCEPT:

a. advertising of "vice products" and pharmaceuticals.
b. comparative advertising.
c. content of advertising messages.
d. advertising towards children.
e. "subliminal advertising."

Answer: (e) Difficulty: (2) Knowledge: (F) Page: 409, 410

24. Ad regulations governing the advertising of cigarettes would probably fall under which of the following advertising regulation categories?
a. advertising of "vice products" and pharmaceuticals.
b. comparative advertising.
c. content of advertising messages.
d. advertising towards children.
e. alcohol advertising.

Answer: (a) Difficulty: (1) Knowledge: (A) Page: 409, 410

25. If advertisers disparage their competition in an advertisement, the regulation category that would govern this practice would probably be:
a. advertising of "vice products" and pharmaceuticals.
b. comparative advertising.
c. content of advertising messages.
d. advertising towards children.
e. alcohol advertising.

Answer: (b) Difficulty: (1) Knowledge: (F) Page: 409, 410

26. An ad ran in Australia that showed a house filling (and finally full of) with water. The ad was banned because it was ruled that it depicted a "wanton and irresponsible use of water." The regulation category that was most probably used to regulate this ad was:

a. advertising of "vice products" and pharmaceuticals.
b. comparative advertising.
c. content of advertising messages.
d. advertising towards children.
e. alcohol advertising.

Answer: (c) Difficulty: (2) Knowledge: (A) Page: 409, 410

27. Given that advertising regulations not only govern advertising in foreign markets but can also create difficulties, how can marketers cope? All of the following are valid suggestions EXCEPT:

a. keep track of regulations and pending legislation.
b. challenge regulations in court.
c. adapt the marketing mix strategy.
d. try to circumvent the regulation by using local advertisers.
e. lobby for favorable regulations or results.

Answer: (d) Difficulty: (2) Knowledge: (F) Page: 410, 411

28. With respect to budget forms for advertising, the _____ method simply sets the overall advertising budget based on either past or expected sales revenue.

a. percentage of sales
b. competitive parity
c. all-you-can-afford
d. objective-and-task
e. marginal increment

Answer: (a) Difficulty: (1) Knowledge: (F) Page: 412

29. The primary appeal of the percentage of sales method of allocating an advertising budget is its:

a. popularity.
b. accounting good sense.
c. control feature.
d. simplicity.
e. accuracy.

Answer: (d) Difficulty: (2) Knowledge: (F) Page: 412

30. The most popular of the budget methods (in fact, two-thirds of respondents in a survey said they had used the method) is the _____ method.

a. percentage of sales
b. competitive parity
c. all-you-can-afford
d. objective-and-task
e. marginal increment

Answer: (d) Difficulty: (2) Knowledge: (F) Page: 412, 413

31. If an advertiser does not want to "rock the boat" and desires to sustain a minimum "share of voice" they will probably choose which of the following advertising budget forms?

    a. percentage of sales
    b. competitive parity
    c. all-you-can-afford
    d. objective-and-task
    e. marginal increment

Answer: (b) Difficulty: (2) Knowledge: (F) Page: 412

32. If an advertiser spells out their goals of their communication strategy and determines what they would like to accomplish with advertising and then plans a budget accordingly, they are probably using the _____ method of budgeting.

    a. percentage of sales
    b. competitive parity
    c. all-you-can-afford
    d. objective-and-task
    e. marginal increment

Answer: (d) Difficulty: (1) Knowledge: (F) Page: 413

33. If an advertiser uses field experiments (such as systematically manipulating the spending amount in different areas within the country to measure the impact of advertising on the brand's awareness, sales volume, and market share) to adjust budget expenditures, they are probably using the _____ method of budgeting for advertising expense.

    a. percentage of sales
    b. competitive parity
    c. all-you-can-afford
    d. objective-and-task
    e. marginal increment

Answer: (d) Difficulty: (2) Knowledge: (A) Page: 413, 414

34. One of the most thorny issues that marketers face when developing a communication strategy is the choice of a:

a. proper media strategy.
b. proper budget method.
c. proper advertising theme.
d. proper position.
e. proper slogan.

Answer: (c) Difficulty: (3) Knowledge: (F) Page: 414

35. The major elements of a campaign are the message (what do we say) and the:

a. headline.
b. body copy.
c. execution.
d. tag line.
e. solution.

Answer: (c) Difficulty: (2) Knowledge: (F) Page: 414

36. A good case can be made for standardizing an ad campaign in the international marketplace. All of the following would be good, justifiable reasons for standardization EXCEPT:
a. scale economics.
b. consistent image.
c. government regulation.
d. global consumer segments.
e. creative talent.

Answer: (c) Difficulty: (2) Knowledge: (F) Page: 414-418

37. Message consistency (an advertising standardization issue) matters a great deal in markets with extensive media overlap or for goods that are sold to "cosmopolitan" customers who travel the globe. An example of a product or service that fits the above would best be described as being:

a. beer.
b. banking.
c. a beef product.
d. an automobile.
e. cosmetics.

Answer: (b) Difficulty: (3) Knowledge: (A) Page: 416

38. In the domain of advertising, _____ means that marketers encourage their affiliates to adopt, or at least consider, advertising ideas that have proven successful in other markets. Which of the following standardization benefits applies?

   a. scale economics
   b. consistent image
   c. cross-fertilization
   d. global consumer segments
   e. creative talent

Answer: (c) Difficulty: (2) Knowledge: (A) Page: 414-418

39. When Proctor & Gamble introduced Pantene shampoo in Latin America, it used a spot that was originally produced in Taiwan (only a few minor changes were made to allow for local and cultural differences). This would be an example of which of the following reasons for using standardization in the foreign market?

   a. scale economics
   b. consistent image
   c. cross-fertilization
   d. global consumer segments
   e. creative talent

Answer: (c) Difficulty: (2) Knowledge: (A) Page: 414-418

40. Research from an advertising agency survey indicates that the number one reason for standardizing multinational advertising was to:

   a. take advantage of demographics.
   b. take advantage of cultural similarities between the countries.
   c. capitalize on the fact that the product was standardized.
   d. make full use of a proven successful idea.
   e. create a single brand image in all markets.

Answer: (e) Difficulty: (3) Knowledge: (A) Page: 418

41. All of the following are barriers to standardization in international advertising EXCEPT:

    a. cultural differences.
    b. budget.
    c. advertising regulations.
    d. differences in the degree of market development.
    e. the "Not Invented Here" syndrome.

Answer: (b) Difficulty: (2) Knowledge: (F) Page: 418

42. As an illustration of a barrier to advertising standardization, Ray-Ban had to re-shoot a sunglasses commercial for Malaysia because the original version had Caucasian actors. In Malaysia, ads featuring Caucasians are not allowed. This example would be an example of which of the following barriers to standardization of international advertising?

    a. cultural differences.
    b. budget.
    c. advertising regulations.
    d. differences in the degree of market development.
    e. the "Not Invented Here" syndrome.

Answer: (c) Difficulty: (2) Knowledge: (A) Page: 420

43. There are a variety of formats for creating international advertising. With _____ advertising, the creative strategy is highly centralized. Universal copy is developed for all markets.

    a. export
    b. import
    c. prototype (pattern)
    d. concept cooperation
    e. psychological

Answer: (a) Difficulty: (2) Knowledge: (F) Page: 421-423

44. Case histories, superior quality, new product/service, and lifestyle are all examples of _____ advertising. This form of advertising has a highly centralized creative strategy and universal copy is developed for all markets.

    a. export
    b. import
    c. prototype (pattern)
    d. concept cooperation
    e. psychological

Answer: (a) Difficulty: (2) Knowledge: (A) Page: 421-423, Exhibit 14-9

45. There are a variety of formats for creating international advertising. With _____ advertising, guidelines are given to local affiliates concerning the execution of the advertising. The guidelines are then conveyed via manuals or tapes.

    a. export
    b. import
    c. prototype (pattern)
    d. concept cooperation
    e. psychological

Answer: (c) Difficulty: (2) Knowledge: (F) Page: 421-423

46. There are a variety of formats for creating international advertising. With _____ advertising, guidelines usually center around the positioning theme to be used in the ads rather than the execution. Responsibility for the execution is left to the local offices.

    a. export
    b. import
    c. prototype (pattern)
    d. concept cooperation
    e. psychological

Answer: (d) Difficulty: (3) Knowledge: (F) Page: 421-423

47. There are a variety of formats for creating international advertising. With _____ advertising, guidelines usually center around the positioning theme to be used in the ads rather than the execution. As an illustration of this technique, Chivas Regal produced twenty-four ads (all using the same slogan) and allowed local affiliates to pick which ads they wanted to run.

a. export
b. import
c. prototype (pattern)
d. concept cooperation
e. psychological

Answer: (d) Difficulty: (3) Knowledge: (A) Page: 421-423

48. Another term to describe the portfolio of media choices (and variations within those choices) is called:

a. media decision making.
b. media super structure.
c. media infrastructure.
d. media bias.
e. media method.

Answer: (c) Difficulty: (1) Knowledge: (F) Page: 423

49. Using the cost-per-thousand (CPM) criterion, research has shown that most expensive TV (peak time period) country market (at over $23 per 1000 reached) is:

a. Italy.
b. United States.
c. Japan.
d. Germany.
e. Switzerland.

Answer: (e) Difficulty: (3) Knowledge: (F) Page: 425, Exhibit 14-12

50. Using the cost-per-thousand (CPM) criterion, research has shown that <u>least</u> expensive TV (peak time period) country market (at under $5 per 1000 reached) is:

a. Italy.
b. United States.
c. Japan.
d. Germany.
e. Switzerland.

Answer: (c) Difficulty: (3) Knowledge: (F) Page: 425, Exhibit 14-12

51. Using the cost-per-thousand (CPM) criterion, research has shown that <u>most</u> expensive newspaper country market (at over $21 per 1000 reached) is:
a. Italy.
b. United States.
c. Japan.
d. France.
e. Switzerland.

Answer: (d) Difficulty: (3) Knowledge: (F) Page: 425, Exhibit 14-12

52. Using the cost-per-thousand (CPM) criterion, research has shown that <u>most</u> expensive magazine country market (at over $18 per 1000 reached) is:
a. Italy.
b. United States.
c. Japan.
d. France.
e. Switzerland.

Answer: (e) Difficulty: (3) Knowledge: (F) Page: 425, Exhibit 14-12

53. All of the following can be characterized as being significant trends or developments in the international media landscape <u>EXCEPT</u>:

a. growing commercialization and deregulation of mass media.
b. shift from radio and print to TV advertising.
c. rise of global media.
d. growing importance of state controlled advertising.
e. improved monitoring.

Answer: (d) Difficulty: (2) Knowledge: (F) Page: 426, 427

54. Informercial marketers now have access to over one-half of Japanese consumers. Which of the following trends would be most representative or closely associated with the above fact?

    a. growing commercialization and deregulation of mass media.
    b. shift from radio and print to TV advertising.
    c. rise of global media.
    d. growing importance of multimedia advertising tools.
    e. improved monitoring.

Answer: (b) Difficulty: (2) Knowledge: (A) Page: 426, 427

55. In Hong Kong, scores of consultants now assist marketers with the set-up and upkeep of Web-sites (especially, in other countries where the client has no expertise). This is an example of which of the following trends?

    a. growing commercialization and deregulation of mass media.
    b. shift from radio and print to TV advertising.
    c. rise of global media.
    d. growing importance of multimedia advertising tools.
    e. improved monitoring.

Answer: (d) Difficulty: (3) Knowledge: (A) Page: 426, 427

56. When screening ad agencies, all of the following criteria might be used EXCEPT:

    a. market coverage.
    b. cost of agency talent and expense.
    c. quality of coverage.
    d. expertise with developing a central international campaign.
    e. scope and quality of support services.

Answer: (b) Difficulty: (3) Knowledge: (F) Page: 428, 429

57. _____ occurs when a firm contributes to the local distributor's advertising spending activities.

    a. Screening advertising
    b. National advertising
    c. Local advertising
    d. Cooperative advertising
    e. Group channel advertising

Answer: (d) Difficulty: (2) Knowledge: (F) Page: 429

58. When dealing with foreign market distributors, Blistex set up an advertising fund from which each distributor could withdraw money up to a certain amount to fund advertising activities. This would be an example of which of the following advertising forms or formats?

    a. screening advertising
    b. national advertising
    c. local advertising
    d. cooperative advertising
    e. group channel advertising

Answer: (d) Difficulty: (2) Knowledge: (A) Page: 430

59. _____ refer(s) to a collection of short-term incentive tools that lead to quicker and/or larger sales of a particular product by consumers or the trade.

    a. Advertising
    b. Sales promotion
    c. Direct marketing
    d. Promotion
    e. Publicity

Answer: (b) Difficulty: (2) Knowledge: (F) Page: 432

60. Sampling, price-offs, coupons, sweepstakes, bonus packs, and trade allowances are all examples of _____.
    a. Advertising
    b. Sales promotion
    c. Direct marketing
    d. Public relations
    e. Publicity

Answer: (b) Difficulty: (2) Knowledge: (A) Page: 432

61. All of the following explain the local nature of sales promotion for the multinational corporation EXCEPT:

    a. economic development.
    b. market maturity.
    c. cultural perceptions.
    d. trade structure.
    e. new product development.

Answer: (e) Difficulty: (3) Knowledge: (F) Page: 432, 433

62. One study of promotional practices in developing countries found above-average use of samples and price-off packs. Which of the following reasons or support for localization of sales promotion for multinational corporations would most likely fit with this example?

    a. economic development
    b. market maturity
    c. cultural perceptions
    d. trade structure
    e. government regulations

Answer: (a) Difficulty: (2) Knowledge: (A) Page: 432, 433

63. If promotional dollars are aimed at the end-user, then the strategy is described as being a _____ strategy.

    a. push
    b. pull
    c. conventional
    d. vertical
    e. horizontal

Answer: (b) Difficulty: (1) Knowledge: (A) Page: 433

64. If promotional dollars are aimed at the trade or distributor, then the strategy is described as being a _____ strategy.
    a. push
    b. pull
    c. conventional
    d. vertical
    e. horizontal

Answer: (a) Difficulty: (1) Knowledge: (A) Page: 433

65. Proctor & Gamble has attempted to cut back on _____ strategy incentives by introducing every-day-low-pricing.

    a. push
    b. pull
    c. conventional
    d. vertical
    e. horizontal

Answer: (a) Difficulty: (1) Knowledge: (A) Page: 433

65. If Heineken brewery sponsors the Rugby World Cup, this would be an example of which of the following promotional forms?

    a. sales promotion
    b. event sponsorship
    c. trade shows
    d. publicity
    e. public relations

Answer: (b) Difficulty: (1) Knowledge: (F) Page: 433

66. Being the official timekeeper (such as TAG Heuer, a Swiss watchmaker) of the Olympics would be an example of which of the following promotional forms?

    a. sales promotion
    b. event sponsorship
    c. trade shows
    d. publicity
    e. public relations

Answer: (b) Difficulty: (1) Knowledge: (A) Page: 433, 434

67. All of the following are risks associated with event sponsorship EXCEPT:

    a. nonsponsors can come in.
    b. too many sponsorships might be sold.
    c. there might be clutter among the sponsors and their messages.
    d. the sponsorship might be to expensive for the number of people that show up.
    e. adequate protection of the sponsorship.

Answer: (d) Difficulty: (3) Knowledge: (F) Page: 434

68. Which of the following promotional forms accounts for one-fifth of U.S. and one-fourth of European firms communications budgets?

    a. sales promotion
    b. event sponsorship
    c. trade shows
    d. publicity
    e. public relations

Answer: (c) Difficulty: (2) Knowledge: (F) Page: 434

69. In a modern sense, the goal of many MNCs is to pursue a(n)_____
    program. In this program, coordination of all communication vehicles would take
    place. Key ideas would be communicated in a unified manner.

    a. vertical communications
    b. horizontal communications
    c. integrated marketing communications
    d. global communications
    e. synergistic communications

Answer: (c) Difficulty: (2) Knowledge: (F) Page: 435

True/False   *Short Answer*

1. The first step in developing a promotional plan in international marketing is to
   set specific campaign objectives (strategic and operational).

Answer: (False) Difficulty: (2) Knowledge: (F) Page: 401, 402

2. Of the five types of constraints that a firm might run into with communicating with
   customers overseas, cultural barriers pose the biggest stumbling block in
   international advertising.

Answer: (True) Difficulty: (1) Knowledge: (F) Page: 405

3. Language barriers can occur through translation problems. The most common of
   these translation difficulties are due to _____ , multiple-meaning
   words, and idioms.

Answer: (simple carelessness) Difficulty: (3) Knowledge: (F) Page: 402

4. Language barriers can occur through translation problems. If the original slogan
   was "Body by Fisher" and the translation was "Corpse by Fisher," the problem with
   translation was probably due to a problem idiom.

Answer: (False) Difficulty: (2) Knowledge: (A) Page: 402

5. Idioms that use slang from one country to another may inadvertently lead to
   embarrassing meanings in the host country.

Answer: (True) Difficulty: (1) Knowledge: (F) Page: 404

6. One obvious cure for misinterpreted meanings of advertising slogans in foreign countries is to reduce the usage of slogans.

Answer: (False) Difficulty: (2) Knowledge: (F) Page: 404

7. With respect to advertising, probably the trickiest of the cultural barriers centers around the host country's religion.

Answer: (True) Difficulty: (2) Knowledge: (F) Page: 405

8. One framework that helps with studying the influence of culture on global advertising is the cultural classification scheme developed by Geert Hofstede. The value system construct that refers to the degree of inequality that is seen as acceptable within the country is called _____.

Answer: (power distance) Difficulty: (3) Knowledge: (F) Page: 405

9. One framework that helps with studying the influence of culture on global advertising is the cultural classification scheme developed by Geert Hofstede. One of these constructs is called power distance. Research has shown that ads that position products or services as status symbols are most likely to be effective in countries with large power distance.

Answer: (True) Difficulty: (2) Knowledge: (A) Page: 405

10. One framework that helps with studying the influence of culture on global advertising is the cultural classification scheme developed by Geert Hofstede. The value system construct that refers to the extent that people within the culture prefer structured situations with clear-cut rules and little ambiguity is called

_____.

Answer: (uncertainty avoidance) Difficulty: (3) Knowledge: (F) Page: 405

11. Ad campaigns that center around the hard-sell approach (such as testimonials) are advisable for cultures with high uncertainty avoidance such as the United States.

Answer: (False) Difficulty: (2) Knowledge: (A) Page: 405

12. An example of a country that scores high of the long-termism construct is Japan. In other words, ads developed with a high amount of this construct would consider projecting long-term oriented values in their message appeals.

Answer: (True) Difficulty: (2) Knowledge: (A) Page: 405, 406

13. Advertising is a primary determinant for consumers choosing a brand leader.

Answer: (True) Difficulty: (1) Knowledge: (F) Page: 406

14. Chinese citizens rank advertising as the chief reason for choosing a brand leader. China ranks ahead of even the United States in this respect.

Answer: (True) Difficulty: (1) Knowledge: (A) Page: 408

15. _____ advertising often disparages the competing brand.

Answer: (Comparative) Difficulty: (2) Knowledge: (F) Page: 409

16. With respect to budget forms that can be used in advertising, the _____ method simply sets the overall advertising budget as a percentage of sales.

Answer: (Percentage of sales) Difficulty: (1) Knowledge: (F) Page: 412

17. With respect to budget forms that can be used in advertising, the _____ method uses competition's spending as a benchmark and provides the measure of the optimal spending amount.

Answer: (competitive parity) Difficulty: (2) Knowledge: (F) Page: 412

18. The most popular budgeting rule is the objective-and-task method.

Answer: (True) Difficulty: (1) Knowledge: (F) Page: 413

19. One of the chief merits of an adaptive advertising campaign is scale economics.

Answer: (False) Difficulty: (2) Knowledge: (F) Page: 414

20. In the domain of advertising, _____ means that marketers encourage their affiliates to adopt, or at least consider, advertising ideas that have proven successful in other markets.

Answer: (cross-fertilization) Difficulty: (3) Knowledge: (F) Page: 417

21. When a marketer provides monetary incentives to their respective distributors to get some level of coordination it is called _____ advertising.

Answer: (cooperative) Difficulty: (3) Knowledge: (F) Page: 429

Essay

1. The steps in developing a promotional plan in international marketing are by and large similar to the sequence in domestic marketing. List each step and comment on which of the steps that you perceive to be the most important.

Answer:

a. Select target audience and positioning theme.
b. Set specific campaign objectives (strategic and operational).
c. Determine the promotional budget.
d. Develop a message strategy.
e. Decide on a media strategy.
f. Monitor and assess campaign effectiveness.

If students are thinking correctly, they should be able to make a case for Step a or b as being the most important. Each answer should be reviewed as to content.

Difficulty: (1) Knowledge: (F) Page: 402

2. List and discuss the major challenges faced by international advertisers.

Answer:

To answer this question, the students should review each of the subjects listed below. These major constraints (challenges) require special attention. Each may be discussed in detail or the students may be assigned individual areas for special study. Additional information is found in the first section of the chapter. Major issues of concern are:

Language Barriers.
Cultural Barriers.
Local Attitudes toward Advertising.
Media Infrastructure.
Advertising Regulations.

Difficulty: (3) Knowlege: (F) Page: 402-411

3. How should marketers cope with advertising regulations?

Answer:

Possible actions include:
   a. Keep track of regulations and pending legislation.
   b. Lobbying activities.
   c. Challenge regulations in court.
   d. Adapt marketing mix strategy.

Difficulty: (1) Knowledge: (F) Page: 410-411

4. What situations are conducive to localization of advertising from the viewpoint of the international advertiser?

Answer:

Several factors entice international advertisers to localize their advertising as opposed to using a standardization policy. The barriers to standardization (promote localization) include:
a. Cultural differences.
b. Advertising regulations.
c. Market maturity.
d. "Not-invented-here" (NIH) syndrome

Difficulty: (2) Knowledge: (F) Page: 418-421

5. Global or pan-regional advertising approaches require a great deal of coordination across and communication among the various subsidiaries of the firm. What are the mechanisms that can facilitate the coordination of global advertising?

Answer:

Mechanisms that facilitate coordination include:
   a. Monetary incentives (cooperative advertising).
   b. Advertising manuals.
   c. Feedback via the Internet.
   d. Lead-country concept.
   e. Global or pan-regional meetings.

Difficulty: (2) Knowledge: (2) Page: 429

Chapter 15

Multiple Choice

1. The form of selling that best describes the way that the majority of cars are sold in Japan is:

   a. at car lots or dealerships.
   b. via the Internet.
   c. by door-to-door salespeople.
   d. direct from the manufacturer.
   e. via used car lots.

Answer: (c) Difficulty: (2) Knowledge: (A) Page: 439

2. All of the following are tasks of the average salesperson <u>EXCEPT</u>:

   a. take orders.
   b. deliver products.
   c. repair products.
   d. educate consumers.
   e. provide technical knowledge.

Answer: (c) Difficulty: (1) Knowledge: (F) Page: 439

3. The salesperson can best be described as being the _____ for the company.

   a. support mechanism
   b. front line
   c. mouthpiece
   d. promoter
   e. educator

Answer: (b) Difficulty: (2) Knowledge: (F) Page: 439

4. Many foreign countries have their own unique adaptations of the selling process. In _____, the primary method for selling cars is to use door-to-door people.

  a. Russia
  b. the United States
  c. Holland
  d. Peru
  e. Japan

Answer: (e) Difficulty: (3) Knowledge: (A) Page: 440

5. When researchers try to put the word international into sales management and personal selling, clarification is needed. _____ considerations include issues that analyze more than one country's assets, strengths, and situations, or that deal directly with cross-border coordination.

  a. International product
  b. International strategy
  c. International mix
  d. Intercultural
  e. Global society

Answer: (b) Difficulty: (1) Knowledge: (F) Page: 440

6. When researchers try to put the word international into sales management and personal selling, clarification is needed. _____ considerations include issues that focus on the culture of the foreign country and its impact on operations within that country.

  a. International product
  b. International strategy
  c. International mix
  d. Intercultural
  e. Global society

Answer: (d) Difficulty: (2) Knowledge: (F) Page: 440

7. All of the following are examples of international sales strategy issues EXCEPT:

   a. sales force skill availability.
   b. selling style differences.
   c. country image.
   d. expatriate recruiting.
   e. centralized training.

Answer: (b) Difficulty: (3) Knowledge: (F) Page: 441, Exhibit 15-1

8. Which of the following is an example of an issue that is addressed by intercultural issues with the foreign country?

   a. sales force skill availability.
   b. selling style differences.
   c. country image.
   d. expatriate recruiting.
   e. centralized training.

Answer: (b) Difficulty: (3) Knowledge: (F) Page: 441, Exhibit 15-1

9. All of the following are examples of intercultural issues with the foreign country EXCEPT:

   a. motivation.
   b. cultural sensitivity.
   c. ethical standards.
   d. relationship building.
   e. home to host communications.

Answer: (e) Difficulty: (2) Knowledge: (F) Page: 441, Exhibit 15-1

10. Which of the following is an example of an issue faced by international sales strategy?

   a. motivation.
   b. cultural sensitivity.
   c. ethical standards.
   d. relationship building.
   e. home to host communications.

Answer: (e) Difficulty: (3) Knowledge: (F) Page: 441, Exhibit 15-1

11. Sales force skill availability, company image, expatriate recruiting, and centralized training are issues relevant to _____ considerations.

   a. international product
   b. international sales strategy
   c. international mix
   d. intercultural issues with the foreign country
   e. global society

Answer: (b) Difficulty: (2) Knowledge: (F) Page: 441, Exhibit 15-1

12. Motivation, cultural sensitivity, ethical standards, fairness, and relationship building are issues relevant to _____ considerations.

   a. international product
   b. international sales strategy
   c. international mix
   d. intercultural issues with the foreign country
   e. global society

Answer: (d) Difficulty: (1) Knowledge: (F) Page: 441, Exhibit 15-1

13. In the sales management "process," the first step is where the manager:

   a. sets objectives and strategy.
   b. determines goals and purposes.
   c. recruits.
   d. trains.
   e. supervises.

Answer: (a) Difficulty: (2) Knowledge: (F) Page: 441

14. A key decision that a market must make with respect to international marketing is _____. This decision limits and defines key underlying aspects of its future sales force management.

   a. which market to enter
   b. how much to spend in a market
   c. how to enter the market
   d. how far should a market be entered
   e. how long to stay in a market

Answer: (c) Difficulty: (3) Knowledge: (A) Page: 441

15. The _____ in(into) a market will determine how large the sales force needs to be, and will influence how much training it will require.

a. form of marketing
b. form of entry
c. form of promotion
d. form of commission
e. form of management

Answer: (b) Difficulty: (2) Knowledge: (F) Page: 441

16. How large a sales force needs to be, how much training the sales force will need, whether the sales force is predominately local or foreign, and the manner of compensation are all issues influenced by the _____ in(into) a market.

a. form of marketing
b. form of entry
c. form of promotion
d. form of commission
e. form of management

Answer: (b) Difficulty: (2) Knowledge: (F) Page: 441

17. With respect to sales and sales management, the entry method in a market is also called the _____.

a. zone process.
b. level of migration.
c. level of expatriation.
d. level of complexity.
e. level of integration.

Answer: (e) Difficulty: (3) Knowledge: (F) Page: 441

18. With respect to sales and sales management entry into a foreign market, _____ integration refers to greater ownership and control of the distribution channel.
a. vertical
b. horizontal
c. forward
d. backward
e. dual

Answer: (c) Difficulty: (2) Knowledge: (A) Page: 441

19. If a company begins its foreign sales by exporting through a merchant distributor who takes title to the product and performs all the necessary foreign sales functions, this would be a form of _____ integration.

 a. vertical
 b. horizontal
 c. forward
 d. backward
 e. dual

Answer: (c) Difficulty: (3) Knowledge: (A) Page: 441

20. If a company begins its foreign sales by exporting through merchant distributors and then purchases a foreign sales subsidiary and locates product warehouses abroad, this would be a form of _____ integration.

 a. vertical
 b. horizontal
 c. forward
 d. backward
 e. dual

Answer: (c) Difficulty: (3) Knowledge: (A) Page: 442

21. All of the following situations indicate that greater forward integration is necessary by the exporting organization, EXCEPT:

 a. the operation is large enough to spread out the overhead costs of owning and maintaining an infrastructure.
 b. the operation is large enough to spread out the costs of training and supervising employees.
 c. the company has an inability to enforce contractual obligations on outside intermediaries.
 d. sales service is needed in the foreign country.
 e. expatriates will not go to a foreign country.

Answer: (e) Difficulty: (2) Knowledge: (F) Page: 442

22. If a company's operation is large enough to spread out the overhead costs of owning and maintaining an infrastructure and training and supervising employees, then the company will probably have a greater _____ integration level.
    a. forward
    b. horizontal
    c. vertical
    d. backward
    e. dual

Answer: (a) Difficulty: (2) Knowledge: (A) Page: 442

23. Which of the following degrees of involvement would probably be in use when Export Management Companies, Export Trading Companies, or direct exporting are being used by the firm?

    a. Limited Foreign Involvement and Visibility
    b. Local Management and Sales Force
    c. Expatriate Management and Local Sales Force (Mixed)
    d. Heavy to Complete Expatriate Sales Force
    e. Maximum Global control and world wide ownership

Answer: (a) Difficulty: (1) Knowledge: (A) Page: 442, Exhibit 15-2

24. Which of the following degrees of involvement would probably be in use when piggybacking and selling through chains are used by the firm?
    a. Limited Foreign Involvement and Visibility
    b. Local Management and Sales Force
    c. Expatriate Management and Local Sales Force (Mixed)
    d. Heavy to Complete Expatriate Sales Force
    e. Maximum Global control and world wide ownership

Answer: (b) Difficulty: (2) Knowledge: (A) Page: 442, Exhibit 15-2

25. Which of the following degrees of involvement would probably be in use when there is a traveling global sales force and high technology experts are used by the firm?

    a. Limited Foreign Involvement and Visibility
    b. Local Management and Sales Force
    c. Expatriate Management and Local Sales Force (Mixed)
    d. Heavy to Complete Expatriate Sales Force
    e. Maximum Global control and world wide ownership

Answer: (d) Difficulty: (2) Knowledge: (A) Page: 442, Exhibit 15-2

26. If the company describes its situation as being concerned with a contract for sales from the U.S., no sales force or representatives abroad, and little or no control over the foreign marketing process, the firm will probably use which form of involvement listed below?

   a. Limited Foreign Involvement and Visibility
   b. Local Management and Sales Force
   c. Expatriate Management and Local Sales Force (Mixed)
   d. Heavy to Complete Expatriate Sales Force
   e. Maximum Global control and world wide ownership

Answer: (a) Difficulty: (2) Knowledge: (A) Page: 442, Exhibit 15-2

27. If the company uses expatriates to oversee sales regions and lead training, the firm will probably use which form of involvement listed below?

   a. Limited Foreign Involvement and Visibility
   b. Local Management and Sales Force
   c. Expatriate Management and Local Sales Force (Mixed)
   d. Heavy to Complete Expatriate Sales Force
   e. Maximum Global control and world wide ownership

Answer: (c) Difficulty: (2) Knowledge: (A) Page: 442, Exhibit 15-2

28. Selling through an Export Management Company (EMC) or an Export Trading Company (ETC) is considered a _____ involvement approach to international sales.

   a. low
   b. middle
   c. high
   d. backward
   e. parallel

Answer: (a) Difficulty: (1) Knowledge: (F) Page: 443

29. _____ serve(s) the needs of their clients in entering a market or sourcing goods from a market. They are characterized by their "service" nature and efforts to interact with and meet the needs of the exporter client.

a. A foreign franchise
b. An Export Trading Company
c. An Export Management Company
d. A Noraizi agent
e. A bulk-breaker

Answer: (c) Difficulty: (2) Knowledge: (F) Page: 443

30. _____ is usually large conglomerates that import, export, countertrade, invest, and manufacture in the global arena.

a. A foreign franchise
b. An Export Trading Company
c. An Export Management Company
d. A Noraizi agent
e. A bulk-breaker

Answer: (b) Difficulty: (2) Knowledge: (F) Page: 443

31. Sogoshosha (such as Mitsubishi, Mitsui, Sumitomo, and Marubeni) are the Japanese equivalents of a(n) _____.
a. a foreign franchise.
b. an Export Trading Company.
c. an Export Management Company.
d. a dealer network.
e. a bulk-breaker.

Answer: (b) Difficulty: (2) Knowledge: (A) Page: 443

32. If a company follows a _____ involvement path, it normally gives up the ability to motivate and monitor the sales force and to train them to better serve the customer.

a. low
b. middle
c. high
d. backward
e. parallel

Answer: (a) Difficulty: (1) Knowledge: (F) Page: 443

33. _____ involvement approaches to foreign sales are those approaches in which the company controls some portion of the distribution process.

    a. Low-level
    b. Mid-level
    c. High-level
    d. Backward level
    e. Parallel level

Answer: (b) Difficulty: (1) Knowledge: (F) Page: 444

34. When a company has the _____ involvement approach, the company (because it uses either host country employees or expatriates) must face the foreign culture and intercultural communication can become an issue that must be dealt with through training.

    a. low-level
    b. mid-level
    c. high-level
    d. backward level
    e. parallel level

Answer: (b) Difficulty: (2) Knowledge: (A) Page: 444

35. When a company has the _____ involvement approach, the company substantially controls the foreign distribution channels.
    a. low-level
    b. mid-level
    c. high-level
    d. backward level
    e. parallel level

Answer: (c) Difficulty: (1) Knowledge: (F) Page: 444

36. As an example of a company that has the _____ involvement approach, the company will generally own warehouses where goods are stored and/or own outlets where products are sold.
    a. low-level
    b. mid-level
    c. high-level
    d. backward level
    e. parallel level

Answer: (c) Difficulty: (2) Knowledge: (A) Page: 444

37. Which of the following forms of company sales involvement generally have the highest involvement of expatriates?

    a. low-level
    b. mid-level
    c. high-level
    d. backward level
    e. parallel level

Answer: (b) Difficulty: (2) Knowledge: (A) Page: 444

38. Which of the following forms of company sales involvement generally have the lowest involvement of expatriates?

    a. low-level
    b. mid-level
    c. high-level
    d. backward level
    e. parallel level

Answer: (a) Difficulty: (2) Knowledge: (A) Page: 444

39. Which of the following statements MOST accurately describes the state of international selling?

    a. At the level of personal selling there is little true international selling.
    b. International selling is a function of the degree of involvement.
    c. Because of the global nature of business today, global selling transcends international boundaries.
    d. International selling will never work.
    e. International selling is tightly monitored by most governments because of the potential for funds outflow.

Answer: (a) Difficulty: (3) Knowledge: (F) Page: 445

40. Which of the following statements MOST accurately describes the state of international selling?

    a. Despite growing "international sales," salespeople typically work only in one region.
    b. International selling is a function of the degree of involvement.
    c. Because of the global nature of business today, global selling transcends international boundaries.
    d. International selling will never work.
    e. International selling is tightly monitored by most governments because of the potential for funds outflow.

Answer: (a) Difficulty: (3) Knowledge: (F) Page: 445

41. Which of the following statements about international selling is LEAST accurately describes the state of international selling?

    a. At the level of personal selling there is little true international selling.
    b. Despite growing "international sales," salespeople typically work only in one region.
    c. Generally, salespeople carry out the majority of their sales within one country.
    d. A salesperson selling big-ticket items such as airplanes may sell to many countries.
    e. Personal selling today (because of the size on most corporations) has become a highly impersonal activity.

Answer: (e) Difficulty: (2) Knowledge: (F) Page: 445

42. A _____ occurs when we group people (from what might appear to us as very similar cultures) together in perhaps an inappropriate manner because those people consider themselves to be different.

    a. cultural onomonopea
    b. cultural adiaphoria
    c. cultural generalization
    d. cultural syncopation
    e. cultural similarity

Answer: (c) Difficulty: (2) Knowledge: (F) Page: 446

43. Germans are typically viewed as scientifically exacting and industrious people. However, the typical German manufacturing work week is only thirty hours and the workers jealously guard their free time and show little interest in working overtime. This would be an example of the dangers of _____.

    a. cultural onomonopea
    b. cultural adiaphoria
    c. cultural generalization
    d. cultural syncopation
    e. cultural similarity

Answer: (c) Difficulty: (2) Knowledge: (A) Page: 446

44. If a marketing manager were to mistakenly group South Koreans and Japanese together (either as a market or by business and labor practices), this would be an example of a _____ problem.

    a. cultural onomonopea
    b. cultural adiaphoria
    c. cultural generalization
    d. cultural syncopation
    e. cultural similarity

Answer: (c) Difficulty: (2) Knowledge: (A) Page: 446

45. Based on Geert Hofstede's cultural dimensions scale, which of the following countries
    most likely scores high on the power distance scale?

    a. Japan
    b. United States
    c. Germany
    d. Australia
    e. Canada

Answer: (a) Difficulty: (1) Knowledge: (A) Page: 447, Exhibit 15-3

46. Based on Geert Hofstede's cultural dimensions scale, which of the following countries

    most likely scores high on the individualism versus collectivism scale?

    a. Japan
    b. United States
    c. China
    d. Mexico
    e. Pakistan

Answer: (b) Difficulty: (1) Knowledge: (A) Page: 447, Exhibit 15-3

47. Based on Geert Hofstede's cultural dimensions scale, which of the following countries

    most likely scores high on the uncertainty avoidance scale?

    a. Hong Kong
    b. United States
    c. Great Britain
    d. Mexico
    e. Pakistan

Answer: (d) Difficulty: (2) Knowledge: (A) Page: 447, Exhibit 15-3

48. Based on Geert Hofstede's cultural dimensions scale, which of the following countries

    most likely scores high on the long-term orientation scale?

    a. Hong Kong
    b. United States
    c. Great Britain
    d. Germany
    e. Pakistan

Answer: (a) Difficulty: (2) Knowledge: (A) Page: 447, Exhibit 15-3

49. The _____ at a company helps to determine the norms of behavior and the mood at the workplace.

    a. office manager
    b. focus

c. objectives

d. corporate culture

e. CFO

Answer: (d) Difficulty: (1) Knowlege: (F) Page: 446

50. If a company attempted to integrate men and women in the sales force in Saudi Arabia, the company would have to deal with _____ problems.

a. focus

b. vision

c. mission

d. corporate culture

e. country culture

Answer: (e) Difficulty: (1) Knowledge: (A) Page: 448

51. One popular tool for characterizing people that addresses their cognitive styles is the _____.

a. Kelsey-Ciebold scale.

b. Johns-Hopkins initial perception scale.

c. Majors-Hawkins Cognitive Indicator.

d. Myers-Briggs Type Indicator

e. Spaniel test.

Answer: (d) Difficulty: (2) Knowledge: (F) Page: 448

52. The _____ classifies people on four personal dimensions. These are extrovert versus introvert, sensing versus intuitive, thinking versus feeling, and judging versus perceiving.

a. Hartman profile

b. Myers-Briggs Type Indicator

c. Majors-Hawkins Cognitive Indicator

d. Spaniel test for concepts

e. Freudian fantasy test

Answer: (b) Difficulty: (2) Knowledge: (F) Page: 448

53. According to the Myers-Briggs Type Indicator test, the _____ tends to rely on the environment for guidance, be action-oriented, sociable, and communicate with ease and frankness.

a. extrovert

b. introvert

c. sensing person

d. intuitive person

e. thinking person

Answer: (a) Difficulty: (2) Knowledge: (F) Page: 448, Exhibit 15-4

54. According to the Myers-Briggs Type Indicator test, the _____ tends to show a greater concern with concepts and ideas than with external events, relative detachment, and enjoyment of solitude and privacy over companionship.

a. extrovert

b. introvert

c. sensing person

d. intuitive person

e. thinking person

Answer: (b) Difficulty: (2) Knowledge: (F) Page: 448, Exhibit 15-4

55. According to the Myers-Briggs Type Indicator test, the _____ tends to focus on immediate experience, become more realistic and practical, and develop skills such as acute powers of observation and memory for details.

a. extrovert

b. introvert

c. sensing person

d. intuitive person

e. thinking person

Answer: (c) Difficulty: (3) Knowledge: (F) Page: 448, Exhibit 15-4

56. According to the Myers-Briggs Type Indicator test, the _____ tends to value the possibility and meaning more than immediate experience, and become more imaginative, theoretical, abstract, and future oriented.
a. extrovert

b. introvert

c. sensing person

d. intuitive person

e. thinking person

Answer: (d) Difficulty: (3) Knowledge: (F) Page: 448, Exhibit 15-4

57. All of the following are steps in the sales force management process EXCEPT:

a. setting sales force objectives.

b. designing sales force strategy.

c. recruiting and selecting salespeople.
d. commission system management.
e. supervising salespeople.

Answer: (d) Difficulty: (2) Knowledge: (F) Page: 450

58. The first step in the sales force management process is best described as being:

a. designing sales force strategy.
b. setting sales force objectives.
c. recruiting and selecting salespeople.
d. commission system management.
e. supervising salespeople.

Answer: (b) Difficulty: (2) Knowledge: (F) Page: 450

59. The _____ state explicitly what the sales force will be asked to do.

a. sales force strategy
b. sales force objectives
c. sales force training procedures
d. sales force recruiting procedures
e. sales force evaluation procedures

Answer: (b) Difficulty: (2) Knowledge: (F) Page: 450

60. Setting sales force objectives internationally will not only depend on the company goals but will also depend on:

a. the training procedures.
b. the recruiting procedures.
c. the evaluation procedures.
d. an analysis of the culture and the values of the country it is entering.
e. management standards for excellence.

Answer: (d) Difficulty: (2) Knowledge: (F) Page: 451

61. _____ addresses the structure, size, and compensation of the sales force.

a. Sales force objectives
b. Sales force goals
c. Sales force strategy
d. Sales force policy
e. Sales force vision

Answer: (c) Difficulty: (2) Knowledge: (F) Page: 451

62. With respect to the functions of sales force strategy, the _____ refers to and determines the physical positioning and responsibilities of each salesperson.

    a. size
    b. structure
    c. compensation procedure
    d. modeling procedure
    e. evaluation procedure

Answer: (b) Difficulty: (1) Knowledge: (F) Page: 451

63. With respect to sales force structure, the _____ sales force has each salesperson responsible for a particular area (reporting up the line to regional sales managers).

    a. territorial
    b. product
    c. customer
    d. matrix
    e. "open plan"

Answer: (a) Difficulty: (1) Knowledge: (F) Page: 451

64. With respect to sales force structure, the _____ sales force has each salesperson sell only one product or product line (even when selling to a single customer).
    a. territorial
    b. product
    c. customer
    d. matrix
    e. "open plan"

Answer: (b) Difficulty: (1) Knowledge: (F) Page: 451

65. With respect to sales force structure, the _____ sales force has account managers responsible for particular clients.

    a. territorial
    b. product

c. customer

d. matrix

e. "open plan"

Answer: (c) Difficulty: (1) Knowledge: (F) Page: 451

66. _____ the sales force means directing and motivating the sales force to fulfill the company's objectives and providing the resources to allow them to do so.

a. Recruiting

b. Training

c. Evaluating

d. Supervising

e. Compensating

Answer: (d) Difficulty: (2) Knowledge: (F) Page: 453

67. With respect to rewarding salespeople, _____ reinforces the negative image of the salesperson benefiting from the sale, with no regard for the purchaser's well-being.

a. the salary system

b. the commission system

c. the motivation system

d. the retainer system

e. the hourly wage system

Answer: (b) Difficulty: (2) Knowledge: (F) Page: 453

68. With respect to evaluating salespeople, _____ evaluations can be in the form of comparisons of sales, of sales percents, or increases in sales.

a. parametric

b. qualitative

c. quantitative

d. nonparametric

e. decisional

Answer: (c) Difficulty: (2) Knowledge: (F) Page: 455

69. _____ are home country personnel sent overseas to manage local operations in the foreign market.

a. Managers

b. International personnel

c. Group managers
d. Expatriates
e. Foreign managers

Answer: (d) Difficulty: (1) Knowledge: (F) Page: 456

70. All of the following are advantages that expatriates have over foreign nationals as managers of MNCs, <u>EXCEPT</u>:

a. more intelligence.
b. better communication.
c. better understanding of office politics.
d. develops better future managers.
e. better relationships with the home office.

Answer: (a) Difficulty: (2) Knowledge: (F) Page: 456

71. All of the following are disadvantages of using expatriates over foreign nationals as managers, <u>EXCEPT</u>:

a. cross-cultural training.
b. motivation.
c. honesty.
d. compensation.
e. family discord.

Answer: (c) Difficulty: (2) Knowledge: (F) Page: 457-459

72. It is widely believed that expatriates are highly paid with respect to average salaries within the MNC. However, approximately _____ percent of the expatriates (results from a recent survey) are dissatisfied with their salary and benefits.

a. 25
b. 50
c. 40
d. 75
e. 60

Answer: (d) Difficulty: (3) Knowledge: (A) Page: 459

73. The single most compelling reason that most expatriates return home early from their tour of duty abroad is:

a. motivation.
b. salary.

c. health.

d. fear of the foreign environment.

e. family discord.

Answer: (e) Difficulty: (2) Knowledge: (F) Page: 459, 460

True/False   Short Answer

1. Unlike the United States, the majority of cars sold in Japan are sold door-to-door.

Answer: (True) Difficulty: (2) Knowledge: (A) Page: 439

2. It is generally believed that the salesperson is the front line for the company.

Answer: (True) Difficulty: (1) Knowledge: (F) Page: 439

3. The primary reason that the United States car makers do not sell their products better in Japan is they don't understand the promotional environment.

Answer: (False) Difficulty: (2) Knowledge: (A) Page: 440

4. When considering international sales management issues, _____ considerations are issues that analyze more than one country's assets, strengths, and situations, or that deal directly with cross-border coordination.

Answer: (international strategy) Difficulty: (3) Knowledge: (F) Page: 440

5. When considering international sales management issues, _____ considerations are issues that focus on the culture of the foreign country and its impact on operations within the country.

Answer: (intercultural) Difficulty: (3) Knowledge: (F) Page: 440

6. Sales force skill availability, country image, and expatriate recruiting are all issues that are relevant as intercultural issues with the foreign country.

Answer: (False) Difficulty: (3) Knowledge: (F) Page: 441, Exhibit 15-1

7. Motivation, cultural sensitivity, ethical standards, and fairness are all issues that are relevant as intercultural issues with the foreign country.

Answer: (True) Difficulty: (2) Knowledge: (F) Page: 441, Exhibit 15-1

8. The question of how to enter the market is central to marketing.

Answer: (True) Difficulty: (1) Knowledge: (F) Page: 441

9. Backward integration refers to greater ownership and control of the distribution channel.

Answer: (False) Difficulty: (3) Knowledge: (F) Page: 441

10. If a firm has limited foreign involvement and visibility, a correct choice for them to use in entering a foreign country would be to develop an expatriate sales force.

Answer: (False) Difficulty: (2) Knowledge: (A) Page: 442, Exhibit 15-2

11. If a firm has limited foreign involvement and visibility, a correct choice for them to use in entering a foreign country would be to enter into an arrangement with an Export Management Company.

Answer: (True) Difficulty: (2) Knowledge: (A) Page: 442, Exhibit 15-2

12. The term sogoshosha in Japan describes an Export Trading Company.

Answer: (True) Difficulty: (2) Knowledge: (A) Page: 443

13. Licensing represents a high-involvement approach to foreign sales.

Answer: (False) Difficulty: (3) Knowledge: (F) Page: 443

14. Expatriate involvement in international sales more likely comes when there is a high involvement entry format.

Answer: (False) Difficulty: (2) Knowledge: (F) Page: 444

15. At the level of personal selling there is little true international selling.

Answer: (True) Difficulty: (3) Knowledge: (F) Page: 445

16. Equating Korean and Japanese consumers and business practices to be the same just because they are in geographic proximity to one another would be a mistake often made because of _____.

Answer: (cultural generalization) Difficulty: (3) Knowledge: (F) Page: 446

17. _____ are home country personnel sent overseas to manage local operations in the foreign market.

Answer: (Expatriates) Difficulty: (2) Knowledge: (F) Page: 456

Essay

1. It has been said that selling is selling the world over. However, there are differences between the way that domestic and international selling efforts occur and are managed. Comment on these differences.

Answer:

Though there are many similarities between domestic and foreign salesforce management there are differences. Some of these differences are: salesforce skill, whether to use expatriates or locals, communication distance and problems, motivation, cultural sensitivity, organizational culture versus local culture, compensation and rewards, expectations and evaluations. There are other differences. The aforementioned areas should provide ample topics for discussion for this question.

Difficulty: (1) Knowledge: (F) Page: 439-431

2. Considering various types of entry formats into the international arena, under what circumstances might it be advisable for the company to attempt a traveling global salesforce?

Answer:

This form of forward integration would be necessary for the firm that desires a great deal of control of the product and channel from beginning to end. Reasons for using the "global approach" might be:

1). The operation is large enough to spread out the overhead costs of owning and maintaining infrastructure and training and supervising employees.
2). An inability to enforce contractual obligations on outside intermediaries or some other need for greater control of the sales process requires a strong presence in the host country.
3). Sales of a service usually require a presence in the country earlier than would otherwise be considered.

Difficulty: (2) Knowledge: (F) Page: 442

3. Not all United States sales methods or systems can automatically be exported abroad. Considering the information provided by research on different cultural dimensions, why might it be difficult to adopt a U.S.-style commission system for salespeople in such countries as Japan or Mexico. Be sure to remember how these two countries might rank on the five cultural dimension scales.

Answer:

Commissions reinforce the negative image of the salesperson benefiting from the sale, with no regard for the purchaser's well-being. Under certain circumstances, large salary discrepancies between employees are not acceptable. In a "collectivist" culture country like Japan, it may not be acceptable that one person should earn substantially more than another in the same position. In countries like Mexico, bribery and ethical behavior might also be considered when examining the compensation issues.

Difficulty: (3) Knowledge: (A) Page: 447, Exhibit 15-3, 453, 454

4. Considering the four major categories of the Myers-Briggs Type Indicator, which of the categories (or combination of categories) best describes you? Explain why.

Answer:

If the instructor chooses to use this question, they should write the four major categories on the board. To judge student response to this question, examine how they justify their pick(s). The justification should give an indication of the definitions found on page 448 in Exhibit 15-4. This question can be modified to suit the instructor's individual purposes.

Difficulty: (2) Knowledge: (A) Page: 448, Exhibit 15-4

5. Why do most firms still consider expatriates to be a valuable extension of their company? What are the advantages and disadvantages of using expatriates?

Answer:

Advantages of expatriates.
   a. Better communication.
      1). They understand the home office better, its politics, and its priorities.
      2). Familiar with products being sold.

b. Development of talent.
   1). These managers can use their international skills at a later point.
   2). They learn home office skills as well as foreign management skills.

Disadvantages or difficulties of using expatriates:

   a. cross-cultural training.
   b. motivation.
   c. compensation.
   d. family discord.
   e. repatriation.

Difficulty: (3) Knowledge: (F) Page: 456-461

Chapter 16

Multiple Choice

1. The concept of business logistics is relatively _____ with the first article on logistics theory being published in _____ .

    a. new/ 1980.
    b. new/1960.
    c. new/1970.
    d. old/1860.
    e. old/1920.

Answer: (b) Difficulty: (3) Knowledge: (F) Page: 465

2. Which of the following famous business thinkers characterized logistics as being "the dark continent of business?"

    a. Philip Kotler.
    b. Stephen Covey.
    c. Michael E. Porter.
    d. Peter Drucker.
    e. Tom Peters.

Answer: (d) Difficulty: (3) Knowledge: (F) Page: 465, 466

3. It is not too difficult to demonstrate the importance of physical handling, moving, storing, and retrieving of material since for almost every product more than _____ percent of product cost is material related.

    a. 20
    b. 30
    c. 40
    d. 50
    e. 70

Answer: (d) Difficulty: (2) Knowledge: (F) Page: 466

4. In the United States, the total logistics cost is estimated to amount to _____ times the current U.S. trade deficit.

    a. 1 to 2
    b. 2 to 3
    c. 3 to 4
    d. 4 to 5
    e. 5 to 6

Answer: (d) Difficulty: (3) Knowledge: (F) Page: 466

5. Two areas that have allowed logistics to make a quantum leap in efficiency are the development of intermodal transportation and _____.

    a. rapid delivery systems (such as UPS).
    b. electronic tracking technology.
    c. the laser.
    d. cellular phones.
    e. jumbo jets.

Answer: (b) Difficulty: (1) Knowledge: (F) Page: 466

6. _____ transportation refers to the seamless transfer of goods from one mode of transportation (such as an aircraft) to another (such as a ship) and vice versa without the hassle of unpacking and repackaging of goods to suit the dimensions of the mode of transportation being used.

    a. Bi-polar
    b. Bi-modal
    c. Intercontinental
    d. Dual-basic
    e. Intermodal

Answer: (e) Difficulty: (2) Knowledge: (F) Page: 466

7. _____ refers to the means of keeping continuous tabs on the exact location of the goods being shipped in the logistics chain.

    a. Electronic data processing
    b. Electronic messaging service
    c. Electronic tracking technology
    d. Computerized messaging
    e. Comp-Track

Answer: (c) Difficulty: (2) Knowledge: (F) Page: 466

8. With electronic tracking technology, shippers are able to quickly react to any disruption in the shipments because the shipper knows where exactly the goods are in real time and:

   a. labor can be adjusted accordingly.
   b. the alternative means can be quickly mobilized should problems develop.
   c. costs can always be evaluated.
   d. losses are rare.
   e. customer service is now at a premium.

Answer: (b) Difficulty: (1) Knowledge: (A) Page: 466

9. _____ is defined as the design and management of a system that directs and controls the flows of materials into, through and out of the firm across national boundaries to achieve its corporate objectives at a minimum total cost.

   a. Global goods flow
   b. Global distribution
   c. Global logistics
   d. Global wholesaling
   e. Global shipping

Answer: (c) Difficulty: (2) Knowledge: (F) Page: 466

10. Global logistics encompasses:

   a. advertising and personal selling.
   b. purchasing and manufacturing.
   c. materials management and trucking.
   d. materials management and physical distribution.
   e. pricing and manufacturing.

Answer: (d) Difficulty: (2) Knowledge: (A) Page: 466

11. _____ refers to the inflow of raw materials, parts, and supplies in and through the firm.

   a. Global logistics
   b. Physical distribution
   c. Materials management
   d. Purchasing processes
   e. Global distribution

Answer: (c) Difficulty: (2) Knowledge: (F) Page: 466

12. The global logistics process begins with which of the following?

    a. materials management
    b. processing and assembly
    c. physical distribution
    d. raw materials, components, and supplies
    e. finished products ready for shipment

Answer: (d) Difficulty: (2) Knowledge: (F) Page: 467

13. When raw materials, components, and supplies are converted or manipulated for processing and assembly by the firm, the process is monitored and controlled by the _____ function of the firm.

    a. physical distribution
    b. purchasing
    c. intermodal transportation
    d. materials handling
    e. materials management

Answer: (e) Difficulty: (3) Knowledge: (A) Page: 467

14. _____ refers to the movement of the firm's finished products to its customers, consisting of transportation, warehousing, inventory, customer service/order entry, and admission.

    a. Physical distribution
    b. Purchasing
    c. Intermodal transportation
    d. Global logistics
    e. Materials management

Answer: (a) Difficulty: (2) Knowledge: (F) Page: 467

15. All of the following are activities that occur during physical distribution EXCEPT:

    a. transportation.
    b. warehousing.
    c. inventory.
    d. order entry.
    e. promotion and advertising.

Answer: (e) Difficulty: (1) Knowledge: (A) Page: 467

16. With respect to distribution costs, a geographically large country such as the United States will normally incur more _____ costs than in smaller countries.

    a. administration
    b. warehousing, customer service/order entry, and general administration
    c. transportation and inventory
    d. materials handling
    e. warehousing and transportation

Answer: (c) Difficulty: (3) Knowledge: (A) Page: 467

17. With respect to distribution costs, a geographically concentrated country such as Japan or England will normally incur more _____ costs than in larger more geographically dispersed countries.

    a. administration
    b. warehousing, customer service/order entry, and general administration
    c. transportation and inventory
    d. materials handling
    e. warehousing and transportation

Answer: (b) Difficulty: (2) Knowledge: (A) Page: 467

18. Which of the following factors contribute significantly to the increased complexity and cost of global logistics as compared to domestic logistics?

    a. domestic intermediaries
    b. service
    c. purchasing
    d. exchange rate fluctuation
    e. materials handling

Answer: (d) Difficulty: (1) Knowledge: (F) Page: 467-469

19. All of the following factors contributed significantly to the increased complexity and cost of global logistics as compared to domestic logistics EXCEPT:

a. exchange rate fluctuation.
b. distance.
c. domestic intermediaries.
d. foreign intermediaries.
e. negotiations with government officials and distributors.

Answer: (c) Difficulty: (2) Knowledge: (F) Page: 467-469

20. There are many differences between the costs of distribution in the United States versus those in Europe. Nowhere is this more apparent than in warehousing. Research has shown that warehousing costs in Europe account for almost _____ of total distribution costs.

a. one fifth
b. one half
c. one fourth
d. one third
e. two fifths

Answer: (d) Difficulty: (3) Knowledge: (A) Page: 468

21. Research has shown that the best description of the European physical distribution system is that it is increasingly:

a. inefficient.
b. based on bribery and graft.
c. based on more direct flow from worldwide manufacturing sites to countries where sales take place.
d. based on indirect flows between member states of the European Union.
e. like the system of the United States.

Answer: (c) Difficulty: (2) Knowledge: (A) Page: 468

22. Recently the U.S. dollar depreciated while the Japanese yen soared in value. Honda found that it was much cheaper to ship its Accord models to Europe from its Ohio plant than from Japan. This could most accurately be classed as a move made because of problems or opportunities with:

a. distance.
b. logistics.
c. exchange rate fluctuations.
d. foreign intermediaries.
e. domestic intermediaries.

Answer: (c) Difficulty: (1) Knowledge: (A) Page: 468

23. The most important factors in determining an optimal mode of transportation for foreign markets are the value-to-volume ratio, perishability of the product, and:

a. the cost of transportation.
b. intermodal ratio.
c. total cost ratio to inventory and warehousing expense.
d. the cost of insurance.
e. the distance to speed relationship.

Answer: (a) Difficulty: (2) Knowledge: (F) Page: 469

24. All of the following are important factors in determining an optimal mode of transportation to be used in foreign markets EXCEPT:
a. the cost of transportation.
b. the value-to-volume ratio.
c. the perishability of the product.
d. obsolescence along the product life cycle.
e. the cost of insurance.

Answer: (e) Difficulty: (3) Knowledge: (F) Page: 469

25. The _____ is determined by how much value is added to the materials used in the product.

a. perishability of the product
b. cost of transportation
c. the cost of insurance
d. the value-to-volume ratio
e. the intermodal ratio

Answer: (d) Difficulty: (1) Knowledge: (F) Page: 469

·26. The _____ of the product refers to the quality degradation over time and/or product obsolescence along the product life cycle.

a. perishability
b. cost of transportation
c. cost of insurance
d. value-to-volume ratio
e. intermodal ratio

Answer: (a) Difficulty: (1) Knowledge: (F) Page: 469

27. All of the following are viable options for shipping products internationally on a global basis (anywhere in the world) EXCEPT:

a. ocean shipping.
b. air freight.
c. cargo liner service.
d. truck.
e. intermodal transportation.

Answer: (d) Difficulty: (2) Knowledge: (A) Page: 469

28. The primary forms of ocean shipping include all of the following EXCEPT:

a. liner service.
b. bulk shipping.
c. tanker shipping.
d. irregular runs.
e. FED EX surface.

Answer: (e) Difficulty: (1) Knowledge: (A) Page: 469

29. If a product were to be categorized as being heavy, bulky, and nonperishable, probably the best form of global shipping would be:

a. ocean shipping.
b. air freight.
c. truck.
d. rail.
e. barge.

Answer: (a) Difficulty: (1) Knowledge: (F) Page: 469

30. If a company wished to ship semiconductor chips abroad, they would probably choose:

    a. ocean shipping.
    b. air freight.
    c. truck.
    d. rail.
    e. barge.

Answer: (b) Difficulty: (1) Knowledge: (A) Page: 470

31. Research has shown that if Nike or Reebok were to be transporting their footwear from plants in Asia to the United States, they would probably choose which of the following transportation modes?

    a. ocean shipping
    b. air freight
    c. truck
    d. rail
    e. barge

Answer: (b) Difficulty: (2) Knowledge: (A) Page: 471

32. The traditional logistics strategy involves _____ based on forecasting and inventory speculation.

    a. supply and demand
    b. anticipatory demand management
    c. inventory volume equations
    d. purchasing ratios
    e. microeconomic principles

Answer: (b) Difficulty: (2) Knowledge: (F) Page: 471

33. Information technology, electronic data interchange, and intermodal transportation have made _____ a reality in physical distribution.

    a. low cost transportation
    b. a "no returns" policy
    c. ultimate distribution service
    d. just-in-time delivery
    e. accurate purchasing management

Answer: (d) Difficulty: (2) Knowledge: (F) Page: 471

34. The European Union has made giant strides in logistics and physical distribution efficiency. All of the following are changes that are reshaping European logistics strategies EXCEPT:

a. customs procedures.
b. harmonized product standards.
c. standardized communication and image messages.
d. transportation deregulation.
e. transportation infrastructure.

Answer: (c) Difficulty: (2) Knowledge: (A) Page: 472

35. Multinational corporations can use _____ as a strategic tool in dealing with currency fluctuations and as a hedge against inflation.

a. buying power
b. just-in-time management
c. just-in-time delivery
d. purchasing management
e. inventory

Answer: (e) Difficulty: (3) Knowledge: (F) Page: 472

36. By increasing _____ before imminent depreciation of a currency instead of holding cash, the firm may reduce its exposure to currency depreciation losses.
a. buying power
b. plant and equipment
c. trucks
d. materials handling equipment (such as forklifts)
e. inventory

Answer: (e) Difficulty: (2) Knowledge: (F) Page: 472

37. _____ refers to coordinating production and distribution across geographic boundaries.

a. Rationalization
b. Utility management
c. Physical distribution management
d. Logistic integration
e. Logistic modeling

Answer: (d) Difficulty: (2) Knowledge: (F) Page: 473

38. _____ means reducing resources to achieve more efficient and cost-effective operations.

   a. Rationalization
   b. Utility management
   c. Physical distribution management
   d. Logistic integration
   e. Logistic modeling

Answer: (a) Difficulty: (2) Knowledge: (F) Page: 473

39. When Baxter Healthcare (a U.S. medical-supplies manufacturer) reorganized its European operations so each of its manufacturing, distribution, and administrative facilities specialized in one type of product and markets that product throughout Europe, it was following what might be called _____.

   a. rationalization
   b. utility management
   c. physical distribution management
   d. logistic integration
   e. logistic modeling

Answer: (d) Difficulty: (2) Knowledge: (A) Page: 473

40. When Baxter Healthcare (a U.S. medical-supplies manufacturer) reorganized its European operations so that the company's warehouses were consolidated in order to serve the entire region from one or a few strategically located distribution centers, it was following what might be called _____.

   a. rationalization
   b. utility management
   c. physical distribution management
   d. logistic integration
   e. logistic modeling

Answer: (a) Difficulty: (3) Knowledge: (A) Page: 473

41. Even though restriction removal is the goal of many international agreements, many countries still erect barriers to protect local interests. Countries often restrict _____ rights of foreign truckers (the right of the trucker to be able to carry goods in an assigned territory).

a. cabrolet
b. freight privilege
c. cabotage
d. duty hauls
e. road

Answer: (c) Difficulty: (3) Knowledge: (A) Page: 474

42. Many top firms consider logistics to be such a specialized task that they use a third party to handle logistical functions for the firm. Research has shown that the reason for this trend may be the result of concentrating on:

a. promotion instead of logistics.
b. core competencies.
c. service instead of purchasing and related functions.
d. domestic rather than international skills.
e. limited management knowledge.

Answer: (b) Difficulty: (2) Knowledge: (F) Page: 474

43. _____ refer(s) to the mix of skills and resources that a firm possesses that enable it to produce one set of goods and/or services in a much more effective manner than another.

a. Management focus
b. Strategic focus
c. Core competencies
d. Leadership vision
e. Purchasing dynamics

Answer: (c) Difficulty: (2) Knowledge: (F) Page: 474

44. Circle International of Canada is a good example of a _____.
They provide logistical information systems, global communications, air freight, ocean freight, customs brokerage, warehousing, and distribution for clients.

   a. freight forwarder
   b. Maquiladora function
   c. free trade zone specialist
   d. third party logistical specialist
   e. Export Management Company (EMC)

Answer: (d) Difficulty: (2) Knowledge: (A) Page: 476

45. All of the following activities are typical of third party logistical specialist EXCEPT:

   a. logistical information system development.
   b. warehousing and distribution.
   c. light manufacturing of component parts.
   d. inventory management.
   e. order tracking.

Answer: (c) Difficulty: (2) Knowledge: (F) Page: 476

46. A _____ is an area that is located within a nation, but is considered outside of the customs territory of the nation.

   a. border zone
   b. red zone district
   c. warehouse district
   d. dock facility
   e. free trade zone

Answer: (e) Difficulty: (1) Knowledge: (F) Page: 477

47. In the United States, a free trade zone is officially called a _____.

   a. Maquiladora operation.
   b. border zone.
   c. red zone district.
   d. Foreign Trade Zone.
   e. Channel Zone.

Answer: (d) Difficulty: (2) Knowledge: (F) Page: 477

48. All of the following are benefits of using a free trade zone <u>EXCEPT</u>:

    a. duty deferral and elimination.
    b. lower tariff rates.
    c. no government interference in intelligence gathering activities.
    d. exchange rate hedging.
    e. "Made in U.S.A." designation.

Answer: (c) Difficulty: (1) Knowledge: (F) Page: 478, Exhibit 16-2

49. Duty deferral and elimination, lower tariff rates, exchange rate hedging, and a "Made in U.S.A." designation are all benefits of using a _____.

    a. Maquiladora operation.
    b. border zone.
    c. red zone district.
    d. Foreign Trade Zone.
    e. Channel Zone.

Answer: (d) Difficulty: (2) Knowledge: (F) Page: 478, Exhibit 16-2

50. Goods in a _____ may be unpacked and repacked, sorted and relabled, inspected and tested, and manipulated in a variety of ways without officially having entered the country where these processes took place.

    a. Maquiladora operation
    b. border zone
    c. red zone district
    d. Foreign Trade Zone
    e. Channel Zone

Answer: (d) Difficulty: (2) Knowledge: (F) Page: 478

51. An example of a product that fits nicely in a _____ is wine. It can be aged for several years without incurring any significant charges from the host country.

    a. vintage zone
    b. Foreign Trade Zone
    c. service zone
    d. commodities zone or border
    e. Channel Zone

Answer: (b) Difficulty: (1) Knowledge: (A) Page: 478

52. When companies like Dell Computer and Chrysler (that rely heavily on components such as auto parts and computer chips are able to take advantage of free trade zones, they usually do it by having:

    a. cheap parts sent to their manufacturing facility from abroad.
    b. their manufacturing facilities designated as subzones of an FTZ.
    c. buying cheap "dumped" products.
    d. creating gray markets.
    e. by passing customs because of being designated a security area.

Answer: (b) Difficulty: (2) Knowledge: (A) Page: 479

53. At the macro-level, benefits of using a free trade zone include all of the following EXCEPT:

    a. increased investment and employment.
    b. more revenue through increased local taxes.
    c. obtaining a beachhead in a foreign market without being in the mainstream distribution process.
    d. the ability to reassemble large shipments into different groupings.
    e. no duties on labor.

Answer: (b) Difficulty: (3) Knowledge: (A) Page: 479

54. The Mexican version of the free trade zone is called the _____.

    a. Maquiladora operation or industry.
    b. border zone.
    c. red zone district.
    d. Foreign Trade Zone.
    e. Channel Zone.

Answer: (a) Difficulty: (2) Knowledge: (F) Page: 480

55. In Mexico another name for the Maquiladora operation or industry is the:

    a. in-bond or twin-plant program.
    b. bonded warehouse.
    c. border zone.
    d. cross border zone.
    e. indentured zone.

Answer: (a) Difficulty: (2) Knowledge: (F) Page: 480

56. In Mexico, the free trade zone program (also called the in-bond or twin-plant program) is called the _____.

   a. Maquiladora operation or industry.
   b. border zone.
   c. red zone district.
   d. Foreign Trade Zone.
   e. Channel Zone.

Answer: (a) Difficulty: (2) Knowledge: (A) Page: 480

57. Mexico allows duty-free imports of machinery and equipment for manufacturing as well as components for further processing and assembly, as long as at least 80 percent of the plant's output is exported. This is called a _____ industry.

   a. moonlighting
   b. cross border
   c. gray market
   d. TRW
   e. Maquiladora

Answer: (e) Difficulty: (2) Knowledge: (A) Page: 480

58. Mexico permits _____ percent foreign ownership of the maquiladora plants in the designated maquiladora zone.

   a. 25
   b. 50
   c. 75
   d. 90
   e. 100

Answer: (e) Difficulty: (2) Knowledge: (F) Page: 480

59. Mexico is an attractive location for _____ intensive assembly.

   a. capital
   b. labor
   c. technology
   d. repair
   e. service

Answer: (b) Difficulty: (1) Knowledge: (A) Page: 480

60. The _____ tariff provisions permit duty-free importation by U.S.-based companies of their components previously sent abroad for further processing or assembly.

   a. 3600
   b. ISO 9000
   c. Millennium 2000
   d. 9802
   e. 8570

Answer: (d) Difficulty: (3) Knowledge: (F) Page: 481

61. Under the _____ tariff provisions, tariffs are assessed only on the foreign value-added portion of imported products that might be used in assembly or processing.

   a. 3600
   b. ISO 9000
   c. Millennium 2000
   d. 9802
   e. 8570

Answer: (d) Difficulty: (3) Knowledge: (F) Page: 481

62. The 9802 tariff provisions have become so popular that _____ of all U.S. imports now fall under the 9802 tariff provisions.

   a. 5%
   b. 10%
   c. 15%
   d. 20%
   e. 50%

Answer: (d) Difficulty: (3) Knowledge: (F) Page: 481

63. To show the increasing power of retailers in today's business world, the traditional supply chain that was once powered by the manufacturer has been turned around. Distribution today is characterized being _____ in nature.

a. push
b. pull
c. vertical shove
d. horizontal slant
e. parallelism

Answer: (b) Difficulty: (2) Knowledge: (F) Page: 482

64. The traditional supply chain powered by manufacturer push is becoming a:

a. demand chain driven by logistics.
b. demand chain driven by advertising.
c. service chain driven by customer service.
d. service chain driven by response time.
e. demand chain driven by customer pull.

Answer: (e) Difficulty: (1) Knowledge: (F) Page: 482

65. With respect to strategies available to the business unit, a _____ strategy appears to be more effective than a _____ strategy in emerging markets.

a. service/product
b. product/service
c. push/pull
d. pull/push
e. pull/parallel

Answer: (c) Difficulty: (2) Knowledge: (A) Page: 483

True/False   Short Answer

1. The concept of business logistics is relatively new.

Answer: (True) Difficulty: (1) Knowledge: (F) Page: 465

2. The first article on logistics theory was published in 1860.

Answer: (False) Difficulty: (2) Knowledge: (F) Page: 465

3. John F. Magee is generally credited with publishing the first article on logistics theory in 1960.

Answer: (True) Difficulty: (2) Knowledge: (F) Page: 465

4. When Peter Drucker described logistics as "the dark continent of business" he probably meant is was _____.

Answer: (underdeveloped or unexplored) Difficulty: (3) Knowledge: (A) Page: 466

5. In almost every product, more than 50 percent of the product cost is material related, while less than 10 percent is labor.

Answer: (True) Difficulty: (1) Knowledge: (F) Page: 466

6. In the United States, total logistical cost is estimated to be about 10 to 11 percent of the country's GNP.

Answer: (True) Difficulty: (2) Knowledge: (F) Page: 466

7. The development of the computer and the Concorde airliner caused a quantum jump in the efficiency of the logistics methods in the latter part of this century.

Answer: (False) Difficulty: (2) Knowledge: (F) Page: 466

8. _____ transportation refers to the seamless transfer of goods from one mode of transport to another and vice versa without the hassle of unpacking and repackaging.

Answer: (Intermodal) Difficulty: (2) Knowledge: (F) Page: 466

9. _____ technology refers the means for keeping continuous tabs on the exact location of the goods being shipped in the logistic chain.

Answer: (Tracking) Difficulty: (2) Knowledge: (F) Page: 466

10. _____ is defined as the design and management of a system that directs and controls the flows of materials into, through and out of the firm across national boundaries to achieve its corporate objectives at a minimum total cost.

Answer: (Global logistics) Difficulty: (1) Knowledge: (F) Page: 466

11. Global logistics, unlike domestic logistics, does not put emphasis on physical distribution.

Answer: (False) Difficulty: (2) Knowledge: (F) Page: 466

12. _____ refers to the inflow of raw materials, parts, and supplies in and through the firm.

Answer: (Materials management) Difficulty: (3) Knowledge: (F) Page: 466

13. _____ refers to the movement of the firm's finished products to its customers, consisting of transportation, warehousing, inventory, customer service/order entry, and administration.

Answer: (Physical distribution) Difficulty: (2) Knowledge: (F) Page: 467

14. Materials management refers to the movement of the firm's finished products to its customers, consisting of transportation, warehousing, inventory, customer service/order entry, and administration.

Answer: (False) Difficulty: (3) Knowledge: (F) Page: 466, 467

15. Physical distribution refers to the inflow of raw materials, parts, and supplies in and through the firm.

Answer: (False) Difficulty: (3) Knowledge: (F) Page: 466, 467

16. One of the greatest disparities between physical distribution in the United States and Europe is in the area of warehousing (in Europe it is over one-third of total distribution cost).

Answer: (True) Difficulty: (1) Knowledge: (A) Page: 468

17. The inventory-to-volume ratio is determined by how much value is added to materials used in the product.

Answer: (False) Difficulty: (3) Knowledge: (F) Page: 469

18. _____ of the product refers to the quality degradation over time and/or product obsolescence along the product life cycle.

Answer: (Perishability) Difficulty: (2) Knowledge: (F) Page: 469

19. Ocean shipping is used extensively for the transport of heavy perishable cargoes.

Answer: (False) Difficulty: (1) Knowledge: (F) Page: 469

20. An example of a product that would probably be air freighted between the United States and Japan is semiconductors.

Answer: (True) Difficulty: (1) Knowledge: (A) Page: 470

21. In intermodal transportation only one mode of transportation is used.

Answer: (False) Difficulty: (1) Knowledge: (F) Page: 470

22. Nike and Reebok often air freight their finished products from Asia to the United States.

Answer: (True) Difficulty: (2) Knowledge: (A) Page: 471

23. _____ refers to coordinating production and distribution across geographic boundaries.

Answer: (Logistic integration) Difficulty: (3) Knowledge: (F) Page: 473

24. A _____ is an area that is located within a nation, but is considered outside of the customs territory of the nation.

Answer: (free trade zone) Difficulty: (2) Knowledge: (F) Page: 477

25. The Mexican version of a free trade zone is called the _____.

Answer: (Maquiladora industry or operation****also known as in-bond or the twin plant program) Difficulty: (2) Knowledge: (F) Page: 480

Essay

1. Explain what the terms global logistics, materials management, and physical distribution mean. Describe the various operations and procedures encompassed by these terms.

Answer:

Global logistics is defined as the design and management of a system that directs and controls the flows of materials into, through and out of the firm across national boundaries to achieve its corporate objectives at a minimum total cost. Global logistics, like domestic logistics, encompasses materials management and physical distribution.

Materials management refers to the inflow of raw materials, parts, and supplies in and through the firm.

Physical distribution refers to the movement of the firm's finished products to customers, consisting of transportation, warehousing, inventory, customer service/order entry, and administration.

Difficulty: (1) Knowledge: (F) Page: 466, 467

2. The global logistics manager must understand the specific properties of the different modes of transportation in order to use them optimally. What the most important factors in determining an optimal mode of transportation? List and briefly describe each of the factors.

Answer:

a. The value-to-volume ratio--this ratio is determined by how much value is added to the materials used in the product.

b. Perishability--perishability of the product refers to the quality degradation over time and/or product obsolescence along the product life cycle.

c. The cost of transportation--this factor should be considered in light of the value-to-volume ratio and perishability of the product.

Difficulty: (2) Knowledge: (F) Page: 469

3. Explain the role that so called "third-party" logistics companies play in contemporary international trade. Cite the advantages of using third-party companies in the trade process.

Answer:

The trend toward third-party logistics may be a result of concentrating on core competencies.

1). Core competencies refer to the mix of skills and resources that a firm possesses which enable it to produce one set of goods and/or services in a much more effective manner than another.
2). Many logistic companies are now providing tailored logistic solutions in international markets for their clients.
3). For smaller firms, however, third-party logistics completely may not be a cost effective alternative because of the relatively lower volumes over which the logistic provider can spread his volumes.

Third-party companies often provide the following services: logistics information systems, global communications, air freight, ocean freight, inland transportation, customs brokerage, warehousing and distribution, and transportation insurance.

Difficulty: (2) Knowledge: (F) Page: 474-477

4. Explain the role of the free trade zone in modern trade. Explain the free trade zone's relationship and benefit to global logistics.

Answer:

A free trade zone (FTZ) is an area that is located within a nation but is considered outside of the Customs territory of the nation. Legally, goods remain in the zone and are counted as international commerce. They are either held or exported.

No taxes are levied until the goods are brought into the country's Customs territory. Operationally, an FTZ provides an opportunity to take advantage of a variety of efficiencies and economies in the manufacture and marketing of their products. Some of the advantages are that the goods can be:
   a. Aged (wine).
   b. Repackaged.
   c. Sorted and labeled.
   d. Tested.
   e. Repaired.
   f. Reprocessed or fabricated.
   g. Assembled.

According to Exhibit 16-2 benefits include:
a. duty deferral and elimination.
b. lower tariff rates.
c. lower tariff incidence.
d. exchange rate hedging.
e. import quota not applicable.
f. "Made in U.S.A." designation.

Difficulty: (2) Knowledge: (A) Page: 477-479, Exhibit 16-2

5. Explain the concept and function of the Maquiladora operation or industry in Mexico.

Answer:

The Maquiladora industry, also known as the in-bond or twin-plant program, is essentially a special Mexican version of a free trade zone.
a. Mexico allows duty-free imports of machinery and equipment for manufacturing as well as components for further processing and assembly as long as at least 80% of the plant's output is exported.
b. Foreign ownership is allowed.
Low wage rates make the program very attractive. Many labor intensive manufacturing concerns have moved to Mexico to take advantage of this opportunity.

The maquiladoras in Mexico are not just encouraged and stimulated by Mexico.
a. U.S. tariff provisions have also encouraged the development of these industries.

Duty importation into the U.S. from these programs have also stimulated growth. The effect is to be able to gain entry into the U.S. market with no real penalty for manufacturing abroad. NAFTA provisions will continue this trend.

Difficulty: (2) Knowledge: (A) Page: 480, 481

Chapter 17

Multiple Choice

1. A recent survey of members of the National Association for Purchasing Managers in the United States showed that _____ of the members (and their companies) were exporting.

   a. 50%
   b. 60%
   c. 70%
   d. 80%
   e. 90%

Answer: (d) Difficulty: (3) Knowledge: (F) Page: 491

2. A significant trend in merchandise exports is the trend toward increasing:

   a. purchasing involvement.
   b. finished goods processing.
   c. intermediate processing.
   d. service delivery.
   e. countertrade requirements.

Answer: (c) Difficulty: (2) Knowledge: (F) Page: 492

3. With respect to merchandise exporting, _____ processing is the process in which goods cross more than one national border in the course of processing and value addition before they reach the final buyer.

   a. finished goods
   b. service
   c. components
   d. materials
   e. intermediate

Answer: (e) Difficulty: (2) Knowledge: (F) Page: 492

4. The new trend toward intermediate processing (with respect to merchandise exporting) seems to be more concentrated in:

   a. NAFTA countries.
   b. the European Union countries.
   c. the Latin American countries.
   d. the Asian countries including China.
   e. most developing countries around the world.

Answer: (d) Difficulty: (2) Knowledge: (A) Page: 492

5. How would you evaluate the following statement? "Developing countries are exporters of raw materials from which they earn revenue to pay for imports of manufactured goods from developed countries."

   a. mostly accurate
   b. totally accurate
   c. partially inaccurate
   d. hopelessly inappropriate
   e. a statement that will not change in its truth

Answer: (d) Difficulty: (3) Knowledge: (A) Page: 492

6. Which of the following percentages accurately describes the amount of exports that is accounted for by manufactured goods from developing countries?

   a. 20%
   b. 30%
   c. 40%
   d. 50%
   e. 60%

Answer: (e) Difficulty: (2) Knowledge: (F) Page: 492

7. For the first time, developing countries (with respect to export and imports in world trade):

   a. are out of debt to the rich world countries.
   b. helped pull the rich world countries out of the recession of the early 1990s.
   c. are beginning to revolt against the domination of the rich world countries.
   d. are beginning to form alliances to rebel against the rich world countries.
   e. are beginning to declare bankruptcies in record numbers.

Answer: (b) Difficulty: (2) Knowledge: (A) Page: 492

8. The world's top six exporters (the United States, Germany, Japan, France, the United Kingdom, and Canada) accounted for _____ percent of the world's exports.

   a. 20
   b. 33
   c. 40
   d. 46
   e. 56

Answer: (d) Difficulty: (3) Knowledge: (F) Page: 492

9. All of the following are among the world's top six exporters EXCEPT:

   a. the United States.
   b. Mexico.
   c. Canada.
   d. Germany.
   e. France.

Answer: (b) Difficulty: (1) Knowledge: (F) Page: 492, Exhibit 17-1

10. At present, the United States is running a exporting trade surplus in which of the following accounts?

   a. merchandise
   b. manufactured goods
   c. light industrial goods
   d. electronic goods
   e. services

Answer: (e) Difficulty: (1) Knowlege: (F) Page: 492

11. According to current research, which of the following countries is the world leader in export trade?

   a. United Kingdom
   b. Germany
   c. Japan
   d. France
   e. United States

Answer: (e) Difficulty: (1) Knowledge: (F) Page: 493, Exhibit 17-1

12. According to current research, the United States is the leader in world export trade. Which of the following countries currently holds the number two (#2) position?

    a. United Kingdom
    b. Germany
    c. Japan
    d. France
    e. Canada

Answer: (b) Difficulty: (3) Knowledge: (F) Page: 493, Exhibit 17-1

13. As an aid to expanding information about world trade, increasingly, international marketing information is available in the form of _____.

    a. CD-ROMs.
    b. electronic encyclopedias.
    c. electronic databases.
    d. CIA reports.
    e. government intelligence reports.

Answer: (c) Difficulty: (2) Knowledge: (F) Page: 493

14. Which of the following countries is the largest participant in database growth?

    a. United Kingdom
    b. Germany
    c. Japan
    d. France
    e. United States

Answer: (e) Difficulty: (1) Knowledge: (A) Page: 493

15. Approximately how many databases (that can be used to help with international trade) are available in the world?

    a. 1,000
    b. 3,000
    c. 4,000
    d. 6,000
    e. 10,000

Answer: (d) Difficulty: (2) Knowledge: (F) Page: 493

16. Conducting export research on China and Russia would best be done by:

   a. doing database research.
   b. doing on-line searches.
   c. doing field work.
   d. using existing government facts and figures.
   e. using data supplied by trade missions.

Answer: (c) Difficulty: (2) Knowledge: (A) Page: 493

17. The identification of an appropriate overseas market and an appropriate segment involves grouping by all of the following criteria EXCEPT:

   a. socioeconomic characteristics.
   b. political and legal variables.
   c. consumer variables.
   d. service variables.
   e. financial variables.

Answer: (d) Difficulty: (2) Knowledge: (F) Page: 493

18. When attempting to identify an appropriate overseas market and an appropriate segment, socioeconomic variables should be considered. All of the following are socioeconomic variables that should be considered EXCEPT:

   a. demographics.
   b. economic.
   c. geographic.
   d. econometrics.
   e. climatic characteristics.

Answer: (d) Difficulty: (2) Knowledge: (F) Page: 493

19. When attempting to identify an appropriate overseas market and an appropriate segment, consumer variables should be considered. All of the following are consumer variables that should be considered EXCEPT:

   a. service quality.
   b. purchase frequency.
   c. lifestyle.
   d. preferences.
   e. purchase behavior.

20. To get an idea of market segments in a foreign country, the marketer can first group regions within countries across the world by macroeconomic variables. An illustration of one of these macroeconomic variables would be:

   a. level of industrial development.
   b. purchase preferences.
   c. services sought.
   d. lifestyles.
   e. purchase frequency.

Answer: (a) Difficulty: (2) Knowledge: (A) Page: 494

21. Data for grouping along macroeconomic criteria are available from international agencies such as:

   a. the CIA.
   b. the World Court.
   c. the World Bank.
   d. the National Geographic Society.
   e. the World Economic Council.

Answer: (c) Difficulty: (2) Knowledge: (F) Page: 494

22. The easiest product to sell abroad with respect to logistics is a(n) _____ product.

   a. differentiated
   b. semi-standardized
   c. clustered
   d. gray market
   e. standardized

Answer: (e) Difficulty: (1) Knowledge: (F) Page: 495

23. _____ exporting involves the use of independent U.S. middlemen to market the firm's products overseas.

   a. Direct
   b. Indirect
   c. Parallel
   d. Synchronized
   e. Dual

Answer: (b) Difficulty: (2) Knowledge: (F) Page: 495

24. When independent U.S. middlemen market a firm's goods in an overseas market, they are called _____. They market through their own network of foreign distributors and their own sales force.

   a. exporters.
   b. export specialists.
   c. export representatives.
   d. distribution specialists.
   e. parallel exporters.

Answer: (c) Difficulty: (2) Knowledge: (F) Page: 495

25. In order to expand their exporting activities, many Japanese firms rely on giant general trading companies known as _____.

   a. keiretsus.
   b. chaebols.
   c. dumcoms.
   d. sogo shoshas.
   e. akimonos.

Answer: (d) Difficulty: (3) Knowledge: (F) Page: 495

26. All of the following are common types of export representatives in the United States EXCEPT:

   a. combination export manager (CEM).
   b. export merchant.
   c. export commission house.
   d. export consortium.
   e. the trading company.

Answer: (d) Difficulty: (3) Knowledge: (F) Page: 495

27. The _____ acts as the export department to a small exporter or a large producer with small overseas sales.

   a. combination export manager (CEM)
   b. export merchant
   c. export commission house
   d. piggyback exporter
   e. trading company

Answer: (a) Difficulty: (2) Knowledge: (F) Page: 495

28. The _____ buys and sells on their own accounts and assumes all the responsibilities of exporting a product. Manufacturers do not control sales activities.

    a. combination export manager (CEM)
    b. export merchant
    c. export commission house
    d. piggyback exporter
    e. trading company

Answer: (b) Difficulty: (2) Knowledge: (F) Page: 496

29. The _____ is someone who brings together an overseas buyer and a U.S. manufacturer for the purpose of an export sale and earns a commission for establishing a contact that results in a sale.

    a. combination export manager (CEM)
    b. export broker
    c. export commission house
    d. piggyback exporter
    e. trading company

Answer: (b) Difficulty: (2) Knowledge: (F) Page: 496

30. A(n) _____ places orders on behalf of its foreign clients with U.S. manufacturers and acts as a finder for its client to get the best buy.
    a. combination export manager (CEM)
    b. export broker
    c. export commission house
    d. piggyback exporter
    e. trading company

Answer: (c) Difficulty: (2) Knowledge: (F) Page: 496

31. _____ are large, foreign organizations engaged in exporting and importing. They buy on their own account and export the goods to their home country.

    a. Combination export manager (CEM)
    b. Export broker
    c. Export commission house
    d. Piggyback exporter
    e. Trading companies

Answer: (e) Difficulty: (2) Knowledge: (F) Page: 496, 497

32. Which of the following are examples of large trading companies?

    a. Ford.
    b. General Motors.
    c. Mitsui.
    d. Volvo.
    e. Louis Dreyfus.

Answer: (c) Difficulty: (1) Knowledge: (A) Page: 497, Exhibit 17-2

33. A(n) _____ refers to the practice where U.S. firms that have an established export departments assume, under a cooperative agreement, the responsibility of exporting the products of other U.S. companies.

    a. combination export manager (CEM)
    b. export broker
    c. export commission house
    d. piggyback exporter
    e. trading company

Answer: (d) Difficulty: (2) Knowledge: (F) Page: 497

34. _____ exporting occurs when a manufacturer or exporter sells directly to an importer or buyer located in a foreign market.

    a. Direct
    b. Indirect
    c. Parallel
    d. Synchronized
    e. Dual

Answer: (a) Difficulty: (2) Knowledge: (F) Page: 497

35. With respect to direct exporting, the primary difference between a foreign sales subsidiary and a foreign sales branch is that the foreign sales branch is:

    a. larger.
    b. smaller.
    c. not a separate legal entity.
    d. uses home country managers.
    e. does not pay taxes.

Answer: (c) Difficulty: (2) Knowledge: (A) Page: 498

36. The following characteristics (low set up costs, credit risk lies with middlemen, and low customer loyalty) apply to which of the following forms of exporting?

a. direct
b. indirect
c. parallel
d. synchronized
e. dual

Answer: (b) Difficulty: (2) Knowledge: (A) Page: 498

37. The following characteristics (high set-up costs, higher credit risks, and higher customer loyalty) apply to which of the following forms of exporting?

a. direct
b. indirect
c. parallel
d. synchronized
e. dual

Answer: (a) Difficulty: (2) Knowledge: (A) Page: 498

38. Once an export contract has been signed, the wheels are set in motion for the process that results in the export contract. The first stage of the process is:

a. to agree to monetary terms.
b. to agree to currency for the contract.
c. to analyze the legality of the transaction.
d. to analyze the profits and value for both parties.
e. to state the time period for completion of the contract.

Answer: (c) Difficulty: (3) Knowledge: (F) Page: 499

39. All exports from the United States (except to Canada and U.S. territories) require a(n) _____.

a. letter of credit.
b. letter of ownership.
c. letter for transportation permission.
d. export license.
e. social security number.

Answer: (d) Difficulty: (2) Knowledge: (A) Page: 502

40. The second pillar of the export transaction is the logistics of the export transaction. Included in this transaction are all of the following EXCEPT:

a. a bill of lading.
b. the terms of sale.
c. the payment.
d. a dispute mechanism.
e. monitoring of the shipment and delivery of the goods.

Answer: (c) Difficulty: (3) Knowledge: (F) Page: 502

41. A(n) _____ is a contract between the exporter and the shipper indicating that the shipper has accepted responsibility for the goods and will provide transportation in return for payment.

a. bill of disclosure
b. term of sale
c. payment statement
d. transportation invoice
e. bill of lading

Answer: (e) Difficulty: (2) Knowledge: (F) Page: 502, 503

42. A(n) _____ is a bill for the goods stating basic information about the transaction, including a description of the merchandise, total cost of the goods sold, addresses of the buyer and seller, and delivery and payment.

a. bill of disclosure
b. term of sale
c. payment statement
d. commercial invoice
e. bill of lading

Answer: (d) Difficulty: (2) Knowledge: (F) Page: 503

43. When the exporter quotes a price for the goods, including charges for delivery of the goods alongside a vessel at a port (the seller covers all costs of unloading and wharfage at the shipment port and the buyer covers all other charges to get the goods to the buyer), this form of terms of shipment is called:

   a. ex-works.
   b. free alongside ship (FAS).
   c. free on board (FOB).
   d. cost and freight (CFR).
   e. Cost, Insurance, and Freight (CIF).

Answer: (b) Difficulty: (3) Knowledge: (A) Page: 504, Exhibit 17-6

44. When the exporter quotes a price for the goods, including charges for delivery of the goods alongside a vessel at a port (the seller covers all costs of unloading and wharfage plus loading the goods on the vessel and the buyer covers all other charges to get the goods to the buyer), this form of terms of shipment is called:

   a. ex-works.
   b. free alongside ship (FAS).
   c. free on board (FOB).
   d. cost and freight (CFR).
   e. Cost, Insurance, and Freight (CIF).

Answer: (c) Difficulty: (3) Knowledge: (A) Page: 504, Exhibit 17-6

45. All of the following are possible payment terms for goods exported to another nation EXCEPT:

   a. cash with order.
   b. third party draft.
   c. confirmed irrevocable letter of credit.
   d. sight draft.
   e. time draft.

Answer: (b) Difficulty: (3) Knowledge: (F) Page: 505, Exhibit 17-7

46. A(n) _____ is a payment form where a shipment is held by the importer until the merchandise has been sold, at which time payment is made to the exporter.

a. cash with order
b. confirmed irrevocable letter of credit
c. sight draft
d. time draft
e. consignment

Answer: (e) Difficulty: (1) Knowledge: (F) Page: 505, Exhibit 17-7

47. A(n) _____ is a payment form where a cash payment occurs when the order is placed.

a. cash with order
b. confirmed irrevocable letter of credit
c. sight draft
d. time draft
e. consignment

Answer: (a) Difficulty: (1) Knowledge: (F) Page: 505, Exhibit 17-7

48. A(n) _____ is a payment form where a draft is so drawn as to be payable on presentation to the drawee (usually the buyer).
a. cash with order
b. third party draft
c. confirmed irrevocable letter of credit
d. sight draft
e. time draft

Answer: (d) Difficulty: (2) Knowledge: (F) Page: 505, Exhibit 17-7

49. The terms of payment between the exporter and importer are a matter of negotiation and depend on a variety of factors. All of the following might be on that list of factors EXCEPT:

a. the buyer's credit standing.
b. the seller's reputation.
c. the amount of the sale transaction.
d. the risks associated with the type of merchandise to be shipped.
e. the usual practice in the trade.

Answer: (b) Difficulty: (2) Knowledge: (F) Page: 504

50. _____ risk is the risk that importer will not pay or fail to pay on the agreed terms.

   a. Credit
   b. Exchange
   c. Transfer
   d. Importer
   e. Exporter

Answer: (a) Difficulty: (1) Knowledge: (F) Page: 504

51. _____ risk exists when the sale is in the importer's currency and that currency depreciates in terms of the dollar, leaving the exporter with a lesser number of dollars.

   a. Credit
   b. Exchange
   c. Transfer
   d. Importer
   e. Exporter

Answer: (b) Difficulty: (1) Knowledge: (F) Page: 504, 505

52. _____ risk refers to the chances that payment will not be made due to the importer's inability to obtain U.S. dollars and transfer them to the exporter.

   a. Credit
   b. Exchange
   c. Transfer
   d. Importer
   e. Exporter

Answer: (c) Difficulty: (1) Knowledge: (F) Page: 505

53. The Exim Bank is described as being a:

    a. bank that lends exclusively to importers.
    b. new name for the old "World Bank."
    c. federally supported bank whose mission is to thwart communism by making loans to anti-communist nations and exporters.
    d. federally supported bank whose mission is to support exporters with necessary credit.
    e. who is not in existence yet. The concept still awaits Congressional approval.

Answer: (d) Difficulty: (2) Knowledge: (F) Page: 508

54. The main emphasis of the Exim Bank's lending practices today is in the area of:

    a. loans to Japan.
    b. loans to Taiwan.
    c. loans to Mexico.
    d. loans for prior bankrupt countries.
    e. project finance (such as infrastructure projects---roads, dams, etc.).

Answer: (e) Difficulty: (2) Knowledge: (A) Page: 508

55. A(n) _____ is a foreign corporation not located in a free trade zone that is allowed to earn some exempt and nontaxable income on its exports from the United States.

    a. export trading company
    b. foreign trading company
    c. foreign sales corporation
    d. foreign sales exporter
    e. free on board carrier

Answer: (c) Difficulty: (2) Knowledge: (F) Page: 510

56. One of the biggest advantages the United States has in importing is that U.S. companies can:

    a. order unlimited amounts of goods.
    b. always sell what they order abroad.
    c. be assured that the government will support their trade efforts.
    d. pay in U.S. dollars--a currency accepted everywhere.
    e. always turn a profit with the goods they buy because of market demand.

Answer: (d) Difficulty: (3) Knowledge: (A) Page: 512

57. About _____ percent of world trade is denominated in U.S. dollars.

   a. 30
   b. 40
   c. 50
   d. 60
   e. 75

Answer: (d) Difficulty: (3) Knowledge: (F) Page: 512

58. Since most world trade is done in dollars, the U.S. importer does not usually need to _____ foreign exchange transactions.

   a. capitalize
   b. hedge
   c. capitate
   d. survey
   e. monitor

Answer: (b) Difficulty: (1) Knowledge: (F) Page: 512

59. Importing any good is predicated upon the existence of a situation where the _____ of the good in question is not sufficient to satisfy demand.

   a. foreign production
   b. world-wide production
   c. domestic production
   d. regional trading bloc production
   e. alliance production

Answer: (c) Difficulty: (2) Knowledge: (A) Page: 512

60. When a model of importer buyer behavior is studied, the decision to source abroad is normally triggered by:

   a. the exporter.
   b. the government.
   c. the importer.
   d. competitive pressures and unavailability.
   e. the consumer alone.

Answer: (d) Difficulty: (2) Knowledge: (F) Page: 513, Exhibit 17-9

61. When an importer searches for a source of supply, they are usually guided by all of the following EXCEPT:

    a. country characteristics.
    b. monetary systems and financial institutions.
    c. vendor characteristics.
    d. choice sets.
    e. screening of information about options available.

Answer: (b) Difficulty: (3) Knowledge: (A) Page: 513, Exhibit 17-9

62. All of the following are activities that an importer would normally go through in order to complete the purchase process. Which of the items listed below does not logically fit?

    a. Find a bank in the exporter's country to handle financial transactions.
    b. Establish a letter of credit to smooth the process.
    c. Decide on the mode of transfer of goods.
    d. Always use an export or import middleman to expedite the process.
    e. Check compliance with national laws.

Answer: (d) Difficulty: (2) Knowledge: (A) Page: 514

63. When a shipment reaches the United States, the consignee (usually the importer) will file _____ with the port director at the port of entry.
    a. visas
    b. product passports
    c. bills of landing
    d. bills of shipping
    e. entry documents

Answer: (e) Difficulty: (2) Knowledge: (F) Page: 515

64. With respect to shipments entering the United States, a(n) _____ is a guarantee by someone that the duties and any potential penalties will be paid to the customs of the importing country.
    a. line of credit
    b. transfer
    c. bond
    d. permit
    e. tariff

Answer: (c) Difficulty: (1) Knowledge: (F) Page: 515

65. Merchandise arriving from Canada and Mexico, trade fair goods, and perishable goods and shipments assigned to the U.S. government almost always utilize the _____ to enable fast delivery after arrival.

    a. quick release form
    b. quick permit form
    c. Customs form 7200
    d. Special Permit for Immediate Delivery
    e. block and load release form

Answer: (d) Difficulty: (2) Knowledge: (A) Page: 515

66. If goods enter a _____, they can be re-exported anytime (up to five years) without payment of duty.

    a. holding pen
    b. corporate security zone
    c. bonded warehouse
    d. wharf zone
    e. parallel import zone

Answer: (c) Difficulty: (2) Knowledge: (F) Page: 515

67. When import duties are paid, the _____ duty is a percentage of the value of the merchandise.

    a. ad valorem
    b. specific
    c. compound
    d. nontariff
    e. import

Answer: (a) Difficulty: (1) Knowledge: (F) Page: 515

68. When import duties are paid, the _____ duty is a specified amount of the per unit weight or other quantity of the merchandise.

    a. ad valorem
    b. specific
    c. compound
    d. nontariff
    e. import

Answer: (b) Difficulty: (2) Knowledge: (F) Page: 515

69. When import duties are paid, the _____ duty is combination of a specified amount of the per unit weight or other quantity of the merchandise plus an ad valorem rate.

   a. bonded
   b. corkage
   c. compound
   d. nontariff
   e. import

Answer: (c) Difficulty: (1) Knowledge: (F) Page: 515

70. _____ duties are assessed on imported merchandise sold to importers in the United States at a price that is less than the fair market value.

   a. Ad valorem
   b. Specific
   c. Compound
   d. Nontariff
   e. Antidumping

Answer: (e) Difficulty: (1) Knowledge: (F) Page: 516

71. _____ duties are duties that are assessed to counter the effects of subsidies provided by foreign governments to goods that are exported to the United States.

   a. Ad valorem
   b. Specific
   c. Compound
   d. Countervailing
   e. Antidumping

Answer: (d) Difficulty: (1) Knowledge: (F) Page: 516

72. _____ channels refer to the legal export/import transaction involving genuine products into a country by intermediaries other than the authorized distributors.

    a. Black market
    b. Gray market
    c. Positioned
    d. Zoned
    e. Red zone

Answer: (b) Difficulty: (2) Knowledge: (F) Page: 516

73. Another name for gray market channels is _____.

    a. positioned imports.
    b. concentric marketing.
    c. strategic entry imports.
    d. parallel imports.
    e. sidebar hedging.

Answer: (d) Difficulty: (2) Knowledge: (A) Page: 516

74. An example of a good that is often sold through gray market channels is:_____.

    a. a camera.
    b. produce.
    c. furniture.
    d. aircraft.
    e. boats.

Answer: (a) Difficulty: (1) Knowledge: (A) Page: 516

75. All of the following conditions lend to the development of gray markets EXCEPT:

    a. the product is available in other markets.
    b. the product has an inelastic demand curve.
    c. trade barriers do not affect the product.
    d. GATT and WTO have reduced entry barriers.
    e. great price differentials between countries.

Answer: (b) Difficulty: (3) Knowledge: (A) Page: 517

1. Since 1945 world exports have expanded steadily ahead of the growth rate of the economic output.

Answer: (True) Difficulty: (1) Knowledge: (F) Page: 492

2. _____ processing is the process in which goods cross more than one national border in the course of processing and value addition before they reach the final buyer.

Answer: (Intermediate) Difficulty: (3) Knowledge: (F) Page: 492

3. Most exports come only from developed countries. Most developing countries have to import manufactured goods and only export raw materials.

Answer: (False) Difficulty: (2) Knowledge: (A) Page: 492

4. Japan is the world's top exporter.

Answer: (False) Difficulty: (2) Knowledge: (F) Page: 493, Exhibit 17-1

5. The identification of an appropriate overseas market and an appropriate segment involves grouping _____ characteristics like demographic, economic, geographic, and climatic characteristics.

Answer: (socioeconomic) Difficulty: (3) Knowledge: (F) Page: 493

6. _____ exporting involves using independent U.S. middlemen to market the firm's products overseas.

Answer: (Indirect) Difficulty: (2) Knowledge: (F) Page: 495

7. The combination export manager buys and sells on their own accounts and assumes all the responsibilities of exporting a product.

Answer: (False) Difficulty: (2) Knowledge: (F) Page: 495, 496

8. Piggyback exporting refers to the practice where U.S. firms that have an established export department assume, under a cooperative agreement, the responsibility of exporting the products of other U.S. companies.

Answer: (True) Difficulty: (2) Knowledge: (F) Page: 497

9. Parallel exporting occurs when a manufacturer or exporter sells directly to an importer or buyer located in a foreign market.

Answer: (False) Difficulty: (1) Knowledge: (F) Page: 497

10. Low set up costs, exporter tends to not gain knowledge of the export markets, and credit risks lie mostly with the middlemen indicates that _____ exporting is occurring.

Answer: (indirect) Difficulty: (3) Knowledge: (A) Page: 498, Exhibit 17-3

11. A bill of lading is a contract between the exporter and the shipper indicating that the shipper has accepted responsibility for the goods and will provide transportation in return for payment.

Answer: (True) Difficulty: (1) Knowledge: (F) Page: 502, 503

12. Exchange risk is the risk that the importer will not pay or fail to pay on the agreed terms.

Answer: (False) Difficulty: (2) Knowledge: (F) Page: 504

13. The World Bank is a federally supported bank whose mission is to support exporters with the necessary credit.

Answer: (False) Difficulty: (2) Knowledge: (F) Page: 508

14. With respect to importing fees, a(n) _____ duty is a percentage of the value of the merchandise.

Answer: (ad valorem) Difficulty: (3) Knowledge: (F) Page: 515

15. Gray market channels are also known as parallel imports.

Answer: (True) Difficulty: (2) Knowledge: (F) Page: 516

Essay

1. Indicate the factors that a prospective exporter might examine to choose an export market.

Answer:

The identification of an appropriate overseas market and an appropriate segment involves grouping by the following criteria:
    a. Socioeconomic characteristics like demographic, economic, geographic, and climatic characteristics.
    b. Political and legal variables.
    c. Consumer variables such as lifestyle, preferences, culture, taste, purchase behavior, and purchase frequency.
    d. Financial variables.

Difficulty: (1) Knowledge: (F) Page: 493, 494

2. Describe the direct and indirect channels of distribution that are available to exporters. As part of the description process, indicate any conditions or advantages that might be present in these channels.

Answer:

The students should be encouraged to summarize the material found in the chapter. Some useful hints for beginning the discussion are listed below.

Indirect exporting involves the use of independent U.S. middlemen to market the firm's products overseas. These export representatives assume responsibility for marketing the firm's products through their network of foreign distributors and their own sales force.

Types include:
    1). The combination export manager (CEM).
        a). Acts as the export department to a small exporter or to a large producer with small overseas sales.
        b). Operates on a commission basis.
        c). Credit support is essential.
        d). This form is diminishing in numbers and usage because of increased involvement in global marketing.
    2). The export merchant.
        a). This person buys and sells on their own account and assumes all the responsibilities of exporting a product.

b). Manufacturers are not in control. The export merchant is.
3). The export broker.
  a). This person brings together an overseas buyer and a U.S. manufacturer for the purpose of an export sale and earns a commission for establishing a contact which results in a sale.
4). An export commission house can place an order on behalf of a client and provides a finder function.
5). A trading company is a foreign organization engaged in exporting and importing. They buy and sell on their own account.
6). Piggyback exporting refers to the practice where U.S. firms that have an established export department assume, under a cooperative agreement, the responsibility of exporting the products of other U.S. companies.

Direct export occurs when a manufacturer or exporter sells directly to an importer or buyer located in a foreign market.
  a. The simplest form is the export manager with some clerical help.
    1). This manager sells and directs the activities of the export process.
  b. As export activities grow, most firms create a separate export department which is largely self-contained and operates independently of domestic operations.
  c. An extension is to form an export sales subsidiary to export separate from the other operations of the firm.
    1). The major difference is that it is a legal entity and can offer tax advantages.
  d. The foreign sales branch is not a separate legal entity. This branch handles all sales, distribution, and promotional work throughout a designated market area and sells primarily to wholesalers and dealers.

Difficulty: (3) Knowledge: (F) Page: 495-498

3. Pick three (3) of the options available to exporters when it comes to terms of payment. Explain each of the options available based on your choice.

Answer:

The terms of payment are outlined in Exhibit 17-7 and should be reviewed by the student when attempting to answer this question. Briefly, three examples of major forms are summarized below (be sure to see Exhibit 17-7 for detail and more variations of the terms):

If the sale is in cash, there is virtually no risk.

Credit letters can be considered.
    a. An unconfirmed letter of credit exposes the exporter to the creditworthiness of the buyer's bank in the foreign country because a U.S. bank is not guaranteeing payment.
    b. A sight draft excludes banks from the process and has less guarantees.
    c. An open account sale is truly one of trust in the buyer's ability to pay.

Difficulty: (2) Knowledge: (F) Page: 504-506, Exhibit 17-7

4. Describe the role the U.S. government plays in maintaining and fostering export activities. Demonstrate this role with specific examples of activities that the government might undertake.

Answer:

Generally, it is believed that governments can perform several roles with respect to export activities. They can do promotion to stimulate exportation, they can develop export strategies, they can aid in the financing of exports, and they can pass legislation that either reduces tariffs or supports exporting activities with constraints against anti-competitive situations. Some of these ideas are summarized below.

Export promotion activities generally comprise:
    a. Export service programs.
    b. Market development programs.

Government expenditures on export promotion seem to make sense.
    a. The government tries to get more firms to export.
    b. The government tries to get firms to overcome the perception of risk in the international area and take the plunge.

Export-import bank (the Exim bank). Promotes exports.
    a. Helps companies get financing for exports.
    b. The bank also works with capital expansion, infrastructure projects, and trade loans.

U.S. tariff concessions.
    a. Free trade zone. Lets businesses store, process, assemble, and display goods from abroad without paying tariff.
    b. Foreign sales corporation. A foreign corporation not located in a free trade zone that is allowed to earn some exempt and non-taxable income on its exports from the United States.
    c. American export trading company. Legislation encourages the formulation of

trading companies for the purpose of exporting.

Export regulations.
    a. The Trade Act of 1974--bars Exim bank from giving credit to most communist countries.
    b. Foreign Corrupt Practices Act of 1977 prohibits influencing overseas officials.
    c. Antitrust laws.
    d. Foreign government laws that affect exports.
    e. Taxes on exports to stimulate domestic consumption first.

Difficulty: (3) Knowledge: (A) Page: 506-511

5. Describe gray markets. Explain how they develop. Describe your feelings about buying from a gray market.

Answer:

Gray market channels refer to the legal export/import transaction involving genuine products into a country by intermediaries other than the authorized distributors.
    a. From the importer's side, this is also called parallel imports.
    b. Since the merchandise is obtained from an unauthorized source, competition and pricing is often affected (especially since the unauthorized distributor usually sells the merchandise below market prices).

Three conditions are necessary for gray markets to develop:
    1). The products must be available in other markets.
    2). Trade barriers such as tariffs, transportation costs, and legal restrictions must be low enough for parallel importers to move the products from one market to another.
    3). Price differentials among various markets must be great enough to provide the basic motivation for gray marketers.

Students may present their own opinions here. Examine the support arguments and merit of their discussion.

Difficulty: (2) Knowledge: (A) Page: 516-519

Chapter 18

Multiple Choice

1. A series of key criteria impact global organizations and their organizational designs. All of the following would be major environmental influences on the organizational design decision and structure EXCEPT:

   a. competitive environment.
   b. rate of environmental change.
   c. product diversity.
   d. regional trading blocs.
   e. nature of customers.

Answer: (c) Difficulty: (2) Knowledge: (F) Page: 524

2. Which of the following would be considered a firm-specific factor that influences global organization design decisions and structure?

   a. competitive environment.
   b. rate of environmental change.
   c. product diversity.
   d. regional trading blocs.
   e. nature of customers.

Answer: (c) Difficulty: (2) Knowledge: (F) Page: 524, 525

3. A series of key criteria impact global organizations and their organizational designs. All of the following would be major firm-specific factors on the organizational design decision and structure EXCEPT:

   a. strategic importance of international business.
   b. product diversity.
   c. company heritage.
   d. regional trading blocs.
   e. quality of local managerial skills.

Answer: (d) Difficulty: (3) Knowledge: (F) Page: 525

4. Which of the following would be considered a key environmental factor that influences global organization design decisions and structure?

    a. strategic importance of international business.
    b. product diversity.
    c. company heritage.
    d. regional trading blocs.
    e. quality of local managerial skills.

Answer: (d) Difficulty: (3) Knowledge: (F) Page: 524, 525

5. Considering the competitive environment area of environmental factors that influence global organization design decisions and structure, which of the following would be most appropriate for an industry where competition is highly localized?

    a. centralized structure.
    b. decentralized structure.
    c. entrepreneurship.
    d. sole proprietorship.
    e. a nonprofit structure.

Answer: (b) Difficulty: (2) Knowledge: (A) Page: 524

6. Typically, when overseas sales account for a very small fraction of the company's overall sales revenues, _____ can easily handle the firm's global activities.

    a. relatively complex organizational structures
    b. complex organizational structures
    c. simple organizational structures
    d. a sole proprietorship
    e. a dual manager system

Answer: (c) Difficulty: (1) Knowledge: (A) Page: 525

7. An example of a simple organizational structure (with respect to global activities) would be the:

    a. export manager.
    b. matrix approach.
    c. country structure.
    d. regional structure.
    e. export department.

Answer: (e) Difficulty: (3) Knowledge: (F) Page: 525

8. With respect to global organizational design, companies with substantial product diversity tend to go for which of the following structures?

   a. global product division configuration.
   b. international division structure.
   c. geographic structure.
   d. regional structure.
   e. matrix structure.

Answer: (a) Difficulty: (2) Knowledge: (A) Page: 525

9. All of the following are examples of the principal designs that firms can adopt to organize their global activities EXCEPT:

   a. an international division.
   b. a city division.
   c. a product-based structure.
   d. a geographic structure.
   e. a matrix structure.

Answer: (b) Difficulty: (2) Knowledge: (F) Page: 525, 526

10. Under the _____ design of global activities organization, the company basically has two entities (the domestic division and the international division).

   a. international division
   b. cryptic division
   c. product-based structure
   d. geographic structure
   e. matrix structure

Answer: (a) Difficulty: (1) Knowledge: (A) Page: 525, 526

11. Under the _____ design of global activities organization, the company is organized along its various product divisions.

   a. international division
   b. cryptic division
   c. product-based structure
   d. geographic structure
   e. matrix structure

Answer: (c) Difficulty: (1) Knowledge: (A) Page: 525, 526

12. Under the _____ design of global activities organization, the company is configured along areas such as countries, regions, or some combination of these two levels.

   a. international division
   b. cryptic division
   c. product-based structure
   d. geographic structure
   e. matrix structure

Answer: (d) Difficulty: (1) Knowledge: (A) Page: 526

13. Under the _____ design of global activities organization, the company use the option of integrating two approaches so there is a dual chain of command.

   a. international division
   b. cryptic division
   c. product-based structure
   d. geographic structure
   e. matrix structure

Answer: (e) Difficulty: (1) Knowledge: (A) Page: 526

14. Most companies that engage in global marketing will initially start off by establishing a(n):

   a. city division.
   b. country division.
   c. international division.
   d. export department.
   e. export commission manager.

Answer: (d) Difficulty: (2) Knowledge: (F) Page: 526

15. Which of the following organizational structures is most appropriate for the company whose product line is not too diverse and does not require a large amount of adaptation to the local country needs?

a. international division
b. cryptic division
c. global product division structure
d. geographic structure
e. matrix structure

Answer: (a) Difficulty: (2) Knowledge: (A) Page: 526

16. Which of the following organizational structures is most appropriate for the company whose is a high-tech company with highly complex product or MNCs with a very diversified product portfolio?

a. international division
b. cryptic division
c. global product division structure
d. geographic structure
e. matrix structure

Answer: (c) Difficulty: (2) Knowledge: (A) Page: 526

17. If Deere & Company organizes itself by breaking into a Worldwide Agriculture Equipment Division, a Worldwide Industrial Equipment Division, and a Worldwide Lawn & Grounds Care Division, which of the following organizational structures would probably be in use?

a. international division
b. customer division
c. global product division structure
d. geographic structure
e. matrix structure

Answer: (c) Difficulty: (2) Knowledge: (A) Page: 527, Exhibit 18-1

18. All of the following are benefits of the global product division structure <u>EXCEPT</u>:

    a. large degree of flexibility in terms of cross-country resource allocation.
    b. large degree of flexibility in terms of cross-country strategic planning.
    c. scale economics.
    d. facilitates a global focus.
    e. easy communication and coordination among the various product divisions without duplication of effort.

Answer: (e) Difficulty: (2) Knowledge: (F) Page: 526, 527

19. Which of the following areas are very difficult for a global product division to accomplish (therefore, this area is a shortcoming)?

    a. large degree of flexibility in terms of cross-country resource allocation.
    b. large degree of flexibility in terms of cross-country strategic planning.
    c. scale economics.
    d. facilitates a global focus.
    e. easy communication and coordination among the various product divisions without duplication of effort.

Answer: (e) Difficulty: (2) Knowledge: (A) Page: 526, 527

20. A(n) _____ is very popular with companies that market closely related product lines with similar end-users and applications around the world.

    a. international division
    b. customer division
    c. global product division structure
    d. geographic structure
    e. matrix structure

Answer: (d) Difficulty: (2) Knowledge: (A) Page: 528

21. All of the following are problems with country-based subsidiaries <u>EXCEPT</u>:

    a. they are too costly.
    b. they have coordination problems with corporate headquarters.
    c. cross-fertilization is hindered.
    d. local market conditions go unnoticed.
    e. a not-invented-here mentality exists.

Answer: (d) Difficulty: (3) Knowledge: (F) Page: 528

22. All of the following are profiles that are suggested for the twenty-first century country manager EXCEPT:

a. the trader.
b. the power broker.
c. the builder.
d. the ambassador.
e. the cabinet member.

Answer: (b) Difficulty: (3) Knowledge: (F) Page: 530

23. As a profile of a twenty-first century country manager, _____ establishes a beachhead in a new market or heads a recently acquired local distributor. They should have an entrepreneurial spirit.

a. the trader
b. the representative
c. the builder
d. the ambassador
e. the cabinet member

Answer: (a) Difficulty: (2) Knowledge: (A) Page: 530

24. As a profile of a twenty-first century country manager, _____ is a team player with profit and loss responsibility for a small- to medium-sized country. Team-manship is key here.
a. the trader
b. the representative
c. the builder
d. the ambassador
e. the cabinet member

Answer: (e) Difficulty: (2) Knowledge: (A) Page: 530

25. As a profile of a twenty-first century country manager, _____ develops local markets. They are entrepreneurs who are willing to be part of regional of global strategy teams.
a. the trader
b. the representative
c. the builder
d. the ambassador
e. the cabinet member

Answer: (c) Difficulty: (2) Knowledge: (A) Page: 530

26. As a profile of a twenty-first century country manager, _____
    is in charge of large and/or strategic markets. Prime responsibilities include handling
    government relations and integrating acquisitions and strategic alliances.

    a. the trader
    b. the power broker
    c. the builder
    d. the ambassador
    e. the cabinet member

Answer: (d) Difficulty: (2) Knowledge: (A) Page: 530

27. With respect to regional structures, a recent survey found that all of the following
    roles were performed EXCEPT:

    a. scouting.
    b. liberating.
    c. strategic simulation.
    d. signaling commitment.
    e. pooling resources.

Answer: (b) Difficulty: (3) Knowledge: (F) Page: 531

28. The _____ structure of organization explicitly recognizes the
    multidimensional nature of global strategic decision making.

    a. international division
    b. customer division
    c. global product division
    d. geographic
    e. matrix

Answer: (e) Difficulty: (2) Knowledge: (F) Page: 531

29. An example of the _____ structure of organization is Siemens AG. This German engineering conglomerate's structure focuses on business and engineering dimensions (with combinations of these divisions).

    a. international division
    b. customer division
    c. global product division
    d. geographic
    e. matrix

Answer: (e) Difficulty: (2) Knowledge: (A) Page: 531, Exhibit 18-3

30. The primary advantages of the matrix structure for organizing is that they represent the growing complexities of the global market arena and:

    a. it fosters team spirit and cooperation among managers.
    b. it secures higher profits.
    c. it does not duplicate efforts.
    d. it has smooth and accurate communications.
    e. it has clear lines of communication with no confusion.

Answer: (a) Difficulty: (2) Knowledge: (F) Page: 533

31. All of the following are considered to advantages of the matrix structure of organizing EXCEPT:

    a. it fosters team spirit.
    b. it fosters cooperation among managers.
    c. it does not duplicate efforts.
    d. it causes managers to think globally.
    e. it causes managers to think globally but act locally.

Answer: (c) Difficulty: (3) Knowledge: (F) Page: 533

32. Which of the following would be considered a disadvantage or drawback of the matrix structure of organizing?

    a. it does not foster team spirit.
    b. it does not foster cooperation among managers.
    c. it does duplicate efforts and can cause confusion.
    d. it prohibits managers from thinking globally.
    e. it causes managers to think locally only.

Answer: (c) Difficulty: (2) Knowledge: (A) Page: 533

33. All of the following are disadvantages or drawbacks of the matrix structure of organizing EXCEPT:

    a. dual reporting leads to conflicts and confusion.
    b. dual profit responsibilities leads to conflicts and confusion.
    c. bureaucratic bloat.
    d. power clashes can occur.
    e. managers think globally and act locally.

Answer: (e) Difficulty: (1) Knowledge: (A) Page: 533

34. The _____ is one solution that has been suggested to cope with the shortcomings associated with the classical hierarchical organization structures.

    a. international division
    b. global network
    c. global product division
    d. geographic
    e. matrix

Answer: (b) Difficulty: (2) Knowledge: (F) Page: 533

35. The _____ model is an attempt to reconcile the tension between the need for local responsiveness and the wish to be an integrated whole.

    a. international division
    b. global network
    c. global product division
    d. geographic
    e. matrix

Answer: (b) Difficulty: (2) Knowledge: (F) Page: 533

36. The networked global organization is sometimes referred to as a(n) _____.

    a. international.
    b. multinational.
    c. transnational.
    d. local-national.
    e. quasi-national.

Answer: (c) Difficulty: (3) Knowledge: (A) Page: 533

37. One of the encouragements for the globally networked organization is to tap into a global knowledge pool. A good metaphor for the global network is the shape depicted by the _____.

   a. square.
   b. polysphere.
   c. atom.
   d. circle.
   e. pentagram.

Answer: (c) Difficulty: (2) Knowledge: (A) Page: 534

38. It has been suggested that global networking (to be successful) is typically coupled with a(n) _____.

   a. profit center.
   b. SBU structure.
   c. pyramid of power.
   d. human investment philosophy.
   e. international leadership model.

Answer: (d) Difficulty: (3) Knowledge: (F) Page: 536

39. It has been suggested that global networking is typically coupled with a human investment philosophy. All of the following are might be considered pillars of this philosophy EXCEPT:
   a. most people want to contribute to the organization (assumption).
   b. most people are trustworthy (assumption).
   c. managers must act as superiors to employees (policies).
   d. managers act as partners to employees (policies).
   e. the more competent an organization is, the more competent will be the network (expectation).

Answer: (c) Difficulty: (3) Knowledge: (A) Page: 536

40. MNCs increasingly rely on international _____ to coordinate their global or pan-regional strategies and operations.
   a. managers
   b. consultants
   c. line personnel
   d. human resource managers
   e. teamwork

Answer: (e) Difficulty: (2) Knowlege: (F) Page: 536

41. _____ often provide the "glue" for network organizations to function properly.

   a. Managers
   b. Consultants
   c. Line personnel
   d. Human resource managers
   e. International teams

Answer: (e) Difficulty: (2) Knowlege: (F) Page: 536

42. All of the following are stages used in the formation of teams EXCEPT:

   a. naming the team.
   b. forming the team.
   c. focusing the team and its mission.
   d. maintaining the team.
   e. transferring learning throughout the organization.

Answer: (a) Difficulty: (1) Knowledge: (F) Page: 537, Exhibit 18-6

43. As part of the team building process, it is necessary for the team to focus and formulate its mission. Which of the following is the most useful step to take in that direction of those described?

   a. senior management sponsorship.
   b. understanding of the business context.
   c. development and accomplishment of team-building exercises.
   d. group memory.
   e. transfer of facilitation skills to team members.

Answer: (c) Difficulty: (3) Knowledge: (F) Page: 537, Exhibit 18-6

44. As part of the team building process, it is necessary for the team eventually maintain the team. Which of the following is the most useful step to take in that direction of those described?

   a. senior management sponsorship.
   b. understanding of the business context.
   c. development and accomplishment of team-building exercises.
   d. cultural sensitivity intervention.
   e. transfer of facilitation skills to team members.

Answer: (e) Difficulty: (3) Knowledge: (F) Page: 537, Exhibit 18-6

45. As part of the team building process, it is necessary for the team to be formed. Which of the following is the most useful step to take in that direction of those described?

    a. senior management sponsorship.
    b. clarification of objectives and performance measures.
    c. development and accomplishment of team-building exercises.
    d. cultural sensitivity intervention.
    e. transfer of facilitation skills to team members.

Answer: (a) Difficulty: (3) Knowledge: (F) Page: 537, Exhibit 18-6

46. With consideration to the team building process, certain leadership roles and team development skills are necessary for success. When a team first starts up _____ skills are needed.

    a. integrative
    b. advocacy
    c. legal
    d. leadership
    e. catalytic

Answer: (b) Difficulty: (2) Knowledge: (F) Page: 538, Exhibit 18-7

47. With consideration to the team building process, certain leadership roles and team development skills are necessary for success. When a team goes through an evolution stage, _____ skills are needed.

    a. integrative
    b. advocacy
    c. legal
    d. leadership
    e. catalytic

Answer: (e) Difficulty: (2) Knowledge: (F) Page: 538, Exhibit 18-7

48. With consideration to the team building process, certain leadership roles and team development skills are necessary for success. When a team reaches maturity, _____ skills are needed.

   a. integrative
   b. advocacy
   c. legal
   d. leadership
   e. catalytic

Answer: (a) Difficulty: (2) Knowledge: (F) Page: 538, Exhibit 18-7

49. Building team legitimacy, linking team mission and company strategy, networking to obtain resources, and bureaucracy busting are all characteristics of _____ skills necessary when a team is first starting up.

   a. integrative
   b. advocacy
   c. legal
   d. leadership
   e. catalytic

Answer: (b) Difficulty: (2) Knowledge: (A) Page: 538, Exhibit 18-7

50. Working with external constituents, differentiating individual roles and responsibilities, building commitment, and rewarding members for valuable contributions are all characteristics of _____ skills necessary when the team is evolving.

   a. integrative
   b. advocacy
   c. legal
   d. leadership
   e. catalytic

Answer: (e) Difficulty: (2) Knowledge: (A) Page: 538, Exhibit 18-7

51. Emphasizing excellence and accomplishment, coordinating and problem solving, and measuring progress and results are all characteristics of _____ skills necessary when teams reach maturity.

    a. integrative
    b. advocacy
    c. legal
    d. leadership
    e. catalytic

Answer: (a) Difficulty: (2) Knowledge: (A) Page: 538, Exhibit 18-7

52. Several management theorists have made an attempt to come up with the "right" fit between the MNC's environment (internal and external) and the organizational setup. One popular model examines the relationship between organizational structure, _____, and the importance of foreign sales to the company (as a share of total sales).

    a. product prices
    b. domestic services
    c. foreign product deliveries
    d. foreign product diversity
    e. purchasing habits

Answer: (d) Difficulty: (3) Knowledge: (F) Page: 539, Exhibit 18-8

53. Research has shown that the key challenge for MNCs is building and sustaining the right _____ instead of looking for the proper organizational structure.

    a. products
    b. prices
    c. distribution network
    d. promotional mix
    e. management process

Answer: (e) Difficulty: (3) Knowledge: (A) Page: 540

54. A(n) _____ can be described as being where country and regional managers look at strategic issues from multiple perspectives.

   a. glocal mindset
   b. global mindset
   c. local mindset
   d. regional mindset
   e. country mindset

Answer: (a) Difficulty: (2) Knowledge: (F) Page: 540

55. With _____ organizations, the national operating companies are highly autonomous. Each one of the local units represents a profit center.

   a. centralized
   b. decentralized
   c. global
   d. international
   e. regional

Answer: (b) Difficulty: (1) Knowledge: (F) Page: 541

56. With _____ organizations, there is a consolidation of most decision-making power at corporate headquarters.
   a. centralized
   b. decentralized
   c. global
   d. international
   e. regional

Answer: (a) Difficulty: (1) Knowledge: (F) Page: 541

57. In practice, most MNCs are somewhere between the extremes of centralization and decentralization. Which of the following tasks are most likely to be centralized by most MNCs?

   a. pricing and advertising
   b. finance and R & D
   c. manufacturing
   d. inventory management
   e. sales management

Answer: (b) Difficulty: (2) Knowledge: (A) Page: 541

58. In practice, most MNCs are somewhere between the extremes of centralization and decentralization. Which of the following tasks are most likely to be decentralized by most MNCs?

a. pricing and advertising
b. finance and R & D
c. manufacturing
d. inventory management
e. sales management

Answer: (a) Difficulty: (3) Knowledge: (A) Page: 541

59. Recently, several management theorists have offered _____ as a way to combine the autonomy of the local units with the benefits of coordination.

a. decentralization
b. centralization
c. parallel management systems
d. federalism
e. oligopoly and alliance

Answer: (d) Difficulty: (3) Knowledge: (F) Page: 542

60. Firms that are able to follow a "federalism" model have all the following characteristics EXCEPT:

a. noncentralization.
b. imbalance of power.
c. negotianalism.
d. constitutionalism.
e. territoriality.

Answer: (b) Difficulty: (3) Knowledge: (F) Page: 542, 543

61. If an organization is described as having noncentralization, negotianalism, constitutionalism, territoriality, and a balance of power, that organization would probably be following which of the following organizational formats?

    a. decentralization
    b. centralization
    c. parallel management systems
    d. federalism
    e. oligopoly and alliance

Answer: (d) Difficulty: (2) Knowledge: (A) Page: 542, 543

62. To make global marketing strategies work, companies need to establish a(n) _____.

    a. career system.
    b. development system.
    c. control system.
    d. appeals system.
    e. listening system.

Answer: (c) Difficulty: (1) Knowledge: (F) Page: 543

63. The main purpose of a _____ is to ensure that the behaviors of the various parties within the organization are in line with the company's strategic goals.
    a. career system
    b. development system
    c. control system
    d. appeals system
    e. listening system

Answer: (c) Difficulty: (1) Knowledge: (F) Page: 543

64. All of the following are parts (or basic building blocks) of a formal control system EXCEPT:

    a. the establishment of control standards.
    b. the measurement of performance against standards.
    c. the evaluation of performance against standards.
    d. perfection training.
    e. analysis and correction of deviations from standards.

Answer: (d) Difficulty: (1) Knowledge: (F) Page: 543

65. Formal control systems are also called _____ control systems.

    a. administrative
    b. conductive
    c. selective
    d. bureaucratic
    e. strategic

Answer: (d) Difficulty: (2) Knowledge: (F) Page: 543

66. The first step in any control process should be to:

    a. clearly establish rewards and punishments.
    b. set standards.
    c. set controls.
    d. set monitoring mechanisms.
    e. establish who the controller is.

Answer: (b) Difficulty: (1) Knowledge: (F) Page: 544

67. The two types of standards are behavior and _____.

    a. outcome-based.
    b. performance.
    c. intellectual.
    d. strategic.
    e. structural.

Answer: (a) Difficulty: (2) Knowledge: (F) Page: 544

68. Although proper reward systems are crucial to motivate subsidiary managers, a recent study has shown the key role played by the presence of _____.

    a. strong leadership.
    b. bonuses.
    c. perks.
    d. due process.
    e. nondiscrimination.

Answer: (d) Difficulty: (3) Knowledge: (F) Page: 544

69. The two most common forms of informal control are human resource development and _____.

    a. outcome-based.
    b. performance.
    c. intellectual.
    d. strategic.
    e. corporate culture.

Answer: (e) Difficulty: (3) Knowledge: (F) Page: 545

70. Corporate cultures can be clan-based or _____.

    a. market based.
    b. leader based.
    c. employee based.
    d. symbol based.
    e. tradition based.

Answer: (a) Difficulty: (3) Knowledge: (F) Page: 545

71. The _____ form of corporate culture is distinguished by an embodiment of a long socialization process, strong and power norms, and a defined set of internalized controls.
    a. market based
    b. leader based
    c. employee based
    d. clan based
    e. tradition based

Answer: (d) Difficulty: (2) Knowledge: (A) Page: 545

72. The _____ form of corporate culture is distinguished by norms that are loose or absent, socialization processes are limited, and control systems are purely based on performance measures.

    a. market based
    b. leader based
    c. employee based
    d. clan based
    e. tradition based

Answer: (a) Difficulty: (2) Knowledge: (A) Page: 545

73. To shape a shared vision, cultural values primarily which of the following properties?

    a. easy to understand in only one way and written in English.
    b. have clarity, continuity, and consistency.
    c. have symbolism, sex-appeal, and sensitivity.
    d. be dynamic, demanding, and declarative.
    e. be global, gifted, and guiding.

Answer: (b) Difficulty: (2) Knowledge: (A) Page: 545

True/False   Short Answer

1. Unlike other global managerial issues, there does seem to be a magic formula that prescribes the "ideal" organizational setup.

Answer: (False) Difficulty: (1) Knowledge: (F) Page: 524

2. In industries where competition is highly localized, a centralized structure where most of the decision making is made at the country level is often most appropriate.

Answer: (False) Difficulty: (2) Knowledge: (F) Page: 524

3. Typically, when overseas sales account for a very small fraction of the company's overall sales revenues, an export department can easily handle the company's global activities.

Answer: (True) Difficulty: (1) Knowledge: (F) Page: 525

4. Companies with substantial product diversity tend to go for a global geographic division configuration.

Answer: (False) Difficulty: (2) Knowledge: (F) Page: 525

5. Under the _____ design, the company basically has two entities: the domestic division and the international division. The _____ is responsible for the company's international operations.

Answer: (international division) Difficulty: (2) Knowledge: (F) Page: 525

6. Under the _____ design, the company's global activities are organized along its various product divisions.

Answer: (product-based structure) Difficulty: (2) Knowledge: (F) Page: 525

7. Under the _____ design, the company configures its organization along geographic areas.

Answer: (geographic structure) Difficulty: (1) Knowledge: (F) Page: 526

8. Under the _____ design, the company integrates two approaches and has a dual chain of command.

Answer: (matrix organization or structure) Difficulty: (2) Knowledge: (F) Page: 526

9. Most companies that engage in global marketing will initially start off by establishing an export department.

Answer: (True) Difficulty: (1) Knowledge: (F) Page: 526

10. The global product structure is most appropriate for companies whose product line is not too diverse and does not need a large amount of adaptation to local country needs.

Answer: (False) Difficulty: (2) Knowledge: (A) Page: 526

11. An advantage of the product structure form of organization is that it offers the company a large degree of flexibility in terms of cross-country resource allocation and strategic planning.

Answer: (True) Difficulty: (2) Knowledge: (F) Page: 526

12. Country-focused organizations can be very good forms of structure because they tend to less costly than other forms.

Answer: (False) Difficulty: (3) Knowledge: (F) Page: 528

13. If a company wants to establish a beachhead in a new market, they should look for _____ manager type.

Answer: (trader or entrepreneur) Difficulty: (3) Knowledge: (F) Page: 530

14. The _____ type of manager is characterized as being in charge of large and/or strategic markets. They also handle government relations.

Answer: (ambassador) Difficulty: (3) Knowledge: (F) Page: 530

15. With respect to organizational forms, the matrix structure explicitly recognizes the multidimensional nature of global strategic decision making.

Answer: (True) Difficulty: (1) Knowledge: (F) Page: 531

16. A typical example of a matrix structure is that of Siemens AG, the German engineering conglomerate who focuses on business and geographic dimensions.

Answer: (True) Difficulty: (2) Knowledge: (A) Page: 531

17. A good metaphor for the global network is the circle.

Answer: (False) Difficulty: (2) Knowledge: (A) Page: 534, Exhibit 18-4

Essay

1. List and briefly discuss the key criteria that impact global organizational design.

Answer:

a. Environmental factors include:
        1). Competitive environment.
        2). Rate of Environmental change.
        3). Regional trading blocs.
        4). Nature of customers.
b. Firm-specific factors:
        1). Strategic importance of international business.
        2). Product diversity.
        3). Company heritage.
        4). Quality of local managerial skills.

Students should review the material in the chapter and briefly comment on each of the factors if the instructor wishes this question to be more discussion-oriented than listing in nature.

Difficulty: (2) Knowledge: (F) Page: 524, 525

2. List and briefly describe the principal organizational design options that firms can use to organize their global activities. Cite the advantages and disadvantages of each form.

Answer:

The principle designs that firms can adopt to organize their global activities are:
- a. International division. Under this design, the company basically has two entities:
  - 1). The domestic division which is responsible for the firm's domestic activities.
  - 2). The international division which is in charge of the company's international division.
- b. Product based structure.
  - 1). Organized along the company's various product divisions.
- c. Geographic structure.
  - 1). The company configures along geographic areas such as countries, regions, or some combination of the two.
- d. Matrix organization.
  - 1). The company integrates two approaches (such as product and geographic boundaries).
  - 2). There is a dual chain of command.

International division structure.
- a. Most companies begin with an export department.
- b. This is usually followed by an international division.
- c. International opportunities are scanned.
- d. This option is suitable for companies that have a product line that is not too diverse and that does not require a large amount of adaptation to local country needs. This also works for companies that are still primarily domestic producers.

Global product division structure.
- a. This option centers around the different product lines or strategic business units of the company. Each SBU is managed separately.
- b. This option is popular among high-tech companies with highly complex products or MNCs with a very different product portfolio.
- c. Benefits include:
  - 1). Large degree of flexibility in terms of cross-country resource allocation and strategic planning.
  - 2). Economies of scale in production.
  - 3). Competitive cost position improvement.
  - 4). Facilitates the development of a global strategic focus to cope with challenges posed by global players.

d. Shortcomings include:
   1). Lack of communication and coordination can lead to needless duplication of tasks.
   2). Can distract from local market needs.
   3). Can scatter company resources--fragmentation.

Geographic structure.
   a. Area structures are especially appealing to companies that market closely related product lines with very similar end-users and applications around the world.
   b. Country-based subsidiaries.
      1). By setting up country affiliates, the MNC can stay in close touch with the local market conditions.
      2). Handicaps include:
         a). Too costly.
         b). Coordination cumbersome.
         c). Leads to a "not-invented-here" bias.
   c. New role of country managers.
      1). Most believe that this is a declining form of organization.
      2). Forces that are leading to a decline include:
         a). Threats by global competitors that must be dealt with globally.
         b). Global customers.
         c). Regional trading blocs.

      3). Factors that still point to the usefulness of this form of manager includes:
         a). Nurturing links with local governments.
         b). Local competitor consideration.
         c). Strong local brands.
         d). Innovative ideas that come from the local environment.

Matrix structure.
   a. Using one structure can often be a disaster.
   b. The matrix structure combines forms and recognizes the multi-dimensional nature of global strategic decision-making.
   c. There is a dual chain of command.
   d. Structures could even be three dimensional.
   e. Advantages include:
      1). Reflect complexities--local and global competitors, customers, and distributors.
      2). Fosters team spirit and cooperation.
   f. Disadvantages include:
      1). Reporting and profit responsibilities are confusing and conflict oriented.
      2). Bureaucratic bloat.

Difficulty: (3) Knowledge: (F) Page: 525-533

3. Explain how a global networked organization might differ from a matrix organizational structure. To answer this question, review the characteristics of both structures carefully.

Answer:

To correctly answer this question, students should re-read the material in the chapter and find information to support their conclusions. Facts that should be considered when making their assessment of the differences are shown below.

The matrix structure:
    a. Using one structure can often be a disaster.
    b. The matrix structure combines forms and recognizes the multi-dimensional nature of global strategic decision-making.
    c. There is a dual chain of command.
    d. Structures could even be three dimensional.
    e. Advantages include:
        1). Reflect complexities--local and global competitors, customers, and distributors.
        2). Fosters team spirit and cooperation.
    f. Disadvantages include:
        1). Reporting and profit responsibilities are confusing and conflict oriented.
        2). Bureaucratic bloat.

The global network solution:
    a. The network model is an attempt to reconcile the tension between two opposing forces--the need for local responsiveness and the wish to be an integrated whole.
    b. This form is a mindset rather than a real structure (in the truest sense of the term). Another term used to describe this form is transnational.
    c. Advocates of this model believe that MNCs should develop processes and linkages that allow each unit to tap into a global knowledge pool.
    d. An international teaming concept can be used to form the network.
    e. The network concept can center around three concepts:
        1). A set of basic assumptions about people.
        2). Assumptions about managerial policies.
        3). Assumptions about certain expectations.

Difficulty: (3) Knowledge: (F) Page: 531-536

4. Describe the five profiles that country managers might need to fit to be able lead their organizations into the challenges of the twenty-first century.

Answer:

To strike a balance, country managers must fit one of these profiles:
- a). Trader--entrepreneurial spirit.
- b). Builder--develops local markets.
- c). Cabinet member--team player.
- d). Ambassador--in charge of large or strategic markets. Good at government relations.
- e). Representative--like Ambassador but in large markets.

Difficulty: (1) Knowledge: (F) Page: 530

5. Explain how a MNC might become a multi-local multinational organization. Include in your answer a discussion of the concept of federalism (as applied to this situation).

Answer:

There can be a variety of creative suggestions to answer this question. To answer, the student must consider the sum of the material in the chapter. This form would really can for a multi-level hybrid of most existing models. The concepts of decentralization and centralization can be part of this answer if the student so chooses.

The concept of so called federalism says companies following this model share these characteristics:
- a. Non-centralization.
- b. Negotianalism.
- c. Constitutionalism.
- d. Territoriality.
- e. Balance of power.
- f. Autonomy.

Difficulty: (2) Knowledge: (F) Page: 538-543